The Pillar New Testament Commentary

General Editor

D. A. CARSON

The Letters
to the
THESSALONIANS

GENE L. GREEN

WILLIAM B. EERDMANS PUBLISHING COMPANY
GRAND RAPIDS, MICHIGAN / CAMBRIDGE, U.K.

APOLLOS
LEICESTER, ENGLAND

© 2002 Wm. B. Eerdmans Publishing Co.

2140 Oak Industrial Drive N.E., Grand Rapids, Michigan 49505 /

P.O. Box 163, Cambridge CB3 9PU U.K.

www.eerdmans.com

First published 2002 in the United States of America by

Wm. B. Eerdmans Publishing Co.

and in the United Kingdom by

APOLLOS

38 De Montfort Street, Leicester, England LE1 7GP

Printed in the United States of America

14 13 12 11 10 09   9 8 7 6 5 4 3

Library of Congress Cataloging-in-Publication Data

Green, Gene L.

The letters to the Thessalonians / Gene L. Green.

p.   cm.   (The Pillar New Testament commentary)

Includes bibliographical references and index.

ISBN 978-0-8028-3738-7 (alk. paper)

1. Bible. N.T. Thessalonians — Commentaries.

I. Title.   II. Series.

BS2725.53.G74   2002

227'.81077 — dc21

2002019444

British Library Cataloguing in Publication Data

A catalogue record for this book is available from the British Library.

A Deborah

mi corazón

y

a Gillian y Christiana

mi sangre

Contents

Series Preface   xi
Author's Preface   xiii
Abbreviations   xvi
Bibliography   xix

INTRODUCTION

   I. RIVERS, ROADS, ROLLING MOUNTAINS, AND
      THE SEA: GEOGRAPHY AND TRAVEL THROUGH
      MACEDONIA AND THESSALONICA   1

  II. A SUMMARY HISTORY OF MACEDONIA AND
      THESSALONICA   8

  III. THE GOVERNMENT OF THESSALONICA   20

  IV. THE SOCIAL AND ECONOMIC WORLDS OF
      THESSALONICA   25

  V. RELIGION IN THESSALONICA   31

  VI. THE GOSPEL AND THE THESSALONIANS   47

  VII. THE AUTHORSHIP OF 1 AND 2 THESSALONIANS   54

     A. 1 Thessalonians   54

     B. 2 Thessalonians   59

        1. *Literary Arguments*   60

        2. *The Argument from Form*   61

        3. *The Theological Argument*   62

VIII. THE ORDER OF THE EPISTLES   64

  IX. THE STRUCTURE OF 1 AND 2 THESSALONIANS   69

CONTENTS

1 THESSALONIANS

I. "PAUL, SILAS AND TIMOTHY, TO THE CHURCH OF THE
THESSALONIANS" — THE EPISTOLARY GREETING (1.1)   81

II. "WE ALWAYS THANK GOD FOR ALL OF YOU" — THE
COMING OF THE GOSPEL AND ITS RECEPTION (1.2-10)   86

III. "YOU KNOW . . ." — THE BODY OF THE LETTER
(2.1–5.22)   111

  A. "Our visit to you was not a failure" — The Gospel
  Arrives in Thessalonica (2.1–3.13)   111

    1. "Our visit" — The Apostolic Entrance (2.1-12)   111

    2. "We also thank God . . . you received the word of God" —
    The Reception of the Gospel (2.13-16)   138

    3. "We were torn away from you" — The Exit of the
    Apostles and the Attempts to Return (2.17-20)   150

    4. "We sent Timothy" — The Mission of Timothy (3.1-5)   156

    5. "But Timothy has just now come to us" —
    Thanksgiving to God for the Thessalonians (3.6-10)   165

    6. "Now may our God . . . clear the way for us to come
    to you" — The Prayer to Return to Thessalonica (3.11-13)   175

  B. "You know what instructions we gave you" —
  The Life That Pleases God (4.1–5.22)   181

    1. "We instructed you how to live in order to please God" —
    The Introduction (4.1-2)   182

    2. "You should avoid sexual immorality" —
    Sanctification (4.3-8)   187

    3. "Now about . . ." — Responses to Questions (4.9–5.11)   202

      a. Fraternal "love" (4.9-12)   202

      b. "Those who fall asleep" (4.13-18)   213

      c. "Times and dates" (5.1-11)   229

    4. "Respect those who work hard among you" —
    The Community and Its Leadership (5.12-13)   246

    5. "Warn . . . encourage . . . help . . . be patient" —
    Life in Community (5.14)   252

    6. "Make sure that nobody pays back wrong for wrong" —
    The Life of Nonretaliation (5.15)   255

    7. "Be joyful . . . pray . . . give thanks" —
    Communion with God (5.16-18)   257

8. *"Do not put out the Spirit's fire"* —
   Prophecy in the Community (5.19-22)   260

IV. "MAY GOD HIMSELF" — THE FINAL PRAYER,
   GREETINGS, AND BLESSING (5.23-28)   266

    A. "May God . . . sanctify you through and through"
   (5.23-25)   266

    B. "Greet all the brothers and sisters" (5.26-27)   270

    C. "The grace of our Lord Jesus Christ be with you" (5.28)   272

2 THESSALONIANS

I. "PAUL, SILVANUS, AND TIMOTHY, TO THE CHURCH
   OF THE THESSALONIANS" — THE EPISTOLARY
   SALUTATION (1.1-2)   277

II. "YOUR FAITH IS GROWING AND YOUR LOVE IS
   INCREASING" — THANKSGIVING AND PRAYERS
   FOR THE FAITH, LOVE, AND STEADFASTNESS OF THE
   PERSECUTED THESSALONIANS (1.3-12)   278

    A. "We must always give thanks to God for you" —
   The First Thanksgiving (1.3-5)   279

    B. "It is indeed just of God to repay with affliction those
   who afflict you" — The Destiny of the Persecutors
   (1.6-10)   286

    C. "To this end we will always pray for you" —
   The Remembrance of Prayers to Be Worthy of
   God's Call (1.11-12)   296

III. "AS TO . . ." — THE BODY OF THE LETTER (2.1–3.15)   300

    A. "As to the coming of our Lord Jesus Christ" —
   The Time of the Day of the Lord (2.1-17)   300

      1. Do not *"be quickly shaken"* — *False Teaching
   about the Day of the Lord (2.1-12)*   300

      2. *"But we must always give thanks to God for you"* —
   The Second Thanksgiving (2.13-14)   325

      3. *"Stand firm and hold fast to the traditions"* —
   Exhortation to Steadfastness — 2.15   329

      4. *"Now may our Lord Jesus Christ himself and
   God our Father"* — *The First Prayer (2.16-17)*   330

CONTENTS

B. "Finally, brothers and sisters" —
   Final Instructions (3.1-15)   334

   1. "Pray for us" — Mutual Prayers (3.1-5)   334

      a. "So that the word of the Lord may spread
         rapidly" — The Prayer Request of the Apostles (3.1-2) 334

      b. "But the Lord is faithful; he will strengthen
         you" — Confidence in the Lord (3.3-4)   337

      c. "May the Lord direct your hearts to the love
         of God" — The Second Prayer (3.5)   339

   2. "Now we command you" — The Problem of the
      Disorderly (3.6-15)   341

      a. "Keep away from believers who are living
         in idleness" — The First Exhortation
         (to the Community) (3.6)   343

      b. "We were not idle when we were with you" —
         The Example of the Apostles (3.7-10)   345

      c. "Work quietly and earn your own living" —
         The Second Exhortation (to the Disorderly) (3.11-12)   350

      d. "Do not be weary in doing what is right" —
         The Third Exhortation (to the Community) (3.13)   353

      e. "Take note of those who do not obey" —
         Discipline in the Community (3.14-15)   354

IV. "NOW MAY THE LORD OF PEACE HIMSELF GIVE YOU
    PEACE" — THE THIRD PRAYER AND FINAL GREETINGS
    (3.16-18)   357

   A. "Now may the Lord of peace himself give you peace" —
      The First Benediction (3.16)   357

   B. "I, Paul, write this greeting" — The Apostolic
      Greeting and Guarantee (3.17)   358

   C. "The grace of our Lord Jesus Christ be with you all" —
      The Final Benediction (3.18)   359

INDEXES

MODERN AUTHORS   361

SUBJECTS   365

SCRIPTURE REFERENCES   367

EXTRABIBLICAL LITERATURE   391

Series Preface

Commentaries have specific aims, and this series is no exception. Designed for pastors and teachers of the Bible, the Pillar commentaries seek above all to make clear the text of Scripture as we have it. The scholars writing these volumes interact with the most important informed contemporary debate, but avoid getting mired in undue technical detail. Their ideal is a blend of rigorous exegesis and exposition, with an eye alert both to biblical theology and the contemporary relevance of the Bible, without confusing the commentary and the sermon.

The rationale for this approach is that the vision of "objective scholarship" (a vain chimera) may actually be profane. God stands over against us; we do not stand in judgment of him. When God speaks to us through his Word, those who profess to know him must respond in an appropriate way, and that is certainly different from a stance in which the scholar projects an image of autonomous distance. Yet this is no surreptitious appeal for uncontrolled subjectivity. The writers of this series aim for an evenhanded openness to the text that is the best kind of "objectivity" of all.

If the text is God's Word, it is appropriate that we respond with reverence, a certain fear, a holy joy, a questing obedience. These values should be reflected in the way Christians write. With these values in place, the Pillar commentaries will be warmly welcomed not only by pastors, teachers, and students, but by general readers as well.

*   *   *   *   *

This commentary by Gene Green is a welcome addition to the series. In addition to his technical competence, especially in helping us to understand the Greco-Roman background of Thessalonica and its bearing on these letters, Dr. Green brings years of teaching experience to his writing, both in Latin America and, more recently, at Wheaton College. The two commentaries he has written in Spanish are highly regarded. Now readers in the Anglo world, not least pastors and missionaries, will be grateful for the clarity and vitality he brings to his exegesis and exposition. The sanity and even-handedness that characterize his interpretation of some of the most hotly disputed passages in the New Testament will be recognized as one of the great strengths of the work.

D. A. CARSON

Author's Preface

The modern city of Thessaloniki, the second largest metropolitan center in modern Greece, stands atop the ruins of the ancient city founded by Cassander in the fourth century BC. When Paul, Silvanus, and Timothy arrived there over three and a half centuries later, they entered a thriving metropolis that was truly the "mother of Macedonia." While archaeologists have unearthed numerous important finds from around that period, recently including a structure that may be the temple of the imperial cult referenced in numerous inscriptions, our understanding of the city remains rather limited, at least in comparison to that of other ancient cities such as Corinth, Athens, Ephesus, and Rome. Yet with the evidence that has survived, we are able to piece together a coherent picture of the character of this provincial capital from inscriptions, archaeological excavations, numismatic evidence, and textual references. Also available is a wealth of information outlining the history of Macedonia, its conquest by the Romans, and its role as a province within the empire. Moreover, students of the classics have enriched our understanding of life within the Mediterranean world during the first century, drawing on the multiplicity of materials that have survived the millennia. We are far from ignorant of governmental and religious institutions and enjoy insight into the structures of economics, the family, and other social institutions. Cultural values and how they differed among people groups are all part of the stock of material handed down to us.

This commentary on 1 and 2 Thessalonians is an attempt to read these letters in the light of relevant materials from the city and world of that era in order to help us better understand the impact of the gospel of Christ on its first readers. Did the special relationship Thessalonica enjoyed with Rome affect the way Christians in the city were handled? Did the outward-looking character of the city as the metropolis of the province influence the Christian mission that emanated from it? How do ancient views of death and comfort inform our reading of 1 Thessalonians 4.13-18? Does the institution of patronage *(clientela)* help clarify why certain individuals within the Thessalonian church refused to work? Was scepticism about prophecy widespread in the first century, and did this trend influence the church?

This commentary explores the relationship between the Thessalonian correspondence and the canon of Scripture, but it also asks questions about how this book was read by first-century Macedonians and Romans living side by side in this city situated along the Via Egnatia. I recognize that this approach necessitates a lengthier than usual section on the history and character of the city, but my hope, dear reader, is that you will take the time to get to know the Thessalonians somewhat before reading about the founding of the church in their city and the believers' subsequent struggles to live out the Christian faith in that context. Reading about the way the gospel impacted them in their context will, in the end, hopefully move us toward a clearer picture of how the gospel is and can be a potent force in our own lives and society at the beginning of the twenty-first century.

This is a rich time for Thessalonian studies, as the bibliography included here and the one published by Stanley Porter and Jeffrey Weima (Brill) attest. I am sorry that the commentary by Abraham Malherbe (Doubleday) came out after this work was finished. Any reader of his previous essays on Thessalonians will recognize my debt to him. We also are looking forward to the commentaries by Jeffrey Weima (Baker) and Greg Beale (IVP) in the near future. Such riches cause us embarrassment.

A project of this type is never undertaken alone, despite the long hours of solitary research. My initial investigation into the social setting of Thessalonica and the Thessalonian letters was undertaken at Tyndale House in Cambridge, England. Many thanks are due to Bruce Winter for his warm encouragement and to David Instone-Brewer for his masterful management of that library. The funding for the research, which also resulted in a Spanish commentary on the letters,[1] was made available through the kindness of our many supporters while we were missionaries with Latin America Mission as well as by The Combs Foundation, The Endowment for Biblical Research, The First Fruit Foundation, and La Iglesia Bíblica Zapote. I am also very grateful to my students of the Seminario ESEPA in San José, Costa Rica, and at Wheaton College for their insights into these letters and for their comments on the perspec-

---

1. Eugenio Green, *1 y 2 Tesalonicenses* (Grand Rapids: Editorial Portavoz, 2001).

tives forwarded in this commentary. Thanks also go to Don Carson, my friend and general editor, whose observations and criticisms have served to improve this work. I am indebted as well to Milton Essenburg of Eerdmans for his careful editing, from which I and a great number of other commentators have benefited over the last thirty years. Hearty thanks also go to my assistants, Sydney Westrate and Jordana Ashman, for helping prepare the first draft of the bibliography and reading and proofing the entire manuscript respectively. Thanks be to God for each of these people!

Finally, I thank my wife, Deborah, and my daughters, Gillian and Christiana, for their encouragement and the way they patiently packed their suitcases one more time so I could complete this project. These three women are the joy of my life, and I will be grateful to God for them throughout eternity. To them this book is lovingly dedicated.

GENE L. GREEN

Abbreviations

ABD	*Anchor Bible Dictionary.* Edited by David Noel Freedman. 6 vols. New York: Doubleday, 1992
AJA	*American Journal of Archaeology*
AJAH	*American Journal of Ancient History*
ANRW	*Aufstieg und Niedergang der römischen Welt: Geschichte und Kultur Roms im Spiegel der neueren Forschung.* Edited by Hildegard Temporini and Wolfgang Haase. Berlin and New York: Walter de Gruyter, 1972-
AR	*Archaeological Reports*
ATR	*Australasian Theological Review*
BA	*Biblical Archaeologist*
BAGD	*A Greek-English Lexicon of the New Testament and Other Early Christian Literature.* Walter Bauer. Translated and edited by William F. Arndt and F. Wilbur Gingrich. Revised by F. Wilbur Gingrich and Frederick W. Danker. Chicago and London: University of Chicago Press, 1979
BASOR	*Bulletin of the American Schools of Oriental Research*
BBR	*Bulletin for Biblical Research*
BCH	*Bulletin de correspondance hellénique*
BDF	*A Greek Grammar of the New Testament.* F. Blass and A. Debrunner. Translated and edited by Robert W. Funk. Chicago and London: University of Chicago Press, 1961
Bib	*Biblica*
BGU	*Berliner Griechische Urkunden*
BJRL	*Bulletin of the John Rylands Library*
BN	*Biblische Notizen*
BR	*Biblical Research*

BRev	*Bible Review*
BSac	*Bibliotheca Sacra*
BT	*The Bible Translator*
CBQ	*Catholic Biblical Quarterly*
Colloq	*Colloquium*
Comm	*Communio*
CP	*Classical Philology*
CT	*Cuadernos de Teología*
DRev	*Downside Review*
EstBíb	*Estudios Bíblicos*
EstEcl	*Estudios Eclesiásticos*
ExpTim	*Expository Times*
GR	*Greece and Rome*
HSCP	*Harvard Studies in Classical Philology*
HTR	*Harvard Theological Review*
Int	*Interpretation*
IG	*Inscriptiones Graecae*
IT	*Inscriptiones Graecae Epiri, Macedoniae, Thraciae, Scythiae, Pars II: Inscriptiones Macedoniae, Fasciculus I: Inscriptiones Thessalonicae et Viciniae.* Edited by C. F. Edson. Berlin: W. de Gruyter, 1972
JBL	*Journal of Biblical Literature*
JETS	*Journal of the Evangelical Theological Society*
JHS	*Journal of Hellenistic Studies*
JPT	*Journal of Pentecostal Theology*
JRA	*Journal of Roman Archaeology*
JRS	*Journal of Roman Studies*
JSNT	*Journal for the Study of the New Testament*
JSOT	*Journal for the Study of the Old Testament*
JTS	*Journal of Theological Studies*
JTSA	*Journal of Theology for Southern Africa*
LAE	*Light from the Ancient East.* Adolf Deissmann. Grand Rapids: Baker, 1978
LSJ	*A Greek-English Lexicon.* Edited by Henry George Liddell and Robert Scott. Revised by Henry Stuart Jones and Roderick McKenzie. Oxford: Clarendon Press, 1968
Lum	*Lumen*
MM	*The Vocabulary of the Greek New Testament.* James Hope Moulton and George Mulligan. Grand Rapids: Eerdmans, 1930
NA	*Numina Aegaea*

ABBREVIATIONS

NBD	*New Bible Dictionary*. Edited by J. D. Douglas. Downers Grove, Ill.: InterVarsity Press, 1982.
NewDocs	*New Documents Illustrating Early Christianity*. Edited by G. H. R. Horsley and S. R. Llewelyn. 8 vols. Grand Rapids: Eerdmans, 1981-98
NIDNTT	*New International Dictionary of New Testament Theology*. Edited by Colin Brown. 4 vols. Grand Rapids: Zondervan, 1975-85
NovT	*Novum Testamentum*
NTS	*New Testament Studies*
OCD	*Oxford Classical Dictionary*. Edited by Simon Hornblower and Antony Spawforth. Oxford and New York: Oxford University Press, 1996
PCPS	*Proceedings of the Cambridge Philological Society*
Presb	*Presbyterion*
Proy	*Proyección*
RB	*Revue biblique*
REG	*Revue des études grecques*
RevBíb	*Revista Bíblica*
RevPhil	*Revue de philologie*
ResQ	*Restoration Quarterly*
RIBLA	*Revista de Interpretación Bíblica Latinoamericana*
RTR	*Reformed Theological Review*
Salm	*Salmanticensis*
SIG³	*Sylloge Inscriptionum Graecarum*. Edited by W. Dittenberger. 4 vols. Leipzig: S. Hirzelium, 1915-24
TDNT	*Theological Dictionary of the New Testament*. Edited by Gerhard Kittel and Gerhard Friedrich. 10 vols. Grand Rapids: Eerdmans, 1964-76
TLNT	*Theological Lexicon of the New Testament*. 3 vols. Ceslas Spicq. Peabody, Mass.: Hendrickson, 1994
TTJ	*Trinity Theological Journal*
TynBul	*Tyndale Bulletin*
VD	*Verbum Domini*
WesTJ	*Wesleyan Theological Journal*
ZNW	*Zeitschrift für die neutestamentliche Wissenschaft*
ZPE	*Zeitschrift für Papyrologie und Epigraphik*
ZTK	*Zeitschrift für Theologie und Kirche*

Bibliography

In addition to the bibliographic references listed below, see:

Weima, Jeffrey A. D., and Stanley E. Porter. *An Annotated Bibliography of 1 and 2 Thessalonians.* Leiden, Boston, and Köln: Brill, 1998.

Ackroyd, Peter R. "*nṣḥ — eis telos.*" *ExpTim* 80 (1968-69) 126.
Adams, J. P. "Toperios Thraciae, the Via Egnatia and the Boundaries of Macedonia." Pages 17-42 in *Ancient Macedonia IV.* Thessaloniki: Institute for Balkan Studies, 1986.
Alcock, Susan E. *Graecia Capta.* Cambridge: Cambridge University Press, 1993.
Arroniz, José Manuel. "La parusía y su hermenéutica (1 Tes 4,13-18)." *Lum* 32.3 (1983) 193-213.
Aune, David E. *The New Testament in Its Literary Environment.* Philadelphia: Westminster Press, 1987.
Aus, Roger D. "The Liturgical Background of the Necessity and Propriety of Giving Thanks according to 2 Thes. 1:3." *JBL* 92 (1973) 432-38.
Aus, Roger D. "The Relevance of Isaiah 66.7 to Revelation 12 and 2 Thessalonians 1." *ZNW* 67 (1976) 252-68.
Baer, David A. *When We All Go Home: Translation and Theology in LXX Isaiah 56–66.* Sheffield: Sheffield Academic Press, 2001.
Bahr, Gordon J. "The Subscriptions in the Pauline Letters." *JBL* 87 (1968) 27-41.
Bailey, J. A. "Who Wrote II Thessalonians?" *NTS* 25 (1978-79) 131-45.
Balch, David L. *Let Wives Be Submissive.* Chico, Calif.: Scholars Press, 1981.
Bammel, Ernst. "Judenverfolgung und Naherwartung: Zur Eschatologie des Ersten Thessalonicherbriefes." *ZTK* 56 (1959) 294-315.

————. "Preparation for the Perils of the Last Days: I Thessalonians 3:3." Pages 91-100 in *Suffering and Martyrdom in the New Testament*. Edited by William Horbury and Brian McNeil. Cambridge: Cambridge University Press, 1981.

Barclay, John M. G. "Conflict in Thessalonica." *CBQ* 55 (1993) 512-30.

————. *Jews in the Mediterranean Diaspora*. Edinburgh: T&T Clark, 1996.

————. "Thessalonica and Corinth: Social Contrasts in Pauline Christianity." *JSNT* 47 (1992) 49-74.

Barr, James. *Biblical Words for Time*. Naperville, Ill.: A. R. Allenson, 1962.

Barrat, Trenchard. *I y II Tesalonicenses*. Madrid: Literatura Bíblica, 1979.

Bassler, Jouette M. "The Enigmatic Sign: 2 Thessalonians 1:5." *CBQ* 46 (1984) 496-510.

Baur, Ferdinand Christian. *Paulus, der Apostel Jesu Christi*. Stuttgart: Becher & Müller, 1845.

Beekman, John, and John Callow. *Translating the Word of God*. Grand Rapids: Zondervan, 1974.

Beauvery, R. "*Pleonektein* in I Thess 4,3-8." *VD* 33 (1955) 78-85.

Bell, Albert A., Jr. *Exploring the New Testament World*. Nashville: Thomas Nelson, 1998.

Benjamin, Anna, and Antony E. Raubitschek. "Arae Augusti." *Hesperia* 28 (1959) 65-85.

Best, Ernest. *A Commentary on the First and Second Epistles to the Thessalonians*. New York: Harper & Row, 1972.

Bjerkelund, Carl J. *Parakalō*. Oslo: Universitetsforleget, 1967.

Blight, Richard C. *An Exegetical Summary of 1 & 2 Thessalonians*. Dallas: Summer Institute of Linguistics, 1989.

Boers, Hendrikus. "The Form-Critical Study of Paul's Letters: 1 Thessalonians as a Case Study." *NTS* 22 (1975-76) 140-58.

Bonnet, Luis, and Alfredo Schroeder. *Epístolas de Pablo*. Vol. 3 of *Comentario del Nuevo Testamento*. El Paso: Casa Bautista de Publicaciones, 1982.

Braund, David. "Function and Dysfunction: Personal Patronage in Roman Imperialism." Pages 137-52 in *Patronage in Ancient Society*. Edited by Andrew Wallace-Hadrill. London and New York: Routledge, 1989.

Brown, Stephen G. "The Intertextuality of Isaiah 66.17 and 2 Thessalonians 2.7: A Solution for the 'Restrainer' Problem." Pages 254-77 in *Paul and the Scriptures of Israel*. Edited by Craig A. Evans and James A. Sanders. Sheffield: JSOT Press, 1993.

Bruce, F. F. *1 and 2 Thessalonians*. Waco: Word, 1982.

————. "Macedonia." Pages 454-58 in Vol. 4 of *Anchor Bible Dictionary*. 6 vols. Edited by David Noel Freedman. New York: Doubleday, 1992.

————. *Paul: Apostle of the Heart Set Free*. Grand Rapids: Eerdmans, 1977.

———. "St. Paul in Macedonia: 2. The Thessalonian Correspondence." *BJRL* 62 (1980) 328-45.

Brunot, Amedee. *Los escritos de san Pablo.* Estella (Navarra): Editorial Verbo Divino, 1982.

Buck, Charles, and Greer Taylor. *Saint Paul: A Study of the Development of His Thought.* New York: Scribner's, 1969.

Butcher, Kevin. "Roman Coinage of Thessalonica." *JRA* 5 (1992) 434-39.

Calderone, Salvatore. *Pistis-Fides: Ricerche di storia e diritto internazionale nell'antichità.* Messina: Università Degli Studi, 1964.

Carrington, Philip. *The Primitive Christian Catechism.* Cambridge: Cambridge University Press, 1940.

Carroll, B. H. *Comentario bíblico; Santiago, 1 y 2 Tesalonicenses y 1 y 2 Corintios.* Barcelona: Clie, 1987.

Casson, Lionel. *Ships and Seamanship in the Ancient World.* Princeton: Princeton University Press, 1971.

———. *Travel in the Ancient World.* Baltimore and London: Johns Hopkins University Press, 1994.

Catling, H. W. "Archaeology in Greece." *AR* 28 (1981-82) 32-36.

Chapa, Juan. "Is First Thessalonians a Letter of Consolation?" *NTS* 40 (1994) 150-60.

Charlesworth, M. P. *Trade Routes and Commerce in the Roman Empire.* Cambridge: Cambridge University Press, 1924.

Chow, John K. *Patronage and Power: A Study of Social Networks in Corinth.* Sheffield: Sheffield Academic Press, 1992.

Clark, Andrew D. *Secular and Christian Leadership in Corinth.* Leiden: Brill, 1993.

Collart, Paul. "Les milliares de la Via Egnatia." *BCH* 100 (1976) 177-200.

———. "Une reflection de la Via Egnatia sous Trajan." *BCH* 59 (1935) 395-415.

Collins, Raymond F. "Apropos the Integrity of 1 Thessalonians." Pages 96-135 in *Studies on the First Letter to the Thessalonians.* Edited by Raymond F. Collins. Leuven: Leuven University Press, 1984.

———. "The Church of the Thessalonians." Pages 285-98 in *Studies on the First Letter to the Thessalonians.* Edited by Raymond F. Collins. Leuven: Leuven University Press, 1984.

———. "I Thessalonians and the Liturgy of the Early Church." Pages 136-53 in *Studies on the First Letter to the Thessalonians.* Edited by Raymond F. Collins. Leuven: Leuven University Press, 1984.

———. "Paul, as Seen through His Own Eyes: A Reflection on the First Letter to the Thessalonians." Pages 175-208 in *Studies on the First Letter to the Thessalonians.* Edited by Raymond F. Collins. Leuven: Leuven University Press, 1984.

————. *Studies on the First Letter to the Thessalonians.* Leuven: Leuven University Press, 1984.

————. "The Unity of Paul's Paraenesis in 1 Thess. 4.3-8; I Cor. 7.1-7: A Significant Parallel." *NTS* 29 (1983) 420-29.

Cormack, J. M. R. "The Gymnasiarchal Law of Beroea." Pages 139-49 in *Ancient Macedonia II.* Thessaloniki: Institute for Balkan Studies, 1977.

Cosby, Michael R. "Hellenistic Formal Receptions and Paul's Use of *apantēsis* in 1 Thessalonians 4:17." *BBR* 4 (1994) 15-33.

Cranfield, C. E. B. "Changes of Person and Number in Paul's Epistles." Pages 280-89 in *Paul and Paulinism.* Edited by M. D. Hooker and S. G. Wilson. London: SPCK, 1982.

Crossland, John, and Diane Constance. *Macedonian Greece.* London: B. T. Batsford Ltd., 1982.

Crouch, James E. *The Origin and Intention of the Colossian Haustafel.* Göttingen: Vandenhoeck & Ruprecht, 1972.

Cullmann, Oscar. *Christ and Time.* Philadelphia: Westminster Press, 1950.

Cuntz, O. *Itineraria Romana.* Leipzig: Teubner, 1929.

Cuss, Dominique. *Imperial Cult and Honorary Terms in the New Testament.* Fribourg: The University Press, 1974.

Danker, Frederick W. *Benefactor: Epigraphic Study of a Graeco-Roman and New Testament Semantic Field.* St. Louis: Clayton Publishing House, 1982.

————, and Robert Jewett. "Jesus as the Apocalyptic Benefactor in Second Thessalonians." Pages 486-98 in *The Thessalonian Correspondence.* Edited by Raymond F. Collins. Leuven: Leuven University Press, 1990.

Davies, P. E. "The Macedonian Scene of Paul's Journeys." *BA* 26 (1963) 91-106.

Deissmann, Adolf. *Bible Studies.* Edinburgh: T&T Clark, 1901.

————. *Light from the Ancient East.* Grand Rapids: Baker, 1978.

————. *Paul: A Study in Social and Religious History.* London: Hodder and Stoughton, 1926.

Dell, Harry J., ed. *Ancient Macedonian Studies in Honor of Charles Edson.* Thessaloniki: Institute for Balkan Studies, 1981.

deSilva, David Arthur. *Despising Shame: Honor Discourse and Community Maintenance in the Epistle to the Hebrews.* Atlanta: Scholars Press, 1995.

Dewailly, L. M. *La joven iglesia de Tesalónica.* Madrid: Studium Ediciones, 1971.

Donfried, Karl P. "The Cults of Thessalonica and the Thessalonian Correspondence." *NTS* 31 (1985) 336-56.

————. "Paul and Judaism: I Thessalonians 2:13-16 as a Test Case." *Int* 38 (1984) 242-53.

————, and Johannes Beutler. *The Thessalonians Debate: Methodological Discord or Methodological Synthesis?* Grand Rapids and Cambridge: Eerdmans, 2000.

————, and I. Howard Marshall. *The Theology of the Shorter Pauline Letters.* Cambridge: Cambridge University Press, 1993.

Doty, William G. *Letters in Primitive Christianity.* Philadelphia: Fortress Press, 1973.

Drummond, Andrew. "Early Roman *clientes.*" Pages 89-115 in *Patronage in Ancient Society.* Edited by Andrew Wallace-Hadrill. London and New York: Routledge, 1989.

Dumais, M. "Cartas a los Tesalonicenses." Pages 37-60 in *Cartas de Pablo y cartas católicas.* Edited by M. Carrey, P. Dornier, and M. Trimaille. Madrid: Ediciones Cristiandad, 1985.

Dunn, James D. G. *Jesus and the Spirit.* Philadelphia: Westminster Press, 1975.

Edson, Charles. "Cults of Thessalonica." *HTR* 41 (1948) 153-204.

————. *Inscriptiones graecae Epiri, Macedoniae, Thraciae, Scythiae, Pars II: Inscriptiones Macedoniae, Fasciculus I: Inscriptiones Thessalonicae et viciniae.* Berlin: W. de Gruyter, 1972.

————. "The Location of Cellae and the Route of the Via Egnatia in Western Macedonia." *CP* 46 (1951) 1-16.

————. "Macedonia, I: A Dedication of Philip V." *HSCP* 51 (1940) 125-26.

————. "Macedonia, II: State Cults of Thessalonica." *HSCP* 51 (1940) 127-36.

————. "Notes of the Thracian *phoros.*" *CP* 42 (1947) 102.

————. "Strepsa (Thucydides 1.61.4)." *CP* 50 (1955) 169-90.

Egenolf, Hans-Andreas. *Segunda carta a los Tesalonicenses.* Barcelona: Editorial Herder, 1980.

Eisenstadt, S. N., and L. Roniger. *Patrons, Clients and Friends.* Cambridge: Cambridge University Press, 1984.

Elgvin, Torleif. "'To Master His Own Vessel': 1 Thess 4.4 in Light of New Qumran Evidence." *NTS* 43 (1997) 604-619.

Ellingworth, Paul. "Which Way Are We Going? A Verb of Movement, Especially 1 Thess. 4:14b." *BT* 25 (1974) 426-31.

————, and Eugene A. Nida. *A Translator's Handbook on Paul's Letters to the Thessalonians.* London, New York, and Stuttgart: United Bible Societies, 1976.

Ellis, E. Earle. *Prophecy and Hermeneutic.* Tübingen: J. C. B. Mohr (Paul Siebeck), 1978.

Epstein, David F. *Personal Enmity in Roman Politics 218-43 BC.* London, New York, and Sydney: Croom Helm, 1987.

Evans, Craig A. "Ascending and Descending with a Shout: Psalm 47.6 and 1 Thessalonians 4.16." Pages 238-53 in *Paul and the Scriptures of Israel.* Edited by Craig A. Evans and James A. Sanders. Sheffield: JSOT Press, 1993.

Fee, Gordon. *The First Epistle to the Corinthians.* Grand Rapids: Eerdmans, 1987.

———. *God's Empowering Presence.* Peabody, Mass.: Hendrickson Publishers, 1994.

———. "Pneuma and Eschatology in 2 Thessalonians 2.1-12: A Proposal about 'Testing the Prophets' and the Purpose of 2 Thessalonians." Pages 196-215 in *To Tell the Mystery: Essays in New Testament Eschatology in Honor of Robert H. Gundry.* Edited by Thomas E. Schmidt and Moisés Silva. Sheffield: JSOT Press, 1994.

Ferguson, Everett. *Backgrounds of Early Christianity.* Grand Rapids: Eerdmans, 1993.

———. "Wine as a Table-Drink in the Ancient World." *ResQ* 13 (1970) 141-53.

Ferreira, Joel A. "Sociologa da comunidade de Tessalônica." *EstBíb* 25 (1990) 9-20.

Finegan, Jack. *The Archeology of the New Testament.* Princeton: Princeton University Press, 1992.

Finley, M. I. *The Ancient Economy.* Berkeley: University of California Press, 1973.

Finn, T. M. "The God-fearers Reconsidered." *CBQ* 47 (1985) 75-84.

Fisher, N. R. E. "Hybris and Dishonour." *GR* 23 (1976) 177-93.

Fishwick, Duncan. *The Imperial Cult in the Latin West.* Leiden: Brill, 1987.

Fitzmyer, Joseph A. "Some Notes on Aramaic Epistolography." *JBL* 93 (1974) 214-16.

Foakes Jackson, F. J., and Kirsopp Lake, eds. *The Acts of the Apostles.* 5 vols. Grand Rapids: Baker, 1979.

Forbes, Christopher. *Prophecy and Inspired Speech in Early Christianity and Its Hellenistic Environment.* Tübingen: J. C. B. Mohr (Paul Siebeck), 1995.

Fraikin, D. "Note on the Sanctuary of the Egyptian Gods in Thessalonica." *NA* 1 (1974) 1-6.

Frame, James Everett. *A Critical and Exegetical Commentary on the Epistles of St. Paul to the Thessalonians.* Edinburgh: T&T Clark, 1912.

Fredricksmeyer, E. A. "On the Background of the Ruler Cult." Pages 145-56 in *Ancient Macedonian Studies in Honor of Charles F. Edson.* Edited by Harry J. Dell. Thessaloniki: Institute for Balkan Studies, 1981.

Fuentes, David Cortés. "El mensaje apocalíptico de Pablo en Primera de Tesalonicenses como un medio de esperanza." *Apuntes* 13 (1993) 190-97.

Fulford, H. W. "Heōs ek mesou genētai, 2 Thes. 2:7." *ExpTim* 23 (1911-12) 40-41.

Furguson, W. D. *The Legal and Governmental Terms Common to the Macedonian Greek Inscriptions and the New Testament.* Chicago: University of Chicago Press, 1913.

Furnish, Victor Paul. "Fellow Workers in God's Service." *JBL* 80 (1961) 364-70.

———. *Theology and Ethics in Paul.* Nashville and New York: Abingdon Press, 1968.

Galánēs, 'Iōannēs. *H Prōtē Epistolē tou Ap. Paulou Pros Thessalonikeis.* Thessalonikē: Ekdoseis P. Pournara, 1985.

García, Miguel Salvador. *San Pablo: Tesalonicenses y grandes cartas.* Madrid: PPC, 1983.

García del Moral, Antonio. "'Nosotros los vivos' ¿Convicción personal de Pablo o reinterpretación de un salmo? (1 Tes 4,13–5,11)." *Comm* 20 (1987) 3-56.

⸻. "La realeza y el señorío de Cristo en Tesalonicenses." *EstBíb* 39 (1981) 63-82.

Gaventa, Beverly Roberts. *From Darkness to Light.* Philadelphia: Fortress Press, 1986.

Gelzer, Matthias. *The Roman Nobility.* Oxford: Blackwell, 1969.

Giblin, Charles H. "2 Thessalonians 2 Re-Read as Pseudepigraphal: A Revised Reaffirmation of *The Threat to Faith.*" Pages 459-69 in *The Thessalonian Correspondence.* Edited by Raymond F. Collins. Leuven: Leuven University Press, 1990.

⸻. *The Threat to Faith: An Exegetical and Theological Re-examination of 2 Thessalonians 2.* Rome: Pontifical Biblical Institute, 1967.

Gillespie, Thomas W. *The First Theologians: A Study in Early Christian Prophecy.* Grand Rapids: Eerdmans, 1994.

Gilliard, Frank D. "Paul and the Killings of the Prophets in 1 Thess. 2:15." *NovT* 36 (1994) 259-70.

Gillman, John. "Signals of Transformation in 1 Thessalonians 4:13-18." *CBQ* 47 (1985) 263-81.

Gilmore, D. D., ed. *Honor and Shame and the Unity of the Mediterranean.* Washington: American Anthropological Association, 1987.

Gold, Barbara K. *Literary Patronage in Greece and Rome.* Chapel Hill and London: University of North Carolina Press, 1987.

Gorrín Castellanos, Obed. *Primera a los Tesalonicenses — una lectura cubana.* La Habana: Consejo Ecuménico de Cuba, 1989.

Goulder, Michael D. "Silas in Thessalonica." *JSNT* 48 (1992) 87-106.

Gounaris, George. *The Walls of Thessaloniki.* Thessaloniki: Institute for Balkan Studies, 1982.

Gow, A. S. F., and D. L. Page. *The Greek Anthology: The Garland of Philip and Some Contemporary Epigrams.* 2 vols. Cambridge: Cambridge University Press, 1968.

Green, Gene [Eugenio] L. "'As for Prophecies, They Will Come to an End': 2 Peter, Paul and Plutarch on 'The Obsolescence of Oracles.'" *JSNT* 82 (2001) 107-22.

⸻. *1 y 2 Tesalonicenses.* Grand Rapids: Editorial Portavoz, 2001.

⸻. *1 Pedro y 2 Pedro.* Miami: Editorial Caribe, 1993.

Grudem, Wayne. *The Gift of Prophecy in 1 Corinthians.* Washington, D.C.: University Press of America, 1982.

———. *The Gift of Prophecy in the New Testament and Today.* Westchester, Ill.: Crossway Books, 1988.

Gruen, Erich S. *The Hellenistic World and the Coming of Rome.* Berkeley, Los Angeles, and London: University of California Press, 1984.

Gundry, Robert H. *The Church and the Tribulation: A Biblical Examination of Posttribulationalism.* Grand Rapids: Zondervan, 1973.

———. *Sōma in Biblical Theology.* Cambridge: Cambridge University Press, 1976.

Guthrie, Donald. *New Testament Introduction.* Downers Grove: InterVarsity Press, 1990.

Hafemann, Scott J. "'Self-Commendation' and Apostolic Legitimacy in 2 Corinthians: A Pauline Dialectic?" *NTS* 36 (1990) 66-68.

Hammond, N. G. L. *A History of Macedonia.* Vol. 1. Oxford: Clarendon Press, 1972.

———. *The Miracle That Was Macedonia.* London: Sidgwick and Jackson; New York: St. Martin's Press, 1991.

——— "The Via Egnatia in Western Macedonia." Pages 246-55 in *Ancient Macedonia IV.* Thessaloniki: Institute for Balkan Studies, 1986.

———. "The Western Part of the Via Egnatia." *JRS* 64 (1974) 185-94.

———, and G. T. Griffith. *A History of Macedonia.* Vol. 2. Oxford: Clarendon Press, 1979.

———, and M. B. Hatzopoulos. "The Via Egnatia I." *AJAH* 7 (1982 = 1985) 128-49.

———. "The Via Egnatia II." *AJAH* 8 (1983=1986) 48-53.

———, and F. W. Walbank. *A History of Macedonia.* Vol. 3. Oxford: Clarendon Press, 1988.

Hanson, Anthony Tyrrell. *The Wrath of the Lamb.* London: S.P.C.K., 1957.

Harrison, R. K. *Major Cities of the Biblical World.* Nashville, Camden, and New York: Thomas Nelson Publishers, 1985.

Hastings, James. *Dictionary of the Apostolic Church.* New York: Charles Scribner's Sons; Edinburgh: T&T Clark, 1919.

Hatzopoulos, Miltiadis. "Greek and International Scholarship on Ancient Macedonia: Some Recent Developments." Pages 109-15 in *Macedonian Hellenism.* Edited by A. M. Tamis. Melbourne: River Seine Press, 1990.

Helliesen, Jean M. "Andriscus and the Revolt of the Macedonians, 149-148 B.C." Pages 307-14 in *Ancient Macedonia IV.* Thessaloniki: Institute for Balkan Studies, 1986.

Helly, Bruno. "Politarques, Poliarques et Politophylaques." Pages 531-44 in *Ancient Macedonia II.* Thessaloniki: Institute for Balkan Studies, 1977.

Hemberg, Bengt. *Die Kabiren.* Uppsala: Almqvist & Wiksells, 1950.

Hengel, Martin. *The Pre-Christian Paul.* Philadelphia: Trinity Press International, 1991.

Hemer, Colin J. *The Book of Acts in the Setting of Hellenistic History.* Winona Lake, Ind.: Eisenbrauns, 1990.

————. "The Name of Paul," *TynBul* 36 (1985) 179-83.

————. "Observations on Pauline Chronology." Pages 3-18 in *Pauline Studies.* Edited by Donald A. Hagner and Murray J. Harris. Grand Rapids: Eerdmans, 1980.

Hendriksen, William. *Exposition of I and II Thessalonians and Exposition of the Pastoral Epistles.* Grand Rapids: Baker, 1979.

Hendrix, Holland Lee. "Beyond 'Imperial Cult' and 'Cults of Magistrates.'" Pages 301-8 in *Society of Biblical Literature Seminar Papers 1986.* Edited by Kent Harold Richards. Atlanta: Scholars Press, 1986.

————. "Thessalonica." Pages 523-27 in Vol. 6 of *Anchor Bible Dictionary.* 6 vols. Edited by David Noel Freedman. New York: Doubleday, 1992.

————. "Thessalonicans Honor Romans." Th.D. diss., Harvard University, 1984.

Herman, Gabriel. *Ritualized Friendship and the Greek City.* Cambridge: Cambridge University Press, 1987.

Hester, James D. "The Invention of 1 Thessalonians: A Proposal." Pages 251-79 in *Rhetoric, Scripture and Theology.* Edited by Stanley E. Porter and Thomas H. Olbricht. Sheffield: Sheffield Academic Press, 1996.

Hill, David. *New Testament Prophecy.* London: Marshall, Morgan & Scott, 1979.

Hock, Ronald F. *The Social Context of Paul's Ministry.* Philadelphia: Fortress Press, 1980.

————. "The Workshop as a Social Setting for Paul's Missionary Preaching." *CBQ* 41 (1979) 438-50.

Holland, Glenn H. *The Tradition That You Received from Us: 2 Thessalonians in the Pauline Tradition.* Tübingen: J. C. B. Mohr (Paul Siebeck), 1988.

Hollander, H. W., and M. De Jonge. *The Testaments of the Twelve Patriarchs.* Leiden: E. J. Brill, 1985.

Horbury, William. "1 Thessalonians ii.3 as Rebutting the Charge of False Prophecy." *JTS* 33 (1982) 492-508.

Horsley, Richard A. *Paul and Empire.* Harrisburg: Trinity Press International, 1997.

Hovey, Alvah. *Comentario expositivo sobre el Nuevo Testamento: I Corintios — 2 Tesalonicenses.* El Paso: Casa Bautista, 1973.

Howell Jr., Don N. "Confidence in the Spirit as the Governing Ethos of the Pauline Mission." *TTJ* 17 n.s. (1996) 203-21.

Hughes, Frank Witt. *Early Christian Rhetoric and 2 Thessalonians.* Sheffield: Sheffield Academic Press, 1989.

―――. "The Rhetoric of 1 Thessalonians." Pages 94-116 in *The Thessalonian Correspondence*. Edited by Raymond F. Collins. Leuven: Leuven University Press, 1990.

―――. "The Social World of 2 Thessalonians." *Listening* 31 (1996) 105-16.

Hunt, A. H., and C. C. Edgar. *Select Papyri*. 3 vols. London and Cambridge: Heinemann and Harvard University Press, 1959.

Isaac, Benjamin. *The Limits of the Empire*. Oxford: Clarendon Press, 1990.

Jensen, Joseph. "Does *Porneia* Mean Fornication? A Critique of Bruce Malina." *NovT* 20 (1978) 161-84.

Jeremias, Joachim. *Unknown Sayings of Jesus*. London: SPCK, 1958.

Jewett, Paul K. *Election and Predestination*. Grand Rapids: Eerdmans, 1985.

Jewett, Robert. "The Agitators and the Galatian Congregation." *NTS* 17 (1970-71) 198-212.

―――. *A Chronology of Paul's Life*. Philadelphia: Fortress Press, 1979.

―――. "The Form and Function of the Homiletic Benediction." *ATR* 51 (1969) 18-34.

―――. *Paul's Anthropological Terms*. Leiden: Brill, 1971.

―――. "Tenement Churches and Communal Meals in the Early Church: The Implications of a Form-Critical Analysis of 2 Thessalonians 3:10." *BR* 38 (1993) 23-43.

―――. *The Thessalonian Correspondence*. Philadelphia: Fortress Press, 1986.

Johanson, Bruce C. *To All the Brethren*. Stockholm: Almquist & Wiksell International, 1987.

Jones, A. H. M. *The Greek City*. Oxford: Oxford University Press, 1940.

Judge, E. A. "The Decrees of Caesar at Thessalonica." *RTR* 30 (1971) 1-7.

―――. "The Regional *kanon* for Requesitioned Transport." Pages 36-45 of Vol. 1 in *New Documents Illustrating Early Christianity*. 8 vols. Edited by G. H. R. Horsley. North Ryde, Australia: Macquarie University, 1981.

Jurgensen, Hubert. "Awaiting the Return of Christ: A Re-Examination of 1 Thessalonians 4.13–5.11 from a Pentecostal Perspective." 4 (1994) 81-113.

Kaye, Bruce N. "Eschatology and Ethics in 1 and 2 Thessalonians." *NovT* 17 (1975) 47-57.

Keener, Craig S. *The IVP Bible Background Commentary: New Testament*. Downers Grove: InterVarsity Press, 1993.

Kemmler, Dieter Werner. *Faith and Human Reason*. Leiden: E. J. Brill, 1975.

Kennedy, George A. *New Testament Interpretation through Rhetorical Criticism*. Chapel Hill and London: University of North Carolina Press, 1984.

Kinman, Brent. *Jesus' Entry into Jerusalem*. Leiden: E. J. Brill, 1995.

Kloppenborg, John S. "Philadelphia, Theodidaktos and the Dioscuri: Rhetorical Engagement in 1 Thessalonians 4.9-12." *NTS* 39 (1993) 265-89.

Knox, A. D. "*To mēdena sainesthai en tais thlipsesin tautais* (I Thess. iii 3)." *JTS* 25 (1924) 290-91.

Koester, Helmut. "I Thessalonians — Experiment in Christian Writing." Pages 33-44 in *Continuity and Discontinuity in Church History: Essays Presented to George Huntston Williams on the Occasion of His 65th Birthday.* Edited by F. F. Church and T. George. Leiden: E. J. Brill, 1979.

———. "From Paul's Eschatology to the Apocalyptic Schemata of 2 Thessalonians." Pages 441-58 in *The Thessalonian Correspondence.* Edited by Raymond F. Collins. Leuven: Leuven University Press, 1990.

———. *History, Culture, and Religion of the Hellenistic Age.* Vol. 1 of *Introduction to the New Testament.* Philadelphia: Fortress Press, 1982.

Kortē-Kontē, Stephē. *H Koroplastikē tēs Thessalonikēs.* Thessaloniki: Paratērētēs, 1994.

Koukouli-Chrysanthaki, Chaïdo. "Politarchs in a New Inscription from Amphipolis." Pages 229-41 in *Ancient Macedonian Studies in Honor of Charles F. Edson.* Edited by Harry J. Dell. Thessaloniki: Institute for Balkan Studies, 1981.

Ladd, George Eldon. *The Blessed Hope.* Grand Rapids: Eerdmans, 1956.

———. *New Testament Theology.* Revised by Donald A. Hagner. Grand Rapids: Eerdmans, 1993.

Larsen, J. A. O. "'Consilium' in Livy 45, 18, 6-7 and the Macedonian Syndria." *CP* 44 (1949) 73-90.

Lattimore, Richmond. *Themes in Greek and Latin Epitaphs.* Urbana: University of Illinois Press, 1942.

Leal, Juan. "Cartas a los Tesalonicenses." Pages 875-952 in Vol. 2 of *La Sagrada Escritura.* Edited by Profesores de la Compañía de Jesús. Madrid: Biblioteca de Autores Cristianos, 1962.

Levinskaya, Irina. *The Book of Acts in Its Diaspora Setting.* Vol. 5 of *The Book of Acts in Its First-Century Setting.* Edited by Bruce W. Winter. Grand Rapids: Eerdmans, 1996.

———. "The Inscription from Aphrodisias and the Problem of God-fearers." *TynBul* 41 (1990) 312-18.

Lightfoot, J. B. *Notes on Epistles of St Paul from Unpublished Commentaries.* London: Macmillan and Co., 1904.

Litfin, A. Duane. *St. Paul's Theology of Proclamation: 1 Corinthians 1–4 and Greco-Roman Rhetoric.* Cambridge: Cambridge University Press, 1994.

Loomis, Julia W. "Cicero and Thessalonica, Politics and Provinces." Pages 183-88 in *Ancient Macedonia II.* Thessaloniki: Institute for Balkan Studies, 1977.

Loubser, J. A. "Media Criticism and the Myth of Paul — The Creative Genius and His Forgotten Co-workers." Paper presented at the annual meeting of the SBL. Orlando, Fla., Nov. 22, 1998.

BIBLIOGRAPHY

Lüdemann, Gerd. *Paul: Apostle to the Gentiles.* Philadelphia: Fortress Press, 1984.

Lund, Nils W. *Chiasmus in the New Testament.* Peabody, Mass.: Hendrickson Publishers, 1970.

Lünemann, Gottlieb. *Critical and Exegetical Handbook to the Epistles of St. Paul to the Thessalonians.* Edinburgh: T&T Clark, 1880.

Lyons, George. "Modeling the Holiness Ethos: A Study Based on First Thessalonians." *WesTJ* 30 (1995) 187-211.

MacMullen, Ramsay. "Roman Attitudes to Greek Love." *Historia* 31 (1982) 484-502.

Makaronas, Charles I. "Via Egnatia and Thessalonike." Pages 380-88 in Vol. 1 of *Studies Presented to David Moore Robinson on His Seventieth Birthday.* Edited by G. E. Mylonas. St. Louis: Washington University Press, 1951.

Malherbe, Abraham J. *Ancient Epistolary Theorists.* Atlanta: Scholars Press, 1988.

―――. "Exhortation in First Thessalonians." *NovT* 25 (1983) 238-56.

―――. "'Gentle as a Nurse': The Cynic Background to 1 Thess ii." *NovT* 12 (1970) 203-17.

―――. *Moral Exhortation: A Greco-Roman Sourcebook.* Philadelphia: Westminster Press, 1986.

―――. *Paul and the Thessalonians.* Philadelphia: Fortress Press, 1987.

Malina, Bruce J. "Does *Porneia* Mean Fornication?" *NovT* 14 (1972) 10-17.

―――. *The New Testament World.* Louisville: Westminster/John Knox, 1993.

―――, and Jerome H. Neyrey. *Portraits of Paul.* Louisville: Westminster/John Knox Press, 1996.

Manson, T. W. *Ethics and the Gospel.* London: SCM Press, 1960.

―――. *Studies in the Gospels and Epistles.* Manchester: Manchester University Press, 1962.

Marín, Francisco. "2 Tes 2,3-12; Intentos de comprensión y nuevo planteamiento." *EstEcl* 54 (1979) 527-37.

―――. *Evangelio de la esperanza, Evangelio de la unidad; Cartas de san Pablo a los tesalonicenses y a los filipenses.* Madrid: Universidad Pontificia Comillas, 1979.

―――. "Pequeña apocalípsis de 2 Tes 2,3-12." *EstEcl* 51 (1976) 29-56.

Marshall, I. Howard. *1 and 2 Thessalonians.* Grand Rapids: Wm. B. Eerdmans Publishing Co., 1983.

―――. "Pauline Theology in the Thessalonian Correspondence." Pages 173-83 in *Paul and Paulinism.* Edited by M. D. Hooker and S. G. Wilson. London: SPCK, 1982.

Marshall, Peter. *Enmity in Corinth: Social Conventions in Paul's Relations with the Corinthians.* Tübingen: J. C. B. Mohr (Paul Siebeck), 1987.

McGehee, Michael. "A Rejoinder to Two Recent Studies Dealing with 1 Thess 4:4." *CBQ* 51 (1989) 82-89.

Mearns, C. L. "Early Eschatological Development in Paul: The Evidence of I and II Thessalonians." *NTS* 27 (1980-81) 137-57.

Meeks, Wayne A. *The First Urban Christians*. New Haven: Yale University Press, 1983.

———. *The Origins of Christian Morality*. New Haven and London: Yale University Press, 1993.

Menken, Maarten J. J. *2 Thessalonians*. London and New York: Routledge, 1994.

———. "Paradise Regained or Still Lost? Eschatology and Disorderly Behaviour in 2 Thessalonians." *NTS* 38 (1992) 271-89.

Mercati, G. "*Sainesthai.*" *ZNW* 8 (1907) 242.

Metzger, Bruce. *A Textual Commentary on the Greek New Testament*. Stuttgart and New York: Deutsche Biblegesellschaft and United Bible Societies, 1994.

Meyer, Marvin W., ed. *The Ancient Mysteries: A Sourcebook*. New York: HarperCollins, 1987.

Míguez, Nestor. "La composición social de la iglesia en Tesalónica." *RevBíb* 51 (1989) 65-89.

———. "La ética cristiana: una opción contrahegemónica." *CT* 10 (1989) 15-25.

———. "Lenguaje bíblico y lenguaje político." *RIBLA* 4 (1991) 65-81.

———. "No como los otros, que no tienen esperanza. Ideología y estrategia del cristianismo paulino en la gentilidad. Lectura socio-política de la Primera Carta de Pablo a los Tesalonicenses." Th.D. diss., Instituto Superior Evangélico de Estudios Teológicos, 1988.

———. "Pablo y la revolución cristiana en el primer siglo." *CT* 10 (1989) 67-80.

———. "Para no quedar sin esperanza — la apocalíptica de Pablo en 1 Ts como lenguaje de esperanza." *RIBLA* 7 (1990) 47-67.

Miller, K. *Itineraria Romana*. Rome: 'L'Erma' di Bretschneider, 1964.

Milligan, George. *St. Paul's Epistles to the Thessalonians*. London: Macmillan, 1908.

Mitchell, Margaret M. "New Testament Envoys in the Context of Greco-Roman Diplomatic and Epistolary Conventions: The Example of Timothy and Titus." *JBL* 111 (1992) 641-62.

———. *Paul and the Rhetoric of Reconciliation*. Louisville: Westminster/John Knox Press, 1991.

Moffatt, J. "2 Thessalonians iii.14, 15." *ExpTim* (1909-10) 328.

Molina Palma, Mario A. "La provisionalidad responsable: el tiempo cristiano en perspectiva escatológica." *EstBíb* 45 (1987) 337-46.

Moore, George Foote. *Judaism in the First Centuries of the Christian Era*. 3 vols. in 2. Peabody, Mass.: Hendrickson, 1997

Morris, Leon. *The Epistles of Paul to the Thessalonians*. Grand Rapids: Eerdmans, 1984.

———. *The First and Second Epistles to the Thessalonians*. Grand Rapids: Eerdmans, 1991.

———. *"kai hapax kai dis." NovT* 1 (1956) 205-8.

Mott, Stephen Charles. "The Power of Giving and Receiving: Reciprocity in Hellenistic Benevolence." Pages 60-72 in *Current Issues in Biblical and Patristic Interpretation*. Edited by Gerald F. Hawthorne. Grand Rapids: Eerdmans, 1975.

Moule, C. F. D. *An Idiom-Book of New Testament Greek*. Cambridge: Cambridge University Press, 1971.

Munck, Johannes. "I Thessalonians 1.9-10 and the Missionary Preaching of Paul." *NTS* 9 (1962-63) 95-110.

Murphy-O'Connor, Jerome. "Lots of God-Fearers? *Theosebeis* in the Aphrodisias Inscription." *RB* 99 (1992) 418-24.

———. *Paul the Letter-Writer*. Collegeville, Minn.: Liturgical Press, 1995.

———. *St. Paul's Corinth: Texts and Archaeology*. Collegeville, Minn.: Liturgical Press, 1983.

———. "Traveling Conditions in the First Century: On the Road and on the Sea with St. Paul." *BRev* 1 (1985) 38-47.

Neil, W. *The Epistles of Paul to the Thessalonians*. London: Hodder & Stoughton, 1950.

Neyrey, Jerome H., ed. *The Social World of Luke-Acts*. Peabody, Mass.: Hendrickson, 1991.

Nigdelis, P. M. "Synagoge(n) und Gemeinde del Juden in Thessaloniki: Fragen aufgrund einer neuen jüdischen Grabinscrift del Kaiserzeit." *ZPE* 102 (1994) 241-49.

Nilsson, Martin P. *The Dionysiac Mysteries of the Hellenistic Age*. Lund: C. W. K. Gleerup, 1957.

Nock, Arthur Darby. "Cremation and Burial in the Roman Empire." *HTR* 25 (1932) 321-59.

———. "A Cabiric Right." *AJA* 45 (1941) 577-81.

Núñez C., Emilio Antonio. *Constantes en esperanza: Primera carta a los Tesalonicenses*. Guatemala: TEMA, 1976.

Nygren, Anders. *Agape and Eros*. 2 vols. London: SPCK, 1938-39.

O'Brien, Peter Thomas. *Introductory Thanksgivings in the Letters of Paul*. Leiden: E. J. Brill, 1977.

O'Sullivan, Firmin. *The Egnatian Way*. Newton Abbot and Harrisburg: David and Charles and Stackpole Books, 1972.

Okeke, G. E. "1 Thessalonians 2.13-16: The Fate of the Unbelieving Jews." *NTS* 27 (1980) 127-36.

Oliver, James H. "Civic Constitution for Macedonian Communities." *CP* 58 (1963) 164-65.

Omanson, Roger L. "Comings and Goings in the Bible." *BT* 46 (1995) 112-19.

Orchard, J. Bernard. "Thessalonians and the Synoptic Gospels." *Bib* 19 (1938) 19-42.

Osiek, Carolyn, and David L. Balch. *Families in the New Testament World. Households and House Churches.* Louisville: Westminster/John Knox, 1997.

Otto, Walter F. *Dionysus: Myth and Cult.* Bloomington and London: Indiana University Press, 1965.

Overman, J. A. "The God-fearers: Some Neglected Features." *JSNT* 32 (1988) 17-26.

Palmer, D. W. "Thanksgiving, Self-Defense, and Exhortation in I Thessalonians 1–3." *Colloq* 14 (1981) 23-31.

Pandermalis, D. "Macedonia under the Romans: Monuments and Art in the Roman Period." Pages 208-21 in *Macedonia: 4000 Years of Greek History and Civilization.* Edited by M. B. Sakellariou. Athens: Ekdotike Athenon S.A., 1983.

Papazoglou, Fanoula. "Macedonia under the Romans: Political and Administrative Developments, Economy and Society, Intellectual Life." Pages 192-207 in *Macedonia: 4000 Years of Greek History and Civilization.* Edited by M. B. Sakellariou. Athens: Ekdotike Athenon S.A., 1983.

———. "Quelques aspects de l'histoire de la province de Macédoine." Pages 302-69 in Vol. 2.7.1 of *Aufstieg und Niedergang der römischen Welt: Geschichte und Kultur Roms im Spiegel der neueren Forschung.* Edited by Hildegard Temporini and Wolfgang Haase. Berlin and New York: Walter de Gruyter, 1979.

Pearson, Birger A. "1 Thessalonians 2:13-16: A Deutero-Pauline Interpolation." *HTR* 64 (1971) 79-94.

Peristiani, J. G., ed. *Honor and Shame: The Values of Mediterranean Society.* Chicago: University of Chicago Press, 1966.

Peterman, Gerald W. *Paul's Gift from Philippi: Conventions of Gift-Exchange and Christian Giving.* Cambridge and New York: Cambridge University Press, 1997.

———. "'Thankless Thanks': The Social-Epistolary Convention in Philippians 4.10-29." *TynBul* 42 (1991) 261-70.

Peterson, Erik. "Die Einholung des Kyrios." *ZTK* 1 (1930) 682-702.

Petsas, Ph. M. "MHTHR THEŌN AYOCHTHŌN: Unpublished Manumission Inscriptions from Macedonia." Pages 229-46 in *Ancient Macedonia III.* Thessaloniki: Institute for Balkan Studies, 1986.

Pfitzner, Victor C. *Paul and the Agon Motif.* Leiden: E. J. Brill, 1967.

Plassart, André. "L'inscription de Delphes mentionnant le proconsul Gallion." *REG* 80 (1967) 372-78.

Pleket, H. W. "An Aspect of the Emperor Cult: Imperial Mysteries." *HTR* 58 (1965) 331-47.

Plevnik, Joseph. "I Thess 5,1-11: Its Authenticity, Intention and Message." *Bib* 60 (1979) 71-90.

———. "The Taking Up of the Faithful and the Resurrection of the Dead in 1 Thessalonians 4:13-18." *CBQ* 46 (1984) 274-83.

Porter, Stanley E. *Idioms of the Greek New Testament.* Sheffield: JSOT Press, 1992.

———. *Verbal Aspect in the Greek of the New Testament, with Reference to Tense and Mood.* New York: Peter Lang, 1989.

Poythress, Vern S. "2 Thessalonians 1 Supports Amillennialism." *JETS* 37 (1994) 529-38.

Purvis, J. D. "The Palaeography of the Samaritan Inscriptions from Thessalonica." *BASOR* 221 (1976) 121-23.

Raditsa, Leo Ferrer. "Augustus' Legislation concerning Marriage, Procreation, Love Affairs and Adultery." Pages 278-339 in Vol. 2.13 of *Aufstieg und Niedergang der römischen Welt: Geschichte und Kultur Roms im Spiegel der neueren Forschung.* Edited by Hildegard Temporini and Wolfgang Haase. Berlin and New York: Walter de Gruyter, 1980.

Ramsay, W. M. "Roads and Travel (in the NT)." Pages 375-402 in Vol. 5 of *A Dictionary of the Bible.* 5 vols. Edited by James Hastings. Edinburgh: T&T Clark, 1904.

Rapske, Brian M. "Acts, Travel and Shipwreck." Pages 1-47 in *The Book of Acts in Its Graeco-Roman Setting.* Edited by David W. J. Gill and Conrad Gempf. Vol. 2 of *The Book of Acts in Its First Century Setting.* Edited by Bruce W. Winter. Grand Rapids: Eerdmans, 1994.

Reiter, Richard R., et al. *The Rapture: Pre-, Mid-, or Post-tribulational?* Grand Rapids: Zondervan, 1984.

Resch, Alfred. *Agrapha.* Darmstadt: Wissenschaftliche Buchgesellschaft, 1974.

Reynolds, Joyce, and Robert Tannenbaum. *Jews and God-fearers at Aphrodisias: Greek Inscriptions with Commentary.* Cambridge: Cambridge Philological Society, 1987.

Richard, Earl J. *First and Second Thessalonians.* Collegeville: The Liturgical Press, 1995.

Rich, John. "Patronage and Interstate Relations in the Roman Republic." Pages 117-35 in *Patronage in Ancient Society.* Edited by Andrew Wallace-Hadrill. London and New York: Routledge, 1989.

———, and Andrew Wallace-Hadrill, eds. *City and Country in the Ancient World.* New York and London: Routledge, 1991.

Richards, E. Randolph. *The Secretary in the Letters of Paul.* Tübingen: J. C. B. Mohr (Paul Siebeck), 1991.

Ridderbos, Herman. *Paul: An Outline of His Theology.* Grand Rapids: Eerdmans, 1975.

Rigaux, Béda. *Saint Paul: Les Épitres aux Thessaloniciens.* Paris: Gabalda, 1956.

Rivera, Luis Fernando. "Cristianismo existencial y expresión eucarística de la religión; 1 y 2 Tesalonicenses." *RevBíb* 41 (1979) 75-89.

————. "Estructuras de la I y II epístola a los tesalonicenses." *RevBíb* 38 (1976) 67-68.

Robert, L. "Les inscriptions de Thessalonique." *RevPhil* 48 (1974) 180-246.

Robinson, J. A. T. *Redating the New Testament.* London: SCM Press, 1976.

Rodríguez Carmona, Antonio. "El nacimiento de una comunidad cristiana entre paganos; El testimonio de 1 Tesalonicenses." *Proy* 25 (1978) 13-22.

Romiopolou, C. "Un noveau milliare de la Via Egnatia." *BCH* 98 (1974) 813-816.

Rousselle, Aline. *Porneia: On Desire and the Body in Antiquity.* Oxford: Blackwell, 1983.

Rowley, H. H. *The Biblical Doctrine of Election.* London: Lutterworth Press, 1950.

Russell, D. A. *Greek Declamation.* Cambridge: Cambridge University Press, 1983.

Russell, Ronald. "The Idle in 2 Thess. 3.6-12: An Eschatological or Social Problem." *NTS* 34 (1988) 105-19.

Ryle, Herbert Edward, and Montague Rhodes James. *Psalms of the Pharisees, Commonly Called The Psalms of Solomon.* Cambridge: Cambridge University Press, 1891.

Ryrie, Charles Caldwell. *First and Second Thessalonians.* Chicago: Moody Press, 1959.

Sakellariou, M. B., ed. *Macedonia: 4000 Years of Greek History and Civilization.* Athens: Ekdotike Athenon S.A., 1983.

Saller, Richard P. *Personal Patronage in the Early Empire.* Cambridge: Cambridge University Press, 1982.

Salvador García, Miguel. *San Pablo: Tesalonicenses y grandes cartas.* Madrid: PPC, 1983.

Sánchez, Benjamín Martín. *Primera carta de San Pablo a los Tesalonicenses.* Madrid: Ediciones Paulinas, 1960.

Sanders, Jack T. "The Transition from Opening Epistolary Thanksgiving to Body in the Letters of the Pauline Corpus." *JBL* 81 (1962) 348-62.

Sarikakis, Theodoros. "Cicero as an Historical Source for Macedonia." Pages 1395-1400 in *Ancient Macedonia V.* Thessaloniki: Institute for Balkan Studies, 1993

Sarikakis, Théodore Chr. "Des Soldats Macédoniens dans L'Armée Romaine." Pages 431-38 in *Ancient Macedonia II*. Thessaloniki: Institute for Balkan Studies, 1977.

Savage, Timothy B. *Power through Weakness*. Cambridge: Cambridge University Press, 1996.

Schaefer, Peter. *Judeophobia: Attitudes toward the Jews in the Ancient World*. Cambridge: Harvard University Press, 1997.

Scherrer, Stephen J. "Signs and Wonders in the Imperial Cult: A New Look at a Roman Religious Institution in the Light of Rev 13:13-15." *JBL* 103 (1984) 599-610.

Schlier, Heinrich. *El apóstol y su comunidad*. Madrid: Ediciones Fax, 1974.

Schippers, R. "The Pre-Synoptic Tradition in 1 Thessalonians II 13-16." *NovT* 8 (1966) 223-34.

Schlueter, Carol J. *Filling Up the Measure: Polemical Hyperbole in 1 Thessalonians 2.14-16*. Sheffield: JSOT Press, 1994.

Schmidt, Daryl D. "1 Thess 2:13-16: Linguistic Evidence for an Interpolation." *JBL* 102 (1983) 269-79.

Schmidt, Johann Ernst Christian. *Vermutungen über die beiden Briefe an die Thessalonicher*. Hadamar: Gelehrtenbuchhandlung, 1801.

Schmithals, Walter. *Paul and the Gnostics*. Nashville and New York: Abingdon Press, 1972.

Schnetz, Joseph, ed., *Itineraria Romana*. Lipsiae: Aedibus B. G. Teubneri, 1940.

Schrader, Karl. *Der Apostel Paulus*. 5 vols. Leipzig: Christian Ernst Kollmann, 1830-36.

Schubert, Paul. *The Form and Function of the Pauline Thanksgivings*. Berlin: Verlag von Alfred Töpelmann, 1939.

Schuler, Carl. "The Macedonian Politarchs." *CP* 55 (1960) 90-100.

Schürer, Emil. *The History of the Jewish People in the Age of Jesus Christ*. Revised and edited by Geza Vermes and Fergus Millar. 3 vols. Edinburgh: T&T Clark, 1973-87.

Scott, James M., ed. *Exile: Old Testament, Jewish and Christian Conceptions*. Leiden and New York: Brill, 1997.

———. "Paul's Use of Deuteronomic Tradition." *JBL* 112 (1993) 645-65.

Selwyn, E. G. *The First Epistle of St. Peter*. Grand Rapids: Baker Book House, 1947.

Sevenster, J. N. *The Roots of Pagan Anti-Semitism in the Ancient World*. Leiden: Brill, 1975.

Sherk, Robert K., ed. *The Roman Empire: Augustus to Hadrian*. Cambridge: Cambridge University Press, 1988.

Sherwin-White, A. N. *Roman Society and Roman Law in the New Testament*. Grand Rapids: Baker, 1963.

Sivignon, Michel. "The Geographical Setting of Macedonia." Pages 12-27 in

Macedonia: 4000 Years of Greek History and Civilization. Edited by M. B. Sakellariou. Athens: Ekdotike Athenon S.A., 1983.

Smith, Clay. *"Adialeiptos Proseuchesthe:* Is Paul Serious?" *Presb* 22 (1996) 113-20.

Spencer, Aída Besançon. *Paul's Literary Style: A Stylistic and Historical Comparison of 2 Corinthians 11:16–13:13; Romans 8:9-39, and Philippians 3:2–4:13.* Jackson, Miss.: Evangelical Theological Society, 1984.

Spicq, Ceslas. *Agape in the New Testament.* 3 vols. St. Louis: B. Herder Book Co., 1963.

————. *Theological Lexicon of the New Testament.* 3 vols. Peabody, Mass.: Hendrickson Publishers, 1994.

St John Parry, R. *"Sainesthai* I Thess. iii 3." *JTS* 25 (1924) 405.

Still, Todd D. *Conflict at Thessalonica: A Pauline Church and Its Neighbors.* Sheffield: Sheffield Academic Press, 1999.

Stott, John. *The Gospel and the End of Time: The Message of 1 and 2 Thessalonians.* Downers Grove, Ill.: InterVarsity Press, 1991.

Stowers, Stanley K. *Letter Writing in Greco-Roman Antiquity.* Philadelphia: Westminster Press, 1986.

Stroker, William D. *Extracanonical Sayings of Jesus.* Atlanta: Scholars Press, 1989.

Sumney, Jerry L. "Paul's 'Weakness': An Integral Part of His Conception of Apostleship." *JSNT* 52 (1993) 71-91.

Tamis, A. M., ed. *Macedonian Hellenism.* Melbourne: River Siene Press, 1990.

Tarazi, Paul Nadim. *1 Thessalonians.* Crestwood, N.Y.: St. Vladimir's Seminary Press, 1982.

Tasker, R. V. G. *The Biblical Doctrine of the Wrath of God.* London: Tyndale Press, 1951.

Tataki, Argyro, B. *Ancient Beroea Prosopography and Society.* Athens and Paris: Kentron Hellenikes kai Romaikes Archaiotetos, Ethnikon Hidryma Ereunon and Diffusion de Boccard, 1988.

Theissen, Gerd. *The Social Setting of Pauline Christianity.* Philadelphia: Fortress Press, 1982.

Thurston, Robert W. "The Relationship between the Thessalonian Epistles." *ExpTim* 85 (1973-74) 52-56.

Touratsoglou, Ioannis. *Die Münzstätte von Thessaloniki in der Römischen Kaiserzeit.* Berlin and New York: Walter de Gruyter, 1988.

Treggiari, Susan. *Roman Marriage.* Oxford: Clarendon Press, 1991.

Trevijano Etcheverría, Ramón. "La misión en Tesalónica (1 Tes 1,1–2,16)." *Salm* 32 (1985) 263-91.

Trilling, Wolfgang. *Untersuchungen zum zweiten Thessalonischerbrief.* Leipzig: St. Benno, 1972.

Trimaille, Michel. *La primera carta a los tesalonicenses.* Estella (Navarra): Verbo Divino, 1982.

Trudinger, Paul. "The Priority of 2 Thesssalonians Revisited: Some Fresh Evidence." *DRev* 113 (1995) 31-35.

Turner, Nigel. *Grammatical Insights into the New Testament.* Edinburgh: T&T Clark, 1965.

Ubieta, José Ángel. *La iglesia de Tesalónica; Una iglesia en proceso de evangelización.* Bilbao: Desclée de Brouwer, 1988.

Unger, Merrill F. "Historical Research and the Church at Thessalonica." *BSac* (1962) 38-44.

Vacalopoulos, Apostolos E. *A History of Thessaloniki.* Thessaloniki: Institute for Balkan Studies, 1993.

van Unnik, W. C. "Teaching of Good Works in 1 Peter." *NTS* 1 (1954-55) 94.

Vawter, Bruce. *Introducción a las cartas paulinas: Primera y Segunda a los Tesalonicenses.* Santander: Editorial "Sal Terrae," 1965.

Velenēs, Giōrgos, and Polyxenē Adam Velenē. *Arjaia Agora Thessalonikēs.* Thessaloniki: University Studio Press, 1997.

Veloso, Mario. "Contenido antropológico de 1 Tesalonicenses." *RevBíb* 41 (1979) 129-40.

Verhoef, Eduard. "Die Bedeutung des Artikels *ton* in 1 Thess 2.15." *BN* 80 (1995) 41-46.

Vickers, Michael. "Hellenistic Thessaloniki." *JHS* 92 (1972) 156-70.

———. "The Date of the Walls of Thessalonica." *İstanbul Arkeoloji Müzeleri Yilliği* 15-16 (1969) 313-18.

———. "The Stadium at Thessaloniki." *Byzantion* 12 (1971): 339-48.

———. "Therme and Thessaloniki." Pages 327-33 in *Ancient Macedonian Studies in Honor of Charles F. Edson.* Edited by Harry J. Dell. Thessaloniki: Institute for Balkan Studies, 1981.

———. "Towards Reconstruction of the Town Planning of Roman Thessaloniki." Pages 239-51 in *Ancient Macedonia I.* Thessaloniki: Institute for Balkan Studies, 1970.

Vokotopoulou, Julia. *Guide to the Archaeological Museum of Thessalonike.* Athens: Kapon Editions, 1996.

VonderLage, Bernard. *Thessaloniki.* Hamburg: Cram, De Gruyter & Co., 1953.

von Dobschütz, Ernst. *Die Thessalonicher-Briefe.* Göttingen: Vandenhoeck & Ruprecht, 1974.

Wainwright, Allan. "Where Did Silas Go? (And What Was His Connection with Galatians?)." *JSNT* 8 (1980) 66-70.

Walbank, F. W. "The Via Egnatia: Some Outstanding Problems." Pages 246-55 in *Ancient Macedonia IV.* Thessaloniki: Institute for Balkan Studies, 1986.

Wallace-Hadrill, Andrew, ed. *Patronage in Ancient Society.* London and New York: Routledge, 1989.

————. "Patronage in Roman Society: From Republic to Empire." Pages 63-87 in *Patronage in Ancient Society*. Edited by Andrew Wallace-Hadrill. London and New York: Routledge, 1989.

Walton, Steve. "What Has Aristotle to Do with Paul? Rhetorical Criticism and 1 Thessalonians." *TynBul* 46 (1995) 229-50.

Wanamaker, Charles. *Commentary on 1 and 2 Thessalonians*. Grand Rapids: Eerdmans Publishing, 1990.

————. "'Like a Father Treats His Own Children': Paul and the Conversion of the Thessalonians." *JTSA* 92 (1995) 46-55.

Ware, James. "The Thessalonians as a Missionary Congregation: 1 Thessalonians 1,5-8." *ZNW* 93 (1992) 126-31.

Weatherly, Jon Allen. "The Authenticity of 1 Thessalonians 2.13-16: Additional Evidence." *JSNT* 42 (1991) 79-89.

Weima, Jeffrey A. D. "An Apology for the Apologetic Function of 1 Thessalonians 2.1-12." *JSNT* 68 (1997) 73-99.

————. *Neglected Endings: The Significance of the Pauline Letter Closings*. Sheffield: JSOT Press, 1994.

Weiss, Johannes. *Earliest Christianity*. 2 vols. New York: Harper and Brothers, 1959.

West, J. C. "The Order of 1 and 2 Thessalonians." *JTS* 15 (1914) 66-74.

Wettstein, J. J. *Novum Testamentum Graecum cum lectionibus variantibus et commentario pleniore opera Jo. Jac. Wetstenii*. Amsterdam: Dommerian, 1752.

White, John Lee. *The Body of the Greek Letter*. Missoula, Mont.: Society of Biblical Literature, 1972.

White, John Lee. *Light from Ancient Letters*. Philadelphia: Fortress Press, 1986.

Wikenhauser, Alfred. *New Testament Introduction*. New York: Herder and Herder, 1958.

Wilcox, Max. "The God-Fearers in Acts — A Reconsideration." *JSNT* 13 (1981) 102-22.

Wiles, Gordon P. *Paul's Intercessory Prayers*. Cambridge: Cambridge University Press, 1974.

Winter, Bruce W. "The Entries and Ethics of Orators and Paul (1 Thessalonians 2:1-12)." *TynBul* 44 (1993) 55-74.

————. "In Public and in Private: Early Christians and Religious Pluralism." Pages 125-48 in *One God, One Lord*. Edited by Andrew D. Clark and Bruce W. Winter. Grand Rapids: Baker Book House, 1993.

————. "Is Paul among the Sophists?" *RTR* 53 (1994) 28-38.

————. "On Introducing Gods to Athens: An Alternative Reading of Acts 17:18-20." *TynBul* 47 (1996) 71-90.

————. *Philo and Paul among the Sophists: A First-Century Jewish and a Christian Response*. Cambridge: Cambridge University Press, 1997. Second edition, *Philo and Paul among the Sophists: Alexandrian and Corinthian Responses to a Julio-Claudian Movement*. Grand Rapids: Eerdmans, 2002.

————. *Seek the Welfare of the City*. Grand Rapids: Eerdmans, 1994.

Wistrand, Erik. *Felicitas Imperatoria*. Göteborg: Acta Universitatis Gothobergensis, 1987.

Witherington, Ben. *Women in the Earliest Churches*. Cambridge: Cambridge University Press, 1988.

Witherup, Ronald D. *Conversion in the New Testament*. Collegeville, Minn.: The Liturgical Press, 1994.

Witt, R. E. *Greece the Beloved*. Thessaloniki: Institute for Balkan Studies, 1965.

————. "The Egyptian Cults in Ancient Macedonia." Pages 324-33 in *Ancient Macedonia I*. Thessaloniki: Institute for Balkan Studies, 1970.

————. "Isis-Hellas." *PCPS* 192 (1966) 48-69.

————. *Isis in the Graeco-Roman World*. London: Thames and Hudson, 1971.

————. "The Kabeiroi in Ancient Macedonia." Pages 67-80 in *Ancient Macedonia II*. Thessaloniki: Institute for Balkan Studies, 1977.

Witton, J. "A Neglected Meaning for *Skeuos* in 1 Thessalonians 4.4." *NTS* 28 (1982) 142-43.

Woodward, A. M. "Inscriptions from Thessaly and Macedonia." *JHS* 33 (1913) 337-46.

Wrede, William. *Die Echtheit des zweiten Thessalonicherbrief untersucht*. Leipzig: Henrichs, 1903.

Yarbrough, O. Larry. *Not like the Gentiles: Marriage Rules in the Letters of Paul*. Atlanta: Scholars Press, 1985.

Zahn, Theodor. *Introduction to the New Testament*, 3 vols. Edinburgh: T&T Clark, 1909.

Introduction

I. RIVERS, ROADS, ROLLING MOUNTAINS, AND THE SEA: GEOGRAPHY AND TRAVEL THROUGH MACEDONIA AND THESSALONICA

After arriving at the port city of Alexandrian Troas on the western coast of the province of Asia, the apostle Paul saw a night vision. A "Macedonian man" was summoning him, saying, "Come over to Macedonia and help us" (Acts 16.9). While the narrative does not indicate how the man was dressed, we may well suppose that this Macedonian wore the traditional garb of the inhabitants of the region. Antipater of Thessalonica, an early first-century epigramist from the capital of the Roman province of Macedonia, spoke of the Macedonians' "broad-brimmed hat, from olden times the Macedonian's comfortable gear, shelter in snow-storm and helmet in war."[1] Who were the people who wore the hat with the "felt-nap"? Where did they live? What was their history? How did the gospel come to these Macedonians? Paul, along with his companions Silas (also known as Silvanus), Timothy, and Luke, crossed the Aegean to begin a significant new stage in the expansion of the gospel. This Macedonian mission must be understood in the setting of Macedonian history, culture, and geography.

"The history of a people is inseparable from the region it inhabits."[2] In order to appreciate the importance of the city of Thessalonica in the Roman Empire and its strategic role in the advance of the gospel we must take into account the geographic location of the city as our first order of business. Thessalonica is located on the eastern coast of Macedonia, the land situated between the Balkan mountain range and the Greek peninsula. Macedonia can also be defined as the region that is drained by two

1. A. S. F. Gow and D. L. Page, *The Greek Anthology: The Garland of Philip and Some Contemporary Epigrams* (2 vols.; Cambridge: Cambridge University Press, 1968), 1.37.
2. Michel Sivignon, "The Geographical Setting of Macedonia," in *Macedonia: 4000 Years of Greek History and Civilization* (ed. Michael B. Sakellariou; Athens: Ekdotike Athenon S.A., 1983), 12.

1

great rivers, the Axius and the Haliacmon.[3] The Roman province of Macedonia was not delimited by the same boundaries as the region of Macedonia, just as the province of Galatia did not exactly correspond to the dimensions of the region of Galatia. According to the Roman geographer Strabo, the province of Macedonia

> is bounded, first, on the west, by the coastline of the Adrias [Adriatic Sea]; secondly, on the east, by the meridian line which is parallel to this coastline and runs through the outlets of the Hebrus River and through the city of Cypsela; thirdly, on the north, by the imaginary straight line which runs through the Bertiscus Mountain [Balkan Mountains], the Scardus, the Orbelus, the Rhodope, and the Haemus; . . . and fourthly, on the south, by the Egnatian Road, which runs from the city of Dyrrhachium towards the east as far as Thessaloniceia. And thus the shape of Macedonia is very nearly that of a parallelogram.[4]

When Cassander, the king of Macedonia, founded the city of Thessalonica in 316 BC, joining together twenty-six villages into one city, he chose an ideal location at the head of the Thermaic Gulf where once stood the ancient town of Therme.[5] In the early fourth century BC when Philip II, the father of Alexander the Great, was the king of Macedonia, his ancient capital city of Pella enjoyed free access to the Aegean via the Loudias River. According to Strabo, the Loudias was "navigable inland to Pella."[6] But the city was surrounded by a swamp,[7] and the river was silting up. By the late fourth century King Cassander needed a port city that would serve all of Macedonia, and the location he chose enjoyed deep anchorage as well as protection from the dangerous southeast winds since it was located in the recesses of the gulf. The hills surrounding the city afforded the harbor additional shelter from the strong northerly winds that blew in from central Europe. The port city of Thessalonica gave the best access via the Mediterranean to the islands and the cities of the Aegean and beyond to the great ports in Syria, Palestine, and Egypt. Cicero mentions that while he resided in Thessalonica he was advised of a plot against his life and so made preparations to "cross over to Asia," using one of the ships that would carry cargo to

---

3. N. G. L. Hammond, *A History of Macedonia* (3 vols.; Oxford: Oxford University Press, 1972), 1.3.

4. Strabo 7, frag. 10.

5. Strabo 7, frags. 21, 24. See the discussion of the relationship between Therme and Thessaloniki on p. 10.

6. Strabo 7, frag. 20. See also Livy 44.46. The Loudias River opened up into a large lake, an area that is currently drained and dry.

7. Livy 44.46.6-7.

the east.[8] The construction of docks during the Roman period greatly accentuated the maritime advantage of the town.

The association of the city with the sea was reflected even in the religious life of the inhabitants. The Vardar Gate, through which passed the great Via Egnatia, held a relief of the gods known as the Dioscuri, the sons of Zeus who were worshiped as saviors from the dangers of the sea. These are mentioned in Acts 28.11 by the names Castor and Pollux, gods who were viewed as the protectors of the Alexandrian ship that sailed under their names. Frequently, ancient mythology associates the Dioscuri with the two deities known as the Cabiri, one of whom, the Cabirus, became the titular deity of the city of Thessalonica.[9] Philip of Thessalonica wrote an epigram that remembered a person named Lysistratus who "implored the spirits that rescue sailors, and they lulled the savage sea." "The spirits" are most likely the Cabiri.[10] Sea travel was dangerous, as Acts 27 and Paul's comment in 2 Corinthians 11.25-26 graphically illustrate: "Three times I was shipwrecked, I spent a night and a day in the open sea. . . . I have been in danger from rivers, . . . in danger at sea." Antipater of Thessalonica, who wrote epigrams in the early part of the first century AD, records the words of a father to his sons, "Approve not the grievous labour of the treacherous ocean or the heavy toil of perilous seafaring. As a mother is more delightful than a step-mother, by so much is the earth more desirable than the gray sea."[11] Another epigram warns, "Trust not the fatal sea, mariner, not even when at anchor."[12]

The location of Thessalonica also gave free access to the hinterland of the city and beyond to the interior of Macedonia, standing as it did at the intersection of the main east-west and north-south trade routes. This ease of access oriented the city more toward the interior of the country than the sea, contrary to the case of ancient Athens. Nicholas Hammond comments that Thessalonica "had a catchment-area of trade which extended westwards to the Adriatic Sea, northwards to the Danube basin, and eastwards into the interior of Thrace."[13] Thessalonica was located near the southern point of the natural route along the Axius River that ran from the Thermaic Gulf northward to the Danube River. Through the Danube basin ran the northern east-west military road of the empire, which stretched to Byzantium. Little is known from ancient sources of the

8. *Pro Cnaeo Plancio* 41.
9. See the discussion of the religious life of Thessalonica on p. 31.
10. Gow and Page, *The Greek Anthology*, 1.329; 2.356.
11. Ibid., 2.57.
12. Ibid., 2.21.
13. Hammond, *History of Macedonia*, 1.3.

north-south road that reached the Danube, but we do know that it ran through Stobi, where a Jewish colony was located. If a group of travelers from Thessalonica wanted to head south instead, they would follow the Via Egnatia westward to a point just east of the ancient capital Pella and would there turn south and pass through Berea (Acts 17.10), Aegae, Dium, and Larissa on the way to cities of the province of Achaia. Ancient itineraries lay out this route and an alternative between Berea and Dium that passed through Alorus.[14]

Although access to the western part of Macedonia from Thessalonica was made difficult by the north-south orientation of the mountains and valleys, the construction of the great military road,[15] the Via Egnatia, gave Thessalonica relatively easy all-weather access direct to the Adriatic.[16] Across this sea lay the southeastern terminus of the Via Appia, the city of Brundisium in Italy. From there it was a fast march up to the heart of the empire, the imperial city of Rome. The Via Egnatia was, in effect, an extension of the Via Appia and so gave Rome quick and easy access to her eastern provinces. This road was constructed between approximately 146 and 120 BC by the Roman proconsul of Macedonia, Cnaeus Egnatius,[17] in order to consolidate Rome's hold on Macedonia. The Via Egnatia began at the Adriatic costal city of Dyrrachium (also called Epidamnus) with a lesser-used southern spur that began at

14. Charles Edson, "Strepsa (Thucydides 1.61.4)," *CP* 50 (1955) 173-82. Strabo traces the route from Maleae up through Thessalonica and Stobi in *Geography* 8.8.5. On Roman itineraries in general see Firmin O'Sullivan, *The Egnatian Way* (Newton Abbot and Harrisburg: David & Charles and Stackpole Books, 1972), 243-46; O. Cuntz, *Itineraria Romana* (Leipzig: Teubner, 1929); K. Miller, *Itineraria Romana* (Rome: 'L 'Erma' di Bretschneider, 1964); Hammond, *History of Macedonia*, 1.19-204, especially p. 131.

15. Cicero calls it "our great military road which goes through Macedonia to the Hellespont." *De Provinciis Consularibus* 2.

16. On the Via Egnatia and other routes see pp. 6-7.

17. C. Romiopolou, "Un noveau milliare de la Via Egnatia," *BCH* 98 (1974) 813-16; P. Collart, "Les Milliares de la Via Egnatia," *BCH* 100 (1976) 395-415. A Roman mile marker found 10 km. outside Thessalonica contains an inscription in both Greek and Latin, with the Latin saying:

CC ↓ X
CN(AEUS).EGNATI(US).C.F(ILLIUS)
PRO.CO(N)S(UL)

The first line indicates that the distance between Dyrrachium and the mile marker was 260 Roman miles (the arrow denotes "50"). Such mile markers or *milaria* were placed every Roman mile (1,000 paces at 1.5 m. each). Strabo (7.7.4) and Polybius (*Histories* 34.12.8) say that the distance between Thessalonica and Apollonia on the Adriatic was 267 roman miles (190 km). The distance could be covered on foot in approximately two weeks at a pace of between 17 and 20 miles per day. Roman troops covered the distance in 15 days, while Cicero took 20.

Apollonia.[18] It passed through Edessa, Pella, and Thessalonica[19] and went from there in a northeasterly direction all the way up to Byzantium. An official messenger could traverse the route from Rome to Byzantium in twenty-one days using the Vias Appia and Egnatia, a trip that would take a normal traveler four to five weeks. The same journey would last two to three months by boat and would be much more dangerous, especially during winter.[20] The Via Egnatia was ten to twelve Roman feet wide but narrowed at times to only six feet. Near cities it widened out to a full twenty feet.[21] This highway was filled with pedestrians, horses, mules, and carts. When Cicero was exiled in Thessalonica, he delayed his departure from the town, complaining about difficulty traveling the Via Egnatia and other routes because of the great volume of traffic.[22]

Travel on the road was not always safe. In the mid-first century BC Cicero accused the Roman proconsul of Macedonia, one L. Calpurnius Piso Caesoninus (57-55 BC), of not maintaining the security of the road and of Thessalonica. He states that Macedonia "is now so harassed by the barbarians, who are not allowed to rest in peace in consequence of the avarice of the late consul, that the people of Thessalonica, placed in the lap as it were of our empire, are compelled to abandon their town and to fortify their citadel, that that military road of ours which reaches all through Macedonia as far as the Hellespont is not only infested by the incursions of the barbarians but is even studded with and divided among Thracian encampments."[23] Upon arrival in Macedonia some one hundred years later, Paul, Silas, Timothy, and Luke traveled this route from the port city of Neapolis to Philippi (Acts 16.11-12), and when they (minus Luke) left Philippi they traversed the road down through Amphipolis and

18. N. G. L. Hammond, "The Western Part of the Via Egnatia," *JRS* 64 (1974) 193; and Strabo 7.7.4.

19. Not through the center of the city like the modern street that bears its name. See Charles I. Makaronas, "The Via Egnatia and Thessalonike," in *Studies Presented to David Moore Robinson on His Seventieth Birthday* (2 vols.; ed. G. E. Mylonas; St. Louis: Washington University Press, 1951), 1.380-88.

20. O'Sullivan, *The Egnatian Way*, 196-200. Strabo 8.6.21 cites the well-known proverb, "But when you double Maleae, forget your home." Maleae was located on the southwest coast of the Peloponnese. However, most shipping along southern Greece navigated the Gulf of Corinth and portaged across the *diolkos* that traversed the narrow isthmus to the shores of the Saronic Gulf, thus avoiding the treacherous waters around Maleae.

21. O'Sullivan, *The Egnatian Way*, 29; Hammond, "Western Part of the Via Egnatia," 185-87.

22. *Ad Atticum* 3.14.

23. *De Provinciis Consularibus* 2.4; see also *In L. Calpurnium Pisonem* 40.

Apollonia on their way to Thessalonica (Acts 17.1). The apostles found themselves alongside Roman soldiers and officials, people involved in trade, Roman colonists, religious heralds, philosophers, pilgrims, and other travelers, all members of a society that had become extremely mobile. The great success of Thessalonica was due in grand part to the union of land and sea, road and port, which facilitated commerce between Macedonia and the entire Roman Empire. No other place in all Macedonia offered the strategic advantages of Thessalonica, a fact not lost on the Christian heralds.

While the land and sea routes gave the city a central place in the expansive empire, the prosperity of the city was also drawn from the tremendous natural resources that surrounded it. Thessalonica was situated on the edge of the great central plain of Macedonia, which boasted fertile soil and abundant rain and rivers. The climate was continental and not Mediterranean, with hot summers and cold winters suitable for growing grain and continental fruits but not crops such as olives and dates.[24] Grazing land was abundant, and fish filled the nearby rivers, lakes, and the Thermaic Gulf. The mountains around the city were forested, providing an abundant source of timber for the construction of houses and boats. The surrounding region was also rich with mines of gold, silver, copper, iron, and lead. Some of the measures the Romans used to break the economy of Macedonia after the conquest of 168 BC were to close the gold and silver mines, prohibit logging, and forbid cultivation of the royal estates.[25] Obviously, Roman rule was liberalized by the middle of the first century AD, but the action of the Romans at the start of their hegemony over Macedonia illustrates the greatness of the economic advantage of Thessalonica.

Thessalonica's location as the best Aegean port along the Via Egnatia gave the city its strategic importance for the empire. It is no surprise to hear Livy say that the city was flourishing in his days or to hear Strabo mention Thessalonica's fame, saying that it had become the greatest city in Macedonia.[26] This city was a hub in the empire that would become the center of the Christian mission in Macedonia. Paul and his company made straight for Thessalonica after the evangelization of Philippi on the second missionary journey. They came down the Via Egnatia (Acts 17.1) alongside other travelers who were engaged in governmental affairs, business, going to festivals and the games, or moving to spread

24. Hammond, *History of Macedonia*, 1.5.

25. Livy 45.18.3-5; N. G. L. Hammond and F. W. Walbank, *A History of Macedonia* (3 vols.; Oxford: Clarendon Press, 1988), 3.564.

26. Livy 45.30.4; Strabo, frag. 7.20-21. Lucian, *Lucius or The Ass* 46.5, also says that Thessalonica is "the largest city in Macedonia."

philosophical and religious ideas. After the turmoil that their visit in Thessalonica generated, they left the city by the same route, this time heading west. Before reaching the city of Pella, they turned south on the road to Berea (Acts 17.10), following the route indicated by the Roman itineraries. The Jews from Thessalonica followed the same route and, due to the uproar they provoked in Berea, Paul escaped to the sea, possibly heading for either Alorus or Dium. From the coast he boarded a ship for Athens (Acts 17.14-15). Later, during his third missionary journey, the apostle and his companions found themselves in Ephesus, a port city of the province of Asia, from which Paul sent Timothy and Erastus on ahead to Macedonia (Acts 19.22). They may have sailed directly from Ephesus to Thessalonica (an established trade route), or possibly they went north to Alexandrian Troas and from there took a boat across to Neapolis as the apostolic team had done during the second missionary journey (Acts 16.11-12). Soon afterward Paul himself set out for Macedonia, undoubtedly following the same route as his associates (Acts 20.1). The apostle went about visiting the churches of Macedonia and then traveled the route outlined in the itineraries down through Macedonia and Achaia (Acts 20.2). He was going to set sail from Achaia (the Corinthian port Cenchrea?) to Syria, but due to a plot against him he decided to return through Macedonia via the same route he traversed to get there. Paul's journey took him through Thessalonica and then northeast to Philippi by the Via Egnatia. He set sail from the port of Philippi, Neapolis, and arrived at Troas (20.5-6).

Not only the apostles but also a number of the new converts from Thessalonica were travelers. Aristarchus and Secundus from Thessalonica accompanied Paul on his journey to Syria and Jerusalem (Acts 20.4). Luke mentions that Aristarchus had been with Paul during his ministry in Ephesus (Acts 19.29). He also set sail with Paul from Caesarea when the apostle was sent bound as a prisoner to Rome to make his appeal to Nero (Acts 27.2). This brother became Paul's "fellow prisoner" in the imperial city (Col. 4.10; Phlm. 24). Jason, one of the first converts of Thessalonica and patron to the apostolic team in the city (Acts 17.6-9), was with Paul at Corinth during his three-month stay in that city (Acts 20.1-3). From there he wrote the Letter to the Romans, which mentions Jason (Rom. 16.21).[27] In 1 Thessalonians 1.8 the apostles praise the evangelistic efforts of the church by saying, "The Lord's message rang out from

27. The Orthodox Church celebrates the feast day of Jason April 29, that of Secundus on December 28, and that of Aristarchus on April 14 and September 27. According to tradition, Aristarchus became the first bishop of Thessalonica. See Apostolos E. Vacalopoulos, *A History of Thessaloniki* (Thessaloniki: Institute for Balkan Studies, 1993), 18.

you not only in Macedonia and Achaia — your faith in God has become known everywhere." Apparently in addition to Aristarchus, Secundus, and Jason, other members of the Thessalonian church participated in the evangelistic mission, using the roads and perhaps even the sea lanes to make sure that the gospel arrived at cities and towns both near and far. The apostles and other Christian travelers also brought the good news of the stability of the Thessalonian church in the midst of persecution to the ears of Christians throughout the provinces of Macedonia and Achaia (1 Thess. 1.7). Moreover, the Thessalonian believers used the routes to the interior of the province to bring aid, most likely financial, to the other churches of Macedonia (1 Thess. 4.9; cf. 2 Cor. 8.1-2). The picture Acts and the first letter to this congregation paint is one of a church that is mobile and expansive, deeply engaged in the mission of the church in its various aspects. This was the church of the metropolis of Macedonia.

II. A SUMMARY HISTORY OF MACEDONIA AND THESSALONICA

The character of a people is inextricably bound with its collective history. Any understanding of the Thessalonian reality at the time of the coming of the gospel of Christ must therefore begin with unearthing the roots of the Macedonians and laying open to view the history of the Thessalonian people. The Thessalonians were sons and daughters of the greatest empire ever known in human history, the Macedonian kingdom of Alexander III, known as "The Great." Before Alexander died, possibly by poisoning, on June 10, 323 BC, at the age of thirty-three, he had succeeded in extending the Macedonian kingdom as far south as Egypt and as far east as the Indus River in India. Alexander the Great was the son of Philip II, the king of Macedonia who had conquered the Greek city-states and had planned the invasion of the territories to the east occupied by the Persians. Before Philip could accomplish his goal, he was assassinated in 335 BC and Alexander inherited his kingdom. Having been educated at the feet of the Macedonian philosopher Aristotle and trained in the art of war on the battlefield from a young age, Alexander led the Macedonian troops in campaign after campaign through Asia Minor, Phoenicia, Palestine, Egypt, Babylonia, and India. Alexander had perfected a type of phalanx formation used by his father that employed a massive block of soldiers who each wielded a four-meter-long, iron-tipped pike called a *sarissa*. Alexander positioned his cavalry to protect the flanks and rear of the formation. Being convinced of his own divinity as the descendant of

Heracles, Perseus, and Zeus, he marched his troops forward to multiple victories and would have continued the expansion had death not vanquished him. In the wake of Alexander's conquests the ancient world became subject to a process of Hellenization (the Macedonians themselves were thoroughly Hellenized) that left profound and deep impressions on the political, religious, and social life of the ancient world.

Alexander was a figure who provoked a great deal of reflection among ancient authors, and he even figures in prophetic and apocryphal literature (Dan. 2.39; 7.6; 8.5-8, 21; 11.3; and possibly Zech. 9.1-8; 1 Macc. 1.1-7; 6.2). Pliny the Elder wrote in his *Naturalis Historia,* "After comes Macedonia, with 150 nations, and famous because of its two kings [Philip and Alexander] and their former world empire."[1] Pliny penned these words in AD 77, showing us that even during the era of Roman domination the Macedonians and others vividly remembered the heritage of Alexander. The *imitatio Alexandri* was a vision that caught more than one ruler's fancy, including not only his successors but also such notables in Roman history as Pompey and the emperor Trajan. Antipater of Thessalonica wrote epigrams during the first decades of the first century AD and left two that shine the glorious light of Alexander on the Roman proconsul of Macedonia, Lucias Calpunius Piso:

> A broad-brimmed hat, from olden times the Macedonian's comfortable gear, shelter in snow-storm and helmet in war, thirsting to drink your sweat, valiant Piso, I come, an Emathian to Italian brows. Take me in friendship; it may be that my felt-nap, which once routed the Persians, will beneath you subdue the Thracians too.[2]

The epigram expresses the idea that as Alexander conquered the Persians wearing the Macedonian hat, so now Piso, donning the same headgear, would subdue the Thracians, who lived north of Macedonia. In another epigram Piso is hailed as the one who metaphorically receives the sword Alexander the Great had held in his hand.

> Macedonia is the sword's iron, and from Alexander's hand it has learnt what makes for valour. And now, Piso, I have reached your hand that I yearn for, and these words I speak: "To my delight I have found the destined hand."[3]

---

1. 4.10.
2. Gow and Page, *A Greek Anthology,* 1.37. "Emathia" was an ancient name for Macedonia according to Strabo 7, frag. 11, and Pliny, *Naturalis Historia* 4.10.
3. Ibid.

Even in the coinage of Macedonia the memory of Alexander lived on well after his death. Following the first century AD, the federation of Macedonian cities, the *koinon,* issued coinage with the idealized image of Alexander with upturned look and flowing hair. For centuries after his death, Alexander was remembered and hailed, especially within Macedonia.

After Alexander's death there was no clear successor to his rule, and the bureaucratic structures were not in place to assure a smooth transition of power. His vast kingdom was divided among his four Macedonian generals, with Antipater receiving the former Macedonian kingdom and Greece. When Antipater died in 319 BC, Cassander managed to wrest the throne from his successor and to establish his connection with the royal family by marrying Thessaloniki, the daughter of Philip II and half sister of Alexander the Great.[4] In 316 BC Cassander founded a new city and named it in her honor — Thessalonica *(Thessalonikeia).* According to Strabo, Cassander joined together the inhabitants of twenty-six towns, and this new city became "the metropolis of what is now Macedonia."[5] The site chosen for the foundation of this new city was the town of Therme, located at the head of the Thermaic Gulf.[6]

The years following the reign of Cassander were turbulent, and Macedonia did not regain its internal stability until Philip V ascended to the throne in 221 BC. Macedonia prospered under his rule, but during this era his kingdom came into conflict with the rising power to the west — Rome. Philip entered into a pact with Hannibal of Carthage in 215 BC, but when Rome was advised of the accord between Macedonia and her archenemy, Rome regarded Macedonia as among her enemies. The First Macedonian War was fought between 214 and 205 BC and ended without significant gains on either side. Rome and Macedonia established a peace

4. Diodorus Siculus, *Historical Library* 19.52.1.

5. Strabo (7, frags. 21, 24) wrote approximately three centuries after this event, and there is some question as to whether these twenty-six towns were "rased to the ground," as he affirms. Vacalopoulos, *History of Thessaloniki,* 6, argues that Strabo's conclusion was based solely on his observation of the ruins around Thessalonica. The normal mode of establishing a new city was rather to abolish the councils and governing authorities of the towns and form a new council that included their leadership. The towns were not destroyed but instead fell into decay and desolation. See also Charles F. Edson, "Notes of the Thracian *phoros,*" *CP* 42 (1947) 102, n. 101; W. G. Cavanagh, "Surveys, Cities and Synoecism," in *City and Country in the Ancient World* (ed. John Rich and Andrew Wallace-Hadrill; New York and London: Routledge, 1991), 97-118.

6. See Michael Vickers, "Therme and Thessaloniki," in *Ancient Macedonian Studies in Honor of Charles F. Edson* (ed. Harry J. Dell; Thessaloniki: Institute for Balkan Studies, 1981), 327-33; Edson, "Notes on the Thracian *phoros,*" 100-104. Contra Hammond, *History of Macedonia,* 1.150-51. Therme may have been a former colony of Corinth. Therme is not to be confused with the modern village outside Thessaloniki that bears the name and that boasts of more than one excellent *taverna.*

accord that ended three brief years later with the beginning of the Second Macedonian War in 200 BC. The conflict culminated with the Roman victory at the Battle of Cynoscephalae. This battle was a resounding defeat for Macedonia and resulted not only in great loss of life but also in the subjection of Macedonia to heavy tribute and the dissolution of Macedonia's authority over Greece. The Roman propaganda machine painted Macedonia as the power that had enslaved the Greek world, and during the Isthmian Games held near Corinth in the summer of 196 BC the Roman Flamininus declared the liberation of the Greeks from Macedonian hegemony. The announcement was met with rousing enthusiasm by the Greeks. Plutarch recounts that when the crowd at the games were quieted so that they could hear the proclamation of the herald, "a shout of joy arose, so incredibly loud that it reached the sea. The whole audience rose to their feet, and no heed was paid to the contending athletes, but all were eager to spring forward and greet and hail the saviour and champion of Greece," that being Titus Flamininus, the proconsular general.[7] Yet the proclamation was hollow since the Romans had also destroyed various Greek communities and had seized a considerable amount of booty. The liberator Rome seemed to have been motivated more by avarice than anything else.[8]

The Third Macedonian War was the most decisive in determining the future of the Macedonian kingdom. The war began in 171 BC during the reign of King Perseus, who had succeeded Philip V in 179 BC. Perseus had renewed relationships with Greece and had entered into a pact with the Seleucids in Asia, events the Romans followed with considerable interest. The Roman senate denounced Perseus and in 172 published charges against him at Delphi, among which was the accusation that Perseus wanted war and was planning to enslave Greece once again under Macedonian rule.[9] In 171 the Romans decided to take action against Perseus and declared war against him. Up to this time Rome had enjoyed great success in conquering her other enemies, but Macedonia continued to present a real and near threat. As the Roman historian Livy tells it, "Only the kingdom of Macedonia remained, both near in situation, and such that, when in any way its good fortune began to fail the Roman people, it might seem able to inspire its kings with the spirit of their ancestors."[10] In a council held at Pella, King Perseus responded to the Roman initiative, declared war against the Romans, and gathered an army so

---

7. Plutarch, *Titus Flamininus* 10.3-5; 9.5.
8. Livy 42.32.6.
9. *SIG*³ 643.
10. 42.50.7.

great that Livy compared it to that of Alexander.[11] Though the Macedonians expected the favor of the gods and Perseus himself offered one hundred sacrifices to Minerva, the deity called the "Defender of the Folk," an eclipse of the moon presaged coming events. The Romans interpreted the wonder as a sign of the eclipse of a king. Commenting on the omen, the Roman Polybius stated, "This, while it lent fresh courage to the Romans, discouraged the Macedonians."[12]

Despite the Macedonian military victory over the Romans in 169,[13] the Romans wasted the Macedonians at the Battle of Pydna in 168 BC. The Macedonian phalanx, which since the time of Philip II and Alexander III had been used with such efficiency to defend and conquer, proved to be ineffective against the Romans led by Aemilius Paulus. The Roman troops managed to open a breach in the phalanx and entered between the four-meter-long pikes *(sarissa)* with swords drawn to shed Macedonian blood. Aemilius broke down the lateral protection of the phalanx by using elephants of war to spook the horses, a tactic the Romans learned from their rival Hannibal. The Macedonian cavalry retreated. The position of Perseus's troops was weakened further by the uneven terrain, which broke up the solid and unified formation of the phalanx. Paulus, a seasoned soldier, "often confessed afterwards to certain persons in Rome that he had never seen anything more terrible and dreadful than a Macedonian phalanx,"[14] yet this powerful and effective instrument of war disintegrated at Pydna. The Macedonians fled the battle, while the Romans pursued and attacked with great viciousness and cruelty. Between 20,000 and 25,000 Macedonians died at Pydna, and another 11,000 were taken captive. Few soldiers escaped of the estimated 35,000 who had been assembled by Perseus. The great city of Thessalonica bowed under the advance of the Roman army. Perseus himself fled the scene of the battle but was eventually captured in the sacred isle of Samothrace where he sought refuge. Polybius accuses Perseus of cowardice since he fled from the beginning of the battle under the pretense of sacrificing to Heracles, "a god who does not accept cowardly sacrifices from cowards, nor accomplish their unnatural prayers."[15] Thus the ancient monarchy and the glorious Macedonian kingdom came to its end. Macedonia became a protectorate of Rome.

The Roman soldiers raped Macedonia, gathering together an immense booty for Rome. So great was the take that Roman citizens were ex-

---

11. 42.51.1-11.
12. *Histories* 29.16.
13. The Greeks applauded this victory according to Polybius, *Histories* 27.9-10.
14. Ibid., 29.17.1.
15. Quoted in Plutarch, *Aemilius Paulus* 19.4-5.

empt from direct taxation for the next hundred years. In a glorious triumphal procession that lasted for days, the booty from Macedonia was displayed to the city of Rome. At the very end of the procession came Perseus in chains and Aemilius Paulus in his chariot.[16] The memory of this victory was etched indelibly in the minds of the Roman people. A centennial-edition denarius minted in 62 BC shows the triumphant Paulus with a victory trophy and the captive Perseus with his two sons. The Romans took 150,000 Macedonian slaves, exiled many of the governors and administrators of the vanquished kingdom, and broke the back of Macedonia's economic power so that the kingdom would never again become a threat to Rome. Roman historians tell the story of the Macedonian defeat over and again, a sure indication that this triumph was a deep well of imperial pride and a clear sign of Rome's universal dominion.[17] At the same time, the conquest of the Macedonians became an object lesson to other peoples concerning Rome's power, a lesson not lost on the Jews (1 Macc. 8.5). The Romans interpreted the defeat of Macedonia as divine judgment on the kingdom,[18] but at the same time Rome proclaimed herself the great liberator of the Macedonians. According to the current Roman perspective, liberty was incompatible with life under the rule of a king. Livy states, "First of all it was voted that the Macedonians and Illyrians should be given their independence, so that it should be clear to all nations that the forces of the Roman People brought not slavery to free peoples, but on the contrary, freedom to the enslaved."[19] The Roman senate gave Macedonia freedom that, according to the Roman propaganda machine, "was assured and lasting under the protection of the Roman People."[20]

But the liberty Rome proclaimed for Macedonia was merely an appearance and not real, as evidenced by the conditions for "liberty" that were instituted. Although Rome retired her troops from Macedonia and allowed the Macedonians to govern themselves by their own laws and elect their own magistrates, measures were instituted to assure the continued weakness of Macedonia. In addition to bringing an end to the monarchy, the Romans prohibited the Macedonians from extracting gold or silver from their mines and did not allow them to cultivate the great estates that had been the source of so much of the kingdom's wealth. Moreover, Rome divided Macedonia into four districts, each with its own legislature and magistrates, so that the Macedonian kingdom could not be reunified under a central government. Trade between the districts was

16. Diodorus Siculus 31.8.9-12.
17. Polybius, *Histories* 31.25.6-7; Pliny, *Naturalis Historia* 4.10.
18. Polybius, *Histories* 36.17.15
19. Livy, 45.18.1-2.
20. Ibid.

prohibited, and even marriage could not be contracted between people of different districts. The Macedonians could no longer cut their forests for shipbuilding. They were obliged to pay tribute to Rome, yet at only half the rate they had previously paid to support their own monarchy. Macedonia was stripped of her imperial powers as all peoples subject to her rule were granted their liberty. Livy commented that "their country seemed as mangled as an animal disjointed into parts." These measures along with others demonstrated that Macedonia was free only to submit to Rome.[21]

When Rome divided Macedonia into four districts (*merides*[22]), Amphipolis was established as the capital of the first district (Acts 17.1), Thessalonica of the second, Pella (the ancient capital of the kingdom) of the third, and Pelagonia of the fourth.[23] Livy dismisses the Macedonian concerns about the division of the kingdom as uninformed whining, stating that each district was sufficient for its own needs. The first district was the home of the Bisaltae, "men of great courage," and enjoyed fertile fields, rich mines, and the great, strategic city of Amphipolis. The second district had the "flourishing cities" of Thessalonica and Cassandrea, fertile lands to the southeast in Pellene, and excellent harbors for trade in the Aegean. The third district was the home of the famous cities of Edessa, Berea (Acts 17.10), and Pella, the "warlike race of the Vettii," and large populations of Gauls (who had aided Perseus) and Illyrians, both known as "industrious farmers." Livy notes that the fourth district was "as a whole cold, difficult to cultivate, and harsh," and it was the home of tribes whose temperament was like the land and who in warfare were made "fiercer by their barbarian neighbours."[24] While Livy argued that the division of the kingdom highlighted her assets, the reality was that the Roman occupation gravely impoverished and weakened the Macedonians.

The degraded existence the Romans imposed on the Macedonians transformed the once powerful kingdom into a region awaiting rebellion. In 149 BC one Andriscus, who bore a distinct resemblance to Perseus, the last king of Macedonia, proclaimed himself to be the son of Perseus and called himself by the great royal name of the father of Alexander III —

21. Ibid., 45.18, 29-30.
22. Acts 16.12; BAGD, p. 505. Although the restrictions on marriage and commerce between the districts had been abandoned by the first century AD, the identification of the districts continued on into the provincial era.
23. Livy 45.29.9; Diodorus Siculus 31.8.8-9; Strabo, *Geography* 7, frag. 47(48). Pelagonia was properly the region's name. Perhaps the city along the Via Egnatia called Heraclea Lyncestius is understood as the capital of the fourth district, or the district was governed by the Pelagonians (as Strabo seems to imply).
24. Livy 45.30.

Philip. Polybius sarcastically remarked, "Here is a Philip fallen from the skies who appears in Macedonia."[25] According to Dio Cassius, Andriscus managed to gather a band of revolutionaries to bring an end to the Roman hegemony over Macedonia. Surprisingly, Andriscus did not receive a complete welcome among the Macedonians at the start, but he did manage to garner sufficient support from surrounding states. With this power he invaded and occupied Macedonia and moved on to kill the Roman praetor Publius Juventius and almost annihilate his entire army. What support Andriscus did receive in Macedonia came from the lower classes, who were more inclined to long for the monarchy rather than those in power who had accommodated comfortably to the new Roman reality.[26] The support Andriscus received among the Macedonians amazed Polybius, who commented on his supporters, "But while they were defeated by the Romans in fighting for Demetrius and Perseus, yet now fighting for a hateful man and displaying great valour in defense of his throne, they worsted the Romans."[27] On the other side, Andriscus attacked the wealthy Macedonians who did not support his claims.[28] The Romans dispatched a more formidable force under the command of Quintus Caecilius Metellus and defeated the troops loyal to Andriscus.[29] Andriscus fled but managed to raise up another army; this army, however, was also defeated by Metellus.[30] Around the same time another "son of Perseus" named Alexander arose making royal claims and, in an attempt to rid Macedonia of the Romans, gathered troops in the region around the Nestus River. But he, too, was defeated by Metellus. These revolutionary movements, spurred on by the monarchal revivals, were justification enough for Rome to establish stronger controls over Macedonia. Rome decided to incorporate the former kingdom into the empire as a province. The provincial era of Macedonia began in 148 BC.[31] But the

25. Polybius 36.10.
26. Fanoula Papazoglou, "Political and Administrative Developments," in Macedonia: 4000 Years of Greek History and Civilization (ed. M. B. Sakellariou; Athens: Ekdotike Athenon, 1983), 193.
27. Polybius 36.17.14.
28. Polybius 36.17.13; Diodorus Siculus 32.9.
29. Dio Cassius 21.28; Diodorus Siculus 32.9, 15; Zonaras 9.28; Erich S. Gruen, The Hellenistic World and the Coming of Rome (Berkeley, Los Angeles, London: University of California Press, 1984), 431-33.
30. For the history of Andriscus, see Jean M. Helliesen, "Andriscus and the Revolt of the Macedonians, 149-148 B.C.," in Ancient Macedonia IV (Thessaloniki: Institute for Balkan Studies, 1986), 307-14.
31. Gruen questions the dating of the organization of Macedonia into a province and underscores the "Roman reluctance to undertake administration" of the region. While the beginning of the "Macedonian era" is marked in the sources by Metellus's de-

end of the kingdom did not completely extinguish the monarchal hopes of some Macedonians. After 148 BC one more rebellion arose under the leadership of a youth named Euphanes, who declared himself to be the "king of the Macedonians." Not a few followed after him, though it appears that many did so more in hopes of receiving the spoils of war than for any more noble concerns. He was subdued by the Romans without much ado.[32] Once more after this another claimant to the throne arose and gathered an army, only to be subdued by the Romans.[33] The dream of the monarchy was not easily shattered.

With the establishment of the province, Rome joined the kingdom of Macedonia with the southern part of Illyria, an act that extended the province as far west as the Adriatic Sea. This union between Macedonia and Illyria did not abolish the cultural differences between the two peoples any more than the Roman occupation of Macedonia erased the unique culture of the Macedonians. Illyria was considered to be a region within the province. When the apostle Paul declared to the Christians in Rome that "from Jerusalem all the way around to Illyricum, I have fully proclaimed the gospel of Christ" (Rom. 15.19), it is possible, if not likely, that he was speaking of the occidental sector of the Macedonian province where the Via Egnatia found its western terminus.[34] In order to govern this vast new province, in 146 BC Rome chose Thessalonica as the capital, giving the city a position of great honor and power. The location of Macedonia as the land link between Rome and her provinces to the east in Asia Minor and beyond gave the province and Thessalonica their strategic advantage in this new Roman order.

Somewhat surprisingly, during the first years of the new Roman era a decidedly pro-Roman attitude arose in strategic Macedonian cities such as Amphipolis and Thessalonica. In one inscription that comes from the new capital, the Thessalonians honor Quintus Caecilius Metellus, the very Roman praetor who had routed Andriscus, saying, "The city honors Quintus Caecilius, son of Quintus Metellus, praetor of the Romans, her savior and benefactor."[35] The Thessalonians viewed Metellus as their

---

feat of Andriscus (148 BC), this date does not mark the inauguration of the province. However, Gruen does not put forward an alternative dating for the *lex provinciae. The Hellenistic World and the Coming of Rome,* 433-36.

32. Diodorus Siculus 37.5.

33. Livy, *Periochae* 53; Gruen, *The Hellenistic World and the Coming of Rome,* 433.

34. Strabo 7.7.4. Illyricum was also the name of the province whose border was just to the north.

35. *IT,* n. 134. The reconstruction is Edson's. On the Romans as benefactors in Thessalonica see Holland Lee Hendrix, "Thessalonicans Honor Romans" (Th.D. dissertation, Harvard University, 1984).

savior from the insurrection of Andriscus, clear evidence that Thessalonica was one of the Macedonian cities that did not support but rather opposed the rebellion.[36] The city's sympathies were with Metellus, who served as proconsul from 147 to 146 BC, and this support possibly resulted in the exemption from paying tribute to Rome and the grant of free-city status to Thessalonica.[37] In 143 a citizen of Thessalonica honored the Roman proconsul with a statue dedicated to Zeus. The attached inscription proclaimed, "Damon, son of Nicanor, Macedonian from Thessalonica; for Quintus Caecilius son of Quintus Metellus, proconsul of the Romans, to Zeus Olympios on account of his *aretē* [virtue] and goodwill which he continues to manifest to myself and to the home city [Thessalonica] and the rest of the Macedonians and the other Greeks."[38] This honorific inscription highlights the fact that not all the Macedonians, especially those with means who lived in Thessalonica, viewed the Roman occupation as an unbearable yoke but rather enjoyed the fruits of Roman benefaction. The inscription makes mention of the "goodwill" *(eunoias)* of Metellus, which is not simply a description of his disposition but of some type of benevolence or benefaction that Metellus granted to Damon and other Macedonians.[39] The benefits Metellus brought extended beyond arresting the rebellion of Andriscus. Pro-Roman attitudes appear over and again in the inscriptions from Thessalonica, a city that appears to have been particularly favored by the Romans. But we should not assume that all those of the city were direct recipients of the Roman benefaction. The ones who appear to have prospered the most came from the higher social strata.[40]

During the following two centuries, Macedonia was integrated completely into the life of the Roman Empire. Toward the middle of the second century BC, the great Roman orator Cicero, who was exiled for almost half a year in Thessalonica, called the Macedonians allies of Rome and affirmed that the province was loyal in its friendship with the Roman people.[41] This strong loyalty, which had developed so quickly, was in part due to the conflicts with the barbarian tribes who lived in the northern part of Macedonia. The protection of the province was one of the chief responsibilities of the Roman governors.[42] In battle after battle, the

---

36. Green, *The Hellenistic World and the Coming of Rome*, 343-44.
37. Ibid., 344-52.
38. *IT*, n. 1031, translation of Hendrix, "Thessalonicans Honor Romans," 23.
39. LSJ, 723.
40. For a full discussion, see Hendrix, "Thessalonicans Honor Romans."
41. *In Pisonem* 34 (84); *Pro Fonteio* 20 (44).
42. *ANRW* 2.7.309-11; Papazoglou, "Political and Administrative Developments," 193; *SIG*[3], nn. 700, 710.

Roman soldiers managed to repel the barbarian incursions into the Macedonian territory. However, at times the Roman leadership was not equal to the task. Cicero complained bitterly against Piso, the Roman proconsul of Macedonia, accusing him of allowing the tribes to accost the Macedonians, especially the city of Thessalonica.[43] He had neglected a fundamental duty.

Macedonia and the city of Thessalonica played an important role during the civil wars in Rome. At the time of the wars between Julius Caesar and Pompey (49-48 BC) the capital of the Roman administration in Macedonia, Thessalonica, became something of a "second Rome" because some two hundred senators along with many knights joined with Pompey in the city. Their place of meeting was consecrated to give the proceedings in the city an air of legitimacy.[44] After the death of Caesar, once again Macedonia became the battleground of the principals who vied for the supreme power of Rome. Brutus and Cassius, who were responsible for the murder of Julius Caesar, received the support of Macedonia and Thessalonica at the outset. In fact, until the Battle of Philippi in 42 BC Brutus exercised sovereign power over the province. He minted gold staters that bore the image of Alexander. But for reasons not explained in the ancient sources, Thessalonica withdrew her support from Brutus, and, in turn, Brutus promised his troops the booty of the city if they won the victory over the rivals to Roman power, Mark Antony and Octavian (who later was to be named Augustus when he became emperor).[45] Brutus and Cassius were defeated at the Battle of Philippi on October 12, 42, Thessalonica was saved from sacking, and from that date forward until 31 BC Macedonia came under the jurisdiction of Antony. The city of Thessalonica showered honors upon the victors, with special honors to Antony, among which was the inauguration of a new era. "In year 'x' of Antony" became the new way to date events.[46]

The accord between Antony and Octavian was not long lived. The conflict between them escalated to a pinnacle at the Battle of Actium where, on September 2, 31 BC, Octavian defeated Antony. In response, Thessalonica gave Octavian the honors, and the city set about erasing the honorific inscriptions that had been erected previously to Antony.[47] Once again a new era was proclaimed, but this time with reference to Octavian and Actium.

Because of its support of Antony and then Octavian, Thessalonica

---

43. *In Pisonem* 34 (84).
44. Dio Cassius 41.18.4-6; 41.43.1-5.
45. Plutarch, *Brutus* 46.
46. Hendrix, "Thessalonicans Honor Romans," 31-37.
47. *IT*, nn. 83, 109.

was recognized as a free city *(Thessalonice liberae condicionis)*.[48] Free-city status normally brought with it exemption from taxation, which was itself an honor of the highest category,[49] along with the privilege of not having Roman troops stationed within the city walls. Moreover, a free city such as Thessalonica could govern itself according to traditional custom and was not obligated to submit to the Roman form of civic government. In the case of Thessalonica, this implied a democratic form of government in which the citizens *(dēmoi)* in assembly would have the highest authority. The daily administration of the city was handled by a council *(boulē)*, and the officials of the city were called "politarchs."[50] Judicial authority in Thessalonica was not in the hands of the Roman governor, as Acts 17.5-9 demonstrates (cf. Acts 18.12-13). Two other cities in the province, Amphipolis and Skotussa, enjoyed the status of *civitas libera*.[51]

In 27 BC Octavian, now the emperor Augustus, placed the province of Macedonia under the control of the Roman senate since it was entirely peaceful and posed no threat to the Roman order.[52] But in AD 15 it was turned into an imperial province, and the emperor Tiberius joined it with Achaia to the south and Moesia to the north, making the three into one extremely large province. Tiberius instituted this change at the petition of Macedonia and Achaia, who argued that the tribute they were paying as senatorial provinces was excessive.[53] In AD 44, during the reign of Claudius, this "super province" was broken up into its component parts once again, and Macedonia was placed back under the authority of the Roman senate.[54]

During the imperial era pro-Roman sentiments in Thessalonica were evident. Macedonia had been incorporated into the empire without the Macedonians losing their historic identity. As the inscriptions in Thessalonica from this era indicate, the natural language of Macedonia, Greek, continued to be used instead of Latin.[55] Even though the memory

48. Pliny, *Naturalis Historia* 4.10.

49. Josephus, *Vita* 429 (76), speaking of his own exemption from taxation, called this "the highest honor." We can suppose that a city would understand the privilege the same way.

50. See "The Government of Thessalonica," p. 20.

51. Pliny, *Naturalis Historia* 4.10; Papazoglou, "Political and Administrative Developments," 198.

52. Imperial provinces were problematic and usually located along the frontiers of the empire. These were under the direct control of the emperor and required one or more legions to maintain security. Senatorial provinces were under the control of the senate. These were peaceful and did not need such a strong military presence.

53. Tacitus, *Histories* 1.76.4; 1.180.1.

54. Dio Cassius 60.24.

55. A few inscriptions are bilingual.

of the monarchy lingered, there was no movement to throw off the Roman yoke. Roman names were included with Greek names among the lists of politarchs of the city and, as Papazoglou comments, "The paradox of this situation is illustrated by the case of a Thessalonian who simultaneously is described as 'Hellene and Philhellene', and bears the *tria nomina* of the Romans."[56] From the Roman perspective, Thessalonica was situated at the heart of Roman power, as Cicero had observed. Loyal to the Romans, the city enjoyed the benefits of the imperial government without the burden of its presence. This relationship was the product of a long historical evolution and left its mark on the political, economic, and religious life of Thessalonica. The situation of Thessalonica gave the city great prestige and presence in the province, so much so that Antipater of Thessalonica could celebrate the defeat of Thrace under the leadership of Lucias Calpurnius Piso, the proconsul of Macedonia, saying, "Thessalonica, the mother of all Macedonia, has sent me to you, the bearer of the spoils of Thrace."[57] As the metropolis of Macedonia, the city extended its power in every direction. On the political as well as the economic and commercial fronts, the city influenced the whole province. The implications of this position for the church in the city and its mission are deep and wide, as we will see presently.

III. THE GOVERNMENT OF THESSALONICA

In Acts 17.5-9 Luke tells his readers that shortly after the arrival of the gospel in Thessalonica the apostles and the newly formed Christian community were drawn into conflict with the governing authorities in the city. We are introduced to the "city officials" (*politarchoi* in vv. 6, 8) and the "assembly of the people" (*NIV* note; *dēmos* in v. 5), who were up in arms because of an accusation leveled against the apostolic team, Jason, and the Christian community. The chilling indictment was, "These men who have caused trouble all over the world have now come here, and Jason has welcomed them into his house. They are all defying Caesar's decrees, saying that there is another king, one called Jesus" (vv. 6b-7). Due to this serious charge, Jason and the others who had been taken were compelled to "post bond" and were subsequently released (v. 9). Paul and the apostolic team fled the city at night (v. 10). From the very beginning, the church in Thessalonica was embroiled in conflict with the government of the city.

56. Papazoglou, "Political and Administrative Developments," 202.
57. Gow and Page, *A Greek Anthology,* 1.13.

Strabo the geographer stated that the city of Thessalonica "is the metropolis (*mētropolis*, or "mother city") of what is now Macedonia," and so signified that it was the capital of the province. Although "metropolis" was not used in the inscriptions of the first century to describe the city, the ascription is found frequently from the second century onward when the city acquired the status of being a "colony" of Rome.[1] During the first century Thessalonica was a "free city," as is testified by both inscriptions and coinage.[2] As previously noted, free cities could govern themselves according to their ancestral custom and were exempt from tribute to Rome. Such communities could mint their own coins and educate their young according to established custom. They were not obliged to garrison Roman troops within their walls. "Such honors were conventionally granted only to people and cities which had displayed remarkable loyalty to the interests of the Roman people."[3] Thessalonica had aligned herself with the interests of Rome and had reaped the benefits. The autonomy and the financial freedom from Rome she enjoyed would have made the citizens and officials jealous to guard her status. The intimation that there was "another king" who challenged Caesar's authority went down hard in Thessalonica. The accusation echoes the Macedonians' longing for and the Romans' fear of a revived monarchy.

The civil administration encountered in the Acts narrative is reflected in the inscriptions of the city. In Acts 17.6 and 8, Jason and the others were dragged before the "city officials" or politarchs. This title appears in inscriptions from Thessalonica[4] and other cities of Macedonia but is unknown outside this region.[5] Normally the city had between five and six politarchs. According to Schuler, politarchs could be found in all four districts of Macedonia but not in the Roman colonies such as Philippi. The number of politarchs varied from city to city, though their number was not consistent throughout the history of any one city. Politarchs were recruited from the upper classes, and one person in the college of politarchs was given the responsibility of presiding. A poli-

1. *IT*, nn. 150, 162-65, 167, 177, and 178.

2. *IT*, n. 6. The name *THESSALONIKEŌN ELEUTHERIAS* appears on the coinage. See Hendrix, "Thessalonicans Honor Romans," 31, 155, 156, 399-464.

3. Ibid., 251.

4. *IT*, nn. 30, 128, 133, and 226. Karl P. Donfried, "The Cults of Thessalonica and the Thessalonian Correspondence," *NTS* 31 (1985) 342-43, comments, "One cannot help but be favourably impressed with the reliability of certain details in Acts when, for example, such a unique term as 'city authorities' *(tous politarchas)*, used in Acts only with regard to Thessalonian authorities (17.8), has been archaeologically verified."

5. A similar title is found in Thessaly just to the south of Macedonia. See Bruno Helly, "Politarques, Poliarques et Politophylaques," in *Ancient Macedonia II* (Thessaloniki: Institute for Balkan Studies, 1977), 531-44.

tarch's term of office was one year, but a person could serve in this capacity more than once. Politarchs could hold other offices at the same time (the inscriptions from Thessalonica refer to one politarch who served also as the municipal high priest and another who was also a high priest). The politarchs were the chief executive and administrative officials of the city, and as such they had the power to convoke the assembly of citizens (known in Thessalonica as the *dēmos*) and to put their seal on decrees and assure that they were executed. They held a certain authority to grant citizenship. Acts 17.5-9 gives clear evidence of their judicial powers.[6] Edwin Judge observes that in the Acts passage the politarchs and not the Roman proconsul were those who took action to assure that the peace was maintained. Although they were given great latitude in their governmental functions, "We must assume that in some respect the politarchs were obliged to take cognisance of offences against the 'decrees of Caesar.'"[7] Protecting Roman interests fell to their lot as well.

The inscriptions from Thessalonica attest to the presence of a council *(boulē)* and assembly of the citizens *(dēmos)*.[8] The council was not the same as the college of politarchs, but the politarchs convoked the council and presided over its meetings.[9] In a number of inscriptions the council and the assembly are mentioned together as joint authors of a proclamation. The more common title for a Greek assembly *(ekklēsia)* is not found in the extant inscriptions until around the year AD 230.[10] Although in most cities *ekklēsia* refers to the assembly proper and *dēmos* to the free citizens who make up that assembly, in Thessalonica *dēmos* refers to both the citizenry and their official assembly. When in Acts 17.5 Luke speaks of the assembly of the Thessalonians citizens he employs the term *dēmos* in accordance with local usage. Among the other governing officials in the city, the inscriptions speak of a treasurer of the

---

6. Carl Schuler, "The Macedonian Politarchs," *CP* 55 (1960) 90-100; and *NewDocs*, 2.34-35; James H. Oliver, "Civic Constitutions for Macedonian Communities," *CP* 58 (1963) 164-65. While the origin of the office is unknown, some speculate that it arose after the Roman conquest of 167 BC, though others argue for a date around the time when Macedonia became a province (148 BC). A third opinion is that the office was established before 167 BC, perhaps from the time of Perseus. An inscription in Amphipolis from this era bears the title. Chaïdo Koukouli-Chrysanthaki, "Politarchs in a New Inscription from Amphipolis," in *Ancient Macedonian Studies in Honor of Charles F. Edson* (Thessaloniki: Institute for Balkan Studies, 1981), 238.

7. E. A. Judge, "The Decrees of Caesar at Thessalonica," *RTR* 30 (1971) 5.

8. *IT*, nn. 5, 6, 7, 14, and 137. The council at times is known as the "most excellent council" *(kratistē boulē)*, a title that indicates the honor associated with this official body (cf. Acts 23.26; 24.3; 26.25).

9. Vacalopoulos, *History of Thessaloniki*, 13; *IT*, nn. 5, 7, and possibly 133.

10. *IT*, n. 1028.

city *(tamias tēs pleōs)*,[11] a magistrate of lesser rank who received taxes according to the laws and decrees, paid the financial obligations of the city, and maintained the accounts.[12] The gymnasiarch *(gymnasiarchos)*[13] was in charge of the gymnasium, the center for the physical training and intellectual development of the citizens of the city.[14] The ephebarch *(ephēbarchos)*[15] functioned as the leader and trainer of the *ephēboi*, the young men between fifteen and twenty-six years old.[16] The architect of the city,[17] the administrator of the market *(agoranomos)*[18] who regulated the buying and selling in the markets, and the president of the games *(agōnothetēs)*[19] all appear in the inscriptions as well. This last official handled the responsibility of contracting the musical artists and athletes, judging the games along with his assistants, and providing hospitality for the participants.[20]

Like any other city in the empire, Thessalonica was subject to the Roman emperor, who at the time of the foundation of this church was Claudius (AD 41-54). However, as we have already seen, during this period Macedonia was a senatorial province and therefore under the direct control of the Roman senate. Since Thessalonica was the capital of the province, it was the home of various Roman officials whose names and titles appear in both the inscriptions and coinage of the city. The proconsul *(anthypatos)*[21] of Macedonia did not intervene in the problems occasioned by the coming of the gospel to Thessalonica, despite the fact that he resided in the town. The politarchs took action (Acts 17.5-9), in stark contrast to the way the proconsul of Achaia, Gallio (AD 50-51), stood to judge the case of the Christians in the Roman colony of Corinth (Acts 18.12-17). We also have evidence of a treasurer of the Romans *(tamias Rōmaiōn)*,[22] an

---

11. *IT*, nn. 31, 50, and 133.

12. A. H. M. Jones, *The Greek City* (Oxford: Oxford University Press, 1940), 241.

13. *IT*, nn. 4, 133, and 201.

14. Jones, *Greek City*, 221-22; *OCD*, 659-70 notes, "As a centre of education it became a focus for the maintenance of Greek identity in the face of non-Greek settlement and Roman political control." We may assume the same function for this Macedonian institution.

15. *IT*, n. 133.

16. J. M. R. Cormack, "The Gymnasiarchal Law of Beroea," in *Ancient Macedonia II*, 143, 148; *OCD*, 527-28; Everett Ferguson, *Backgrounds of Early Christianity* (Grand Rapids: Eerdmans, 1993), 101-2.

17. *IT*, nn. 31, 128, and 133.

18. *IT*, nn. 7, 26; LSJ, 13. A post equivalent to that of the aedile in Roman cities.

19. *IT*, nn. 132, 226.

20. Jones, *Greek City*, 234.

21. *IT*, n. 31.

22. *IT*, nn. 29, 135. The title in Latin would have been *quaestor*.

official in the senatorial provinces who was responsible to supervise the financial affairs.[23]

Apart from the Roman administration and the governing officials of this free city stood a provincial council *(koinon makedonōn)* whose administrative center was Berea.[24] The members of this council were drawn from the various cities of the province and served as a channel of communication between the upper classes and the emperor that bypassed the provincial governor. In fact, the council could present complaints against the proconsul if he engaged in bad administration. The Macedonian *koinon* organized games in Berea at the time of the annual assembly (Thessalonica also celebrated games and sought to assure that theirs surpassed those in Berea), and these events served to focus the national sentiments of the Macedonians. The council had the authority to mint coins, minting some issues that celebrated the memory of Alexander III. On the Roman side, the *koinon* promoted the imperial cult, and the leader of the council also served as the high priest in the cult of Augustus.[25]

The political life of Thessalonica was characterized by the tension between the freedom the city enjoyed and the source of that liberty, their loyalty to Rome. Not only in civic honors but also in the civic cult, Rome received the adulation of the city for the benefits its citizenry received. As we have already observed, this loyalty became the axis around which the conflict with the Christians revolved according to the Acts narrative and became an even greater powder keg as Christians abandoned the civic cult and imperial honors in their loyalty to Christ.[26] Both imperial worship and the civic cult to the titular deity of the city were tied in intimately with the function of the government and loyalty to the same. As we can imagine, in this atmosphere where religion and government intertwined, abandonment of the cult could be understood as opposition to the existing political structures. Here is the flashpoint between the church and the community. The proclamation of "another king" by the name of Jesus would have aroused the deepest concerns among the Romans that the Macedonian monarchy was once again on the rise. The royal theology of the Christians clashed with the

---

23. Cicero, *Pro Cnaeo Plancio* 41, enjoyed the hospitality of the *quaestor* Plancius in his residence, the *quaestorium,* when he arrived in Thessalonica in the mid-first century BC.

24. Similarly, Acts 19.31 introduces the Asiarchs ("officials of the province"), who were members of the *koinon* of the province of Asia.

25. Papazoglou, "Political and Administrative Developments," 199; Ferguson, *Backgrounds of Early Christianity,* 43, Vacalopoulos, *History of Thessaloniki,* 13; Fanoula Papazoglou, "La Province de Macédoine," *ANRW* 2.7.1.351-69.

26. See the commentary on 2 Thessalonians 2.

imperial claims of Rome and the emperor while it resonated with the ancient aspirations of the Macedonian people.

IV. THE SOCIAL AND ECONOMIC WORLDS OF THESSALONICA

After the defeat at the hands of the Romans (168 BC), Macedonia entered a period of deep poverty. The Romans carried off the riches of the kingdom to Rome and instituted a series of economic measures that assured that Macedonia could not recover and once again become a threat to the Roman power, such as the division of Macedonia into four districts, the prohibition of commerce between the districts, and the closure of the mines. The economic force of the region did not recover even after Macedonia's incorporation as a Roman province. One official Thessalonian inscription, which comes from the last part of the second century or the first part of the first century BC, was executed with a crude and inexpert hand, leaving an enduring testimony of the economic plight of the early provincial years. The inscription "suggests a time when Thessalonica was impoverished and demoralized."[1]

In spite of the economic weakness of the province during the republican era, Macedonia managed to recover much of the prosperity it had enjoyed during the imperial epoch due to the new politic toward the province.[2] The city of Thessalonica was a key player in the economic recovery. The town's location at the head of the Thermaic Gulf and along the great Via Egnatia, its intimate relationship with the interior of Macedonia with its rich agricultural land, and the reopening of mines and forests as sources of raw materials all contributed to the creation of a new, robust economic climate, adding to the peace in the region. But the development is also attributed to the favorable policies Rome exercised toward the city, which had roots in the support Thessalonica had extended to Rome at critical moments in their intertwined histories. The laws of reciprocity assured that Rome would not, and indeed could not, forget. A community of Romans immigrated to the city to reside there, and testimony of their presence is recorded in multiple inscriptions and funeral reliefs.[3] Numerous members of this community facilitated the economic and commercial de-

---

1. Schuler, "The Macedonian Politarchs," 92.
2. Papazoglou, "Economy and Society," 199.
3. For example, *IT*, n. 38, which comes from the last part of the first century BC, makes mention of the Romans residing in the city.

velopment of this and other cities of the province. Many of those who emigrated to the city were from the upper strata of Roman society, people who had the economic power to own slaves.[4] The names of prominent Italians appear in the sarcophagi from this period.[5] Not a few of these immigrants went beyond taking advantage of the opportunities the city afforded and so became contributors to its development. A conspicuous number of inscriptions honor the "Roman benefactors" *(Rōmanoi euergetoi)*[6] alongside of *thea Rōma* (the goddess Rome) and refer to a priesthood that functioned in their honor. The Thessalonians offered these public honors to the group of Roman benefactors without specifying the exact nature of the service they had rendered to the community. However, since the inscriptions are official, we may conclude that the city recognized that the well-being of the community depended in part on the economic contributions these Romans made.[7] The inscriptions do, however, name certain individuals who were benefactors to the city along with their specific deeds.[8] The civic cult in honor of these Roman benefactors was a symbol of the great gratitude and the loyalty the Thessalonians felt toward the Romans because of these benefits. The imperial cult itself is a manifestation in grand scale of these honors given to the Romans since the emperor was the benefactor of the city par excellence.[9]

The relationship between Thessalonica and the Roman benefactors is a specific example of a wide-ranging social institution of the era, the system of patronage or *clientela*.[10] Roman society, with its vast social and economic differences, maintained its social equilibrium in part on the basis of this social institution. The relationship between a patron and his or her client had fundamentally three characteristics. In the first place, the patron/client relationship implied an interchange of goods and services.

---

4. Papazoglou, "Political and Administrative Developments," 196; "Economy and Society," 201.

5. Robert Jewett, *The Thessalonian Correspondence* (Philadelphia: Fortress Press, 1986), 121.

6. *IT*, nn. 4, 31, 128, 133, and 226.

7. On the nature of public benefaction see the literature in n. 10 and p. 41, n. 54.

8. *IT*, nn. 136 and 225.

9. See pp. 38-42.

10. See Richard P. Saller, *Personal Patronage under the Early Empire* (Cambridge: Cambridge University Press, 1982); Andrew Wallace-Hadrill, ed., *Patronage in Ancient Society* (London and New York: Routledge, 1989); Barbara K. Gold, *Literary Patronage in Greece and Rome* (Chapel Hill and London: University of North Carolina Press, 1987); S. N. Eisenstadt and L. Roniger, *Patrons, Clients and Friends* (Cambridge: Cambridge University Press, 1984); Gabriel Herman, *Ritualized Friendship and the Greek City* (Cambridge: Cambridge University Press, 1987); John K. Chow, *Patronage and Power: A Study of Social Networks in Corinth* (Sheffield: Sheffield Academic Press, 1992).

Secondly, the bond between a patron and client was personal and lasted for an indefinite period of time. Finally, the relationship was asymmetric in the sense that the patron and the client were not of equal social status and different types of goods and services were exchanged between them.[11]

The patron/client relationship functioned on almost every level of society and even became an essential component of the Roman bureaucracy. As Wallace-Hadrill comments, "Patronage was central to the structure of Roman society as feudalism was to medieval: it constituted the dominant social relationship between ruler and the ruled."[12] Under this system the emperor was understood as the principal patron in the empire. Far from being an administrator who distributed goods and privileges to all members of the society equally, the emperor granted access to his person and power through a network of patronage relationships. Impartiality did not characterize the system. The distribution of goods and privileges was made through those who had access to his person, and it was expected that he would be especially liberal in his treatment of family and friends along with others who were granted access.[13] The general expectation was that public officials, especially the emperor, would use their power in favor of those who where closest to them. Their role was more patronal than administrative.

Since cities like Thessalonica depended on the emperor and his benefaction, they established two means to secure his patronage. In the first place, the imperial cult in the city, with its temple and priesthood, was on the one side a form of thankfulness for past benefits received and on the other served as a means of soliciting future benefits for the client city. Secondly, the city depended on the good relationships with the Roman citizens resident there, who served as channels to the imperial power by means of the network of patron/client relationships. Even a city as grand and prosperous as Thessalonica needed its patrons in order to gain access to the emperor as well as the Roman senate.[14] In order to utilize this system, through honorific inscriptions Thessalonica publicly recognized the

11. Saller, *Personal Patronage under the Early Empire,* 1; Andrew Drummond, "Early Roman Clients," in *Patronage in Ancient Society* (ed. Wallace-Hadrill), 101.

12. Wallace-Hadrill, "Patronage in Roman Society: From Republic to Empire," in *Patronage in Ancient Society* (ed. Wallace-Hadrill), 68.

13. Saller, *Personal Patronage under the Early Empire,* p. 32.

14. "The Roman political system at all times avoided any sort of direct regional representation in government. Instead, access was mediated through individuals. It was this inaccessibility of the centre except through personal links that generated the power of patronage." Wallace-Hadrill, "Patronage in Roman Society: From Republic to Empire," in *Patronage in Ancient Society* (ed. Wallace-Hadrill), 74.

benefits the city received via the Roman elite. This elite not only gave direct benefits to the city but also served as channels of access to the central power of the government. Through this group of Roman benefactors the emperor could express his patronage. Dionysius of Halicarnassus, who wrote his *Roman Antiquities* during the reign of Augustus, explained the power of the elite in the Roman provinces during an earlier era, saying, "The patronage of the patricians was not restricted to the city and the common people, but each of Rome's colonies, the cities that became her friends and allies and those subjugated in war, had Romans of their own choosing as their protectors and patrons. Indeed, the senate often referred the disputes which came from these cities or peoples to their patrons and regarded their decisions as binding."[15] Though the patricians had diminished radically in number by the time of the empire, the role of the Roman elite in the provinces undoubtedly continued into this era.

The importance of these observations in relationship to the church in Thessalonica is evident as we consider how the apostles and fledgling church in the community were accused of being part of a seditious movement (Acts 17.6-7). The denunciation could produce grave consequences with respect to the favored position the city enjoyed before the imperial power. The apparent proclamation of a rival rule to that of the emperor would have been viewed not only as seditious but also as a grave violation of the delicate and privileged relationship of this client city with her patron the emperor. We can easily understand why the politarchs of the city were anxious to eliminate the problem as quickly as possible. These tensions are sufficient to explain why the church continued to suffer persecution after the apostolic team left the city. In addition, the imperial cult, which was a component of the system of patronage, appears to be a hermeneutical key to unlock the problematic passage of 2 Thessalonians 2.[16]

The patron/client relationship also helps illuminate the problem of work among certain members of the Thessalonian church, an issue Paul addressed in both letters to this community (1 Thess. 4.11-12; 2 Thess. 3.6-13).[17] A number of Thessalonian Christians maintained their client status, with both believers and the unconverted serving as patrons, and Paul strongly opposed the practice: "For even when we were with you, we gave you this rule: 'If a man will not work, he shall not eat'" (2 Thess. 3.10). We should not conclude, however, that those who enjoyed client status among the Thessalonian Christians came from the lowest strata of

---

15. *Antiquitates Romanae* 2.11.1.
16. See pp. 309-13.
17. See pp. 208-13, 341-56.

society. Traditionally clients were those who had been freed and could enhance the status of the patron.[18] Paul prescribed labor and not patronage as the means by which Christians were to support themselves (1 Thess. 4.11; 2 Thess. 3.7-12), yet he recognized that aid should be extended to those with genuine need and commended and encouraged the Thessalonians for so acting (1 Thess. 4.9-10; 2 Thess. 3.13). Such benefaction had deep roots within Christian teaching (e.g., Gal. 6.10; 1 Pet. 2.12; 1 John 3.17). While Paul opposed the institution and the entailments of *clientela*, he affirmed the church's responsibility to help those in need both within and outside its membership.

According to the evidence that has survived in the inscriptions, the Romans in Thessalonica belonged to the upper social strata. There were, of course, Macedonians who were of the same social status. Those who occupied administrative posts, such as politarchs and members of the council, came from the aristocracy, as also those who served as priests in the various cults celebrated in the city. Within the Thessalonian church we encounter a number of people who also came from the higher social classes. In the Acts narrative, Luke makes mention of many "prominent" or noble women who had converted at the hearing of the gospel (Acts 17.4), and Jason was sufficiently rich to offer hospitality to the apostolic team and prominent enough to be recognized by many persons (Acts 17.5-7, 9). He served as a benefactor within the Christian community. It has been suggested that Aristarchus of Thessalonica (Acts 19.29; 20.4) was the same person who appears in a list of politarchs from the city and as such would have been one of Thessalonica's most prominent and well-to-do citizens.[19] In addition, certain members of the congregation had sufficient means to serve as benefactors (1 Thess. 4.10; 2 Thess. 3.13).

The city of Thessalonica was also the home of many people of the working and artisan class. The epigrams of Philip of Thessalonica (first century AD) mention a large number of them as well as their trades. In

18. Bruce W. Winter, *Seek the Welfare of the City* (Grand Rapids and Carlisle: Eerdmans and Paternoster, 1994), 45; Peter Garnsey and Greek Woolf, "Patronage of the Rural Poor in the Roman World," in *Patronage in Ancient Society* (ed. Wallace-Hadrill), 153; Chow, *Patronage and Power*, 41-64. In his rather idealized description of the patron/client relationship, Dionysius of Halicarnassus makes mention of the reciprocal relationship between patron and client that included economic aid for the patron in times of necessity (*Antiquitates Romanae* 2.9-11). Whatever the reality of the situation was, his description of patronage presupposes that most clients did not come from the poorest classes. Although clients could be found among the poor, the system especially favored those who were of higher social levels.

19. Colin J. Hemer, *The Book of Acts in the Setting of Hellenistic History* (Tübingen: J. C. B. Mohr, 1989), 236.

them we meet the fisherman, the farmer, the carpenter, the cook, the scribe, the hunter, the weaver, the miller, the rhetor, and the temple servant.[20] Various of these people dedicated the tools of their trade to their patron deity at the end of their life, such as the oars and nets of the fisherman that were dedicated to Hermes and Poseidon and the sack, mallet, sickle, threshing implements, and plow that the plowman dedicated to Demeter.[21] These persons did not separate their religion from their labor. A large number, if not most, of the members of the Christian community in Thessalonica came from this class, among whom were many who had taken on the role of clients. Paul himself was an artisan and exhorted such people in the church "to work with your hands" (1 Thess. 4.11) and so follow his own example: "we worked night and day, laboring and toiling so that we would not be a burden to any of you" (2 Thess. 3.8; 1 Thess. 2.9). The economic situation of Thessalonica allowed these people to earn the bread they ate (2 Thess. 3.12). Whatever the economic situation of other cities in Macedonia and Achaia, Thessalonica offered the majority of the population both work and food.[22]

However, not everyone in the city managed to obtain the basics of life. Philip wrote an epigram describing the fortune of Aristides, a poor man, who "used to count up his great wealth, reckoning his one sheep as a flock, his cow as a herd. Then he lost both: a wolf killed the sheep, pangs of birth the cow; his poverty's consolation perished. He fastened a knot against his neck with his wallet-binding strap, and died in his misery beside the cabin where no cattle lowed."[23] Paul acknowledged that some within the Thessalonian and other Macedonian churches were in a precarious economic situation, and promoted and commended the church's response to their necessity (1 Thess. 4.10; 2 Thess. 3.13). But, commenting on the economic situation of the city, Jewett incorrectly concludes, "it appears that the converts derived from a stratum of the population suffering from a degree of relative deprivation."[24] Clearly there were those who needed the support of the community, but to say that the majority were in that position is an erroneous conclusion. The members of this church had the power to support themselves and, in fact, were even able to become benefactors to needy members among them and in other Christian communities in Macedonia (1 Thess. 4.9-10). The fundamental problem of the congregation was that certain people wanted to

---

20. Gow and Page, *Greek Anthology,* 1.269-351.

21. Ibid., 1.328.

22. Cf. Ronald F. Hock, *The Social Context of Paul's Ministry* (Philadelphia: Fortress Press, 1980), 34-37.

23. Gow and Page, *Greek Anthology,* 1.329.

24. Jewett, *Thessalonian Correspondence,* 121.

maintain a client status instead of working and not that they could not gain a living (1 Thess. 4.11-12).

In these letters, Paul does not mention the social classifications of slaves, freed persons, and the free, nor does he allude to the citizens and those noncitizens and foreigners among them (cf. Eph. 6.5-9; Col. 3.22–4.1). In a city like Thessalonica all these groups would have been represented, but there is no evidence from the letters themselves of how the social stratification and tensions affected the Christian community. The great social differences among the members of the church are given expression only in the problems that arise out of the patron/client relationship and the exhortations concerning benefaction. Repeatedly Paul praises the mutual love of the members of the community and encourages them to grow in the same (1 Thess. 1.3; 3.6, 12; 5.8, 13; 2 Thess. 1.3). The church expressed its desire to learn more about fraternal love (1 Thess. 4.9-10). Whatever social and economic differences existed among this congregation, the Thessalonian Christians had learned the fundamental lesson of Christian love among themselves. The church was a testimony to the miracle of community in diversity.

V. RELIGION IN THESSALONICA

When Paul, Silas, and Timothy arrived in Thessalonica to preach the gospel, they did not enter into a religious vacuum. The Thessalonians were worshipers of a plethora of deities. The gospel proclamation was an ardent call to abandon the worship of images, but at the same time the message answered the people's deepest religious desires and concerns. According to the narrative in Acts 17, the apostles entered the Jewish synagogue to begin the Thessalonian mission. Among this assembly of descendants of Abraham were some "God-fearing Greeks" and "prominent women," Macedonians who had integrated with the monotheistic Jewish community without becoming full proselytes to their way of life. Such people had some kind of affinity for Judaism, ranging from those who admired Jewish thought and life to those who abandoned the idol cult and adopted monotheism, stopping short of full conversion, which entailed circumcision.[1] These and the rest of the

---

1. See especially Irina Levinskaya, *The Book of Acts in Its Diaspora Setting* (Grand Rapids and Carlisle: Eerdmans and Paternoster, 1996), 78-79; and Kirsopp Lake, "Proselytes and God-Fearers," in *The Acts of the Apostles* (eds. F. J. Foakes-Jackson and Kirsopp Lake; Grand Rapids: Baker, 1979), 5.74-96; Max Wilcox, "The God-Fearers in Acts — A

Thessalonians who became Christians forsook their idols as part of their new allegiance to the living God: "You turned to God from idols to serve the living and true God" (1 Thess. 1.9). On the pagan side, the instruction concerning the "man of lawlessness" in 2 Thessalonians 2 alerts us to the religiously charged atmosphere in which the Thessalonians lived, where a human being could receive worship as if divine: "He will oppose and will exalt himself over everything that is called God or is worshiped, so that he sets himself up in God's temple, proclaiming himself to be God" (2 Thess. 2.4). Far from being indifferent about religious questions, the Thessalonians who listened to the gospel were submerged in a world that Paul elsewhere describes as filled with "so-called gods, whether in heaven or on earth" (1 Cor. 8.5). The gospel of the "living and true God" was proclaimed to these who floated in a sea of great religious pluralism and confusion. If we are going to understand the gospel's impact on the Thessalonians, a careful examination of their religious world is necessary.[2]

Any analysis of the religious environment of Thessalonica during the first century AD will necessarily be incomplete due to the limited number of sources that detail the cults and their activities. Although Charles Edson published an ample collection of inscriptions from the city,[3] the information gives little insight into the daily practices of the several religious centers. Moreover, archaeologists have not been able to excavate the city extensively since the ancient remains are buried beneath the modern city of Thessaloniki, the second largest metropolis in modern Greece. The end result is that we do not possess a balanced catalog of information concerning many aspects of daily life in the city, including the religious milieu with its multiple gods and temples. The majority of the inscriptions that have been preserved surfaced as chance finds or came from rescue excavations. Although a number of primary texts that de-

Reconsideration," *JSNT* 13 (1981) 102-22; T. M. Finn, "The God-fearers Reconsidered," *CBQ* 47 (1985) 75-84; Joyce Reynolds and Robert Tannenbaum, *Jews and God-fearers at Aphrodisias: Greek Inscriptions with Commentary* (Cambridge: Cambridge Philological Society, 1987); J. A. Overman, "The God-fearers: Some Neglected Features," *JSNT* 32 (1988) 17-26; Irina Levinskaya, "The Inscription from Aphrodisias and the Problem of God-fearers," *TynBul* 41 (1990) 312-18; Jerome Murphy-O'Connor, "Lots of God-Fearers? *Theosebeis* in the Aphrodisias Inscription," *RB* 99 (1992) 418-24.

2. Donfried, "The Cults of Thessalonica and the Thessalonian Correspondence," 336, presents the fundamental concern: "The basic question we propose to ask is simply this: what was Thessalonica like when Paul first visited and established a Christian community there and what impact does this information have for understanding 1 and 2 Thessalonians?"

3. *IT*. The Archaeological Museum of Thessalonica is planning to publish a supplement to this collection.

scribe the dynamics of many cults in antiquity have been passed down to us, little information has survived concerning how these cults functioned in Thessalonica itself. A delightful exception to this rule was the excavation of the Serapeum, which yielded a rather full picture of the role of the Egyptian gods in the city. Despite the generally scanty and eclectic nature of the evidence for other cults, some sound observations can be made based on the historical data that have fortunately survived. Epigramists such as Philip and Antipater of Thessalonica preserve for us hints of the beliefs and the religious longings of the Thessalonians during the first century when they wrote. The inscriptions that have come to light, the coinage, and the excavations that have been undertaken give us hints about aspects of the history that can be joined together to help us pry open the historical window at least partially.

The ancient sources testify clearly that Athens was not the only city "full of idols" (Acts 17.16). Thessalonica was host to multiple deities who were objects of genuine religious devotion. In his extant epigrams, Philip of Thessalonica, for example, makes mention of more than twenty deities who played more than a formal role in people's lives. He recorded a supplication to Artemis for the emperor that asked for his recovery, "Artemis . . . dispatch this very day that hateful sickness away from the best of Emperors. . . . For Philip will offer the smoke of frankincense above your altars, and will make splendid sacrifice of a mountain-roaming boar."[4] In another prayer a sailor offers a barley cake and a libation to Apollo with the petition, "Be gracious in return, and send upon the sails a favourable breeze running with us to the harbours of Actium."[5] Antipater of Thessalonica composed an epigram for a statue of Aphrodite that expressed the simple desire of a woman, "Bithynian Cythera dedicated me, the marble image of your form, Cyprian goddess [Aphrodite], according to her vow. Do you make a large gift in return for a small one, as your custom is; a husband's loving heart is all she asks."[6] Another woman, both sterile and blind, wanted to give birth and to have her sight restored and, according to an epigram, received both: "Both prayers were heard by Artemis, midwife in child-bearing and light-bringer of white-gleaming rays."[7] The relationship with the gods was viewed as a transaction: "Do this for me, and I'll do that for you." One inscription mentions a votive offering to "the great gods" in anticipation of some benefit to be re-

---

4. The emperor in this case was Augustus or possibly Gaius (Caligula), who suffered from a grave illness at the beginning of his reign (October/November, AD 37). Gow and Page, *Greek Anthology*, 2.331; 1.299.

5. Ibid., 1.303.

6. Ibid., 1.19.

7. Ibid., 1.79.

ceived.[8] In a prayer to Isis, the suppliant asks for salvation from poverty and, in exchange, "he will sacrifice a kid with golden horns."[9] The Thessalonians dedicated offerings and prayed to their deities, and they expected something in return.

Alongside these petitions a number of religious inscriptions preserve the thanksgivings of devout people. According to one worshiper, the highest god (Zeus), who was also called "the great savior," had saved him from disaster at sea in response to his prayer. He therefore dedicated a public inscription to the god as a way to offer thanks.[10] Without specifying the reason, another devotee presented his thanks to the Egyptian gods — Serapis, Isis, and Anubis — and to "the gods of the same temple."[11] Although we do not doubt the sincerity of those who erected such public monuments in thanksgiving to the deities, the function of inscriptions dedicated to benefactors, be they human or divine, was not simply to recognize their beneficence but also to solicit future benefits.

The Thessalonians did not always perceive the gods as benevolent. They could bring both benefits and tragedy to a person's life. An epigram from Antipater records the tragic history of Cyllenē, an athlete who was on his way home from the Olympic games when ill fortune befell him: "He was travelling at night-time from Pisa when lightning fell from Zeus and killed him."[12] Hermocrateia, a woman who gave birth to twenty-nine children, was fortunate enough to have them all survive. She knows, however, the dark power of the gods and says, "Neither Apollo shot my sons down, nor Artemis bereaved me of my daughters to my sorrow. Rather the one came and eased my travail, while Phoebus brought my boys to young manhood unharmed by sickness."[13] Her relief betrays her belief that the gods were capable of doing her ill as well as good. Over the tomb of Polyxenus, who had slipped and died because of his fall, someone placed the following epigram: "I know not whether to blame the wine-god [Dionysus] or the rain from Zeus; both are slippery for the feet."[14] One never knew what to expect from the gods. They could bring both blessing and disaster to a person, as in the case of a woman who

---

8. *IT*, n. 51. Greek *euchēn.* So n. 80 dedicated to Serapis, Isis, Anubis, and the gods of the same temple (Gk. *synnaois*).

9. Gow and Page, *Greek Anthology,* 1.312.

10. *IT*, n. 67.

11. *IT*, n. 78. So the thanksgivings in nn. 81 (to Isis and Harpocrates), 85 (to Serapis, Isis, Harpocrates, and the gods "of the same temple and the same altar"), and 87 (to Eros, Isis, Serapis, and Harpocrates).

12. Gow and Page, *Greek Anthology,* 1.50.

13. Ibid., 1.52.

14. Ibid.

died while giving birth to triplets, "One and the same god [*daimōn*] took life from her and gave life to them."[15]

In antiquity, ethics was the domain of the philosophers and not of the gods. Normally religion did not have anything to do with the morality of the worshipers. In fact, a number of cults promoted a lifestyle that would have been viewed as immoral from a Christian perspective. Dionysus, the god of wine and drunkenness, is depicted in reliefs, statues, and mosaics with a vine and grapes laced through his hair and a down-turned empty cup in his hand, a symbol of drunkenness. In an epigram from Antipater a person is chastised for being sober, having drunk only water: "I had drunk my fill of undiluted water, when Bacchus stood beside my bed, yesterday, and spoke thus: 'You sleep the sleep of those whom Aphrodite hates; tell me, my sober friend, have you heard of Hippolytus? You should be afraid of suffering a fate like his.' Thus he spoke, and went away; and since then water is no longer any pleasure to me."[16] The god promoted drinking wine and encouraged this solitary sober man to seek the sexual pleasures Aphrodite brings. Aphrodite was herself the symbol of sexual license and the patroness of the prostitutes. Philip commemorates a boat whose construction costs were underwritten by the proceeds from a bordello: "I, a ship built from the Cyprian's trade, have come to the sea that gave that goddess [Aphrodite] birth. A trafficker in beauty wrought me and called me 'Courtesan', for I am all men's friend. Board me cheerfully, I ask no heavy fee. I welcome all comers; I carry the foreigner [and citizens alike]. As once on land, so row me on the deep."[17] Aphrodite was among the most popular deities in Thessalonica, as witnessed by the preponderance of small, household cult images of her that have been found among the clay figurines excavated principally from the cemeteries of the ancient city.[18]

Among various religions of Thessalonica the phallus was a cult object. For example, the image of Priapus was an enlarged phallus with a small, grotesque body attached.[19] According to mythology, the Egyptian

15. Ibid., 1.77.

16. Ibid., 1.35. Wine and water were normally mixed. The dilution at times was one part wine to twenty parts water, though the more common mix was three of water to one of wine or five of water to two parts wine. The moralists of the day recognized the danger of one-to-one mixing, although drinking unmixed wine was well attested. See Everett Ferguson, "Wine as a Table-Drink in the Ancient World," *ResQ* 13 (1970) 141-53.

17. Gow and Page, *Greek Anthology,* 1.333. Clement of Alexandria condemned Aphrodite as the "lover of the virilia" and said that a lump of salt and a phallus were given to the initiates. *Exhortation to the Heathen,* ch. 2.

18. Stephē Kortē-Kontē, *H Koroplastikē tēs Thessalonikēs* (Thessaloniki: Paratērētēs, 1994).

19. Ibid., 1.308.

god Osiris was dismembered, and Isis formed a phallus for him and consecrated it.[20] The phallus was honored and even borne aloft in processions. In the worship of Dionysus the phallus became a symbol of the power to give life, and in the cult to this god the phallus was revealed and carried in processions with appropriate hymns intoned to it.[21] In the Serapeum in Thessalonica archaeologists discovered a small image of Dionysus that accommodated a removable phallus.[22] The phallus was also employed in the cult of Aphrodite[23] and in the worship of the Cabirus, a principal deity of the city of Thessalonica.[24] It comes as no surprise to find that the Christians in Thessalonica, the majority of whom had been converted out of idolatry, needed special and strong instruction concerning sexual purity (see the commentary on 1 Thess. 4.3-8).

Alongside the grand temples dedicated to house the images of the deities, the religion of the common folk combined the worship of the traditional gods with superstitions and mysticism. Philip of Thessalonica speaks of an idol dedicated to Pan that was no more than an oak image with bark attached to which he offered an old goat with milk in hopes of obtaining two kids in the womb of each goat.[25] Antipater wrote an epigram for a poplar tree that came to life and said, "A holy tree am I; when you pass by, beware of harming me."[26] The reason for the plea was simply that the Sun-god was its protector. Astrology appears among the religious mix of the city as a significant factor in determining the destiny of people. Antipater speaks of a person who lived in light of the prognostication of the astrologers: "The experts in astrology tell of an early death for me; though it be so, I care nothing for that, Seleucus. All men have the same way down to Hades; if mine is quicker than others', I shall be face to face with Minos the sooner. Let us drink, for surely it is a true saying that wine is like a horse for the highway, while your foot-traveller must go to Hades by a lane."[27] Revelations from the gods were communicated to the devout

20. Plutarch, *De Iside et Osiride* 358A-B, 365C.

21. Walter F. Otto, *Dionysus: Myth and Cult.* Bloomington and London: Indiana University Press, 1965), 164-65; Martin P. Nilsson, *The Dionysiac Mysteries of the Hellenistic Age* (Lund: C. W. K. Gleerup, 1957), 44-45.

22. Holland Lee Hendrix, "Thessalonica," in *ABD*, 6.525. On the Serapion, see Vacalopoulos, *History of Thessaloniki*, 8; R. E. Witt, "The Egyptian Cults in Ancient Macedonia," in *Ancient Macedonian Studies I* (Thessaloniki: Institute of Balkan Studies, 1970), 324-26; Donfried, "Cults of Thessalonica," 337.

23. Clement of Alexandria, *Exhortation to the Heathen*, ch. 2.

24. Ibid.; Bengt Hemberg, *Die Kabiren* (Uppsala: Almqvist & Wiksells, 1950), 205-7.

25. Gow and Page, *Greek Anthology*, 1.306.

26. Ibid., 1.62.

27. Ibid., 1.35, and see 1.16. Cf. 1 Cor. 15.32. While astrology has its roots deeply embedded in Babylonian religion, the Greeks also made their contribution. In the ancient

by means of dreams or visions[28] that were often part of the ceremonies of religious initiation or "incubation."[29] "Demons" *(daimōn)*, spirits that occupied the intermediate space between gods and humans, filled the surrounding air.[30] All these aspects of religious life were combined and bound together into a confused and complex weave of beliefs and faith.

Religion in Thessalonica was linked intimately with the affairs of daily life. The inscriptions tell us about religious associations in the city, such as that of the worshipers of Dionysus who joined together to celebrate the mysteries and organize funeral rites.[31] The city was also the host of associations dedicated to the worship of "the highest god" (Zeus) that organized common meals for their members.[32] In a cosmopolitan city such as Thessalonica, such associations would offer many people a sense of belonging and community.[33]

---

world no clear distinction was made between astronomy and astrology as is done today. It was believed that the stars influenced nature, and from that belief grew the idea of their influence over human life. One papyrus presents detailed instructions concerning how to interpret astrological information:

> If in addition Mercury is in conjunction, and Saturn is irregularly situated, . . . from an unfavorable position; if at the same time Mars is in opposition to Saturn, the aforesaid position being maintained (he will destroy?) profits of transactions. Saturn in triangular relation to Mars signifies (bad) fortune. Jupiter in triangular relation to Mars or in conjunction makes great kingdoms and empires. Venus in conjunction with Mars causes fornications and adulteries; if in addition Mercury is in conjunction with them, they in consequence make scandals and lusts. If Mercury is in conjunction with Jupiter or appears in triangular relation, this causes favorable actions of commerce, or a man will gain his living by . . . or by reason, and. . . . If Mars appear in triangular relation to Jupiter and Saturn, this causes great happiness, and he will make acquisitions and. . . . If while Jupiter and Saturn are in this position Mars comes into conjunction with either, . . . after obtaining (wealth) and collecting a fortune he will spend and lose it. If Jupiter, Mercury, and Venus are in conjunction, they cause glories and empires and great prosperity; and if the conjunction takes place at the morning rising (of Venus), they cause prosperity from youth upwards. *P. Tebtunis* 276

The twelve constellations and the wandering stars or planets determined destiny.

28. *IT*, nn. 67, 82, 88, and 99.

29. R. E. Witt, *Isis in the Graeco-Roman World* (London: Thames and Hudson, 1971), 54, 135, 185, and 189.

30. *NIDNTT*, 1.449-50; *OCD*, 426; *IT*, n. 108; Gow and Page, *Greek Anthology*, 1.328.

31. Papazoglou, "Intellectual Life," in *Macedonia* (ed. Sakellariou), 205; Vacalopoulos, *History of Thessaloniki*, 14; Charles F. Edson, "Cults of Thessalonica," *HTR* 41 (1948) 154-60. The *thiasoi* were often associations of foreigners. See Ferguson, *Backgrounds of Early Christianity*, 131.

32. *IT*, nn. 68, 70; Hendrix, "Thessalonica," 6.525.

33. R. K. Harrison, ed., *Major Cities of the Biblical World* (Nashville: Thomas Nelson, 1985), 264; Ferguson, *Backgrounds of Early Christianity*, 131-36.

In the political sphere religion played a principal role. The politarchs of the city, for example, dedicated an inscription to Serapis and Isis, rather striking evidence of the civic importance of the Egyptian cult in this city during the first century.[34] The council *(boulē)* of Thessalonica erected another inscription (first century BC or AD) dedicated to Apollo, and in 60 BC this same group, along with the assembly of the people *(dēmos)*, makes mention of Dionysus in an honorific inscription.[35] Edson observes that the epigraphic evidence points to the presence of a state cult to Dionysus that was celebrated since Hellenistic times: "The city to Dionysus, Aristandros son of Aristonos, Antimachos son of Aristoxenos, politarchs."[36] Since Thessalonica was a free city that had the right to mint its own coins, the numismatic evidence fills out the picture of the relationship between civic government and certain cults. The images and symbols of gods such as the Dioscuri, Heracles, Nike, Dionysus, Apollo, and, somewhat later, the Cabirus all appear in the official coinage.[37]

The adoration and honor of the gods was not simply a private but a civic affair. Cities in the ancient world normally had their patron deities and honored them by establishing their cults. In this Thessalonica was no exception. Sacrifices, prayers, and images of the gods were common elements in meetings of the official assembly or the governing council. Inscriptions testify of the presence of priests whose position in the society paralleled that of the civic magistrates, while public funds were used to defray the costs of the civic cults. The "pious" in the community were those who upheld the civic cults as well as the traditional gods. Participation in the civic cult was one of the fundamental obligations of the population.[38] The government celebrated festivals and consecrated games to gods such as Apollo, as was the practice in other cities as well.[39] The games began with sacrifices, prayers, and votive offerings to the gods. The administrator of the games *(agōnothetēs)*, who could either inherit or be elected to the post, was a high official of the city.[40]

The union between religion and government reached its climax in

---

34. *IT,* n. 86. In n. 109 (39-38 BC) the politarchs made a dedication to Osiris and "to the other gods."

35. Ibid., nn. 52, 5.

36. Edson, "Cults of Thessalonica," 160-61.

37. Ioannis Touratsoglou, *Die Münzstätte von Thessaloniki in der Römischen Kaiserzeit* (Berlin and New York: Walter de Gruyter, 1988); Kevin Butcher, "The Roman Coinage of Thessalonica," *JRA* 5 (1992) 434-39; Hendrix, "Thessalonicans Honor Romans," 188.

38. Ferguson, *Backgrounds of Early Christianity,* 170-85.

39. Papazoglou, "Intellectual Life," 204; Vacalopoulos, *History of Thessaloniki,* 14.

40. Jones, *The Greek City,* 234; *IT,* nn. 31, 32, 132, 133, and 201.

the imperial cult. The worship of the king as a god enjoyed a long history in the East. In Macedonia itself, Alexander the Great received divine honors that were related to the "revelations" he received concerning his own divinity at Delphi in Greece and Siwa in Egypt.[41] Not only Alexander but also his father Philip had sought divine honors, and the evidence appears to support the theory that he attempted to establish a dynastic cult.[42] A number of inscriptions from the second and third centuries AD testify not only of the divine status of Alexander but also of a priesthood who serviced his cult in Thessalonica. The myth of the divine Alexander persisted long after the ruler's death.[43] With this tradition firmly established, the imperial cult was introduced into Thessalonica early in the Roman period with relative ease. During the last part of the first century BC a temple was erected to the emperor, and a surviving inscription commemorates the event:

> . . . proconsul . . . of Latomia[44] buil[t the] tem[ple] of Caesar. In the time of priest and *agōn*[*othete* of Im]perator Caesar Augustus son [of god] . . . -ōs son of Neikopol[eōs, priest] of the gods, Dō[. . . son of . . .] -pos, and (priest) of Roma a[nd Roman] benefactors, Neik[. . . son of] Paramonos. In the term of the Politarchs Diogenēs son [of . . .] Kleōn son of P . . . , Zōpas son of Kal . . . , Eulandros son of . . . , Prōtogenēs son of . . . , and the superin[tendent] of the work, trea[surer of the city] Sōsōnos s[on of . . .] [In the term of the] architec[t] Dionysiu[s son of . . .].[45]

Titles such as *sebastos* (a religious term, translated "Augustus," that indicated that the bearer was something more than human) and "son of god" (that is, of the divinized Julius Caesar) appear in a number of inscriptions dedicated to Octavian (Augustus). Other inscriptions testify to the importance of the priests of the imperial cult and of the administrator of the games dedicated to the divine emperor.[46] There was also a priestess associated with this cult.[47] The numismatic evidence confirms that both Julius

41. See E. Badian, "The Deification of Alexander the Great," and E. A. Fredricksmeyer, "On the Background of the Ruler Cult," in *Ancient Macedonian Studies in Honor of Charles F. Edson* (ed. Harry Dell; Thessaloniki: Institute for Balkan Studies, 1981), 27-71, 145-56.

42. Ibid., 146-47.

43. *IT*, nn. 275, 276, and 278. The coinage from the Macedonian *koinon* centered in Berea features the idealized image of the divinized Alexander.

44. A region of the city.

45. *IT*, n. 31 (27 BC–14 AD). Translation of Hendrix, "Thessalonicans Honor Romans," 107-8.

46. *IT*, nn. 31, 32, 132, and 133. Elsewhere in the Strymon River valley an inscription was found indicating that the "gods *sebastoi*" (Julius Caesar and Augustus) were

and Augustus received divine honors in the city, with titles such as "god" and *sebastos* attributed to them. One emission replaced the head of Zeus with that of Augustus.[48] Philip of Thessalonica wrote about "Caesar's altar" from which Daphne "has now raised up her dark-leafed bough." According to Greek mythology, Daphne was pursued by Apollo but in response to her supplication was rescued by Zeus, who turned her into a bay tree. But Philip now sees her growing from the imperial altar and says, "She cast her root not from mother-earth but from rock; not even stone can refuse to be fertile for Caesar."[49] The altar in Thessalonica was one of the many dedicated to the imperial cult throughout the eastern empire.[50] A statue of Augustus, possibly produced during the reign of Tiberius, was found in 1939 and presents the deceased emperor in a divine posture.[51] Although Augustus received divine honor during his lifetime, the evidence does not point to a similar exaltation of succeeding emperors.

With the ascension of Augustus to the position of supreme power in the empire, the city of Thessalonica honored him in a number of ways. Augustus ushered in a new era of security and peace that was celebrated not only in Thessalonica but throughout the empire. The *Res Gestae Divi Augusti* recorded the achievements of Augustus, and this litany of his accomplishments was on display at Rome and elsewhere for all to see and read. It begins, "The accomplishments of the deified Augustus, by which he subjected the whole world to the empire of the Roman people," and continues, "My name by decree of the senate was included in the Salian Hymn, and the fact that I should be sacrosanct forever and that as long as I live the tribunician power should be mine, was sanctioned by law." Again, "In return for this service of mine by senatorial decree I was called

---

venerated as *synnaoi* along with the Egyptian deities Serapis and Isis. Papazoglou, "Intellectual Life," 540, n. 111.

47. Michael Vickers, "Town Planning in Roman Thessaloniki," in *Ancient Macedonia I* (Thessaloniki: Institute for Balkan Studies, 1970), 247. Vickers also discusses the possible location of the temple (247-49), though archaeologists have not been able to locate the remains of this structure. Recent excavations in the agora of the city have uncovered a first-century imperial monumental structure that may be the remains of an altar.

48. Hendrix, "Thessalonicans Honor Romans," 188.

49. Gow and Page, *Greek Anthology*, 1.301.

50. Anna Benjamin and Antony E. Raubitschek, "Arae Augusti," *Hesperia* 28 (1959) 65-85. They comment, "There exists, however, a large group of dedications, mainly, though perhaps not exclusively, altars, which have the name of the emperor (or of another person) in the dative case, indicating, as in the case of dedications to the gods, that the monument is set up to the emperor" (67).

51. Archaeological Museum of Thessaloniki, n. 1065. See Julia Vokotopoulou, *Guide to the Archaeological Museum of Thessalonike* (Athens: Kapon Editions, 1996), 85-86.

Augustus."[52] Augustus had established peace, inaugurated an era of economic prosperity, brought in stable government, improved the means of transportation and communication, pacified the seas and the provinces, and accomplished a multitude of other great deeds that generated adulation throughout the empire. The expressions of thanks and loyalty reached their pinnacle in the imperial cult that was celebrated in Thessalonica along with its rival Berea, the seat of the confederation of Macedonian cities or *koinon*. The impact of the imperial cult on the Christian community in Thessalonica is not hard to imagine. Paul had proclaimed in Thessalonica that "there is another king, one called Jesus" (Acts 17.7), and the royal imagery in the Thessalonian letters is significant (e.g., 1 Thess. 1.10; 4.16; 2 Thess. 1.5-10; 2.8). The proclamation of Christ was the counterpoint to imperial claims as well as a rekindling of traditional Macedonian monarchal longings.

We should not imagine, however, that the imperial cult in Thessalonica and elsewhere was nothing more than an expression of religious devotion. The celebration of the cult was a political and diplomatic act that was intimately intertwined with the economic realities of the relationship between Thessalonica and Rome. Hendrix has argued that the imperial cult in Thessalonica was an extension of the custom of honoring benefactors, such as those Roman benefactors whose names appear over and again in the inscriptions that honor them for their beneficence to the city. One inscription mentions "the gods and the Roman benefactors," while others speak of the "priest of Roma and the Roman benefactors," and "the priest of the gods . . . and of the priests of Roma and the Roman benefactors."[53] In that era, benefactors were those who made contributions, constructed buildings, saved communities from adversity, canceled debts, or offered aid to the population in a number of ways.[54] Without specifying the precise nature of the benefits conferred by the Roman benefactors, the inscriptions give ample evidence of their generosity to the city. Public recognition of these benefactors was, on the one hand, an act of thanksgiving but, on the other, served as an implicit request for fur-

52. Robert K. Sherk, ed., *The Roman Empire: Augustus to Hadrian* (Cambridge: Cambridge University Press, 1988), 41-50.

53. *IT*, nn. 4, 31, and 133 and see nn. 32, 128, and 226.

54. On benefaction in antiquity, see Winter, *Seek the Welfare of the City*; idem, "The Public Honouring of Christian Benefactors," *JSNT* 34 (1988) 87-103; idem, " 'Seek the Welfare of the City': Social Ethics according to 1 Peter," *Themelios* 13 (1988) 91-94; Frederick W. Danker, *Benefactor: Epigraphic Study of a Graeco-Roman and New Testament Semantic Field* (St. Louis: Clayton Publishing House, 1982); Stephen Charles Mott, "The Power of Giving and Receiving: Reciprocity in Hellenistic Benevolence," in *Current Issues in Biblical and Patristic Interpretation* (ed. Gerald F. Hawthorne; Grand Rapids: Eerdmans, 1975), 60-72; and the literature in n. 10, p. 26.

ther benefits and as an inspiration to others to imitate their example. Thessalonica owed a debt of gratitude that was so great that the recognition of these individuals extended beyond the normal inscriptions, generating a whole cult and priesthood dedicated to "Roma and the Roman benefactors."

The emperor was seen as the supreme Roman benefactor; for that reason the honors that were given to him were extremely high. Religion, political well-being, and economic benefits were inseparably intertwined at this point.[55] Hendrix defines the imperial cult almost exclusively with reference to the practices related to benefaction, and even questions whether terms such as "cult" and "worship" should be used to speak of this institution. However, the altars dedicated to Caesar in this and other cities, the divine titles, the temple, and the priesthood all point to the presence of genuine religious sentiments. Signs and wonders were not infrequently associated with the imperial cult, and these served as a means of inspiring awe.[56] In the Greek worldview the line between the human and the divine was fuzzy. The gods were viewed as little more than beings elevated somewhat above humans because of their great virtues and immortality. Therefore those humans who did those things that appeared divine could expect corresponding honors. Moreover, the distinction between honors and adoration was not clearly marked.[57]

Thessalonica enjoyed great benefits from her privileged relationship with Rome and the Romans, and the imperial cult was the supreme manifestation of the city's response to those benefits. As in other cities of the empire, those who benefited most from this relationship were the upper classes of the society, which included those who were leaders both politically and economically.[58] Any threat to this relationship would be challenged. Most likely the persecution of the Christian community in the city should be understood, at least in part, in light of the unique connection the city had with Rome (Acts 17.6-9; 1 Thess. 2.14). Moreover, given the centrality of the imperial cult in the city, the Thessalonian believers would have understood clearly what the apostles meant when they wrote about the "man of lawlessness" who "will oppose and will exalt himself over everything that is called God or is wor-

55. Holland Hendrix, "Beyond 'Imperial Cult' and 'Cults of Magistrates,'" in *Society for Biblical Literature Seminar Papers 1986* (ed. Kent Harold Richards; Atlanta: Scholars Press, 1986), 301-8; idem, "Thessalonicans Honor Romans."

56. Steven J. Scherrer, "Signs and Wonders in the Imperial Cult: A New Look at a Roman Religious Institution in the Light of Rev 13:13-15," *JBL* 103 (1984) 599-610.

57. Ferguson, *Backgrounds of Early Christianity,* 185-98.

58. Ibid., p. 198.

shiped, so that he sets himself up in God's temple, proclaiming himself to be God" (2 Thess. 2.4).

The religious world of Thessalonica included traditional cults alongside foreign religions. The evidence handed down to us tells of the worship of many members of the Greek pantheon, such as Zeus "the highest god,"[59] who was also called Eleutheros ("Free"),[60] Apollo,[61] Athena,[62] Heracles,[63] Aphrodite,[64] Demeter and Persephone,[65] Poseidon,[66] Pan,[67] and Hades,[68] among others. Occasionally the inscriptions speak about "the gods" without specifying which gods are in mind. Although this general title is often found in inscriptions that refer to the Egyptian deities, "the gods" do not appear to be identified with them.[69] Most likely "the gods" are those of the classical pantheon, and, if this is the case, these inscriptions point to their importance in the religious life of the city.

A number of deities enjoyed special prominence in Thessalonica, such as the Cabirus, Dionysus, and the Egyptian gods. The center of the cult of the Cabiri was the island of Samothrace[70] (Acts 16.11), and the religion most likely arrived in Thessalonica directly from that city. The cult of the two Cabiri (father and son) was celebrated in Samothrace, where they were known as "the great gods." However, the city of Thessaloniki celebrated only one of the Cabiri, the Cabirus. The literature sometimes identifies the Cabiri with the sons of Zeus known as the Dioscuri, while

59. *IT*, nn. 67, 72.

60. *IT*, n. 32. See Charles Edson, "Macedonia, II: State Cults of Thessalonica," *HSCP* 51 (1940) 134. *IT*, n. 1031, speaks of "Zeus Olympia." On a clear day Mt. Olympus can be seen from Thessalonica.

61. *IT*, n. 85.

62. Philip of Thessalonica in Gow and Page, *The Greek Anthology*, 1.308, 312.

63. Antipater and Philip in ibid., 72, 346; Hendrix, "Thessalonica," 525.

64. *IT*, n. 965; Kortē-Kontē, *H Koroplastikē tēs Thessalonikēs*, 172. A grotesque of Aphrodite is one of the more unique treasures of the collection in the Archaeological Museum (116-17, 200-201).

65. Antipater and Philip in Gow and Page, *The Greek Anthology*, 1.63, 302; Kortē-Kontē, *H Koroplastikē tēs Thessalonikēs*, 172.

66. Philip in Gow and Page, *The Greek Anthology*, 1.302-4.

67. See p. 36.

68. Philip in Gow and Page, *The Greek Anthology*, 1.313-15, 328.

69. Contra Hendrix, "Thessalonicans Honor Romans," 128. *IT*, nn. 77, 78, 109, and 80 are dedicated to "Isis, Serapis, Anubis and the gods of the same temple." See also n. 85, dedicated simply to "the gods," and nn. 4, 31, 133, 32, and 132 where "the gods" appear in the context of the imperial cult and in association with the priests of the goddess Roma and the Roman benefactors.

70. Arthur Darby Nock, "A Cabiric Right," *AJA* 45 (1941) 577-81; Strabo, frag. 7.50 (51), notes the identification of the gods worshiped in Samothrace with the Cabiri. Also see Hemberg, *Die Kabiren*.

Clement of Alexandria later linked them with the nature spirits called the Corybantes.[71] The exact date when this cult was established in Thessalonica cannot be determined with precision, but an inscription from Samothrace contains a list of pilgrims from Thessalonica who arrived in the holy island between 37 BC and AD 43.[72] An important inscription from the second century AD refers to the Cabirus as "the most holy and *ancestral* god, Cabirus."[73] A number of centuries earlier, the last king of Macedonia, Perseus, fled to Samothrace at the time of the battle fought with the Romans at Pydna (168 BC), while even earlier the parents of Alexander the Great met at a rite of initiation that was being celebrated on that island.[74] The relationship that existed between Samothrace and Macedonia was quite old, and we may assume that the cult of the Cabirus was established in Thessalonica at least by the first century BC. During the second century AD the Cabirus begins to appear in the coinage of the city, and his image greeted those who entered Thessalonica through the Vardar Gate along the Via Egnatia. The Cabirus had been elevated to the position of titular deity in the city.[75] Edson argues that this accession happened as early as the first century.

Diverse stories about the Cabiri appear in the mythology of the cult. Clement of Alexandria relates that there were three brothers and that two of them murdered the other and buried his head at the foot of Mt. Olympus in Macedonia. "These mysteries are, in short, murders and funerals."[76] Clement adds that the cult was associated with the phallus of Dionysus, which had been cut off and preserved in a box. Diodorus Siculus identified the Cabiri with the Dioscuri and attributed to them the power to save from maritime disaster. This salvation, in turn, was offered to the initiates of the cult.[77] Strabo describes the worshipers in this and similar cults "as a kind of inspired people and as subject to Bacchic frenzy, and, in the guise of ministers, as inspiring terror at the celebration of the sacred rites by means of war-dances, accompanied by uproar and noise and cymbals and drums and arms, and also by flute and outcry."[78] Exactly how the Cabirus was celebrated in Thessalonica cannot

71. Pausanias 10.38.7; Clement of Alexandria, *Exhortation to the Heathen*, ch. 2.

72. Edson, "Cults of Thessalonica," 189; R. E. Witt, "The Kabeiroi in Ancient Macedonia," in *Ancient Macedonia II* (Thessaloniki: Institute for Balkan Studies, 1977), 78.

73. Edson, "Cults of Thessalonica," 193.

74. See p. 12; Witt, "The Kabeiroi in Ancient Macedonia," 73-74.

75. Hendrix, "Thessalonica," 525; Edson, "Cults of Thessalonica," 188-200.

76. Clement of Alexandria, *Exhortation to the Heathen*, ch. 2. The story is of the Corybantes, but Clement goes on to say, "those Corybantes also they call Cabiric; and the ceremony itself they announce as the Cabiric mystery."

77. Diodorus Siculus 5.49.5-6; 4.43.1-2.

78. Strabo 10.3.7.

be determined, but it appears that the phallic symbol was at the heart of the celebrations.[79] We can assume that not a few of the converts to Christ in Thessalonica had previously participated in these ceremonies (1 Thess. 1.9).

The worship of Dionysus was prominent in Thessalonica since it is mentioned in the official inscriptions of the city alongside the Egyptian gods Serapis, Isis, and Anubis, as well as the Dioscuri and Zeus.[80] This cult was established at the time of the founding of the city by Cassander,[81] and by the time the gospel came to Thessalonica it had become one of the most well-rooted religions in the city. This state cult included a priesthood, an association of devotees known as the *thiasoi* and officials who were in charge of an unknown type of water ceremony that was part of the cult *(hydroskopoi)*. The ritual license, ecstasy, and drunkenness associated with this cult were legendary.[82]

The Egyptian gods found a central place in the religious life of Thessalonica, as the discovery of the Serapeum with its multiple inscriptions testifies. Serapis, Isis, Anubis, and other Egyptian deities appear in the inscriptions, both private and official, giving ample evidence of the vitality of their cult in Thessalonica. In addition to the public celebrations of the cult, the evidence points to the existence of associations of worshipers who gathered for common meals. A house had been established for them by one of their members, while their association was known as "the companions at table" *(synklitai)*.[83] The members of this group were those who had participated in its mysteries. They did not make racial or social distinctions among the membership because of the universality of Isis, a perspective also shared by the Christians. Part of their responsibility was to bear the sacred objects to the cult.[84] Although we do not know the precise nature of the mysteries of Isis, we understand that the goddess offered healing, salvation, and immortality to the initiated and required humility and confession before the nocturnal rite of initiation.[85]

Isis, who was becoming the supreme feminine deity, was seen as a nurse and maternal figure and was known for her wisdom.[86] In an in-

---

79. Hemberg, *Die Kabiren,* 203; Witt, "The Kabeiroi in Ancient Macedonia," 72-73.

80. *IT,* nn. 5, 12, 28, 259, 56, and 77.

81. Vacalopoulos, *A History of Thessaloniki,* 5-6.

82. *OCD,* 479-82 and bibliography.

83. Edson, "Cults of Thessalonica," 184; also see R. E. Witt, "The Egyptian Cults in Ancient Macedonia"; idem, "Isis-Hellas," *PCPS* 192 (1966) 48-69; idem, *Isis in the Graeco-Roman World* (London: Thames and Hudson, 1971).

84. Plutarch, *Moralia* 352B.

85. Donfried, "Cults of Thessalonica and the Thessalonian Correspondence," 337.

86. Plutarch, *De Iside et Osiride* 351F, 372E.

scription from Thessalonica that celebrates her virtues[87] she is attributed with the great works of the creation of the sun, the moon, and the sea and is proclaimed as the one who put the stars on their course. Her power over nature is symbolized in the sistrum, a metal instrument that makes noise and appears in a multitude of reliefs and pictures that depict her worship. In his exploration of the cult, Plutarch explains that the sistrum "makes it clear that all things in existence need to be shaken, or rattled about, and never to cease from motion but, as it were, to wake up and [be] agitated when they grow drowsy and torpid. They say that they avert and repel Typhon by means of the sisturms, indicating thereby that when destruction constricts and checks Nature, generation releases and arouses it by means of motion."[88] Isis not only had power over the cosmos but was also credited with bringing men and women together and with creating the family. She is said to have taught her worshipers the mysteries. One inscription from the city records a mission to Opus, instigated by a dream, which was undertaken to promote the cult of Serapis and Isis and bring salvation.[89] The greatness of the goddess and Serapis motivated the worshipers to take the message of this now universal deity to other peoples who were in need. The Christian church was not the only missionary religion operating in Macedonia.

Finally, Judaism had established itself as part of the religious milieu of Thessalonica (Acts 17.1-4). In his journey through Macedonia Paul stopped and preached in those communities where there was a Jewish presence (such as Philippi, Thessalonica, and Berea), while he simply passed over those cities, both great and small, where there was no Jewish cult, such as Neapolis (Acts 16.11), Amphipolis, and Apollonia (17.1). The fact that there was no Jewish community in Pella possibly explains Paul's reason for heading off the Via Egnatia when he fled Thessalonica and turned south on a side road that led him to Berea. His choice of centers for evangelization was motivated by the theological concern expressed in Romans 1.16, "I am not ashamed of the gospel, because it is the power of God for the salvation of everyone who believes: first for the Jew, then for the Gentile." Moreover, the hospitality he would have received in the Jewish communities may have been another factor in selecting these cities as a base of operations (Acts 16.15; 17.7).

The sources do not preserve any evidence concerning when or how the Jewish community was established in Thessalonica. A bilingual inscription from between the fourth to sixth centuries AD gives surprising

---

87. *IT*, n. 254, her *aretalogiae*.
88. Plutarch, *De Iside et Osiride* 376C-D.
89. *IT*, n. 255.

evidence of a Samaritan community in the town.[90] An earlier inscription from the third Christian century makes reference to "the synagogues" in the city, showing us that there was a rather sizable Jewish community in Thessalonica by this date.[91] A number of inscriptions are dedicated "to the highest god," likely a reference to Zeus. However, the title is given to Yahweh in the LXX (Gen. 14.18; Deut. 32.8), and it is possible that at least one of these inscriptions is Jewish due to the lack of distinctly pagan elements.[92]

The religious milieu of Thessalonica was complex, as it was in any city of the ancient world. Those who were called and responded to the gospel (2 Thess. 2.14) did so in opposition to their culture, which considered piety and religious traditionalism to be great virtues. The Thessalonians' problem was not simply that they adopted a new deity. To add one more god to a person's or family's pantheon was no cause for concern. Rather, the Christians abandoned those gods who were considered to be patrons of both their families and city (1 Thess. 1.9). To break from them was a civic and not simply a private and personal act. The strong reaction of the community to them is understandable in this context. But the conversion to the living God left the Thessalonians bewildered with their state of affairs, and, for this reason, eschatological concerns are so dominant in these letters. If Jesus is truly the king, when will he exercise his kingly rule? Why is there death and suffering among us if he is the exalted one over death and over all political powers? Answers to these concerns are highlighted especially in 1 Thessalonians 4 and 5 as well as 2 Thessalonians 1 and 2. Jesus will come and reign. The Risen One will return (1 Thess. 1.10)!

VI. THE GOSPEL AND THE THESSALONIANS

During his second missionary journey, the apostle Paul, along with his coworkers Silas and Timothy (Acts 15.40; 16.1-3),[1] arrived at the populous city of Alexandrian Troas in the region of Mysia after being prohib-

---

90. *IT*, n. 789. See J. D. Purvis, "The Palaeography of the Samaritan Inscriptions from Thessalonica," *BASOR* 221 (1976) 121-23; *New Docs*, 1.108-10.

91. P. M. Nigdelis, "Synagoge(n) und Gemeinde del Juden in Thessaloniki: Fragen aufgrund einer neuen jüdischen Grabinschrift del Kaiserzeit," *ZPE* 102 (1994) 241-49.

92. *IT*, n. 72.

1. Timothy appears to have continued on with the apostolic team in Thessalonica, although Acts 17.1-9 does not mention his participation in the ministry there (see 17.14-15 and 1 Thess. 1.1; 2.7, 13).

ited by the Spirit from preaching in the provinces of Asia and Bithynia (16.6-7).[2] One night during their stay Paul had a vision of a Macedonian man who begged him to "Come over to Macedonia and help us" (16.6-10). This vision, as well as the previous prohibition to engage in an Asian or Bithynian ministry, led Paul and his team[3] to the conclusion that God had called them to preach the gospel to the Macedonians. They left the port of Troas and sailed the Aegean to the island of Samothrace, where they spent their first night (Acts 16.11). This island frames the history of Macedonia. Here at the sanctuary of the Cabiri, Philip II met his wife Olympias, while centuries later the last king of Macedonia, Perseus, fled to the island for refuge after his defeat at the Battle of Pydna.[4] After a night on the island, Paul and the apostolic team made their way to Macedonia, making landfall at the port city of Philippi called Neapolis, the same harbor where Brutus had anchored his ships when he waged war against Antony and Octavian. A second Paulus had now come to Macedonia, but this one did not come under the standard of Rome as Aemilius Paulus had some two centuries earlier but under the authority of Christ.[5] Paul and his associates followed the Via Egnatia inland to Philippi, where they managed to establish a church despite the opposition and humiliation they faced in this Roman colony (16.16-40; 1 Thess. 2.2).

After their imprisonment in the city, Paul and Silas took leave of Philippi and continued down the Via Egnatia, only passing the night in the cities of Amphipolis and Apollonia where apparently no Jewish communities were resident (Acts 17.1).[6] Paul's strategy was to preach the gospel first to the Jews (see Rom. 1.16-17); after being rejected by them, he directed his preaching to the Gentiles (Acts 18.5-6; 19.8-10). Upon arriving in Thessalonica, Paul found a synagogue and there discussed the gospel with the Jews and God-fearers on three Sabbaths, interpreting the Scrip-

---

2. Silas, being a prophet, was the likely channel for these directions. See Acts 15.32.

3. The narrative in Acts changes at this point from the third person to the first person plural "we" (v. 10), most likely an indication that the author of Acts, Luke, accompanied the group to Philippi. The return to the third person in v. 40 implies that Luke remained in Philippi while the others continued down the Via Egnatia. During the third missionary journey the narrative changes once again to the first person plural precisely at the time when Paul was passing back through Macedonia where Philippi was located (20.1-6). A useful discussion of the "we" sections in Acts in relationship to authorship can be found in Hemer, *The Book of Acts in the Setting of Hellenistic History*, 312-34.

4. See Strabo, frag. 7.50(51); *IG*, 12.8.195; Hammond, *History of Macedonia*, 3.558; Edson, "Cults of Thessalonica," 188-94; Nock, "A Cabiric Right," 577-81; Witt, "The Kabeiroi in Ancient Macedonia," 69-79; *ABD*, 6.524; *OCD*, 1352.

5. See "A Summary History of Macedonia and Thessalonica," 3.

6. On the Jewish communities in Macedonia, see Levinskaya, *The Book of Acts in Its Diaspora Setting*, 153-57.

ture and using it as evidence to persuade them that "the Christ had to suffer and rise from the dead" (cf. Luke 24.45-46; 1 Cor. 1.23; 15.3-4) and that, "This Jesus I am proclaiming to you is the Christ" (Acts 17.2-3; cf. 9.22; 18.5, 28; Matt. 16.16). The response to Paul's rhetoric was mixed (17.4). Only a few Jews were persuaded, so few that they are not even referred to in the first letter to this church, which came to be populated overwhelmingly with Gentiles (1 Thess. 1.9; 2.14). The narrative in Acts informs us that "a large number of God-fearing Greeks and not a few prominent women" were persuaded and attached themselves to the apostles (Acts 17.4). This group was composed of women who were of the elite of the city (cf. 17.12), wives of the principal men of the city,[7] and the God-fearers. These people were Gentiles who, while sympathetic to Judaism, did not become proselytes and so did not undergo the rite of circumcision.[8] 1 Thessalonians 1.9-10 describes the conversion of the Thessalonians from idolatry, which most likely implies that the apostles also successfully developed a ministry directly to the Gentile populace of the city. Acts does not elaborate the details of this part of the apostolic mission.

The number of people who exited from the synagogue provoked an understandably strong reaction among the Jews who were not persuaded by Paul's proclamation (Acts 17.5). Filled with envy due to the loss of so many God-fearers,[9] Luke tells us that the Jews "rounded up some bad characters from the marketplace, formed a mob and started a riot in the city." These "bad characters" were those who hung around the central market and were of the lowest class. Their presence in the cities was commonplace, and even Plutarch notes how easy it was to get them agitated: "When, therefore, Appius saw Scipio rushing into the forum attended by men who were of low birth and had lately been slaves, but who were frequenters of the forum[10] and able to gather a mob and force all issues by means of solicitations and shouting, he cried with a loud voice and said. . . ."[11] The Jews managed to form a mob of these people who then

---

7. *Tōn prōtōn.* See 13.50; Mark 6.21.

8. See p. 31, n. 1, especially Levinskaya, *The Book of Acts in Its Diaspora Setting*, 51-126. God-fearers were not a monolithic but rather an amorphous group. As Levinskaya notes, "Some of the God-fearers were only one step from becoming converts, while others just added the Jewish God to their pantheon. So long as they showed some kind of sympathy with the Jewish religion they were considered God-fearers" (p. 78). See Juvenal's estimation of them his *Satires* 14.96-106.

9. The defection of these people would have meant not simply a depletion of the roles for the Sabbath celebrations but more pointedly a loss of income (see Acts 10.2; Luke 7.1-5) and of those who were significant liaisons with the wider Gentile community, especially the nobility.

10. The term here is the same as the one used by Luke, *agoraious.*

11. *Aemilius Paulus* 38.4.

caused a civil disturbance and even attacked the house of Jason, a man who had extended hospitality to the apostles and so served as their patron during their stay in the city. The mob wanted to take Paul and Silas before the assembly of the city,[12] but when they did not find the apostles they dragged away Jason and some other Christians, bringing them before the politarchs or governing officials of the town[13] and shouting out, "These men who have caused trouble all over the world have now come here, and Jason has welcomed them into his house" (17.6b-7a).

The news that civil disturbances had surrounded the preaching of the gospel had already arrived in Thessalonica, perhaps coming from Philippi from those who had traveled down the Via Egnatia.[14] The accusation was not only that the apostles caused civic unrest but that "They are defying Caesar's decrees, saying that there is another king, one called Jesus." The charge was not simply one of treason, which would have been based on public law and not imperial "decrees." Under the administrations of Augustus and Tiberius, imperial decrees were emitted that made it illegal to inquire about or predict the death of any person by means of divination, especially if that person was the emperor.[15] These decrees restricted divination to such an extent that the apostolic announcement of the coming of a new sovereign Lord would have been viewed as a daring violation (see 1 Thess. 4.16; 5.2-3; 2 Thess. 2.3-8). What is more, the royal theology of the kingdom proclaimed by Paul would have been heard by Macedonians and Romans alike as setting flame to the ancient Macedonian kindling, the longing for the revival of the monarchy.

12. *Dēmon.* On the *dēmos* as the assembly of citizens in Thessalonica, see p. 22.

13. *Politarchas.* See p. 21.

14. The reputation of the Christians in the eyes of the Romans is reflected in Tacitus, *Annals* 15.44.2-8 and Suetonius, *Nero* 16.2. Similar negative sentiments are expressed by Pliny the Younger during the second decade of the second century in *Epistulae* 10.96.

15. See Judge, "The Decrees of Caesar at Thessalonica," 3-5. The decree under Augustus is noted by Dio Cassius (56.25.5-6, as cited by Judge), ". . . the seers were forbidden to prophesy to any person alone or to prophesy regarding death even if others should be present. Yet so far was Augustus from caring about such matters in his own case that he set forth to all in an edict the aspect of the stars at the time of his own birth. Nevertheless, he forbade this practice." The Tiberian decree, according to Dio (57.15.8, as Judge), contained the following: "But as for all the other astrologers and magicians and such as practised divination in anyway whatsoever, he put to death those who were foreigners and banished all the citizens that were accused of still employing the art at this time after the previous decree *(dogma)* by which it had been forbidden to engage in any such business in the city. . . ." These decrees stayed intact even as late as the third-century jurist Ulpian. The *Comparison of the Mosaic and Roman Laws* 15.2 (recorded in Judge) states, "For those who have sought advice about the health of the emperor suffer either capital punishment or some other heavy penalty."

When we take into account the special relationship that existed between the free city of Thessalonica and Rome, it becomes easy to understand the strong impact of this calculated accusation. The politarchs were responsible to maintain local loyalty to the emperor. The charge threw them and the wider populace into disorder (Acts 17.8). But it was not the apostles but rather the populace and even the officials who caused the unrest, according to Luke's reading of the situation! Since Paul and his associates were not found (were they hiding?), the politarchs made Jason and the other Christians with him "post bond," which was most likely a guarantee that they would not allow the Christian messengers to cause any more trouble in the city nor would they be a party to any trouble (17.9).[16] The only option left for Paul, Silas and Timothy was to leave the city. The brothers and sisters of the church sent them away by cover of night down the Via Egnatia toward Pella, then south to Berea (17.10). This new Thessalonian church was left without leadership and without having received all the instruction they needed (cf. 1 Thess. 4.13). Moreover, the persecution that was directed primarily at the apostles overflowed to the church. These new believers suffered much at the hands of their contemporaries (1 Thess. 1.6; 2.14; 3.3-4).

After a short period of evangelization in Berea, Paul was sent off to Athens (17.14-15). Apparently Silas and Timothy arrived in that city on a trip that is not mentioned in Acts, and from there Timothy was sent back to Thessalonica (see 1 Thess. 3.1-2, 5 and commentary). On more than one occasion Paul himself attempted to return to Thessalonica but was hindered from doing so by some kind of opposition that he identifies as being satanically generated (2.17-18). In light of the tender age of this congregation and the persecution that rolled over them, the apostles feared the worst. Had Satan brought their work to nothing (1 Thess. 3.5)? Had the church committed the sin of apostasy?[17] The concerns that Paul and the others had for this congregation were so overwhelming (3.1, 5) that they decided to send Timothy back to the city "to strengthen and encourage" the believers in their faith and "to find out about" their faith (3.2, 5). While Timothy journeyed to Thessalonica, Paul himself moved south to Corinth, where he waited for news of the Thessalonian church. 1 Thessa-

---

16. A. N. Sherwin-White, *Roman Society and Roman Law in the New Testament* (Grand Rapids: Baker, 1963), 95-96. Of the bond, Sherwin-White notes, "The term is the equivalent of the Latin *satis accipere*, correlate of *satis dare*, in connexion with the offering and giving of security, in civil and criminal procedures. . . . What is happening to Jason is clear enough: he is giving security for the good behaviour of his guests, and hence hastens to dispatch Paul and Silas out of the way to Berea. . . ." The observation unfortunately does not take into account that not only Jason but also the others posted bond.

17. See the commentary on 1 Thess. 3.5.

lonians was written shortly after Timothy's arrival at Corinth (3.6; Acts 18.5). He brought with him the "good news" of the faith, love, and steadfastness of this congregation despite all their hardships (1 Thess. 3.6-8). 1 Thessalonians is a letter of thanksgiving to God for them (3.6-10; 1.3; 2.13) as well as a letter of encouragement for this church in the midst of all their sufferings (1.6; 2.14-16; 3.3-4).

But Timothy also brought disturbing news from Thessalonica. It appears that concerns about the apostles' integrity were circulating and questions were raised concerning why Paul especially had not returned to the church (2.1-12 and commentary). For this reason the author included an extensive explanation about both their desire and attempts to return to the city (2.17-20), the mission of Timothy (3.1-5), the overwhelming joy the good news about the congregation brought them (3.6-9), and a record of their earnest prayers to God about their return (3.10-11). There should be no doubt about their true concerns and motives. The report Timothy brought also included the disturbing news that some in the congregation were not heeding the moral teaching on sexuality (4.1-8) and work (4.11-12; 5.14; 2 Thess. 3.10) that the founders of the church had previously given them. The Christian ethic on these matters was quite distinct from their traditional values and was not readily embraced by these new believers. The last section of the letter reflects some of the other problems that entwined this new Christian community. Problems surrounding the emergent leadership (5.12-13), reactions to various persons both within and outside the congregation (5.14-15), and the rejection of prophecy (5.19-20) were all matters that called for apostolic intervention. On the other hand, the church appears to have sent a letter with Timothy that included a series of questions on fraternal Christian love (4.9), the destiny of the deceased in Christ (4.13), and the time when the day of the Lord would arrive (5.1-2). In response to all the foregoing issues Paul and his coworkers wrote 1 Thessalonians. How the letter arrived in the Thessalonians' hands is unknown.

The argument of this commentary is that 2 Thessalonians was written after 1 Thessalonians. How much time elapsed between the composition of these two communications cannot be determined with any precision, nor can we ascertain with any certainty where Paul and his associates were when it was penned. Due to the similarity of themes between the two letters, the most likely scenario is that the second letter to the church was written during the eighteen-month period that Paul spent in the city of Corinth on his second missionary journey (Acts 18.11).[18] We

---

18. The issue of the order of the epistles is discussed on pp. 64-69. The occasion of both 1 and 2 Thessalonians would be evaluated somewhat differently were their chrono-

must assume that some additional news about the state of the church reached the ears of the apostles and the second book was a response to the same. Wanamaker suggests that members of the Philippian church, which maintained close contact with Paul, were the source of the information,[19] but it is just as likely that the messenger who carried 1 Thessalonians to the church now returned with further information about the congregation.

Some of the key themes that dominated the first letter are strikingly absent from the second, indicating that they were no longer a major concern. There is no discussion that would suggest that the integrity of the Christian heralds continued to be at issue (cf. 1 Thess. 2.1-12) and no further explanation was needed concerning why they had not returned to the city (cf. 2.17–3.13). Also absent is any further discussion on sexual morality (cf. 4.3-8), fraternal love (cf. 4.9-10), or church leadership (cf. 5.14-15). On other fronts the situation of the church had deteriorated. The persecution against the church continued and had possibly intensified, although the believers were persevering through the hostility (2 Thess. 1.3-5). The first section of the letter responds to the situation by laying out the destiny of both the persecutors and the Christians (1.6-10) and assures the church of the constant prayers of the founders on their behalf (1.11-12).

Secondly, the letter takes up the issue of eschatology. This theme dominates much of 1 Thessalonians, but the question in the second book is not about the fate of the dead in Christ (cf. 1 Thess. 4.13-18) but rather the advent of the day of the Lord. The church had previously inquired about the time when that day would appear (5.1-2), but now the believers were destabilized by a teaching they had received from some source unknown to Paul to the effect that the day of the Lord had "already come" (or, perhaps, was "at hand"; 2 Thess. 2.1-2 and commentary). The deceptive teaching (2.3) found fertile ground among these Christians who were already living in the midst of great uncertainty and who had so many questions about Christian eschatology. This new doctrine threatened the stability of the congregation, and so in response Paul reminded the church of the tradition they had already received (2.5), which had included instruction concerning the events that would precede that day (2.3). The bulk of the response elaborates the coming and the destruction of the "man of lawlessness" (2.4-8) as well as explains the power of deception by which this figure is able to persuade (2.9-12). While many will

logical order reversed. See Charles A. Wanamaker, *Commentary on 1 and 2 Thessalonians* (Grand Rapids: Eerdmans, 1990), 53-63.

19. Ibid., 58-59.

believe his deception and will suffer judgment since they have not embraced the truth, Paul calls the church to stand firm in the apostolic tradition already handed down to them (2.13-17).

After asking for the church's prayers (3.1-2), Paul and his companions affirm their confidence both in God's strength and protection for the believers and in their obedience to the apostolic teaching (3.3-5). The third major theme the letter addresses is one that was already taken up in the first letter (1 Thess. 4.11-12; 5.14). Some in the congregation refused to obey the apostolic teaching (2 Thess. 3.10) and follow their example (3.7-9) about work and were continuing as dependent clients instead of working to earn their own food (3.6-15). Despite the repeated teaching, both in person and by letter, these members of the congregation refused to heed the instruction. Paul responded with an extremely strong exhortation concerning the need to earn one's own food, underlining the measures the church should take to bring disorderly members into line with apostolic teaching on this matter.

VII. THE AUTHORSHIP OF 1 AND 2 THESSALONIANS

A. 1 Thessalonians

Since ancient times few have questioned the view that 1 Thessalonians is an authentic letter of the apostle Paul. In 1.1 Paul's name appears in the epistolary greeting, alongside that of his companions Silas and Timothy, and then again in 2.18. Although the role of Silas and Timothy in the composition has been the theme of some modern discussion, virtually no one has argued that the letter is pseudonymous, save for some scholars of the nineteenth century. The verdict of one modern Thessalonian scholar, Charles Wanamaker, stands: "No contemporary scholars of repute seem to doubt the authentic Pauline character of the letter."[1] The language and style are that of the apostle Paul, and the external evidence from the early church is unanimous in favor of Pauline authorship.

The early external evidence that supports the authenticity of 1 Thessalonians is monolithic though not extensive.[2] Eusebius, the early church historian (d. 341/342), was careful to distinguish between those

---

1. Wanamaker, *Commentary on 1 and 2 Thessalonians*, 17.
2. Two full summaries are found in George Milligan, *St. Paul's Epistles to the Thessalonians* (London: Macmillan, 1908), lxxii-lxxiii; Béda Rigaux, *Les épîtres aux Thessaloniciens* (Paris: Gabalda, 1956), 112-20.

letters that were genuine and undisputed and those that were not. He included 1 Thessalonians among the authentic Paulines.[3] Allusions to the letter appear as early as the *Didache* (late first or early second century; 16.6 with 1 Thess. 4.16), while Ignatius (d. 135) echoes the book in his letters to the Romans (2.1 with 1 Thess. 2.4) and the Ephesians (10.1[4] with 1 Thess. 5.17). In the *Shepherd of Hermas* (*Vision* 3.9.10; beginning of the second century) we hear a reference to 1 Thessalonians 5.13, "Be at peace among yourselves." Tertullian even notes that the reduced canon of Marcion included this book as an authentic letter of Paul (*Against Marcion* 5.15, AD 207/208), while Tertullian himself quotes 1 Thessalonians on a number of occasions (e.g., *On the Resurrection of the Flesh* 24). The Muratorian Canon (second part of the second century) includes 1 Thessalonians, and Irenaeus (end of the second century) cites 1 Thessalonians 5.23 as the words of the apostle (*Against Heresies* 5.6.1). No ancient voice was raised against the authenticity of 1 Thessalonians.

Despite this strong and early attestation, during the nineteenth century some scholars raised questions concerning the authenticity of 1 Thessalonians. In 1836 Karl Schrader was the first to doubt that the apostle Paul had written this book, and just a few years later F. C. Baur continued the attack.[5] The objections of Baur and others who followed him revolved around four considerations. First, he observed that the character of the book was inferior to the genuine Paulines. 1 Thessalonians was a collection of general instructions and exhortations that did not reflect the doctrinal depth of the authentic Pauline letters. Furthermore, it appeared that 1 Thessalonians did not have a specific purpose or definite occasion. Second, the letter seemed to contain echoes of Pauline books as well as Acts, and these were understood as clues that the letter was an imitation. Third, while 1 Thessalonians presented itself as a document that was written in the months after the founding of the church, the description of the Christian community in the book showed a church that had progressed much more than would have been possible in that short a time. Finally, the exposition concerning the coming of the Lord in 4.13-18 was much more concrete and detailed than the other Pauline passages that treat the same subject.

---

3. *Historia Ecclesiastica* 3.3.5. At the end of his brief summary of canonical evidence he says, "This will serve to show the divine writings that are undisputed as well as those that are not universally acknowledged."

4. J. B. Lightfoot, *The Apostolic Fathers* (London: Macmillan, 1889), 2.2.58, comments that "unceasingly" is not found in the Syriac and Armenian versions of Ignatius.

5. Karl Schrader, *Der Apostel Paulus* (5 vols.; Leipzig: Christian Ernst Kollmann, 1830-36), 5.23ff.; Ferdinand Christian Baur, *Paulus: Der Apostel Jesu Christi* (Stuttgart: Becher & Müller, 1845), 480-85.

The response to the objections was strong and decisive, as well as instructive for us, despite the fact that this issue is not one of current scholarly debate.[6] In the first place, the literary works of Paul are occasional documents that respond to specific situations and therefore touch on those doctrinal and practical matters that arise from the needs of the moment. They can hardly be construed as systematic theological treatises but rather elaborate themes that address the concerns of the moment, such as the questions the Thessalonians entertained about the fate of deceased Christians or the time of the coming day of the Lord (4.13-18; 5.1-11). Secondly, the supposed dependency on other Pauline letters and Acts can alternatively be interpreted as evidence that the same author wrote the letters to the Corinthians and 1 Thessalonians and that the author of our letter was one of the principals in the history described in Acts 17. Third, the evidences of the "maturity" of the congregation, such as their evangelistic zeal (1.8) and their love and generosity (4.9-10), can be understood as signs of a true conversion (1.9-10) that was the fruit of having received the gospel as the word of God that worked powerfully in them (2.13). Finally, Paul was completely capable of giving detailed instruction concerning the coming of the Lord in one place and then treating the subject in a more summary way in another (compare Rom. 8.23 with 1 Cor. 15). Although the objections to the authenticity of 1 Thessalonians are hardly strong enough to topple the ancient testimony, they do alert us to some problems of interpretation that will be explored within this commentary.

The more vexing problem centers on the respective roles of Silvanus and Timothy in the composition of the letter (1.1).[7] In only three passages do the verbs appear in the first person singular (2.18; 3.5; 5.27; cf. 2 Thess. 2.5; 3.17), while other passages use the first person plural. Should we understand the frequently occurring "we" as an epistolary plural that functions as a formal variant of the less frequent "I"? Paul appears to make reference to himself in Romans using the plural "we" (Rom. 1.5; 3.8-9), and this custom was not unknown in the literature of the era.[8] But unlike ancient custom, Paul includes the names of two others in the introduction, leaving the impression that in one way or another they participated in the composition. Possibly Paul included their names as a formal courtesy since, as we know, Silvanus and Timothy were with Paul both at the

---

6. See Gottlieb Lünemann, *The Epistles to the Thessalonians* (Edinburgh: T&T Clark, 1880), 10-15; James Everett Frame, *A Critical and Exegetical Commentary on the Epistles of St. Paul to the Thessalonians* (Edinburgh: T&T Clark, 1912), 37-38; Rigaux, *Les épîtres aux Thessaloniciens*, 120-22.

7. The same issue arises in 2 Thess. 1.1.

8. Milligan, *St. Paul's Epistles to the Thessalonians*, 132.

time of the founding of the church and at the time of composition. However, Richards notes that the available evidence from ancient writings is not sufficiently strong to warrant the conclusion that including names of persons in a letter heading as a courtesy was a known custom.[9] On the other hand, writing correspondence in conjunction with others was indeed practiced. In Cicero's *Ad Atticum* (11.5.1) we gain some insight into joint authorship when he states, "For my part I have gathered from your letters — both that which you wrote in conjunction with others and the one you wrote in your own name — " (cf. Acts 15.23-29). At times, however, Paul includes the names of associates in his letter openings and then proceeds to write the bulk of the correspondence in the first person singular. But even if this evidence is put forward as proof that Paul might break with convention and include names as a courtesy, the statistics demonstrate that the Thessalonian letters present a unique situation. In 1 Thessalonians 96 percent of the first person verbs appear in the plural, and in 2 Thessalonians the ratio is similarly high at 89.5 percent. These figures are disproportionately high in comparison with the other Paulines where the apostle includes the name of another person in the opening greeting.[10]

Doty observes that in Hellenistic letters an author will sometimes name the messenger who carried the letter as a guarantee that what the messenger says as he interprets the correspondence comes with the sanction of the author.[11] However, Doty's observation does not explain the inclusion of their names in the opening salutation since the messenger's name is commonly used after the final salutation.[12] In light of all this evidence, the presence of the names of Silvanus and Timothy in the opening greeting of these letters should be understood as reflecting some real participation in the composition. In the three verses where the first person singular appears Paul comes forth from the group to express his particu-

---

9. E. Randolph Richards, *The Secretary in the Letters of Paul* (Tübingen: J. C. B. Mohr [Paul Siebeck], 1991), 153-54.

10.

	1st person sing.	1st person pl.
1 Cor. (with Sosthenes)	73.0%	27.0%
2 Cor. (with Timothy)	60.5%	39.5%
Phil. (with Timothy)	94.0%	6.0%
Col. (with Timothy)	70.0%	30.0%
1 Thess. (with Silvanus and Timothy)	4.0%	96.0%
2 Thess. (with Silvanus and Timothy)	10.5%	89.5%
Phlm. (with Timothy)	100%	0.0%

11. William G. Doty, *Letters in Primitive Christianity* (Philadelphia: Fortress Press, 1973), 30.

12. See the examples in A. H. Hunt and C. C. Edgar, *Select Papyri* (3 vols.; London and Cambridge: Heinemann and Harvard University Press, 1959), 1.296-97, 300-301.

lar desires. His raised voice at these moments in no way drowns out those of his associates in the rest of the letter. In 2.18 the founders' desire to get back to the church is underlined, "For we wanted to come to you — certainly I, Paul, did, again and again — but Satan stopped us." In 3.5 the emphatic "and I"[13] highlights the particular plans and desires of Paul without negating the anxiety that the others experienced concerning the well-being of this church (3.1-2). The use of the singular in these verses does not annul the reality of the plural in other verses but rather demonstrates that they truly express the views and opinions of the whole group.

Silvanus and Timothy were co-founders of this congregation (1.5, 9; 2.9; Silas in Acts 17.4; Timothy in Acts 16.3 and 18.5). Both exercised an apostolic ministry (1 Thess. 2.7), and Timothy had just returned from the church when this letter was written (3.6). Their participation in the composition of the letter should not be surprising. In fact, the idea of a strictly individual authorship has been brought into question recently, being viewed as a product "of a typical Western individualistic bias."[14] We may speak of an authorial community that includes both those responsible for the composition and the messengers who would give an oral interpretation and explanation of the concerns of the author or authors, a procedure we see functioning in the letter of the Jerusalem council (Acts 15.23-29), which is then read publicly in Antioch (15.30-31) and augmented by the oral intervention of Judas and Silas (15.32). The way an authorial community functioned should be understood in the context of community life. Dictation was known in the ancient world, but so also was a form of composition that included interaction between author and scribe.[15] In addition, a group could express its concerns and have one person bring them together in a letter, as was the case of the letter from the Jerusalem council. Is it also possible that one member of the group became the channel for the voices of the many while at the same time being the dominant player in both forming and expressing the desire of the group? This appears to be the role James played in the composition of the letter from the leadership of the Jerusalem council (cf. Acts 15.19-21 and 15.28-29). In accordance with common custom, the original composition

---

13. *Kagō.*

14. J. A. Loubser, "Media Criticism and the Myth of Paul — The Creative Genius, and His Forgotten Co-workers" (Pauline Epistles Group, SBL Annual Meeting, Orlando, Fla., 22 Nov. 1998). Loubser makes the case that "It is not the 'we' in the Pauline letters that are in need of explanation, but rather the 'I' of the authorial voice that surfaces regularly."

15. Aída Besançon Spencer, *Paul's Literary Style: A Stylistic and Historical Comparison of 2 Corinthians 11:16–13:13; Romans 8:9-39, and Philippians 3:2–4:13* (Jackson, Miss.: Evangelical Theological Society, 1984), 84-86.

of the letter was likely done on wax tablets before it was transcribed to papyrus. This process facilitated a form of composition that went beyond dictation, allowing for easy editing before the final composition was put to papyrus. We should most likely understand the process as one of collaboration but in which Paul gave the group's thoughts their final form, as is suggested by the Pauline style and vocabulary of this document. Paul was clearly the leader of this apostolic team and served as the principal authority and guarantor of the letter's contents (5.27; 2 Thess. 3.17). Whatever conclusions may be reached concerning the participation of Silas and Timothy in the composition, the primary voice and the apostolic authority that undergird it are Paul's.

B. 2 Thessalonians

In 2 Thessalonians 1.1 Paul's name appears, along with those of Silvanus and Timothy, as the author of the letter, and in 3.17 he includes a subscript, originally written in his own hand, to confirm the document's authenticity. The language and the style of the letter are distinctly Pauline,[16] but, as in the first letter, first person plural verbs dominate (we encounter the first person singular only in 2.5 and 3.17).[17] Like 1 Thessalonians, this book appears to be written by Paul, with some collaboration by his associates in ministry.

The ancient church was unanimous in its acceptance of this book as an authentic work of the apostle Paul.[18] In fact, the external evidence in favor of its authenticity is even stronger than that of 1 Thessalonians. Various ancient Christian authors allude to it, such as Ignatius (d. ca. 107; *Romans* 10.3 with 2 Thess. 3.5), Polycarp (d. ca. 155; *Philippians* 11.3 and 4 with 2 Thess. 1.4 and 3.15), and Justin (d. 165; *Dialogue with Trypho* 32.12 and 110.6 with 2 Thess. 2.3). Polycarp even attributes the words he quotes to the apostle Paul. Irenaeus (*Against Heresies* 3.7.2) refers to 2 Thessalonians 2.8 and specifies that the words were taken from the Second Letter to the Thessalonians.[19] Clement of Alexandria (d. 220) quotes 2 Thessalonians 3.1, 2 (*Stromata* 5.3) and attributes what is said to Paul. Tertullian (d. ca. 220) uses 2 Thessalonians on a number of occasions (e.g., *De Anima* 57 with 2 Thess. 2.4; *Against Marcion* 5.16 with 2 Thess. 1.6-9; 2.3-4, 9-12; and

---

16. Rigaux, *Les Épitres aux Thessaloniciens*, 80-94; Frame, *Epistles of St. Paul to the Thessalonians*, 28-37.

17. See the previous discussion on the first person plural and singular and its implication for authorship.

18. See the bibliography, p. 54, n. 2.

19. "Et iterum in secunda ad Thessalonicenses."

3.10) and even claims that his source was "the apostle." Marcion accepted the book in his New Testament, as he had 1 Thessalonians, and the Muratorian Canon places 2 Thessalonians among the books accepted by all. Not a single voice in the ancient church was raised against the authenticity of 2 Thessalonians.

In spite of the positive opinion of the church fathers regarding the paternity of this letter, from the nineteenth century onward not a few scholars have found sufficient evidence to put the letter's authenticity in doubt.[20] The debate began in the nineteenth century with J. E. C. Schmidt, who argued that although the letter was composed principally by the apostle Paul, the section from 2.1 to 2.12 was a non-Pauline interpolation. Schmidt observed a contradiction between the eschatological vision presented in that section and 1 Thessalonians 4.13–5.11. In 2 Thessalonians 2 certain events precede the end, while in 1 Thessalonians 4.13–5.11 the final day is presented as an event that arrives suddenly without any prelude.[21] Following after Schmidt, William Wrede published an attack against the authenticity of this letter based on the literary dependence he observed. According to Wrede, the author of the second letter was a copyist who imitated Paul's style (he regarded 1 Thessalonians as authentic) and repeated the themes found in 1 Thessalonians in almost the same order as they were presented there.[22]

In the modern era, the most influential authors who have argued against authenticity are Wolfgang Trilling and John Bailey.[23] Trilling and Bailey base their case on the following considerations:

1. Literary Arguments

Trilling comments that the vocabulary and style of 2 Thessalonians imitate that of 1 Thessalonians and so betray the hand of a copyist behind the writing. Bailey observes the same phenomenon and argues that the vocabulary and the style of 2 Thessalonians are so similar to 1 Thessalonians and so unoriginal that it is hard to believe that the writing was

20. On the history of the debate see especially Alfred Wikenhauser, *New Testament Introduction* (New York: Herder and Herder, 1958), 368-72; Rigaux, *Les Épitres aux Thessaloniciens*, 120-24; I. Howard Marshall, *1 and 2 Thessalonians* (Grand Rapids: Eerdmans, 1983), 28-45; and Wanamaker, *Commentary on 1 anad 2 Thessalonians*, 17-28.

21. Johann Ernst Christian Schmidt, *Vermutungen über die beiden Briefe an die Thessalonicher* (Hadamar: Gelehrtenbuchhandlung, 1801).

22. William Wrede, *Die Echtheit des zweiten Thessalonicherbrief untersucht* (Leipzig: Henrichs, 1903).

23. Wolfgang Trilling, *Untersuchungen zum zweiten Thessalonischerbrief* (Leipzig: St. Benno, 1972); John A. Bailey, "Who Wrote II Thessalonians?" *NTS* 25 (1978-79) 131-45.

penned by the apostle. But even Trilling recognizes that the argument based on vocabulary is not decisive. Moreover, they put forward no objective criteria regarding what types of stylistic variations would indicate that the two writings did not come from the same hand. The similarity of the two letters could just as well be an argument for the authenticity of 2 Thessalonians, especially if both books were written at around the same time during the apostle's ministry.

Bailey adds that the tone of 1 Thessalonians is much more personal and not as formal or official as 2 Thessalonians. 2 Thessalonians does not mention any of Paul's travel plans, and instead of saying "We always thank God for all of you" (1 Thess. 1.2; 2.13), 2 Thessalonians includes the more formal "We *ought* always to thank God for you" (2 Thess. 1.3; 2.13). But Bailey himself mentions the personal notes in 1.7 and 3.1, and what could be more personal than Paul's report about how he gloried in the Thessalonian believers among the other churches (2 Thess. 1.4)? While we would grant that 1 Thessalonians is more intensely personal, the distinct tone of the second letter arises from the different situation that letter addresses. 1 Thessalonians expresses the profound relief and joy of the apostle when Timothy returned with good news about the Thessalonian church (2.17–3.13). 2 Thessalonians, on the other hand, contains a more sustained reflection on the persecutions the church was enduring (1.3-12), corrects a doctrinal error concerning the timing of the day of the Lord (2.1-12), and strongly admonishes the unruly in the church who refused to work (3.6-15). The tone is different from that of 1 Thessalonians because the concerns of the letters are different. Bailey adds that the inclusion of a postscript to authenticate the letter (2 Thess. 3.17) was part of the mechanism of pseudepigraphy, a shallow attempt to promote the letter's authenticity. But this final note should be understood against the backdrop of the suspicion that someone had circulated a letter under Paul's name that contained false teaching about the day of the Lord (2 Thess. 2.2). The inclusion of the postscript in no way advances the argument against authenticity.

2. *The Argument from Form*

Trilling observes that the heading of 2 Thessalonians is almost identical to that of 1 Thessalonians, a phenomenon not observed in any other letter of Paul. Moreover, the thanksgiving in 2 Thessalonians 1.3-12 is so general in nature that it gives no evidence of having been written for any community in particular. Trilling's argument about the thanksgiving in 2.13-14 is similar. Concerning the apocalyptic section in 2.1-12, he notes that the author uses traditional material, something that would not be expected of Paul. Trilling also regards the prayer in 3.1-5 as being dependent on

1 Thessalonians 3.11-13 and observes that, unlike the prayer in 1 Thessalonians, it does not respond to any concrete situation. The prayer in 2 Thessalonians is more formal and general. He comments on the parenetic section concerning labor in 2 Thessalonians 3.6-15, saying that it does not respond to a real and concrete situation either. The letter was not directed to any congregation in particular, whatever the heading may indicate (1.1). On the basis of these arguments, Trilling comes to the conclusion that the person who wrote this book was not Paul.

Do Trilling's arguments support his conclusion? First, Paul could well have used a similar introduction in both letters. Second, as we will see in the commentary proper, all three chapters of the letter contemplate a real and concrete situation. This was a persecuted community that was also confused on the issues of eschatology and work. Third, the use of traditional material in 2.1-12 is not an argument against apostolic authorship because in 1 Thessalonians 4.13-18 Paul drew from traditional eschatological material that came from Jesus. Why would its inclusion here argue against Pauline authorship? In such passages as 1 Corinthians 11.23-26; 15.3-7; and Philippians 2.6-11 Paul shows no reservation about using material handed down to him as part of the tradition. Fourth, Trilling's evaluation of 3.1-5 is suspect. The prayer is born out of the situation of conflict that embroiled both the apostle and the church. Finally, the section 3.6-15 contradicts Trilling's thesis, and for that reason he must conclude that the section was included *to give the appearance* that the letter was written to a specific congregation. This is hardly a sound approach. The arguments against Pauline authorship based on the form of the letter simply do not convince.

3. The Theological Argument

Trilling points out that the theology of the letter includes Pauline elements but lacks certain themes that are commonly identified with the apostle. Moreover, he argues that the theology of the book is post-Pauline. However, as Jewett and Wanamaker have demonstrated, the supposed evidences of a post-Pauline author are also found in 1 Thessalonians and other letters that are undoubtedly Pauline. For example, Jewett comments on Trilling's perspective regarding the use of the word "gospel" in 2 Thessalonians, saying, "That 'gospel' is used in 2 Thess 1:8 without the theological sophistication of Romans and 2 Corinthians is an accurate perception, but the same is true for 1 Thess 1:5; 2:2, 4, 8, 9; and 3:2."[24] Trilling also criticizes the eschatology of the letter because the ex-

24. Jewett, *The Thessalonian Correspondence*, 13.

pectation and joy of genuine Pauline theology are absent when the author treats this theme. But the seriousness of the tone in the sections on eschatology in 2 Thessalonians is due to the severe persecution the believers faced (1.5-12) and the error about the time of the day of the Lord that had infiltrated the congregation and threatened to destabilize their faith (2.1-11). Moreover, Trilling tags the "tradition" mentioned in 2.15 as an indication that the book was written during the post-Pauline period. This argument is rather surprising since the apostle also affirms the necessity of maintaining the apostolic "tradition" in 1 Thessalonians (2.13; 4.1-2).[25] The theological arguments Trilling presents do not prove that 2 Thessalonians was composed during the post-Pauline period.

Bailey also comments on the theological questions, saying that the eschatology of 2 Thessalonians differs from and even contradicts that found in 1 Thessalonians. In 1 Thessalonians Paul deals with the question of the dead in Christ (1 Thess. 4.13-18) and the fact that the day of the Lord will come at an unexpected moment like a thief in the night (1 Thess. 5.1-11). But the eschatology of 2 Thessalonians is quite different in that, in his correction of the false teaching regarding the time of the day of the Lord, the author indicates that certain signs will occur before that great event (2 Thess. 2.1-12). However, as Marshall observes, in Jewish eschatology we encounter the same juxtaposition of the conviction that the end will come at an unexpected moment and the affirmation that there will be signs before the end.[26] The same tension is found in the eschatological teaching of Jesus (see Mark 13).

Not one of the arguments put forward by these authors is sufficiently strong to cast doubt on the traditional ascription of Pauline authorship, a fact that even Trilling recognizes. His verdict against Pauline authorship finds its support exclusively in the collective force of various weak arguments. We must ask whether this methodology is acceptable. If the foundations are weak, can the structure stand? The majority of the problems concerning authorship arise out of the relationship between this book and 1 Thessalonians. But if we suppose that the two books were written around the same time and that the second book is a response to fresh news about the worsening conditions that assailed the church, we can explain both the similarities and the differences between 1 and 2 Thessalonians. Without adequate warrant to reject the authenticity of this letter, our best approach is to follow the unanimous opinion of the ancient fathers of the church and receive this book as a genuine composition of the apostle Paul. In it we hear the authentic voice of the one com-

25. See above and the comments on these verses.
26. Marshall, *1 and 2 Thessalonians*, 37.

missioned by the Lord Jesus himself, the person who calls himself an "apostle of Jesus Christ." The apostolic authorship of the book is, in the end, the guarantor that the authority behind the book is not simply some community heavyweight such as Paul but rather Jesus himself. His voice is heard here, through his authoritative messenger, and so his words are taken as "gospel," even without being written in red letters.

VIII. THE ORDER OF THE EPISTLES

If we attempt to reconstruct the history of the gospel in Thessalonica and the chronology of the relationship between the apostolic team and the church, we need a clear understanding of which of these two letters was written first. F. F. Bruce rightly observes that the canonical order of the books is attributed to the fact that 1 Thessalonians is the longer of the two books and has nothing to do with which of the two was written first.[1] We should not be surprised that a number of modern authors have questioned the traditional order, arguing that there are clear evidences that demonstrate the priority of 2 Thessalonians. They propose that the relation between the two books is better explained if we acknowledge that 2 Thessalonians was the first letter written to this church.[2]

The first argument[3] in favor of the priority of 2 Thessalonians states that the persecutions reflected in 1 Thessalonians are part of the church's past experience whereas those of 2 Thessalonians were a present reality when that book was written. In 2 Thessalonians 1.4-7 the verbs used to describe their tribulations are all in the present tense (v. 4, "the persecutions and trials *you are enduring*"; v. 5, "for which *you are suffering*"; v. 6, "those *who trouble* you"; v. 7, "you *who are troubled*"). On the other hand, sufferings are only a memory in 1 Thessalonians 2.14 and 3.4 ("*You suffered* from your own countrymen"; "we kept telling you that we would be

---

1. F. F. Bruce, *1 and 2 Thessalonians* (Waco: Word, 1982), xli.

2. See J. C. West, "The Order of 1 and 2 Thessalonians," *JTS* 15 (1914) 66-74; Johannes Weiss, *Earliest Christianity* (2 vols.; New York: Harper and Brothers, 1959), 1.289-91; T. W. Manson, *Studies in the Gospels and Epistles* (Manchester: Manchester University Press, 1962), 259-78; Charles Buck and Greer Taylor, *Saint Paul: A Study of the Development of His Thought* (New York: Scribner's, 1969), 140-45, 149-62; Robert W. Thurston, "The Relationship between the Thessalonian Epistles," *ExpTim* 85 (1973-74) 52-56; Wanamaker, *Commentary on 1 and 2 Thessalonians*, 37-45.

3. Although Wanamaker, *Commentary on 1 and 2 Thessalonians*, presents the most recent defense of the priority of 2 Thessalonians, his arguments follow those of Manson, *Studies in the Gospels and Epistles*, with some additions. Wanamaker also evaluates the defense of the traditional understanding laid out by Jewett, *The Thessalonian Correspondence*.

persecuted. And *it turned out* that way"). Wanamaker adds that the situation 2 Thessalonians addresses is the same one that prevailed when Paul sent Timothy back to the city after the apostles' inopportune departure. As a result, Timothy's mission and the purpose of 2 Thessalonians were one and the same. Paul sent Timothy "to strengthen and encourage you in your faith" (*stērixai . . . kai parakalesai,* 1 Thess. 3.2). 2 Thessalonians expresses the same desire that God would "encourage your hearts and strengthen you" (*parakalesai . . . kai stērixai,* 2 Thess. 2.17). Timothy went to Thessalonica "so that no one would be unsettled by these trials" (1 Thess. 3.3), which is the same concern expressed in 2 Thessalonians 2.2, where the authors urge the church "not to become easily unsettled or alarmed." Wanamaker not only concludes that 1 Thessalonians was the second letter but also contends that when Timothy traveled to Thessalonica he took with him the book we know as 2 Thessalonians. The mission of Timothy and the purpose of this letter were identical.

While the arguments of Wanamaker and others are strong, they are not devoid of problems. In the first place, the believers were presently suffering persecution when 1 Thessalonians was written, as was the case when 2 Thessalonians was sent to them. While it is true that the verbs that describe the persecution are in the aorist indicative in some of the verses in 1 Thessalonians (see 1.6; 2.14; 3.2-4), we should be cautious about observing the verbs' tense while neglecting the context in which each of the verbs is located. In these verses the apostles narrate the history of the gospel's advent to the Thessalonians and how they had received it in the midst of great affliction (1.6). In their experience of suffering they followed the example of the churches in Judea (2.14). In 3.2-4 the apostles recount how the Thessalonians continued suffering during the time when Timothy visited them. What determines the verbs' tense in these sections is the narrative of the history of their conversion and their subsequent experience. The tense of the verbs does not imply that the sufferings had come to an end when 1 Thessalonians was written.

On the other hand, there are indications that Paul was conscious of continuing persecution when 1 Thessalonians was written. Timothy arrived from Thessalonica after his mission with the good news that the church continued on in faith and love, and so Paul and the rest were able to exclaim, "For now we really live, since you are standing firm in the Lord" (1 Thess. 3.8). "Standing firm" (*stēkō*) is frequently the verb used to describe stability in the midst of persecutions (Phil. 1.27, 28; 2 Thess. 2.15), and it is exactly this type of situation that the narrative in 1 Thessalonians 3.1-10 reflects.[4] The fact that they are "standing firm" implies that they

4. See the comments on 3.8.

faced opposition that threatened to destabilize them. Moreover, the teaching about revenge (1 Thess. 5.15) became an aspect of the apostolic exhortation given to communities that faced persecution (as, e.g., 1 Pet. 3.9),[5] though the source of the corrective was traditional (Prov. 20.22). And although 1 Thessalonians 3.3 specifically mentions the situation of the church when Paul sent Timothy to them (3.2), the reference to "*these* trials" implies that the unbelievers continued to accost the church up through the time that 1 Thessalonians was written. The Thessalonians' sufferings were not simply a memory when 1 Thessalonians was composed.

Wanamaker argues that Timothy carried the letter known as 2 Thessalonians in his mission to the church described in 1 Thessalonians 3.1-5. But it is quite curious that 1 Thessalonians makes no mention of a previous written communication when the apostles narrate the history of that mission. Wanamaker explains this omission by saying that Timothy had the responsibility of interpreting the letter, and for that reason it was not necessary to mention it. While it is true that ancient messengers were charged with adding and clarifying information contained in the letters they carried, their role was supplementary to that of the letters themselves.[6] We would expect that Paul would have mentioned the letter and its contents and not simply the previous visit of Timothy. As noted above, Wanamaker also maintains that the purpose of sending Timothy and the letter known as 2 Thessalonians was "to strengthen and encourage" the Thessalonians (1 Thess. 3.3; 2 Thess. 2.17). This argument in no way proves that Timothy carried that letter to the church. The combination of "strengthen and encourage" was a standard description of what we might call the "ministry of follow-up" for new churches, especially those that were undergoing persecution (cf. Acts 14.22; 15.32; *stērizō* in 18.23; 1 Pet. 5.10; and *parakaleō* in Acts 11.23). The inclusion of this common language to describe the visit of Timothy and the purpose of 2 Thessalonians is not an important factor in determining whether or not both these events occurred at the same time. Both the letter and the visit were aspects of standard operating procedure in this ministry of establishing the new congregations. Paul employs traditional language, and not language specific to the situation, to describe both the visit and the letter. Moreover, similar exhortations using the same verbs are found in 1 Thessalonians 3.13 and 5.11. We cannot arrive at the conclusion that Timothy carried 2 Thessalonians on the basis of these verbs.

The second argument in favor of the priority of 2 Thessalonians

---

5. Eugenio Green, *1 Pedro y 2 Pedro* (Miami: Editorial Caribe, 1993), 197-98.

6. John Lee White, *Light from Ancient Letters* (Philadelphia: Fortress Press, 1986), 216.

states that the internal problems of the church, such as the issue of the disorderly (2 Thess. 3.11-12), are new concerns in 2 Thessalonians, whereas 1 Thessalonians presupposes that everyone already understood both the problem and the apostolic response. In 1 Thessalonians Paul exhorts them "to work with your hands, just as we told you" (4.11), a supposed reference to the previous letter 2 Thessalonians (cf. also 1 Thess. 5.14). But this teaching was a point in the apostolic instruction given orally to the Thessalonians soon after the apostles founded the church (2 Thess. 3.6-10). The allusion in 1 Thessalonians to the instruction about work could just as easily be to the oral instruction the church had received and not to the teaching contained in 2 Thessalonians.

Another argument put forward in favor of the priority of 2 Thessalonians is the unlikelihood that 1 Thessalonians was the first letter written since 2 Thessalonians 3.17 inserts an authenticating note saying, "I, Paul, write this greeting in my own hand, which is the distinguishing mark in all my letters." This manner of indicating authorship and authenticity would make sense only in the first letter to the church and not in the second. However, as we will see in the comments on this verse and 2 Thessalonians 2.2, the authenticating subscript became necessary because of the suspicion of the circulation of a letter or letters falsely written under the name of Paul ("letter supposed to have come from us").

A fourth reason why some consider 2 Thessalonians to be the first letter is that 1 Thessalonians 5.1 ("Now, brothers, about times and dates we do not need to write to you") seems appropriate only if the church already had the teaching of 2 Thessalonians 2.1-12 in hand. However, 2 Thessalonians 2.5 discloses that this eschatological instruction was also part of the apostolic teaching given orally that the church had received while Paul was with them. The reference in 1 Thessalonians 5.1 could simply be a reference to the teaching they had already received orally.

Similarly, some argue that 2 Thessalonians was the first letter because at a number of points 1 Thessalonians alludes to teaching the church had already received in 2 Thessalonians (1 Thess. 4.9-10 and 2 Thess. 3.6-15; 1 Thess. 4.13 and 2 Thess. 2.1-12; 1 Thess. 5.1 and 2 Thess. 2.1-12). This teaching led the Thessalonians to ask Paul a number of questions that arose out of each point, to which the apostle replies in 1 Thessalonians, the second letter to the church. Although it is possible that Paul responds to the concerns of the Thessalonians in 1 Thessalonians 4.9, 13 and 5.1,[7] communicated orally or in written form to the apostle, it is not entirely certain that these questions arose as a reaction to a previous letter. As shown above, the teaching in 4.11 had to do with the previous oral

_____

7. See the comments on these verses.

instruction about labor. The concern expressed in 4.13 was generated by the fact that some members of the church had died before the day of the Lord and the church did not fully understand the implications of this situation. The problem that stands behind 2 Thessalonians 2 is completely different from that of 1 Thessalonians 5.1 (see 2 Thess. 2.2). Moreover, their questions about the "times and dates" arose out of the same complex of teaching on eschatology that they had received orally soon after the church was founded (2 Thess. 2.5).

None of the arguments that Manson and Wanamaker put forward in favor of the priority of 2 Thessalonians is decisive. In fact, the evidence flows in the opposite direction. 2 Thessalonians 2.15 refers to a previous letter written to the church: "stand firm and hold to the teachings we passed on to you, whether by word of mouth or *by letter.*"[8] The verb "we passed on" (*edidachthēte*; NRSV, "you were taught") is not an "epistolary aorist" that makes reference to the teaching contained in this letter, as Wanamaker suggests, because the verb is linked not only with a written correspondence but also with the teaching they had received orally in the past. Nor can it be proved that the sense of the verb is a perfect passive that included both the previous oral teaching and the letter itself (1 Thessalonians).[9] Rather, both the oral instruction and the letter were previous communications. It is possible that the reference is not to 1 Thessalonians but to some other letter. But this letter is the only known and extant candidate. We have no warrant to suggest the existence of another letter.

1 Thessalonians makes no mention of any previous written communication with the church but repeatedly looks back to more recent events in the common experience of the Thessalonians and the apostles: the entrance of the apostles and founding of the church, the exit of the apostolic team, the concern for the church's well-being, the attempts by Paul to return, and the mission of Timothy to Thessalonica. 1 Thessalonians sees the conversion of these believers as an event of the recent past (2.17 and comments). This letter responds to the necessities of this new community, which Timothy related to Paul and Silvanus when he returned from the city (1 Thess. 3.6). 2 Thessalonians touches on a number of the same problems, which had gone from bad to worse, such as the persecutions they had endured and the refusal of some members to work, while at the same time answering a threat to the stability of the church, the entrance of a novel and erroneous teaching concerning the day of the Lord (2 Thess.

---

8. 2 Thess. 2.2 and 3.17 are not evidences of a previous letter, as Wanamaker correctly observes. See the comments on these passages.

9. See the comments on 2 Thess. 2.15.

2.2). 2 Thessalonians comes from the period in the relationship between the community and the apostle when Paul was convinced of the "perseverance and faith" of the Thessalonians in the midst of their persecutions (2 Thess. 1.4). But when Timothy was sent to Thessalonica, doubts about their ability to endure caused no end of anxiety (1 Thess. 3.1-5), and therefore it is difficult to imagine that 2 Thessalonians was the letter Timothy carried with him on his mission. Although the traditional order of the letters in the canon was due originally to their relative size, this order best explains the historical phenomena here observed.

IX. THE STRUCTURE OF 1 AND 2 THESSALONIANS

In recent years, scholars have generated a considerable amount of discussion concerning the literary analysis of 1 and 2 Thessalonians. Quite a few authors have attempted to analyze these and other NT letters with reference to the canons of rhetoric that prevailed during the era when they were written. Rhetoric was studied in the schools of the rhetoricians, while experts in rhetorical technique arrived at the cities of the Roman Empire to promote their ideas and to acquire students, and through them their livelihood. Those who practiced the art of rhetoric followed the principles and techniques laid out by writers like Aristotle in his famous *Ars Rhetorica*. He defined rhetoric as "the faculty of discovering the possible means of persuading in reference to any subject whatever."[1] Rhetoricians gave public lectures in various locations in the cities, such as public buildings (both governmental and religious), the odeon, or the theater. Those who sought their instruction had the ambition of entering public office or wanted to become professionals in rhetorical technique. Such people were also equipped to serve as ambassadors or legal counsel. Those who belonged to the social elite were expected to have undergone training in rhetoric.[2] Since public rhetoric was a fixture in ancient Greek and Roman society, not a few authors have asked whether Paul employed rhetorical methodology in his letters and whether the principles of rhetoric can help us to understand the purpose and structure of his

---

1. Aristotle, *Ars Rhetorica* 1.2.1.
2. See Bruce W. Winter, "Entries and Ethics of Orators and Paul (1 Thessalonians 2:11-12)," *TynBul* 44 (1993) 57-60. For introductory discussions on rhetoric and the NT, see George A. Kennedy, *New Testament Interpretation through Rhetorical Criticism* (Chapel Hill and London: University of North Carolina Press, 1984); A. Duane Litfin, *St. Paul's Theology of Proclamation: 1 Corinthians 1–4 and Greco-Roman Rhetoric* (Cambridge and New York: Cambridge University Press, 1994).

writings. 1 and 2 Thessalonians occupy center stage in this contemporary debate.[3]

Aristotle classified public discourse into three categories: deliberative, judicial, and epideictic rhetoric.[4] Deliberative rhetoric was used in discourses that had to do with the future, and its purpose was to exhort or dissuade. Judicial rhetoric, on the other hand, was oriented to the past, and its purpose was to accuse or defend. The context of judicial rhetoric was the tribunal. Epideictic rhetoric concerned the present; its purpose was to praise or blame.[5] Aristotle held the opinion that the epideictic style was especially suited for written compositions,[6] and a number of modern authors have identified 1 Thessalonians as an example of this kind of rhetoric due to its praise of good conduct and censure of bad behavior.[7] At the same time, a number of authors argue that 2 Thessalonians is a good example of deliberative rhetoric.[8] These authors proceed to analyze the structure of the argument in these letters using rhetorical categories, dividing the letters according to the components of rhetorical discourse as discussed by Aristotle, Cicero, and others who gave instruction on the use of rhetoric. Their analysis attempts to identify elements such as the *exordium*, the *narratio*, the *partitio*, the *probatio*, and the *peroratio*. The *exordium* is the beginning or prologue of the discourse, the *narratio* is the exposition of events that have occurred, the *partitio* pre-

---

3. Summaries of the recent debate can be found in Steve Walton, "What Has Aristotle to Do with Paul? Rhetorical Criticism of 1 Thessalonians," *TynBul* 46 (1995) 229-50; Frank Witt Hughes, *Early Christian Rhetoric and 2 Thessalonians* (Sheffield: Sheffield Academic Press, 1989), 19-50; Jewett, *The Thessalonian Correspondence*, 61-87; Wanamaker, *Commentary on 1 and 2 Thessalonians*, 45-52; and more recently Karl P. Donfried and Johannes Beutler, *The Thessalonians Debate: Methodological Discord or Methodological Synthesis?* (Grand Rapids and Cambridge: Eerdmans, 2000). From ancient times it has been recognized that Paul used rhetorical elements on the syntactic level (such as the *gradatio* in Rom. 5.3-5), but recent discussion has focused on the use of rhetorical categories to analyze the structure of entire documents.

4. Aristotle, *Ars Rhetorica* 1.4-10.

5. Ibid., 1.3.3-4.

6. Ibid., 3.12.5-6.

7. For example, Jewett, *The Thessalonian Correspondence*, 71; Walton, "What Has Aristotle to Do with Paul?" 234-38, 249-50; Karl P. Donfried and I. Howard Marshall, *The Theology of the Shorter Pauline Letters* (Cambridge: Cambridge University Press, 1993), 4; F. W. Hughes, "The Rhetoric of 1 Thessalonians," in *The Thessalonian Correspondence* (ed. R. F. Collins; Leuven: Leuven University Press, 1990), 97. But cf. Bruce C. Johanson, *To All the Brethren* (Stockholm: Almqvist & Wiksell International, 1987), 189, who opts for the position that the letter is an example of deliberative rhetoric.

8. Hughes, *Early Christian Rhetoric and 2 Thessalonians*, 73-74; Donfried and Marshall, *The Theology of the Shorter Pauline Letters*, 84; Jewett, *The Thessalonian Correspondence*, 82; Glenn H. Holland, *The Tradition That You Received from Us: 2 Thessalonians in the Pauline Tradition* (Tübingen: J. C. B. Mohr [Paul Siebeck], 1988), 6.

sents the problem, and the *probatio* is the proof and, therefore, the most important part of the rhetorical discourse. The *peroratio* is added as the finale of the speech.[9] The following chart presents the analysis of several authors who have attempted to identify these rhetorical structural components in 1 and 2 Thessalonians:[10]

1 Thessalonians:

	Hughes	Jewett	Wanamaker
Prescriptio	—	—	1.1
Exordium	1.1-10	1.1-5	1.2-10
Narratio	2.1–3.10	1.6–3.13	2.1–3.10
Partitio	3.11-13	—	—
Transitus	—	—	3.11-12
Probatio	4.1–5.3	4.1–5.22	4.1–5.22
Peroratio	5.4-11	5.23-28	5.23-28
"Exhortation"	5.12-22	—	—
Conclusion	5.23-28	—	—

2 Thessalonians:

	Hughes	Jewett	Wanamaker	Holland
Prescriptio	—	—	1.1-2	1.1-2
Exordium	1.1-12	1.1-12	1.3-12	1.3-4
Narratio	—	—	—	1.5-12
Partitio	2.1-2	2.1-2	2.1-2	—
Probatio	2.3-17	2.3–3.5	2.3-15*	2.1-17
Exhortatio	3.1-15	3.6-15	3.1-15*	3.1-13
Peroratio	3.14-15	3.16-18	2.16-17*	—
Postscript	3.16-18	—	3.16-18	3.16-18

In spite of the similarity of analysis at a number of points, the differences between these authors' perceptions of the structure give us pause. Did Paul and his associates really have these rhetorical categories in mind when they composed the letters? Is this a "good fit," or one that is forced upon the letter? But beyond this concern we must ask if it is legitimate to analyze the *letters* of the NT using the categories of *oral rhetorical discourse.* Aristotle, Cicero, and others who wrote extensively about rhetoric focused

9. For a fuller analysis of the various components of rhetorical discourse, see Aristotle, *Ars Rhetorica* 3.14-19; Cicero, *De Inventione* 1.19; *De Partitione Oratoria* 27; and the summary in Hughes, *Early Christian Rhetoric and 2 Thessalonians*, 30-43.

10. Jewett, *The Thessalonian Correspondence*, 221, 225; see also Donfried and Marshall, *The Theology of the Shorter Pauline Epistles*, 6-7, 83-84; Wanamaker, *Commentary on 1 and 2 Thessalonians*, 48-52. The strong influence of Hughes is evident in these recent studies.

their discussion on oral discourse and not principally on written communication. The counterargument has been raised that those who discussed rhetoric were the same ones who taught about epistolary forms, and at times comparisons were made between oral and written communication. For example, Demetrius in his tract *De Elocutione* echoed Artemon, the editor of letters of Aristotle, who said "that a letter should be written in the same manner as a dialogue,"[11] and Cicero compared written communication with conversation.[12] Seneca likewise wanted his letters to read like conversations.[13] However, we note that the comparison these authors make is consistently between letters and conversation and not between letters and formal rhetorical discourse. In fact, they state explicitly that the style of a written composition should not be the same as that of formal discourse. Aristotle himself indicated that the style of written composition should differ from the style of a debate. He expounds rather extensively on the differences between the type of rhetoric that is appropriate for a debate and that which one should use in a letter.[14] Letters could be read out loud to their recipients (Diodorus Siculus 15.10.2; cf. 1 Thess. 5.27), but this act did not transform them into formal discourses.

Despite this differentiation between formal discourse and letters, some comparisons were made between types of discourse and categories of letters. Aristotle even said that epideictic rhetoric was most in harmony with the purposes of a letter. Moreover, later manuals written on the composition of letters[15] included categories that came from the discussions on rhetoric, such as "praise" and "blame."[16] However, nowhere can we find an analysis of the structure of letters that is analogous to the teaching on the structure of oral discourse. While there exists a general relationship between the types of letters and rhetoric, the norms for the elaboration of these two genres were distinct. Letters were more like conversation and less like formal discourse.

Recent studies on the composition of letters in antiquity provide us with a much more useful analysis of these letters.[17] Manuals on episto-

11. Demetrius, *De Elocutione* 223. He goes on to clarify, "The letter should be a little more formal than a dialogue, since the latter imitates improvised conversation, while the former is written and sent as a kind of gift" (224). But Demetrius differentiates between the style of "oral delivery" and letters (226).

12. Cicero, *Ad Atticum* 8.14.1; 9.10.1; 12.53.

13. Seneca, *Epistulae Morales* 75.1.

14. Aristotle, *Ars Rhetorica* 3.12.1-3.

15. See Abraham Malherbe, *Ancient Epistolary Theorists* (Atlanta: Scholars Press, 1988).

16. Pseudo-Demetrius, cited in Malherbe, *Ancient Epistolary Theorists,* 32-33.

17. See, e.g., John Lee White, *The Body of the Greek Letter* (Missoula, Mont.: Society of Biblical Literature, 1972); idem, *Light from Ancient Letters* (Philadelphia: Fortress Press,

lary theory identified various types of letters, such as the one written by Pseudo-Demetrius, who identified twenty-one types: "friendly, commendatory, blaming, reproachful, consoling, censorious, admonishing, threatening, vituperative, praising, advisory, supplicatory, inquiring, responding, allegorical, accounting, accusing, apologetic, congratulatory, ironic, thankful."[18] A number of centuries later, Pseudo-Libanius managed to identify some forty-one types of letters.[19] Many of the categories which Pseudo-Libanius presented were already discussed by Pseudo-Demetrius. One type of composition in his list was called the "mixed" letter. Its content was a combination of various types of letters. 1 Thessalonians could well be classified as this kind of correspondence since it includes elements that identify the letter as "thankful" (1.2-3; 2.13-16), "commendatory" (1.4-10), "apologetic" (2.1-12), "friendly" (2.17–3.13), "admonishing" (4.1-12; 5.12-23), and "consoling" (4.13–5.11). 2 Thessalonians combines a number of letter types in the same way. To identify these writings as a single kind of letter ignores the fact that they respond to a variety of necessities within the community to which they were written. The Thessalonians needed the affirmation of the friendship of the apostles but also consolation in the face of the death of loved ones and exhortation regarding their moral life. These letters are of the "mixed" type, and any attempt to categorize the whole any more narrowly fails in the light of their many facets.[20]

A number of studies on ancient letters have isolated their fundamental components: (1) the introduction (including the name of the author, the recipients, a greeting, and frequently additional greetings or a wish that the recipient would be in good health); (2) the body (introduced with some characteristic formula); and (3) the conclusion (including greetings, wishes, and a final greeting or prayer).[21] Studies on the form of the Pauline letters reveal that the apostle followed this basic outline with

---

1986); William G. Doty, *Letters in Primitive Christianity* (Philadelphia: Westminster Press, 1986); David E. Aune, *The New Testament in Its Literary Environment* (Philadelphia: Westminster Press, 1987); Malherbe, *Ancient Epistolary Theorists*.

18. Pseudo-Demetrius, "Epistolary Types," in Malherbe, *Ancient Epistolary Theorists*, 31.

19. Pseudo-Libanius, "Epistolary Styles," 4, in Malherbe, *Ancient Epistolary Theorists*, 66-67.

20. For example, Aune, *The New Testament in Its Literary Environment*, 206, and Stanley K. Stowers, *Letter Writing in Greco-Roman Antiquity* (Philadelphia: Westminster Press, 1986), 96, say that 1 Thessalonians is a "parenetic" letter (one of the categories mentioned in Pseudo-Libanius). Stowers contends that 2 Thessalonians is a letter of praise and blame (80, 128).

21. Doty, *Letters in Primitive Christianity*, 14; White, *Light from Ancient Letters*, 194-213.

certain modifications. After the introduction (which includes the names of the author and the recipients with a greeting) comes a thanksgiving or a blessing.[22] The body of the letter follows, introduced by a standard form and including notes about the apostolic *parousia* or coming, which is then followed by a parenetic section. The closing consists of greetings, a doxology, and a benediction.[23] Aristotle compared letters with epideictic rhetoric, as noted above.[24] Their function was to combine praise and blame, and this is precisely the combination that is characteristic of Pseudo-Libanius's "mixed" type of letter.[25] I would suggest that the parenetic sections of Paul's letters should therefore be understood as integral parts of the body of the letter and not as appendixes to it. In any case, the letters to the Thessalonians conform to this standard format, with the body of the letter taking up the major portion of the composition. Therefore, apart from the observations we can make about the general structure of these compositions, we should examine these letters thematically. What guides the apostle in the development of the structure of these letters are the events and situations that arose out the realities the Thessalonians faced, including the distance of the founders from the church, the persecution, the moral lapse of certain members, the death of some believers, and doctrinal confusion.[26] Their concerns are pastoral, and these are what give the body of the letter its character and form. The following outlines are presented in light of these observations:

22. On this section, see Paul Schubert, *The Form and Function of the Pauline Thanksgivings* (Berlin: Alfred von Töpelmann, 1939); Jack T. Sanders, "The Transition from Opening Epistolary Thanksgiving to the Body in the Letters of the Pauline Corpus," *JBL* 81 (1962) 348-62. I do not accept the conclusion of Schubert (pp. 16-27) that the thanksgiving of the letter extends all the way to 3.13. Paul includes a formula in 2.1 to signal the start of the body of the letter: "You yourselves know, brothers. . . ." See White, *The Body of the Greek Letter*, 115-20.

23. Doty, *Letters in Primitive Christianity*, 27; White, *Light from Ancient Letters*, 71, 112.

24. See p. 70, n. 6.

25. Pseudo-Libanius, "Epistolary Types," 92, in Malherbe, *Ancient Epistolary Theorists*, 80-81.

26. Hendrikus Boers, "The Form Critical Study of Paul's Letters: I Thessalonians as a Case Study," *NTS* 22 (1976) 142, commenting on the comparison between the structure of 1 Thessalonians and that of Hellenistic letters, cautions that "one should be careful not to assume that Paul's letters had to conform to a particular pattern. Paul was undoubtedly, consciously and subconsciously, influenced by the conventions of Hellenistic letters, but it would be a mistake to assume that his letters had to follow a given pattern."

1 THESSALONIANS

I. **"PAUL, SILAS AND TIMOTHY, TO THE CHURCH OF THE THESSALONIANS" — THE EPISTOLARY GREETING (1.1)**

II. **"WE ALWAYS THANK GOD FOR ALL OF YOU" — THE COMING OF THE GOSPEL AND ITS RECEPTION (1.2-10)**

III. **"YOU KNOW . . ." — THE BODY OF THE LETTER (2.1–5.22)**
    A. "OUR VISIT TO YOU WAS NOT A FAILURE" — THE GOSPEL ARRIVES IN THESSALONICA (2.1–3.13)
        1. "Our visit" — The Apostolic Entrance (2.1-12)
        2. "We also thank God . . . you received the word of God" — The Reception of the Gospel(2.13-16)
        3. "We were torn away from you" — The Exit of the Apostles and the Attempts to Return (2.17-20)
        4. "We sent Timothy" — The Mission of Timothy (3.1-5)
        5. "But Timothy has just now come to us" — Thanksgiving to God for the Thessalonians (3.6-10)
        6. "Now may our God . . . clear the way for us to come to you" — The Prayer to Return to Thessalonica (3.11-13)
    B. "YOU KNOW WHAT INSTRUCTIONS WE GAVE YOU" — THE LIFE THAT PLEASES GOD (4.1–5.22)
        1. "We instructed you how to live in order to please God" — The Introduction (4.1-2)
        2. "You should avoid sexual immorality" — Sanctification (4.3-8)
        3. "Now about . . ." — Responses to Questions (4.9–5.11)
          a. Fraternal "love" (4.9-12)
          b. "Those who fall asleep" (4.13-18)
          c. "Times and dates" (5.1-11)
        4. "Respect those who work hard among you" — The Community and Its Leadership (5.12-13)
        5. "Warn . . . encourage . . . help . . . be patient" — Life in Community (5.14)
        6. "Make sure that nobody pays back wrong for wrong" — The Life of Nonretaliation (5.15)
        7. "Be joyful . . . pray . . . give thanks" — Communion with God (5.16-18)
        8. "Do not put out the Spirit's fire" — Prophecy in the Community (5.19-22)

IV. "MAY GOD HIMSELF" — THE FINAL PRAYER, GREETINGS, AND BLESSING (5.23-28)
  A. "MAY GOD . . . SANCTIFY YOU THROUGH AND THROUGH" (5.23-25)
  B. "GREET ALL THE BROTHERS AND SISTERS" (5.26-27)
  C. "THE GRACE OF OUR LORD JESUS CHRIST BE WITH YOU" (5.28)

2 THESSALONIANS

  I. "PAUL, SILVANUS, AND TIMOTHY, TO THE CHURCH OF THE THESSALONIANS" — THE EPISTOLARY SALUTATION (1.1-2)

 II. "YOUR FAITH IS GROWING AND YOUR LOVE IS INCREASING " — THANKSGIVING AND PRAYERS FOR THE FAITH, LOVE, AND STEADFASTNESS OF THE PERSECUTED THESSALONIANS (1.3-12)
  A. "WE MUST ALWAYS GIVE THANKS TO GOD FOR YOU" — THE FIRST THANKSGIVING (1.3-5)
  B. "IT IS INDEED JUST OF GOD TO REPAY WITH AFFLICTION THOSE WHO AFFLICT YOU" — THE DESTINY OF THE PERSECUTORS (1.6-10)
  C. "TO THIS END WE WILL ALWAYS PRAY FOR YOU" — THE REMEMBRANCE OF PRAYERS TO BE WORTHY OF GOD'S CALL (1.11-12)

III. "AS TO . . ." — THE BODY OF THE LETTER (2.1–3.15)
  A. "AS TO THE COMING OF OUR LORD JESUS CHRIST" — THE TIME OF THE DAY OF THE LORD (2.1-17)
    1. Do not "be quickly shaken" — False Teaching about the Day of the Lord (2.1-12)
    2. "But we must always give thanks to God for you" — The Second Thanksgiving (2.13-14)
    3. "Stand firm and hold fast to the traditions" — Exhortation to Steadfastness (2.15)
    4. "Now may our Lord Jesus Christ himself and God our Father" — The First Prayer (2.16-17)
  B. "FINALLY, BROTHERS AND SISTERS" — FINAL INSTRUCTIONS (3.1-15)
    1. "Pray for us" — Mutual Prayers (3.1-5)

      a. *"So that the word of the Lord may spread rapidly"* — *The Prayer Request of the Apostles (3.1-2)*

      b. *"But the Lord is faithful; he will strengthen you"* — *Confidence in the Lord (3.3-4)*

      c. *"May the Lord direct your hearts to the love of God"* — *The Second Prayer (3.5)*

  2. "Now we command you" — The Problem of the Disorderly (3.6-15)

      a. *"Keep away from believers who are living in idleness"* — *The First Exhortation (to the Community) (3.6)*

      b. *"We were not idle when we were with you"* — *The Example of the Apostles (3.7-10)*

      c. *"Work quietly and earn your own living"* — *The Second Exhortation (to the Disorderly) (3.11-12)*

      d. *"Do not be weary in doing what is right"* — *The Third Exhortation (to the Community) (3.13)*

      e. *"Take note of those who do not obey"* — *Discipline in the Community (3.14-15)*

IV. "NOW MAY THE LORD OF PEACE HIMSELF GIVE YOU PEACE" — THE THIRD PRAYER AND FINAL GREETINGS (3.16-18)

A. "NOW MAY THE LORD OF PEACE HIMSELF GIVE YOU PEACE" — THE FIRST BENEDICTION (3.16)

B. "I, PAUL, WRITE THIS GREETING" — THE APOSTOLIC GREETING AND GUARANTEE (3.17)

C. "THE GRACE OF OUR LORD JESUS CHRIST BE WITH YOU ALL" — THE FINAL BENEDICTION (3.18)

1 THESSALONIANS

I. "PAUL, SILAS AND TIMOTHY, TO THE CHURCH OF THE THESSALONIANS" — THE EPISTOLARY GREETING (1.1)

1 The function of ancient letters, especially those that could be classified as letters of friendship,[1] was to shorten the distance between the author and the recipients. In one correspondence, Seneca the philosopher wrote, "I never receive a letter from you without being in your company forthwith."[2] In the case of Paul and the Thessalonians, the agony of separation was acute while the desire to be reunited burned brightly (2.17-18; 3.6, 10, 11). In the gap between the present and that reunion, the letter lays bare the heart of the author to the church and serves as a means to communicate his care and concern as well as to pass on the teaching that the believers were lacking (2 Thess. 2.15; cf. 1 Thess. 3.10).

The form of the letter follows the conventions of the time. Unlike modern letters, Greek correspondence began with the name of the author followed by the name of the recipient and a salutation.[3] For example, one letter from the first century begins, "Sarapion to our Heraclides, greeting." Frequently letters added greetings at the end of the correspondence as well. The same letter ends by saying, "Salute Diodorus heartily. Goodbye. Salute Harpocration."[4] In a similar way, 1 Thessalonians begins with the names of the authors and the recipients and ends with a greeting to all the brothers and sisters (5.26). Although the format of 1 Thessalonians

---

1. See the comments on the structure and genre of this letter, pp. 69-74.

2. Seneca, *Epistulae Morales* 40.1; and see 75.1; Cicero, *Epistulae ad Familiares* 2.4.1. Pseudo-Libanius, "Epistolary Styles" 2, similarly states some centuries later, "A letter, then, is a kind of written conversation with someone from whom one is separated, and it fulfills a definite need. One will speak in it as though one were in the company of the absent person" (quoted in Malherbe, *Ancient Epistolary Theorists*, 67).

3. White, *Light from Ancient Letters*, 194-97. White gives examples of letters that diverge from this norm, such as those of petition that first name the recipient, then insert a greeting and, at the end of the salutation, the name of the author.

4. Hunt and Edgar, *Select Papyri*, 1.297, 299. Examples from the NT can be found in Acts 15.23-29 and 23.25-30.

is similar to that of ordinary letters of the era, it is much longer and the content much more substantial. This and other NT letters rise above the literary level of common correspondence but do not approach the rhetorical sophistication of the letter-essays of an author such as Cicero.[5] Rather, 1 Thessalonians is a pastoral letter whose aim is to respond to the needs that resulted from the acute situation of the congregation and the distance that separated the church from its founders.

Paul, Silas and Timothy are the three authors of this letter,[6] although Paul appears to be the principal person responsible for its composition.[7] These three were the founders of the church and were together in Corinth when they wrote this correspondence shortly after Timothy had arrived with news of the believers' faith, love, and steadfastness in the midst of the persecutions they were facing (3.6, 8). *Paul* (the Greek name *Paulos* is a transliteration of the Latin *Paulus*) is the Roman name of Saul (Acts 13.9).[8] Unlike the majority of his letters, this one does not include the name of his office, "apostle," in the greeting (cf. Rom. 1.1; 1 Cor. 1.1; 2 Cor. 1.1; Gal. 1.1; Eph. 1.1; Col. 1.1; 1 Tim. 1.1; 2 Tim. 1.1; Tit. 1.1). Although conscious of his apostolic authority (1 Thess. 2.7), he does not insert the title either here, in 2 Thessalonians, or in Philippians. Apparently Paul did not feel the necessity of emphasizing his apostolic authority to these churches, which is perhaps a testament of the good relationship that existed between him and the Macedonian believers. In 2.7 he similarly ex-

---

5. Stowers, *Letter Writing in Greco-Roman Antiquity*, 25.

6. Current scholarship on letter writing in antiquity makes no distinction between "letters" and "epistles." See Stowers, *Letter Writing in Greco-Roman Antiquity*, 17-21; Aune, *The New Testament in Its Literary Environment*, 160; Jerome Murphy-O'Connor, *Paul the Letter-Writer* (Collegeville, Minn.: Liturgical Press, 1995), 42-45.

7. See p. 59.

8. As a Roman citizen (Acts 22.25-29), Paul would have had at least three names: "forename" *(praenomen)*, family name *(nomen gentile)*, and additional name *(cognomen)*. Of these we know only his *cognomen*, Paullus" (F. F. Bruce, *Paul: Apostle of the Heart Set Free* [Grand Rapids: Eerdmans, 1977], 38). To this *tria nomina* could be added the father's name and the tribe to which a Roman citizen belonged. During the imperial period, the *cognomen* was increasingly used as the principal name. Paulus (or its variant Paullus) was a common name among the upper classes, and Paul's family, being Roman citizens, may well have been of the social elite of Tarsus (Acts 22.3). The use of double names was popular during this era, so it does not surprise us to discover that he was called both Paul and the Hebrew Saul (his *supernomen,* a kind of *cognomen; Saulos* being the Greek transliteration of Heb. *Sha'ul*). The common way of indicating that a person had two names is found in Acts 13.9 *(A. ho kai B.),* and this most likely indicates that he had both names from his birth. See *New Docs,* 1.94; also *OCD,* 1024-26. On the names of Paul, see Colin J. Hemer, "The Name of Paul," *TynBul* 36 (1985) 179-83; *New Docs,* 1.89-96; 2.106-8; Adolf Deissmann, *Bible Studies* (Edinburgh: T&T Clark, 1901), 313-17; Martin Hengel, *The Pre-Christian Paul* (Philadelphia: Trinity Press International, 1991), 105-6.

presses his reservation about making full use of his apostolic authority with this congregation.[9]

Silas (NIV), or rather "Silvanus" in the Greek text (see the *NIV* note), is the *cognomen* or surname of this Roman citizen (Acts 16.37). This is the Latinized form of the Semitic *Silwani*. *Silas* is his other Greek name, which itself is a transliteration of the Aramaic form of the name "Saul."[10] Silvanus had been a leader in the Jerusalem church and exercised a prophetic ministry (Acts 15.22, 32). The Jerusalem council had appointed him sometime previously, along with Judas, to accompany Paul and Barnabas when they delivered the decision of that body to the church of Antioch (Acts 15.22, 27, 32). After the division between Paul and Barnabas, Paul chose Silvanus to become his coworker during his second missionary journey. Silvanus was possibly left at Corinth, where he had participated in the evangelistic ministry alongside Paul and Timothy (Acts 18.5; 2 Cor. 1.19). 1 Peter 5.12 indicates that he eventually arrived at Rome, where he became Peter's secretary, being responsible for penning that letter or perhaps even for the translation of Peter's thoughts into Greek.[11] According to Acts 17.4, Silvanus was one of the founders of the church in Thessalonica.

Timothy, whose name was common among both the Greek-speaking Gentiles and the hellenized Jews, appears for the first time in the Acts narrative in 16.1. He was a native of Lystra in Galatia whose mother was a Jewess and his father a Greek (Acts 16.1, 2; cf. 2 Tim. 3.10-11). He was well spoken of by the believers who lived near his home. He may have come to faith through his mother and grandmother (Acts 16.1; 2 Tim. 1.5) or possibly through Paul's preaching during his first missionary journey. Paul considered Timothy his spiritual son (1 Cor. 4.17; Phil. 2.19-22; 1 Tim. 1.2; 2 Tim. 1.2) as well as his fellow worker (Rom. 16.21). Acts 16.1 implies that his father was not a believer. Since Paul had great confidence in Timothy, he sent him on various critical missions to tend to the affairs of the young churches (Acts 19.22; 1 Cor. 4.17; 16.10; Phil. 2.19; 1 Thess.

---

9. To the contrary, Ernest Best, *A Commentary on the First and Second Epistles to the Thessalonians* (New York: Harper & Row, 1972), 60, suggests that during this stage of his ministry Paul was not conscious of the necessity of making his apostolic authority explicit. On the other hand, Wanamaker, *Commentary on 1 and 2 Thessalonians*, 68, explains the omission with reference to the situation. There was no need to emphasize his authority because it was not questioned.

10. BAGD, 750; MM, 574; *ABD*, 6.22; Hemer, *The Book of Acts*, 230. Alternatively, *Silas* may be the shortened form of the Greek *Silvanus (Silouanos)*. The name *Silas* appears only in Acts (15.22, 27, 32, 40; 16.19, 25, 29; 17.4, 10, 14, 15; 18.5), while *Silvanus* is used exclusively in the letters (2 Cor. 1.19; 2 Thess. 1.1; 1 Pet. 5.12). It is doubtful that *Silas* and *Silvanus* are two distinct individuals.

11. BAGD, 750.

3.2, 6). His name appears as co-author alongside Paul's in the heading of a number of Paul's letters (1 Cor. 1.1; Phil. 1.1; Col. 1.1; 1 Thess. 1.1; 2 Thess. 1.1; Phlm. 1). The narrative in Acts tells how he accompanied Paul from near the beginning of the second missionary journey through the time when Paul returned to Jerusalem at the end of his third missionary tour (Acts 20.4). The presence of his name in the heading of the letters written during Paul's first Roman imprisonment suggests that he accompanied Paul to the imperial city. According to 1 and 2 Timothy, he eventually assumed the role of pastor in the Ephesian church (1 Tim. 1.3; 2 Tim. 1.18). Timothy also receives mention in Hebrews 13.23 as one who had been imprisoned.

The recipients of this letter are the members of *the church of the Thessalonians*. This letter was written to the whole church and not a subgroup within the larger congregation. To assure that all the members of the church would be familiar with its contents, Paul concludes with a solemn charge to the recipients "to have this letter read to all the brothers" (5.27). The term *church (ekklēsia)* commonly designated the popular governing assembly of free citizens *(dēmos)* in a Greek city such as Corinth or Athens (note this use in Acts 19.32, 39, 41). Those who participated were males, and commonly the lower social classes were excluded even if they enjoyed citizenship. This assembly had the power to propose changes in laws, elect officials, decide political questions, and administer justice. Since there was no separation between religion and politics, the assembly gathered in the presence of the titular deity of the city, to whom appropriate sacrifices and prayers were offered.[12] However, the power of the Greek *ekklēsia* was greatly diminished during the era of Roman imperialism. In the LXX the term *ekklēsia* translated the Hebrew *qahal* and so designated the assembly of Yahweh, the people of God (Deut. 9.10; 18.6; 31.30; Judg. 20.2; 1 Kings 8.14). For this reason, Stephen uses *ekklēsia* to refer to the people of Israel during the wilderness wanderings in Acts 7.38. Most certainly the Christian use of this term of self-identity finds its deepest roots in this soil. *Ekklēsia* could refer to the totality of the Christian community in a city (Rom. 16.23; 1 Cor. 1.2; 14.23) or to the basic cell group that met in the house of one of the members (Rom. 16.5; 1 Cor. 16.19). On rare occasions it could designate the totality of the Christian community in any and every place (Eph. 1.22, 23; Col. 1.18).[13] Calling the Christians in Thessalonica a *church* shows their continuity with the an-

---

12. *OCD*, 514-15; *NIDNTT*, 291-92; *TDNT*, 3.513-14. The assembly in Thessalonica was called the *dēmos*. See p. 22.

13. Never in Greek, Hellenistic Jewish, and Christian literature of the era did the term designate a building, contrary to popular modern usage.

cient people of God and at the same time establishes an alternative form of social identity that stands as a challenge to existing structures of power whose god is another.

But insofar as this title *church of the Thessalonians* echoed common Greek usage, clarification was necessary to distinguish this assembly, and so the apostles added that this is the *ekklēsia in God the Father and the Lord Jesus Christ.* In his homily on the epistle, Chrysostom comments, "For there were many assemblies, both Jewish and Grecian; but he says, 'to the (Church) that is in God.' It is a great dignity, and to which there is nothing equal, that it is 'in God.'" While some would understand *in* as instrumental ("God establishes the church"), others interpret the preposition as locative/spatial ("the church that is in the presence of God" or "that is in union with him"). Best argues that the spatial sense is never communicated by the expression "in God" in the NT, but Bruce responds by observing that the phrase should be understood in line with Paul's normal use of "in Christ" and its variants ("in Christ Jesus," "in the Lord," "in him"). In this sense the meaning would be that the believers participate "in Christ's risen life or their membership in his body."[14] The *church of the Thessalonians* finds its unique identity in its union or relationship with *God the Father* and the exalted *Lord Jesus Christ.* The social dimension (*church*; cf. 5.26-27) and the vertical *(in God the Father and the Lord Jesus Christ)* are thus inseparably joined. The importance of this dual relationship is highlighted by their alienation from their contemporaries in the city (2.14) and the abandonment of their ancestral and civic deities (1.9).

The epistolary salutation ends with a blessing, *Grace and peace to you.*[15] Greek letters commonly included the word "Greetings"[16] at this point, while Jewish correspondence tended to prefer expressions such as "Mercy and peace" or "Greetings and peace" (*2 Bar.* 78.2; 2 Macc. 1.1). The apostles created a Christianized greeting that, while echoing common greetings, became a blessing that expressed the essence of the gospel.[17] *Grace* summa-

---

14. Best, *First and Second Epistles to the Thessalonians*, 62; Bruce, *1 and 2 Thessalonians*, 7. "In Christ" expresses both the sphere of salvation (Rom. 3.24; 8.1; 1 Cor. 15.22; Gal. 2.16; Phil. 3.14) and the unity of believers (Gal. 3.26-28; Rom. 12.5).

15. Some ancient manuscripts add, "from God our Father and the Lord Jesus Christ" (‫א‬, A, I), while others include the similar phrase, "from God the Father and the Lord Jesus Christ" (D, 1050). The strong evidence for the reading reflected in our translation from the Alexandrian and Occidental families (B, G, Ψ, 1739), in addition to the unlikelihood that a scribe would have left out the words of the longer reading, favors the shorter reading. The longer reading reflects an attempt to harmonize this greeting with that of 2 Thess. 1.2.

16. *Chairein.*

17. Cf. Rom. 1.7; 1 Cor. 1.3; 2 Cor. 1.2; Gal. 1.3; Eph. 1.2; Phil. 1.2; Col. 1.2; 2 Thess. 1.2; Phlm. 3; 1 Pet. 1.2; 2 Pet. 1.2; and Rev. 1.4. The variation "Grace, mercy and peace" is

rizes the saving work of God through Jesus Christ (Rom. 3.24; 5.15; Eph. 2.8; 2 Thess. 2.16). But "grace" embraces not only the gift of salvation but also the continuous divine action by which he enables his people to do his will (Acts 15.40; 2 Cor. 8.1, 7; Gal. 2.9). *Peace* was the common greeting among the Jews *(shalom)*.[18] It did not express the wish that the other would have inner, emotional tranquility but rather points to the core of the saving relationship between God and a people or person. Paul, for example, tells the Roman church that "we have *peace with God* through our Lord Jesus Christ" (Rom. 5.1). We could say that the *grace* of God results in *peace* with God. Far from being a mere formality, in Paul's hands the common letter greeting becomes a blessing that embraces the totality of the divine benefits he and his associates desire for the Christians in Thessalonica.

II. "WE ALWAYS THANK GOD FOR ALL OF YOU" — THE COMING OF THE GOSPEL AND ITS RECEPTION (1.2-10)

A common convention in ancient letters was to include a prayer to a deity after the salutation in which a petition was made for the recipient. Most frequently the request was for the health of the person. Occasionally a note about offering thanks to the god or gods was added. In this letter Paul, Silvanus, and Timothy place their thanks to God for the church in the primary position (1.2a) but then quickly mention their prayers for the congregation (1.2b). To give thanks for benefits received was an important social obligation, whether one's benefactors were human or divine.[1] In his study on Paul's use of the thanksgivings in his letters, Schubert has demonstrated that the main themes of the letter are introduced in these thanksgivings.[2] In this letter the extensive thanksgiving (1.2-10) summarizes the themes of the coming of the gospel to Thessalonica (vv. 5a, 9a), the character of the gospel messengers (v. 5b), the conversion of the Thessalonians (vv. 6, 9-10), the results of their conversion (vv. 3, 7-8), the sufferings they and the apostles endured (v. 6), the mission of the church

---

found in 1 Tim. 1.2; 2 Tim. 1.2; and 2 John 3. Since greeting conventions were flexible, the identification of the exact prototype for the Christian form appears to be a fruitless quest.

18. Joseph A. Fitzmyer, "Some Notes on Aramaic Epistolography," *JBL* 93 (1974) 214-16.

1. *TDNT*, 9.407-10.

2. Schubert, *Pauline Thanksgivings*, 180; and Peter O'Brien, *Introductory Thanksgivings in the Letters of Paul* (Leiden: E. J. Brill, 1977), 262. Unlike these authors, I argue that the thanksgiving ends at 1.10. See p. 74.

(v. 8), and their eschatological hope (v. 10). Each of these themes is addressed at greater length in the remaining chapters of the book.

2 By means of this opening thanksgiving, Paul and his associates show that they are conscious of the fact that the benefits the Thessalonians received and the conversion they experienced were due to God's action. God, and not the Christian heralds nor the good efforts of the Thessalonians themselves, was the source of their salvation. Their faith, love, and hope were evidence of this salvation (1.3), which was rooted in God's election (1.4). In this letter, as in many of Paul's other letters, Paul and his associates note that they constantly give thanks to God for the Christian community (1 Cor. 1.4; Col. 1.3; 2 Thess. 1.3; 2.13; Phlm. 4)[3] by saying, *We always thank God for all of you.* Later on in the letter Paul will call the church to a similar life of thanksgiving (5.17). The author's thanksgivings were frequent and embraced all the members of the community (cf. Rom. 1.8). While Paul commonly informs the churches of his constant thanks and prayers for them, the language is more than conventional and truly reflects his practice. Undoubtedly Paul and his companions could remember both the faces and the names of the members of this church whom they had to abandon just a short time previously (2.17).

The occasions when these thanksgivings were offered were the periods of corporate prayer that Paul and his associates enjoyed: *mentioning you in our prayers* (prayer and thanksgiving are also linked in Phil. 4.6; Col. 1.3; 4.2; 1 Tim. 2.1; 2 Tim. 1.3; Phlm. 4). While some versions translate *mentioning* as "to remember" *(NAB, Challoner-Rheims)*, the Greek phrase translated "making mention"[4] is commonly used in the NT of the act of offering petitions by means of prayer (Rom. 1.9-10; Eph. 1.16; Phil. 1.3-4; Phlm. 4). The emphasis is not merely on the fact that they remembered the Thessalonians (a thought that instead appears in the following phrase), but that they presented them before God in these sessions of prayer. The adverb "continually," which is found in the following verse in the *NIV* where it modifies "remember," should most likely be understood with *mentioning* in the present verse. Where this word appears elsewhere in the NT it is invariably associated with prayers (Rom. 1.9; 1 Thess. 5.17; also the adjective in 2 Tim. 1.3) or with thanksgiving (1 Thess. 2.13). Given Paul's common usage, the *RSV* translates the clause, "constantly mentioning you in our prayers."[5] This sentiment parallels the first clause of the verse, *We always*

---

3. A variation of this thanksgiving is found in Eph. 5.20, where the apostle notes that he is "always giving thanks to God the Father *for everything.*"

4. *Mneian poioumenoi. Mneian* can mean either "remembrance, memory" or "mention" (BAGD, 524; and see MM, 414).

5. Paul could place the adverb *adialeiptōs* either before the verb (Rom. 1.9) or after it (1 Thess. 2.13).

thank God for all of you, which itself emphasizes their constancy in thanksgiving for the Thessalonians. We should not, however, think that these men prayed for the church with every breath. They are hardly saying that they "kept on babbling like pagans" (Matt. 6.7). The adverb "continually" expresses the thought that they were persistent in their prayers, as Jesus taught in Luke 18.1 when he told his disciples that "they should always pray and not give up" (cf. 1 Thess. 5.17). While prayers were normally offered daily among the Greeks, Paul and his associates' prayers for the church were a constant in their lives.[6] They were diligent and consistent in this labor of prayer. Greek prayer was self-interested and included an argument with the deity that put forth why the prayer should be answered (e.g., the piety of the petitioner expressed in some deed that merited a response, or the character of the god).[7] In contrast, this is a model of Christian prayer that puts thanksgiving to God and the interests of others in first place.

3 If the occasions of thanksgiving to God for the believers in Thessalonica were the times of prayer (v. 2), the motivation for the thanksgiving was the memory of the Christian virtues that were clearly evidenced in these believers' lives. *We . . . remember* does not introduce a petition, as is the case in Colossians 4.18 where Paul calls the church to "remember" his chains, but rather indicates that they brought to mind and even mentioned in their prayers the *faith . . . love . . . and . . . hope* of the Thessalonians as the ground of their thanksgiving to God (v. 2).[8] The memory of the church was recent and was refreshed by the news Timothy brought of their faith and love (3.6) and their steadfastness that sprang from their hope in God (3.8). Paul had feared for their faith and constancy because of the persecutions they were enduring (2.14; 3.2-5), and for this reason the report from Timothy was received with abundant thanksgiving (3.6, 9). The grammar of the Greek sentence might suggest that the *work . . . labor . . . and . . . endurance* of the Thessalonians, or possibly only their *endurance inspired by hope,* were done *before our God and Father,* that is, in consciousness of his presence, since this phrase appears at the very end of the verse in the Greek text. But the thought here is the same as in 3.9-10. There the news Timothy brought of their faith, love, and steadfastness issued in thanks and joy "in the presence of God."[9] So in those periods of prayer *before our God and Father* the founders remem-

---

6. *TLNT,* 1.32-34.
7. *OCD,* 1242.
8. BAGD, 525.
9. Although the expression "before God" also appears in eschatological contexts (2 Cor. 5.10; 1 Thess. 2.19; 3.13), in this verse the reference is rather to the thanksgiving offered in God's presence.

bered the active Christian virtues that were strongly evidenced in the corporate life of this church.

Paul, Silas, and Timothy remembered their *work produced by faith, . . . labor prompted by love, and . . . endurance inspired by hope in our Lord Jesus Christ*. They found in these believers the trinity of classic Christian virtues: faith, love, and hope.[10] These three appear repeatedly in early Christian teaching wherever the ideal Christian character is described (5.8; Rom. 5.1-5; 1 Cor. 13.13; Gal. 5.5-6; Col. 1.4-5; 1 Pet. 1.21-22; Heb. 10.22-24). In a number of verses, faith and love are joined together with the fruit of hope, that being perseverance (2 Thess. 1.3-4; 1 Tim. 6.11; 2 Tim. 3.10), while the fruits of all three virtues — works, labor, and perseverance — appear together in Revelation 2.2. Timothy had returned from Thessalonica with a report of the faith and love of the Thessalonians (3.6) and news of their steadfastness in hope (3.8). In spite of the disadvantages of being a young and persecuted congregation, these believers gave clear evidence of possessing genuine and recognizable Christian character.

Far from being passive or hidden virtues, their faith, love, and hope could be witnessed in the Thessalonians' conduct. Paul and the others remembered their *work produced by faith*. Although the object of their faith was God (1.8), this faith was given active expression in their work. Paul states categorically that salvation is by faith and not by human works (Eph. 2.8-9), but he also interjects that faith has its fruit in good works (Eph. 2.10). The apostle speaks in one place of "every work of faith" (2 Thess. 1.11), and in another of "faith that works through love" (Gal. 5.6). The Roman and Greek understanding of *fides/pistis* (faith) can help clarify the close association between faith and works in these verses. In the relationship between patrons and clients, the client was said to be in the *fides/pistis* of the patron, for their part clients owed *fides/pistis* or loyalty to their patron, and this was shown in their actions.[11] The type of work that flowed out of the Thessalonians' faith is not specified. The

---

10. Cf. the cardinal classical virtues of "prudence, justice, temperance, and fortitude." Bruce J. Malina and Jerome H. Neyrey, *Portraits of Paul* (Louisville: Westminster/John Knox Press, 1996) 44.

11. "The client should be marked by dependability, one for whom the patron can pledge his faith *(fides)*." Andrew Wallace-Hadrill, "Patronage in Roman Society: From Republic to Empire," in *Patronage in Ancient Society* (ed. Andrew Wallace-Hadrill; London and New York: Routledge, 1989), 64. On *fides/pistis* see John Rich, "Patronage and Interstate Relations in the Roman Republic," in *Patronage in Ancient Society* (ed. Andrew Wallace-Hadrill; London and New York: Routledge, 1989), 118-35; E. S. Gruen, "Greek *pistis* and Roman *fides*," *Athenaeum* 60 (1982) 50-68; Salvatore Calderone, *Pistis-Fides: Ricerche di storia e diritto internazionale nell'antichità* (Messina: Università Degli Studi, 1964); Malina and Neyrey, *Portraits of Paul*, 167-68. For a fuller discussion of patronage in the ancient world, see pp. 26-28.

word used for *work* could refer to manual labor (1 Thess. 2.9; 4.11; 2 Thess. 3.8, 10; 1 Cor. 4.12; 9.6) and elsewhere described the ministerial labors of ecclesiastical leaders (1 Thess. 5.12-13; Rom. 15.23; 16.3, 6, 9, 12, 21; 1 Cor. 3.13; 15.10; 16.9-10; 2 Cor. 6.5; Phil. 2.22; Col. 4.17). But the reference here appears to be to "good works," as in 2 Thessalonians 1.11 and other texts (2 Cor. 9.8; Eph. 2.10; 4.12; Col. 1.10; 2 Tim. 2.21). In the Jewish community "good works" were acts such as charity to the poor, visitation of the sick, hospitality to strangers, comfort for the downtrodden, and other helpful activities that especially benefited those who were poor or afflicted. On the other hand, the Greek concept of "good works" was somewhat broader. One could do "good works" on behalf of family, friends, the community, or the state. This was the virtue of rendering aid to others without distinction,[12] a broad sense that is reflected in the phrase "for each other and for everyone else" in 1 Thessalonians 3.12 (cf. Gal. 6.10). It was understood that a person could be known by his or her work, this being an evidence of virtue and a person's character (cf. Luke 6.43-45).[13]

Paul and his associates also remembered the Thessalonians' *labor prompted by love.* The objects of this love were the other members of the Christian community in Thessalonica (2 Thess. 1.3) and the leadership of the church (1 Thess. 5.13), as well as Christians in other locations such as Philippi and Berea (4.9-10). They also taught that the church's love should extend to the unconverted, and they prayed to that end (3.12). The Thessalonians had learned the lesson of love from God himself (4.9), who demonstrated his love toward them (1.4; 2 Thess. 2.13, 16). The love of the Thessalonian believers expressed itself in hard, strenuous, and exhausting labor.[14] Far from being simply an emotion, love sought the best for the other and labored for the other's benefit (cf. Eph. 4.16; Heb. 6.10). As in the previous clause, Paul does not explain what type of labor the Thessalonians undertook. He frequently used the term to refer either to his ministerial labors (e.g., 1 Cor. 3.8; 15.58; 2 Cor. 6.5; 11.23, 27; 1 Thess. 3.5) or to manual labor (1 Thess. 2.9; 2 Thess. 3.8). But here the word most likely refers to any kind of self-sacrificing labor the believers engaged in as they served those both inside and outside the community. Both their faith and love generated labors that were for the benefit of others.

The believers' *endurance inspired by hope in our Lord Jesus Christ* was also brought to mind and mentioned before God. Endurance becomes the ability to remain steadfast and persevere in the face of suffering or temp-

---

12. W. C. van Unnik, "Teaching of Good Works in 1 Peter," *NTS* 1 (1954-55) 94-97.

13. *NIDNTT,* 3.1148.

14. *Kopos;* BAGD, 443; *NIDNTT,* 1.262-63. Note, however, that in 1 Cor. 15.58 *kopos* is synonymous with the word previously used for "work" in this verse *(ergon).*

tation (Luke 21.19; Rom. 5.3-5; 2 Cor. 1.6; 6.4; Col. 1.11; 2 Thess. 1.4; 1 Tim. 6.11; Titus 2.2; Heb. 12.1; Jas. 1.3-4; Rev. 2.2-3). This was the virtue of martyrs, according to Jewish thought (4 Macc. 1.11; 17.4; *T. Jos.* 10.1),[15] and it became one of the most valued virtues of the early church, which was beset by adversity on every side. Paul had become greatly concerned for the stability of the Christian community in Thessalonica because of the persecutions they endured and the temptations of Satan to apostatize from the faith (3.1-5; 2.14; and cf. 2 Tim. 2.11-12). But the Thessalonians had shown tenacious endurance in the face of extreme opposition and hostility (3.8). The source of this perseverance was not some inner resolve or personal strength but their hope in the Lord Jesus Christ (the same union of steadfastness and hope appears in Rom. 5.3-4; 8.25; 15.4). In contrast to their unconverted contemporaries, the Christians possessed hope[16] (4.13; Eph. 2.12) in the Lord Jesus Christ. The Christians' hope was bound up with the coming of the Lord Jesus Christ, an event that is mentioned frequently in these letters (1.10; 2.19; 3.13; 4.15; 5.23; 2 Thess. 1.7-10; 2.1; and cf. 1 Thess. 5.8). The hope they held was not some vague expectation about a better future but rather solid confidence rooted in the expectation of Christ's coming. This was the strong foundation that gave the Thessalonians the power to endure and persevere in the face of the tremendous hostility leveled against them.

4 Paul declared that he and his companions offered thanks to God for the Thessalonians in their times of prayer (v. 2) and indicated that the ground for their gratitude was the authentic Christian character of these believers (v. 3). Now he presents the second and most profound reason for their thankfulness to God: *For we know, brothers loved by God, that he has chosen you.* The *NIV* mistakenly places a paragraph break at this point despite the fact that vv. 2-4 string together three adverbial participles ("mentioning," "remembering," and "knowing") that all modify the verb found in the main clause of v. 2, "We always thank God for all of you." Therefore we should understand v. 4 as part of the sustained thanksgiving of the opening section of this book. Furthermore, Paul was convinced that God had chosen the brothers and sisters in Thessalonica because of the way the gospel had come to them (as explained in the following verse: "because our gospel came to you not simply with words, but also with power, with the Holy Spirit and with deep conviction") and because of the manner in which they received its message (as noted in v. 6, "You became imitators of us and of the Lord. . . . you welcomed the

---

15. MM, 659.

16. This means the subjective experience of hope and not the objective hope itself, as in Col. 1.5, "the hope that is stored up for you in heaven."

message with the joy given by the Holy Spirit"). God had spoken to them in the apostolic proclamation of the gospel, and they had heard the message as God's word (cf. 2 Thess. 2.13-14; 1 Thess. 2.13). Paul and his associates saw in all this clear evidence of their election.[17]

Paul mentions the root cause of the Thessalonians' election as he calls them those who are *loved by God* (cf. 2 Thess. 2.13; Rom. 1.7; Jude 1).[18] Frequently, biblical authors affirm that God chose his people Israel, and now the church, because of his own love for them (cf. Deut. 4.37; 7.7-8; 10.15; Pss. 47.4; 78.68; Isa. 42.1; Matt. 12.18; Rom. 11.28; Eph. 1.4; Col. 3.12).[19] In other words, God's election is not based on human merits or virtue (2 Tim. 1.9), but instead his decision and initiative are rooted solely in his love. In the Greek world the election or recruitment of political and military leaders had to do with the merits and the character of the persons chosen.[20] But in God's community, nothing less than the love of God is the cause of election, regardless of the positive or negative character or achievements of a person (Rom. 5.7-8). This much is assumed and not debated, as is often the case today. The purpose of the declaration is to provide assurance and comfort and not to fuel theological controversy, however important such discussions might be.

The relationship people had with the gods of the ancient pagan pantheon was not based on the love the deity demonstrated to them. Much to the contrary, the primary concern was to placate the gods and to solicit fa-

---

17. Some have suggested that the certainty that the apostles had concerning their election stemmed from the evidence of the Christian virtues in their conduct (v. 3; Marshall, *1 and 2 Thessalonians*, 52; Wanamaker, *Commentary on 1 and 2 Thessalonians*, 76-77; Best, *First and Second Epistles to the Thessalonians*, 70. However, the following verse, which begins with *hoti* ("because"), explicitly points to the ground of their confidence.

18. On the love of God, see *TLNT*, 1.8-22; Anders Nygren, *Agape and Eros* (2 vols.; London: SPCK, 1938-39); C. Spicq, *Agape in the New Testament* (3 vols.; St. Louis: B. Herder Book Co., 1963).

19. At times the basis of God's election is said to be his divine grace (Rom. 11.5; 2 Tim. 1.9) or his sovereign purpose (Eph. 1.5; Rom. 9.11).

20. "Prudence and experience, appropriate standing in society or sufficient wealth, courage and suitability constitute the conditions necessary in each instance, if a person is to be considered for election. But it is the election itself which makes it possible for him to take up his function and which at the same time lays an obligation upon him. For election, whether of individuals or of a group, is regarded as a distinction. . . . It is usually conducted in a manner in keeping with the concept of an aristocratic élite. It is always, however, accompanied by some kind of obligation or task concerned with the well-being of all the other members of the community of which the one elected forms a part." *NIDNTT*, 1.536. See also H. H. Rowley, *The Biblical Doctrine of Election* (London: Lutterworth Press, 1950); Paul K. Jewett, *Election and Predestination* (Grand Rapids: Eerdmans, 1985); I. Howard Marshall, "Election and Calling to Salvation in 1 and 2 Thessalonians," in *The Thessalonian Correspondence* (ed. Collins), 259-76.

vors without any security concerning whether they would be disposed to a person favorably or otherwise.[21] People believed that a god's influence over a human being could be either positive or negative;[22] the God of Christians, however, always works for the good of those whom he chooses and calls (Rom. 8.28). In 1.4, as in 2 Thessalonians 2.13, the implication is that this divine love also transforms these people from different sectors of society into a family of brothers and sisters. The Christian community is not simply an association, guild, or fraternity but a brotherhood/sisterhood (cf. 1 Pet. 2.17; 5.9; cf. this use in the Jewish community in Rom. 9.3; Exod. 2.11; Hos. 2.1; 2 Macc. 2.1; 1QS 6.10, 22), where familial love dominates (1 Thess. 4.9-10) among those who together call God their Father (Gal. 4.6; Rom. 8.15; Jude 1). In this letter Paul calls the Christians "brothers and sisters" *(adelphoi)* nineteen times, while in 2 Thessalonians he refers to the believers in this manner nine times, giving us one of the most important windows into the early church's self-identity. The recipients of this letter are those who have been alienated from their society due to their new religious allegiance (1 Thess. 1.9; 2.14) but whose new social identity is forged by the One who is their Father. This patriarchal family "is concerned with 'nurturing' or social support, concern, interest, help, and the like."[23] God's election resulted in a new layer of social relationship that could be most closely described as that of siblings.

5 After affirming his confidence in the fact that the believers in Thessalonica are God's elect, Paul presents the first foundation of this conviction: *because our gospel came to you not simply with words, but also with power, with the Holy Spirit and with deep conviction.* The word translated "because" *(hoti)* may denote a causal relationship and thus presents the reason why he and his fellow missionaries were sure of the Thessalonians' election (so the *NIV*). On the other hand, some commentators have understood the word here as epexegetic or explanatory, introducing the occasion or way in which they were chosen.[24] On this reading, vv. 4-5 would mean something like, "We know how God chose you, that

21. An exception to this general observation was Isis, who was considered tender, but the benefits she conferred can in no way be compared to the self-sacrificial love of God. See *IT*, n. 254; Witt, "The Egyptian Cults in Ancient Macedonia," 330; *TLNT*, 1.17-18.

22. See p. 34.

23. Malina and Neyrey, *Portraits of Paul*, 160; Wayne Meeks, *The First Urban Christians* (New Haven and London: Yale University Press, 1983), 75-77, 86-87. Meeks notes a similar use of *adelphoi* among some pagan religious groups (p. 225, n. 73).

24. J. B. Lightfoot, *Notes on the Epistles of St Paul from Unpublished Commentaries* (London: Macmillan, 1904), 12; Milligan, *St. Paul's Epistles to the Thessalonians*, 8; Best, *First and Second Epistles to the Thessalonians*, 73; Gordon Fee, *God's Empowering Presence* (Peabody, Mass.: Hendrickson Publishers, 1994), 40; Heinrich Schlier, *El apóstol y su comunidad* (Madrid: Ediciones Fax, 1974), 27.

is to say, we know that our gospel came to you not simply with words, etc." However, Paul does not explain the occasion or manner of the Thessalonians' election, nor does he elaborate on its nature, but instead he tells why he knew that these believers were counted among the elect.[25]

The message brought to Thessalonica is summarized as *our gospel* (cf. 2 Thess. 2.14; 2 Cor. 4.3).[26] Elsewhere in these letters the *gospel* is called "the gospel of God" (2.2, 8, 9), "the gospel of Christ" (3.2), and "the gospel of our Lord Jesus" (2 Thess. 1.8). This is the proclamation of the good news of Jesus Christ and his salvation.[27] This term was very well known in the cities of the Roman Empire, and it appears frequently in the context of the imperial cult.[28] The news of the transcendent events in the life of the emperor, as well as his decrees and discourses, was proclaimed throughout Italy and the provinces as his "gospel." A frequently cited inscription that dates from 9 BC celebrates the birth of Augustus as a "gospel":

> It is a day which we may justly count as equivalent to the beginning of everything — if not in itself and in its own nature, at any rate in the benefits it brings — inasmuch as it has restored the shape of everything that was failing and turning into misfortune, and has given a new look to the Universe at a time when it would gladly have welcomed destruction if Caesar had not been born to be the common blessing of all men. . . . Whereas the Providence . . . which has ordered the whole of our life, showing concern and zeal, has ordained the most perfect consummation for human life by giving to it Augustus, by filling him with virtue for doing the work of a benefactor among men, and by sending him, as it were, a saviour for us and those who come after us, to make war to cease, to create order everywhere . . . and whereas the birthday of the God [Augustus] was the beginning for the world of the glad tidings [in the Greek the "Evangel"] that have come to men through him. . . .[29]

The church countered such imperial claims with the announcement of the gospel of Jesus Christ (Mark 1.1), whose coming was understood as

25. So Gottlieb Lünemann, *Critical and Exegetical Handbook to the Epistles of St. Paul to the Thessalonians* (Edinburgh: T&T Clark, 1880), 26; Frame, *St. Paul's Epistles to the Thessalonians*, 78; Leon Morris, *First and Second Epistles to the Thessalonians* (Grand Rapids: Eerdmans, 1991), 445; Wanamaker, *Commentary on 1 and 2 Thessalonians*, 78.

26. See *TLNT*, 2.82-92; *TDNT*, 2.721-36; *NIDNTT*, 2.107-14; *LAE*, 366-67.

27. We should not understand the "gospel" here as the act of proclamation (2 Cor. 8.18), a rather rare use of the term, but as the content of the message the apostles proclaimed.

28. Richard A. Horsley, *Paul and Empire* (Harrisburg: Trinity Press International, 1997), 140-41, 148-49. The fragmentary inscription (*IT*, n. 14) from Thessalonica uses this term, though not in the context of the imperial cult.

29. *SIG*³ 458, cited in *NIDNTT*, 2.108.

the "good news" of the fulfillment of the hope of Israel for the victory of God and the establishment of his universal sovereignty (Isa. 40.9; 52.7; 61.1-2). People believed that the "gospel" of the emperor was much more than a proclamation since it also brought to pass the new era that was proclaimed. The same kind of link between proclamation and act is evident in the apostolic proclamation to the Thessalonians, which was powerful (v. 5) and effected changes in the lives of those who responded to its claims (vv. 6-10).

Paul reminds the Thessalonians that the proclamation of the gospel came to them *not simply with words, but also with power, with the Holy Spirit and with deep conviction.* "Words" in the Greek text is singular *(logō)*, so the disclaimer may have to do with the mode of proclamation ("not simply with words"), as the *NIV* suggests, or perhaps with the message itself ("not simply with the Word"). To put the question another way, Is the contrast in this verse between rhetorical methodology and the proclamation of the gospel that comes accompanied with divine power (as in 1 Cor. 2.1-5; cf. 1.17; 4.19), or is the thought that the gospel not only comes as a message but is also accompanied by divine manifestations? As we will observe shortly in 2.1-12, Paul and his associates distance themselves from the ancient rhetors and their methodology. Moreover, 1 Corinthians 2.4 appears to explain the sense of 1 Thessalonians 1.5, using as it does much of the same vocabulary: "My message and my preaching were not with wise and persuasive words, but with a demonstration of the Spirit's power." But the contrast in that verse is absolute ("not . . . but"), while that in 1 Thessalonians 1.5 is relative ("not simply . . . but also"). And while in 1 Corinthians 2.4 Paul completely rejects the methodology of the rhetoricians,[30] here he affirms that they preached the message (cf. v. 6) and *also* that they did so in divine power.[31] This type of affirmation is made over and again in the NT, where the authors describe how the proclamation of the gospel was confirmed powerfully by the miracles wrought through the Holy Spirit (Rom. 15.18-19; 1 Cor. 1.6-7; 2 Cor. 6.7; 12.12; Heb. 2.3-4). This is the way the gospel came to Thessalonica and so was recognized and received by them as a divine message, "you accepted it not as the word of men, but as it actually is, the word of God, which is at work in you who believe" (2.13).

The way in which the gospel came to the Thessalonians was *with power, with the Holy Spirit and with deep conviction.* Fee suggests that Paul

30. Gordon Fee, *The First Epistle to the Corinthians* (Grand Rapids: Eerdmans, 1987), 94-96. Cf. Diodorus Siculus (1.2.5-6), who spoke of the "power" of "rhetoric" *(logos)*.
31. See Dieter Werner Kemmler, *Faith and Human Reason* (Leiden: E. J. Brill, 1975), 149-68.

qualifies "power" by adding "that is, with the Holy Spirit and deep/full conviction," while Bruce understands "power" and "conviction" as further clarifying the way the Holy Spirit manifests himself.[32] On the other hand, Marshall and Best link only "power" and not "deep conviction" with the "Holy Spirit."[33] However, the three elements "power . . . Holy Spirit . . . deep conviction" are in a parallel construction, as the NIV shows,[34] and so no attempt should be made to understand any element of the clause as subordinate to another. The verse recalls how miracles were manifested along with the preaching of the gospel in Thessalonica (*power*, as in Mark 6.5; Acts 2.22; 1 Cor. 2.4; 2 Cor. 12.12; Heb. 2.4; and cf. 2 Thess. 2.9). Moreover, the *Holy Spirit* accompanied the gospel proclamation as the one who convinced the hearers of its truth (Luke 24.46-49; Acts 1.8; 5.23; 1 Cor. 2.4-5; 1 Pet. 1.12). Finally, Paul states that the gospel came *with deep conviction,* an expression that possibly refers to the way he and his associates themselves were convinced of the truth of the message (cf. Col. 2.2; Heb. 6.11; 10.22; *1 Clem.* 42.3; and the verb in Luke 1.1; Rom. 4.21; 14.5) or to the Thessalonians' own conviction on hearing it. But the word found here *(plērophoria)* can also signify "complete fullness," in this case the fullness of the divine work, and this appears to be the sense in the present verse.[35] In this context the focus is on the divine operation in the apostolic preaching ("power . . . Holy Spirit") and not on the conviction of the missionaries nor on the way the Thessalonians received the message (cf. 2.13). The proclamation of the gospel came "with miraculous power, with the Holy Spirit and with great fullness." The Thessalonians heard the message of God and saw his power in the apostolic proclamation.

Turning from the miraculous proclamation of the gospel, the final affirmation of the verse highlights the character of the messengers, *You know how we lived among you for your sake.* This declaration is taken up again and elaborated in 2.1-12 (see especially 2.1-2, 5, 11), which reflects on the heralds' character, conduct, and methods, which the Thessalonians witnessed while they were with them. There was great harmony between the character of the missionaries and the message they preached, as the Thessalonians themselves could testify. They knew what

32. Fee, *God's Empowering Presence,* 44; Bruce, *1 and 2 Thessalonians,* 14.

33. Marshall, *1 and 2 Thessalonians,* 53-54; Best, *First and Second Epistles to the Thessalonians,* 75.

34. *Kai en . . . kai en . . . kai [en].*

35. So *TDNT,* 6.310-11; *TLNT,* 3.120, "every kind of richness." Spicq notes that had Paul intended to say "complete assurance" he would have written *en pasē parrēsiā* (Phil. 1.20; cf. 2 Cor. 2.13; 7.4; 1 Tim. 3.13; or *meta pasēs parrēsias,* Acts 28.31) instead of *en plērophoriā pollē.*

kind[36] of persons they were and not simply what manner of message they preached. The powerful presentation of the gospel was in no way contradicted by the conduct of its messengers, a point that should be taken to heart by ministers of all eras. Far from being a question of little importance, the character of the messengers was part of the message they preached. The Thessalonians could hear the proclamation, see its power, and observe how the message was lived. In all this, the concern of the evangelists was for the well-being of the Thessalonians themselves — *for your sake* — and not for the glory of the messengers (2.6-12). Paul, Silas, and Timothy did not minister among the Thessalonians to receive benefits from them but rather preached for the benefit of their hearers.

6 The evidence of these believers' election (v. 4) could be found not only in the proclamation of the gospel (v. 5) but also in the Thessalonians' reception of it (vv. 6-10): and[37] *you became imitators of us and of the Lord; in spite of severe suffering you welcomed the message with the joy given by the Holy Spirit.* The sentence begins with an emphatic "you" that highlights the shift of emphasis from the apostolic proclamation (v. 5) to the reception of the message by the Thessalonians (v. 6). As a consequence of their reception of the Christian message (*logon,* as in v. 5), the Thessalonians became *imitators* of the apostles and *of the Lord,* becoming people who followed their model of suffering in adversity. The clause, which can be translated "having received the message in much affliction," begins with an adverbial participle and thus shows how[38] they became imitators of the apostles and their Lord. Unlike many modern students, the ancients deeply appreciated the value of imitating model lives as a means of moral education, whether those models were parents, heroes, or teachers. Xenophon, for example, described the role of the teacher, saying, "Now the professors of other subjects try to make their pupils copy their teachers."[39] In Jewish literature the imitation of model lives was a commonplace in moral instruction, whether one imitated the conduct of a person (Wis. 4.2; *T. Ben.* 3.1; 4.1), a person's sufferings (4 Macc. 13.9), or the character of God himself (*T. Asher* 4.3; *Ep. Arist.* 188, 210, 280-81). In the NT we

---

36. *Hosios,* used often with reference to questions of character (2 Cor. 10.11; 12.10). BAGD, 562.

37. Verse 6 begins with the word "and" *(kai),* left untranslated in the *NIV.* The structure of the thought of vv. 5-6 is, "because our gospel came to you . . . and you became imitators." The previous clause ("You know how we lived among you for your sake") is parenthetical.

38. Or perhaps "when."

39. Xenophon, *Memorabilia* 1.6.3. Xenophon uses the term *mimētas,* as does our verse. See also Epictetus, *Dissertationes* 2.14.12-13; Plutarch, *De Sera Numinis Vindicta* 550E; *Demetrius* 1.4-6; Lucian, *Demonax* 1-2; Pliny, *Epistulae* 8.13.

find repeated exhortations to imitate the leaders of the church (1 Cor. 4.16; 11.1; Gal. 4.12; Phil. 3.17; 4.9; 2 Thess. 3.7, 9; 1 Tim. 4.12; Titus 2.7; 1 Pet. 5.3), other members of the community of faith (Phil. 3.17; Heb. 6.12; 11; 13.7), and "what is good" (3 John 11), as well as God and Jesus Christ (Eph. 5.1; 1 Cor. 11.1). In the patristic literature, the fathers of the OT (*1 Clem.* 9–12, 17–18), Christian leaders (*1 Clem.* 19), and Christ himself (Pol. *Phil.* 8) are all put forward as examples to follow.

But in 1 Thessalonians, as in Polycarp (*Phil.* 9), Paul refers specifically to the imitation of the sufferings of Christian leaders. The Thessalonians, as well as the churches of Judea (2.14), became imitators of the Lord's sufferings in that they "received the message in much affliction." The emphasis here appears to fall on the condition they were in when they received the message ("in much affliction"), and not on the reception itself. Only in this way can we understand how the Lord was a model whom they imitated. According to many texts of the NT, suffering is a component of Christian discipleship (Matt. 8.18-22; 10.22-25; Mark 8.34; John 15.18-21; 16.33; Acts 9.15-16; 14.21-22). As the Lord suffered, so did his followers (Rom. 8.17; 2 Cor. 1.5; Phil. 3.10; 1 Pet. 2.21; 3.17-18; 4.12-13). Paul had warned the new believers in Thessalonica that they were going to suffer for their faith, and this was already happening (1 Thess. 2.14; 3.3-4; and 2 Thess. 1.4-7; 3.3-5). This same instruction about suffering was a fundamental part of the teaching given to new believers (Acts 14.22). The Thessalonians had witnessed the sufferings of the apostles and had heard of their rejection in Philippi before coming to their city (2.2), and Paul informed them of the sufferings he and his associates were enduring in Corinth, the place from which they sent this letter (3.7). This was their lot as they continued their mission (2 Thess. 3.2). The Thessalonian believers came into this common Christian experience, but, because of the way they responded to their sufferings, they themselves became an example to the rest of the believers in the provinces of Macedonia and Achaia (v. 7). The *severe suffering* they endured is not a reference to their emotional state or anguish of heart, but rather speaks of the opposition they faced from their contemporaries in the city (2.14; 3.3, 7; 2 Thess. 1.4, 6; cf. Rom. 8.35).[40] The intensity of the persecution is underlined (*severe*). The miracle of the Thessalonians' conversion is that they received the gospel message (2.13; cf. Acts 8.14; 11.1; 17.11; Luke 8.13; and 2 Thess. 2.10) in the midst of the persecutions described in Acts 17.5-9 and those that continued after Paul and his companions left the city.

But despite the sufferings that came upon them because of the gos-

---

40. *Thlipsei.* See BAGD, 362. Contra Malherbe, *Paul and the Thessalonians,* 48, who contends that the word describes their emotional state.

pel, these new believers also received the message *with the joy given by the Holy Spirit*. The theme of "joy in suffering" appears in Jewish literature (*2 Bar.* 52.6), but the source of this teaching in the NT is the Lord himself (Matt. 5.11-12; Luke 6.22-23; 21.28). The apostles and the Christian churches faced horrible opposition because of their faith, but found joy in their sufferings since they knew that they shared the sufferings of Christ (Acts 5.41; Rom. 12.12; 2 Cor. 4.8-10; 7.4; Phil. 2.17; Col. 1.24; Jas. 1.2; 1 Pet. 1.6; 4.13-14). Paul even informed the Corinthian church that joy in suffering characterized the Macedonian churches (2 Cor. 8.2). The source of this joy was not the agony of the suffering itself (cf. 1 Pet. 1.6) but rather the Holy Spirit who produced joy in these believers as a fruit of his presence (Acts 13.52; Rom. 14.17; Gal. 5.22; 1 Pet. 4.13-14; cf. Luke 10.21). Joy was one of the chief outcomes of people's conversion to Christ, and the strength of this joy was such that the adversity they faced could not destroy it. What determined these Christians' attitude in their persecutions was not their circumstances but rather their experience of the Holy Spirit.

7   As a result[41] of their reception of the gospel in the midst of great suffering and the abundant joy they experienced because of the Spirit's presence in their lives, this young congregation became an example for the rest of the Christian churches in the region: *And so you became a model to all the believers in Macedonia and Achaia*. Those who had imitated the Lord and his heralds were now a *model*[42] for other believers. The term *model* appears at various stages in the moral teaching of the NT, signifying that which one imitates (Phil. 3.17; 2 Thess. 3.9). In a number of places the apostles and the leaders of the churches are presented as models whom the believers should imitate (2 Thess. 3.9; 1 Tim. 4.12; Titus 2.7; 1 Pet. 5.3), but mature members of the congregations could fulfill the same function (Phil. 3.17). Verse 7 is the only text in the NT where a whole congregation is viewed as a *model* for other churches. This was an exceptional church in the way they responded to persecution. Molded by the example of the Lord, Paul, Silvanus, and Timothy, they themselves now become a model for others.

The term *model (typos)* could mean various things, such as the example or model that would be used to produce clay pots,[43] or a relief carving or painting that represented not only the one depicted but also the person's character.[44] It could also denote the seal that leaves an impression

41. *Hōste* introduces the result of the events in v. 6. BAGD, 890.
42. Some mss. evidence is strong in supporting the plural *typous* (ℵ A C D² F G Ψ), but the editors of NA²⁷ and UBS⁴ favor the singular *typon* (B D*).
43. MM, 645.
44. *TDNT*, 8.247. Antipater of Thessalonica (n. 39) uses the term in this way.

or the mold by which some material, such as soft clay, was shaped.[45] It was used metaphorically in ethical teaching as the "model" of conduct to which a person should, or should not, conform.[46] The church in Thessalonica was a model Christian community for other congregations (2 Thess. 1.3-4). In his homily on 1 Thessalonians, Chrysostom comments on this verse, saying, "illustrious and admirable men do not shut up their virtue within themselves, but by their good report benefit many, and render them better" *(Homily 2)*. They were a model *to all the believers*, or Christians (Rom. 3.22; 1 Cor. 1.21; Gal. 3.22; 1 Thess. 2.10, 13; 2 Thess. 1.10), *in Macedonia and Achaia*. This is not hyperbole. At this time the churches in these provinces were few in number (Philippi, Berea, Athens, Corinth, and perhaps Cenchrea, since at a later date Rom. 16.1 mentions a church there; see Rom. 15.26; 2 Cor. 1.1; 8.1-2; 9.2, 4). Paul, Silvanus, and Timothy spoke about the Thessalonians to these churches (Acts 17.15; 18.6), explaining how they showed faith, love, and steadfastness in the midst of their persecutions (2 Thess. 1.3-4). Moreover, members of the Thessalonian congregation themselves traveled, and the other churches could see firsthand the character of that community (1 Thess. 1.8; 4.10). Their reputation was known everywhere.

In spite of being young in the faith and having to endure so much adversity, the church of Thessalonica was active in the extension of the gospel and in supplying relief to other congregations (see 1.8; 4.10 and commentary). Thessalonica was located along the Via Egnatia, which gave the city access to the entire province of Macedonia and beyond. The major north-south road from the Danube basin to the Peloponnese ran just west of the town, while Thessalonica had sea access to the north, south, and east due to its excellent port.[47] The city was the capital of the province and Macedonia's "metropolis."[48] This city exercised political and economic control over a vast region. This, as any other city, should not be viewed as an island but rather as a hub that radiated its governmental, economic, social, and religious influence over a vast region.[49] City and hinterland cannot be separated. Thessalonica's natural orientation outward was set aflame in the lives of those touched by the gospel. The apostle Paul's strategy was to reach not just cities but entire provinces; indeed, the evangelization of a single city could result in the diffu-

---

45. *New Docs*, 1.77-78; *TDNT*, 8.247.

46. See *NIDNTT*, 3.903-4; *TDNT*, 8.246-59; *TLNT*, 3.384-87; BAGD, 830. The negative sense is found in 4 Macc. 6.19 ("model of impiety"). Cf. 1 Cor. 10.6. MM, 645, cites an inscription that speaks, on the other hand, of a "model of piety."

47. See p. 2.

48. See pp. 10, 21.

49. See pp. 1-47.

sion of the gospel throughout a whole province (cf. Acts 19.10, where the establishment of the church in Ephesus began the evangelization of the province of Asia). Paul could boldly state that he had filled the whole region from Jerusalem to Illyricum with the gospel, even though he had evangelized only principal cities. Since establishing a church in a city meant reaching the province where it was located, a city could represent the whole of the province (Philippi and Macedonia — Phil. 4.15; Corinth and Achaia — 1 Cor. 16.15; 2 Cor. 1.1; Ephesus and Asia — 1 Cor. 16.19; 2 Cor. 1.8; Rom. 16.5).[50] Thessalonica is a best-case scenario of this vision. The reach of this church followed the natural lines of communication and influence throughout Macedonia and even to Achaia in the south and beyond (1.8), showing itself in both evangelistic efforts and support for other churches. The first manifestation of this influence was that they *became a model to all the believers in Macedonia and Achaia* in their sufferings.

8 In the Greek text, v. 8 begins with a conjunction (*gar*), which may denote the reason for what was previously affirmed. On this reading, the Thessalonian believers would be an example for the other churches of the region because *the Lord's message rang out* from them. But Paul had already stated why they were examples in v. 6 (see vv. 6-7). We should therefore understand the conjunction as a continuation of what was stated previously about the wide geographical impact of this congregation.[51] Not only were the Thessalonians an example but *the Lord's message rang out from you not only in Macedonia and Achaia — your faith in God has become known everywhere. The Lord's message* ("the word of the Lord") is a reference to the gospel itself (Acts 8.25; 13.44, 48-49; 15.35-36; 19.10; 2 Thess. 3.1). The term translated *rang out* (*exēchētai*) appears only here in the NT, but in other literature of the era it could be used to describe a clap of thunder (Sir. 40.13), the loud cry of a multitude (Philo, *In Flaccum* 39), a rumor that runs everywhere (3 Macc. 3.2), or, as Chrysostom suggests, "every place near is filled with the sound of a loud trumpet" (Chrysostom, *Homily on 1 Thessalonians* 2). The proclamation from Thessalonica was set at high volume and went out with great force over a large area. While some commentators would say that those who undertook this proclamation are Paul and his companions themselves,[52] the focus of these verses is on the activity of the church and

50. Bruce, *1 and 2 Thessalonians*, 16.

51. So Wanamaker, *Commentary on 1 and 2 Thessalonians*, 82; contra Best, *First and Second Epistles to the Thessalonians*, 80.

52. Milligan, *St. Paul's Epistles to the Thessalonians*, 12; Lünemann, *The Epistles to the Thessalonians*, 32. Milligan comments that had the Thessalonians been the agents of the proclamation, the text would likely have read *hyph' hymōn* ("by your instrumentality") rather than *aph' hymōn* ("from you as the center"). But *aph' hymōn* may imply simply that some but not all the members of the church went out on the evangelistic mission.

not that of the messengers. A number of persons from this church had gone out to proclaim the gospel, a few of whom are mentioned at a later stage in the NT. Aristarchus and Secundus of Thessalonica traveled with Paul and arrived with him in Syria and Jerusalem (Acts 20.4). Aristarchus also went with Paul to Ephesus on the second missionary journey (Acts 19.29), and he even accompanied him to Rome (Acts 27.2; Col. 4.10; cf. Phlm. 24). Jason, who had served as the patron for the apostles during the time of the initial evangelization of the city, traveled with Paul to Corinth (17.6-9; 18.1; Rom. 16.21, written at a later date from Corinth). These and possibly other members of the church were responsible for bringing the gospel to all the surrounding regions. 1 Thessalonians 1.8 speaks of a tremendous effort by the Thessalonian believers to carry the word of the Lord to all parts.

The influence of the capital city of Thessalonica over the province of Macedonia was enormous, as noted in the comments on the previous verse and in the Introduction.[53] The Macedonians in Thessalonica were the descendants of the great empire, once governed by Alexander, that lasted up to the time of King Perseus some two hundred years before the coming of the gospel. Once conquered by the Romans, Thessalonica became the capital of the newly formed province and enjoyed the economic and political benefits that came with being classified as a free city. It was a powerful metropolis with easy access to the interior and the northern frontier by means of good roads, and it lay not far from Asia and other Roman provinces by way of the sea. The Via Egnatia would take a person up to Byzantium or east to the region of Illyricum and from there on to Rome across the Adriatic. The Thessalonians looked outward. These were not a rustic people who were occupied only with local concerns but a city of great influence in all spheres, not only the political and economic but also the religious. Therefore it comes as no surprise to hear that when the Thessalonians turned from their idols to the true and living God (1.9-10), they themselves became the ones who brought the gospel to Macedonia, Achaia, and *everywhere* (v. 8).

The reference to *everywhere* is a hyperbole, but this should not diminish our understanding of the way this church spread the gospel over a vast area and even beyond Macedonia and Achaia. Chrysostom, on the other hand, questions whether Paul's speech is really hyperbolic. He is one of the few authors to link this great effort on the part of the Thessalonian believers with their heritage:

> And whence know we, says one, that the words were not hyperbolical? For this nation of the Macedonians, before the coming of Christ,

53. Pp. 1-47.

was renowned, and celebrated everywhere more than the Romans. And the Romans were admired on this account, that they took them captive. For the actions of the Macedonian king exceeded all report, who, setting out from a little city indeed, yet subdued the world. Wherefore also the Prophet saw him, a winged leopard, showing his swiftness, his vehemence, his fiery nature, his suddenly in a manner flying over the whole world with the trophies of his victory. And they say, that hearing from a certain philosopher, that there were infinite worlds, he groaned bitterly, that when they were numberless, he had not conquered even one. So high-minded was he, and high-souled, and celebrated everywhere. And with the fame of the king the glory of the nation also kept pace. For he was called "Alexander, the Macedonian." So that what took place there was also naturally much talked of. For nothing can be concealed that relates to the illustrious. The Macedonians then were not inferior to the Romans. And this has also arisen from their vehemence. For as if he were speaking of something living, he introduces the word "gone forth"; so vehement and energetic was their faith. "So that we need not to speak anything," says he, "for they themselves report concerning us what entering in we had unto you." *(Homily II on 1 Thessalonians)*

So great was the Thessalonians' evangelistic effort that Paul could proclaim, *your faith in God has become known everywhere. Therefore we do not need to say anything about it.* The grammar of the Greek is somewhat difficult at this point, in part due to the lack of punctuation in the original. The *NIV* understands the words translated *everywhere* as part of the thought that begins, *your faith in God has become known.* However, the words that could be translated "but in every place" are in relative contrast with the words *not only in Macedonia and Achaia.*[54] The point is that the gospel went forth from the Thessalonians "not only in Macedonia and Achaia but in every place."

The whole of v. 8 is a chiasmus that has the structure *a b/a′ b′*, where the third element restates the thought of the first element and the fourth element contrasts the thought of the second.[55] The structure of the verse can be presented in the following manner:

---

54. This is evident in the Greek, which says *ou monon en tȩ̄ Makedonią̄ kai [en tȩ̄] Achaią̄, all' en panti topǭ.*

55. Chiasmus is a rhetorical style in which two parts of a literary unity (e.g., a sentence or paragraph) are a reflection of each other. The common chiastic scheme is *a b/b′ a′*, but many variants have been identified in Hebrew, Greek, and Latin literature, such as *a b c/c′ b′ a′* and *a b c/a′ b′ c′*. See BDF, §477; John Beekman and John Callow, *Translating the Word of God* (Grand Rapids: Zondervan, 1974), 226-28; Nils W. Lund, *Chiasmus in the New Testament* (Peabody, Mass.: Hendrickson Publishers, 1970).

> *a* The Lord's message rang out from you
>> *b* not only in Macedonia and Achaia but in every place.
> *a'* Your faith in God has gone out;
>> *b'* Therefore we do not need to say anything.

The elements *a* and *a'*. present complementary ideas (they proclaimed the message), while the elements *b* and *b'* are contrasting elements (the evangelization of the Thessalonians was so extensive that the apostles did not have to preach in certain places).

The majority of the commentators understand the words translated *Your faith in God has become known* as a reference to the reputation of the Thessalonians, which had been noised abroad on all sides, an idea similar to what Paul said about the Romans (Rom. 1.8). But was it the reputation of the church or the gospel itself that went out? 2 Thessalonians 1.3-4 notes that the Paul and his associates spoke much about the reputation of this church in a statement that appears to be a contradiction of the affirmation of v. 8, *Therefore we do not need to say anything about it*.[56] This would incline us to the position that the reference here is to the gospel itself that went out of the city. Moreover, the word translated *has become known (exelēlythen)* is in the active voice in the Greek and means "has gone out." The term appears over and again in those texts that speak about the proclamation of the message of God (Mic. 4.2; Ps. 18.5; Rom. 10.18; 1 Cor. 14.36), although it may also be used to speak of rumors or reports (Matt. 9.26; Luke 4.14; 7.17; Mark 1.28; John 21.23). The content of what is proclaimed is specified as *your faith in God*[57] in contrast to their previous faith in idols (v. 9).[58] It is unlikely that the expression means "the report about your faith" since these words are used in the chiasmus as another way of saying "the Lord's message." What has gone out from Thessalonica was the proclamation of their faith whose object was God and not idols.

The result of this great evangelistic effort on the part of the Thessalonians was that *Therefore we do not need to say anything about it*. The words *about it* are not part of the Greek sentence and need not be supplied in translation to clarify the sense. Following the previous interpretation of this verse, the idea is not that Paul did not have to say anything about the reputation of the Thessalonians (cf. 2 Thess. 1.3-4) but rather

---

56. Wanamaker, *Commentary on 1 and 2 Thessalonians*, 84, solves this problem by saying that 2 Thessalonians was the first letter written to this church. See the discussion of the order of the letters on pp. 64-69.

57. This expression is found elsewhere in the NT, although Rom. 5.1 ("peace with God"; *eirēnēn . . . pros ton theon*) is similar.

58. So Milligan, *St. Paul's Epistles to the Thessalonians*, 13; Morris, *First and Second Epistles to the Thessalonians*, 51.

that they did not find it necessary to preach in certain places because of the previous evangelistic efforts of this church.[59] So understood, *to say (lalein)* is a reference to the apostolic preaching, as in 2.2, 4, and 16.

9 In this and the following verse Paul moves on to explain how he and the others came to know about the evangelistic efforts of the Thessalonian congregation:[60] *for they themselves report what kind of reception you gave us. They tell us how you turned to God from idols to serve the living and the true God. They* refers to those in Macedonia and Achaia who heard the gospel from the Thessalonians (v. 8). These people now report to Paul about what kind of "entrance" the apostolic team had in Thessalonica (v. 9a; cf. v. 5) and, secondly, how the Thessalonians had converted to God from idolatry (v. 9b; cf. v. 6). The *NIV* understands the first part of the verse as an explanation of how the Thessalonians had received the apostolic team.[61] But the term translated reception *(eisodon)* can just as well mean the act of entering a place, or even the place through which one enters, the entrance.[62] The same word is found in 2.1, where it clearly speaks of the messengers' entrance into the city, and we should understand it the same way here. The first part of v. 9 is a reference to the news about the nature of the heralds' "entrance" to Thessalonica. The ones who had heard the gospel from the Thessalonians also heard the narrative about this grand entrance of the apostolic band to the capital city, and now they play back the story to Paul and company. Interpreted this way, we can understand why the content of the report is "about us" *(peri hēmōn;* "For the people of those regions report about us," *NRSV).*

The "entrance" of the heralds is the principal theme of 2.1-12, which can best be interpreted as a contrast to the way that ancient philosophers would enter a city, at times with great pomp and questionable motives.[63] The "entrance" of an orator to a city could be a grand event, such as when Aristides entered Smyrna, "Before I even entered the city, there were people coming to meet me because they had heard about me, the most distinguished of the young men were giving themselves to me, and there was already a definite plan for a lecture. The invitation list was being arranged."[64]

---

59. So Paul Ellingworth and Eugene A. Nida, *A Translator's Handbook on Paul's Letters to the Thessalonians* (London, New York, and Stuttgart: United Bible Societies, 1976), 14.

60. Understanding *gar* (for) as explanatory.

61. An option presented in BAGD, 233.

62. BAGD, 233; MM, 188.

63. See Bruce W. Winter, "The Entries and Ethics of Orators and Paul (1 Thessalonians 2:1-12)," *TynBul* 44 (1993) 55-74, and the present commentary on 2.1-12.

64. Quoted in D. A. Russell, *Greek Declamation* (Cambridge: Cambridge University Press, 1983), 76.

Dio Chrysostom (47.22) speaks of the counsel he had received to "visit the greatest cities, escorted with much enthusiasm and éclat, the recipients of my visits becoming grateful for my presence and begging me to address them and advise them and flocking about my doors from early dawn." Paul and his associates' entrance to Thessalonica was not accompanied by all this ceremony, and, as we will see in 2.1-12, Paul was careful to distinguish between their "entrance" and those of the common stock philosophers. The character of the apostolic "entrance" was something that the Thessalonians not only witnessed (v. 5b) but also spoke about to others. These "others" are the ones who heard the story from the Thessalonians and who now retell it to Paul (v. 9a). However, we should not miss the fact that the purpose of a good "entrance" was to gain hearers and disciples. Although the evangelists did not come seeking glory, their entrance was accompanied with the divine message and power and fulfilled the objective of gaining converts to the living God, as noted in v. 9b.

The second part of the report given to Paul was about how the Thessalonians themselves had *turned to God from idols.* The account of the Thessalonians turning to God and abandoning idols echoes the missionary preaching *(kerygma)* of the apostles among the Gentiles (cf. Acts 14.15).[65] These believers had made a true response that was a reflection of their conviction that what they heard from Paul was the word of God (2.13). The first movement of this conversion was *to God,* and as a result they turned *from idols.* There was no syncretism between their new faith and old religious loyalties. Nor did they take half a step by adopting God into their pantheon, placing him alongside their other religious loyalties. They took the radical step of abandoning those gods that were part of the worship of their family and their community. When the Christian faith arrived in the cities and towns of the empire, its presence was rightly perceived as an attack on the images of the gods (Acts 14.11-18; 17.22-31; 19.23-41). The church resoundingly condemned the worship of idols and pointed people to the true God who created all things (Rom. 1.22-25; 1 Cor. 5.11; 6.9; 10.14-22; Gal. 5.20-21; Eph. 5.5; Col. 3.5; 1 John 5.21; Rev. 21.8; 22.15). Conversion meant not only abandoning the idol cult but also forsaking the immoral practices associated with it (1 Pet. 4.3). The gospel was not viewed in a favorable light in Greek and Roman society, which accepted polytheism and pluralism but did not tolerate the abandonment of one's traditional religious loyalties, whether of the civic or family deities.

The term Paul uses to refer to the Thessalonians' conversion, "to

65. See Johannes Munck, "I Thessalonians 1.9-10 and the Missionary Preaching of Paul," *NTS* 9 (1962-63) 95-110.

turn" *(epistrephō)*, implies not simply a change in attitude but also action.[66] This is true repentance. Conversion is described in biblical and Jewish literature as a turning to God (Hos. 14.2; Joel 2.19; Amos 4.8; Philo, *Quod Deus Sit Immutabilis* 17; Acts 14.15; 15.19; 2 Cor. 3.16) or as a turning to some quality of the moral life such as justice or the light (Philo, *De Somniis* 2.174; Acts 26.18). But on the other side, it is also understood as abandoning idols (Josephus, *Antiquitates* 10.53; Acts 14.15), Satan (Acts 26.18), sins (2 Chr. 6.26), or darkness (Acts 26.18).[67] Over against a philosophic perspective, conversion is not the progressive realization of virtue in a person's life (cf. Epictetus 1.4.1, 18-21)[68] but a radical reorientation of the heart of a person's existence. There was no mixing of indigenous religious practices with the new Christian worship. The Thessalonians came to the one God (implied by the use of the article before *God — ton theon*) and abandoned the multiplicity of *idols*. In Judaism, the description of pagan gods as *idols* did not imply that they were alternative gods but rather that they were not truly gods (cf. 1 Cor. 8.5),[69] a perspective that Paul heartily embraced.

We cannot specify exactly which idol cults the Thessalonians in the church had abandoned but can only refer to the general religious milieu of the city.[70] The Thessalonians worshiped a variety of gods, some being traditional and others being imports from Samothrace, Egypt, and Rome. "Atheists" were a very rare breed during this era. Religion was part of the warp and woof of society and had both political and economic ties. For this reason, the conversion of the Thessalonians had social and political implications and was not simply a personal matter. Most likely, their abandonment of idols, including the imperial cult, was the root cause of the social tension between the Christians and their contemporaries (2.14).

The implication of this verse is that the converts to the faith in

---

66. BAGD, 301; *TDNT,* 7.722-29; *NIDNTT,* 1.353-55. The Greek translates the Hebrew *shub* in the LXX (Deut. 30.2; 1 Sam. 7.3; 1 Kings 8.33; Tob. 14.61; Isa. 6.10 — cited in Matt. 13.15; Mark 4.12; John 12.40; Acts 28.27; Jer. 24.7; Joel 2.12-14; Zech. 1.3; Mal. 3.18), and the word is found repeatedly in Jewish literature where an author speaks of a return to God or to justice (Josephus, *Antiquitates* 10.53 [10.4.1]; Philo, *De Iosepho* 87; *Quod Deus Sit Immutabilis* 17; *De Confusione Linguarum* 131; *De Somniis* 2.174; *De Specialibus Legibus* 2.256). On conversion, see A. D. Nock, *Conversion* (Oxford: Clarendon Press, 1933); Beverly Roberts Gaventa, *From Darkness to Light* (Philadelphia: Fortress Press, 1986); Ronald D. Witherup, *Conversion in the New Testament* (Collegeville, Minn.: The Liturgical Press, 1994).

67. Interestingly, apostasy is described using the same verb since it is a turning from God to sin or idols. Philo, *De Confusione Linguarum* 131; Gal. 4.9; 2 Pet. 2.22.

68. In 2.20.22 Epictetus does use *epistrephō* with reference to the progress of the moral life as the fruit of philosophy.

69. *TDNT,* 2.377.

70. See pp. 31-47.

Thessalonica were not Jewish but Gentile, or at least that the vast majority of the church was Gentile. From the Acts narrative we learn that there were a few Jews from the synagogue in the city who converted to the faith (Acts 17.4) and that the majority of the Jews resisted the message that Jesus was the Messiah (17.3, 5). Their numbers appear to be so small that they are not even referred to in the description of the conversion of the Thessalonians in 1.9. Many of the "God-fearing Greeks" in the same synagogue accepted the Christian message. "God-fearers" were a rather amorphous group, some of whom had abandoned their gods but others who had simply added the Jewish God to their pantheon.[71] 1 Thessalonians 1.9 embraces the conversion of these people and implies a wider evangelistic campaign to the Gentiles outside the synagogue, carried on by the apostles or the new converts out of the synagogue or both. These would have been converted directly out of paganism.

As Israel was called not to serve the false gods (Exod. 23.33; Deut. 28.64; Judg. 10.13; 1 Sam. 8.8; cf. Gal. 4.8) but to serve God (Judg. 10.16; 1 Sam. 7.3-4), so, too, the conversion of the Thessalonians was so that they might *serve the living and the true God* (cf. Heb. 9.14). This service included not only the worship of God but also doing that which was good and just (Rom. 6.6, 16-20).[72] The description of God as *the living and true God* presents a striking contrast with idols, which have no life and can therefore do nothing (Deut. 5.26; Josh. 3.10; 1 Sam. 17.36; 1 Kings 17.1; 2 Kings 19.4; Ps. 42.2; Isa. 37.4, 17; Dan. 6.26; Acts 14.15; 2 Cor. 3.3; 6.16) and which are not real or genuine[73] (2 Chr. 15.3; Isa. 65.16; John 17.3; Rom. 3.4; 1 John 5.20, and especially Jer. 10.10, where the prophet describes God as "living" and "true" in contrast to idols). God is the only deity with life and the only one who is real.

10 The "blessed hope" of the church was the coming of the Lord Jesus Christ (Titus 2.13; 1 Cor. 1.7; Phil. 3.20), a hope that burned brightly in the Thessalonian believers (1 Thess. 2.19; 2.13; 2 Thess. 1.7-10; 2.1, 8). The Thessalonians were confused about what would happen to those of their number who died before the Lord's coming (4.13-18), and they had questions concerning the time of the coming of the day of the Lord (5.1-11), which was associated with his coming (2 Thess. 2.1-2). They became greatly shaken by a false teaching regarding the imminence of the day of the Lord (2 Thess. 2.1-12). Despite the confusion that arose regarding the teaching about the coming of the Lord, the hope that the church em-

71. See p. 49.

72. Best, *First and Second Epistles to the Thessalonians*, 83; Marshall, *1 and 2 Thessalonians*, 58.

73. *Alēthinŏ* denotes "real" or "genuine," in contrast to that which is not real. BAGD, 37.

braced was solid. Paul and his companions not only heard how the conversion of the Thessalonians resulted in their service to God (v. 9b) but also learned of their disposition *to wait for his Son from heaven*. The word translated *wait (anamenein)* appears only in this text in the whole of the NT, but it is found frequently in the LXX,[74] where at times, as in our present verse, it refers to the hope the people of God have for the salvation or mercy of God (Isa. 59.11; Jdt. 8.17; Sir. 2.7). How this hope was manifested is not specifically stated, but we should not assume that it was passive. The expectation of the Lord's coming is linked strongly with their moral life (3.13; 5.6-8, 23; cf. Titus 2.12-13)[75] and with their steadfastness in the face of great persecution, a point that is especially emphasized in this chapter (1.3; and 3.8). Serving God and holding fast to a strong eschatological expectation were not antithetical but complementary (vv. 9b-10a).

The object of their expectation, God's *Son*, is described in four ways in this verse. First, he is the *Son* who comes *from heaven*, an event referred to elsewhere in this letter as his royal coming (*parousia*; 2.19; 3.13; 4.15). This is the only place in the Thessalonian correspondence where Jesus is called God's *Son*, although the title is very common in Paul's writings (cf. Rom. 5.10; 8.3, 29, 32; 1 Cor. 1.9; 2 Cor. 1.19; Gal. 1.16; 4.4, 6; etc.). The coming of the *Son* will be *from the heavens*,[76] an affirmation that appears elsewhere in these letters (4.16; 2 Thess. 1.7) and that means that Jesus will come from the place of God the Father (Matt. 3.17; 16.1; 21.25; Luke 11.13, 16; John 1.32; 3.13, 27, 31; 6.31-33; Acts 2.2; 9.3; 11.9; 2 Pet. 1.18) and denotes his sovereignty (Eph. 1.20-21; 1 Pet. 3.22). This expectation presupposes that the Thessalonians were aware of the ascension of Jesus to the heavens (Acts 1.11; 2.34; Eph. 1.20; 2.6; Heb. 4.14; 9.24; 1 Pet. 3.22). His presence in the heavens (Acts 7.55) was linked tightly with their hope (cf. Matt. 26.64; Phil. 3.20). Certain verses of this letter imply that they expected this coming during their lifetime (4.15, 17; 5.4).

Second, the *Son* is described as the one whom God *raised from the dead*, or, more exactly, "from among the dead" (plural). This affirmation implies that they understood the preaching about the cross and the death of Jesus (4.14). The resurrection of Jesus was at the core of the apostolic proclamation in Thessalonica and the universal confession of the church (4.14; Acts 3.7, 15; 4.10; 5.30; 10.40; 13.30, 37; Rom. 4.24; 6.4, 9; 8.11, 34; 10.9; 1 Cor. 6.14; 15; 2 Cor. 4.14; Gal. 1.1; Eph. 1.20; Col. 2.12; 2 Tim. 2.8; 1 Pet. 1.21). The expectation concerning the coming of Jesus would have been impossible

---

74. Job 2.9a; 7.2; Isa. 59.11; Jer. 13.16; Jdt. 7.12; 8.17; Sir. 2.7; 5.7; 6.19; 2 Macc. 6.14.

75. So Marshall, *1 and 2 Thessalonians*, 58.

76. There does not seem to be any special significance to the plural here since our authors use this interchangeably with the singular (cf. 4.16; 2 Thess. 1.7).

without the resurrection from the dead. The past is linked intimately with the future in God's saving history, while the hope of the Thessalonians lives between these two poles. The Gentiles did not hope for a resurrection from the dead. For example, Pliny the Elder (*Natural History* 2.5.27) affirmed that it was not possible for the gods to do such things as bring the dead back to life, and Herodotus (*History* 3.62) understood the natural order of things to preclude the resurrection of the dead. Although Osiris could be called the lord of the dead (Plutarch, *De Iside et Osiride* 382F), this belief did not approach the Christian doctrine of the resurrection of the dead, of which Jesus was the firstfruits (1 Cor. 15.20; 1 Thess. 4.14-18).

Third, the *Son* who is raised is named — *Jesus,* none less than the person whose history had become known through the apostolic proclamation. This historic person, Jesus of Nazareth, is the same one who died, was raised, and will come from the heavens (cf. Acts 1.11). Over and again in this letter Jesus is the one who is said to have died (2.15; 4.14; 5.9-10) and who will come again (1.3; 2.19; 3.13; 4.14; 5.9, 23).

Finally, the last part of the verse describes Jesus as the one *who rescues us from the coming wrath.* The wrath of God is not simply the impersonal law of sowing and reaping or the outbreak of a negative emotion. God's wrath is the execution of his just judgment against those who violate and oppose his law.[77] Although the NT proclaims the love of God (John 3.16), this aspect of his character does not negate his judgment (Matt. 3.7; Luke 3.7; Rom. 2.5; Eph. 5.6; Col. 3.6; Rev. 6.16-17; 11.18; 16.19; 19.15). The wrath of the gods was a concept that was well known among the pagans and was believed to be seen in natural disasters.[78] Their wrath could be inexplicable and capricious.[79] But the wrath of God is an eschatological event that is directed toward those who do not know and obey God (2 Thess. 1.6-10; Rom. 1.18). Paul assures the Thessalonians that they will not suffer this wrath because Jesus, the one who was raised from the dead, will deliver them from it (5.9; cf. Rom. 5.9).[80] But Jesus is also the very one who will execute the divine wrath against those who disobey God (2 Thess. 1.6-10; Rev. 6.16). For their part, the Thessalonians should not confuse their sufferings with the wrath of God. The present tense of the verb *rescues* may imply that this deliverance has already begun. The wrath of God will be seen not simply at some future time (1 Thess. 5.9;

---

77. Marshall, *1 and 2 Thessalonians,* 59; *NIDNTT,* 1.105-13; R. V. G. Tasker, *The Biblical Doctrine of the Wrath of God* (London: Tyndale Press, 1951); Anthony Tyrrell Hanson, *The Wrath of the Lamb* (London: S.P.C.K., 1957).

78. *NIDNTT,* 1.107-8.

79. See the Introduction, p. 34.

80. In 1.10 Paul uses the verb *rhyomai,* which emphasizes more the aspect of rescue from disaster than *sōzō,* which can include the idea of the end for which one is saved.

2 Thess. 1.6-10; Rom. 5.9) but as an eschatological event that has already begun in the present (1 Thess. 2.16; Rom. 1.18). However, the emphasis in this verse is on the future or *coming wrath,* which is certain if not also near at hand (Matt. 17.11; John 4.21; 14.3; Eph. 5.6; Col. 3.6). The Thessalonian believers were undergoing persecution at this time and are here assured not only of their own liberation (1 Thess. 5.9) but also of the judgment of God that will come upon those who afflict them (2 Thess. 1.6-10). Whatever the agony and shame of the present, in the end God will reverse their fortunes. Those who are without power now will participate in the final victory, while those who have power over them now will have to meet the Judge, the God of the Christians.

III. "YOU KNOW . . ." —
THE BODY OF THE LETTER (2.1–5.22)

A. "Our visit to you was not a failure" —
The Gospel Arrives in Thessalonica (2.1–3.13)

1. "Our visit" — The Apostolic Entrance (2.1-12)

Paul ended the initial thanksgiving (1.2-10) and now pens the body of the letter.[1] The opening thanksgiving recounted the heralds' coming to the city (1.3-5) and the Thessalonians' reception of the gospel (1.6-10). These themes are once again taken up and elaborated, with 2.1-12 explaining the character of the preachers and their entrance to the city, and 2.13-16 recalling the Thessalonians' response to their message in the midst of great persecution.

At first glance, 2.1-12 appears to be an apologetic that counters some form of negative criticism of the character of the messengers and their mission. In light of the Jewish community's hostility against Paul and his associates at the beginning (Acts 17.5) and the strong words against those Jews who oppose the faith (1 Thess. 2.14-16), it may be that the criticisms to which he responds came from that source.[2] However, he notes that the Gentiles in Thessalonica and not the Jews were the primary perpetrators of the persecution against the church (2.14), which may imply that the response in 2.1-12 is to the Gentile tongue wagging against the apostolic band. Walter Schmithals, who interprets much of the NT in light of what

---

1. See the Introduction, p. 74.
2. See Frame, *Epistles of St. Paul to the Thessalonians,* 90.

he considers to be an emergent Gnosticism in the first century, proposes another scenario, arguing that in this section Paul defends his ministry against rival Gnostics.[3] But the absence of a distinctly anti-Gnostic polemic in this book (such as a response to Gnostic dualism, which identified the physical with evil and the spiritual with good), plus the abiding question of whether or not there even existed a full-blown pre-Christian Gnosticism, gives us doubt about the viability of Schmithals's proposal.

On the other hand, it is possible that the opposition that moved Paul to include this apologetic section came from within the Thessalonian church itself. Had not he and his associates departed from the city precipitously, leaving the church to face adversity alone? Did they "preach and run" at the first sign of trouble? Why had Paul not returned? But notice that although Paul and his companions left this fledgling congregation to face great trouble on their own (2.17-18), there is no compelling evidence from this letter that the church criticized them. Timothy was sent to the town after they departed, and when he arrived in Corinth he gave this report: "He has told us that you always have pleasant memories of us and that you long to see us, just as we also long to see you" (3.6). Another possible motivation for including an apologetic section might be that those Gentiles who persecuted the church criticized the founders, characterizing them as charlatans whose motivations were nothing more than their own personal interests for fame and fortune. As attractive as this suggestion is, 2.1-12 does not appear to be a mirror that reflects the criticisms against the heralds that came from outside the church. There is no reference to "them" in this section. We do not hear the voices of outsiders being mentioned or alluded to. What is more, the defense contains elements that could be called "traditional" and not specific to the situation, as we will see shortly.

In light of the difficulty of reconstructing the situation behind 2.1-12 in terms of an apologetic, Abraham Malherbe suggests that there was not a specific accusation against Paul and the others, either from within or outside the community, and therefore we should not read this section as a defense of their ministry.[4] Malherbe compares the language and thought of these verses with the way Dio Chrysostom distinguishes himself from other Cynic philosophers, without having specifically been accused of acting like them. Dio criticizes various types of Cynics and then presents a picture of the ideal Cynic using language similar to Paul's to show the difference between himself and others. For example, Dio says,

3. Walter Schmithals, *Paul and the Gnostics* (Nashville and New York: Abingdon Press, 1972), 139-51.
4. Abraham J. Malherbe, "'Gentle as a Nurse': The Cynic Background to 1 Thess ii," *NovT* 12 (1970) 203-17.

But to find a man who in plain terms and without guile speaks his mind with frankness, and neither for the sake of reputation nor for gain makes false pretensions, but out of good will and concern for his fellow-man stands ready, if need be, to submit to ridicule and to the disorder and the uproar of the mob — to find such a man as that is not easy, but rather the good fortune of a very lucky city, so great is the dearth of noble, independent souls and such the abundance of toadies [flatterers], mountebanks, and sophists. (32.11)

The parallels between 1 Thessalonians and the style and language of Dio, in this and other passages, are noteworthy. According to Malherbe, the purpose of this type of teaching was not apologetic but parenetic. The philosopher presented himself as a moral example to follow.[5] But despite the vivid examples Malherbe presents, we have to wonder whether Paul is really presenting himself and his companions as the ideal Christian philosophers, just as Dio Chrysostom did in his vocation as a Cynic philosopher. Moreover, while the philosophers used this type of teaching to present themselves as moral examples, in 1 Thessalonians 2.1-12 the author nowhere suggests that the Thessalonians are to imitate his character (although the imitation of his character does appear as a theme elsewhere in this letter, as we saw in 1.6). Even 2.12, which concludes this section with an ethical note, makes reference to the exhortation they had given the church while they were with them and not to the review of their conduct just presented.

Bruce Winter presents another analysis of 2.1-12 that, like the thesis of Malherbe, takes into account the practices of the ancient moralists. Winter compares 2.1-12 with the customs of orators upon their "entry" into a city.[6] His argument is that, far from identifying himself with the philosophic traditions of his days, Paul instead distances himself from the habits of the sophists, who entered the cities of the empire with great pomp in order to gain an audience and disciples for their teaching. What motivated them, according to ancient sources, was money, fame or glory, praise, or simply the desire to deceive. Paul distinguishes his "entry" (2.1; 1.9) from that of those moralists *in anticipation of* problems in Thessalonica like those he encountered in Corinth, where he wrote 1 Thessalonians. The parallels between the argument in 2.1-12 and the moral problems associated with the "entry" of those orators, in addition to Paul's own declaration in 2.1 about the character of his own "entry," supports the analysis of Winter, as we will see in the interpretation of this passage.

5. Idem, *Moral Exhortation: A Greco-Roman Sourcebook* (Philadelphia: Westminster Press, 1986), 135-38; idem, "Exhortation in First Thessalonians," *NovT* 25 (1983) 240-41.
6. Winter, "Entries and Ethics of Orators and Paul."

However, it is questionable whether Winter has correctly identified the reason for the inclusion of this material. He states that Paul distances himself from the norms of the philosophers in anticipation of problems arising in Thessalonica similar to those in Corinth (1 Cor. 2.1-5). While this may be a possibility, Winter does not prove his point. He is unable to show that the teaching here is a vaccination against future problems.

Both Winter and Malherbe correctly identify the relationship between this section and the less desirable practices of itinerant philosophers. Paul distinguishes his approach from their ways and reminds the Thessalonians once and again of his genuine concern for their well-being. I would suggest that the way the apostolic band left so quickly from the city plus the fact that Paul, the leader of the group, had not returned was reason enough to include this section. The following context suggests that this was the issue (chapters 2 and 3 cohere together as a whole). Paul explains in detail why he did not return to Thessalonica (2.17-20) and recounts the measures he undertook to assure that the church would be strengthened in their time of adversity (3.1-5). At the end of that section, he again expresses his desire to see the church (3.6-12). The situation in and of itself demanded an explanation of their actions, especially in light of the questionable character and methods of many of the philosophers of their day. There is no need to project the situation of Corinth onto Thessalonica. In the end, due to the intimate relationship between Paul and the message he preached, what was at stake was not simply the reputation of the Christian messenger among the believers but rather the Thessalonians' continuation in the faith (3.5).

1 Paul again takes up the theme of his "entry" into the city, which he had already touched upon in 1.5 and 9, by saying, *You know, brothers, that our visit to you was not a failure.* The relationship between this verse and the preceding is signaled by the word "for" *(gar)*, left untranslated in the *NIV*. The Thessalonians knew what kind of persons Paul and the others were (1.5b), and this section now helps them to remember in detail the blameless character they exhibited. The call to remember what they already knew appears frequently in this section (2.1-2, 5, 9, 10, 11) and at other points in this letter (1.5; 3.3-4; 4.2; 5.2; and cf. 2 Thess. 2.5-6; 3.7). In ancient ethical instruction, moralists commonly called their readers to remember what they already knew (e.g., Dio Chrysostom 17.1-6), and Paul repeatedly does the same, bringing to mind not only the teaching he had previously given the church but also helping them recall his character upon his "entry" to the city (see 1.9 and the commentary there). He reminds the Thessalonians that his entry was not a *failure.* The term translated *failure (kenē)* can in some contexts mean "empty" or "vain" (1 Cor. 15.14; Eph. 5.6; Col. 2.8; Jas. 2.20), and if this is the meaning in 2.1, the emphasis would be upon the character of the apostolic mission. Understood in this way, the thought would be that Paul's "entry" was not without sound motives (cf. 2.2-12) or not without power (cf. 1.5). On the other hand, the word possibly refers to the results of the apostolic mission, stating that the entry was not "in vain" or *not a failure,* as the *NIV* translates (1 Cor. 15.10, 58; 2 Cor. 6.1). Paul uses the term in this second sense in 3.5, where he also speaks about his fears concerning the possible results of his mission in the city: "and our efforts might have been useless." The theme of 2.1-12 is the character of the messengers' mission and not the results of their labors. But while the primary emphasis appears to be on the apostolic mission, the missionary character was bound up with the results of the mission. The philosophic tradition underlines the union between these two. Dio Chrysostom railed against those philosophers who would roll into a town "with a view to their own profit and reputation, and not to improve you" (32.10). Malherbe notes, "Consequently, since they lacked substance and did not result in anything positive, they were described as vain or empty."[7] Character and results could not be separated. Sound character produced credible results.

2 Verse 2 begins with the adversative "but" *(alla),* left untranslated in the *NIV.* If the thought in the previous verse is that the motives of Paul and his companions' entry was not "empty," the contrast presented in this verse would be that the true character of the missionaries is that they preached even though they had previously suffered for doing so in Philippi. If, on the other hand, the emphasis of the previous verse is on the results of their preaching, what kind of contrast would be presented in v. 2? Verse 2 does not present any kind of contrast with that idea, which again supports our understanding of v. 1 as a reference primarily to the charter of the mission. Paul declares that instead of having an "entry" that was "vain" with wrong motives, *We had previously suffered and been insulted in Philippi, as you know, but with the help of our God we dared to tell you his gospel in spite of strong opposition.* The fact that they preached in Thessalonica despite the opposition they faced before and during their ministry there was strong evidence of their genuine and pure motives. Once more the appeal is to what the Thessalonians already knew about their character *(as you know),* this time reminding them of the missionaries' experience in Philippi, the Roman colony along the Via Egnatia that they had evangelized before coming to Thessalonica. In Acts 16 Luke describes the evangelization (16.11-18) and the conflict the evangelists endured in that city (16.19-24; Phil. 1.30). On order of the city's magistrates, the lictores used their bundle of rods (Latin *fasces*) to beat Paul and Silas

---

7. Malherbe, "Gentle as a Nurse," 207.

publicly, having stripped them of their robes (Acts 16.22, 35, 37-38, translated "officers"). This punishment was undertaken without trial, and afterward the heralds were thrown into jail. Roman law prohibited this type of treatment of Roman citizens (v. 37), exempting them from degrading punishment.[8] The news of this scandal in Philippi had arrived in Thessalonica (Acts 17.6; 1 Thess. 2.2a). Paul remembers this unjust treatment in 2.2 by saying, *We had previously suffered.* But he adds that they were also *insulted in Philippi.* The insult was a theme that was frequently touched upon by ancient moralists. Aristotle, for example, comments on insults *(hubris),* saying, "For insult consists in causing injury or annoyance whereby the sufferer is disgraced."[9] So grave were insults that the victim could take legal action against the person who caused the insult,[10] similar to the way we could take a person to court for defamation of character. The authorities in Philippi had abused their power and had insulted and shamed Paul and Silas publicly, exposing them to dishonor, disgrace, and humiliation in the eyes of everyone.[11] When Paul recalls that they had suffered physically and had been humiliated socially in Philippi, it was evident to all that they had to overcome a great social obstacle in order to preach the gospel in Thessalonica.

Paul recounts to the Thessalonians how, despite the ill treatment and humiliation the heralds had suffered previously, *with the help of our God we dared to tell you his gospel in spite of strong opposition.* One of the Cynic ideals was to possess the ability to speak to an audience with boldness *(parrēsia),* even in the face of severe criticism by the audience. The verbal form of this term is found here in v. 2b *(eparrēsiasametha),* translated *we dared.*[12] The Cynic's words could be hard or even severe, but this was acceptable only if his motivation was the love of the people whom he wished to help. In other instances the Cynic could use language that was softer and more tender (cf. 2.7).[13] This confidence was a function of the self-understanding that came in response to the well-known dictum,

8. Cicero, *Pro Rabirio Perduellionis Reo* 12. The beating the apostles endured was called the *verberatio,* a type of punishment given out to those of low status who would be considered guilty on the basis of an accusation alone, without a trial.

9. Aristotle, *Ars Rhetorica* 2.2.5-6.

10. See the discussion of *hybris* in Peter Marshall, *Enmity in Corinth: Social Conventions in Paul's Relations with the Corinthians* (Tübingen: J. C. B. Mohr [Paul Siebeck], 1987), 183-218; N. R. E. Fisher, "Hybris and Dishonour," *Greece and Rome* 23 (1976) 177-93.

11. On the abuse of power as a source of *hybris,* see Marshall, *Enmity in Corinth,* 188-89.

12. So Acts 9.27-28; 13.46; 14.3; 18.26; 19.8; Eph. 6.20; and the substantive in Acts 4.13; Eph. 6.19; Phil. 1.20.

13. On *parrēsia* in public discourse, see Dio Chrysostom 12.9; 32.11; and the discussion in Malherbe, "Gentle as a Nurse," 208-16.

"Know thyself."[14] Paul and his companions demonstrate their knowledge of themselves in this section (vv. 1-12), but the source of their confidence was not themselves but God, with whom they were in relation ("we had boldness in our God"). For this reason, they confidently proclaimed "the gospel of God" in the city (cf. Mark 1.14; Rom. 1.1; 15.16; 2 Cor. 11.7; 1 Thess. 2.9; 1 Pet. 4.17; and the commentary on 1 Thess. 1.5). The words "of God," translated by the word *his* in the *NIV*, indicate that the source of the good news they proclaimed was God himself. They demonstrated their love for the Thessalonians by speaking the gospel to them boldly, despite the fact that they had suffered in Philippi and endured the same while ministering in Thessalonica, as the last words of the verse indicate, *we dared to tell you his gospel in spite of strong opposition.* The rhetoricians who spoke publicly in ancient cities could be the object of much abuse by their audience[15] (much like the ridicule leveled at many speakers at Hyde Park's Speaker's Corner in London), and the Christian heralds suffered the same type of abuse and more. The term translated *opposition (agōni)* could denote anxiety or concern in the face of conflict or problems (Col. 2.1), but it is doubtful that the word carries this meaning here in a context where the author recalls their boldness in the face of conflict. The term could also denote the strong efforts of an athlete (Heb. 12.1), but here, as in Philippians 1.30, the reference is to the great effort one puts out in the presence of opposition.[16] Preaching was no easy task. The heralds struggled forward with their ministry in Thessalonica in spite of the opposition, and they displayed great boldness as they proclaimed the gospel, even after having suffered ill treatment and infamy in Philippi. Their actions showed that they spoke without any interest in personal gain.

3 Paul continues to detail the pure character of their motives[17] when they preached to the Thessalonians by saying, *For the appeal we make*

14. Plutarch, *Quomodo Adulator ab Amico Internoscatur* 65F; *Quomodo Quis Suos in Virtute Sentiat Profectus* 81C-D.

15. For example, Dio Chrysostom 9.9 tells of Diogenes' public speaking, saying, "to others he seemed crazy, many scorned him as a beggar and poor good-for-nothing, some jeered at him, others tried to insult him grossly by throwing bones at his feet as they would to dogs, yet others would approach him and pluck at his cloak, but many could not tolerate him and were indignant. It was just like the way in which Homer says the suitors made sport of Odysseus; he too endured their riotous conduct and insolence for a few days, and Diogenes was like him in every respect."

16. BAGD, 15; Victor C. Pfitzner, *Paul and the Agon Motif* (Leiden: E. J. Brill, 1967), 112-14. Cf. Col. 1.29, where the verb *agōnizomai* is used in the same way.

17. This appears to be the sense of "for" *(gar)*, continuing the thought begun in 2.1. Less likely is the view that *gar* introduces the reason for their boldness (v. 2) since the authors already rooted that confidence in their relationship with God ("in our God").

does not spring from error or impure motives, nor are we trying to trick you. The *appeal* to which he refers is the preaching they undertook in the city (v. 2) and not the current teaching, as the present tense in the *NIV* may imply. The term they use to speak of their proclamation of the gospel (*paraklēsis*) may mean, depending on the context, "comfort" (Luke 6.24; Acts 9.31; 15.31; 2 Cor. 1.4-7; 4.13; 7.7; Phil. 2.1; 2 Thess. 2.16; Phlm. 7), "petition" (2 Cor. 8.4), or "exhortation" in the realm of moral teaching (1 Cor. 14.3; 1 Tim. 4.13; Heb. 12.5; and possibly Phil. 2.1).[18] But 1 Thessalonians 2.3 is the only place where it refers to Christian proclamation, although the verbal form of the word is used in this manner in Luke 3.18 and Acts 2.40, similar to the common Greek sense of "to call" or "to summon."[19] The gospel is not simply an announcement of the good news but also a call to respond to the divine initiative contained in it.

Paul declares that in their evangelistic campaign in the city both their motives and their methods were pure.[20] Their proclamation did *not spring from error*, which means that the doctrine they preached was not false but true.[21] This was the "gospel of God" (v. 2), the message that God communicated (v. 13), and as such it was not false teaching but true (Col. 1.5; 1 John 4.6). The teachers of error assailed many of the early churches (Eph. 4.14; Col. 2.8; 1 John 2.26; 3.7; 4.6; 2 Tim. 3.13; 2 Pet. 2.18; 3.17), just as numerous philosophers of those days were accused of teaching error.[22] Paul and his companions were not like those whose motivation was to corrupt the minds of the hearers with false or heterodox ideas. Moreover, they were not driven by *impure motives (akatharsias)*. Although this word may refer to ceremonial impurity, the sense here is moral.[23] In the vast majority of the NT texts where it appears, it denotes "sexual impurity" (Rom. 1.24; 2 Cor. 12.21; Gal. 5.19; Eph. 5.13; Col. 3.5; and 1 Thess. 4.7).

18. BAGD, 618; *TDNT*, 5.773-99.

19. *TDNT*, 5.774-75; Epictetus, *Dissertationes* 3.23.27-28. Horbury suggests that Paul counters the charge that he is a false prophet and not that he is distancing himself from the habits of some philosophers. His argument is based on the use of *paraklēsis, planē*, and *akatharsia* in the denunciation of false prophecy. Although Horbury demonstrates that the vocabulary fits nicely into that context, the argument fails by not taking into account the full scope of this passage that over and again counters the excesses within the philosophic tradition. William Horbury, "I Thessalonians ii.3 as Rebutting the Charge of False Prophecy," *JTS* 33 (1982) 492-508.

20. The motives are expressed by the first two elements of the verse, introduced by *ek* ("from"), while their method is underlined in the third element of the verse and introduced by *en* ("in" or "by means of").

21. The word *planēs* does not signify "deception," which would refer to the method of preaching, but rather "error," with emphasis on the content of the message. See *New Docs*, 2.94-95.

22. See Malherbe, "Gentle as a Nurse," 214.

23. BAGD, 28-29.

Some commentators believe that Paul uses the word in this way, distancing himself and his associates from the various cults in Thessalonica that gave place to and even promoted sexual license.[24] But what element in the immediate context would lead the Thessalonians to believe that this is what Paul had in mind? The word had a broader range of meaning and could simply refer to any kind of moral impurity (Rom. 6.19; Eph. 4.19), and it is precisely this wider sense that is found in Dio Chrysostom when he speaks of the type of purity of mind that the true philosopher should possess.[25] No impure motive brought these gospel messengers to town, whether it were greed or glory (vv. 5-6).

Finally, the author reminds the Thessalonians that not only their motives but also their methods were upright: *nor are we trying to trick you.* They did not deceive the Thessalonians by using the bait of rhetorical tricks (cf. 1 Cor. 2.4) in order to gain disciples for their cause. The NT classifies deception as a sin (Mark 7.22; John 1.47; Acts 13.10; Rom. 1.29; 1 Pet. 2.1, 22; 3.10), and for this reason the Christian preachers shunned it as a legitimate means to gain converts (cf. 2 Cor. 12.16). In the philosophic tradition, Dio Chrysostom advised those who wanted to speak with boldness against both impurity and deception.[26] In the gospel appeal to the Thessalonians, the message was not false, the motivations were not impure, and the methods were not deceptive. The heralds were not hucksters who hustled these people!

4 After declaring that their motives and methodology were not corrupt, Paul proceeds to present their credentials as those whom God had approved to participate in the evangelical ministry: *On the contrary, we speak as men approved by God to be entrusted with the gospel.* The verb *approved (dokimazō)* may mean "to prove" or "to examine" in order to determine the quality of something or someone, a sense found in the last part of this verse where the term is again used ("who *tests* our hearts"; see also Luke 14.19; 1 Cor. 3.13; 11.28; 2 Cor. 13.5; Gal. 6.4; 1 Thess. 5.21; 1 Tim. 3.10). In other contexts, as here in v. 4a, the verb means "approve," the successful result of examining something or someone (Rom. 2.18; 14.22; 1 Cor. 16.3; 2 Cor. 8.22).[27] Paul himself calls the churches to examine those who will serve as their leaders (Rom. 14.18; 2 Cor. 13.7; 1 Tim. 3.10) and states that only those who have passed the exam should be given responsibility (1 Cor. 16.3; 2 Cor. 8.22). But here in v. 4a it is God himself who, having tested, approved the apostles for this ministry (cf. 2 Cor. 10.18;

24. Milligan, *St. Paul's Epistles to the Thessalonians,* 18; Morris, *First and Second Epistles to the Thessalonians,* 62; Frame, *Epistles of St. Paul to the Thessalonians,* 95-96.

25. Dio Chrysostom 32.11-12; Malherbe, "Gentle as a Nurse," 214-15.

26. Ibid.

27. See BAGD, 202; MM, 167; *TLNT,* 1.353-361; *NIDNTT,* 3.808-10.

2 Tim. 2.15; and Rom. 16.10). The verb, which here is in the perfect tense in the Greek, implies that there was a time of testing prior to their being entrusted with the gospel, but we may only speculate about when and how this happened in the lives of Paul and his associates. In Paul's case, could the time of testing have been during his three-year sojourn in Arabia (Gal. 1.16-18)? Despite the fact that he was chosen by God to be an apostle even before his birth (Gal. 1.1, 15), there was a period during which he was tested and after which God set his seal upon him as one *approved* for the ministry. Cultural norms of the day required that a person be tested and approved before being commissioned for some office. Not only the inscriptions but also a number of texts indicate that those who served as public officials should first be approved for the post. Xenophon, for example, says that Socrates asked about the membership of the Areopagus in Athens (cf. Acts 17.19, 22, 34), "But what of the Court of the Areopagus, Pericles? Are not its members persons who have won approval?"[28] Josephus notes that, under Moses, the tribal chiefs were those "approved by the whole multitude as upright and just persons."[29] Having been approved by God, the apostles were *entrusted with the gospel* by God himself. In a number of ancient writings, the naming of officials to their post or giving a person a position of responsibility was described using the same verb "entrust." Josephus, for example, wrote about Beryllus, "who was Nero's tutor and who had been *appointed* secretary of Greek correspondence."[30] What Paul points out in our verse is that he and his companions had received their commission from God to proclaim the gospel (1 Cor. 9.17-18; Gal. 2.7; 1 Tim. 1.11-12; Titus 1.3; cf. Luke 16.11; Rom. 3.2). They were faithful to this commission and so had proclaimed this good news: *so we speak (houtōs laloumen)*. "To speak" refers to their evangelistic proclamation (as in 1.8; 2.2, 16). In the Greek text this declaration is placed after the statement about God's approval and commission. The heralds had carried out the mission for which God had commissioned them.

Since they were commissioned by God, their ardent desire was to

28. *Memorabilia* 3.5.20; Lysias, *Against Alcibiades* 15.6: "But I say it is monstrous, gentlemen, that although the generals themselves, who have been duly elected by the people, would not dare to take command of us before they had passed their scrutiny in compliance with the laws, Alcibiades should dare to take his rank from them in violation of the laws of our city"; Plato, *Leges* 6.765C-D; "Three shall be appointed: twenty having been first selected by show of hand, three out of the twenty shall be chosen by lot; and they shall be subject also to the approval of the scrutineers"; Demosthenes, *Against Midias* 21.111, "Lastly, when I was made senator by lot, he denounced me at the scrutiny"; MM, 167; Milligan, *St. Paul's Epistles to the Thessalonians*, 18; *TLNT*, 1.354-55.

29. Josephus, *Antiquitates* 3.71 (3.4.1).

30. Ibid., 20.183 (20.8.9); *LAE*, 374; MM, 514; Xenophon, *Memorabilia* 4.4.17.

serve him: *We are not trying to please men but God, who tests our hearts.* Paul is in no way saying that in pleasing God he and his companions were somehow displeasing to people (cf. Rom. 15.1-3; 1 Cor. 9.22; 10.33). The point is rather that the fundamental motivation in their ministry was to please God rather than people (Gal. 1.10; 2 Tim. 2.4; cf. Rom. 8.8; 1 Cor. 7.32-34; Col. 1.10; 3.22; 1 Thess. 4.1; 1 John 3.22; and 1 Thess. 2.15). Milligan reminds us that *to please (areskontes)* does not simply mean "seek to please" but points to the idea of rendering service in the interest of another. The term appears with frequency in inscriptions that publicly testified to the good service officials or citizens rendered to the state, the people, or the governing council of a city.[31] Similarly, the heralds were not seeking the praise and approval of their hearers (v. 6); rather, their motivation was to serve God, who had chosen, tested, approved, and commissioned them (2 Tim. 2.4).

While Paul has made various declarations about his and his associates' character, it is apparent that only God knows what transpires in a person's mind. He is the one *who tests our hearts.* With these words Paul invokes God himself as witness to their integrity since he is the one who examines where no human can see — the inner workings of the heart.[32] Biblical literature is replete with the same thought that God tests the heart of each human (1 Sam. 16.7; 1 Chr. 28.9; Pss. 7.9; 139.23; Prov. 17.3; Jer. 11.20; 12.3; 17.10; Acts 1.24; 15.8; Rom. 8.27; Rev. 2.23). The present tense of the verb *tests* suggests that the One who tested and approved the apostles in the past (v. 4a) continues to examine their character in the present. He continually examines the motives of his messengers.

5 As a further explanation of the integrity of the messengers' motives, the author states, *You know we never used flattery, nor did we put on a mask to cover up greed — God is our witness.* As the Thessalonians could testify from their own knowledge of the heralds' conduct ("You know"; cf. 2.1), Paul and his coworkers at no time employed flattering speech[33] to gain converts for themselves. The ancients wrote frequently about flattery and how to identify it. Milligan defines the notion of flattery during this era in this way: "The word carries with it the idea of the tortuous methods by which one man seeks to gain influence over another, generally for his own ends, and when we keep in view the selfish conduct of too many of the heathen rhetoricians of the day . . . we can easily understand how such a charge might come to be laid against the Apostles."[34] Flattery was com-

---

31. Milligan, *St. Paul's Epistles to the Thessalonians,* 19; MM, 75.
32. Bruce, *1 and 2 Thessalonians,* 27.
33. "Word of flattery" or "flattering speech" *(en logō kolakeias).*
34. MM, 352.

monly viewed as a way to get money out of others, so the double denial of flattery and greed in this verse does not surprise. Aristotle distinguishes between friends and flatterers, saying, "The man who always joins in the pleasures of his companions, if he sets out to be pleasant for no ulterior motive, is Obsequious; if he does so for the sake of getting something by it in the shape of money or money's worth, he is a Flatterer."[35] Eupolis gives voice to the flatterer's intentions, saying, "And when I catch sight of a man who is rich and thick, I at once get my hooks into him. If this money-bags happens to say anything, I praise him vehemently and express my amazement, pretending to find delight in his words."[36] The very fact that Paul denies flattery and greed implies that within this church there were some people with sufficient economic means to be desirable objects of flattery. The ancients recognized that flattery was evidence of the bad character of the person who used it to persuade or move others to action.[37] It was a way to gain the favor of someone, equal to the way one could gain another's favor through giving gifts or entertaining the person one wished to influence.[38] Plato advised that one should shun any kind of flatterer, while sometime later Plutarch stated that a flatterer corrupts the morals of the young and only pretends to be a friend.[39] Dio Chrysostom warned that flattery was a characteristic of charlatans and sophists. Plutarch was so concerned about flatterers that he wrote a whole treatise about how to distinguish between them and true friends.[40] As communicators of the truth of God and as those who sincerely cared for the well-being of their hearers, the apostles never flattered their audience in an attempt to gain something for themselves. The Thessalonians knew this well.

What motivated the evangelists was not their greed for financial gain either: *nor did we put on a mask to cover up greed*. They did not use a false front (*prophasei*, meaning "pretext" or "false excuse") to cover up their true motivation (Matt. 23.14; Mark 12.40; Luke 20.47; Acts 27.30; Phil. 1.18).[41] In no way did they use flattery, or even their preaching, to cover up greed as their driving force (*pleonexias*; Mark 7.22; Luke 12.15; Rom. 1.29; 2 Cor. 9.5; Eph. 4.19; Col. 3.5; 2 Pet. 2.3, 14).[42] *Greed* is the insa-

---

35. Aristotle, *Nicomachean Ethics* 1127a.
36. Eupolis, 236-37. Cited in Paul Millett, "Patronage and Its Avoidance in Classical Athens," in *Patronage in Ancient Society* (ed. Andrew Wallace-Hadrill; London and New York: Routledge, 1989), 31.
37. Josephus, *Antiquitates* 16.301 (16.10.1); *Bellum Judaicum* 4.231 (4.4.1).
38. Dio Cassius 71.35.
39. Plato, *Gorgias* 527C; Plutarch, *De Liberis Educandis* 13A-B.
40. Dio Chrysostom 32.11; Plutarch, *Quomodo Adulator ab Amico Internoscatur*.
41. BAGD, 722.
42. See BAGD, 667; MM, 518; *TLNT*, 3.117-19; *TDNT*, 6.266-74; *NIDNTT*, 1.137-39.

tiable and excessive desire to have more and more money; it thinks nothing of using another person or another's property to gain its own ends.[43] Dio Chrysostom's Seventeenth Discourse was devoted entirely to the subject of avarice, and both he and Plutarch condemn those rhetoricians who are motivated simply by financial gain.[44] Dio declares at the opening of his Thirty-Fifth Discourse, "Gentlemen, I have come before you not to display my talents as a speaker nor because I want money from you, or expect your praise" (35.1). He classifies greed as one of the greatest evils (17.6) and declares that the avaricious do damage to themselves and to their neighbors (17.7). In his opinion, the majority of people suffer from this vice, not simply the itinerant philosophers (17.16). But Paul declares that they did not preach among the Thessalonians in order to shake out whatever financial gain they could from them, trying all the while to hide this motive. Instead, Paul worked with his own hands while among the Thessalonians, and nobody could accuse him of greed (2.9; 2 Thess. 3.8; 1 Cor. 4.12; Acts 20.34). He made sure that his handling of monies from the churches was always upright (2 Cor. 8.20-21), and insisted that all church leaders be above reproach in their financial affairs (1 Tim. 3.3; Titus 1.7; and cf. 1 Pet. 5.2). Not everyone, however, followed his example (1 Tim. 6.5; Titus 1.11; Jude 11; *Did.* 11.5-6, 12), either in those days or ours. God himself is invoked as witness to their absence of greed — *God is our witness* (cf. Rom. 1.9; 2 Cor. 1.23; Phil. 1.8; and Gen. 31.50; Judg. 11.10; 1 Sam. 12.5; 20.42; Job 16.19; Jer. 29.23; 42.5; Mic. 1.2). There are now two witnesses to the heralds' integrity — the Thessalonians and God himself — and with this their blameless character becomes established fact (cf. 2.4, 10; 2 Cor. 13.1; 1 Tim. 5.19; and Heb. 10.28; Deut. 17.6; 19.15).

6   In the third negation that clarifies the motivations of the messengers (cf. v. 5) Paul declares, *We were not looking for praise from men, not from you or anyone else.*[45] They did not try to obtain (*zētountes*) glory or honor from the Thessalonians nor anyone else (the verb is used similarly in John 5.44; 7.18; 8.50a; Rom. 2.7). On the other hand, in other contexts this verb "seek" can have the more forceful sense of "demand" or "require" (Mark 8.11-12; Luke 11.16; 12.48; 1 Cor. 1.22; 2 Cor. 13.3). Is this, then, a denial that they made any such demand upon their hearers by wielding apostolic authority over them (cf. vv. 6b-7)?[46] Since the quest for glory was

---

43. Sir. 14.9; Philo, *De Praemiis et Poenis* 121; Plutarch, *Agis and Cleomenes* 3.1; and 16.1, which speaks of the avarice of the rich and of the Macedonians.

44. Dio Chrysostom 32.11; Plutarch, *Moralia* 131A.

45. The standard critical editions of the Greek text (*Nestle*[27], UBS[4]) end the verse at this point, contrary to the *NIV,* and place a comma at the end of the verse instead of a full stop. Neither edition places a paragraph break after v. 6.

46. So Wanamaker, *Commentary on 1 and 2 Thessalonians*, 98.

such a common activity of itinerant philosophers and since NT teaching repeatedly warns against this desire, the first rendering of the verb is to be preferred. The gospel heralds did not come to town looking for special honors from the Thessalonians themselves *or anyone else.* Who are these others?[47] These are most likely the people in Thessalonica who heard the gospel from Paul and his associates but did not respond to it as did the believers. The reference is not to Christians in other cities (cf. 4.12) since the whole focus of this passage is upon the heralds' "entrance" to Thessalonica (2.1).

The *praise (doxan)* to which Paul refers is the honor, prestige, or fame that so many rhetoricians and sophists sought in those days before Hollywood.[48] Orators were akin to the rock music legends or Hollywood stars in ancient society. Plutarch tells of those who were motivated not simply by money but also by honor *(doxa)* and a public reputation. Dio Chrysostom decried those Cynics who would declaim publicly just for the glory they would receive and "who are lifted aloft as on wings by their fame and disciples." Dio ridiculed one sophist named Prometheus who was "being destroyed by popular opinion *(doxa)*; for his liver swelled and grew whenever he was praised and shriveled again when he was censured."[49] Epictetus railed against the sophists who sought glory at the expense of their disciples, saying, "And so it's for this, is it, that young men are to travel from home, and leave their parents, their friends, their relatives, and their bit of property, merely to cry 'Bravo!' as you recite your clever little mottoes?"[50] In his opinion, some orators made an exhibition of their ingenious way of speaking for no other reason than to gain the praise of their hearers: "'But praise me.' What do you mean by 'praise'? 'Cry out to me, "Bravo!" or "Marvellous!"'"[51] Paul and his fellows did not come to Thessalonica in order to gain this type of public praise from anyone. They were not looking for cheering crowds who would be awed at their oratory.

7 Verse 7 in the Greek text begins with an adverbial participle (concessive; *dynamenoi*) that closely ties the thought with the previous declaration (cf. the NRSV, "though we might have made demands as

---

47. The prepositions *ek* (*"from* you") and *apo* (*"from* others") were frequently used interchangeably in Hellenistic Greek. See James Hope Moulton, ed., *A Grammar of New Testament Greek* (4 vols.; Edinburgh: T&T Clark, 1908-76), vol. 3, Nigel Turner, *Syntax,* 259.

48. BAGD, 204; *TLNT,* 1.362-79; *TDNT,* 2.233-53; *NIDNTT,* 2.44-48.

49. Plutarch, *Moralia* 131A; Dio Chrysostom 32.11; 12.5 (cf. Plutarch, *Moralia* 78A); 8.33; and 77/78.27.

50. Epictetus 3.23.32.

51. Epictetus 3.23.23-24. On this theme, see especially Winter, "Entries and Ethics of the Orators and Paul," 61-63; Malherbe, "Gentle as a Nurse," 214.

apostles of Christ"). The *NIV*, on the other hand, puts a full stop and a paragraph break at this point and connects the participle with the following statement that the messengers *were gentle among you*. Although the grammar will allow for either of these interpretations, the beginning of v. 7 rounds out the negative assertions that Paul had been making in the preceding verses (vv. 4b-6). In v. 7b the argument takes a decidedly positive turn. The thought is this: they did not seek glory from the Thessalonian believers or from others (v. 6), although *As apostles of Christ we could have been a burden to you*. What type of *burden (en barei)* do they have in mind? It may be that he is saying that they could have been an economic *burden* to the church but chose not to do so. If this is the sense of the word, it would be the only place in the NT where it conveys this meaning (cf. Matt. 20.12; Acts 15.28; 2 Cor. 4.17; Gal. 6.2; Rev. 2.24), although a cognate verb found in 2.9 and 2 Thessalonians 3.8 means "to be a financial burden" *(epibarēsai)*. In 2 Corinthians 11.9 Paul also declares that he was not an economic burden *(abarēs)* upon that church, again using a cognate of the word found in 1 Thessalonians 2.7. Another related verb appears in 2 Corinthians 12.13, where the apostle affirms the same *(katabarein)*. Moreover, the term *burden* was used in the literature of the day to speak of an economic burden, such as the burden of paying taxes, a heavy weight well known in all generations.[52] We understand that Paul's usual habit was to shun offerings for his support, and when he did receive offerings he demonstrated a degree of discomfort (1 Cor. 9.12b, 15-18; Phil. 4.10-19). In the case of the Thessalonians, he and his associates did not depend upon the new converts for their sustenance (2.9; 2 Thess. 3.8; Phil. 4.16). In light of all this, v. 7a may well refer to their decision not to be a financial *burden* to the church. However, over and again in ancient texts the term *burden* speaks of the weight of authority of a city or a person due to their character or importance.[53] Although the financial interpretation of *burden* is attractive, in vv. 6-8 the argument does not revolve around their financial relationships with the church. This point is not taken up until v. 9. Here the thought is that Paul and his associates did not come to town seeking glory (v. 6), although they could have wielded their apostolic authority (v. 7a).

In v. 7a the plural *apostles* indicates that not only Paul but also Silas and Timothy, co-founders of this church, were apostles. We know that

---

52. MM, 103-4; *TDNT*, 1.554.

53. Plutarch, *Pericles* 37, "The city made trial of its other generals and counsellors for the conduct of the war, but no one appeared to have *weight* that was adequate or authority that was competent for such leadership"; Diodorus Siculus 4.61.9; Polybius 4.32.7; and Plutarch, *De Catone Minore* 1.4; 20.1; Diodorus Siculus 19.70.8. See BAGD, 134; *TDNT*, 1.554, 556.

the circle of apostles was larger than the twelve and Paul (Acts 14.14; 1 Cor. 15.5b, 7b),[54] although these occupied a unique place in the history of salvation as the authoritative witnesses of the resurrection of Christ (1 Cor. 9.1). Paul possibly had only Silas in mind at this point and not Timothy since wherever Timothy is mentioned elsewhere in Paul's writings he is never designated an "apostle" (2 Cor. 1.1; Phil. 1.1; Col. 1.1). The title "apostle" refers to one who is sent in the authority of another. Behind NT apostleship is the Jewish institution of the *shaliach,* an authoritative messenger who spoke and acted in the authority of another. *Mishnah Berakhot* illustrates the point, saying, "the one sent by a man is as the man himself" (5.5).[55] The apostles were more than simply messengers or missionaries but people who carried out a mission in the authority of another and under that authority. In this case, the "other" was none other than Christ himself. For this reason they could have made the weight of their authority felt.

Paul declares that they did not impose the weight of their authority on the Thessalonians but states that *we were gentle among you, like a mother caring for her little children.* A text-critical issue confronts us here that, surprisingly, is not mentioned in a footnote in the *NIV.* While some ancient manuscripts read "gentle" (*ēpioi*),[56] others insert a word that differs by only one letter in the Greek, "infants" (*nēpioi*).[57] The evidence from the manuscripts themselves favors the reading "infants," but many commentators and translators prefer the reading "gentle" since it makes what appears to be better sense of the verse. How could we understand the logic of the argument if the apostles claimed to be "infants" among the Thessalonians and then compare that state with maternal care: "like a mother caring for her little children"?[58] Moreover, while Paul frequently talks in his letters about those who are "infants" (Rom. 2.20; 1 Cor. 3.1; 13.11; Gal. 4.1, 3; Eph. 4.14), he speaks about ministers being "gentle" (2 Tim. 2.24) while never comparing himself with an "infant." Gentleness, on the other hand, was a virtue that characterized wet-nurses, parents, and certain deities (such as Isis and Zeus), as well as some political leaders[59] and philoso-

---

54. See Ernest De Witt Burton, *A Critical and Exegetical Commentary on the Epistle to the Galatians* (Edinburgh: T&T Clark, 1920), 364-78; *TDNT,* 1.422-23.

55. Ibid., 1.414-20.

56. א^c, A, C², D², Ψ^c.

57. 𝔭^65, א, B, C, D, F, G, I, Ψ.

58. See the discussion in Bruce M. Metzger, *The Text of the New Testament* (Oxford: Oxford University Press, 1992), 230-33; idem, *Textual Commentary,* 629-30.

59. The LXX of Esth. 3.13 reads, "Ruling over many nations, and having obtained dominion over the whole world, I was minded (not elated by the confidence of power but ever conducting myself with great moderation and with gentleness). . . ."

phers.[60] It was the virtue of being tender and considerate, concerned for the well-being of the other, instead of being severe, brusque, or hard. This meaning would fit well between the denial that the heralds imposed the weight of their apostolic authority and the affirmation that they were like a mother with them.

However, as attractive as this reading is, the manuscript evidence clearly favors the reading "infants," as recent editions of the Greek critical texts recognize.[61] Moreover, a basic canon of textual criticism is that the more difficult reading is to be preferred (scribes had the tendency to clarify words or grammar that was difficult to understand). Since this evidence points in the direction of the reading "infants" (*nēpioi*), how should we understand the thought? Paul and his associates appear to be saying that they did not come as those who imposed the weight of their authority but, in fact, were among the Thessalonians in a way that was just the opposite. They were like babes among them, hardly those who throw their weight around. But this metaphor was inadequate, and may even call to mind wrong associations if one remembers an infant's cries, and so in a lightning shift of imagery the thought moves from infants to those who care for them, *like a mother caring for her little children.*[62]

Paul freely uses both masculine (v. 11) and feminine imagery (v. 7b; Gal. 4.19) to describe his care for the churches. Here he compares himself to a wet-nurse (*trophos*), a woman who was contracted to suckle and care for the child of another person. One ancient text, which is strikingly similar to v. 7, records the words of a mother-in-law or possibly father-in-law of a new mother who demands that "the infant have a wet-nurse, because I do not permit my daughter-in-law to suckle him."[63] Contracts between families and wet-nurses were common[64] because suckling one's own

---

60. Homer, *Odyssey* 2.46-47; Herodotus, *History* 3.89; Aratus, *Phaenomena* 5; MM, 281; *New Docs,* 4.169-70; *TLNT,* 2.174-77; Malherbe, "Gentle as a Nurse," 210-17.

61. *Nestle*[27], *UBS*[4].

62. See Stephen Fowl, "A Metaphor in Distress: A Reading of *NHPIOI* in 1 Thessalonians 2.7," *NTS* 36 (1990) 469-73; Beverly Roberts Gaventa, *First and Second Thessalonians* (Louisville: John Knox Press, 1998), 27. Crawford understands *nēpioi* as the proper reading, but solves the problem of the logic of the passage by arguing that the word is vocative, "But we, O Children, were among you as a nurse nourishes her own children." Charles Crawford, "The 'Tiny' Problem of 1 Thessalonians 2,7: The Case of the Curious Vocative," *Bib* 54 (1973) 69-72. Another solution to this interpretive quandary may be to note that the text does not simply say that the apostles were "like (*hōs*) a mother" but rather "as when (*hōs ean*) a mother cares for her own children." Under this reading, the apostles affirm that they did not impose their weight but rather were like babes when they are been suckled by their very own mothers.

63. MM, 643.

64. *New Docs,* 2.7-10 and bibliography. From Thessalonica, see *IT,* nn. 330, 517.

child was not as common as might be imagined. The wet-nurse was in charge of feeding the child, but her job also included caring for and even educating the infant. She became a person in whom the child had great confidence throughout his or her lifetime.[65] But Paul's declaration was not that they were like a hired wet-nurse but rather one who "cared for her *own* children" *(ta heautēs tekna)*. They nurtured and cared for the Thessalonians believers, not as hired help, as tender as such people might be, but as a nurse would do when she cares for the fruit of her own womb.[66] The disposition of the apostles was not to throw their weight around with these Thessalonians but to care for them tenderly and warmly.

8 The metaphoric affirmation about their care and love for the church in v. 7b is now explained in plain language: *We loved you so much that we were delighted to share with you not only the gospel of God but our lives as well, because you had become so dear to us.* The language Paul uses to speak of their love for the congregation is not found elsewhere in the NT, and is even rare in the literature of the era. The Greek term *(homeiromenoi)* means "desire greatly" or "long for," a word found in such contexts as a funerary inscription that tells how the parents long for their deceased son.[67] The messengers' affectionate disposition toward the Thessalonians was an earnest longing for them, as a parent would long for an absent child. Because of this attitude toward the Thessalonians, Paul states that they decided to commit to them not only the gospel but themselves. *We were delighted* does not mean simply that they took pleasure in this, as the *NIV* implies (cf. 1 Cor. 10.5; 2 Cor. 12.10; 2 Thess. 2.12; Heb. 10.6, 8, 38; 2 Pet. 1.17), but rather that by an act of will they decided to make a commitment to the Thessalonians (cf. 3.1; Luke 12.32; 1 Cor. 1.21; Gal. 1.15-16).[68] They decided to share what they had with them *(metadounai;* Luke 3.11; Rom. 1.11; Eph. 4.28), which was, in the first instance, the *gospel of God* himself (see 1.5; 2.2, 4, 9; 2 Thess. 2.14).[69] But unlike those orators who would swing into a town to declaim and gain praise for themselves, these messengers gave both the message and themselves to their hearers.

65. Paul Veyne, ed., *A History of Private Life*, I: *From Pagan Rome to Byzantium* (Cambridge, Mass. and London: Harvard University Press, 1987), 14.

66. On the verb "care" *(thalpē),* see BAGD, 350; MM, 283; *TLNT,* 2.184-85; and cf. Eph. 5.29.

67. MM, 447; BAGD, 565; Job 3.21. Hesychius says that the meaning of the word is the same as that of *epithymein* ("desire" or "long for").

68. *Eudokeō* with a verb in the infinitive means "to decide to," "resolve." See BAGD, 319; MM, 260; *TLNT,* 2.99-106; *NIDNTT,* 2.817-29; and, e.g., Polybius 1.78.8, ". . . not only did he *consent* to associate him in his undertakings but. . . ."

69. For a discussion of the verb, see MM, 402. It can be used to speak of the sharing of goods or the sharing of information (Wis. 7.13).

The *lives* they gave them are "their own souls," the "soul" signifying not simply their inner life but rather the whole of their person.[70] Paul and his coworkers had decided to give to the Thessalonians everything they were (cf. 2 Cor. 12.15; Phil. 2.17), and the Thessalonians responded to them in the same way (1 Thess. 3.6; 2 Cor. 8.1, 5). Part of the evidence of their decision to give themselves as well as their message was the way they had proclaimed the gospel even in the face of great hostility and opposition (2.2), as well as their willingness to work with their own hands so as not to be any kind of financial burden to the Thessalonians (2.9). Their rapid departure from the city should not be construed as evidence that they did not really care about these new believers.

The verse ends as it began with a declaration of the reason why they were willing to commit all to the Thessalonians: *because you had become so dear to us.* The Thessalonians are "beloved" (*agapētoi*) by these ministers, a term that speaks of a close and intimate relationship like that between members of a family (1 Cor. 4.14, 17; Eph. 5.1; Phil. 2.12; 4.1; Phlm. 16).[71] Malherbe has noted that 1 Thessalonians overflows with family language. God is the Father of the members of the community (1.3; 3.11, 13), and Paul, Silas, and Timothy relate to them like a father and like a nursing mother with their own children (2.7, 11). They are beloved by God (1.4) and the apostles (2.8). Over and again they are called "brothers and sisters" (1.4; 2.1, 9, 14, 17; 3.2, 7; 4.1, 6, 10, 13; 5.1, 4, 12, 14, 25-27). These new believers were at variance with their compatriots in the city (2.14), and the conflict likely descended to the members of their families as well (cf. Mark 10.29-30; Luke 12.51-53).[72] Those who are alienated and outcast now find their identity in this new family of God, both in Thessalonica and in other cities of Macedonia (4.9-10), with the "mothers/fathers" who love them, the apostles themselves.

9 In v. 9 Paul presents one of the evidences that they were disposed to give their lives to the Thessalonians:[73] *Surely you remember, brothers, our toil and hardship; we worked night and day in order not to be a burden to anyone while we preached the gospel of God to you.* The church could *remember* (a variation of the refrain "you know"; 2.2; 2 Thess. 2.5) the manual labor that occupied Paul and his associates during their stay in the city, and how in the midst of these exhausting labors they proclaimed the gospel

---

70. *Psychas.* The anthropology is not dualistic, but rather, as in Gen. 2.7, the "soul" identifies the person as a psychosomatic unit. See Matt. 16.25-26; Heb. 10.39; 1 Pet. 3.20. A good discussion can be found in George Eldon Ladd, *A Theology of the New Testament* (ed. Donald Hagner; Grand Rapids: Eerdmans, 1993), 499-520.

71. See Homer, *Odyssey* 4.817 (of a "beloved" son); BAGD, 6; *New Docs* 4.250-55.

72. Malherbe, *Paul and the Thessalonians*, 48-52.

73. *Gar,* translated "Surely" in the *NIV,* is explanatory.

of God to them. We know that during Paul's stay in Thessalonica, the Philippians had sent offerings for his support (Phil. 4.15-16).[74] But these donations were not adequate to permit Paul and his companions to devote themselves completely to the evangelistic mission. For this reason they engaged in manual labor, and in doing so they also left an example for the Thessalonian believers to follow (v. 9; 2 Thess. 3.8-9). In a similar way, while Paul was in Corinth he spent long hours working as a tent maker (Acts 18.1-4).[75] But when Timothy and Silas arrived there from Macedonia, they brought sufficient funds with them that Paul could leave this labor and dedicate himself completely to the ministry of the word of God (Acts 18.5; cf. 1 Cor. 4.12; 2 Cor. 11.8). Acts indicates that the apostle supported himself in the same way while in Ephesus (Acts 20.33-35; 19.12 refers to the "handkerchiefs and aprons" he used in his work, the one to wipe the sweat from his brow and the other to protect his clothing). The common opinion is that Paul, as a rabbinic student of Gamaliel (Acts 22.3), was obliged to learn a vocation. But evidence of this practice is late (mid-second century AD),[76] and it is much more likely that Saul learned this vocation from his father.[77] Labor as an artisan was generally looked down upon in the Greek-speaking world, and the general disdain for such work is reflected in 2 Cor. 11.7 and possibly 1 Cor. 9.19. The labor an artisan undertook did not guarantee good income, and for this reason the apostle suffered deprivation despite his abilities (Phil. 4.12; 1 Cor. 4.11; 2 Cor. 6.5, 10; 11.27). Hock has argued that some orators adopted a vocation to sustain themselves and has also demonstrated that the workplace was an acceptable forum for philosophical discourse.[78] Paul's pattern was strikingly similar.

Paul reminds the Thessalonians how hard he and his companions worked by speaking of their *toil and hardship*. The first term is the same

74. Leon Morris, *"kai hapax kai dis,"* *NovT* 1 (1956) 205-8, argues that the expression "once and twice" denotes that the Philippian church sent various offerings to Paul and may even imply that they sent an offering while he was in Thessalonica and other support during his mission in other cities.

75. For a discussion of the materials he used in this work, see Hock, *The Social Context of Paul's Ministry,* 20-25.

76. Mishnah, *Aboth* 2.2, "Excellent is study of the Law together with worldly occupation, for toil in them both puts sin out of mind."

77. Talmud, *Qiddushin* 29a; Hock, *Social Context of Paul's Ministry,* 22-25. The practice of teaching your son a trade was not limited to the Jewish community but was a general practice throughout the Greek and Roman world.

78. Hock, "The Workshop as a Social Setting for Paul's Missionary Preaching," *CBQ* 41 (1979) 438-50; idem, "Paul's Tentmaking and the Problem of His Social Class," *JBL* 97 (1978) 555-64; Abraham Malherbe, *Social Aspects of Early Christianity* (Philadelphia: Fortress Press, 1983), 23-28.

one we encountered in 1.4 ("your *labor* prompted by love"). Elsewhere it could denote "trouble" or "difficulty" (e.g., Matt. 26.10; Mark 14.6; Luke 11.7; 18.5; Gal. 6.17), but here the focus is on the type of work that results in fatigue and exhaustion (2 Cor. 6.5; 11.23; Rev. 2.2; 14.13).[79] The second term, *hardship (mochthon)*, refers to the kind of labor that is a genuine hardship.[80] These terms are often combined (e.g., 2 Cor. 11.27; 2 Thess. 3.8); together, they simply speak of hard and exhausting labor. This description echoes what we know about the labor of those who made tents. This was no cushy desk job! These men wore themselves out as they worked long hours, *night and day*. The order of the words may indicate that they rose up to work before the sun and that their labors continued throughout the day.[81] Labor contracts normally indicated the period of labor as "from sunrise to sunset," but these men went beyond the norm, rising before the dawn. Paul, Silas, and Timothy put in long, laborious hours *in order not to be a burden* to anyone in the church. Unlike v. 7, this verse refers to an economic burden (cf. 2 Thess. 3.8). Some preachers exploited their congregations (2 Cor. 11.20), but this was not the practice of Paul's team (cf. 2.5). Paul himself taught that the church had the responsibility to sustain its leadership (1 Cor. 9.7-14; 1 Tim. 5.17-18), but he himself chose not to place any heavy economic obligation on the churches for his own support. We know that some members of the Thessalonian congregation were persons of means (Acts 17.5, 7, 9) and could serve as patrons (see 2 Thess. 3.6-13), but it appears that many suffered extreme poverty (2 Cor. 8.1-2) and gravitated toward the role of clients (1 Thess. 4.11-12; 2 Thess. 3.6-15). Although the Christian messengers stayed in the house of Jason during their visit to the city (Acts 17.5-7), they avoided a patronal relationship (2 Thess. 3.8). They were not a burden *to anyone*, whatever their economic situation. Their goal in coming to town was not to find rich patrons to support them! In the midst of all their long hours of hard manual labor, they *preached the gospel of God* to the Thessalonians. If Hock is correct, the main venue for this preaching was the workplace where Paul made and sold his tents. Manual and gospel labor were integrated. In the workplace they *preached*, or rather "proclaimed," the gospel as would a herald.[82] In this humble context Paul and his associates would proclaim the glorious message — *the gos-*

---

79. BAGD, 443; *TLNT*, 2.322-29. It may be used of the labors one undertakes in preaching the gospel (John 4.38; 1 Cor. 3.8; 2 Cor. 10.14-15), but v. 9 refers to manual labor.

80. BAGD, 528; *TLNT*, 2.526-27.

81. Hock, *Social Context of Paul's Ministry*, 31-32. "Night and day" (3.10; Acts 20.31; 2 Thess. 3.8; 1 Tim. 5.5; 2 Tim. 1.3) may simply be a variation of "day and night" (Luke 18.7; Acts 9.24; Rev. 4.8; 7.15; 12.10; 14.11; 20.10), as Cole Porter reminds us.

82. BAGD, 431; *NIDNTT*, 3.48-57.

pel of God (cf. vv. 2, 8; and 1.5; 2.4; 3.2). They were without hopes of financial gain for their efforts.[83]

10 The *NIV* places a paragraph break at the end of v. 9. However, v. 10 continues the previous discourse concerning the integrity of the messengers, and this may indicate that the placement of a paragraph break here is not warranted. In v. 9 Paul said the church could remember their labors among them, and now in v. 10 the church is reminded that they were witnesses of the heralds' conduct. On the other hand, there is a slight shift of emphasis from what precedes to what follows. In vv. 1-9 the primary focus was on the conduct of the apostolic team during their evangelistic ministry in Thessalonica, while vv. 10-12 speak of their integrity during the short time of their pastoral ministry there.

Paul declares, *You are witnesses, and so is God, of how holy, righteous and blameless we were among you who believed.* As in v. 5, Paul invokes two witnesses, the Thessalonians and God himself, to give testimony to their character ("A matter must be established by the testimony of two or three witnesses," Deut. 19.15; 2 Cor. 13.1). The idea of bearing witness was found not only in juridic contexts but also, as here, where the character of a person was being established. For example, in Acts 6.3 the apostles tell the Jerusalem church to "select from among yourselves seven men of good standing" *(NRSV)*, or seven to whom they bear witness *(martyroumenous)*. The Thessalonians could bear witness to what they had seen. God could bear witness to what they had not seen. The invocation of a deity to bear witness was not unknown even among the Gentiles.[84] The preachers' rapid leave-taking from the city was sufficient cause to include a solemn declaration such as this one.[85]

The Thessalonian believers and God himself bore witness *of how holy, righteous and blameless* the messengers were while *among you who believe*. They acted in a *holy* manner (adverb *hosiōs*). This term is not the same as that which is commonly translated "holy" *(hagios)*, but rather speaks of the way people conformed to what was ordained or permitted

---

83. In Plato, *Apology* 31B-C, Socrates declares that he would not get rich nor receive pay for his exhortations and, as a testimony, says, "but now you yourselves see that my accusers, though they accuse me of everything else in such a shameless way, have not been able to work themselves up to such a pitch of shamelessness as to produce a witness to testify that I ever exacted or asked pay of anyone. For I think I have a sufficient witness that I speak the truth, namely, my poverty."

84. Pindar, *Pythian Odes* 4.167. Apollo could even present a witness, according to Aeschylus, *Eumenides* 664.

85. See p. 51. Marshall, *1 and 2 Thessalonians*, 73, says that the solemnity of the affirmation presupposes an accusation against the character of the apostles, while, on the other hand, Wanamaker, *Commentary on 1 and 2 Thessalonians*, 104, argues that the function is parenetic.

by the deity. Such people acted "piously."[86] This word appears frequently, along with its cognates, in combination with "righteous" (adverb "righteously," *dikaiōs*) and related terms to describe that conduct which conforms to both divine and human laws. For example, Socrates was said to have been "satisfied with being just *(dikaios)* in his dealings with men and religious *(hosios)* in his attitude towards the gods."[87] By making use of this common combination, Paul and his coworkers declare that there was solid testimony that they acted in conformity with both God's law and human law while they were in Thessalonica. The initial accusation that was leveled against them in Thessalonica was that these men were "defying Caesar's decrees," that is, they acted "unjustly." Moreover, their preaching led people to abandon the civic and family cults, and so opened them up to the charge of acting impiously against the gods (1.9; cf. 1 Pet. 1.18). But Paul emphatically states that their actions conformed to both divine and human law and that, in all this, they were *blameless* or acted "blamelessly" (adverb *amemptōs*). The testimony that a person lived blamelessly appears frequently in ancient epigraphs, and especially in funerary inscriptions, to describe people who had faithfully fulfilled their obligations throughout their life.[88] The heralds had fulfilled their obligations to God and human laws without fail. This they did while they were *among you*, the Thessalonians, *who believed* (cf. 1.7; 2.13; 2 Thess. 1.10). These are the people who had put their faith in the apostolic confession (1 Thess. 4.14), in contrast to those who did not respond to the message in faith (2 Thess. 2.12).

11 Paul once again reminds the Thessalonians of what they knew about the heralds' conduct (cf. v. 1 and commentary): *For you know that we dealt with each of you as a father deals with his own children.* The verse in the Greek text does not have a principal verb, and so the *NIV* has supplied "we dealt" and "deals." Since the sentence really runs from v. 10 through the end of v. 12, it may be that "we were" *(egenēthēmen)* of v. 10 should be understood as the main verb. Another possibility is that the author carried along the thought at such a clip that the main verb was simply dropped and the original readers/hearers were meant to supply it.[89] In

---

86. BAGD, 585-86; MM, 460-61; *NIDNTT*, 2.236-38; *TDNT*, 5.489-92.

87. Marcus Aurelius 7.66; *SIG*[3] 800.20-21, of a priest who lived piously and justly toward the gods and the people; Plato, *Gorgias* 507B, "as regards men, his actions will be just, and as regards the gods, pious; and he who does what is just and pious must needs be a just and pious man; Luke 1.75; Titus 1.8; Eph. 4.24; *TDNT*, 5.490; *NIDNTT*, 2.236.

88. *IT*, n. 215; *New Docs*, 4.141; *TDNT*, 4.572.

89. An example of anacoluthon. BDF §67. Milligan, *St. Paul's Epistles to the Thessalonians*, 25, suggests that the supplied verb could be "we admonished" *(enouthetoumen)*, whereas Wanamaker, *Commentary on 1 and 2 Thessalonians*, 106, suggests "we brought

either case, in vv. 11-12 the messengers are compared to a father who instructs his children in the fundamentals of Christian ethics so that they might lead a life "worthy of God."

Previously Paul compared their ministry among the Thessalonians to that of a nursing mother who suckles her own children (v. 7), but now he speaks of this relationship metaphorically as that between a father and *his own children,* not those whom he has adopted (cf. v. 7b). Paul elsewhere compares himself with a father when he speaks about the Christians under his care. At times he is like a father who sires children (1 Cor. 4.15b; Phlm. 10), an allusion to his evangelistic ministry, but in other contexts he is like a father who instructs his children in the fundamentals of the moral life (1 Cor. 4.14-15a; 2 Cor. 6.11-13). In Roman families, the image of the father was severe and harsh, especially when he warned his children against the temptations of life.[90] But the Greek moralist Plutarch had another approach. He said that a father should not use beatings but rather reason, exhortation, counsel, and praise of good conduct to instruct his children to follow virtue and shun vices. There are occasions when a father has the responsibility to reprove his child, but the correction should be coupled with kindness. In all cases, the father should be an example to his children.[91] Aristotle's advice was that a father should not rule as a tyrant over his children. Instead, "The relationship of father to sons is regal in type, since a father's first care is for his children's welfare."[92] These sentiments are echoed in the Jewish author Philo of Alexandria, who urged that a father should teach the law to his children.[93] His responsibility was not simply to give them knowledge of certain subjects but also to instruct them "on the most essential questions of what to choose and avoid, namely, to choose virtues and avoid vices and the activities to which they lead."[94] At

---

up" or "we trained" *(anethrepsamen).* Milligan also offers the suggestion that this may be an example of the Hellenistic participle functioning as an indicative verb, in which case the three participles of the following verse would constitute the main verbs. In any case, this sentence, like so many in Paul's letters, is an example of what Aristotle called the "continuous" style, as opposed to the periodic. "The continuous style is an ancient one. . . . It was formerly used by all, but now is used only by a few. By a continuous style I mean that which has no end in itself and only stops when the sense is complete. It is unpleasant, because it is endless, for all wish to have the end in sight" *(Ars Rhetorica* 3.9.1-3). Not a few Greek students have struggled with this "unpleasant" aspect of Paul's style.

90. Dionysius of Halicarnassus, *Antiquitates Romanae* 2.27.1-5, compares the severity of the Roman father with the laxity of his Greek counterpart. See Veyne, *A History of Private Life,* 1.16.

91. Plutarch, *De Liberis Educandis* 8F-9A, 13D, 14A.

92. Aristotle, *Nicomachean Ethics* 1160b.

93. Philo, *De Hypothetica* 7.14.

94. Philo, *De Specialibus Legibus* 2.228.

the same time he speaks of the right fathers have to correct and admonish their offspring.[95] Philo's teaching also finds roots in the Pentateuch (Deut. 4.9; 6.7; 11.19; 32.46; cf. Exod. 10.2).

Since one of the prime obligations of a father was the moral instruction of his children, the moralists metaphorically compared their work to that of a father.[96] In the same way, Paul understands his didactic role as a paternal obligation, one that is carried out in the tenderness of a Greek father. The moral instruction he and his associates gave them was public (4.2, 6) but also individual, as 2.11 indicates: *we dealt with* each of you *as a father* (cf. Acts 20.31). Possibly this instruction was given in the various houses of the members of the new Christian community (see Acts 20.20) or in the workplace where Paul made tents for sale (2.9 and commentary). The moralists recognized the value of private as well as public instruction. Plutarch relates how Socrates dealt with a person rather severely near the place where people change money. Plato corrected him, saying, "Were it not better that this had been said in private?" To this Socrates responded, "Should you not have done better if you had addressed your remark to me in private?"[97] But the main concern of v. 11 is not so much public versus private instruction as the fact that Paul and the others were concerned about the moral well-being of the individual members of the church and not only the church as a whole. Their instruction, therefore, was individual as well as corporate.

12 The form and content of the moral instruction the Thessalonians' "fathers" gave them is described in this verse: *encouraging, comforting and urging you to live lives worthy of God, who calls you into his kingdom and glory*. The three participles[98] that begin the verse appear frequently in the moral instruction of the era, including biblical literature. *Encouraging* translates the participial form of one of the principal verbs used in the moral instruction of the NT (*parakalountes*; 3.2; 4.1, 10; 5.11, 14; 2 Thess. 3.12; Rom. 12.1; 1 Cor. 1.10; Eph. 4.1; Phil. 4.2; 1 Pet. 2.11; 5.1). In some contexts the verb may signify "to console" or "to comfort" (1 Thess. 3.7; 4.18; 2 Thess. 2.17), but in the context of moral instruction, such as here in v. 12, it conveys the meaning of "to exhort" or "to urge" a person to follow a certain mode of conduct.[99] The sense is much stronger and more di-

---

95. Ibid. 2.232.

96. Dio Chrysostom 77/78.42; Epictetus 3.22.82; Malherbe, "Exhortation in First Thessalonians," 244-245.

97. Plutarch, *Quomodo Adulator ab Amico Internoscatur* 70F; Dio Chrysostom 77/78.38; Malherbe, "Exhortation in First Thessalonians," 244.

98. The three adverbial participles are parallel in the Greek, as the *NIV* indicates, and show the manner in which the moral instruction was given.

99. Frequent in the Maccabean literature: 2 Macc. 2.3; 6.12; 7.5, 21; 8.16; 9.26; 12.42;

rective than the *NIV's encouraging*. Wherever the following verb *comforting* (adverbial participle; *paramythoumenoi*) appears in the NT (1 Thess. 5.14; John 11.19, 31), it conveys the idea of "to console" one who has suffered some kind of tragedy or the death of a loved one.[100] But over and again outside the NT this word is encountered in contexts where one person seeks to encourage or persuade another to a certain type of action. For example, Plutarch notes how that when Demetrius was about to kill himself "his friends encompassed him, and with encouraging words *(paramythoumenoi)* persuaded him to do as the man had said."[101] Since the concern of 2.12 is the moral teaching the Christian teachers had given the church, this second meaning of the word is most likely what they intended. The last participle of the trio, *urging (martyromenoi)*, is the strongest of the three, since it suggests the idea of insisting or requiring that a certain course of action be adopted.[102] These three together summarize the exhortation, persuasion, and insistence with which the apostolic team delivered the moral instruction to *each one* of the members of this church (v. 10). The strong language of this instruction was borne out of their fatherly concern.

In 4.1-2 Paul reminds the church once more of the moral teaching that he and the others had previously given and of their exhortation to follow it (cf. 2 Thess. 3.6). Teaching on the moral life was not a secondary consideration well after this church was established, but a primary concern for its founders. Those who came into the church knew from the start what was required of them by God. Both the visit of Timothy (3.2) and these two letters underlined and augmented that fundamental teaching. In the second part of v. 12 we catch a glimpse of the transcendent importance of this instruction. The church was exhorted *to live lives worthy of*

13.14; 15.8, 17; 3 Macc. 1.4; 5.36; 4 Macc. 8.17; 10.1; 12.6; 16.24. The same sense is found outside Jewish and Christian literature: Xenophon, *Memorabilia* 1.2.55; MM, 484; BAGD, 617; *New Docs*, 6.145-46; *NIDNTT*, 1.569. See the comments on 1 Thess. 4.1.

100. BAGD, 620; MM, 488; *TLNT*, 3.30-35; *New Docs*, 4.166, includes an inscription erected in honor of a young person who died in order to "console" his parents and grandfather: "providing efficacious honour for the dead and consolation for the living and unfortunate." Similarly, a letter preserved for us reads, "but we did greatly console Marcus who was grieving." Wanamaker, *Commentary on 1 and 2 Thessalonians*, 106-7, suggests that this is the sense conveyed here since many in the church were suffering for their faith.

101. Plutarch, *Demetrius* 49.5; so Philo, *De Vita Mosis* 2.50; see *TDNT*, 5.818; *TLNT*, 3.33. Note the combination of *parakaleō/paraklēsis* and *paramytheomai/paramythia/paramythion* in 2 Macc. 15.8-9; 1 Cor. 14.3; Phil. 2.1; 1 Thess. 5.14.

102. Eph. 4.17; Gal. 5.3; Jdt. 7.28; Josephus, *Antiquitates* 10.104 (10.7.2); Polybius 13.8.6. In other contexts the verb means "to bear witness," as in Acts 20.26; 26.22; Gal. 5.3; Eph. 4.17. See BAGD, 494; *TDNT*, 4.510-12.

God. The moral life of a person was frequently described as the way one "walked" (*peripatein,* here translated *to live*), both in the OT (2 Kings 20.3; Prov. 6.22; 8.20; Eccl. 11.9) and in Hellenistic literature (Epictetus 1.18.20; Philodemus, *De Libertate* 23.3). This language is adopted in the NT, especially in the Pauline letters, to speak of the way one conducts oneself — either before God or in sin (Rom. 6.4; 8.4; 13.13; 14.15; 1 Cor. 3.3; 7.17; 2 Cor. 4.2; 5.7; 10.2-3; 12.18; Gal. 5.16; Eph. 2.2, 10; 4.1, 17; 5.2, 8, 15; Phil. 3.17-18; Col. 1.10; 2.6; 3.7; 4.5).[103] Paul reminds the church how they were exhorted to "walk" so as "to please God" (4.1) and to "win the respect of outsiders" (4.12). In 2 Thessalonians Paul calls the members of the church to separate themselves from every brother who does not walk "according to the teaching you received from us" (2 Thess. 3.6; cf. v. 11). The norm that should govern the Christian's walk is the life lived *worthy of God.* In a similar way Ephesians exhorts its readers/hearers "to live a life worthy of the calling you have received" (Eph. 4.1), and Philippians calls believers to "conduct yourselves in a manner worthy of the gospel of Christ" (Phil. 1.27). Similarly, Colossians reminds believers to "live a life worthy of the Lord" (Col. 1.10).[104] To live in a way *worthy (axios)*[105] *of God* was a well-known idea within Judaism (Wis. 3.5; 7.15; Sir. 14.11) and appears also in the moral teaching of Jesus (Matt. 10.37-38). The inscriptions and writings of the era also give us a window into the lives of those people who had conducted themselves in a way that was "worthy" of some deity, of a city, or of the council of a city.[106] Such persons had lived according to a very high standard, which was implicit in the relationship with some exalted figure, be it the deity or the city. Similarly, the Christians in Thessalonica were called to live in conformity to the dictates of their relationship with the one who was most exalted, God himself, imposing over this relationship the highest norm of morality in existence. What Paul has in mind is the "holy" life (Col. 1.10), one that honors God in all its relationships and activities.

At the conclusion of this verse and this section, God is described as the one *who calls you into his kingdom and glory.* God, who is known as "the One who calls" his people (cf. Rom. 9.1; Gal. 5.8; 1 Thess. 5.24), called the Thessalonians to himself through the preaching of the gospel (2 Thess. 2.14). This call was also to a life of holiness (1 Thess. 4.7) and to "share in the glory of our Lord Jesus Christ" (2 Thess. 2.14; cf. 1 Pet. 5.10). In the teaching of Jesus, as in the preaching of Paul, the *kingdom* of God is not a

---

103. BAGD, 649; MM, 507; *TDNT,* 5.940-45; *NIDNTT,* 3.943-45.
104. Cf. the use of the verb *axioō* ("to consider worthy") in 2 Thess. 1.11.
105. BAGD, 78-79.
106. MM, 51; Deissmann, *Bible Studies,* 248.

territory, but the rule of God that has begun to be exercised in the present time (Matt. 11.12; Mark 1.15; Luke 11.20; Rom. 14.17; 1 Cor. 4.20; Col. 1.13) and that will be revealed in the future in all its fullness and glory at the time of Christ's royal coming (2 Thess. 1.5; Matt. 6.10; Mark 9.1; 1 Cor. 6.9; 15.50; Gal. 5.21; 2 Tim. 4.1, 18; cf. 2 Thess. 1.9-10). Paul here speaks about the future coming of this *kingdom,* the time when God's glory will be revealed (2 Thess. 2.14; Rom. 5.2; 8.17-18; Col. 1.27), as a reality in which outsiders do not take part (2 Thess. 1.9). This teaching was a piece of the royal theology that had been presented to the Thessalonians when the heralds first arrived in the city (Acts 17.7; cf. 1 Thess. 2.19; 3.13; 4.15; 5.23; 2 Thess. 1.7-10; 2.1, 8), a theology that resonated with the monarchal longings of the Thessalonian people.[107] God is the one who will bring in this *kingdom* and will make them participants in the coming *glory.*[108] The Thessalonians' present conduct is oriented toward this high calling to participate in God's *kingdom and glory.*

2. "We also thank God . . . you received the word of God" — The Reception of the Gospel (2.13-16)

This section is the second thanksgiving of the letter (cf. 1.2-10) and not the continuation of an extensive thanksgiving that began in 1.2.[109] The section leaves behind the explanation of the apostolic mission and character (2.1-12) and moves on to speak of the Thessalonians' reception of the gospel (v. 13) and the sufferings they endured as a consequence of their conversion (v. 14). The discussion of their trials carries Paul on to compare the Thessalonians' sufferings with the persecutions the Judean churches endured at the hands of the Jewish community (v. 14). This provokes him to denounce the Jewish opposition to the gospel that began with the crucifixion of Jesus and ran through their hostility to the apostolic mission to the Gentiles in cities throughout the empire such as Thessalonica (vv. 15-17). This polemic was likely a response to the opposition to the gospel generated by the Jewish community in Thessalonica (Acts 17.5).

13 As observed previously, to offer thanksgiving to a deity was

107. See pp. 14-16.
108. Note the relationship between kingdom and glory in 1 Chr. 29.11; Ps. 145.11-12; Dan. 7.14; and cf. Esth. 1.4; Isa. 13.19; Dan. 4.36.
109. See p. 74. Note that 2.1-12 is not a digression but rather an integral part of the argument. The initial thanksgiving (1.2-10) introduced the themes of the evangelism of Thessalonica (1.5) and the reception of the gospel message in that city (1.6-10). These themes are readdressed in ch. 2, with vv. 1-12 recapping the apostolic ministry among them and vv. 13-16 recalling their reception of the gospel. The third thanksgiving begins at 3.9.

commonplace in ancient letters.[110] In fact, people recognized the social obligation of offering thanks to whoever acted as one's benefactor, whether the benefactor was human or divine.[111] Kings were the supreme human benefactors, and so the previous note about the Thessalonians' calling to God's kingdom would naturally give rise to thanksgiving. But Paul is not merely following a convention of the day; rather, he expresses sincere and profound gratitude to God for the members of the church in Thessalonica, who filled the apostles with joy because of their reception of the word of God and their faith, love, and hope that made them stand firm (1.3-4; 2.13; 3.6-9). The thanksgiving begins, *And we also thank God continually*. The Greek sentence begins with the words "And for this reason" *(kai dia touto)*. For which reason do they give thanks? Was it for the evangelization of the Thessalonians previously discussed (vv. 1-12) or for the way the Thessalonians responded to the gospel (v. 13b)? Although the expression may refer either to what precedes or what follows, the following clause begins with "because" *(hoti)*, which introduces the reason for their thanksgiving.[112] The founders thanked God *continually (adialeiptōs;* cf. 1.2; 5.7 and commentary; 1 Cor. 1.4; Eph. 5.20; 2 Thess. 1.3; 2.13; Phlm. 4) for the church, so great was their gratefulness to God for the Thessalonians' reception of the gospel.

The reason for this thanksgiving was the way the believers had responded to the apostolic preaching, *because, when you received the word of God, which you heard from us, you accepted it not as the word of men, but as it actually is, the word of God*. The reception of teachings from a teacher by a student was commonly described using the word employed here *(paralabontes)*, whether the teachings were those of the teacher himself (as in the case of Alexander the Great, who "received from his master [Aristotle] his ethical and political doctrines")[113] or those of an infallible tradition (as in the case of disciples, who received the Law from the rabbis).[114] The word is employed in this latter sense in the NT in relation to the transmission of the apostolic doctrine (1 Cor. 11.23; 15.1, 3; Gal. 1.9, 12; Phil. 4.9;

---

110. See p. 86.

111. To humans, see Xenophon, *Memorabilia* 2.2.13-14; to the gods, see Epictetus 1.4.31-32.

112. In 3.5 and 2 Thess. 2.11 the expression refers to what precedes and not to what follows.

113. Plutarch, *Alexander* 7.5.

114. *TDNT*, 4.11-14; *NIDNTT*, 3.748, *paralambanō* "indicates the way one takes over a tradition, whether it is the teaching and training of a philosopher, or the mysteries and rites of the mystery religions. In Judaism, tradition limited itself to the Torah and its exegesis (cf. Mk. 7:4). . . . The rabbis, too, passed on certain subject matter in teaching . . . under conditions of strict secrecy in order to prevent misunderstandings amongst the religiously impure."

Col. 2.6; 1 Thess. 4.1; 2 Thess. 3.6), which is here described as *the word of God* (cf. 1.6, 8; 4.15; 2 Thess. 3.1). Although they received this sacred message from the hands of Paul and his companions *(from us)*, there was a recognition on the Thessalonians' part that what was received was sacred and much more transcendent than some philosophy or *word of men*. Paul describes the word of God as that which they *heard (akoēs)*, which may refer to the act of hearing (as in the *NIV*) or to that which is heard, "the message" (John 12.38; Rom. 10.16-17; Isa. 53.1; and Gal. 3.2, 5).[115] In combination with *word*, as here and in Hebrews 4.2, the sense is most likely active. They heard the message from the apostolic messengers. Upon hearing it, they *accepted it not as the word of men, but as it actually is, the word of God.* While *accepted (edexasthe)* is almost synonymous with *received* of the previous clause, the verb commonly places more emphasis on personal appropriation. In other words, they solemnly received the sacred message and appropriated it for themselves.[116] The methodology of the heralds was unlike that of the philosophers of their day (vv. 1-12), and the content of their message was not simply human but divine (cf. Gal. 1.11-12). The Thessalonians recognized this, having seen the way this message came powerfully to their city (1.5). They had listened to the voices of Paul, Silas, and Timothy, but they heard what their proclamation *actually* was, the *word of God.* God spoke to them in this proclamation (2 Thess. 2.14; 2 Cor. 5.20), and their reception of the message was the moment of their conversion (Acts 8.14; 1 Thess. 1.5).

The confirmation that this message was truly the *word of God* came from the way that it *is at work in you who believe.* Frequently biblical authors use the word *is at work (energeitai)* to talk about God's activity in the human realm (Matt. 14.2; Mark 6.14; 1 Cor. 12.6, 11; Gal. 2.8; 3.5; Eph. 1.11, 20; 3.20; Phil. 2.13; Col. 1.29).[117] The Thessalonians embraced the message as the word of God, and now this gospel brings about a divine work within their lives (cf. Heb. 4.12; 1 Cor. 1.18; Jas. 1.21). Paul does not specify what kind of activity they have in mind, but most likely he is thinking of the conversion of the Thessalonians from idolatry (1.9-10) and the production of the fruit of the Spirit in their lives (1.3). Although the founders of the church were absent from the Thessalonians, the *word of God* contin-

115. See the discussion in O'Brien, *Introductory Thanksgivings in the Letters of Paul,* 155; *TDNT,* 1.221; BAGD, 30-31.

116. 1.6; 2 Thess. 2.10; Acts 8.4; 11.1; 1 Cor. 2.14; 2 Cor. 6.1; 8.17; 11.4; Gal. 4.14. See Bruce, *1 and 2 Thessalonians,* 45; Milligan, *St. Paul's Epistles to the Thessalonians,* 28; Wanamaker, *Commentary on 1 and 2 Thessalonians,* 111; Lightfoot, *Notes on the Epistles of St. Paul,* 30; Frame, *Epistles of St. Paul to the Thessalonians,* 107.

117. Note also its use to describe supernatural activity which is not from God in Eph. 2.2 and 2 Thess. 2.7.

ued its work in them, the believers (see 2.10). Their initial acceptance of the message was an act of faith, and now, in the midst of their persecutions, they continued in the same faith as the word of God continued its work in them. This message was not a philosophical discourse on the means to the virtuous life (or a self-help seminar on how to overcome personal and social issues, as the gospel is frequently portrayed in our era). It was the *word of God,* which powerfully transformed their lives.

14 Verse 14 presents one of the evidences of their reception of the word of God — the persecutions they endured.[118] As part of the fundamental instruction of the church, Paul and his companions had taught the Thessalonians the theology of suffering, and as they had taught, so it happened (3.3-4; 1.6). Now Paul adds that what the church was enduring was the common experience of the churches in Judea as well: *For you, brothers, became imitators of God's churches in Judea, which are in Christ Jesus.* Paul had already framed the Thessalonians' sufferings as an "imitation" of the apostles and the Lord in 1.6, where the term "imitators" does not denote active but rather passive imitation. In their experience of suffering they were made like the apostles and the Lord.[119] So here, the church is told that they not only share the sufferings of the messengers and the Lord but also those *of God's churches in Judea.* They are not actively seeking martyrdom as the many who sought to imitate the martyr Polycarp at a later date.[120] The experience of the churches in Judea was the pattern that was duplicated in Thessalonica — they suffered for their faith, and the Thessalonians experienced the same. *Judea* at times refers to that part of the territory of Palestine which is distinguished from Samaria and Galilee to the north (e.g., Matt. 4.25; Acts 9.31), but here, as in many other texts, Judea stands for the whole area, which includes these northern regions (e.g., Luke 1.5; 4.44; 23.5; Acts 10.37; Josephus, *Antiquitates* 1.160 [1.7.2]; Tacitus, *Histories* 5.9). The churches in Judea are mentioned as a group elsewhere (Acts 9.31; 11.1, 29; Gal. 1.22), and included Christian communities in such places as Jerusalem, Caesarea, and Capernaum. Exactly why these particular churches are singled out is difficult to ascertain since the experience of suffering for the faith was common among a large number of churches (see Acts 14.22; 1 Pet. 5.9). I would suggest that the Judean churches were recognized to be the

---

118. The verse begins with *gar* ("for"), that introduces the reason why the apostles believed they received the gospel (v. 13a). Alternatively, *gar* may introduce the grounds for saying that the word of God was at work in them (v. 13b), these being that they suffered and endured. Since persecution is linked with the reception of the gospel (1.6; cf. Acts 14.22), the first reading is preferred.

119. *TDNT,* 4.667. Cf. the active moral imitation in 2 Thess. 3.7, 9.

120. *Martyrdom of Polycarp* 19.1, "he was not only a famous teacher, but also a notably martyr, whose martyrdom all desire to imitate, for it followed the Gospel of Christ."

"first fruits" of God's work in establishing the new covenant (Rom. 15.26-27; Gal. 1.17-24; 2.1-10) and enjoyed a certain status among the rest of the Christian churches throughout the empire (cf. the Jerusalem council in Acts 15). They now become the paradigm for other congregations, even in this matter of sufferings. The churches of Judea are described in two ways here: they are *God's churches* (cf. Acts 20.28; 1 Cor. 1.2; 10.32; 11.16, 22; 15.9; 2 Cor. 1.1; Gal. 1.13; 2 Thess. 1.4; 1 Tim. 3.5, 15), and they are *in Christ Jesus* (cf. Gal. 1.22; 1 Thess. 1.1; 2 Thess. 1.1). Both these ascriptions underline the churches' union with God and Christ Jesus and distinguish them from any other human assembly (*ekklēsia;* see 1.1 and commentary). This form of identification also highlights the unity between those churches and the one in Thessalonica, which was also "in God the Father and the Lord Jesus Christ" (1.1; 2 Thess. 1.1). Paul drives the Thessalonians to see their situation from a larger perspective and to strengthen their sense of being part of a larger movement. They are not alone in their difficulties, and their experience is not unique.[121]

Exactly how the church in Thessalonica imitated the churches in Judea is explained in the last part of the verse: *You suffered from your own countrymen the same things those churches suffered from the Jews.* The persecution against the Thessalonian church began during the time when the heralds were in the city. The trouble was provoked by the Jewish community but spilled over to the Gentile populace, including the civic assembly and the city officials, the politarchs (Acts 17.5-9).[122] The Thessalonians' *countrymen* are identified as those responsible for carrying out the persecution. This English term does not define a people racially but embraces all who live within a locality, and so we might understand that it was not only the Gentiles but also the Jews who continued to oppress the church.[123] However, the Greek word that underlies the translation *countrymen (symphyletōn)* singles out those who are "of the same race,"[124] and so we should understand the Gentile populace as those who were now the perpetrators of the persecution that was originally fired by those from the synagogue. The emphasis of the verb *suffered* falls on the experience of suffering the believers bore as a result of the rejection and hostility

---

121. See Meeks, *First Urban Christians,* 107-10. The Thessalonians understood their union with the other believers in Macedonia and Achaia according to 1.7 and 4.10.

122. See pp. 49-51.

123. See Milligan, *St. Paul's Epistles to the Thessalonians,* 29; Lightfoot, *Notes on the Epistles of St. Paul,* 32; Marshall, *1 and 2 Thessalonians,* 78-79. The causes of the persecution are explored on pp. 28, 42, 51.

124. The word is equivalent to *homoethnōn* and *syngenōn* ("of the same race"), according to the lexicons of Suda (1411.1) and Hesychius (2368.1). See also Eustathius (364.16).

against them.[125] While the letter does not give us details concerning the form the persecution took, we can suppose that it included social rejection, including verbal abuse and accusations (cf. Acts 17.5-9), and possibly came to the point of physical attacks that resulted in martyrdom (1 Thess. 4.13).

The sufferings of the churches in Judea to which Paul compares those of the Thessalonians were well known to him since he was formerly a perpetrator of the attacks (Acts 8.3; Gal. 1.22-23; 1 Tim. 1.13). Beginning with the martyrdom of Stephen, the churches in Judea suffered greatly (Acts 8.1-3; 9.1), although they experienced a time of peace after the conversion of Saul (Acts 9.31). However, Herod Antipas renewed the persecutions (Acts 12.1-5) and saw how these attacks brought him favor among the populace (Acts 12.3). Jewett has brought together evidence to demonstrate that during the period when Ventidius Cumanus was the procurator of Judea (AD 48-52) another persecution broke out against the Judean church, provoked by the Zealot movement. Paul may have this specific event in mind as he tells the Thessalonians about the sufferings of the churches in Judea.[126] This should not lead us to the conclusion that the reference to the *Jews* means simply "the Judeans" (the term could be translated this way) because the following accusation is a general indictment of Paul's kin and not just of those who resided in Palestine.

15 Having compared the persecutions the Thessalonians suffered at the hands of their compatriots with the way the Jews persecuted the Judean churches, the apostle launches a strong polemic against the Jewish people. Since it is difficult to reconcile vv. 14-15 with Paul's deep concern for his people in Romans 9–11, a number of authors have argued against the authenticity of this section, saying that it is an interpolation into the letter.[127] There is no textual evidence to support this conclusion,

---

125. BAGD, 634.

126. Robert Jewett, "The Agitators and the Galatian Congregation," *NTS* 17 (1970-71) 204-6.

127. See R. F. Collins, "Apropos the Integrity of 1 Thessalonians," in *Studies on the First Letter to the Thessalonians* (ed. R. F. Collins; Leuven: Leuven University Press, 1984), 96-135; Birger A. Pearson, "1 Thessalonians 2:13-16: A Deutero-Pauline Interpolation," *HTR* 64 (1971) 79-94; Daryl D. Schmidt, "1 Thess 2:13-16: Linguistic Evidence for an Interpolation," *JBL* 102 (1983) 269-79; J. M. Scott, "Paul's Use of Deuteronomic Tradition," *JBL* 112 (1993) 645-65; Jon Allen Weatherly, "The Authenticity of 1 Thessalonians 2.13-16: Additional Evidence," *JSNT* 42 (1991) 79-89. The bibliography on this section is legion. See, e.g., George E. Okeke, "1 Thessalonians 2.13-16: The Fate of the Unbelieving Jews," *NTS* 27 (1980-81) 127-36; Karl Paul Donfried, "Paul and Judaism: I Thessalonians 2:13-16 as a Test Case," *Int* 38 (1984) 242-53; Frank D. Gilliard, "Paul and the Killing of the Prophets in 1 Thess. 2:15," *NovT* 36 (1994) 259-70; Carol J. Schlueter, *Filling Up the Measure: Polemical Hyperbole in 1 Thessalonians 2.14-16* (Sheffield: JSOT Press, 1994).

which arises simply out of discomfort with the strong accusations Paul levels against his own. But the pointed rhetoric is not unique in Paul's writings, for in Romans itself Paul points out that the Jews were in rebellion against God and that only a remnant of them were being saved in his days (Rom. 9.27; 11.15). The majority were hardened (Rom. 11.7), a situation that gave rise to the inclusion of the Gentiles in the people of God (Rom. 11.11ff.). God has not rejected his people, however, as was evident from the salvation of this remnant (Rom. 11.1-5), and the apostle held out hope that all his people would be saved (Rom. 11.23-26). Far from being anti-Jewish, Paul loved his own and longed for their salvation (Rom. 9.1-5; 10.1; 1.16). The accusations we encounter in these verses in 1 Thessalonians should be read in light of the larger context of Paul's teaching. The negative tone at this point is due, in part, to the persecutions the apostle and his coworkers endured at the hands of their countrymen in city after city throughout the empire. We should also remember that Paul was unsparing in his critique of the Gentile populace as well, for they had given themselves over to idolatry and all manner of debauchery that resulted from their rejection of God's revelation (Rom. 1.18ff.). Paul is, at times, a bit less "politically correct" than we would like him to be. This section, however, does not justify any form of anti-Semitism among Christians (see below).

The accusation against the Jewish opposition is laid out in six points (vv. 15-16a) and culminates with the announcement that the judgment of God has come upon them (v. 16b). First, the author declares that the Jews are those *who killed the Lord Jesus.* Although Jesus died under the Roman procurator Pontus Pilate, as the Gospels and the Apostles' Creed declare (1 Tim. 6.13), over and again the Gospels and Acts show the responsibility of the Jewish community in Jerusalem for this deed, including both the religious authorities and the populace in general (Mark 3.6; 14.1; 15.14-15; John 5.18; 7.1; 8.59; 11.45-53; Acts 2.23, 36; 3.13-15; 4.10; 5.30; 7.52). However, this verse is the only place in the Paulines where this frank accusation appears. Not only were the Jewish people responsible for the death of Jesus but they also had a long history of opposition to the messengers of God — they had killed *the prophets.* In both the OT (1 Kings 19.10, 14; Neh. 9.26) and the NT (Matt. 23.31, 34, 37; Luke 11.47-51; 13.33-34; Acts 7.52; Rom. 11.3) the rejection and martyrdom of the prophets are presented as the archetypical evidence of the rebellion of God's people against his plan. In the third place, in the present time the Jews oppose this plan, as evidenced in their persecution of the apostles — they *also drove us out.*[128] The verb *drove us out* (*ekdiōxantōn;*

---

128. Note the union of apostles and prophets in Eph. 2.20.

aorist participle) may mean only that they were "persecuted severely,"[129] but the term more commonly means that someone was "expelled" or "driven out."[130] Paul and his fellow ministers of the gospel were persecuted in city after city and, as a result, were driven out of town (Acts 8.1; 9.28-30; 13.50; 14.5-6; 16.39; 17.14), as the Thessalonians knew since they were likewise driven out of their city (Acts 17.10). Acts shows how in many cities the Jews instigated the populace against Paul and were key players in his expulsion (Acts 9.23-25, 29; 13.45, 50; 14.2, 4-6, 19-20; 17.5, 13; 18.6, 12-17; 19.9; and cf. 2 Cor. 11. 24, 26). Paul may refer here specifically to the way he and his companions were driven out of Thessalonica. This put an end to their proclamation of the gospel in that city.

The fourth accusation is that *they displease God.* "To please God" is a moral concept rooted in the OT (Num. 23.27; 1 Kings 3.10; Ps. 69.31); it arises frequently in Paul's ethical teaching (2.4; 4.1; 1 Cor. 7.32; Gal. 1.10; Col. 1.10; 2 Tim. 2.4; and cf. 1 John 3.22). Rebellion against God and his law is characteristic of those who do not please God (Rom. 8.8). The fact that the Jews do not please God is evident from their opposition to God's messengers (vv. 15a, 16a) and their sin (v. 16b). Not only do they oppose God, but they also turn against those who are not of their race — they *are hostile to all men.* The hostility of the Jews against the rest of humanity was a characterization that frequently appeared in ancient authors. Tacitus, the Roman historian, says that they were loyal to one another "but toward every other people they feel only hate and enmity" (*Histories* 5.5). Philostratus similarly states, "For the Jews have long been in revolt not only against the Romans, but against humanity; and a race that has made its own a life apart and irreconcilable, that cannot share with the rest of mankind in the pleasure of the table nor join in their libations or prayer or sacrifices, are separated from ourselves by a greater gulf than divides us from Susa or Bactra or the more distant Indies" (*Vita Apollonii* 5.33). Diodorus Siculus observed that the Jews "alone of all nations avoided dealings with any other people and looked upon all men as their enemies" and that "the Jews had made their hatred of mankind into a tradition" (34.1.1-2; and see 40.3.4-5; Juvenal, *Satires* 14.96-106). Jewish separateness and nonparticipation in civic cults was largely responsible for such strong criticism against them rather than overt acts of hostility. The Jewish historian Josephus responded to these invectives, calling them

---

129. Josephus, *Contra Apionem* 1.292 (1.32).
130. Ps. 119.157; *T. Judah* 18.4; Sir. 30.19; Aristotle, *Historia Animalium* 612b.12; Lucian, *Timon* 10. See MM, 193; LSJ, 504; BAGD, 239. *diōkō* may also mean "cast out" (Matt. 23.34; 10.23).

"false accusations."[131] But Paul does not join in the general and broad-ranging denunciation of the Jews, but limits the critique to Jewish opposition to God's mission. This is even the case in this final accusation of the verse, which is clarified in the following clause. Their opposition to humanity stems from the way they blocked the preaching of the gospel (v. 16).

16 In the sixth denunciation of the Jews, the apostle states that their "hostility to all men" (v. 15) is seen *in their effort to keep us from speaking to the Gentiles so that they may be saved.* From what we observe in Acts, the Jewish community in many cities not only made an effort to keep Paul and his coworkers from speaking to the Gentiles but managed to silence them on more than one occasion (Acts 13.48-51; 14.2, 19). In Thessalonica itself their efforts resulted in a truncated ministry to the Gentiles (Acts 17.5-10). In fact, the verb Paul uses to describe their efforts *(kōlountōn)* places emphasis not so much on their efforts as on their success — "by *hindering* us from speaking to the Gentiles" *(NRSV).*[132]

Paul and his team tried to "speak," or preach the gospel *(lalēsai;* see 1.8; 2.2, 4 and comments), *to the Gentiles so that they may be saved.* Salvation and the proclamation of the gospel are intertwined and can not in any way be separated. The gospel is not a philosophy that leads to a better way of life or a therapy that promotes inner harmony and well-being, but rather "the power of God for the salvation of everyone who believes: first for the Jew, then for the Gentile" (Rom. 1.16-17). For this reason it is called "the gospel of your salvation" (Eph. 1.13). God has chosen "through the foolishness of what was preached to save those who believe" (1 Cor. 1.21), that is, through the "message of the cross" that "to us who are being saved is the power of God" (1 Cor. 1.18). Without this proclamation, people will not be saved (Rom. 10.8b-13). The opposition of the Jews to the apostolic proclamation was not only a personal attack against the apostles or opposition to the purposes of God (v. 15) but also an attack against humanity, blocking the way to the hope of salvation. In this way they are *hostile to all men.*

Before their conversion to the living God the Thessalonians, like the rest of the Gentiles, believed that the hope of salvation was linked with

---

131. "Then he attributes to us an imaginary oath, and would have it appear that we swear by the God who made heaven and earth and sea to show no goodwill to a single alien, above all to Greeks. Having once started false accusations. . . ." *Contra Apionem* 2.121 (2.10). On anti-Semitism in the ancient world see J. N. Sevenster, *The Roots of Pagan Anti-Semitism in the Ancient World* (Leiden: E. J. Brill, 1975); Peter Schaefer, *Judeophobia: Attitudes toward the Jews in the Ancient World* (Cambridge: Harvard University Press, 1997).

132. BAGD, 461; MM, 366-67; *NIDNTT,* 2.221-23.

the cult of certain deities.[133] For example, an inscription from Thessalonica (first century AD) preserves a thanksgiving to the "highest god," Zeus, who is called "the great savior" because in answer to a prayer he saved Julios Orios "from the great danger of the sea."[134] But the salvation the apostles offered to the Gentiles was, in the first place, the future hope (Rom. 8.24; 1 Cor. 3.15; Phil. 1.28) of deliverance from the wrath of God (Rom. 5.9; 1 Thess. 5.9) and of the glorification of the saints (Rom. 8.18-25). This future salvation had already been inaugurated in the present as salvation from sin (Matt. 1.21; 1 Tim. 1.15), the regeneration of those who believe (Eph. 2.5; Titus 3.5), and sanctification by the Holy Spirit (2 Thess. 2.13).[135] The opposition the Jewish community posed to the preaching to the Gentiles recalls Jesus' denunciation of the teachers of the Law and the Pharisees: "You shut the kingdom of heaven in men's faces. You yourselves do not enter, nor will you let those enter who are trying to." They not only hinder the salvation of the Gentiles but oppose the plan of God to save them. God announced through the prophets his intention to extend his salvation to the Gentiles (Isa. 49.6), and this plan was realized through the apostolic mission to the Gentiles that became one of the most significant and problematic issues in the early church (Acts 13.26, 47; 28.28; Rom. 1.16; 11.11; 1 Cor. 10.32-33). To prohibit the preaching to the Gentiles was to stand in the way of the plan of God.

Paul declares that the Jewish opposition to the preaching is the conclusion[136] of a long history of sin: *In this way they always heap up their sins to the limit.* The point is that throughout their history *(always)* they have resisted the divine initiative.[137] Therefore this affirmation is really the conclusion of everything that has been said previously in vv. 15-16a concerning their opposition to the divine plan going back to the time of the prophets. The statement echoes a theme that appears over and again in biblical and extrabiblical literature, namely that the sins of a people come up to their complete measure before divine judgment is poured out upon them. In the OT, God permitted the Amorites to continue to live in Canaan for four more generations, "for the sin of the Amorites has not yet reached its full measure" (Gen. 15.16; cf. 6.11-13). Afterward judgment

---

133. See the Introduction, pp. 31-47.

134. *IT,* n. 67; and see n. 134.

135. See *NIDNTT,* 3.205-16; *TDNT,* 7.965-1003.

136. *Eis to* introduces either the purpose or the result of an action. Although Paul most frequently uses this expression to express purpose, the results are introduced here. BAGD, 229; BDF, §402(2).

137. Frame, *Epistles of St. Paul to the Thessalonians,* 113, notes that although the infinitive *anaplērōsai* is aorist ("heap up") it points to an action that is logically progressive, and the aorist views the process as a whole, a series of actions taken as a whole unit.

came, and they were exiled from the land. According to the LXX version of Daniel's vision, the final judgment will come after the sins of the kingdoms are filled up (Dan. 8.23). Similarly, the apocryphal book 2 Maccabees 6.14 declares, "For in the case of the other nations the Lord waits patiently to punish them until they have reached the full measure of their sins; but he does not deal in this way with us, in order that he may not take vengeance on us after our sins have reached their height." Paul does not agree. Judgment will come upon them, as upon the other nations, when they "fill up the measure of their sins." This perspective is based on the teaching of Jesus, who said, "So you testify against yourselves that you are the descendants of those who murdered the prophets. Fill up, then, the measure of the sin of your forefathers!" He followed these words with the warning, "You snakes! You brood of vipers! How will you escape being condemned to hell? Therefore I am sending you prophets and wise men and teachers. Some of them you will kill and crucify; others you will flog in your synagogues and pursue from town to town" (Matt. 23.31-32). The source of Paul's teaching is the gospel tradition, for Matthew and 1 Thessalonians both speak of the murder of the prophets, the persecution of God's messengers, the sins that are brought to full measure, and the final judgment.[138] The announcement here is that their sins have come to the full measure. Can judgement lag far behind?

The shocking response to this question is found in the last part of this verse, the conclusion of the paragraph: *The wrath of God has come upon them at last.*[139] In 1.10 and 5.9 (see comments) Paul assures the Thessalonians that they will escape from the wrath of God. But those Jews who have opposed the divine plan and who have filled up the measure of their sins will in no way escape his judgment. The translation of the verb *has come (ephthasen)* is the key to understanding what event in mind. It may mean "has just arrived" or "arrive," but followed by the preposition *epi* as in this verse it means "come upon" or "overtake."[140] Since the verb is an aorist indicative, the translation should be "arrived" or, rather, "came upon."[141] The surpris-

---

138. J. Bernard Orchard, "Thessalonians and the Synoptic Gospels," *Bib* 19 (1938) 19-42; R. Schippers, "The Pre-Synoptic Tradition in 1 Thessalonians II 13-16," *NovT* 8 (1966) 223-34.

139. The same affirmation is found in *T. Levi* 6.11, although it is not entirely correct to say that Paul depended on this book since *T. Levi* shows clear evidences of Christian influence. See H. W. Hollander and M. De Jonge, *The Testaments of the Twelve Patriarchs* (Leiden: E. J. Brill, 1985), 67-68, 82-85.

140. BAGD, 856-57. Six times in the NT: Matt. 12.28; Luke 11.20; Rom. 9.31; 2 Cor. 10.14; Phil. 3.16; and see 1 Thess. 4.15 and commentary.

141. Marshall, *1 and 2 Thessalonians*, 80, correctly notes that it cannot be construed as a future. Okeke, "The Fate of the Unbelieving Jews," 130, argues that the inclusion of *eis telos* (*at last* in the *NIV*) frustrates every attempt to understand the verb as if it were a

ing conclusion is that, in some way, the wrath of God has already come upon them.

The measure of this wrath is expressed in the words translated *at last (eis telos)*, which may mean "finally" (Gen. 46.4), "eternally" or "forever" (1 Chr. 28.9; Pss. 9.18; 77.8), or "completely" (Josh. 8.24; 2 Chr. 12.12; T. *Levi* 6.11).[142] This final rendering of the phrase is not likely since, although Paul understands that the future wrath has already begun to be realized in the present (Rom. 1.18), the final culmination of this wrath is still a matter for the future (2 Thess. 1.7-10). For the same reason we should question the second interpretation. Moreover, in spite of the strong curse language of this passage, Paul continues to hold out hope for the conversion of his people (Rom. 11.25-27). Therefore, the first interpretation is preferable, and the *NIV* concurs. The apostle is not speaking prophetically about the future judgment, whether it be the destruction of the temple in AD 70 or the final judgment that will occur when Christ returns. Rather, the reference is to some manifestation of this wrath in the present time that even the readers of this letter could perceive. A number of authors have noted that during AD 49 the Jewish people suffered greatly, including their expulsion from Rome by Claudius's decree[143] and the massacre of thousands of Jews in the temple during the Passover of 49.[144] These events, although not the fullness of the divine judgment, were an inauguration of the wrath that will find its culmination at the time of Christ's coming. They could already witness the divine retribution in the present.

We should bear in mind that Paul and his companions are not fomenting anti-Semitism with the strong rhetoric of this passage. They stand in the prophetic tradition, and that of Jesus, by announcing judgment on those who stood firmly opposed to the new thing God was doing among the Gentiles. The opposition to the Gentile mission was one of the most bitter moments of the early church, and this issue not only pressed in from without but even threatened the very unity of the early

---

future. On the other hand, Wanamaker, *Commentary on 1 and 2 Thessalonians*, 117, notes that apocalyptic language is poetic; the Thessalonians therefore possibly understood the wrath of God to be at the point of being manifested. However, Wanamaker does not take into account the combined weight of the tense and sense of the verb.

142. BAGD, 812; BDF, §207.3; Peter R. Ackroyd, *"nṣḥ — eis telos,"* *ExpTim* 80 (1968-69) 126.

143. Mentioned in Acts 18.2 and Suetonius, *Claudius* 25.4. See Ernst Bammel, "Judenverfolgung und Naherwartung: Zur Eschatologie des ersten Thessalonicherbriefes," *ZTK* 56 (1959) 295, 306.

144. Josephus, *Bellum Judaicum* 2.224-27 (2.12.1), calculates that 30,000 were massacred; cf. *Antiquitates* 20.105-12 (20.5.3), where the number is put at 20,000. Jewett, "The Agitators and the Galatian Congregation," 205, n. 5; Bruce, *1 and 2 Thessalonians*, 49.

church. The response to the repeated and hostile attacks that Paul and others faced is found here. At the same time, this very man continued to go "to the Jew first" since they had, and continue to have, a priority in God's plan and purposes. Paul's language concerning the pagan opposition to the spread of the gospel is equally strong, and the consequences he lays out are as severe (as, e.g., in Rom. 1.18ff.). But at the end of the day, we must always remember that God is the Judge of all humanity, both of the Jews and of the Gentiles. And that very Judge is the one who is the Savior who extends his hand to both the Jew and the Gentile. All should respond. None should resist. Both the divine call and warning are clear.

3. "We were torn away from you" — The Exit of the Apostles and the Attempts to Return (2.17-20)

Paul summarized the character of the apostolic ministry among the Thessalonians in 2.1-12, and then in the following paragraph (2.13-16) he reflected on the reception of the gospel by these believers, including a digression on the Jewish opposition to the Gentile mission. Now he returns to the theme of the relationship between themselves and the Thessalonians, focusing on the anguish of their separation and the desire and attempts to return. This theme occupies the rest of this major section of the letter up to 3.13.

17 The change of theme is signaled by an emphatic discourse marker, "But we, brothers and sisters" (*hēmeis de, adelphoi*). In spite of the opposition the heralds faced at the hands of those who opposed the proclamation of the gospel (vv. 15-16), their intention was to return to Thessalonica: *But, brothers, when we were torn away from you for a short time (in person, not in thought), out of our intense longing we made every effort to see you.* In Acts 17.10 Luke relates how the gospel messengers were obliged to leave the city because of the rising movement against them. This separation was extremely painful for the founders of the church and is described here as "being made orphans" (*aporphanisthentes*). Unlike the modern term, the word "orphan" could refer to the child who had lost his or her parents or the parents who were bereft of their child, with the pain of this loss at the forefront.[145] Paul uses the verbal form of the word in this latter sense and does not introduce a new metaphor by calling themselves "orphaned children." Although this separation was painful, just a little time had passed since they were in the city with the church, that is,

---

145. *TDNT*, 4.487-88; Philo, *De Specialibus Legibus* 2.31.1; Euripides, *Hecuba* 149; Sophocles, *Antigone* 425.

for a short time.[146] Paul and his companions do everything within their power to assure the Thessalonians of their continued friendship with them and to explain why the fact that they had not returned should not be counted as evidence of his lack of concern or care for them. The separation was really rather short and, what is more, it was *in person, not in thought* (literally, "in face, not in heart"). Although they were absent physically, they carried the church in their hearts or thoughts (Phil. 1.7; 2 Cor. 8.16; and with other vocabulary, 1 Cor. 5.3; Col. 2.5).[147] The burning desire of Paul, Silas, and Timothy was to be with the Thessalonians in person, seeing their faces (cf. 2.17b; 3.10; and Col. 2.1). According to what we know from Paul's writings, he felt a great tension between his mission, which demanded that he travel from city to city, and his pastoral concerns that filled him with profound longings to return to the ones he had left (cf. Gal. 4.20). In friendly letters it was common for ancient authors to state that physical separation did not mean emotional or mental separation.[148] Although this was a common convention, the reality of their longing should not be minimized. The apostles had not forgotten the Thessalonians and made real efforts to return after their importune departure, *out of our intense longing we made every effort to see you.* This great *longing*[149] issued in action. They took great pains,[150] and this in the extreme,[151] in their effort to return to the church. The founders not only carried them around in their hearts and intensely wanted to see them, but they also made plans and put them into action. But the opposition was formidable. Satan himself stepped in and frustrated their plans (v. 18). It was for this reason that they sent Timothy back to the church (3.1) and continued praying that God would grant them the opportunity to be with them again to "supply what is lacking in your faith" (3.10).

18 Although the heralds had attempted to return to Thessalonica, they had not been able to make it back. The reason why is now explained:

---

146. The expression *pros kairon hōras* is a combination of *pros hōras* ("for a moment," "for a while" — John 5.35; 2 Cor. 7.8; Gal. 2.5; Phlm. 15) and *pros kairon* ("for a limited time," "for the present moment" — Wis. 4.4; Luke 8.13; 1 Cor. 7.5). BAGD, 896, 394.

147. In this context, the "heart" is the center of the mental and emotional life of the person and not simply his or her inner life. BAGD, 403-4; *NIDNTT*, 2.182; 1 Sam. 16.7; 1 Thess. 2.4. See also 2 Cor. 5.12, where the contrast between "face" and "heart" also appears.

148. Malherbe, *Ancient Epistolary Theorists*, 32-33, 74-75; Stowers, *Letter Writing in Greco-Roman Antiquity*, 58-60.

149. *Epithymia*, "desire," is here used in a positive sense instead of the more commonly known "sinful desire." See Phil. 1.23; Luke 22.15; BAGD, 293.

150. *Espoudasamen*, not meaning "to make haste" but rather "to make every effort." BAGD, 763.

151. *Perissoterōs*, BAGD, 651; MM, 509.

For we wanted to come to you — certainly I, Paul, did, again and again — but Satan stopped us. Their desire to return was not simply a passive wish that they expressed in casual conversation, but rather they made plans and put forth effort to return, as we saw in v. 17.[152] They put into action their plans to return, but their attempts were frustrated. At this point in the narrative, Paul steps out from the authorial community and speaks on his own, as he does at a number of points in this and the following letter (3.5; 5.27; 2 Thess. 2.5; 3.17), and expresses his personal attempts: *certainly I, Paul, did, again and again.* As was already shown in the Introduction, both Silas and Timothy participated with Paul in writing this letter, with Paul being the principal author. Interjections like this one do not deny joint authorship but rather highlight it. Paul wants to make sure that the church was clear about his own personal desires, which were in complete harmony with those of the rest.[153] He tells the Thessalonians that he tried to return on more than one occasion[154] but that he and the apostolic team could not reach their goal because *Satan stopped us.* So great was their effort that only Satanic opposition could explain why they did not return! *Stopped* is a term that comes from the military. In order to stop the advance of enemy armies, soldiers would tear up and destroy the road to hinder their passage.[155] Warfare imagery is embedded in the metaphor, Satan himself being their adversary. The battle was over the souls of the Thessalonian believers whom Satan tempted to commit the sin of apostasy (3.5 and comments; 1 Pet. 5.8). One of his tactics was to bar the way so the apostles could not return to the church. In spite of the opposition, they did manage to send Timothy back (3.1), and the church itself continued on in faith and love (3.5, 6). Sometime later Paul was able to return to Macedonia and Thessalonica (Acts 19.21-22; 20.1-6; 1 Cor. 16.5; 2 Cor. 1.16; 2.13; 7.5; 1 Tim. 1.3). God responded to their fervent prayers (1 Thess. 3.10-11). In this spiritual warfare, Satan is hardly an omnipotent adversary. But he is a real adversary.

Paul does not attribute to Satan every obstacle in the way of his plans (Rom. 1.13; 15.22; and cf. Acts 16.6-7; 2 Cor. 1.15–2.4). However, at a number of points in his writings Paul reflects on the conflict with Satan,

---

152. Note that the verb "we wanted" (*ēthelēsamen*) may mean simply "wish" but can also convey the idea of resolve or purpose. BAGD, 354-55.

153. See the Introduction, pp. 56-59.

154. The expression *hapax kai dis* ("once and twice") means "more than once," but not necessarily "repeatedly." See Morris, *"kai hapax kai dis,"* 205-8. See Deut. 9.13; 1 Sam. 17.39; Neh. 13.20; 1 Macc. 3.30; Phil. 4.16; *1 Clem.* 53.3.

155. *NIDNTT,* 2.222-23; *TDNT,* 3.855; Milligan, *St. Paul's Epistles to the Thessalonians,* 34. See Acts 24.4; Rom. 15.22; Gal. 5.7; 1 Pet. 3.7. The blockage does not have to be permanent, as Rom. 15.22-23 demonstrates.

the "adversary,"[156] who wages war against him and the Christians (Rom. 16.20; 1 Cor. 7.5; 2 Cor. 2.11; 11.14; 12.7; 2 Thess. 2.9). This is the one who is also called "the devil" (Eph. 4.27; 6.11; 1 Tim. 3.6-7; 2 Tim. 2.26), "the ruler of the kingdom of the air" (Eph. 2.2), and "the tempter" (1 Thess. 3.5). He tempts Christians (1 Cor. 7.5; 2 Cor. 2.11; Eph. 6.10-17; 1 Thess. 3.5) and takes advantage of them (2 Cor. 2.11), while his own "apostles" distort the gospel and walk about like honorable preachers (2 Cor. 11.3, 14). One of Satan's messengers tormented Paul, though exactly how is left a mystery to us (2 Cor. 12.7). In the present verse, the Thessalonians are not informed concerning how Satan managed to impede the founders' return to the city. Possibly sickness brought them low (2 Cor. 12.7; Phil. 2.25-30; 2 Tim. 4.20), or perhaps the Jewish opposition mentioned previously was at work here as well (1 Thess. 2.15-16). The bond Jason and others in Thessalonica were required to post may have served as a guarantee to the officials that Paul and company would not return (Acts 17.9). In truth, we do not know how Satan frustrated their plans to return before the writing of this letter. All we can say is that the opposition was formidable enough to put a halt to their best efforts.

19 So that there could be no doubt about the sincerity of their desire and attempts to see the Thessalonians again, in this and the following verse the Paul and his companions explain one of the reasons why they wanted to see them. The church is the source of their joy, both now in the present (2.20; 3.9) and in the future when Christ returns (2.19). *For what is our hope, our joy or the crown in which we glory in the presence of our Lord Jesus when he comes?* The answer, which is placed in the middle of the Greek sentence, is nobody less than the Thessalonians themselves: *Is it not you?* The sentence begins by asking, *What is our hope?* The way they speak of *hope* is a bit unusual, although not without precedent. In 1 Timothy 1.1 Christ is called "our hope" (cf. Col. 1.27), while in Jeremiah 17.7 (LXX) God is the "hope" of the person who is blessed.[157] But here the Thessalonians, rather than God, are called their hope. These were the ones in whom they placed their hope, without in any way implying that they did not hope in God himself.[158] They place hope in the Thessalonians in expectation of the time when they will present the church *in the presence of our Lord Jesus when he comes* (cf. 2 Cor. 11.2; Col. 1.28). The apostolic minis-

156. *NIDNTT*, 3.468-71.
157. In a similar way, the Egyptian deity Isis is called "the great hope." *New Docs*, 2.77; Plutarch, *Moralia* 169C.
158. Cf. Thucydides, *Histories* 3.57.4, "So that we Plataeans, after exertions beyond our power in the cause of the Hellenes, are rejected by all, forsaken and unassisted; helped by none of our allies, and reduced to doubt the stability of our only hope, yourselves."

try will be put to the test in that day, and they hope to receive a reward (1 Cor. 3.13-15). Their hope is that their labors will not be in vain (Phil. 2.16; 1 Thess. 3.5). Whatever fears (3.5) and frustrations face them now (vv. 15, 18), their hope in this church remains strong.

Moreover, the brothers and sisters in Thessalonica will be their *joy*. As the following verse and 3.9 show us, the Thessalonians are already the joy of the founders (cf. 2.20; Rom. 16.19; 2 Cor. 2.3; 7.4, 7; Phil. 2.2; Phlm. 7; and Phil. 4.1, which calls the Philippians "my joy and crown"). But the orientation of this verse is eschatological. Paul and his companions will have *joy* in the coming of the Lord (cf. 1 Pet. 4.13; Jude 24; Rev. 19.7) because of the Thessalonians and their faith. As if that were not enough to convince the church of their feelings toward them, they proclaim that the Thessalonians are the *crown in which we will glory*. The *crown* was the wreath of laurel, pine, celery, or, in the case of Macedonia, oak leaves that was given to the person who received grand civic honors. For example, an inscription from Thessalonica declares, "Those of the gymnasium decided to praise Paramenos for his aspiration to obtain (public recognition) and to honor him with a crown and a bronze image, natural size and painted, and the (honorific) decree inscribed in this stele will have a prominent place in the gymnasium."[159] Athletes, for example, would receive their "crown" when they won an athletic contest that was a recognition not only of their victory but also of their efforts and labor (cf. 1 Cor. 9.25; Phil. 4.1; 2 Tim. 4.8; 1 Pet. 5.4). Frequently these crowns were then dedicated to the deity (cf. Rev. 4.10).[160] Paul, Silvanus, and Timothy hope for a *crown in which we will glory*, or "crown of boasting" *(NRSV)*.[161] In the OT the critique of those who boast in their own achievements is quite severe (Ps. 12.3; Prov. 25.14; 27.19) because boasting characterizes those who are impious (Pss. 49.6; 52.1; 74.4; 94.3). Therefore, human boasting should be in God himself (Pss. 34.2; 44.8; Jer. 9.23-24; cited in 1 Cor. 1.31). Paul adopts this perspective (Phil. 3.3; Gal. 6.14), and if he boasts, it is because of what the Lord has accomplished through him (Rom. 15.17-18; 2 Cor. 10.13; cf. 1 Cor. 15.10). But the apostle also boasted in the churches themselves (2 Cor. 8.24; 2 Thess. 1.4), in the same way that he and his associates anticipate an eschatological time of boasting in the Thessalonians. At the time of the coming of the Lord, they will receive a *crown* in which they will *boast*. But what is the honor in which they will boast? Not their own achievements, but the Thessalonians themselves! *Is it not you?* (Cf. 2 Cor. 1.14; Phil. 2.16.)

---

159. *IT*, n. 4; cf. nn. 5, 11.

160. Xenophon, *Historia Graeca* 3.4.18. See *TDNT*, 7.615-36.

161. See ibid. 3.645-53; *TLNT*, 2.295-302; *NIDNTT*, 1.227-29. Expressions similar to "crown of boasting" are found in Prov. 16.31; Ezek. 16.12; 23.42.

Paul and his coworkers will rejoice and glory in the Thessalonians *in the presence of our Lord Jesus when he comes.* In the present time, they are conscious that their prayers are offered "before our God" (1.3), and they now rejoice "in the presence of our God" because of the Thessalonians (3.9). But they also recognize that in the final judgment both they and the Thessalonians will have to present themselves "in the presence of our God and Father" (3.13; 2 Cor. 5.10; cf. Luke 21.36). The heralds anticipate having joy and receiving an honorific crown at that time when they present the Thessalonians before the Lord. The time of this event will be when the Lord Jesus comes, in his *parousia.* The "coming" of the Lord Jesus is a theme referred to over and again in these letters (3.13; 4.15; 5.23; and 1.9; 2 Thess. 2.1, 8). Teaching about this coming was part of their initial proclamation in the city and became the principal cause of the hostilities against them (Acts 17.6-7). A *parousia* could mean the coming of a deity to a person (as Asclepius supposedly came to the sick in his temple), or it could refer to the coming of some dignitary, especially the coming of the emperor, to a city. Therefore, Josephus could use the term to talk about the "coming" of God to Moses or Israel,[162] and the word appears in 2 Maccabees 3.17 in reference to the "coming" of King Ptolemy. In memory of the *parousia* of Nero to Corinth that city minted new coins that proclaimed in Latin, *Adventus Aug(usti) Cor(inthi)* (*adventus* is the Latin equivalent of *parousia,* "coming").[163] While in his royal coming the emperor would receive a crown, Christ is the one who will give a crown to the apostles upon his advent (2.19a; 2 Tim. 4.8). The *parousia* of the Lord Jesus is part of the royal theology of these letters and was a chief component of the hope the church embraced as they faced opposition from their contemporaries (cf. 1.3, 9). Although the purpose of mentioning the royal coming at this point is not to encourage the Thessalonians in their afflictions, it does help them to focus on the ultimate and glorious realities that will sustain them in the present time. Paul's main point is that their own ultimate joy and hope is bound up with the well-being of the Thessalonian church. Their absence from the Thessalonians should not be construed as a lack of care or even benign neglect.

20 In language that is both clear and direct, Paul again highlights their true feelings about the Thessalonians. Now, and not just in the future, he emphatically exclaims, *Indeed, you are our glory and joy. Glory* is not the same term we encountered in v. 19. This *glory (doxa)* is the

162. Josephus, *Antiquitates* 3.80 (3.5.2); 3.203 (3.8.5); 9.55 (9.3.3).
163. See *LAE*, 368-72; *NIDNTT*, 2.898-901; *TDNT*, 5.858-71; Milligan, *St. Paul's Epistles to the Thessalonians*, 145-48.

"fame" or "renown" (2.6; John 5.44; 7.18; 8.50)[164] that a person receives when honored by others. Whatever honor or recognition the founders receive does not accrue to them because of their rhetorical acumen as they travel the cities of the empire; rather, the believers themselves, the Thessalonians, are their "fame" or source of honor. Bruce and Wanamaker suggest that *glory* in this context is that in which one glories or boasts[165] and as such would be a repetition of the idea that the Thessalonians are their "crown of boasting" (v. 19). However, the common use of the term *glory* to denote "fame" argues for the first interpretation. Whatever honor is ascribed to them has its source in the Thessalonians themselves. Similarly, the Thessalonians are their source of *joy* (cf. 3.9). In the midst of all their afflictions and distress, this church filled them with overabundant joy.

4. "We sent Timothy" — The Mission of Timothy (3.1-5)

The plans that Paul and his coworkers tried to carry out were frustrated. They made more than one attempt to return to Thessalonica, but they were blocked from reaching their goal by Satan himself (2.17-20). Since the group could not return, they decided to send Timothy, the junior member of the apostolic team, back to the city "to strengthen and encourage you in your faith" (v. 2) and "to find out about your faith" (v. 5). Satan had blocked the founders' continuing pastoral ministry. Had he led the Thessalonians away from the faith as well (v. 5b)? The danger was real.

1 The founders' painful separation from the congregation (2.17) and their frustrated attempts to return to the church (2.18) should be kept in mind as we read the opening and final verses of the paragraph (3.1, 5). The anxieties brought about by being torn from the church and thwarted in their continued ministry, along with the knowledge that the Thessalonians were undergoing persecution (3.2-4), were too much to bear: *So when we could stand it no longer, we thought it best to be left by ourselves in Athens.* Since they could no longer bear up under the agony and the weight of their concern for the church, they took action.[166] These men did not love the church only when they were face to face with them. They carried these believers in their hearts (2.17).

---

164. BAGD, 204.

165. Bruce, *1 and 2 Thessalonians*, 57; Wanamaker, *Commentary on 1 and 2 Thessalonians*, 126; cf. 1 Cor. 11.7?

166. The depth of the emotion expressed by the principal verb is illustrated in a papyrus that says, "For my father did many evil things to me, and I bore them until you came" (MM, 587). See Philo, *In Flaccum* 64. Polybius 18.25.4 uses the verb to describe the inability to ward off an attack. *TLNT*, 3.289-90.

When they could stand it no longer, *we thought it best to be left by ourselves in Athens,* and as a result they sent Timothy back to Thessalonica (vv. 2, 5). The verb *we thought it best* is the same as that found in 2.8, and the first person plural indicates that this decision was collective. If the plural is real and not editorial (*we* for "I"),[167] the implication is that at some point Silvanus and Timothy traveled from Macedonia to Athens. Paul expresses his own, particular sentiments in v. 5, but the inclusion of this personal note does not negate the collective nature of the concern or the decision indicated in v. 1. According to the narrative in Acts 17.14, Paul departed from Macedonia and traveled on to Athens, leaving Silvanus and Timothy in Berea. When he arrived, those who accompanied him went back to Macedonia "with instructions for Silas and Timothy to join him as soon as possible" (Acts 17.15). It appears that they did precisely this. After coming to Athens, Timothy was sent back to Thessalonica, at which time Paul and Silas were "left behind" in Athens.[168] Silas himself returned to Macedonia as well, though this is not specifically mentioned but only implied from the Acts narrative. Paul left Athens and headed south to Corinth where Silas and Timothy caught up with him upon their return from Macedonia (Acts 18.1, 5).[169] Acts does not include all the details of the comings and goings of several people who appear in the narrative, so the omission of some movements of the characters does not surprise us.[170] In any case, the

167. See pp. 56-59. Note the plural "by ourselves" *(monoi)* in Mark 4.10; 9.2; Luke 9.18; John 6.22; 1 Cor. 14.36. Allan Wainwright, "Where Did Silas Go? (And What Was His Connection with *Galatians?*)," *JSNT* 8 (1980) 66-70, suggests that Paul was left by himself in Athens while Silas went on to Galatia. The reconstruction presented in this commentary presents a more plausible explanation of the apostles' movements.

168. The verb *kataleiphthēnai* means "to leave behind" (Matt. 16.4; 21.17; Acts 18.19; Titus 1.5), and so in the passive voice "to be left behind" (John 8.9; Xenophon, *Anabasis* 5.6.12. BAGD, 413; MM, 329; Deissmann, *Bible Studies,* 190). It does not mean simply "to remain." See Lightfoot, *Notes on the Epistles of St Paul,* 40.

169. So Lightfoot, *Notes of the Epistles of St Paul,* 40; Bruce, *1 and 2 Thessalonians,* 60. Contra Morris, *First and Second Epistles to the Thessalonians,* 95; Wanamaker, *Commentary on 1 and 2 Thessalonians,* 95; Marshall, *1 and 2 Thessalonians,* 90. Best, *First and Second Epistles to the Thessalonians,* 131, discusses the problems of the several interpretations of the data.

170. On the question of the historicity of Acts, see Hemer, *The Book of Acts in the Setting of Hellenistic History.* We should bear in mind that Luke's presentation of early Christian history in Acts is by no means complete at every point, and often we find lacunae in the narrative as we attempt to trace the movements of certain people. Timothy, e.g., appears just before the Macedonian ministry (Acts 16.1, 3) but is not mentioned again until Paul and Silas leave Berea (Acts 17.14). By ancient classification, Luke-Acts would be a *bios* ("life") instead of a history, and in such literature the concern of the author was not to chronicle all events. Commenting on his method for writing the lives of Alexander, Caesar, and Pompey, Plutarch states that "the multitude of their great actions affords so large a field that I were to blame if I should not by way of apology forewarn my reader

opposition to the apostolic mission (3.7) was just cause to keep all the members of the apostolic team together. Travel itself was hard and dangerous labor, so staying with the group that would give protection and help carry the stuff was always desirable.[171] But these itinerant missionaries' well-being took second place to concerns about the welfare of the Thessalonian church. Timothy was sent back. It was preferable to be left alone than to leave the Thessalonians alone.

2 The Thessalonians should gauge the true nature of Paul's and the others' concern for them by the fact that Timothy was sent back: *We sent Timothy.* From v. 5 we learn that Paul was the principal person responsible for this mission, which was carried out with the consent of Silvanus. Paul subsequently sent this young minister on other missions to the churches at Corinth (1 Cor. 4.17; 16.10-11) and Philippi (Phil. 2.19-24), and then on to pastor the church in Ephesus (1 Tim. 1.3). Such visits, however, were never a substitute for the coming of the apostle himself (Phil. 2.24; 1 Cor. 16.7; 4.18-19; 1 Thess. 3.10-11). The mission to Thessalonica was the first recorded ministry that Timothy carried out on his own. Despite the fact that he enjoyed the confidence of Paul (Phil. 2.20-22), his youth and his temperament were such that he did not always receive honor (1 Cor. 16.10-11; 1 Tim. 4.12; 5.23). He was under the authority of the apostle Paul as one who was "sent" (see 1 Cor. 4.17; Phil. 2.19) instead of simply being "asked" to go (cf. Apollos and Titus in 1 Cor. 16.12; 2 Cor. 8.6; 12.18).[172]

In the case of the Thessalonians, Timothy was sent *to strengthen and encourage you in your faith* (v. 2) and "to find out about your faith" (v. 5). However, his visit did not meet all the needs of this congregation, and for that reason Paul expresses his own desire to return to them to "supply what is lacking in your faith" (v. 10). Timothy returned from his visit to the church with questions that the Thessalonians posed (4.9, 13; 5.1 and comments) and a report that appears to have indicated that the church needed special exhortation concerning sexual ethics (4.2-8). Why was Timothy unable to respond to their questions and give them an adequate corrective to their moral problems? In spite of his qualifications, at this stage Timothy was a very junior member of the apostolic team, the youngest member among them. Since his status was not equal to that of Paul

---

that I have chosen rather to epitomize the most celebrated parts of their story, than to insist at large on every particular circumstance of it. It must be borne in mind that my design *is not to write histories, but lives*" (*Vita Alexander* 1).

171. A very accessible and fascinating study of ancient travel is Lionel Casson, *Travel in the Ancient World* (Baltimore and London: Johns Hopkins University Press, 1994).

172. Best, *First and Second Epistles to the Thessalonians*, 132.

or even Silas, there may have been questions concerning why the apostle Paul himself did not return to the city. Therefore, Paul expresses his personal sentiments concerning his desire to return (2.18), and how he himself orchestrated Timothy's journey (3.5). This mission was called for by the situation of both the missionaries and the Thessalonians.

The titles that are ascribed to Timothy not only showed how esteemed he was but also served to elevate his status in the eyes of the Thessalonians. He is *our brother and God's fellow worker in spreading the gospel of Christ*. Although *brother* is a name that could be ascribed to any member of the Christian family, at times Paul uses the term to refer specifically to those who are engaged in ministry with him (Sosthenes in 1 Cor. 1.1; Apollos in 1 Cor. 16.12; Timothy in 2 Cor. 1.1 and Phlm. 1; Onesimus in Col. 4.9; and an unnamed group in 2 Cor. 8.22-23; 12.18).[173] Timothy is hereby included in the ministerial circle, giving him a certain elevated status, as does the title *God's fellow worker in spreading the gospel of Christ*. As the note in the *NIV* indicates, the textual variants in some Greek manuscripts read that he is "God's servant"[174] instead of *God's fellow worker*,[175] while others say that he is "God's servant and our fellow worker."[176] Although the evidence favors the reading that underlies the NIV, the rather uneven textual tradition at this point shows the discomfort that some scribes had with the idea that Timothy could be called *God's fellow worker*, and their apparent alteration of the sense. We can understand why the change would readily present itself, since Paul commonly talks about his associates in ministry as his "fellow workers" (Rom. 16.3, 9, 21; 2 Cor. 1.24; 4.3; 8.23; Phil. 2.25; Col. 4.11; Phlm. 1, 24). A "fellow worker" is a work companion, or, in a negative sense, it could refer to an accomplice.[177] The additional problem is whether *God's fellow worker* means that Timothy collaborated with God in the spread of the gospel or whether he collaborated with Paul and Silas *for* God (the same interpretive puzzle presents itself in 1 Cor. 3.9). While both readings are possible, it appears that the early scribes understood the expression according to the first interpretation.[178] However, since Paul commonly uses this word to speak of those who are his own companions in ministry and

---

173. Contra Marshall, *1 and 2 Thessalonians*, 90; See E. Earle Ellis, *Prophecy and Hermeneutic* (Tübingen: J. C. B. Mohr [Paul Siebeck], 1978), 13-22.

174. א A P Ψ.

175. D 33 B, without "God's." F and G say, "servant and God's fellow worker."

176. D² 075 0150.

177. Josephus, *Bellum Judaicum* 2.102 (2.7.1); *Antiquitates* 7.346 (7.14.4); see BAGD, 787-88; *New Docs*, 3.154; MM, 605.

178. On the interpretation of the title here and in 1 Cor. 3.9, see Victor Paul Furnish, "Fellow Workers in God's Service," *JBL* 80 (1961) 364-70.

since the combination of "brother and fellow worker" appears as a designation of Epaphroditus in Philippians 2.25, Paul likely has the second sense in mind. Timothy is not only their "brother" but also their "fellow worker" in the service of God. The service they have in mind is that of evangelism, as the *NIV* implies, *in spreading the gospel of Christ* (1.5; 2.4; 2 Thess. 2.14). In a number of verses in this letter the *gospel* is "of God" (2.2, 8, 9), since it has its origin in him. But here the object or center of this gospel is in view — it is the *gospel of Christ* (cf. 2 Thess. 1.8; cf. Mark 1.1).

In 3.5 Paul indicates that the mission of Timothy was "to find out about your faith," but in v. 1 the other purpose of the visit is revealed: *to strengthen and encourage you in your faith*. The verb *to strengthen* means "to establish" and is employed frequently in those contexts where someone is in danger of falling in some way or another. For example, "When the rich person totters," Sirach says, "he is supported by friends" (13.21). *2 Clement* 2.6 speaks of how it is a great thing to establish those things that are falling, while Philo comments that those who are carried in different directions in their life are those who cannot be established.[179] Diogenes Laertius refers to those people who are never firmly established in any dogma.[180] In the NT "to strengthen" points to the process of establishing someone in the faith, especially in the face of apostasy or persecution (Luke 22.32; Acts 18.23; Rom. 16.25; 1 Thess. 3.13; 2 Thess. 3.3; 1 Pet. 5.10; 2 Pet. 1.12; Rev. 3.2). Therefore, the choice of this term *(stērizō)* to describe the character of the ministry to new converts is natural (Acts 18.23; and *epistērizō* in Acts 14.22; 15.32, 41). In the same way, *encourage (parakalesai)* not only appears in the context of moral instruction (2.12; 4.1) but also describes how Christian leaders encouraged or exhorted new converts to persevere or "to remain true to the faith" (Acts 14.22; and 11.23; 16.40; 20.1). In this verse and in Acts 15.32, *to strengthen and encourage* are placed together, as also in 2 Thessalonians 2.17. These words summarize the "ministry of follow-up" to those new believers who faced opposition for their faith, and appear to be part of the common stock of early Christian teaching on this matter. We understand the mission of Timothy in light of the dangers of persecution and falling away that they faced (3.2-5). Timothy went to them in order to help assure that they would stay firm and press on ahead in their faith. Although Timothy's mission did not bring a resolution to all their problems, the fundamental objective was realized (3.6).

---

179. Philo, *De Somniis* 2.11; and see *De Congressu Quaerendae Eruditionis Gratia* 58; *De Fuga et Inventione* 49; *De Specialibus Legibus* 2.202; *De Praemiis et Poenis* 30.

180. Diogenes Laertius 2.136. See also Ps. 111.8; Sir. 24.10; 38.34; 40.19; 42.17; *TLNT*, 3.291-95; BAGD, 768.

3 The mission of Timothy to Thessalonica was calculated to establish them firmly in the faith *so that no one would be unsettled by these trials.* The exact nuance of the verb translated *be unsettled* has, surprisingly, been the issue of some debate (*sainesthai,* only here in the NT).[181] While originally meaning "to wag the tail," the term passed over from the canine to the human realm, where it suggests the idea of fawning over or flattering someone. Morris believes that this is precisely the sense in 3.3: "Here Paul seems to have in mind the possibility that, while the Thessalonians were in the middle of their troubles, some of their enemies might by fair words wheedle them out of the right way."[182] While the verb may permit this interpretation, Morris interjects elements that are not hinted at in the context (such as the suggestion that the Jews were trying to get these Christians to convert to Judaism). But the verb may also be used to describe some kind of profound emotional agitation, or it may speak of being moved from one place to another. Both possibilities are suggested in the ancient lexicon of Hesychius,[183] but the second suggestion is more likely in this context where the concern is for the stability of the Thessalonian church and not their emotional state (v. 2; cf. v. 8). Timothy's mission was to strengthen the foundations of the Thessalonians so that they would be stable, firm, and unmoved from the faith *by these trials.* The *trials* to which they refer are the persecutions the Thessalonians faced at the hands of their contemporaries (1.6; 2.17; 3.7; 2 Thess. 1.4, 6), which were themselves evidence of the nearness of the end (2 Thess. 1.4-12).[184] Their continuance in the faith and not simply their emotional well-being was at stake. The possibility of apostasy was very real in this toxic environment (3.5).

At this point Paul reminds the Thessalonians once more about that which they already knew (cf. 2.1) because of the teaching they had received (3.4): *You know quite well that we were destined for them.* Part of the basic catechism for new believers was instruction concerning the sufferings they were going to endure (3.4; Acts 14.22), and for that reason no one should have been surprised when it happened. The author reminds

181. Apart from the standard commentaries, see Eberhard Nestle, "Ein neues Wort für das Wörterbuch des Neuen Testaments," *ZNW* 7 (1906) 361-62; G. Mercati, "*Sainesthai,*" *ZNW* 8 (1907) 242; A. D. Knox, "*To mēdena sainesthai en tais thlipsesin tautais* (I Thess. iii 3)," *JTS* 25 (1924) 290-91; R. St John Parry, "*Sainesthai,* I Thess. iii 3," *JTS* 25 (1924) 405; *TDNT,* 7.54-56; BAGD, 740; MM, 567.

182. Morris, *First and Second Epistles to the Thessalonians,* 96.

183. He says it signifies *kineisthai* ("to be moved"), *tarassesthai* ("to be confused, agitated"), and *saleuesthai* ("to be moved," "to oscillate from one side to another").

184. Ernst Bammel, "Preparation for the Perils of the Last Days: I Thessalonians 3:3," in *Suffering and Martyrdom in the New Testament* (ed. William Horbury and Brian McNeil; Cambridge: Cambridge University Press, 1981), 91-100.

them of an aspect of the "theology of suffering" that said *we were destined* to face such suffering. At this point Paul and his companions identify with the Thessalonians by stating that *we* were going to face such trials (cf. 3.7). Suffering persecution was not understood as an extraordinary event but that to which they were called or *destined*.[185] When the apostolic team arrived in Thessalonica, they taught in the synagogue that it was necessary for the Messiah to suffer (Acts 17.3; cf. Luke 24.26; 1 Pet. 1.10-11). Moreover, Christ not only suffered but also became the paradigm for those who follow him (2.14) — as he suffered, so would his disciples (Rom. 8.17; 2 Cor. 1.5; cf. 1 Pet. 4.12), including Paul himself (Acts 9.16). The promise given to the church was, "Everyone who wants to live a godly life in Christ Jesus will be persecuted" (2 Tim. 3.12). Such suffering is a component of the Christian life (Acts 14.22; 1 Pet. 1.6) that God himself has allowed (Phil. 1.29; 1 Pet. 2.20-21; 3.17; 4.19). Best rightly comments, "Paul is not thinking of a period of persecution which will pass and the church return to normality; normality is persecution (cf. Acts 14.22)."[186] The theology of suffering was a centerpiece in early Christian teaching, unlike many muddled modern theologies that promise prosperity and the absence of trouble as the fruits of true faith.

4 During their stay in Thessalonica, the founders of the church taught the new believers over and again that they were all going to suffer persecution. As they taught, so it happened. So Paul says, *In fact, when we were with you, we kept telling you that we would be persecuted.* He refers back to the catechetical instruction he and his companions had given the church (cf. 2 Thess. 2.5; 3.10). Although they had not remained in the city long enough to instruct them in all the fundamental aspects of the Christian faith (cf. 4.13), the founders at least gave them basic teaching on the theology of suffering that was part of the diet for new converts. This instruction was given as a form of prophecy. The verb *we kept telling you (proelegomen)* means "to announce beforehand" and frequently appears in those contexts where a prophecy or oracle about the future is given.[187] The note about fulfillment at the end of this verse gives weight to this "prophetic" reading of the verb. Prophecy had a didactic function in the church (1 Cor. 14.31), and Silas, one of the founders of this community, was known as a prophet (Acts 15.32). The verb is in the imperfect tense, which here is iterative — over and again they returned to this theme.

185. Cf. the use of this verb in Luke 2.34; Phil. 1.16. BAGD, 426-27; MM, 339; *TDNT*, 3.654.

186. Best, *Commentary on the First and Second Epistles to the Thessalonians*, 135.

187. BAGD, 708. See 4.6b; 2 Cor. 13.2; Gal. 5.21; *1 Clem.* 34.3; Appian, *Bella Civilia Romana* 1.71; Herodotus 1.53. The verb is not used exclusively in the context of prophecy. See Appian, *Bella Civilia Romana* 2.139; MM, 542-43.

What the apostles predicted was that *we would be persecuted*. The grammatical construction may be interpreted as a simple future (*mellomen thlibesthai*, where *mellō* plus the infinitive is a substitute for the future). But the same construction may also point to that which *must* happen, especially where events that are within the divine plan are concerned. In fact, in many NT texts that speak about the sufferings of Christ and of the Christians, the same structure appears (Matt. 17.12, 22; Luke 9.44; John 11.51; 12.33; 18.32; and cf. Mark 10.32; Luke 9.31; John 7.39; Heb. 11.8). The teaching is that they were destined to suffer.[188] *We would be persecuted* may point to the emotional affliction they would have to endure ("we would be afflicted"), but in this context the focus is rather upon the external reality of persecution rather than their inward experience (cf. v. 3). Moreover, the passive voice implies that the oppression or affliction would come from without.[189]

In the second letter sent to this church, the afflictions the Thessalonians endured are framed as tribulations that anticipate the end (2 Thess. 1.4-10).[190] But here in v. 4 the concern is to remind the church that what was predicted has now come to pass: *And it turned out that way, as you well know*. They were destined to suffer (3.3b, 4b), Paul and his associates predicted that this would happen (3.4a), and as they predicted so it happened (3.4c). Why the emphasis on the fulfillment of this prophecy? Jewett suggests the following: "It seems to imply . . . that the Thessalonians were for some reason surprised or perturbed that persecution would be a part of their life in the new age, and that its presence cast doubt on the validity of their faith."[191] The Thessalonian congregation had a number of concerns about the "last things" (4.13; 5.1; 2 Thess. 2.2), and we can well imagine how their present experience clashed with their ultimate hopes (cf. 1 Pet. 4.12). But the confusion may not have its roots in the apparent clash between their present experience and future hope. The very fact that they had met with dishonor as a result of their faith would be cause enough for confusion. A person who was given the evil eye, insulted, or beaten publicly suffered great dishonor in a society where one's honor was held by the community to which one belonged. The loss of honor due to the conversion to the true and living God would have resulted in profound confusion (see 2.2 and commentary). As a counterpoint, the authors remind the church of the instruction they received and

---

188. So BAGD, 501.

189. Ibid., 362. See 2 Thess. 1.7; 1 Tim. 5.10; 2 Cor. 1.6; 4.8; 7.5 (where the objective and subjective aspects are combined). MM, 292; *New Docs*, 4.155.

190. See Wanamaker, *Commentary on 1 and 2 Thessalonians*, 131; Best, *First and Second Epistles to the Thessalonians*, 136.

191. Jewett, *The Thessalonian Correspondence*, 94.

how the things that were predicted have now come to pass. They could witness their fulfillment in their own lives. The God who called them is the one who let them know through his messengers that they would suffer. Validation of their experience came from understanding it both within God's plan and as a fulfillment of prophecy.[192]

5 After the digression of vv. 3b-4 on persecution as taught and experienced, the initial theme of the paragraph is taken up again (3.1-3a). Since the founders could not bear the agony of not having news about the church, they took action. But in this verse Paul steps forward from the group to express his own personal concern: *For this reason, when I could stand it no longer, I sent to find out about your faith.* The inclusion of "I also" (*kagō*, a combination of *kai* and *agō*) at the head of this verse highlights Paul's role in sending Timothy while at the same time keeping the other members of the team in view (3.1). The change to the singular signals to the Thessalonians the depth of his own concern for their well-being in light of the fact that he had not returned (cf. 2.18). Because of the persecutions the Thessalonians were enduring, Paul sent Timothy not only to "strengthen and encourage" the Thessalonians (cf. v. 2) but also *to find out about your faith.*[193] Though Paul was absent from this and other congregations he founded, he carried the believers in his heart (2 Cor. 11.28-29). Here his concern is for the *faith* of the Thessalonian believers. Does he mean here *faith* as their confidence in God, Christ, or the gospel (2 Thess. 2.13), or is the *faith* the corpus of revealed truth (Rom. 1.5; Gal. 1.23)? Where the object of faith is not specified it may also mean "true piety" or "genuine religion," and thus becomes an equivalent of "being a Christian" (see 3.2, 7, 10; 2 Thess. 1.3, 11; 3.2). This is the sense here. Timothy was sent back to find out whether they continued their allegiance to Christ. Was there anyone who had defected due to the enormous pressure of persecution?

The possibility of apostasy is expressed in the final part of the verse: *I was afraid that in some way the tempter might have tempted you and our efforts might have been useless.* Paul expresses his apprehension,[194] which was rooted in his knowledge of Satanic activity. Although the Thessalonians' contemporaries were driving the persecution forward, the power of the tempter orchestrated this battle for their souls (cf. Eph. 6.11-12). He had impeded the return of Paul and his associates to the city (2.18) and now converted the persecution into a temptation. In Matthew 4.3, Satan is known as "the tempter" whose mission is to tempt people to

192. Validation by fulfillment is a key theme in Cicero's *De Divinatione.* See, e.g., 1.19.37-38.

193. *Gnōnai,* "to know," here meaning "to ascertain"; Mark 5.43; Luke 24.18; Acts 21.34; 22.30; Col. 4.8 (BAGD, 161).

194. Expressed by *mē pōs* and translated *I was afraid.* See BDF, §370.

sin (*epeirasen;* see Matt. 4.1; Mark 1.13; Luke 4.2; 1 Cor. 7.5; Rev. 2.10).[195] The temptation of the tempter was not simply to commit some sin or sins but rather to commit the sin of apostasy (Luke 8.12; 1 Pet. 5.8), which is implied in this context by the references to their stability and continuance in the faith (3.2, 6, 8).[196] The issue is not only moral lapse but continuance in faith. What was at stake was the salvation of the Thessalonians. Paul knew the machinations of Satan (2 Cor. 2.11), *the tempter,* but he was unsure whether he had met with success in Thessalonica *(and our efforts might have been useless).*[197] The temptation, while inevitable, was resistible. But the possibility of apostasy was a clear and present danger.

The apostolic *efforts* were, in fact, difficult labor (the same word is used in 1.3b and 2.9). Here the labor is not that of making tents but the hard work associated with disseminating the gospel (cf. 2 Cor. 6.5; 11.23, 27). The focus, however, is on the fruit of this labor, which was in danger because this young church, bereft of leadership and struggling without full Christian instruction, faced Satan-inspired persecution that was designed to lead them to give up and abandon their alliance with the living God. So would the apostolic labors *have been useless* (cf. 2.1, where the same term appears)?[198] Paul could speak of "labor in vain" (1 Cor. 15.58; Phil. 2.16; cf. Isa. 65.23; 49.4), "running in vain" (Gal. 2.2; Phil. 2.16), or "receiving his grace in vain" (1 Cor. 15.10; 2 Cor. 6.1). The athletic imagery of Philippians 2.16 (along with "labor") and Galatians 2.2 describes the runner who makes an effort but becomes exhausted in the race. He does not win, and his efforts are for naught. A similar idea is found here. Paul entertained the fear that his labors to establish a church in that city might have been futile. The question was whether they had abandoned their new loyalty or whether they had continued firm and stable (3.2, 6, 8). Would the pressures lead them to defect? Not knowing was more than he could stand: *I sent to find out about your faith.*

5. "But Timothy has just now come to us" — Thanksgiving to God for the Thessalonians (3.6-10)

Undoubtedly the wait was agonizing. Paul and Silas had sent Timothy from Athens to Thessalonica to establish the believers and to find out

---

195. The verb may mean "to test" the character of a person (John 6.6; Heb. 11.7), but here it rather means "induce to sin" (as Gal. 6.1; 1 Chr. 21.1). In Greek literature the verb can convey either of these senses (Homer, *Odyssey* 9.281; Epictetus, *Dissertationes* 1.9.29). BAGD, 640; *TLNT,* 3.80-90; *NIDNTT,* 3.798-808.

196. *TLNT,* 3.88; *NIDNTT,* 3.803.

197. Hence the subjunctive *genētai,* "our efforts *might have been* useless."

198. *TLNT,* 2.303-10.

about their continuation in the faith (3.1, 5). From Athens, Silas himself had returned to the province of Macedonia while Paul remained alone in the city (Acts 17.16-34). From there Paul went on to Corinth (Acts 18.1), where he continued to wait for news of the condition of the church in Thessalonica. Eventually Timothy and Silas arrived (Acts 18.5). We cannot be sure whether Timothy traveled by land or sea, but whatever his route and means of transport the journey was not a short one. The trip from Athens to Thessalonica was approximately 220 miles (350 km.) overland, a journey that would have taken ten to eleven days. If Timothy had remained there for a minimum of a week, the whole trip from Athens to Thessalonica and then to Corinth beyond Athens would have taken approximately a month. 1 Thessalonians 2.17 notes that the time between leaving the church and writing this letter was relatively short, but whatever time elapsed between the apostles' exit and the news Timothy brought, the wait would have been long and agonizing. Timothy has just now arrived, with "good news," and the letter all but explodes with joy and thanks to God.

6 *But Timothy has just now come to us from you.* This letter was penned right after Timothy's arrival.[199] On more than one occasion, Paul sent Timothy on missions to the churches and then waited for his return with news about the congregations (1 Cor. 16.10-11; Phil. 2.19; 2 Tim. 4.9, 13; so Titus in 2 Cor. 12.18; 7.6). But none of those journeys was as charged with emotion as this one.

How could Timothy return *to us* since Acts 18.5 appears to indicate that they arrived together to Corinth from Macedonia? Acts 18.5 may be a condensed version of that history. Alternatively, Timothy may have met up with Silas at some point on the way to Corinth, and so the coming *to us* mentioned here would be a compressed version of the meeting first with Silas and then with Paul. In any case, when Timothy arrived he *brought good news about your faith and love.* Paul had feared the worst (3.5), but the news was the best. The verb "announced good news" (*euangelisamenou,* adverbial participle) in the NT commonly means "to proclaim the gospel [good news]" of salvation (Rom. 1.15; 10.15; 1 Cor. 1.17; etc.), but here the basic idea of announcing news that is good and joyful is in mind (Luke 1.19).[200] The announcement came in two parts. First, Timothy

---

199. *Arti* points to an event in the immediate past, but it may also mean simply "now." BAGD, 110; MM, 80. The first translation is in harmony with the pathos of the section.

200. BAGD, 317; *TLNT*, 2.82-92; *NIDNTT*, 2.107-8. See Aristophanes, *Equites* 643; Demosthenes, *De Corona* 323. Marshall, *1 and 2 Thessalonians,* 94; and Best, *First and Second Epistles to the Thessalonians,* 139-40, understand the verb here in its Christian sense, saying that the announcement of Timothy was like the proclamation of the gospel to

brought the good tidings of the *faith* and *love* of the Thessalonian believers. These virtues characterized the Thessalonian church (1.3 and commentary; 5.8; 2 Thess. 1.3; and note their "faith" in 1.8; 3.2, 5, 7, 10;
2 Thess. 1.4, 11; 2.13; and their "love" in 3.12; 4.9; 5.13; 2 Thess. 3.5). These
were, and still are, the distinctive characteristics of those who are true
members of the community of the redeemed (Gal. 5.6; Eph. 1.15; Col. 1.4-
5; 1 Tim. 1.14; Phlm. 5; Rev. 2.19).[201] When Timothy witnessed the
Thessalonians' faith in God (1.8), their mutual love (3.12; 4.9; 5.13; and
2 Thess. 1.3), and their love for God (2 Thess. 3.5), it was evident that they
had not yielded to the tempter but had tenaciously held to the gospel
(3.2-5, 8). They had the marks of true Christianity. The tempter's scheme
was unfruitful, and the apostle's fears were not realized.

The *NIV* starts a new sentence at this point, contrary to the Greek
syntax: *He has told us that you always have pleasant memories of us and that
you long to see us, just as we also long to see you.* This is the second aspect of
the "good news" Timothy brought to the ears of his companions.[202] Far
from having a bad memory of Paul and his companions or hostility toward them for leaving, they had warm and kindly *memories.*[203] Their separation from the church was only physical and not emotional. There was
no animosity but only "pleasant memories," which were constant *(always).* It is possible to understand *always* with the following clause in
which Paul mentions that the Thessalonians "always long to see us."
While either understanding of the adverb is possible, the numerous references to the desires and attempts to be united with the congregation incline us to the second reading (2.17-18; 3.10-11). As the founders wanted
to see the Thessalonians, so they *always* wanted to see the apostles. The
verb that expresses this longing for reunion means "to desire intensely"
and communicates something of the anxiousness and discontent that
come with not getting what one desires.[204] It appears frequently in those
texts where Paul expresses his desire to see fellow Christians from whom
he is separated (Rom. 1.11; Phil. 2.26; 2 Tim. 1.4; cf. Rom. 15.23). This desire motivated these missionaries, especially Paul, to return to the city

---

them. But this understanding of the verb ignores the common use of the term, which
would be the most accessible understanding for the readers/hearers.

201. On this essential combination of Christian virtues, see 1 Cor. 13.2, 13; 2 Cor.
8.7; Eph. 3.17; 1 Tim. 1.5; 2.15; 4.12; 6.11; 2 Tim. 1.13; 2.22; 3.10; Titus 2.2; 3.15; Jas. 2.5;
1 Pet. 1.8; 1 John 3.23.

202. The Greek syntax makes clear that the announcement of Timothy was both
about the Thessalonians' faith and love and their kind memory of and longing to see the
apostles.

203. *Agathos.* So 2 Macc. 7.20; and cf. Rom. 5.7; Titus 2.5; 1 Pet. 2.18. BAGD, 3.

204. *TLNT,* 2.58-60. Note its use in Jas. 4.5; 2 Cor. 5.2. In other contexts it may refer
to affection (2 Cor. 9.14; Phil. 1.8).

(2.17-18) and drove them to join together in intense prayer for a reunion with the church in Thessalonica (3.10-11). But what encourages them (3.7) is the mutuality and reciprocity in this relationship. The Thessalonians had not abandoned God, nor had they rejected the founders of the church! It would have been difficult to think of better news than this.

The theme of separation and statements that physical distance did not mean emotional distance were part of the "friendly" letter type known in antiquity. Talk about reunion was common in such correspondence (cf. 2 Cor. 1.16; Phlm. 22; 2 John 12; 3 John 14). This type of letter would also strike the chord of mutuality or reciprocity that characterized the relationship between friends and that lay at the very core of the concept of friendship.[205] In some way the letter itself was as the presence of the person who sent it; as Seneca says, "I never receive a letter from you without being in your company forthwith" (*Epistulae* 40.1). But the letter was never a full and adequate substitute for the presence of an absent friend. While this correspondence has the marks of a "friendly letter," it also mixes admonition and thanksgiving with expressions of friendship. The relationship between Paul, his coworkers, and the churches was a complex one. While Paul follows the epistolary conventions of the day, this in no way diminishes the sincerity of his longings for this church.

7 The news Timothy brought was encouraging beyond measure: *Therefore, brothers, in all our distress and persecution we were encouraged about you because of your faith.* For Paul and his associates, the ministry in Macedonia and Achaia had been extremely difficult. They were beaten, jailed, and defamed in Philippi (Acts 16.22-24; Phil. 1.30; 1 Thess. 2.2), and persecuted and expelled from Thessalonica (Acts 17.10; 1 Thess. 1.6) and Berea (Acts 17.13-14), and Paul was rejected and scorned in Athens (Acts 17.32). He describes how he was in Corinth "in weakness and fear, and with much trembling" (1 Cor. 2.3; Acts 18.9-10). In 2 Corinthians he details the adversity he faced (2 Cor. 6.3-10; 11.16-29), all in fulfillment of the revelation of the Lord about the sufferings he would have to endure (Acts 9.15-16). His coworkers shared in the same, and the adversity they experienced is summarized as *all our distress and persecution. Distress* is not the emotional reaction to adversity but rather the afflictions and calamities themselves that they faced on their journeys (2 Cor. 6.4; 12.10).[206] *Persecution* is roughly equivalent, referring also to the afflictions they endured, especially since they were the objects of oppression (Acts 14.22; Rom. 5.3;

---

205. On this type of letter, see Stowers, *Letter Writing in Greco-Roman Antiquity*, 58-70; Malherbe, *Ancient Epistolary Theorists*, 33, 69.

206. *Anankē*. See also Diodorus Siculus 10.4.6; Appian, *Bella Civilia Romana* 5.40; Josephus, *Bellum Judaicum* 5.571 (5.13.7); *Antiquitates* 2.67 (2.5.2); 16.253 (16.8.4); BAGD, 52; MM, 31-32.

8.35; 12.12; 2 Cor. 1.4, 8; 4.17; 6.4; 7.4; 8.2; Eph. 3.13; Phil. 1.17; 4.14; Col. 1.24; 1 Thess. 1.6; 3.3; 2 Thess. 1.4, 6).[207] The term may refer to the inner distress a person experiences (2 Cor. 2.4), but in this context in combination with *afflictions* the emphasis is on their outward experience and not their inner reaction. Elsewhere these two terms appear together (2 Cor. 6.4; Job 15.24; Ps. 119.143). Best and Wanamaker suggest that the description of their experience as "distress and persecution" would bring to mind the adversity the people of God face before the final end.[208] Although the NT ties together adversity and eschatology (see 3.3), the point here is other. Paul simply relates to the Thessalonians that he and his associates were also suffering for their faith. They shared this common experience.

But in the midst of all the adversity, Paul was able to say, *we were encouraged about you because of your faith.* Timothy had been sent to Thessalonica to "encourage" the Thessalonians in their faith (v. 2),[209] but now in return the apostles themselves are encouraged upon hearing the news about the church. Were they encouraged "about them," as opposed to being concerned about whether or not the Thessalonians had continued in the faith (v. 5), or were they encouraged "because of them," finding encouragement in their own trials because of the good news Timothy brought from Thessalonica?[210] In a passage strikingly similar to this one, Paul speaks about his own afflictions and how the coming of Titus with news from the church brought him encouragement because of the way Titus was encouraged about them (2 Cor. 7.6-7). We should probably understand our present verse similarly, that is, Paul and company were encouraged "about them." The reason they were encouraged about them was *because of your faith.* Such news brought great joy (v. 9), as their fears were put to rest. Timothy had gone to the church to strengthen and encourage them "in their faith" (v. 2) as well as "to find out about their faith" (v. 5), but now the founders are encouraged "about their faith" since it held and was intact. But since this verse begins by speaking about the troubles of the messengers themselves, the implication would also be that the news about the church brought some measure of relief to them in the middle of all the trouble they themselves faced, a point more

207. BAGD, 362; MM, 292; Josephus, *Antiquitates* 4.108 (4.6.3). The word is not limited to those sufferings that are due to persecution. See *New Docs*, 1.84.

208. Best, *First and Second Epistles to the Thessalonians*, 141; Wanamaker, *Commentary on 1 and 2 Thessalonians*, 135.

209. The verb *pareklēthēmen* may denote "to console" (Gen. 37.35; Matt. 5.4; 1 Thess. 4.18), but here it has the sense of "encourage" (2 Cor. 1.4, 6, 7; 7.6, 13; 2 Thess. 2.17). See BAGD, 617; *NIDNTT*, 1.570-71.

210. *Eph' hymin* can bear either sense.

clearly brought out in v. 8. Reciprocity characterized true friendship, and Paul and his companions not only gave but received (cf. 2 Cor. 1.7; Rom. 1.10-11; 2 John 2-4). They and the Thessalonians shared faith, afflictions, and now encouragement. The continuing faith of the Thessalonians (vv. 6a, 7b) is also bound tightly with the relationship this church enjoyed with the founders (vv. 6b, 7a). This shared faith was the foundation on which their relationship rested. True faith and true community go hand in hand.

8 In the midst of all the oppression they endured, Paul and his co-workers can now exclaim, *For now we really live, since you are standing firm in the Lord. Now* can be understood with all its temporal force.[211] Timothy has just arrived from the church (v. 6), and the others were encouraged about the Thessalonians because of the news he brought (v. 7). *Now,* in contrast to their previous state, they *really live.* How should we understand this declaration? Obviously, the assertion is not that they were alive physically (4.15). This much was obvious! Is the idea rather that they have been able to "recover" due to this news (cf. Mark 5.23; John 4.50, 51, 53; Josephus, *Vita* 421 [75]), speaking figuratively? They were both oppressed by their circumstances (v. 7) and distressed by their concerns for the church (vv. 1, 5). Now they recover from their anxiety and have renewed hope in the middle of their own afflictions, all because of the Thessalonians. While this understanding of *we really live* is possible, we should bear in mind that Paul over and again faced the danger of death (1 Cor. 15.31), which became a metaphor in his life: "We always carry around in our body the death of Jesus . . . we who are alive are always being given over to death for Jesus. . . . Though outwardly we are wasting away, yet inwardly we are being renewed day by day" (2 Cor. 4.10-11, 16). Given that Paul counted himself among those who were "considered as sheep to be slaughtered" (Rom. 8.36), we can understand that in the midst of persecution and the dangers of death the image of life would spring to mind. For him and his companions the good news about this church was like a resurrection.

The reason for this renewal was *since you are standing firm in the Lord.* The verb means "to be constant and stable,"[212] whether in the faith (1 Cor. 16.13), in the community of faith (Phil. 1.27), in the doctrine received (2 Thess. 2.15), or, as here, *in the Lord* (Phil. 4.1). They maintained their solidarity with the Lord despite the persecutions (2.14) and in the face of Satanic attacks, which were designed to separate them from their faith in

211. *Nyn* may mean "at the present time" or "in these circumstances." BAGD, 545-546.

212. BAGD, 767-68; *TNDT*, 7.636-38.

the Lord (3.5). In the opening thanksgiving of the letter (see 1.3 and commentary), the "endurance produced by hope" that characterized the Thessalonian believers is underscored. This constancy in the midst of trial was the true fruit of hope, and we may suppose that the same idea underlies v. 8. In v. 6 Timothy brought the report of their "faith and love," and now we see the fruit, hope, completing the trilogy of Christian virtues. However, the final clause of the verse is a conditional construction *(ean* with the indicative *stēkete)* found infrequently in the NT. It poses a type of exhortation — they *should* stand firm in the Lord. Paul's hope is that the stability that Timothy had witnessed and reported, and that he and his companions knew well (1.3), would continue. Their action is also an obligation.

9   At this point the letter bursts with emotion as Paul realizes that the Thessalonians kept faith, love, and hope. Their thankfulness to God and their overwhelming joy are expressed in the form of a rhetorical question, a literary technique sometimes used to convey vivid emotion (cf. Rom. 8.31):[213] *How can we thank God enough for you in return for all the joy we have in the presence of our God because of you?* This is the third thanksgiving to God in this letter (see 1.2; 2.13 and commentary). The thanksgiving indicates that Paul realized that although Timothy did his part to establish the Thessalonians in the faith (v. 2) and the Thessalonians themselves continued on in faith and love (v. 6), all the while standing firm in the Lord (v. 8), God himself was active within their lives to produce this kind of spiritual tenacity in the midst of so much opposition. To him go the thanks! The question that is poised is strikingly similar to that of the psalmist, who asked, "How can I repay the LORD for all his goodness to me?" (Ps. 116.12). The thanksgiving to God, both in our text and in the psalm, is viewed as a debt that is impossible to pay.

A more literal rendering of the verse would be: "What thanksgiving are we able to return to God?" The verb *antapodounai* means "to repay," in either a positive (1 Macc. 10.27; Luke 14.14; Rom. 11.35) or a negative sense (Prov. 24.22; Sir. 30.6; 2 Thess. 1.6; Rom. 12.19). It frequently appears in Greek literature in the context of returning thanks for some benefit received. For example, Josephus transcribes a letter from Julius Caesar to the Jewish high priest Hyrcanus in which the emperor wanted to "return" to Hyrcanus, the Jewish nation, and Hyrcanus's sons, "a token of gratitude worthy of their loyalty to us and of the benefits which they have conferred upon us."[214] The principle of reciprocity

213. BDF, §496.
214. Josephus, *Antiquitates* 14.212 (14.10.7).

was bound up with Caesar's show of gratitude. This principle is what Thucydides described, using the same verb, in the statement "return us like for like."[215] In the same way, Herodotus made note of another act of reciprocity, saying, "these lent their aid in return for a similar service done for them."[216] The principle of reciprocity was part of the fabric of Greek and Roman culture. Reciprocity placed a strong social obligation on those who received benefits to demonstrate their gratitude. Seneca said, "Not to return gratitude for benefits is a disgrace, and the whole world counts it as such."[217] Thanksgiving was understood as a debt that one owed to one's benefactor. This principle was at the heart of Paul's thanksgiving to God for the Thessalonians. Paul and his coworkers have received a great gift from God — the news that the Thessalonians stood firm in their faith — and now in response to that benefit they seek a way to repay the debt of thanks adequately. But how? The question implies that Paul and his companions could not find an adequate way to thank God, so great was their joy! This was a conventional way of saying that the gift exceeded all bounds. Seneca says that one should respond to a great benefit received in a similar way: "I shall never be able to repay you my gratitude, but, at any rate, I shall not cease from declaring everywhere that I am unable to repay it."[218]

The Thessalonians themselves were the reason why they wanted to offer thanks to God (*for you, peri hymōn*) as well as the cause of their joy (*because of you, di' hymas*).[219] Over and again Paul and other church leaders point to those Christians who are faithful to God as the source of their joy (Rom. 16.19; 2 Cor. 7.4; Phil. 1.4-5; 2.2; 4.1; 1 Thess. 2.20; 2 Tim. 1.4; Phlm. 7; Heb. 13.17; 1 John 1.4; 2 John 4, 12; 3 John 3, 4). The Thessalonians were no exception to this rule (2.19-20). Paul lets the Thessalonians know about the intensity of their joy in two ways. First, he makes mention of *all the joy* they had, and, second, he emphasizes the abundance of their joy by using a redundant expression, "all the *joy* with which we *rejoice*" (not reflected in translation; cf. a similar construction in 1 Pet. 1.8; 4.13). They could not find an adequate way to thank God for

215. Thucydides, *Histories* 1.43.2
216. Herodotus 1.18. See also Thucydides 4.19.3; Aristotle, *Rhetorica* 2.2.16-17.
217. Seneca, *De Beneficiis* 3.1.1. See 2.31; 2.33.1-2; 2.35.1. On the theme see Gerald W. Peterman, "'Thankless Thanks.' The Social-Epistolary Convention in Philippians 4.10-29," *TynB* 42 (1991) 261-70; idem, *Paul's Gift from Philippi: Conventions of Gift-Exchange and Christian Giving* (Cambridge and New York: Cambridge University Press, 1997).
218. See Seneca, *De Beneficiis* 2.24.4.
219. Their special affection for the Thessalonians is highlighted throughout vv. 6-10 where "you" (*hymeis*) is used ten times. Milligan, *St. Paul's Epistles to the Thessalonians*, 42.

the overflowing joy they experienced.[220] This joy was expressed *in the presence of our God.* Previously Paul spoke of the eschatological joy they anticipated "in the presence of our Lord Jesus when he comes" (2.19; cf. 2 Cor. 5.10; 1 Thess. 3.13). But the joy they now have (2.20) is part of their communal times of prayer *in the presence of our God* (as in 1.3) when they also offered petitions (3.10). The theme of their present communion with God is taken up and expanded through the end of the chapter. Thanks, joy, petition, and blessings for the Thessalonians mark these times in the very presence of the living God.

10 Verse 10 records how the founders moved from thanksgiving and joy in the presence of God to petition that they might be reunited with the Thessalonians and complete the ministry they had begun among them: *Night and day we pray most earnestly that we may see you again and supply what is lacking in your faith.* Paul tells about their prayers to see the Thessalonians in this verse, while in the following the prayer itself is recorded. He highlights the intensity of their prayers for reunion with the church in three ways. First, they prayed *night and day,* that is, they prayed constantly and insistently (see 2.9; 1.2-3). Marshall believes that the mention of prayers at night shows how profound their concern for the church became.[221] However, the phrase *night and day* was quite common and communicated the idea of long hours and great exertion in prayer, which was a response to a critical situation (cf. 2 Macc. 13.10, "But when Judas heard this, he ordered the people to call upon the Lord day and night"). Second, Paul states how intense their prayers were. The adverb *most earnestly (hyperekperissou),* which appears infrequently in Greek literature (see 5.13; Eph. 3.20; *T. Joseph* 17.5), is the highest form of comparison that can be expressed.[222] Their prayers were intense beyond measure. Third, their prayers were not simple requests since the verb (participle) translated *we pray (deomenoi)* means "to pray with insistence" or "implore" (cf. 2 Cor. 8.4; and the prayers in Matt. 9.38; Luke 10.2; Acts 4.31; 8.24).[223] As they had made a great effort to return to Thessalonica (2.17-18a), so, too, they invested great energy in prayer so that they could see the church and help them. They were not about to give up in the face of the obstacles Satan had thrown in their way (2.18b).

The prayers focused on two objectives. First, Paul notes that they prayed that God would permit them to see the Thessalonians again, *to see your face (eis to idein hymōn prosōpon;* cf. 2.17 and comments). The NT let-

---

220. *Epi* plus the dative *(epi pasę tę charą)* indicates that on which an action or state of being is based. BAGD, 287.

221. Marshall, *1 and 2 Thessalonians,* 98. See Pss. 42.8; 63.6; 77.2; 1QS 6.6-8.

222. BAGD, 840; *NIDNTT,* 1.728, 730.

223. BAGD, 175; Milligan, *St. Paul's Epistles to the Thessalonians,* 42.

ters contain a number of similar notes about authors' desires to see their readers' faces (2 Cor. 1.16; Phlm. 22; 2 John 12; 3 John 14), and this was a standard theme in letters of friendship.[224] Absence does not mean indifference! Some centuries later Basil wrote, "And I wish my difficulties to be known for no other object than your pardon in the future, that we may not be condemned for indifference if we do fail to pay you the visit."[225] The reality of this longing should not be minimized simply because of the literary parallels that can be found. The letter is replete with genuine concern for the church. Had not Paul tried to return but was stopped by Satan (2.17-18)? Had not he also sent Timothy to look in on them and do what he could for them (3.2, 5)? But he could not fulfill all their needs. Though the Thessalonians would have recognized that the letter could cut the distance between the author and the recipients (cf. 2 John 12; 3 John 13-14), there would still be something lacking. The situation demanded more than a letter — a visit was necessary, especially from Paul (cf. 2.18). Did he eventually see them again? The narrative in Acts and the geographical notes in the Pauline letters give abundant evidence that God truly did grant this request, since Paul returned to Macedonia (Acts 19.21-22; 20.1-6; 1 Cor. 16.5; 2 Cor. 1.16; 1 Tim. 1.3).

The second concern the prayers addressed was that God would give Paul and the others the opportunity to *supply what is lacking in your faith*. *Supply (katartisai)* could mean "to restore" or "to put in order" (Matt. 4.21; Mark 1.19; 2 Cor. 13.11; Gal. 6.1), but here the idea is not repairing that which needs restoration but "to put in its proper condition" or "to make complete" (Luke 6.40; 1 Cor. 1.10; Heb. 13.21).[226] The verb commonly surfaces in educational contexts to talk about training and completing the education the student receives (Luke 6.40; and the substantive in Eph. 4.11-12). For example, Plutarch takes up the verb to describe the training Alexander the Great received from Aristotle.[227] The teacher had the responsibility of completing the instruction given to the student so that the pupil could live as an adult. In spite of the Timothy visit (3.2), the operation of the grace of God in their lives (3.9), and the intent to fill the gaps in their moral and theological training by means of this letter (4.1–5.22), Paul well knew that their personal training would be necessary to *supply what is lacking in your faith*. There were deficiencies *(hysterēmata)* in their faith (see 3.2, 5 and commentary). Because of the short time the apostolic team spent in the city, it appears that they had insufficient opportunity to impart all the

---

224. Stowers, *Letter Writing in Greco-Roman Antiquity,* 60, 65, 68-69, 75-76, 82, 159.
225. Ibid., 68.
226. BAGD, 417-18; MM, 332; *TLNT,* 2.18-20, 271-74. At times the verb is synonymous with *exartizō* (2 Tim. 3.17).
227. Plutarch, *Alexander* 7.2; Themistocles 2.5-6; Polybius 5.2.11.

Christian instruction the believers needed (4.13). What is more, the Thessalonians had not been fully mindful of the teaching they had already received (5.1-2). They did not take to heart or accept all the teaching on sexuality (4.3-8), and they needed to progress in a Christian approach to labor (4.11-12). A visit to the church was called for because Paul was an essential instrument in the process of spiritual maturation (cf. Eph. 4.11-16, where this idea is expanded to include all Christian ministers).

6. "Now may our God . . . clear the way for us to come to you" — The Prayer to Return to Thessalonica (3.11-13)

Paul concludes the first section of the body of the letter (2.1–3.10) with a prayer (3.11-13) instead of a doxology (cf. Rom. 11.33-38; Eph. 3.20-21; Heb. 13.20-21; 1 Pet. 4.11). Jewett has suggested that this type of ending has its roots in "homiletic settings." Normally, a preacher would conclude his homily with a prayer, and this custom was transferred to the letters.[228] Similarly, Wiles comments that this kind of prayer came out of a liturgical context, but he traces its origin both to the worship in Israel as presented in the OT and the practice in the synagogue.[229] He notes that the prayer in 3.11-13, like that in 5.23-24, carried out a number of functions. First, it summarized the central message of the letter (in this case, the return to Thessalonica and the spiritual progress of the congregation in light of the prospect of the coming of the Lord Jesus). Second, the prayer had a parenetic purpose: it is an implicit exhortation to continue in love and to remain firm. Third, the prayer was didactic in that it served as a model for the church's own prayers. This, however, does not appear to be one of the primary purposes of the prayer in 3.11-13. Fourth, Wiles points to the liturgical purpose. After hearing the letter read in the meeting of the congregation (5.27), the church would participate in the Lord's Supper. But again, the lack of evidence makes us wonder if this purpose is a true reflection of what happened or was expected. More to the point is Wiles' fifth suggestion, that the prayer is what it appears to be — a prayer (cf. 5.23; 2 Thess. 3.5, 16; Rom. 15.5-6, 13)! Now Paul and his co-workers offer their prayers to God for their journey back and for the Thessalonians, while allowing the church to listen in.

11 The prayer, which is in the form of a wish,[230] begins, *Now may*

228. Robert Jewett, "The Form and Function of the Homiletic Benediction," *ATR* 51 (1969) 18-34; idem, *The Thessalonian Correspondence*, 188-89.

229. Gordon P. Wiles, *Paul's Intercessory Prayers* (Cambridge: Cambridge University Press, 1974), 22-71; and see O'Brien, *Introductory Thanksgivings in the Letters of Paul*, 160-64.

230. Optative mood *(kateuthynai)*.

our God and Father himself and our Lord Jesus clear the way for us to come to you. The prayer in the Greek text begins with the word *himself* (*autos;* so 5.23), which was likely liturgical language, as Wiles suggests.[231] The prayer is directed in the first place to "God himself and our Father" (*autos de ho theos kai patēr hēmōn; NIV, our God and Father himself*),[232] an invocation that echoes the prayer that Jesus taught his disciples and that gave definition to their understanding of God and their relationship with him (Matt. 6.9; Luke 11.2; Mark 14.36; cf. 1 Pet. 1.17). Over and again in these letters, Paul refers to God as the Father of the Christians (1 Thess. 1.1, 3; 3.13; 2 Thess. 1.1-2; 2.16). He is the object of both the heralds' thanks (1 Thess. 1.2; 2.13; 3.9; 2 Thess. 1.3; 2.13) and their prayers (1 Thess. 1.3; 3.11-13; 5.23; 2 Thess. 1.11-12; 2.16). But in this prayer, as in 2 Thessalonians 2.16-17, the *Lord Jesus* is the one to whom prayers are directed alongside God the Father. To address prayers to the *Lord Jesus* (so 2 Thess. 3.5, 16) in the same breath with God the Father implies a very high Christology. This prayer would be proper only if the apostles held to the divinity of Christ.[233] This point is even clearer in the prayer of 2 Thessalonians 2.16, where the order of the names is reversed, "May our Lord Jesus Christ and God our Father."

The prayer itself requests that God their Father and the Lord Jesus Christ *clear the way for us to come to you.*[234] The phrase *clear the way* (or, "make straight the way") alludes to an experience of daily life in those lands where there were few straight paths to follow. The expression took on a metaphorical sense in Jewish literature (1 Sam. 6.12; Pss. 5.8; 118.5; Prov. 4.26-27; 9.15; 29.27; Ezek. 18.25; Jdt. 12.8) and was also known in Greek writings (Plato, *Leges* 8.847A; Plutarch, *Alexander* 33.2). The basic idea was to keep on the path, not turn aside (see especially 1 Sam. 6.12; Prov. 4.26-27); metaphorically, this meant not to deviate from some kind of moral conduct or, as in the present case, from some activity. The prayer was that God and the Lord Jesus would facilitate the founders' return to the Thessalonians without impediment and without any change in plans. As such, the petition is the counterpoint to the Satanic opposition that impeded their return previously (2.18).

12 The prayer for the Thessalonians continues with a petition for

---

231. Wiles, *Paul's Intercessory Prayers,* 30-31.

232. *Autos* may be either reflexive ("May God himself") or emphatic ("May he, God") and may be understood with either "God" alone or both titles, "God and Father." Similarly, "our" may be understood with both "God and Father" or only "Father." The use of the formula "God himself" in 5.23 and the echo of the Lord's Prayer's "our Father" lead us to modify the *NIV*'s rendering slightly.

233. See Marshall, *1 and 2 Thessalonians,* 100.

234. Singular verb with plural subject.

the abundant growth of their love: *May the Lord make your love increase and overflow for each other and for everyone else, just as ours does for you.* The prayer in the Greek texts begins with an emphatic "you" and the adversative "but" (*de*; "But may the Lord make *you* increase and overflow in love"). The point of the construction seems to be that whatever happened to Paul and the others (v. 11), their desire was that the love of the believers would increase abundantly. This second part of the prayer is directed specifically to Jesus, the Lord (cf. v. 11, "our Lord Jesus"; 2 Thess. 3.5, 16), as the one who would infuse them with this love (cf. 4.9). As we saw previously, the Thessalonian church was noteworthy for the fraternal love they showed each other (1.3; 4.9), such that Timothy was able to bring back a firsthand report of the evidences of this love among them (3.6) and for the believers in other parts of Macedonia (4.9-10). They had received the love of God (1.4; 2 Thess. 2.13, 16; 3.5), and he was the very one who taught them to love (4.9-10). The church was so exemplary in this regard that the apostle put them forward as a model for other Christians (2 Thess. 1.3-4). This love was not simply affective, made up of warm feelings, but rather that which bound them together in a form of a kinship group.[235] Despite the love they already exhibited, Paul voices the desire that the Lord would make their love *increase and overflow*. The first verb is usually intransitive, but when used transitively it means "to increase abundantly" (*pleonasai*; Num. 26.54; 2 Chr. 31.5; Ps. 71.21), even to the point of overflowing.[236] The following verb is almost synonymous (*perisseusai*) and as a transitive verb means "to cause to abound" or "to provide in superabundance" (4.1, 10; Rom. 15.13; 1 Cor. 14.12; 15.58; Phil. 1.9; 2 Cor. 8.2), to the point of having more than enough (Xenophon, *Symposium* 4.35).[237] Taken together, the verbs show the superlative degree to which the apostles wanted the church's love to grow. The prayer is not simply that their love increase but that it abound beyond limits, being exceedingly great and overflowing. In his homily on Thessalonians, Chrysostom captures the sense, "Do you see the unrestrainable madness of love that is shown by his words? 'Make you to increase and abound,' instead of cause you to grow."[238] The strong love for one another within the community was the counterpoint to the rejection they faced from their contemporaries. The Lord evidently answered this prayer since in the second letter Paul comments that "the love every one of you has for each other is increasing (*pleonazei*)" (2 Thess. 1.3).

---

235. Malina and Neyrey, *Portraits of Paul*, 196-97.
236. BAGD, 667; MM, 517; *TDNT*, 6.263-66; *NIDNTT*, 2.130-31.
237. BAGD, 650-51; *TDNT*, 6.58-61; *NIDNTT*, 1.728-31.
238. Chrysostom, *Homilies on 1 Thessalonians* 4.

The objects of this love were, in the first instance, the other members of the Christian community in Thessalonica, *for each other*. The commandment of the Lord Jesus to love one another echoes throughout the NT as well as here (John 13.34-35; 15.12, 17; Rom. 12.10; 13.8; 1 Thess. 4.9; 2 Thess. 1.3; 1 Pet. 1.22; 4.8; 1 John 3.11, 23; 4.7, 11-12; 2 John 5; and cf. Gal. 5.13; Eph. 4.2) and constitutes the virtue that, more than any other, defines the relationship between members of the Christian community. It is truly reciprocal.[239] The Thessalonians even extended their love to Christians in other places throughout Macedonia (4.9-10). The prayer continues that their abundant love would be not only for other Christians but also *for everyone else*. Although Paul could speak of the totality of the Christian community similarly with the inclusive "all the brothers and sisters" (4.10; 5.26-27), the reference here is rather to the people who were not members of the church. In the same way, 5.15 calls the Thessalonians "to be kind to each other and *to everyone else*," and in Galatians 6.10 Paul exhorts the churches to "do good to all people, especially to those who belong to the family of believers." In his teaching about how to relate to those outside the Christian community, Paul tells Timothy that the servant of the Lord "must be kind to everyone" (2 Tim. 2.24), while Titus is urged to remind the believers "to show true humility to all men" (Titus 3.2). Paul regularly shows his concern for the relationships Christians have with fellow believers as well as with "outsiders" (1 Thess. 4.12; Col. 4.5; cf. 1 Cor. 5.12-13). The call to love all people finds its roots in the teaching of Jesus (Matt. 5.43-48; 22.39; Mark 12.31-33; Luke 10.27-37), though at times the commandment to "love your neighbor" was converted into a teaching that governed the internal relationships in the church (Rom.13.8-10; Gal. 5.14-15; Jas. 2.8-9). However, since Jesus is the "Lord of all" (Rom. 10.12), the church kept one eye on the mission to those "outside," which included both the proclamation of the gospel (1.8) and good works done for all (5.15 and commentary).

The prayer presents a model or example of the kind of overflowing love that Paul wants the Thessalonians to have for each other and for all people, *just as ours does for you*. He calls the believers those who are "be-

---

239. Contra Wanamaker, *Commentary on 1 and 2 Thessalonians,* 143; Gerd Theissen, *The Social Setting of Pauline Christianity* (Philadelphia: Fortress Press, 1982), 106-10, speaks about "love-patriarchalism" where the socially superior are called to "love and respect" while the socially inferior are exhorted to "subordination, fidelity, and esteem." The context of the love command in 1 Thessalonians is the kinship relationship (4.9), and the primary concern is mutuality in love, both here and in 2 Thess. 1.3. Each one gives, each one receives. Nobody is excluded as either subject or object of love. The power of the Christian ethic is that even those on the lowest level of society are called to the highest level of morality.

loved" (2.8), while the whole section from 2.1 through 3.10 speaks eloquently of the love Paul and his companions had for them. They were a true Christian example, which the Thessalonians imitated (1.6 and commentary; 2 Thess. 3.7-9; and Acts 20.35; 1 Cor. 4.16; 11.1; Phil. 3.17; 4.9). In his other letters Paul makes known his love for both individuals (Rom. 16.8; 1 Cor. 4.17) and churches (1 Cor. 4.21; 16.2; 2 Cor. 2.4; 6.6; 11.11; 12.15; Phil. 4.1). His writings give clear evidence that his love was one of the key motivating factors in his ministry to the churches. So great and genuine was his and his associates' love that they could come before the Lord in prayer and ask that the Thessalonians have the same love that they had for the Thessalonians.

13 In the beginning of this prayer, Paul asked that God would facilitate their return to Thessalonica so that they might "supply what is lacking" in the Thessalonians' faith (vv. 10-11), after which he prayed that the believers' love would increase superabundantly (v. 12). The prayer now concludes with his gazed fixed on the final events when the church will come before *the presence of our God and Father* at the time of the Lord's coming: *May he strengthen your hearts so that you will be blameless and holy in the presence of our God and Father when our Lord Jesus comes with all his holy ones.* Verse 13 is really a continuation of the prayer offered in v. 12. The grammar implies that establishing the believers as those who are blameless in holiness is the fruit of their mutual love for one another and "for everyone else."[240] The first part of the verse could be translated, "so that your hearts might be established blameless in holiness." Their growth in love for each other and for all people contributes to their holiness, a thought similar to Paul's teaching in Romans 13.8-10, which concludes, "Love does no harm to its neighbor. Therefore love is the fulfillment of the law."

Paul's concern is that the Thessalonians' *hearts* might be established *blameless in holiness.* In 3.2 the same verb *(stērizō)* appears, which, as we observed previously, was used to speak of establishing that which was in danger of falling or moving in one way or another. Previously, Timothy was sent to the church "to establish" them in their faith so they would not fall. But the concern of the present verse is the last judgment, as we will see presently, and therefore this establishing refers to that future time when they will appear *in the presence of our God and Father* (cf. 1 John 2.28; 3.21; Phil. 1.20). Paul's desire is that their *hearts* may be established *blameless in holiness* in that eschatological moment (see Jas. 5.8). *Heart* in some

---

240. *Eis to* with the infinitive *stērixai* ("to establish") indicates either the result of the Lord's action of making them abound in love or the purpose of the prayer for their increase in love. In either case, the connection with the preceding is clear. BDF, §402 (2).

contexts refers to the inner life of a human being (see 2.4, 17 and comments), but elsewhere it designates the center of a person's life and moral decisions (Matt. 5.8; Acts 15.9; Heb. 10.22; and Rom. 2.5; Heb. 3.12; 2 Pet. 2.14).[241] Paul has this second sense in mind here, since his desire is that their *hearts* may be established *blameless in holiness.* The moral life of the believers is his primary concern, and the prayer he offers is that in the last judgment the Thessalonians might be found *blameless* (see 2.10 and comments). *Blameless* is a term that arises frequently as a description of the moral conduct of a person, especially from the perspective of the final evaluation of someone's life (for this reason it appears frequently in funeral epitaphs).[242] But the word also appears, as we might expect, in judicial contexts where the verdict of the accused is pronounced (Plato, *Leges* 11.945D). The hope of the founders of the church is that in the final assize the Thessalonians will not be found guilty in any way (cf. Phil. 1.10; 2.15).

The norm by which God would judge their *hearts* is *holiness. Holiness (hagiōsynē),* which is the condition and not the process of sanctification,[243] was one of the author's chief concerns for this congregation (4.3, 4, 7; 5.23; 2 Thess. 2.13). This is the state of being consecrated or separated to God and, as a result of this relationship, being separated from sin.[244] The process of sanctification began with their conversion (1.9), was the will of God for their lives in the present (4.3a; 2 Thess. 2.13), included the separation from the sinful practices that characterized their former life (4.3b), and becomes a reality in their lives through the activity of God (5.23).

At the end of the prayer, Paul refers to the context of the final evaluation. First, it will take place *in the presence of our God and Father* (see 3.11). Paul previously made known the apostolic company's prayers before God (1.3; 3.9), but he also anticipates that eschatological moment when they shall rejoice "in the presence of our Lord Jesus" (2.19). But the same expression also appears in judicial contexts that are similar to this verse (Matt. 27.11; and 25.32; Luke 21.36; 2 Cor. 5.10). Their *God and Father* is, at the same time, their judge (cf. 4.6; 1 Pet. 1.17). The time when they will appear before the presence of God is *when our Lord Jesus comes* (see 2.19 and comments; 4.15; 5.23; 2 Thess. 2.1, 8). This divine and royal event will take place at the final moment of history as we know it (1 Cor. 15.23-24) and will usher in a time of terrible judgment for those who do not obey the gospel (2 Thess. 1.5-9; 2.1-12). But the destiny of the Christians will be

241. BAGD, 404.

242. Plutarch, *Sulla* 35.5; Xenophon, *Cyropaedia* 7.3.10; Luke 1.6; Phil. 2.15; 3.6; Heb. 8.7; and see 1 Thess. 5.23. BAGD, 45; MM, 668; *New Docs,* 4.141; *TDNT,* 4.572.

243. Milligan, *St. Paul's Epistles to the Thessalonians,* 44. Only here and in Rom. 1.4 and 2 Cor. 7.1.

244. *TDNT,* 1.114-15; BAGD, 10.

different since they are not objects of the wrath of God, a promise repeated more than once in these letters (1 Thess. 5.9; 2 Thess. 1.10; 2.13-14). The prayer and confidence of the founders of the church is that the brothers and sisters in Thessalonica will be firmly established in that eschatological moment, with a life that is truly blameless in holiness before the presence of God.

The coming of the Lord Jesus, according to this verse, will be *with all his holy ones.* Are these deceased Christians (4.16) or celestial angelic beings (see 2 Thess. 1.10 and comments)? *Holy ones* or "saints" is a common way in which Christians are described in the NT (1 Cor. 1.2; 2 Cor. 1.1; Eph. 1.1; Phil. 1.1), and so it appears possible that deceased Christians are those who will accompany Jesus in his coming. However, the author alludes to Zechariah 14.5 at this point: "Then the LORD my God will come, and all the holy ones with him." While in the OT "holy ones" may refer to human beings (Lev. 21.7-8; Num. 16.5, 7), in Zechariah and other OT texts they are the celestial beings who accompany Yahweh (Deut. 33.2; Job 5.1; 15.15; Ps. 89.5, 7; Dan. 4.13; 8.13). Elsewhere in the NT the celestial beings, called either "angels" or "holy ones," will accompany the Lord in his coming (Matt. 13.41; Mark 8.38; 13.27; 2 Thess. 1.7; Jude 14-15; and cf. *1 Enoch* 1.9). 1 Thessalonians 3.13 reflects this hope. The Lord Jesus will come with power and glory, as a warrior on the day of the Lord (Zech. 14.1-9), and his *holy ones* will come with him. Here at the close of this section of the letter, Paul's prayer introduces one of the great themes of the second part of this letter, the coming of the Lord.[245] He will come with armies greater than those of Alexander III or the Romans. He is the coming King whom they await!

B. "You know what instructions we gave you" — The Life That Pleases God (4.1–5.22)

At this point Paul begins the second section of the body of the letter, which is oriented principally toward giving moral instruction to the church. Since the teaching the founders had handed over to this young congregation included the fundamentals of Christian moral teaching, Paul now exhorts the believers to progress in what they already know and put in practice what they were taught. But he also adds correctives and new teaching in accordance with the needs of the church. This sec-

---

245. Some mss. end the prayer with a final "Amen" (א, A, D, 81), while others omit it (א¹, B, D¹, F, G, Ψ). The manuscript evidence is not decisive in either direction. See Metzger, *Textual Commentary*, 563.

tion deals with the specific issues that were raised by the report from Timothy when he arrived at Corinth, such as sexual ethics (4.3-8) and labor (4.11-12). Moreover, this part of the letter responds to a number of questions the church appears to have put to Paul, such as their concern for fraternal love (4.9-10), the destiny of the dead in Christ (4.13-18), and the time of the day of the Lord (5.1-12). The second major section of the body of the letter concludes with a number of exhortations that center around their relationship with the emergent leadership in the church (5.12-13) and with other members of the congregation (5.14-22).

1. "We instructed you how to live in order to please God" — The Introduction (4.1-2)

The first verses of this section are an introduction both to the teaching on sexual ethics (4.3-8) and to the rest of the moral instruction of the letter. The principal verbs that begin this section are "to ask" (erōtaō) and "to exhort" (parakaleō; both in 4.1), and these are repeated further on in this major section (5.12; and 4.10; 5.11, 14). So, too, Paul reiterates the opening affirmation that the Thessalonians have, indeed, put into practice the apostolic teaching, at least in part (4.1, 10; 5.11). The exhortation to progress in Christian virtue is signaled as a theme in this opening paragraph (4.1), and is later taken up in the exhortation about fraternal love in the community (4.10). In the introduction they are reminded about the knowledge they already have concerning the commands of the Lord (4.2), and at other points in the exhortation they are again reminded of what they have learned (4.9; 5.1-2). The introduction of 4.1-2 is bound closely with the following section (4.3-8) and with the rest of the body of the letter.

1 The new section of exhortations and teaching begins with the words translated in the *NIV* as "finally" (loipon oun), which are included in the argument as a rhetorical marker to transition to a new theme (Phil. 3.1) and not, as in other contexts, to indicate that the author has reached the end of the discourse (cf. 2 Cor. 13.11; Phil. 4.8; 2 Thess. 3.1). The appeal Paul makes is, *Finally, brothers, we instructed you how to live in order to please God, as in fact you are doing. Now we ask you and urge you in the Lord Jesus to do this more and more.* Those addressed are called "brothers and sisters" (adelphoi) or those whose identity as Christians is formulated in terms of a kinship unit (see 1.4 and commentary). On first glance, the exhortation they receive as members of this family does not appear to be official and formal but rather familial and informal. The appeal begins with two verbs that appear frequently in the exhortations contained in personal letters of the era, translated in the *NIV* as *we ask you and urge* *you.*[1] The first of these verbs in other contexts means simply "to make a request" *(erōtōmen)*, but in exhortations the meaning is the much stronger "beseech" or "entreat" (Phil. 4.3; 1 Thess. 5.12; 2 Thess. 2.1; 2 John 5).[2] The second verb means "exhort" *(parakaloumen)* and appears in these letters where the authors strongly urge the believers to adopt some kind of conduct (5.14, in combination with *erōtaō* in 5.12; 2.12; 3.2, 7; 4.10; 2 Thess. 2.17; 3.12).[3] Bjerkelund has shown that Paul is following a common formula used to ask that a certain course of action be taken. This formula included: (1) the verb "exhort" *(parakalō)* or another synonym in the first person plural (here "beseech and exhort"); (2) the identification of the person or persons to whom the exhortation is addressed, placed in the vocative ("brothers and sisters"); (3) in official letters, a prepositional phrase is included ("in the Lord Jesus"); and (4) a request or command that appears as an infinitive or a clause that begins with "in order that" *(hina;* "to do this more and more").[4] Bjerkelund observes that the formula appears in personal letters between persons of similar status, but the inclusion of the prepositional phrase (number 3) is normally reserved for official documents in which the one in authority addresses those who are partially subject and whom the authority exhorts but does not command. Therefore, the *form* of the exhortation in 4.1 should not be classified as simply familiar or personal but rather diplomatic, while including personal and familial notes alongside another element that underscores Paul's apostolic authority. However, the authority behind the exhortations is not that of Paul himself but rather derived: *in the Lord Jesus* (cf. 2 Thess. 3.12; Rom. 14.14). This point is again highlighted in v. 2, "For you know what instructions we gave you by the authority of the Lord Jesus." Over and again in this and the following sections the divine authority of the Lord Jesus is put forward as that which gives weight to the apostolic exhortations (4.3, 5, 6, 7, 8 and commentaries). What follows is more than "good advice" or "friendly suggestions."

The exhortation proper is that they continue to progress in their moral development *(do this more and more)*. The exact same appeal ap-

---

1. See *New Docs*, 6.145-46. The verbs in 4.1 are those that normally appear in personal letters *(erōtaō* and *parakaleō)*. For example, in the *Oxyrhynchus Papyri* 744.6 (first century BC) we read, "I ask and exhort that you take care of the child," and in 294.28 (AD 22), "I ask and exhort you to send me an answer concerning what happened." For a collection of other examples see Carl J. Bjerkelund, *Parakalō* (Oslo: Universitetsforlaget, 1967), 35-39.

2. BAGD, 311-12; MM, 255.

3. See also Rom. 12.1; 15.30; 16.17; 1 Cor. 1.10; 4.16; 16.15; 2 Cor. 2.8; 6.1; 10.1; Eph. 4.1; Phil. 4.2; 1 Tim. 2.1; Phlm. 9-10; Heb. 13.19, 22; 1 Pet. 2.11; 5.1; Jude 3.

4. Bjerkelund, *Parakalō*, 109-11, 188-90. Cf. Rom. 12.1-2; 15.30-32; 1 Cor. 1.10; 4.16; 16.15-16; 2 Cor. 10.1-2; 1 Thess. 4.10b-12; 5.14.

pears in 4.10, but there with reference to their growth in love for each other. Paul used this verb previously in 3.12 *(perisseuēte)*, and here, as there, it means "to abound" or "overflow." The verb is followed by *mallon*, "to a greater degree," which highlights how dramatic their progress should be in living in such a way as to *please God.*[5] The way of life they have adopted is to give way to ever increasing excellence in their moral conduct. Paul recognizes and commends the Thessalonians for already living according to the moral teachings the founders had given them, *as in fact you are living.* The commendation for their good conduct surfaces at other points in these letters (4.10; 5.11; 2 Thess. 3.4). Such praise for someone's conduct was understood as another type of moral instruction that could be used alongside exhortation and other means of moral formation.[6] The commendation becomes an implicit exhortation. However, despite this praise of their conduct, the Thessalonians showed deficiencies in their moral life, as we will see presently.

The fact that the Thessalonians have already put into practice aspects of the Christian ethic and are now exhorted to progress in the same implies that they had already received the fundamentals of moral instruction. The exhortation *to do this more and more* is based on the premise, *we instructed you how to live in order to please God.* The verb *instructed* has to do with the Thessalonians' reception of the apostolic teaching *(parelabete).* It commonly appears in those contexts where an author wishes to speak about the reception of some authoritative and sacred tradition (see 2.13 and commentary; Rom. 6.17; 1 Cor. 11.23; 15.1, 3; Gal. 1.9, 12; Phil. 4.9; Col. 2.6-7; 4.17; 2 Thess. 3.6). They received from the apostles something more than classroom instruction that students could choose to ignore if they so desired (although *praxis* was expected of students of the philosophers). The message the Thessalonians had received was, in the first instance, the call of God to salvation (2.13; 2 Thess. 2.14), but it also included the divinely inspired moral teaching that was to be an authoritative guide for their conduct. The content of that sacred moral tradition was that it was necessary for them *(dei,* "it is necessary"; not translated in the *NIV) to walk and please God.* Frequently this verb appears where an author wants to highlight an obligation or duty, even that which is imposed by God (Matt. 18.33; Luke 2.49; 15.32; 18.1; Acts 5.29; Titus 1.11).[7] Such conduct was not optional but obligatory since the

---

5. BAGD, 489. See Phil. 1.12, 9; 3.4; and used pleonastically with verbs that contain the sense of "more" (Matt. 6.26; Luke 12.24; 1 Thess. 4.10).

6. Cicero, *Epistulae ad Familiares* 6.10b.4; Seneca, *Epistulae Morales* 1.1; 25.4. Seneca includes the *adhortatio* and the *laudatio* as types of moral exhortation (94.39).

7. See also Wis. 12.19; 16.28; Tob. 12.1. BAGD, 172; MM, 137. *Dei* is also used to refer to those events that must occur because of the divine will (Herodotus 8.53; Josephus,

source of the teaching was not simply human but divine (as implied by the verb "received" and the following verse). They received the authoritative teaching concerning how *to walk* (see 2.12; 4.12; 2 Thess. 3.6, 11) or conduct themselves in a way that would *please God* (see 2.4, 15 and comments; Rom. 8.8; 15.1-3; 1 Cor. 7.32-34; 10.33; Eph. 5.10; 2 Tim. 2.4). "Pleasing God" does not mean anything so mundane as "being pleasant" toward him but rather points to serving him in a way that makes his interests a person's primary ambition. For example, those who rendered civic service to the council and free citizens of a city could be said "to please" those people.[8] According to Xenophon, Socrates asked, "Or are you set on trying *to please* nobody, and *obeying* neither general nor other ruler?" (*Memorabilia* 2.2.11). A slave who renders true service will similarly "please" his master (Gal. 1.10). Since Christians are those who come to serve God as his slaves (1.9), the norms that govern their conduct are those that he establishes and not those that the society considers acceptable (4.5).

2   In ancient letters, occasionally an author would remind the recipient of things the person already knew, at times indicating that such things should be put into practice.[9] Reminders and repetition of what people had learned were considered essential for moral progress. In the same way, once more Paul reminds the Thessalonians of the teaching they had received: *For you know what instructions we gave you by the authority of the Lord Jesus.* Over and again he urges the Thessalonians to recall what they already knew (cf. 1.5; 2.1, 2, 5, 11; 3.3, 4; 5.2), and when his teaching was remembered, his hope was that the Thessalonians would not ignore it but would put it into practice. The orientation the author had given this congregation went beyond the fundamental teaching on the nature of God and the work of Christ to embrace the ethics that were to guide the Christian's conduct.[10] It was not assumed, however, that

---

Antiquitates 10.142 [10.8.3]; and Matt. 17.10; 24.6; 26.54; Mark 9.11; 13.7, 10; Luke 4.43; 21.9; John 3.14, 30; 9.4; 10.16; 20.9; Acts 1.16; 3.21; 4.12; Rom. 1.27; 1 Cor. 15.53; 2 Cor. 5.10; Rev. 1.1; 4.1; 22.6).

8. MM, 75.

9. For example, Cicero, *Epistulae ad Familiares* 1.4.3; Seneca, *Epistulae Morales* 13.15; Pliny, *Epistulae* 8.24; Pseudo-Diogenes 32; Dio Chrysostom 17.1-11. Dio Chrysostom remarks, "For instance, just as we see physicians and pilots repeating their orders time and again to those under their command, although they were heard the first time — but still they do so when they see them neglectful and unattentive — so too in life it is useful to speak about the same things repeatedly, when the majority know what is their duty, but nevertheless fail to do it" (17.2). See Stowers, *Letter Writing in Greco-Roman Antiquity*, 103-4; Malherbe, *Moral Exhortation: A Greco-Roman Sourcebook*, 125.

10. On the nature of the early Christian instruction of new believers, see David L. Balch, *Let Wives be Submissive* (Chico, Calif.: Scholars Press, 1981); Philip Carrington, *The*

they inherently knew what the right course of conduct should be. Paul would hardly agree with Dio Chrysostom, who said, "However, since I observe that it is not our ignorance of the difference between good and evil that hurts us, so much as it is our failure to heed the dictates of reason on these matters and to be true to our personal opinions, I consider it most salutary to remind men of this without ceasing, and to appeal to their reason to give heed and in their acts to observe what is right and proper" (17.2). In the following matter of Christian sexual ethics, the Thessalonians had rejected and not simply ignored reason or forgotten the exhortations the apostles had given them, and for that reason they are warned that "he who rejects this instruction does not reject man but God" (4.8).

The *instructions* they received were not mere guidelines that could be ignored but, more precisely, "commands" or "orders" (*parangelias*; Acts 5.28; 16.24; 1 Tim. 1.5, 18; and cf. the verb in 4.11; 2 Thess. 3.4, 6, 10, 12). As such, they should not be glibly put aside or ignored according to the whims of those in the church. When an ancient author wanted to speak of an authoritative command that should be obeyed, such as that of a military commander, a philosopher, or a deity, this is a term that was readily at hand.[11] Therefore, when the Thessalonians accepted the apostolic proclamation as the word of God (2.13), they also came under obligation to obey the moral commandments that accompanied it.

The authority behind the moral teaching was not that of the apostles themselves, as is clear from 4.8. Rather, Paul and his coworkers were only the messengers who had delivered the commands *by the authority of the Lord Jesus (dia tou kyriou Iēsou,* "through the Lord Jesus"). This may mean that the commandments they gave came through the revelation of the Lord Jesus (John 1.17; Gal. 1.12; cf. 1 Cor. 14.37) or that the source and foundation of their authority was the Lord Jesus (Rom. 15.30; 1 Cor. 1.10). In this context where the necessity of obedience is highlighted, the latter rather than the former sense is primarily in view. The Thessalonians had experienced a genuine conversion that became a dramatic theological and moral revolution (1.9-10). What they needed was to progress more and more in what already had begun in their lives (4.1, 10) and to submit

---

Primitive Christian Catechism (Cambridge: Cambridge University Press, 1940); James E. Crouch, *The Origin and Intention of the Colossian Haustafel* (Göttingen: Vandenhoeck & Ruprecht, 1972); Wayne A. Meeks, *The Origins of Christian Morality* (New Haven and London: Yale University Press, 1993); E. G. Selwyn, *The First Epistle of Peter* (Grand Rapids: Baker Book House, 1947).

11. BAGD, 613; MM, 480-481; *TLNT,* 3.9-11; *NIDNTT,* 1.340-41; *TDNT,* 5.761-65. See Diodorus Siculus 4.12.3; Polybius 6.27.1; Xenophon, *Hellenica* 2.1.4; Philo, *In Flaccum* 141; Josephus, *Antiquitates* 16.241 (16.8.3); Jdt. 7.1; 1 Macc. 5.58; 2 Macc. 5.25.

certain areas of their lives, such as their sexuality (4.3-8) and their habits concerning labor (4.11-12), to the lordship of Jesus.

2. "You should avoid sexual immorality" — Sanctification (4.3-8)

In this section of the letter Paul addresses the problem of sexual ethics in the Thessalonian church. Evidently, he and his fellows had instructed the new believers in the divine norms that should govern their sexuality (4.1-2, 6b), but certain members of the church had rejected their teaching (4.8). Most likely, Timothy had reported to Paul and Silas that certain members had yielded to their sexual passions in a way that was characteristic of those "who do not know God" (4.5). Since they had not separated themselves from "sexual immorality" (4.3), Paul calls them once again to sanctification, underlining repeatedly that this is the very will of God (4.3, 4, 7, 8). God will judge all who give themselves over to their passions (4.6), but he is also the one who gives the Thessalonians his Holy Spirit so that they might do God's will (4.8).

The apostle joins together their relationship with God, inaugurated at their conversion (1.9-10; cf. 4.5b, "the heathen, who do not know God"), with morality in a way that was unknown in the religions that dominated the landscape in Thessalonica, except in the Jewish synagogue. Far from prohibiting sexual immorality, the cults of Dionysus, Aphrodite, Osiris and Isis, the Cabirus, and Priapas promoted sexual license.[12] The Gentile members of the Thessalonian church would have found it difficult to understand how their conversion to the living God necessitated abandoning those pleasures that their previous religious alliances had approved or ignored. Moreover, the social norms of the day permitted those practices that the Christian ethic prohibited. For example, it was socially acceptable for young men to have sexual relationships before marriage. Cicero, who spent some time in Thessalonica during the mid-first century BC, argued in favor of this freedom for youths. He commented, "Let not pleasures always be forbidden. . . . let desire and pleasure triumph sometimes over reason," but only if these pleasures do not do damage to oneself or others. He went on to argue that after hearing the voice of pleasure and concupiscence, the empty desires of youth, the young person could give himself to the interests of both domestic and public life.[13]

In Greek society, a man who owned female slaves could use his "hu-

---

12. See the Introduction, pp. 35-36.
13. Cicero, *Pro Caelio* 18.42.

man property" to satisfy his sexual desires, while prostitutes were at the service of any man. Antipater of Thessalonica commented on the price of love with prostitutes, saying, "Homer said all things well, but best of all that Aphrodite is golden. For if you bring the cash, my friend, there is neither porter in your path nor dog chained at the door. But if you come otherwise, Cerberus himself is there."[14] Not only the single person but also the married man could avail himself of her services. A number of centuries earlier, Demosthenes expressed the social opinion regarding male sexuality that continued to prevail: "For this is what living with a woman as one's wife means — to have children by her and to introduce the sons to the members of the clan and of the deme, and to betroth the daughters to husbands as one's own. Mistresses we keep for the sake of pleasure, concubines for the daily care of our persons, but wives to bear us legitimate children and to be faithful guardians of our households."[15] At times a voice arose against sexual relationships outside of marriage, but in such cases the concern was only that illegitimate children might be sired in such liaisons who would then be the cause of shame.[16] Plutarch's advice was that a wife should not be angry if her husband sought sexual pleasure with another woman.[17]

The practice that was roundly and universally condemned was having sexual relations with the wife of another man. However, violations of even this social norm were well known. Dio Chrysostom commented, "Yes, the seduction of women — especially, one might almost say, of the freeborn and virgins — has been found easy and no task for a man who pursues that kind of game with money; and even against the highly respected wives and daughters of men really respected, the libertine who attacks with the device of Zeus and brings gold in his hands will never fail."[18] On the other hand, the married woman should never have sexual relations with anyone but her husband. In marital contracts the husband was prohibited from taking another wife, while the restrictions for the wife were more limiting. For example, one such contract stipulated, "Isidora will neither sleep apart nor be absent for a day from Dionysios' house without his knowledge nor will she ruin his house nor live [or, 'have sexual intercourse'] with another man or if she is convicted of do-

---

14. Antipater of Thessalonica, n. 6, in Gow and Page, *The Greek Anthology*, 1.16-17. Aphrodite was the patroness of prostitutes, while Cerberus was the multi-headed "dog of hades" who guarded the way to the Underworld.

15. Demosthenes 59.122.

16. Plutarch, *Moralia* 144B. See also Susan Treggiari, *Roman Marriage* (Oxford: Clarendon Press, 1991), 199-210.

17. Plutarch, *Moralia* 140B; Treggiari, *Roman Marriage*, 201.

18. Dio Chrysostom 7.150.

ing any such thing she will be deprived of her dowry, etc."[19] This kind of disparate norm prevailed in Greek as well as Roman society.[20] However, there were women who ran the risk. In one of his epigrams, Philodemus records the comments of a woman who engaged in adultery, "I have defrauded my husband and came at midnight, wet from the torrential rain. Should we only sit, doing nothing, not talking and not sleeping as lovers should sleep?"[21] It appears, however, that Paul addresses the men in this section instead of the women as those in the Thessalonian church who were resisting the apostolic teaching on sexuality (see commentary). In the context of the sexual mores of the era, these new believers found it difficult to comprehend and practice the strict sexual ethic the apostles taught.

3 Paul explains (*gar*, "for," is explanatory here) one aspect of the "instructions" or commands he and his coworkers had given this church (4.2), that being: *It is God's will that you should be sanctified*. This is just one dimension of God's will (cf. 5.18), a point that is highlighted in the Greek by the absence of the definite article before the word *will*.[22] Unlike Greek ethics, Jewish and Christian ethics were not organized around a collection of ideals or virtues but rather centered on "the will of God."[23] Here, as at a number of points in the NT, the "will of God" is God's moral plan for human beings that should be both known and put into practice (Matt. 7.21; 12.50; 21.31; Mark 3.35; Luke 12.47; John 7.17; 9.31; Acts 13.22; Rom. 12.1-2; Eph. 6.6; Heb. 10.36; 13.21; 1 John 2.17). Doing this *will* is the counterpoint to being carried along by "passionate lust like the heathen" (4.5; 1 John 2.17), while positively it constitutes that which pleases God (4.1; Col. 1.9-10). The moral will of God for the church was laid out in the apostolic teaching the Thessalonians had received (4.1-2, 6b).

The aspect of God's will that the apostle brings into view is *that you should be sanctified*,[24] a call that is at the very heart of God's plan for his people (1 Pet. 1.15-16; Lev. 19.2). The sanctification of the Thessalonian believers is his principal concern (vv. 3, 4, 7), and here this sanctification is defined as purity in sexual relationships as opposed to being "impure"

19. *New Docs*, 6.4.

20. See Treggiari, *Roman Marriage*, 199-201, 299-309; and O. Larry Yarbrough, *Not like the Gentiles: Marriage Rules in the Letters of Paul* (Atlanta: Scholars Press, 1985); Aline Rousselle, *Porneia: On Desire and the Body in Antiquity* (Oxford: Blackwell, 1983); Albert A. Bell Jr., *Exploring the New Testament World* (Nashville: Thomas Nelson, 1998), 227-38.

21. Philodemus, n. 7, in Gow and Page, *The Greek Anthology*, 1.354-55.

22. BDF, §252. Contra Bruce, *1 and 2 Thessalonians*, 81, who argues that the "will of God" can be fully summarized as "sanctification" and that the anarthrous noun merely shows that it is a predicate.

23. T. W. Manson, *Ethics and the Gospel* (London: SCM Press, 1960), 18.

24. The text reads, "For this is the will of God, your sanctification, etc."

(v. 7). The term used to reflect on their "sanctification" is not the same as in 3.13, which focuses on the state rather than the process of sanctification (see comments). Here "sanctification" (*hagiasmos*; cf. vv. 4, 7; Rom. 6.19, 22; 1 Cor. 1.30; 2 Thess. 2.13; 1 Tim. 2.15; Heb. 12.14; 1 Pet. 1.2) means the process of sanctification[25] that began in their conversion and that is made a living reality in their lives through the power of the Holy Spirit (v. 8; 2 Thess. 2.13; 1 Pet. 1.2).

Although the sanctification of their entire lives progresses only through divine agency (5.23), the Thessalonians have the responsibility of aligning their conduct with the will of God. In the present situation this means *that you should avoid sexual immorality.* The language is traditional Jewish (cf. *T. Levi* 9.9-10; Tob. 4.12), but it made its way into the teaching of the church through the decree of the Jerusalem council (Acts 15.20, 29) that Paul and Silas had delivered to Antioch and other churches of the Gentiles (Acts 15.22, 40; 16.4; 21.25). It is most likely that Paul had included the decree as part of the moral instruction delivered to the new believers in Thessalonica (4.1-2, 6b). The command to *avoid,* or "abstain" from, certain practices was commonly sounded both in Jewish and Greek moral teaching,[26] and it also appears in the early church's moral code to introduce those practices that believers were prohibited from doing (1 Thess. 5.22; 1 Pet. 2.11).[27] The Thessalonians should specifically abstain from *sexual immorality. Sexual immorality (porneias)* meant any kind of sexual relation outside of heterosexual marriage, whether it was fornication, adultery, homosexuality, incest, prostitution, or bestiality.[28] In certain contexts the term had a more restricted use and was distinguished from "adultery" (Philo, *De Vita Mosis* 1.300; Matt. 15.19; Mark 7.21), but elsewhere, as in v. 3b, it embraced all forms of *sexual immorality,* including adultery (Sir. 23.23; Hermas, *Mandates* 4.1.5; Matt. 5.32; 19.9). Paul does not call the church to partial moderation of their sexual impulses but to

---

25. *TDNT,* 1.113; BDF, §109.1; cf. BAGD, 9.

26. *Apechesthai;* of abstaining from sexual relations (Homer, *Iliad* 14.206, 305-6); from seductive clothing (Plutarch, *Moralia* 144E); from robbery (Josephus, *Bellum Judaicum* 2.142 [2.8.7]); from wine (2.313 [2.15.1]); from blasphemy (Josephus, *Contra Apionem* 1.164 [1.22]); from the tree of wisdom (Josephus, *Antiquitates* 1.20 [1.1.4]); from shedding blood (1.102 [1.3.8]); from doing evil (Philo, *Legum Allegoriae* 1.102); from all sins (Philo, *De Virtutibus* 163); and from improper conduct (Philo, *De Specialibus Legibus* 2.15).

27. See Selwyn, *The First Epistle of Peter,* 369-75; *TLNT,* 1.162-68; BAGD, 84-85; MM, 87-88.

28. Bruce Malina, "Does *Porneia* Mean Fornication?" *NovT* 14 (1972) 10-17, does not include "fornication" under the definition of *porneia.* Malina's conclusion is contested by Joseph Jensen, "Does *Porneia* Mean Fornication? A Critique of Bruce Malina," *NovT* 20 (1978) 161-84; and *TDNT,* 6.579-95; BAGD, 693; *NIDNTT,* 1.497-501.

abstain completely from all forms of *sexual immorality* (Eph. 5.3). This was God's will for them and what distinguished them from the people around them as those whom God had separated for himself.

4 This verse is the most problematic of this section. The *NIV* translates it, *that each of you should learn to control his own body in a way that is holy and honorable.* The *NIV* also suggests two alternative translations in a note, the first being that a man should "learn to live with his own wife" in sanctification and honor, and the other that a man should "learn to acquire a wife" in sanctification and honor. Is this teaching about how a man should live with or acquire a spouse or about how he should take control of his own sexual desires? The interpretive problem centers around the verb, which means either *to control* or "to acquire," and the noun, translated alternatively as *body* and "wife." This latter term may be translated in other contexts as "vessel" or "implement" *(skeuos),* such as any kind of pottery vessel, tools, baggage, or equipment, but is employed in v. 4 in a metaphorical sense. Whatever the correct interpretation of this noun and the verse as a whole, Paul puts forward his antidote to "sexual immorality (v. 3). This teaching is not directed at a select group within the church but rather is for all or *each of you* (2.11; 2 Thess. 1.3), although it appears that the author principally has in mind all the male members of the congregation, as we will see presently. Moreover, the following teaching is something they should know *(eidenai),* in the sense of learning how something is done and being able to do it (1 Tim. 3.5; Jas. 4.17; 2 Pet. 2.9).[29] The church's knowledge of this issue needs to be more than theoretical. The author's expectation is that the sexual ethic they prescribe will be put into practice *in a way that is holy and honorable.*

Does this verse say that the Thessalonians should exercise control over their *own bodies* or that, in order to avoid sexual immorality, the single men should acquire wives? Or is this a teaching about how married men are to live with their wives in sanctification and honor? The verb translated *to control (ktasthai)* in classical Greek ranged in meaning from being proficient in something, such as music or poetry, to exercising lordship over slaves.[30] The mastery one has over something is communicated by this word, making possible the translation *to control,* although we need to observe that there do not appear to be any exact parallels to the idea of "having control" over a person's passions.[31] On the other hand, the word may convey the sense of "to procure" or "to acquire" (i.e., "to get control"), whether the thing that is acquired is money, a salary, horses, books,

29. BAGD, 556.
30. Plato, *Leges* 829C; LSJ, 1001.
31. BAGD, 455; MM, 362.

understanding, the favor of others, or friends.[32] A few texts exist in which the verb means "to acquire" a wife (Ruth 4.10; Sir. 36.24; Xenophon, *Symposium* 2.10). Does the verb in our verse talk about an established state ("to hold, possess"), or is the emphasis on the process of getting something ("to acquire, obtain")? While it may clearly be used to speak about the state of having and holding (Isa. 26.13; Sir. 22.23; Luke 21.19), whenever it appears in the context of the marital relationship it conveys the latter sense of "to acquire."[33]

The noun translated *body* in the *NIV* (*skeuos*) was understood as any type of instrument that one could use to accomplish some work, including both furniture and implements. It could mean "vessel" or, metaphorically, the human body or the human person.[34] The term could, in rare contexts, refer even to the male sexual organ.[35] But the literature of the era also shows us that "vessel" could refer metaphorically to a man's wife. In 1 Peter 3.7 not only the husband but also the wife is a "vessel," while the woman is called "the weaker vessel."[36] 1 Peter exhorts the husband to "show honor" to his wife, a thought strikingly similar to the apostles' exhortation in 4.4, which promotes the relationship with the one's own "vessel" as defined by "sanctification and honor." Moreover, in a number of references in rabbinic literature the woman is referred to as a type of "vessel," at times with sexual connotations.[37] If it is objected that the Thessalonians could not have understood this opaque allusion to the woman, we should remember that the teaching that is presented in this paragraph is not the "first round" with the Thessalonians over this

32. LSJ, 1001; BAGD, 455; MM, 361-62. Josephus, *Bellum Judaicum* 2.285 (2.14.4); *Antiquitates* 1.284 (1.19.2); Plutarch, *Moralia* 189D; Herodian 2.6.5; Xenophon, *Memorabilia* 1.6.3; Matt. 10.9; Luke 18.12; Acts 1.18; 8.20; 22.28.

33. See the contours of the debate in *TDNT*, 7.365-67; Yarbrough, *Not like the Gentiles*, 68-72.

34. Matt. 12.29; Mark 3.27; 11.16; Luke 17.31; and "vessel," Luke 8.16; John 19.29; 2 Tim. 2.20. Paul is a "chosen instrument" (Acts 9.15); the body is a "jar of clay" (2 Cor. 4.7); the devil inhabits a person as "his own instrument" (*T. Naph.* 8.6); the body is the habitation of the Holy Spirit (Hermas, *Mandates* 5.1.2); and the person is an instrument of evil (Polybius 15.25.1) or a useless instrument (13.5.7). BAGD, 754.

35. J. Witton, "A Neglected Meaning for *Skeuos* in 1 Thessalonians 4.4," *NTS* 28 (1982) 142-43; so Wanamaker, *Commentary on 1 and 2 Thessalonians*, 152-53; Torleif Elgvin, "'To Master His Own Vessel': 1 Thess 4.4 in Light of New Qumran Evidence," *NTS* 43 (1997) 604-19. See 1 Sam. 21.5.

36. Plutarch, *Moralia* 138E, compares the man and woman with "vessels." However, Bruce, *1 and 2 Thessalonians*, 83, observes that nowhere is a man's wife called "his own vessel." But *T. Naph.* 8.6 does make mention of the body of another as "his own vessel," opening up the possibility that Bruce rejects.

37. SB, 3.632-33; Yarbrough, *Not like the Gentiles*, 72-73; cf. *TDNT*, 7.361-62. For example, *m. Ket.* 3.4-5; *b. Pes.* 112a-b; *b. Sanh.* 152a; and cf. Prov. 5.15-18.

issue but rather a reminder of what they had already learned (v. 2). Whatever the interpretation of the word, we can assume that the Thessalonians knew what Paul was talking about.

Despite these observations, the linguistic evidence in favor of one or another of these interpretations is, at best, ambiguous. Is it possible to find some other texts that might help illuminate or clarify the sense in the present verse? Some have observed that in 1 Corinthians 7.2 Paul presents what appears to be a teaching that is strikingly similar to 1 Thessalonians 4.3-4, "But since there is so much immorality (*porneias*, 'sexual immorality' as in 1 Thess. 4.3), each man should have his own (*heautou*, as in 1 Thess. 4.4) wife, and each woman her own husband" (cf. 1 Cor. 7.8-9). Yarbrough argues that the same exhortation appears at two points in Jewish literature. Tobit 4.12 exhorts, "Beware, my son, of every kind of fornication (*porneias*). First of all, marry a woman from among the descendants of your ancestors." In the same way, the *Testament of Levi* 9.9-10 urges, "Be on guard against the spirit of promiscuity (*porneias*). . . . Therefore take for yourself a wife while you are still young." These texts suggest that the traditional Jewish teaching, which then seems to be embraced by Paul, was that one way to avoid sexual immorality (*porneia*) was to marry. However, it is not certain that Paul promotes marriage as the antidote to sexual sin in 1 Corinthians 7.2. The verb "to have" found in that verse is never employed to convey the idea "to get a wife."[38] In 1 Corinthians 7, Paul argues that the context of sexual expression should be the marriage bond, and not that one should get married to avoid sexual immorality (see 1 Cor. 7.2-7). Whatever the Jewish teaching on this matter, we cannot say that Paul prescribed marriage to avoid this vice.

On the other hand, where Christian teaching concerning the problem of sexual immorality arises, the common call is to abstinence and self-control (Acts 15.20, 29; 21.25; 1 Cor. 6.12-20; Eph. 5.3; Col. 3.5). In a passage strikingly similar to 1 Thessalonians 4.4-5, Paul explains to Timothy, "If a man cleanses himself from the latter, he will be an instrument (*skeuos*) for noble (*timēn*, as in 1 Thess. 4.4b) purposes, made holy (*hagiasmenon*; cf. *hagiasmō* in 1 Thess. 4.4b)" (2 Tim. 2.21). The following verse, just like 1 Thessalonians 4.5, is a call to reject a life dominated by passions: "Flee the evil desires (*epithymias*, as in 1 Thess. 4.5a) of youth" (2 Tim. 2.22). Similarly, 1 Thessalonians 4.4 reminds the Thessalonians to exercise control over their own bodies and thus avoid "sexual immorality." While it may be that the call is to exercise control over the male sexual organ, the metaphorical meaning that would have been most readily

---

38. See Gordon Fee, *The First Epistle to the Corinthians* (Grand Rapids: Eerdmans, 1987), 278.

accessible was the more common Christian use of "vessel" as a way to allude to the body. The repetition of this teaching later in 2 Timothy 2.21-22 points strongly in this direction.

Paul makes very clear that the kind of control he has in mind is that which is in accord with the will of God: *in a way that is holy and honorable.* "Sanctification" (the same word is used here as in 4.3 and 7) should dominate every aspect of the Christian's character (5.23). "Sanctification" should define how believers exercise their sexuality, which means abstaining from all forms of "sexual immorality" (v. 3) and not being carried along "in passionate lust like the heathen, who do not know God" (v. 5). "Honor," on the other hand, is the respect and recognition a person receives from the community because of his or her position or achievements.[39] In the societies surrounding the Mediterranean, "honor" was a high cultural value; for that reason the moralists frequently persuaded their audiences by showing them which deeds would assure them of receiving "honor."[40] The expression "in honor" *(en timē; honorable* in the *NIV)* appears in Greek literature, where one may be said to be "in honor" or be recognized "in honor."[41] Christians were not to seek this honor from the members of the surrounding Gentile community but rather from the Christian community (Rom. 12.10) or from God (Rom. 2.7; 9.21 — with "vessel"; 1 Pet. 1.7; 2.7). The concern of this passage is how the "will of God" should govern the sexuality of believers; thus the "honor" that Paul reminds the Thessalonians about is that which they will receive from God himself. Christians should exercise control over their bodies as those who hope to receive "honor" from God.

5 Paul advises the Thessalonians to exercise control over their own bodies "in a way that is holy and honorable" instead of giving themselves over to "sexual immorality" as is the habit of their unbelieving neighbors: *Not in passionate lust like the heathen, who do not know God.* What the author has in mind when he advises against *passionate lust (en pathei epithymias)* is the lasciviousness that arises out of sexual desire. This is the erotic "passion" that Paul elsewhere warns against (Rom. 1.24; Col. 3.5) and is spoken

---

39. MM, 635, e.g., quotes a papyrus that tells of the provisions being made for the visit of a senator, a man who was "occupying a position of highest rank and honour," and another that, in recognition of public honors received, reads, "I acknowledge with great pleasure the honour which you do me." See *TDNT*, 8.169-180; *NIDNTT*, 2.48-51.

40. See David A. deSilva, *Despising Shame: Honor Discourse and Community Maintenance in the Epistle to the Hebrews* (Atlanta: Scholars Press, 1995), 1-144; D. D. Gilmore, ed., *Honor and Shame and the Unity of the Mediterranean* (Washington: American Anthropological Association, 1987); Jerome H. Neyrey, ed., *The Social World of Luke-Acts* (Peabody, Mass.: Hendrickson, 1991), 25-65.

41. Lucian, *De Mercede Conductis* 17; Homer, *Iliad* 9.319; Xenophon, *Anabasis* 2.5.38; Arrian, *Anabasis* 4.21.10; Dio Chrysostom 7.150; cf. Col. 2.23.

about in other literature of the era.[42] This passion is the fruit of "desire" (*epithymias*), a term that may be used to speak about neutral or positive desires (Luke 22.15; Phil. 1.23; 1 Thess. 2.17). Most frequently in the NT, however, the "desires" spoken of are those that are sinful (Mark 4.19; Rom. 7.7-8; Gal. 5.16-17; 1 Tim. 6.9; Titus 3.3; 1 Pet. 1.14; 2.11). At times these desires are identified as sexual, as here in v. 5 (Matt. 5.28; Rom. 1.24; 1 Pet. 4.3; and Plutarch, *Moralia* 525A-B; Josephus, *Antiquitates* 4.130 [4.6.6]). The sexual conduct of the believers in Thessalonica should not be governed by the burning passions that arise out of their sexual desire, *as the heathen are*. While *heathen (ethnē)* is a term that most commonly identifies those who are not Jews by birth, the Gentiles (Acts 11.18; 13.46; Rom. 11.11; Gal. 1.16; 3.14), here they are those people who are not Christians (1 Cor. 12.2; 1 Pet. 2.12; 4.3). As the new people of God, these who were converted out of idolatry (1.9) should demonstrate their new community identity in their lifestyle. The apostle calls the believers not to imitate the sexual conduct of their contemporaries. They had been converted from such practices not so many months previously (1 Cor. 5.1; Eph. 4.17; 1 Pet. 4.2-3).

The lifestyle of the *heathen* who were given over to sexual passions was evidence of the distance between them and God. Such people are here further described as those *who do not know God* (Jer. 10.25; Ps. 79.6; 1 Cor. 1.21; Gal. 4.8; 2 Thess. 1.8). According to Paul, ignorance of God, or the absence of a relationship with him, was understood as the prime cause of immorality among the Gentiles (Rom. 1.18-32; Eph. 4.17-18). The implication for the church is clear. Faith and Christian ethics are bound together in such a way that the person who knows God will not be driven by sexual passions but will rather live according to the will of God (cf. 1 Cor. 15.34). What determines the sexual conduct of the pagans is their desire to satisfy their sexual passions, but the guide to Christian sexuality is knowing God and longing to serve him (4.1).

6 Previously in vv. 3-5 Paul addressed the general problem of "sexual immorality," while in v. 6 he specifies the issue that motivated him to write this section, that being adultery between members of the Christian community in Thessalonica. As we saw, sexual excesses were commonly tolerated in Greek society, even those of married men. However, adultery with the wife of another man was roundly condemned. Musonius Rufus, a conservative Stoic of the time, said, "But of all sexual relations those involving adultery are most unlawful."[43] Musonius was

---

42. Josephus, *Antiquitates* 2.53 (2.4.5); *T. Joseph* 7.8. BAGD, 603; MM, 473; *TDNT*, 5.926-30; LSJ, 1285.

43. Musonius Rufus, frag. 12. Cited in Malherbe, *Moral Exhortation: A Greco-Roman Sourcebook*, 153.

so conservative that he criticized the common opinion of the day that, in his words, claimed, "unlike the adulterer who wrongs the husband of the woman he corrupts, the man who has relations with a Courtesan or a woman who has no husband wrongs no one, for he does not destroy anyone's hope of children."[44] In AD 18 Augustus established the Julian Law, which prohibited adultery, but its effectiveness in restraining the practice was questionable, especially in the provinces.[45] At best, the Augustan legislation turned a private practice into a public concern. In a city like Thessalonica adultery would have been viewed dimly among the general populace, and such activity within the church no doubt would have damaged the Christians' reputation severely. However, the apostle makes no appeal to the social conventions of the day to enforce Christian morality (cf. 1 Cor. 5.1), but rather explains how this sexual sin destroys community and will be severely judged by the Lord.

The apostle's exhortation is *that in this matter no one should wrong his brother or take advantage of him.* Some have suggested that Paul changes his theme at this point and addresses the problem of commercial exploitation of other members of the church (implied in the translation "defraud" in the *KJV* and *NASB*).[46] But the topic of this section is "sexual immorality," and the language that is used to censure this practice is appropriate to that subject and does not demand that we view the problem addressed as some kind of economic fraud. The first verb, "to wrong" *(hyperbainein),* could be used by an author to talk about "overstepping the bounds" and thus, as here, "to transgress" or "to break" laws or commandments. The word is frequently found in combination with the verb "to sin" and is almost its synonym.[47] Someone or some persons had overstepped the boundary set by the divine command and had transgressed against fellow Christians. This transgression is also condemned as an exploitation of another member of the church. The second verb, *take advantage (pleonektein),* meant "to exploit" another, whether the exploitation was political, economic, military, or, as in this case, sexual.[48] Some had exploited their fellow believers *in this matter (en tō pragmati),* which, in this context, is a euphemistic reference

---

44. Ibid.

45. See Treggiari, *Roman Marriage,* 277-98; Leo Ferrero Raditsa, "Augustus' Legislation concerning Marriage, Procreation, Love Affairs and Adultery," in *ANRW,* 2.13.

46. R. Beauvery, *"Pleonektein* in I Thess 4,3-8," *VD* 22 (1955) 78-85; and see *NIDNTT,* 3.1158.

47. Homer, *Iliad* 9.501; Plato, *Republic* 2.366A; Josephus, *Antiquitates* 8.318 (8.13.1); MM, 652; *TDNT,* 5.743-44; BAGD, 840; LSJ, 1850; *NIDNTT,* 3.583-84.

48. BAGD, 667; MM, 517; *NIDNTT,* 1.137-39; *TDNT,* 5.266-74; Dionysius of Halicarnassus 9.7.1; Dio Chrysostom 17.8; Plato, *Symposium* 182D; *Leges* 10.906C.

to sexual relationships.[49] In the intimate meetings held in the tight confines of the home or homes of fellow believers, Christians of both sexes were thrown together in a close, interpersonal setting that could easily have given rise to relationships that were outside the lines of morality. Such offenders went beyond the bounds and so sinned against both the Lord and the spouse of the person with whom they had an affair. Sexual sin was not simply about a sinful liaison between two people. Their relationship with God and the community was prejudiced.

The gravity of adultery as well as the consequences of this sin is highlighted in the following sentence: *The Lord will punish men for all such sins.* The *Lord* is the Lord Jesus[50] in his judicial capacity, who is here called an "avenger" *(ekdikos)* or one who chastises those who do evil, executing the judicial decision. The title is distinctly legal. Civic officials and others who punished those who violated the law were "avengers" (Rom. 13.4),[51] while God himself was known as the ultimate "Avenger" (Deut. 32.35; Ps. 94.1; Sir. 5.3; and cf. 2 Thess. 1.9).[52] The apostle reminds the sexual offender that it is not the officials of the city, nor the spouse of the one with whom he or she committed adultery, but rather the Lord himself who is the Avenger "in all these things" *(NRSV, peri pantōn toutōn,* without the word *sin* as in the *NIV)*, again speaking euphemistically of sexual transgression itself. These final words join the warning with the argument of the previous verses. The Lord is the one who will chastise those who commit adultery or any other type of "sexual immorality." Those who engage in sexual sin will not merely endure the "consequences of their actions," such as begetting children outside the bounds of marriage and inheritance, but will be subject to the judgment of the Lord (1 Cor. 10.1-13; 6.9-10). The issue is more than property and public shame. The Lord is the avenger "in all these things," whether or not the protagonists are members of the church! What many would view in our day as a strictly "personal" issue is understood by the apostle as a community issue that has eternal consequences.

This warning is not something new to the ears of the Thessalonians, since the founders of the church had included this solemn teaching on sexuality and judgment in the cycle of instruction which they had previously given these new believers. Once more Paul reminds them of this teaching, *as we have already told you and warned you.* While the term trans-

---

49. BAGD, 697; MM, 532.

50. Cf. 1.1, 3, 6, 8; 2.15, 19; 3.8, 11-13; 4.1-2, 15-17; 5.2, 9, 12, 23, 27-28; and see 2 Thess. 1.7-9.

51. Plutarch, *Moralia* 509F; Herodian 2.14.3; 7.4.5; *TDNT,* 2.444-45.

52. See also Appian, *Bella Civilia Romana* 2.85; Josephus, *Bellum Judaicum* 5.377 (5.9.4); BAGD, 238; MM, 193; *NIDNTT,* 3.97.

lated *we have already told you* meant "to announce beforehand" and could refer to prophetic speech (Acts 1.16; 1 Thess. 3.4), here it has to do simply with a warning they had previously given to the church (Gal. 5.21; 2 Cor. 13.2). No one in the congregation could claim that he or she was not given previous notice of the consequences of his or her actions. Paul, Silas, and Timothy had placed great stress on this teaching (cf. 2.12), as the following verb indicates. They had given the new believers a solemn warning that some had ignored to their own peril (Luke 16.28; 1 Tim. 5.21; 2 Tim. 2.14; 4.1).[53] The disobedience of these members of the church is all the more surprising in light of the clear, emphatic, and solemn teaching they had already received condemning "sexual immorality."

7   After laying out the negative consequence of divine judgment for sexual immorality, Paul reminds the Thessalonians of the positive motivation for eschewing adultery and all forms of sexual immorality: *For God did not call us to be impure, but to live a holy life*. The Thessalonians' calling is a primary topic that appears repeated in the Thessalonian correspondence. At the beginning of his treatise, Paul noted that the believers in Thessalonica were chosen by God (1.4), and they will be reminded that he had called them through the proclamation of the gospel (2 Thess. 2.13-14). They were chosen for salvation so that they might "share in the glory of our Lord Jesus Christ." In 1 Thessalonians 2.12 the apostle highlights the fact that the sovereign God's had called them "into his kingdom and glory," a call that embraced the gift of eternal life (1 Tim. 6.12). But the divine call to salvation and this glorious future hope were at the same time a call to sanctification (cf. 1 Pet. 1.15-16). In 2.12 Paul reminded the Thessalonians that they had been exhorted "to live lives worthy of God, who calls you into his kingdom and glory," while in 5.23-24 the God who called them is also the one who will "sanctify" the members of the church "through and through." Their sanctification was not separated from their election to salvation, and so in the second letter to the church the apostle spoke to the Thessalonians of how "God chose you to be saved through the sanctifying work of the Spirit" (2 Thess. 2.13). Paul's aim was that divine salvation might become a present, living reality in these believers through their moral sanctification. Their election and calling not only graced them with a secure eternal hope but also effected a moral transformation in their daily lives. Holiness in their sexual conduct was part of God's eternal plan, which was bracketed in the past by his eternal election and in the future by his eternal glory.

Paul joins with the Thessalonians, therefore, as he reminds them

---

53. BAGD, 186; MM, 152. In other contexts, the term could even be used of preaching the gospel (Acts 2.40; 8.25; 10.42; 18.5; 20.21, 24; 23.11; 28.23).

that *God did not call* us *to be impure.*[54] "Impurity" is the opposite of "sanctification" or "holiness" (Rom. 6.19) and may denote either ceremonial or moral impurity, depending on the context (2.3; Rom. 6.19; Eph. 4.19; Epictetus 2.8.12-13; 4.11.5). In this present verse, as in a number of other NT texts, sexual "impurity" is in mind (Rom. 1.24; 2 Cor. 12.21; Gal. 5.19; Eph. 5.3; Col. 3.5; and see *1 Enoch* 10.11; Plutarch, *De Othone* 2.2); it embraces all forms of "sexual immorality."[55] Sexual impurity should never characterize the conduct of those who have been called by God (Eph. 5.3) because they have been called *to live a holy life* (*hagiasmǭ*, as in 4.3-4; 2 Thess. 2.13).[56] This holiness is now the goal of their lives instead of the sexual "impurity" that had previously dominated their existence.[57] God is the one who sanctifies the Christian at conversion through the agency of the Holy Spirit (2 Thess. 2.13; 1 Cor. 1.30) and who continues the process of sanctification in all aspects of their lives until the coming of the Lord Jesus Christ (1 Thess. 5.23-24), and this also through the Holy Spirit (4.8). But those who are called must, at the same time, align their conduct with their holy calling. They are summoned by God to sexual purity, and they must respond. The believers not only receive the call to salvation from the wrath of God (5.9) but are also called to abandon sexual impurity and embrace holiness. Sanctification is at the same time both a divine work and a human obligation that can only be met through the power of the Holy Spirit (v. 8).

8 Throughout this section Paul has made every effort to underscore the fact that the teaching the Thessalonians had received concerning sexuality found its source in God himself and was therefore an expression of his will (4.3-4). The Thessalonians were called by God to obey his commandments (v. 7), and he is the one who will judge those who embrace sexual immorality (v. 6). As the proclamation of the gospel was divinely inspired as God's message (1.5; 2.13), so, too, was the moral teaching they received. The author introduces the conclusion of their argument with the emphatic *Therefore*[58] — in light of what has been laid out previously about the character of the moral teaching — *he who rejects this instruction does not reject man but God.* In the Greek text, the verb *rejects*

54. *Epi akatharsia,* where *epi* with the dative denotes the purpose or the object to which someone is, or is not, called (Gal. 5.13; Eph. 2.10; 2 Tim. 2.14).

55. BAGD, 28-29; *TDNT*, 3.427-29.

56. Sanctification is the *goal* of their calling (1 Cor. 7.14; Eph. 4.4) rather than the sphere in which they were called (2 Thess. 2.13).

57. On this reading, the difference between *epi* plus the dative *akatharsiǫ* ("to impurity") and *en* plus the dative *hagiasmǭ* ("to holiness") is purely stylistic.

58. *Toigaroun,* a compound and emphatic particle that presents the inference of an argument. In the NT, it is found only here and in Heb. 12.1. BAGD, 821; MM, 637.

does not have an object, and so our translators have supplied the words *this instruction*. But the emphasis in this verse is not placed upon *what* but rather *who* is rejected by these disobedient Christians. Truly, the apostolic teaching was rejected, but in the end what was at issue was their relationship to God. The person who puts him aside is here called "the rejecter" *(ho athetōn)*. There was either one person ("the rejecter") or possibly more than one ("whoever rejects")[59] who had embraced sexual immorality and is therefore advised that he or they "do not reject man but God" (an echo of Luke 10.16; cf. John 12.28; 1 Sam. 8.7; Isa. 21.2 LXX). They had rejected God by their disobedience, but he, on the other hand, is the one who *gives you his Holy Spirit!*

Someone or some members of the church had continued their pre-Christian sexual habits (4.5), and therefore the situation called for correction that was at once strong, firm, and public (5.27). The verb "reject" (used both as a substantive participle and the principal verb; *ho athetōn . . . athetei*) is used in biblical literature to speak of infidelity to and rejection of authority, whether the authority was human or divine (Isa. 24.16; 33.1; Jer. 12.1; and Judg. 9.23; 2 Kings 1.1; 18.7; 1 Chr. 5.25; Isa. 1.2; Ezek. 39.23).[60] When the apostle affirms that these people's rejection was not of *man*, the point may be simply that they have not rejected something human. But keeping in mind the personal nature of the rejection, the *man* referred to may be more specifically Paul himself, the leader of the apostolic team.[61] If this observation is correct, it would uncover someone or some people in the church who had questioned the apostle's authority, and therefore his teaching, in spite of the generally positive attitude this congregation displayed toward the apostolic team (3.6). Such people would have distinguished between the gospel proclamation, which they received as divine (2.13), and the moral teaching on sexuality, which they rejected as coming simply from a man. Those who had engaged in this selective acceptance and rejection of certain points of Christian teaching are reminded that they had not rejected a man but God, and the consequence of their action was fearful (v. 6).

At the end of this section, God is identified as the one *who gives you*[62]

---

59. The participle with the article may point to an individual, or the use may be generic (cf. Eph. 4.28). BDF, §413.1.

60. *TLNT*, 1.39-40; BAGD, 21; MM, 12. It is used with reference to the rejection of divine revelation (Mark 7.9; Luke 7.30) or of the grace of God (Gal. 2.21), but also of infidelity (1 Tim. 5.12; Mark 6.26).

61. So Marshall, *1 and 2 Thessalonians*, 113; Wanamaker, *Commentary on 1 and 2 Thessalonians*, 158; Schmithals, *Paul and the Gnostics*, 157.

62. Some Greek mss. read "us" instead of "you" (A, 6, 365, 1505, 1739, 1881), but the textual evidence favors the reading used in the *NIV*.

his Holy Spirit. The promise of the OT was that God would enter into a new covenant with his people and that as part of this new alliance he would put his Spirit in their hearts so that they could walk in his statutes (Ezek. 36.27; 37.6, 14), a promise that has now been fulfilled. Sanctification, which includes the conquest of passions that are motivated by sexual desire (4.5) and the embrace of conduct that conforms to the will of God (4.3), becomes a reality in believers' lives only through the agency of the Holy Spirit (cf. Rom. 8.4; Gal. 5.16; 1 John 3.24; cf. 1 Thess. 5.23). For this reason, the presence of the Holy Spirit in the life of a believer is antithetical to a life given over to sexual immorality (1 Cor. 6.15-20). The emphasis in the Greek text is on the character of the Spirit as holy *(to pneuma autou to hagion)*, and as such he is understood not simply as the one who motivates but also as the one who makes possible their sanctification (cf. the other motivations of "the will of God" and judgment in vv. 3 and 6). God, who is known here as "the one who gives" *(ton [kai] didonta)*[63] in contrast to "the one who rejects" at the head of this verse, supplies his Holy Spirit to his people as a sign of his acceptance of them (Acts 11.17; 15.8; Rom. 8.9; 1 Cor. 1.22; and 1 John 3.24; 4.13). The Christian ethic has its foundation in God, who not only makes his will known but whose presence is powerful in their lives through the Holy Spirit. Therefore, disobedience to the divine imperative was a negation of the indicative of their relationship with God. They had rejected him in order to pursue their sexual passions.

The message of sexual purity was a "hard sell" in Thessalonica, and, clearly, the first round of teaching on this matter was not sufficient for some members of the church. The language of this passage could not be weightier or more emphatic. Though Paul employs euphemisms in describing sexual sin, he speaks with great plainness about what God expects and the consequences of disobedience. But the passage is also filled with positive words about God's will and calling, as well as his empowerment through the Holy Spirit. From Paul's perspective Christians *must* and *can* lead a life that conforms to God's and not society's norms. The present passage speaks loudly and directly to the church of our day, which is still working through the implications of the "sexual revolution." In the contemporary perspective, sexual license is viewed as "natural," and the only concern is that sex be "safe." The Christian ethic challenges this contemporary lack of moral norms, which, unfortunately, has

63. The present participle means simply that God is the source of the Spirit as the "one who gives" and should not be pressed to mean that God constantly supplies them with the Holy Spirit (cf. Gal. 3.5; Phil. 1.19). Some mss. substitute an aorist participle (A, Ψ, 0278, 33, 1739, 1881).

infiltrated the church. The situation of the Thessalonians was similar to ours, and the apostolic response to them and to us is the same.

3. "Now about . . ." — Responses to Questions (4.9–5.11)

Verse 9 begins with the words "now about" *(peri de)*, which possibly indicate that Paul begins to respond to a letter (or, less likely, an oral communication) that Timothy had brought from the Thessalonian church. The same words appear in the introduction to the section on the day of the Lord (5.1) and, without the preposition *(peri)*, at the head of the teaching on the destiny of those who were deceased (4.13). In 1 Corinthians 7.1 the same expression appears where Paul begins to respond to a series of questions the Corinthians had put to him in a letter (see also 1 Cor. 7.25; 8.1; 12.1; 16.1, 12). Most likely, in 1 Thessalonians Paul responds similarly to queries sent to him by the church. When we consider how valuable messengers were during this era, we can understand that the Thessalonians would have wanted to take advantage of the forthcoming trip of Timothy back to Paul and Silas by sending a letter with him. In a letter to Atticus, Cicero once commented that he did not have any news to send; however, "I cannot refrain from entrusting letters to folk who are bound for Rome, especially when they are members of my household."[64] He could not let a good messenger go to waste! The issues that concerned the Thessalonians and that called for clarification were fraternal love (4.9-10), the destiny of the dead in the Lord (4.13-18), and the time of the day of the Lord (5.1-11). After addressing the issue of fraternal love among the members of the church, the apostle widens the discussion by adding instruction concerning the Christians' relationship with the wider community in which they lived (4.11-12; cf. 3.12; 2 Pet. 1.7).

a. Fraternal "love" (4.9-12)

9 The first question Paul addresses is about fraternal love *(philadelphia)*. Over and again in these epistles, the apostle commends the members of this congregation for their mutual love and exhorts the believers to an ever increasing love for one another (1.3 and commentary; 3.6, 12; 5.8, 13; 2 Thess. 1.3; 3.5). Since love was a characteristic virtue of this church (3.6) that the Thessalonians had managed to extend even beyond the confines of the city to Christians in other locations (4.10), it comes as a surprise to discover that questions arose about fraternal love. Although there was clear evidence of love among them, however, apparently cer-

---

64. Cicero, *Epistulae ad Atticum* 8.14.1.

tain tensions existed within the Christian community. As observed in the previous section (4.3-8), someone or some members of the church had engaged in sexual immorality and had wronged and taken advantage of fellow believers (v. 6). Moreover, questions had arisen about the emerging leadership in the church (5.12-13), and some members of the church had eschewed work and were acting in a disorderly manner (4.11-12; 5.14a). Other believers were, frankly, difficult to help (5.14b). There were questions in this church regarding the proper place of prophecy in the assembly (5.19-20) that could have been another source of tension among them. While there is no evidence of grave division among the members of this church, as is the case with the Corinthians, it appears that the Thessalonians were properly aware of their own failings in the area of fraternal love.

The Thessalonians were subject to social rejection due to their new faith (2.14), while Christian conversion generally brought instability to the traditional family unit (cf. Matt. 10.21; Mark 13.12; Luke 21.16), realities that highlight the importance of the believers' mutual love as members of the same kinship group. Since the family (the "household") was the fundamental social unit, privation of acceptance and status within it would have brought grave consequences to the individual. The church assumed the function of a family, while the place of meeting, the house, served to reinforce the reality of Christians becoming members of the same brotherhood and sisterhood (Rom. 16.5; 1 Cor. 16.19; Col. 4.15; Phlm. 2).[65] Moreover, within the Christian community itself the question of fraternal love was of paramount importance since the church was open to people of all social classes and any ethnic background. Both the free and the slave were welcome, while Greeks, Romans, Macedonians, Jews, and barbarians gathered together to share the same cup in the worship of their one Lord. Men and women had equal status, as did citizens and foreigners in this community where common social boundaries were crossed as a fruit of their common salvation (Gal. 3.23; Rom. 1.16-17; Col. 3.11). In such a community, it would not be surprising for questions to surface about the meaning of "fraternal love."

The apostle's response to the Thessalonians' query was, *Now about brotherly love we do not need to write to you, for you yourselves have been taught by God to love each other. Brotherly love (philadelphia)* normally referred to the love members of a family held for each other and would not normally be used to describe the love between members of different fam-

---

65. See Meeks, *First Urban Christians*, 75-77; Carolyn Osiek and David L. Balch, *Families in the New Testament World: Households and House Churches* (Louisville: Westminster/John Knox, 1997), 91ff.

ilies.[66] Ancient authors who discoursed on fraternal love emphasized the collaboration, solidarity, and harmony or concord that existed between siblings, while recognizing that these relationships were not always what they should be.[67] Siblings should be best friends, and, as Plutarch said, "Most friendships are in reality shadows and imitations and images of that first friendship which Nature implanted in children toward parents and in brothers toward brothers," a thought that is echoed in Hierocles as well.[68] This fraternal love is a paradigm for the relationship between Christians who have become brothers and sisters in the community of faith (they are called "brothers and sisters" nineteen times in 1 Thessalonians alone).[69] In the NT the term "fraternal love," while not appearing frequently, describes the relationship between those who are brothers and sisters due to their common faith in Christ (Rom. 12.10; Heb. 13.1; 1 Pet. 1.22; 2 Pet. 1.7; cf. Matt. 23.8; Mark 3.32-35) and is understood as the fruit of the new birth (1 Pet. 1.22; 1 John 4.17). Epictetus had taught that all humans were brothers and sisters and, for that reason, worthy objects of love,[70] but there is no hint of a "universal brotherhood/sisterhood" in the apostle's thinking.

With regard to this fraternal love, Paul affirms that *we do not need to write to you* (cf. 5.1-2; 2 Cor. 9.1).[71] The apostle had already reminded the church of some matters they had previously learned through the apostolic teaching (3.3-4; 4.2; cf. 2 Thess. 2.6; 3.7). The stress here is not on the

---

66. 4 Macc. 13.23, 26; 14.1; Philo, *De Legatione ad Gaium* 87; Josephus, *Antiquitates* 4.26 (4.2.4); Plutarch, *De Fraterno Amore*. The use in 2 Macc. 15.14 is similar to that in the NT, "This is a man who loves the family of Israel and prays much for the people and the holy city — Jeremiah, the prophet of God."

67. Plutarch, *De Fraterno Amore* 478E-F, 479D, 482E-F; 2 Macc. 13.19–14.1; Hierocles, *On Duties* 4.27.20.

68. Plutarch, *De Fraterno Amore* 479D; Hierocles, *On Duties* 4.27.20. Both argue that it is absurd to form friendships with others and not with those of one's own family.

69. So, too, the Israelites could use fraternal language to speak of fellow Israelites (Deut. 15.2; Hos. 1.2). *NIDNTT*, 1.255.

70. Helmut Koester, *Introduction to the New Testament: History, Culture and Religion of the Hellenistic Age* (2 vols.; Philadelphia: Fortress Press, 1982), 1.354.

71. Wanamaker, *Commentary on 1 and 2 Thessalonians*, 159, observes that this is an example of the rhetorical technique called paralipsis *(praeteritio)*, which is employed when a orator wishes to touch on a point but pretends to pass over it (see BDF, §495.1). For example, in his letter to Maximus, Pliny says, "Pliny to his own Maximus, greeting. I know you need no telling, but my love for you prompts me to remind you to keep in mind and put into practice what you know already, or else it would be better for you to remain ignorant" (8.24). Less convincing is the position of Johanson, *To All the Brethren*, 114-15, who argues that this is not a typical example of this technique. The affirmation that *we do not need to write to you* is calculated rather to avoid the impression that the apostles were censuring the church when they exhorted them, "Yet we urge you, brothers, to do so more and more."

apostle's agency, although certainly the Thessalonians learned something of this theme through the apostolic instruction, but rather on God's instruction of the church: *for you yourselves have been taught by God to love each other.* The statement echoes Isaiah 54.13, "All your sons will be taught by the LORD," which is taken up in the teaching of Jesus recorded in John 6.45 (cf. Pss. 25.5; 71.17; 143.10; Isa. 2.3; Jer. 31.33-34; Mic. 4.2; *Pss. Sol.* 17.32; and 1 John 2.27). The verb itself is not found elsewhere in biblical literature *(theodidaktoi).*

Malherbe suggests that the apostles contrast the divine teaching on love that the Thessalonians had received with the Epicurean ideal of being self-taught *(autodidaktos)* by developing the understanding that lies inherently within each person.[72] But there is no evidence in the immediate context that Paul is in any way engaging in an anti-Epicurean polemic (although a refutation of Epicurean teaching may well stand behind the teaching about prophecy in 5.19-22). But even Malherbe is aware that it might be "a bit too much to speculate that Paul has Epicurus or Epicureans in mind."

In any case, the apostle wanted to underscore the fact that the fraternal love they had was the result of divine teaching on this matter, although he does not specify how this teaching was mediated to them. He may have in mind the teaching the church had received through the activity of the indwelling Holy Spirit who produced the fruit of love (Rom. 5.5; Gal. 5.22), or the instruction may have come via the example of the love of God in the cross of Christ that became the paradigm for Christian love (John 3.16; Rom. 5.8; Eph. 5.1-2). But the command *to love one another* was a hallmark of Jesus' teaching to the disciples as he called them to imitate the type of love he demonstrated toward them (John 13.34-35; 15.12, 17; cf. Lev. 19.18).[73] The teaching was picked up and repeated frequently by the apostles (Rom. 12.10; Gal. 6.2; 1 Pet. 1.22; 1 John 3.11, 23; 4.7, 11; 2 John 5). This message would have been a piece of the apostolic instruction that this church received and that had a divine source (4.1-2; cf. 2.13). For that reason, Paul could say, *for you yourselves have been taught by God to love each other.* They already had in hand the teaching they needed.

10 The second reason[74] why the believers in Thessalonica do not need further instruction about fraternal love is that they already demonstrated clear evidences not only of loving one another but also of extending their love to other Christians who lived outside the confines of Thes-

---

72. Malherbe, "Exhortation in First Thessalonians," 253-54.

73. Is this an echo of Jesus' teaching independent of the Johannine tradition?

74. The words *kai gar,* translated in the *NIV* as "and in fact," introduce the second reason for saying "we do not need to write to you" (v. 9). Cf. *gar* in v. 9b.

salonica: *And in fact, you do love all the brothers throughout Macedonia*. The main clause of sentence could be rendered, "you do *(poieite)* the same for all the brothers and sisters throughout Macedonia." The author implies that what they *do* for the other believers in Macedonia is an extension of their love to them (v. 9; cf. the same expression in Gal. 2.10). As they did for one another, so they did for believers throughout the province. How was this love demonstrated? Possibly the thought is that the Thessalonians showed hospitality to believers from other parts of Macedonia who traveled through the city (Rom. 16.1-2), or perhaps they gave economic support to the Christian mission (Phil. 4.14-16). On the other hand, they may have offered financial aid to those Christians who were in need (2 Cor. 8.1-5), or perhaps the manner they expressed this love was a combination of these three.[75] But the extension of love to other believers throughout Macedonia is the point the apostle wishes to make, and so the offer of hospitality to those passing through is the least likely suggestion.

Moreover, the Thessalonians' support of the mission is not the thought since the object of this love is *all the brothers throughout Macedonia* and not only those who participate in the mission. Most likely, Paul is reflecting on the way the Thessalonian church lent economic aid to needy believers in other parts of the province. He notes elsewhere that the Macedonian Christians were known for their poverty (2 Cor. 8.1-2); yet despite this, they gave! In fact, the way the author speaks about "doing this" is similar to how he describes giving economic aid for the saints in Jerusalem (2 Cor. 8.8, 10-11, 24, in light of the context of 2 Cor. 8–9; cf. 1 John 3.17-18).

What is more, the following verse presents the counterpoint to this note about the generosity of love, that one should work for one's own support and should not position oneself as a dependent client before rich patrons, whether they be inside or outside the congregation (see v. 11 and comments). In the same way, in 2 Thessalonians 3 praise for the generous is counterbalanced by the exhortation to others about their obligation to work for their food (2 Thess. 3.6-15, especially vv. 10, 13). Therefore, although we may not conclude that the expression of love was limited to economic aid (cf. Rom. 13.10; 14.15; 1 Thess. 1.3), this appears to be the prominent aspect of showing love that is addressed in this verse. This type of aid would include the distribution of food as well (2 Thess. 3.10).[76] The

---

75. Wanamaker, *Commentary on 1 and 2 Thessalonians,* 161, mentions hospitality; Best, *First and Second Epistles to the Thessalonians,* 173, points to economic aid to propagate the gospel and hospitality; Marshall, *1 and 2 Thessalonians,* 115-16 opts for both the proposals of Best and adds aid for those in need.

76. See Susan E. Alcock, *Graecia Capta* (Cambridge: Cambridge University Press, 1993), 113-14, 116.

church in Thessalonica became a benefactor to the brothers and sisters who belonged to other churches throughout the province of Macedonia.[77]

The extension of the Thessalonians' love was notable since its objects were *all* the brothers and sisters (2 Thess. 1.3; 1 Thess. 5.14, 26-27), however low on the social scale they might be, throughout the whole (*holē*)[78] of Macedonia. While Paul employs hyperbole to make his point, the extensiveness of the Thessalonians' concerns for believers elsewhere is impressive. The churches in Philippi and Berea would have been included, as well as other congregations established by the missionary efforts of the Thessalonians (1.8) and the apostolic foundations not mentioned in the narrative in Acts. This generosity was evidence of the emerging solidarity between congregations in distinct localities.[79] A major city would have its own region or *chōra* (Latin *territorium*; cf. Acts 13.49), which extended approximately 110 miles (180 km.), sometimes larger and sometimes smaller, and which served the economic interests of the city by providing the grain and livestock the city consumed.[80] But the city also served the surrounding region by providing a market to sell its goods and generate capital. This church, however, did not see other congregations as sources for its own benefit (as a consumer) but rather reversed the flow by extending love in the form of economic benefit to others in its hinterland and even beyond to the whole of the province.

As we saw previously, Thessalonica was the capital of the province of Macedonia and served as the geographic, economic, and political hub

---

77. On the economic condition of this church, see pp. 25-31. We need not conclude that the other congregations became clients of the Thessalonian church (a relationship viewed dimly by the apostles in 4.11-12 and 2 Thess. 3.6-15). In Greek vocabulary, the relationship between patron and client (Latin *patroni* and *clientes*) was expressed by the term *philoi*, "friends" (John 19.21). But the paradigm for the relationship between Christians is the family since all are "brothers and sisters" (*adelphoi*). See Herman, *Ritualized Friendship and the Greek City*, 38; Meeks, *The Origins of Christian Morality*, 40; and on benefaction, Winter, *Seek the Welfare of the City*; Danker, *Benefactor*; Wallace-Hadrill, *Patronage in Ancient Society*; Richard P. Saller, *Personal Patronage under the Early Empire* (Cambridge: Cambridge University Press, 1982).

78. Note the use of this term with geographic units — Matt. 14.35; Mark 6.55; Acts 9.31; 10.37; 13.49; 19.27; Rom. 1.8; 2 Cor. 1.1; Rev. 3.10.

79. Wanamaker, *Commentary on 1 and 2 Thessalonians*, 161, points out how Paul sought to establish relationships at the regional level between congregations (1 Cor. 16.1, 19; 2 Cor. 1.1; Gal. 1.2). Meeks, *First Urban Christians*, 110, notes that economic aid was evidence of the consciousness of the churches that they were part of a brotherhood/sisterhood that was much larger than the local congregation (Rom. 15.26-27; Gal. 2.10).

80. See Ian Morris, "The Early Polis as City and State," in *City and Country in the Ancient World* (ed. John Rich and Andrew Wallace-Hadrill; London and New York: Routledge, 1991), 90, and other articles of this anthology; M. I. Finley, *The Ancient Economy* (Berkeley: University of California Press, 1973), 123-49.

and the "mother of Macedonia." This city was oriented to the interior and not toward the sea as was Athens, despite its excellent harbor.[81] Thessalonica developed its principal relationships with the interior of the province, and the members of the church shared the same provincial orientation. The church in this city was expansive and mobile, participating in the Christian mission toward the world that did not know Christ as well as toward other believers who were in need (1.7-8; 4.10; and later it contributed to the Jerusalem church, according to Rom. 15.26-27). There was sufficient economic power within this church to facilitate this extensive generosity, although the grace of giving was not always an indicator of the possession of great economic resources (2 Cor. 8.2).[82]

After praising the church for the demonstration of its fraternal love and the extension of the same to all the believers throughout Macedonia, Paul exhorts the believers, *Yet we urge you, brothers, to do so more and more.* The call is the same as that found in 4.1 (see commentary), where the apostle urged them to "abound" or "overflow" to an even greater degree in that conduct which pleased God. The founder of the church exhorts them to abound ever more greatly in their love, which is both mutual (v. 9) and extensive (v. 10a; cf. 3.12; 5.11). The apostle had every confidence that this church would respond positively to the exhortation (cf. 2 Thess. 3.4; Phlm. 21).

11 Having touched on the theme of benefaction in the previous verses, Paul fixes their attention on those in the church who received support from their patrons, whether these were inside or outside the Christian community. This passage, like 2 Thessalonians 3.6-15, demonstrates that the apostle was opposed to the economic and social dependence that characterized the institution of patronage.[83] Clients were attached to patrons of higher status and economic solvency, hoping to receive from them benefits such as food and representation, while they gave their patrons honor and augmented their status in society by showing up for the morning greeting at their home and giving them public support. The more clients a person would have, the more important he or she would appear to others. Honor was the name of the game. Perseus (1.54-55) satirizes a patron, saying, "You know how to present a shivering client with a threadbare cloak, and then you say, 'I love the Truth; tell me the truth about myself!'" But the benefits were not every-

---

81. See the Introduction, pp. 3-4, and the commentary on 1.7-8 on the relationship between the city and its hinterland.

82. On the economic situation of this church, see pp. 25-31.

83. For an idealized description of patronage, see Dionysius of Halicarnassus, *Antiquitates Romanae* 2.9-11. On the other hand, Juvenal, *Satire* 5, lampoons this social institution.

thing that a client might expect since not a few patrons treated their clients in a less than respectful way and would offer them food of quite questionable quality.[84]

Not everyone views the teaching about work in these letters as an apostolic response to the widespread institution of patronage. Many have advocated a reading that states that the Thessalonians had abandoned work as part of their eschatological expectation. Why work if Jesus was coming soon? Since they anxiously awaited the "day of the Lord" (5.1) and at a later point some came to believe that it was right at hand (2 Thess. 2.2 and commentary), they ceased working and began to depend on other Christians for daily maintenance.[85] But we should observe that although the eschatological expectation concerning the coming of the Lord was vivid in this church, Paul does not link his thought about the day of the Lord with the question of labor, neither in this passage nor in 2 Thessalonians 3.6-15. His teaching at these points adheres closely to what we know about the patron/client relationship that the apostle rejects as a proper manner of economic maintenance.[86] Moreover, behind the author's concern was the persecution this church endured, which profoundly complicated the established commitments certain Thessalonian believers had with their patrons.

In the previous verse Paul urged the believers to abound in love. Now, as a second point in his exhortation, he says, *Make it your ambition to lead a quiet life, to mind your own business and to work with your hands,*[87] *just as we told you.* While the *NIV* indicates a paragraph break at this point, the thought of v. 11 is a continuation of the previous argument, as signaled by the word "and" at the head of the verse (left untranslated in the *NIV*). If the economic issue is kept in mind, the link between vv. 11-12 and the preceding becomes clear and the temptation to place a paragraph break here diminishes. The verb rendered *make it your ambition* appears in a number of inscriptions meaning "consider it an honor" or even "act with a public spirit," but with the three following infinitives it simply states that they should aspire or strive eagerly to adopt the lifestyle here prescribed.[88]

---

84. Ibid.

85. For example, Bruce, *1 and 2 Thessalonians*, 91; Marshall, *1 and 2 Thessalonians*, 117; Best, *First and Second Epistles to the Thessalonians*, 175; Frame, *Epistles of St. Paul to the Thessalonians*, 161.

86. See Winter, *Seek the Welfare of the City*, 41-60.

87. Some Greek manuscripts include the word "own" *hands (idias)*, a reading favored by the editors of the *UBS*[4] text, though one not followed by the *NIV* nor the *NRSV*.

88. BAGD, 861; *New Docs*, 1.88; MM, 672. The word is used in a number of ways and need not be understood as a mark of those who are benefactors, as Winter suggests

The first exhortation, *to lead a quiet life* (*hēsychazein*; cf. 2 Thess. 3.12), elsewhere means simply "to keep quiet" (Luke 14.4; Acts 11.18; 21.14) or "to rest" (Luke 23.56). However, here the idea is quite different. At times the theme of "being quiet" appears in the literature of the era in the description of those respectable people who do not cause problems in the community. Philo, for example, contrasted the "quiet" person with someone who was evil: "Besides, the worthless man whose life is one long restlessness haunts market-places, theatres, law-courts, council-halls, assemblies, and every group and gathering of men; his tongue he lets loose for unmeasured, endless, indiscriminate talk, bringing chaos and confusion into everything, mixing true with false, fit with unfit, public with private, holy with profane, sensible with absurd, because he has not been trained to that silence (*hēsychian*) which in season is most excellent."[89] Philo and others contrast the "quiet" life with the public life, while Philo even observes that being "quiet" is a mark of nobility.[90] At times the thought of leading the quiet life is found in combination with the words of the following clause in our text, *to mind your own business* (*prassein ta idia*). This combination had to do with retiring from public activity, whether from the tribunal or from politics in general.[91] In fact, *to mind your own business* was the exact opposite of "participating in public affairs" (*prassein ta koina*).[92] We can safely assume that the apostle is calling believers to stay out of public/political affairs.[93]

However, this interpretation has been questioned since those who would need the following exhortation, *to work with your hands*, would be those of the artisan class, people who would not wield political power nor have the social status to engage in the political process.[94] But Paul is addressing those who, as clients, had become attached to prominent patrons, whether inside or outside the church. Central to the politics of the era was this relationship between patron and client. The client who had citizenship could support the patron's cause and vote in the assembly

---

(*Seek the Welfare of the City*, 48). See Josephus, *Bellum Judaicum* 1.206 (1.10.5); *Antiquitates* 3.207 (3.8.6), 15.330 (15.9.5); *Ep. Arist.* 79; and cf. *SIG*³ 956.2, 915.16, 850.7, 1099.31, 304.65, and 362.24.

89. Philo, *De Abrahamo* 20.

90. Philo, *De Vita Mosis* 1.49; *De Abrahamo* 27, 216; Plutarch, *Moralia* 53B; and Epictetus 1.10.2.

91. Xenophon, *Memorabilia* 2.9.1.

92. Dio Cassius 60.27.4; Dio Chrysostom 34.52; Plutarch, *Moralia* 798E-F; Plato, *Republic* 6.496D, 4.433A.

93. So Hock, *The Social Context of Paul's Ministry*, 46-47; Winter, *Seek the Welfare of the City*, 48-50.

94. Marshall, *1 and 2 Thessalonians*, 116; Best, *First and Second Epistles to the Thessalonians*, 175.

(*dēmos* in Thessalonica),[95] but to have real access to power the intervention of the patron was needed. Commenting on the patron/client relationship in the Roman Empire, Gelzer observes, "These relationships determined the distribution of political power. To maintain their rights citizens and subjects alike were constrained to seek the protection of powerful men."[96] Given the institution of patronage, we can well understand why the apostles would call the Thessalonians to retire from public life, especially in this context where the civil rights of the Christians were threatened due to persecution.[97] In other words, Paul does not want the brothers and sisters to utilize the "normal" channels of public debate and judicial defense to resolve the tension between the members of the church and the rest of the Thessalonians (2.14). They had another solution.

The counterpoint to patronage was labor, *to work with your hands.* Manual labor was generally despised by those of the Greek aristocracy and by those who aspired to a higher social status. *To work with your hands* was something that slaves and artisans did (the work of the artisan was compared with that of a slave),[98] but those of high social rank and wealth lived "knowing nothing of labor," according to Philo.[99] Plutarch commented, "while we delight in the work, we despise the workman, as, for instance, in the case of perfumes and dyes; we take a delight in them, but dyers and perfumers we regard as illiberal and vulgar folk," while at the same time observing that those who labored with their own hands were indifferent to higher things.[100] Dio Chrysostom, however, counters this opinion with the pragmatic dictum that labor was better than poverty, a point that was not entirely evident to everyone.[101] Therefore, to call those who had lived as clients to engage in manual labor to gain their living was shocking. Although the apostle promoted benefaction toward those in need (4.10; 2 Thess. 3.13), he opposed the dependency of clients on patrons. For that reason they presented themselves as examples of those who labored for their own bread (2.9; 2 Thess. 3.7-9; Acts 20.34; 1 Cor. 4.12) and instructed the Thessalo-

95. Winter, *Seek the Welfare of the City,* 50.

96. Matthias Gelzer, *The Roman Nobility* (Oxford: Blackwell, 1969), 139; Dionysius of Halicarnassus, *Antiquitates Romanae* 2.10.

97. Wanamaker, *Commentary on 1 and 2 Thessalonians,* 163, is one of the very few to read these verses in light of the persecution. See Xenophon, *Memorabilia* 2.9.1. On the defense of the client by the patron, see also Chow, *Patronage and Power,* 75-80.

98. Hock, *Social Context of Paul's Ministry,* 35-36.

99. Philo, *Quod Deterius Potiori Insidiari Solet* 34.

100. Plutarch, *Pericles* 1.4–2.2.

101. Dio Chrysostom 7.103-32. He was not alone in promoting this perspective. See again Hock, *Social Context of Paul's Ministry,* 44.

nians about the necessity of working (4.11b; 2 Thess. 3.6, 10). The author reminds the church of the directives on this matter that they had previously given (v. 11b; cf. 4.1), *just as we told you,* or, rather, "just as we commanded you" (*parēngeilamen;* 2 Thess. 3.4, 6, 10). The founders' word about work was more than information or a mere suggestion but an authoritative, apostolic command![102] But the institution of patronage was so imbedded that, despite this strong language, some in the church did not respond but continued as clients. In the second letter the apostle found it necessary to censure this conduct in terms that were both strong and severe (2 Thess. 3.6-15).

12 Evidently, the way some Christians participated in public affairs and their economic dependence on their clients did not aid the cause of the church in the community. The solution Paul presents is to retire from public debate and to quit receiving support from patrons, cutting the economic ties by taking up manual labor instead: *so that your daily life may win the respect of outsiders and so that you will not be dependent on anybody.* Paul wants the Thessalonians to "walk" (*peripatēte;* see 2.12; 4.1; 2 Thess. 3.6, 11) or conduct themselves with "decorum" (*euschēmonōs,* translated *may win the respect*) among the unbelievers, who are here called *outsiders* (*tous exō;* Mark 4.11; 1 Cor. 5.12-13; Col. 4.5; and see 1 Tim. 3.7). They should conduct themselves "decently" or "in a fitting manner" (Rom. 13.13; 1 Cor. 14.40; and the adjective in 1 Cor. 7.35),[103] a word that is also used to describe those in the community who acted nobly and worthily and who would even receive public recognition for their conduct.[104] Conduct of this type was highly valued in the ancient world. As Pseudo-Musonius said, "The true end of our being born into the world is to live orderly and with decorum, our minds being furnished by nature with reason as overseer and guide for this purpose."[105] Christians should work and conduct themselves in the community in such a way that they received the "respect" and not the censure of "outsiders" (cf. 1 Pet. 2.11-17; Titus 2.4-10; 3.1-2).[106] They should be regarded as excellent members of the surrounding society, with their conduct being a key element of their testimony (1 Tim. 3.7).

The apostle concludes the section by saying that the Thessalonians

---

102. BAGD, 613; MM, 481; LSJ, 1306.

103. Diodorus Siculus 19.33.2; Epictetus 4.1.163.

104. *TLNT,* 2.139-42; *New Docs,* 2.86; BAGD, 327; MM, 266; Malherbe, "Exhortation in First Thessalonians," 252.

105. Cited in Malherbe, "Exhortation in First Thessalonians," 252.

106. Dio Chrysostom, 7.125, says that poverty is not hopeless since there were "many opportunities of making a living that are neither unseemly nor injurious to men who are willing to work with their hands."

should *not be dependent on anybody*. Self-sufficiency was another ideal that was a commonplace and was especially promoted by the Stoics.[107] The demonstration of this virtue by the Christians, as opposed to being dependent clients, would enhance their status among the unbelievers in their city. While this passage reflects the Christian ethic of work that is rooted in the creation mandate (Gen. 1.28), it would be unwise for us to understand the prohibition as a call to us to abandon any form of involvement in politics. What the apostle warns against is becoming dependent as well as disruptive members of society whose reputation in no way enhances the gospel.

b. "Those who fall asleep" (4.13-18)

In this section Paul responds to the second question of the Thessalonians. What will happen to "the dead in Christ"? The reply implies that between the foundation of the church and the return of Timothy, some member or members of the church had died, an event that caused much sorrow among them (v. 13). The author of the letter encouraged the believers to comfort one another with the teaching on the coming of the Lord and the resurrection of the dead in Christ (v. 18). The possible cause of death was the persecution the church endured, although the text may only hint that some had met martyrdom (see the commentary on v. 15). What is not clear is why the church did not understand the fundamental points of Christian eschatology.

Various reconstructions of the situation have been suggested: (1) Had Paul and his fellows neglected to teach the Thessalonians about the resurrection of the dead? We find it hard to imagine that they had omitted a point so fundamental as this, especially in light of the intimate relationship between the resurrection of believers and the resurrection of Christ (Rom. 8.11; 1 Cor. 15), a doctrine they heartily confessed (1 Thess. 4.14; 1.10). Moreover, since the apostles included the teaching about the coming of Christ as part of their initial instruction for the church (1.10; 2.19; 3.13; 5.23), it is unlikely that they would have neglected to explain the relationship between this event and the destiny of the "dead in Christ." In 4.14 and again in 4.16 the author declares that "the dead in Christ will rise" without any explanation about what this means, implying that the church already knew what he was talking about. The concern of the Thessalonians was not simply wrapped around the destiny of the

---

107. Ferguson, *Backgrounds of Early Christianity*, 303, 346, 355; Malherbe, "Exhortation in First Thessalonians," 252; idem, *Moral Exhortation*, 13, 40, 112-14, 120, 145, 154, and 157.

deceased but rather the relationship between the resurrection and the "rapture" of living believers (vv. 15-17).[108]

(2) Alternatively, it has been suggested that a false doctrine had infiltrated the church that placed in doubt the reality of the resurrection. Schmithals, for example, sees Gnostic influence in this church that threatened their faith in the apostolic doctrine concerning the destiny of the dead.[109] But apart from the fact that Gnosticism as a movement was a late development, the passage does not display evidence of being a polemic against false doctrine. The purpose of the author is to clarify and not to defend a fundamental doctrine of the Christian faith.

(3) Another option is that the problem did not have to do with the reality of the resurrection but with the loss of hope in the coming of the Lord due to the death of certain members of the community. However, Paul does not defend the doctrine of Christ's coming, neither here nor elsewhere in the letter. Far from having lost faith in this event, it formed the foundation for their hope (1.10).

(4) A fourth reconstruction of the problem proposes that the Thessalonians had received instruction about the resurrection but in the moment of confronting the reality of death became consumed with grief. Their theology did not inform their emotional reaction. Morris forwards a variation of this interpretation, explaining that the Thessalonians saw death before the imminent coming of the Lord as chastisement for sin (see 1 Cor. 11.30) and therefore believed that those who had died before this event would be excluded from final salvation.[110] But this interpretation does not adequately explain the discussion in vv. 15-17 about the relationship between the resurrection of the dead in the Lord and the catching away of living believers at the moment of the Lord's coming.

(5) On the other hand, it may be that the Thessalonians thought that the dead were in a disadvantaged situation with regard to the coming of the Lord. They believed that the living believers would see the Lord at the moment of his coming but that the resurrection of the dead would occur after that event. While this interpretation has the advantage of giving an explanation for the discourse about the relationship between the coming of the Lord and the resurrection (vv. 14-17), it does not clarify the reason for the overwhelming grief the church experienced as they struggled with the death of some members (v. 13). According to their perspective,

---

108. Summaries of the various positions are also found in Best, *First and Second Epistles to the Thessalonians*, 180-84; Marshall, *1 and 2 Thessalonians*, 120-22; Wanamaker, *Commentary on 1 and 2 Thessalonians*, 164-66; Earl J. Richard, *First and Second Thessalonians* (Collegeville, Minn.: The Liturgical Press, 1995), 231-32.

109. Schmithals, *Paul and the Gnostics*, 160-64.

110. Morris, *First and Second Epistles to the Thessalonians*, 134-35.

the dead would be raised, although somewhat later, and this would be a true hope for the living despite the confusion about the timing.

(6) A sixth alternative argues that the fundamental problem had to do with the assumption of the dead and not with the resurrection. According to OT and Jewish apocalyptic literature, only the living could be translated to the heavens, and therefore the dead could not participate in this event.[111] But we raise the objection that the Thessalonians were new believers and would not have been acquainted with fine details of Jewish apocalyptic literature. There is little probability that the histories of such figures as Enoch and Elijah would have been the root of their theological problems as they faced the issue of death.

In the end, not one of these explanations regarding the situation that gave rise to the Thessalonians' concerns about the dead is completely satisfactory. The reconstruction of greatest merit argues that at the moment of confronting the reality of death, the Thessalonians did not allow their confession to inform their reaction to this human tragedy. Alternately, they may simply have not understood fully the reality of the resurrection from the dead, especially in light of the general Gentile consensus that such things simply do not happen. However, these proposals do not clarify why it was that Paul needed to discuss at such length the relationship between the resurrection of the dead and the assumption of the living and the dead. What is quite clear is that the Thessalonians were experiencing great grief because of the death of one or more of their members, and the apostle needed to respond with the appropriate teaching so that they would not be overwhelmed with grief like the unbelievers "who have no hope" (v. 13). His purpose was distinctly pastoral as he urged the church to use this teaching to comfort one another (v. 18). The passage was clearly not designed to satisfy idle speculative curiosity about the last things; its purpose was to encourage those who were facing the most profound grief that a human could experience.

Paul's teaching about the dead echoes a number of characteristics that were commonly contained in ancient letters of consolation, a literary genre well known in antiquity. In his discussion of various letter types, Demetrius says:

> The consoling type is that written to people who are grieving [*eis lypēs*] because something unpleasant has happened (to them). It is as follows:
> When I heard of the terrible things that you met at the hands of

---

111. See Joseph Plevnik, "The Taking Up of the Faithful and the Resurrection of the Dead in 1 Thessalonians 4:13-18," *CBQ* 46 (1984) 274-83.

thankless fate, I felt the deepest grief, considering that what had happened had not happened to you more than to me. When I saw all the things that assail life, all that day long I cried over them. But then I considered that such things are the common lot of all, with nature establishing neither a particular time or age in which one must suffer anything, but often confronting us secretly, awkwardly and undeservedly. Since I happened not to be present to comfort [*parakalein*] you, I decided to do so by letter. Bear, then, what has happened as lightly as you can, and exhort yourself just as you would exhort someone else. For you know that reason will make it easier for you to be relieved of your grief with the passage of time.[112]

Stowers isolates six characteristics of these letters of consolation: "1. Death is inevitable. 2. Death is the fate of all, kings and beggars, rich and poor. 3. The person's memory and honor will live on in spite of death. 4. Death releases one from the evils of life. 5. The funeral and the tomb are a great honor to the deceased. 6. Either death is nonexistence and does not matter to the dead or it leads to some happier state of existence."[113] The consolation Paul extends to the Thessalonians shares a number of traditional elements, such as the call to minimize grief (v. 13), the need for mutual comfort (v. 18), and the explanation about the happy state of the dead (vv. 14-17).[114] But unlike the common letters of consolation, Paul roots his consolation in the resurrection of Jesus and his coming. His resurrection is the paradigm of the destiny of the deceased believer (v. 14), and at the moment of his coming the dead will be raised, and they, in the company of the living believers, will be taken up to meet him (vv. 15-17).

13 The consolation begins with a declaration of pastoral concern for the church: *Brothers, we do not want you to be ignorant about those who fall asleep.* The statement implies that this was one of the areas where their understanding of the faith was deficient (3.10). The initial affirmation may suggest that they were completely ignorant about the following matter (cf. the same expression in Rom. 1.13; 11.25; 1 Cor. 10.1; 2 Cor. 1.8), or that they needed more orientation about a theme with which they were already acquainted (cf. 1 Cor. 12.1). At a number of points in this section of the letter, the author refers the Thessalonians back to what they already knew (4.1-2, 6, 9; 5.1-2). But the change of language in 4.13 may

112. Cited in Malherbe, *Ancient Epistolary Theorists,* 34-35 and see 70-71. On this letter type, idem, "Exhortation in First Thessalonians," 254-55; Stowers, *Letter Writing in Greco-Roman Antiquity,* 142-52.

113. Stowers, *Letter Writing in Greco-Roman Antiquity,* 142.

114. See especially Malherbe, "Exhortation in First Thessalonians," 255.

imply that they had not received previous instruction about this theme or that they needed more instruction concerning what they already knew. In this latter case, the change from "remember" to *we do not want you to be ignorant* would be more stylistic than substantial. In either case, the use of the preposition "concerning" (*peri,* left untranslated in the *NIV*) appears to indicate that Paul is responding to a concern that the church had communicated to him and his companions (see 4.9; 5.1 and commentary; cf. 1 Cor. 12.1).

The apostle refers to the deceased using the euphemistic *those who fall asleep* (as in 4.14-15; 5.10), although he has no reservations about calling them "the dead" (4.16). This euphemistic way of speaking about the dead appears in both Jewish and Christian texts and implies nothing about the intermediate state.[115] Some have erroneously concluded that this epithet for the dead implies that the soul sleeps after death, but the NT teaching clearly points to a conscious existence during the intermediate state (Luke 16.19-31; 23.39-43; Acts 7.55-60; 2 Cor. 5.6-10; Phil. 1.20-24; Rev. 6.9-11). At times the dead are described as "those who sleep" with a view to the anticipated resurrection of their body (Dan. 12.2; 4 Ezra 7.32; Matt. 27.52; Mark 5.39-42; 1 Cor. 15.20). But the deceased are also referred to as "those who sleep" in Greek and Latin literature and inscriptions,[116] and for that reason we should understand the term as a simple synonym for "the dead" without reading into it a more profound theological meaning. This was a common and universal way to speak of those who had died.

The reason why Paul does not want the Thessalonians to be ignorant about the destiny of the deceased Christians is that they may not *grieve like the rest of men, who have no hope.*[117] As we saw previously, the desire to minimize grief was a common theme in letters of consolation as well as in epigrams. One inscription said, "My mother, leave off lamenting, cease to mourn and cut yourself; Hades turns pity aside,"[118] while another exhorted, "do not grieve over the departed."[119] The idea was not that death was welcome but rather that no human reaction to death could

---

115. Gen. 47.30; Deut. 31.16; 1 Kings 2.10; 11.43; Isa. 14.8; 43.17; Jer. 51.39; 2 Macc. 12.45; *As. Mos.* 1.15; 10.14; *1 Enoch* 100.5; *T. Joseph* 20.4; John 11.11-14; Acts 7.60; 13.36; 1 Cor. 7.39; 11.30; 15.6, 18, 51; 2 Pet. 3.4.

116. Homer, *Iliad* 11.241; Sophocles, *Electra* 509; Catullus 5.4-6; Richmond Lattimore, *Themes in Greek and Latin Epitaphs* (Urbana: University of Illinois Press, 1942), 59, 164-65; BAGD, 437; MM, 350; LSJ, 967.

117. *Hina mē ktl.* presents the reason why the apostles do not want them to be ignorant and does not introduce a coordinate clause, as the *NIV* implies.

118. Cited in Lattimore, *Themes in Greek and Latin Epitaphs,* 218.

119. MM, 382.

change that which destiny dictated. Plutarch added in a letter sent to console Apollonius, "Indeed, though there are many emotions that affect the soul, yet grief *(lypē)*, from its nature, is the most cruel of all" (102C). But he continues his argument by saying that although grief is a natural reaction to death and that humans cannot be indifferent in the face of death, one should not be overcome by grief because this is contrary to nature and causes damage. It is also bad and improper for a diligent person (102C-D). But the apostle in no way prohibits grief in the face of death (see John 16.6, 20; Acts 8.2; Phil. 2.27; cf. 1 Pet. 1.6; Rom. 12.15) but only advises that grief should not be overwhelming so that they do not *grieve like the rest of men, who have no hope. The rest (hoi loipoi)* is a reference to those who are not Christians (5.6; Eph. 2.3), who in the previous verse are called "outsiders."

The Gentile unbelievers are further described in this verse as those *who have no hope* (Eph. 2.12). We cannot say that the Gentile world was entirely devoid of hope. According to Greek mythology, when Pandora opened her large jar and released all the evils upon the world, Hope remained (Hesiod, *Opera et Dies* 90-105). Various philosophers spoke of the immortality of the soul, and certain religions affirmed existence after death. The tombs of the deceased, both of those who were buried and those who were cremated, had holes in them so that the living could pass them foodstuffs.[120]

However, at the popular level desperation in the face of death reigned. E. Hoffmann comments, "Living hope as a fundamental religious attitude was unknown in Gk. culture. . . . But in the final analysis men had to stand without hope before the hostile forces of guilt and death. Sophocles' chorus lamented, 'The highest remains, never to be brought to life.' Seneca called hope the definition of 'an uncertain good.' But deification and immortality promised by the mystery religions were human pipe dreams."[121] Theocritus reflected on the absence of hope, saying, "Hopes are for the living; the dead are without hope" (*Idyll* 4.42). Both Greek and Latin inscriptions have been found that read, "I was not, I was, I am not, I care not."[122] In a second-century letter of consolation from Irene to Taonnophris and Philo who were in mourning we read, "I am as sorry [*elypēthēn*] and weep over the departed one as I wept for Didymas. . . . But nevertheless, against such things one can do nothing.

---

120. Arthur Darby Nock, "Cremation and Burial in the Roman Empire," *HTR* 25 (1932) 321-59.

121. *NIDNTT*, 2.239. On death in general, see Ferguson, *Backgrounds of Early Christianity*, 228-34, and the literature cited.

122. Latin: *non fui, fui, non sum, non curo.* Greek: *ou ēmēn kai egenomēn, ouk eimi kai ou lypoumai.* See Ferguson, *Backgrounds of Early Christianity*, 232; MM, 382.

Therefore comfort ye one another."[123] In the epigrams of Philip and Antipater of Thessalonica we encounter similar sentiments. One of Antipater's epigrams shows the same spirit of resignation in the face of death, "The experts in astrology tell of an early death for me; though it be so, I care nothing for that, Seleucus. All men have the same way down to Hades; if mine is quicker than others', I shall be face to face with Minos the sooner."[124] In an inscription that tells of the death of a person drowned at sea, Philip reflects the belief in the futility of life, "See on the beach this body of a man all-unfortunate, with scattered limbs, washed forth from the sea-beaten rocks. . . . This man in many parts was once a whole; happy are those who saw not the sunlight after the birth-pangs."[125]

In part, the lack of hope was linked to the belief that the stars fixed a human's fate,[126] while the gods were capable of doing a person both evil and good. Commenting on the death of a woman who just gave birth to triplets, Antipater says, "One and the same god took life from her and gave life to them."[127] Death was filled with tragedy and irony, and the human response was overwhelming grief.[128] Philip comments on the grief of Agathanor's father, a stone mason, who built a tomb with his grief, "this sorrowful grave-stone not cut by the iron but worn by floods of fast-falling tears."[129]

As the Christians in Thessalonica faced the death of those whom they loved, they are called not *to grieve like the rest of men, who have no hope.* Their grief should be tempered and informed by the hope they held, based on the resurrection of Christ and the promise of his coming. The apostles preached hope in a world where even hope seemed to have flown out of the jar.

14 The reason why Christians should not despair in the face of death as do those "who have no hope" is found in the fundamental confession of the church, *We believe that Jesus died and rose again.* In the Greek text, this clause is the protasis of a conditional sentence that presents an assumption that is considered to be certain, "For since we believe that Je-

---

123. Cited in Deissmann, *LAE*, 176.

124. Antipater, n. 38, in Gow and Page, *The Greek Anthology*, 1.35.

125. Philip, n. 32, in Gow and Page, *The Greek Anthology*, 1.319.

126. Antipater, nn. 5, 38, in Gow and Page, *The Greek Anthology*, 17, 35.

127. Antipater, n. 102. So also nn. 62, 65, 67, and 68, and Philip, n. 30, in Gow and Page, *The Greek Anthology*, 1.77, 51, 53, 54, 317.

128. Tragedy — Antipater, nn. 53, 64, 66, 68, 68a, 69; Philip, nn. 25, 28, 29, 31, 37; irony — Antipater, nn. 26, 34, 58, 102, 107; Philip, n. 39; grief — Philip, n. 37, in Gow and Page, *The Greek Anthology*, 1.29, 33, 45, 47, 53, 55, 77, 79, 315, 317, 319, 323, 325.

129. Philip, n. 27, in Gow and Page, *The Greek Anthology*, 1.315.

sus died and rose again . . ." *(NRSV)*.[130] The clause is a repetition of the creed the apostles had taught the church at the time of its foundation (Acts 17.3). The confession, which begins with the words *we believe that*, includes a verb that Paul does not normally employ when he speaks about the resurrection (*rose again* is *anestē* instead of the more common *egeirein*, used some thirty-seven times). These characteristics suggest that the apostle appeals to a pre-Pauline creed that had been handed over to the church and that both the apostolic company and the Thessalonians confessed. The centrality of the death and resurrection of Jesus as the cornerstone of the apostolic proclamation can hardly be disputed (1 Cor. 15.1-11).

Upon this foundation was built the hope in the resurrection of the dead. Over and again in the apostolic teaching, the resurrection of Jesus is put forward as the guarantee of the resurrection of believers. So intimately connected are these events in the history of salvation that Paul could even dare to proclaim to the Corinthians that denial of the resurrection of the dead constituted a *de facto* denial of the resurrection of Christ (1 Cor. 15.12-28; and see Acts 26.23; Rom. 8.11; 1 Cor. 6.14; 2 Cor. 4.14; Col. 1.18). The author introduces the second part of the confession as an inference drawn from the resurrection of Christ: *and so we believe that God will bring with Jesus those who have fallen asleep in him*. The verb translated *will bring* in the NIV (*axei*, from *agō*) may mean either "bring" or "take," depending on the point of view of the person who observes the action. Only the context can determine which sense the author had in mind. The verse may mean, on the one hand, that *God will bring* from heaven *with Jesus* the souls of *those who have fallen asleep in him*. On the other hand, the verse may mean that God will take *with Jesus* the deceased. This second interpretation understands the verb as a reference to the resurrection or even the ascension, which presupposes the resurrection.[131] This second interpretation is preferable since the concern of this verse and of vv. 15-16 is to show that the death and resurrection of Christ becomes the paradigm and foundation for the destiny of believers. As Jesus died and was raised, so "God will take with Jesus those who have fallen asleep in him." However, inasmuch as the resurrection of the believer and the ascension cannot be separated (vv. 16-17), the verb "take" most likely embraces both events. The hope in the resurrection of believers is based on the resurrection of Christ, an event that will take place in union *with Jesus*.

Another problem of interpretation that this verse presents is how to

---

130. BDF, §371.1, *ei* with the indicative.

131. See Ellingworth and Nida, *A Translator's Handbook*, 94-99; Paul Ellingworth, "Which Way Are We Going? A Verb of Movement, Especially 1 Thess. 4:14b," *BT* 25 (1974) 426-31.

understand the description of deceased Christians as *those who have fallen asleep in him*. We have already observed that ancient authors frequently described the dead as *those who have fallen asleep* (see v. 13 and comments). But what does Paul mean by saying that these have died *in him* or rather "through Jesus" (*dia tou Iēsou*)?[132] The preposition (*dia* plus the genitive) may introduce the agent of an action, but it would be most difficult to understand the sense if interpreted this way.[133] In what way could it be said that Jesus was the agent of their death? Moule offers the more attractive possibility that this preposition with the genitive presents an attendant circumstance (cf. Acts 15.32; 2 Cor. 2.4; Eph. 6.18; Heb. 13.22 and especially 2 Tim. 2.2) and would thus be simply a way of saying that these believers died as Christians in union with him.[134] In death, believers are not separated from Jesus. This phrase then becomes an implicit affirmation that those who die as Christians do not cease to exist between the time of their death and the resurrection.

15 Having demonstrated on the basis of the death and resurrection of Christ that the dead in Christ will be raised, the apostle elaborates this doctrine with reference to the teaching of the Lord himself. His intention is not merely to reaffirm the reality of the resurrection but rather to show the relationship between this event and the destiny of Christians who are found alive at the moment of the coming of the Lord. The teaching is introduced with the solemn, *According to the Lord's own word, we tell you*. . . . At the start, Paul clarifies that the teaching that follows is inspired by the Lord Jesus ("the word of the Lord") and, for that reason, authoritative for the church. In the OT, "the word of the LORD" was the typical designation of the prophetic oracles (Isa. 1.10; Jer. 1.4; Ezek. 1.3; Hos. 1.1; Joel 1.1; Amos 5.1; Mic. 1.1), and for that reason we might conclude that the author is about to present some prophecy that was given through a Christian prophet such as Silas. But in the NT, the "word of the Lord" is not used this way. Instead of designating that which the Lord Jesus says through prophetic inspiration, the phrase refers to the message of the gospel that is proclaimed (Acts 12.24; 13.49; 14.35-36; 19.10; 1 Thess. 1.8; 2 Thess. 3.1) or to a teaching that was given by the Lord Jesus during his earthly ministry (Acts 20.35), whether or not this teaching was incorporated into the Gospels.[135] Most likely, Paul has in mind a teaching they

---

132. It is unlikely that we should understand this phrase as modifying the principal verb "to take," an event that is said to occur "with Jesus."

133. See Best, *First and Second Epistles to the Thessalonians,* 188-89, for a discussion of the various interpretive possibilities.

134. C. F. D. Moule, *An Idiom-Book of New Testament Greek* (Cambridge: Cambridge University Press, 1971), 57.

135. On the teaching of Jesus that did not make its way into the Gospels, see

had received from the Lord himself as part of the Christian tradition (cf. 1 Cor. 7.10, 25; 9.14; 11.23-25) that now becomes the foundation for the following teaching. The problem with this conclusion is that the Gospels nowhere record a teaching from Jesus that conforms exactly to the instruction given in the following verses. However, the declaration of vv. 15-17 corresponds in many respects with Matthew 24.29-31, 40-41, thus making it possible that Jesus' eschatological discourse was the source of this instruction. The teaching was not then presented in its original form but was summarized and clarified in light of the situation the apostles addressed with the Thessalonians.

The teaching that the Lord gave and that the apostle now presents to the Thessalonians is that *we who are still alive, who are left till the coming of the Lord, will certainly not precede those who have fallen asleep*. At this point in his ministry, it appears that Paul believed that he was going to remain alive until the *coming of the Lord* (cf. 1 Cor. 15.51-52), although he admits that he did not know exactly when the day of the Lord would come (1 Thess. 5.1-2). However, later in his ministry he no longer expected to be alive to witness that grand event (2 Cor. 4.14; 5.1), although he believed in the imminent coming of the Lord to the end of his life (Phil. 4.5). This vivid expectation resounds throughout the NT (Rev. 22.20), although the church maintained an agnosticism about the timing of the final events (Acts 1.6-7) and an antagonism toward those who tried to fix the time (2 Thess. 2.1-12 and commentary; 2 Tim. 2.16-18). The word translated *we . . . who are left (hoi perileipomenoi)* appears over and again in the literature of the era and refers to those who had survived a tragedy that left others dead, though the word does not convey this sense in every context.[136] The use of this description of the living believers may imply that some Christians in Thessalonica had died tragically in the persecution driven forward by their unconverted contemporaries (2.14).

The apostle states emphatically[137] that those who survive *till the coming of the Lord* (see v. 16; and 2.19; 3.13; 5.23; 2 Thess. 2.1, 8 and comments) *will certainly not precede those who have fallen asleep* (cf. 4.13-14 and comments). For some reason or other the Thessalonians needed to know that at the time of the Lord's coming the living believers would not precede the

---

Joachim Jeremias, *Unknown Sayings of Jesus* (London: SPCK, 1948). Jeremias notes that 1 Thess. 4.16-17a is this type of teaching. See also William D. Stroker, *Extracanonical Sayings of Jesus* (Atlanta: Scholars Press, 1989); Alfred Resch, *Agrapha* (Darmstadt: Wissenschaftliche Buchgesellschaft, 1974).

136. 4 Macc. 12.6; 13.18; Euripides, *Helena* 426; Herodian 2.1.7; Josephus, *Contra Apionem* 1.35 (1.7); and the references in MM, 506.

137. *Ou mē* with the aorist subjunctive *phthasōmen* is the most emphatic way to state a negation about the future. BDF, §365.

dead. The verb Paul uses *(phthasōmen)* appears in other texts with the meaning of "to arrive" or "to come" (Matt. 12.28; Luke 11.20; Rom. 9.31; 2 Cor. 10.14; Phil. 3.16; 1 Thess. 2.16), while only here in the NT does it carry the sense of "precede." However, this second sense is quite common in Greek literature,[138] while the meaning "to have advantage over" is not attested in the sources. The point Paul makes is simply that the dead in Christ will be raised first (v. 16b), and then the living and the dead will be taken up to meet the Lord (v. 17). The question we are left to ponder is why the Thessalonians needed such strong assurance that the living were not going to precede the dead in Christ. Some have suggested that Jewish apocalyptic literature at times projects the idea that the living will be in a more advantageous position when the kingdom of God is inaugurated (Dan. 12.12; *Pss. Sol.* 17.50; *4 Ezra* 13.24), and that this teaching had affected the Thessalonians.[139] However, the possibility that this young gentile congregation would have read and understood this obscure point in Jewish theology is remote. More likely, the Thessalonians understood that only the living would have the honor of going out to meet the Lord in his royal and triumphal *parousia* *(coming;* see vv. 16 and 17 and comments), and the apostle responds by saying that the dead will rise first and will have this place of honor in the procession. The dead in Christ will in no way be excluded from the grand celebration that will surround the *parousia* of the Lord but will enjoy a place of honor. Recognition of this fact would give the living believers great comfort in their grief (vv. 13, 18).

16 In v. 15 Paul referred to the coming of the Lord as his *parousia*, a term that commonly meant the glorious "coming" of a deity or the official visit of a sovereign to a city, who himself was often honored as divine. An imperial visit was an event of great pomp and magnificent celebrations, with rich banquets, speeches that praised the imperial visitor, a visit to the local temple, rich donations, celebration of games, sacrifices, statues dedicated, and arches and other buildings constructed. Money was minted to commemorate the event, crowns of gold might be given, and at times a new era was inaugurated. As we will see in the exposition of v. 17, the officials and a multitude of people would head out of the city to receive the one who came, all dressed with special clothing.[140] In v. 16

---

138. Wis. 4.7; 6.13; 16.28; Diodorus Siculus 15.16.4; Appian, *Bella Civilia Romana* 5.30; Josephus, *Antiquitates* 7.24 (7.10.4); and see MM, 666-67; BAGD, 856.

139. Milligan, *St. Paul's Epistles to the Thessalonians*, 59; Best, *First and Second Epistles to the Thessalonians*, 195; Marshall, *1 and 2 Thessalonians*, 127; Wanamaker, *Commentary on 1 and 2 Thessalonians*, 172.

140. *TLNT*, 3.53-54; *LAE*, 368-73; Brent Kinman, *Jesus' Entry into Jerusalem* (Leiden: E. J. Brill, 1995), 25-47; Erik Wistrand, *Felicitas Imperatoria* (Göteborg: Acta Universitatis Gothobergensis, 1987).

the apostle describes the glory and the pomp that will accompany the *parousia* of the Lord, while assuring the Thessalonians that all Christians, both the living and the dead, will participate in this grand event. The author declares, *For the Lord himself will come down from heaven, with a loud command, with the voice of the archangel and with the trumpet call of God, and the dead in Christ will rise first.* The visit of other high-ranking officials to a city could also be called a *parousia*, such as the advent of the governor of a province,[141] but in the grand event here described it is *the Lord himself* who comes *down from heaven* (see 1 Thess. 1.10 and commentary; 2 Thess. 1.7) in this divine epiphany (cf. Mic. 1.3), and not just his representatives such as the angels (cf. 3.13; Isa. 63.9 LXX). They will accompany him, but he is the protagonist.

Far from being a secret event, the coming of the Lord will occur amid a great amount of noise as God gives his order that the dead be raised.[142] First, there will be *a loud command (en keleusmati),* which is a cry or command that must be obeyed.[143] Philo used the word when speaking about how God, "with a single call [*heni keleusmati*], may easily gather together from the ends of the earth to any place that He wills the exiles dwelling in the utmost parts of the earth" (*De Praemiis et Poenis* 117; cf. Matt. 24.31). Although our text does not indicate who issues this *loud command,* we should probably understand that it is God who orders *the dead in Christ* to rise.

The royal *parousia* of the Lord is also accompanied by *the voice of the archangel.* Jude 9 names one of the archangels, Michael, but in Jewish literature other names are mentioned besides his.[144] Michael may not be the archangel whom the apostle has in mind. According to Jewish thought, the archangels are the rulers of the angels or the principal messengers among the multitude of angels.[145] In Jesus' eschatological discourse, the angels play an important role in the moment when the chosen of God are gathered together (Matt. 24.31), but here only the chief among the angels is mentioned as the one who adds his voice to the command of God.

The third great sound at this event is *the trumpet call of God.* The trumpet was not primarily a musical instrument during this era but

---

141. See Kinman, *Jesus' Entry into Jerusalem,* 34-39.

142. Michael R. Cosby, "Hellenistic Formal Receptions and Paul's Use of *apantēsis* in 1 Thessalonians 4:17," *BBR* 4 (1994) 15-33.

143. Philo, *De Abrahamo* 116; Josephus, *Antiquitates* 17.199 (17.8.3); Herodotus 4.141; *TDNT,* 3.656-659; BAGD, 427.

144. See, e.g., *1 Enoch* 20.1-7, which names Suru'el, Raphael, Raguel, Saraqa'el, and Gabriel, as well as Michael.

145. Philo, *De Confusione Linguarum* 146; *Quis Rerum Divinarum Heres* 205; *De Somniis* 1.157.

found its place rather in military exercises, cultic events, and funeral processions. In the Roman army nothing happened without sounding the trumpet. In funeral processions the trumpets were sounded, and so common was this custom that when the emperor Claudius died the sound of the trumpets was so deafening that it was thought that the dead could hear them.[146] But the idea of this verse is not simply that the dead will hear the great sound of the *trumpet call of God*, but that they will respond to the command to rise. According to the OT, the trumpet of God would announce the coming of the day of the Lord (Joel 2.1; Zeph. 1.15-16) and the time when the dispersed people of God would be gathered and God would bring them salvation (Isa. 27.13; Zech. 9.14-16), events that in Jewish literature were also associated with the sounding of the trumpet of God.[147] Not only in our text but also in 1 Corinthians 15.52 the trumpet of God announces or commands the resurrection of the dead, while in Matthew 24.31 the trumpet of God calls together the dispersed people of God.

By means of these agents God gives his command, and *the dead in Christ will rise first*. Not all the dead will be raised at this time, but only those who have entered into a relationship with Christ before their death (cf. "the dead in Christ" in 1 Cor. 15.18; Rev. 14.13). The point Paul wished to drive home with the Thessalonians, however, is not simply that *the dead in Christ will rise* but that this event will occur *first*. The dead will not remain in their tombs and lose the opportunity of going out to receive their sovereign Lord, but before the grand entourage goes out they will be raised. They will have a place of privilege, if not preeminence, in this grand procession, which is described in the following verse.

17 After the resurrection the living believers will be joined with those who are raised, and together they will go out in procession to meet their Sovereign at the time of his *parousia*. This grand event, frequently called the "rapture" (from the Latin *rapio*), is described in the following manner: *After that, we who are still alive and are left will be caught up together with them in the clouds to meet the Lord in the air.* Once again, Paul emphasizes the order of the events: "The dead in Christ will rise first" (v. 16); *After that, we who are still alive and are left will be caught up together with them.*[148] The use of the first person plural *we* most likely indicates that Paul and his associates anticipated being alive at the moment of the *parousia* (see v. 15 and commentary). As in v. 15, the living are called "we

---

146. *TDNT*, 7.72-88.

147. Ibid., 7.84.

148. The expression "first . . . then" (*prōtos . . . epeita*) was a common way to describe orderly succession. 4 Macc. 6.2-3; 1 Cor. 15.46 (and 15.6-7, 23); Xenophon, *Anabasis* 3.2.27; Diodorus Siculus 16.69.4.

who are still alive and are left" (see commentary), and these will be *caught up together* with the resurrected believers. From the author's perspective, the primary group is the resurrected, with whom the living are then joined. This theology is a long way from the idea that the deceased will stay in their tombs or are somehow disadvantaged. When the living have been joined together with the resurrected, both *will be caught up together*. This verb, which appears in a number of texts in the NT, means either to take someone by force or violence (Matt. 11.12; 12.29; 13.19; John 6.15; 10.12, 28-29; Acts 23.10; Jude 23), or to catch someone away to a celestial place (Acts 8.39; 2 Cor. 12.2, 4; Rev. 12.5). In some descriptions of the rapture of Enoch the same verb appears (Wis. 4.10-11; 2 *Enoch* 3.1), as it does in classical myths that describe how some persons were snatched away by the gods.[149] In all of these cases, whether in biblical history or mythology, only some people are caught away. So the striking revelation for the Thessalonians would have been to hear how all the resurrected dead along with the living believers would be snatched away. Never had such a glorious event been contemplated.

The medium into which the resurrected and the living will be caught away is *the clouds,* which are a common element in divine theophanies (Matt. 17.5; Mark 9.7; Luke 9.34-35; 1 Cor. 10.1-2) as well as in the ascension of Christ and of the two witnesses in Revelation (Acts 1.9; Rev. 11.12). But *the clouds* also accompany the Lord at his return (Matt. 24.30, 64; Mark 13.26; 14.62; Luke 21.27; Rev. 1.7; 14.14-16), a reality that finds its theological roots in Daniel's vision of "one like a son of man, coming with the clouds of heaven" (Dan. 7.13-14). *The clouds* are the place of meeting between humans and the divine.

The purpose of the catching away underlines this divine/human encounter, *to meet the Lord in the air. To meet (eis apantēsin)* was almost a technical term that described the custom of sending a delegation outside the city to receive a dignitary who was on the way to town. In Acts 28.15 Luke utilizes this word in his description of the way a delegation of Christians from Rome went out to receive Paul and his companions when he approached the imperial city, "The brothers there had heard that we were coming, and they traveled as far as the Forum of Appius and the Three Taverns to meet us" *(eis apantēsin).* The customary procedure was for the delegation to return to the city with the visiting dignitaries (Acts 28.16; also Matt. 25.6). The OT texts where the verb is used are numer-

---

149. As Persephone by Pluto (Apollodorus 1.5.1) and Aeneas by Aphrodite (Quintus Smyrnaeus 11.289-90). See also Homer, *Odyssey* 15.250-51; Plutarch, *Moralia* 591C; and Apollonius Rhodius 3.1114, who talks about how the winds caught someone away and took him to another place.

ous,[150] while in Greek and Roman culture the custom was well established, especially when persons of high political rank came to town. Polybius spoke of the great pomp of such occasions (5.26.8), and author after author described how not only certain officials but also all the population would file out of the city to meet the emperor in his *parousia*. Josephus, for example, tells how the citizens of Rome went out to meet Vespasian as their new emperor (who, by the way, had just come from leading the Roman troops in the battles to quell the Jewish rebellion that began in AD 66):

> Amidst such feelings of universal goodwill, those of higher rank, impatient of awaiting him, hastened to a great distance from Rome to be the first to greet [*hapantōn*] him. Nor, indeed, could any of the rest endure the delay of meeting, but all poured forth in such crowds — for to all it seems simpler and easier to go than to remain — that the very city then for the first time experienced with satisfaction the paucity of inhabitants; for those who went outnumbered those who remained. But when he was reported to be approaching and those who had gone ahead were telling of the affability of his reception of each party, the whole remaining population, with wives and children, were by now waiting at the road-sides to receive him; and each group as he passed, in their delight at the spectacle and moved by the blandness of his appearance, gave vent to all manner of cries, hailing him as "benefactor," "savior," and "only worthy emperor of Rome." The whole city, moreover, was filled, like a temple, with garlands and incense.[151]

In this entourage, those who went out first to meet Vespasian were those of the highest rank, and we most likely hear an echo of this custom in vv. 16b-17a: "the dead in Christ rise first." In formal receptions, the leaders of the city and all the population would go out, including the soldiers, the gymnasiarch and the students, and the priest with cultic objects, all dressed with special clothing and garlands. The city would greet the dignitary upon entry with songs, loud cries, and sacrifices. Cosby correctly observes that the characteristics of these receptions do not correspond one for one with the reception the Lord shall receive when the resurrected and the living are caught away to meet him.[152] However, since the context of this formal reception is the time of the royal *parousia* of the

---

150. LXX Judg. 4.22; 1 Sam. 9.14; 13.10; 25.20, 32, 34; 2 Sam. 19.15, 16, 20, 24-25; 2 Kings 4.26; 5.21; 8.8-9; 2 Chr. 15.2; 19.2; 28.9).

151. Josephus, *Bellum Judaicum* 7.68-72 (7.4.1). See also *Antiquitates* 11.329-36 (11.8.5); Dio Cassius 62.4.1-2; Polybius 5.26.8-9.

152. Cosby, "Hellenistic Formal Receptions," 20-32. See also Erik Peterson, "Die Einholung des Kyrios," *ZST* 1 (1930) 682-702.

Lord (v. 15), there remains little doubt that this custom formed the background of this teaching, although with some notable modifications (for example, the time of the day of the Lord is unknown — 5.1-11).

The place of this meeting is *in the air*.[153] At times this expression *(eis aera)* means simply "up" (Achilles Tatius 7.15.3; Josephus, *Antiquitates* 7.327 [7.13.3]), and it may be that the apostle has nothing more in mind here. On the other hand, *the air* was understood as the habitation of malignant supernatural powers (Eph. 2.2), and, according to the common conception of the day, *the air* was "filled with gods and spirits" (Plutarch, *Moralia* 274B). But there does not appear to be any connection between this statement and that belief. It was also believed that *the air* was filled with "souls" (Diogenes Laertius 8.31-32), and by way of contrast the extraordinary affirmation of the apostle was that the resurrected and the living believers, and not simply their souls, will meet the Lord *in the air.* Paul does not elaborate how this could happen, but we know from his other writings that he expects a transformation of the mortal human body to a state of immortality (Phil. 3.20-21; 1 Cor. 15.35-37).

The result of this whole process of resurrection, catching away, and meeting is described in the final sentence, *And so we will be with the Lord forever.* Although the soul of the believer is united with the Lord at the time of death (Phil. 1.23; 2 Cor. 5.6-9), the security the Thessalonians needed was that the dead in their community would not be separated from the Lord in his glorious coming and beyond. The security of union with him is given to this and other churches on more than one occasion (5.10; 2 Thess. 2.1; John 12.26; 17.24; Col. 3.3-4). What the apostle does not explain at this point is where they *will be with the Lord forever.* The custom that forms the background of the previous verse, that of going out to meet a visiting dignitary, implies that the delegation that goes out will return with the one who comes. Since no other explanation is offered of the events after the meeting, we may assume that the Thessalonians would have understood that the Lord would continue his *parousia* until he arrived at the final destination of the city or the earth. But the concern of the teachers was not to explain all the details of Christian eschatology but rather to console members of the church in their moment of agony, as the final verse once again clarifies.

18 The paragraph concludes as it began, on a pastoral note (v. 13), *Therefore encourage each other with these words.* The verb is the same one that is used at a number of points in this letter to mean "exhort" (2.12; 3.2, 7; 4.1, 10; 5.11, 14), but here it means "to console" or "to comfort" (3.7; 2 Cor. 1.4; 7.6-7). The Thessalonians grieved profoundly over the death of some

---

153. See BAGD, 20; *New Docs,* 4.28-29.

of their community, but the hope that the dead would not be excluded from the great meeting with the Lord was a reality that would bring great comfort. The truth of the Lord (v. 15) opens the door to true comfort. But Paul does not put himself forward as one who comforts the grieving; rather, he urges the members of the church to use *these words* to comfort *each other* (see 3.12; 4.9; 5.11, 15). The development of a true pastoral concern among the members of the congregation was a fundamental goal. The preceding teaching would serve as an instrument in this ministry of mutual comfort, but it was not designed to be a substitute for it.

The previous passage has suffered much ill as it has been mined to provide clues concerning the timing of the "rapture" of the church. Will this great event occur before seven years of tribulation, in the middle of this period, or at the very end? In the haste to answer this question, the real purpose of 1 Thessalonians 4.13-18 is overlooked. This teaching was presented to comfort those in grief by connecting the confession of the creed ("Jesus died and rose again") with the reality of the resurrection of the dead in Christ. This is not the stuff of speculative prophecy or bestsellers on the end times. The text is located at the funeral home, the memorial service, and the graveside. It is placed in the hands of each believer to comfort others in their time of greatest sorrow. The decidedly bizarre pictures of airplanes dropping out of the sky and cars careening out of control as the rapture happens detract from the hope that this passage is designed to teach. The picture presented here is of the royal coming of Jesus Christ. The church, as the official delegation, goes out to meet him, with the dead heading up the procession as those most honored. One coming is envisioned, which will unite the coming King with his subjects. What a glorious hope!

c. "Times and dates" (5.1-11)

In this section of the letter Paul responds to the third question the Thessalonians addressed to him (cf. 4.9, 13 and comments). When would the day of the Lord arrive (vv. 1-2)? This theme continued to dominate the thought of the Thessalonian congregation, as evidenced by their facile adoption of an erroneous teaching about the "when," an issue addressed in the second letter (2 Thess. 2.1-2). The persecution they suffered motivated their concern about the timing of this event. The apostle replies by assuring them that God will certainly judge their persecutors (v. 3; cf. 2 Thess. 1.3-10).[154] But it is also evident that the brothers and sisters enter-

---

154. The purpose of the section is not to revive a sense of imminency with regard to the day of the Lord, as Wanamaker suggests (*Commentary on 1 and 2 Thessalonians*, 177).

tained doubts about how they might be prepared for that day and how its advent might affect them (vv. 4-10). Paul answers this concern by teaching that living in faith, love, and hope is the proper way to be prepared so that the day of the Lord will not surprise them "like a thief." On the other hand, the destruction of the final judgment will come upon those who have rejected the gospel, and they will not be able to escape (v. 3). But the divine wrath will not be poured out upon the church, which will instead be saved from that event (v. 9). In fact, throughout the passage the contrast between the church and unbelievers is maintained, not only with regard to their destiny (vv. 3, 9) but also touching their conduct (vv. 4-8). The purpose of the whole discussion of this theme is pastoral and not speculative (v. 11; cf. 4.13, 18). Paul demonstrates no interest in fueling an apocalyptic perspective in order to hypothesize about the end nor to foster escapism. The teaching about final events is meant to inform and encourage them in their daily life and conduct. Clear thinking about the end is designed to help them live as true Christians in the present.

1 The section begins with the words "now concerning" (*peri de* as in 4.9; cf. 4.13), which indicate that the apostle is responding to yet another question the Thessalonians had asked, most likely through a letter they sent via Timothy: *Now, brothers, about times and dates we do not need to write to you.* Using the same words as in 4.9, the author assures the church that they did not need to add anything to the instruction they already possessed on this theme. What they knew they should remember and put into practice. This type of affirmation was well known in ancient parenetic teaching. In Dio Chrysostom's seventeenth discourse he states, "However, since I observe that it is not our ignorance of the difference between good and evil that hurts us, so much as it is our failure to heed the dictates of reason on these matters and to be true to our personal opinions, I consider it most salutary to remind men of this without ceasing."[155] The appeal the apostle makes is not to reason or personal opinion, as if proper knowledge of these issues were inherent in his readers, but the present teaching hearkens back to that which they had already received (v. 2; 2 Thess. 2.5). The affirmation that they knew these things is at the same time a call to put them in practice. Moreover, the denial that they needed teaching about the *times and dates* gently opens the door for Paul to add new points or perhaps simply to develop the teaching they already had.

Wanamaker presupposes the priority of 2 Thessalonians and therefore argues that this passage balances the instruction given in 2 Thess. 2.1-12. On the order of the letters, see pp. 64-69.

155. Dio Chrysostom 17.2. See Malherbe, *Moral Exhortation: A Greco-Roman Sourcebook,* 125. This is an example of paralipsis, in which "The orator pretends to pass over something which he in fact mentions." BDF, §495.1.

Since the apostle had included teaching on the "day of the Lord" in his initial package of instruction to the church (v. 2), he denies that he really needs to write to the church *about times and dates*. The words *times and dates* (*tōn chronōn kai tōn kairōn*; Acts 1.7) could be distinguished in classical Greek, but during the Hellenistic period they were synonymous.[156] The combination of the two words denoted an indefinite time or period in the future. They are even found in secular literature, where they refer to a time that is not fixed. Diogenes Laertius, for example, said, "Whatever money remains over, Arcesilaus shall take over from Olympichus, without however pressing him as to times and seasons."[157] The apostle affirms that they already had the teaching they needed about when this event was going to happen (cf. 2 Thess. 2.5).

Preoccupation with the timing of the day of the Lord arose frequently in biblical and Jewish literature; thus the question the Thessalonians raised is hardly surprising. In Daniel 12.6 the prophet asks, "How long will it be before these astonishing things are fulfilled?" In *4 Ezra* 4.33, which was written late in the first century AD, the same concern appears: "How long and when will these things be?" On more than one occasion the disciples inquired about the time of the end (Matt. 24.3; Luke 17.20; Acts 1.6), and Peter declares that this was the question that occupied the ancient prophets (1 Pet. 1.10-11). But in the face of so many concerns about when the end would come, the NT maintains an agnosticism about the time of the day of the Lord (Matt. 24.36; Mark 13.32; Acts 1.7). In the following verse the Thessalonians are reminded that they cannot know when this grand event will occur but that they should be prepared for it at all times. In our day the same question arises frequently, while not a few have promoted themselves as "date setters" who have supposed special insight into the answer. When will we hear the biblical response?

2 The reason why Paul does not need to pen a response about the "times and dates" is that *you know very well that the day of the Lord will come like a thief in the night*. Once again the apostle appeals to what the Thessalonians already knew (1.4, 5; 2.1, 2, 5, 11; 3.3, 4; 4.2; 5.12; and see 2 Thess. 2.6; 3.7). Here they affirm emphatically that because of the instruction previously received they knew *very well*, or certainly *(akribōs)*,[158]

---

156. Contra Oscar Cullmann, *Christ and Time* (Philadelphia: Westminster Press, 1950), 40. See BDF, §446; James Barr, *Biblical Words for Time* (Naperville, Ill.: A. R. Allenson, 1962), 21-49.

157. Diogenes Laertius 5.64; and Dan. 2.21; 7.12; Neh. 10.34; 13.31 (LXX 2 Esdr. 20.35; 23.31); Eccl. 3.1; Wis. 8.8; Sir. 29.5; Acts 3.19-21.

158. Epictetus 1.27.17; 2.22.36; Herodotus 7.32; BAGD, 33. Marshall, *1 and 2 Thessalonians*, 132-33, wisely observes that Paul did not have any more detailed information

the teaching about the *day of the Lord*. A "day" at times means something other than a twenty-four-hour period; it may even indicate the "day" when a judge decides to give his judgment (1 Cor. 4.3).[159] Therefore, the *day of the Lord* becomes that eschatological event when the Lord comes to judge the inhabitants of the earth and to pour out his wrath because of sin (Isa. 13.6, 9; Ezek. 13.5; 30.3; Joel 1.15; 2.1, 11; 3.14; Amos 5.18, 20; Zeph. 1.7, 14; Zech. 1.14; Mal. 4.5; Acts 2.20; 1 Cor. 5.5; 2 Thess. 2.2; 2 Pet. 3.10). However, for the people of God, the *day of the Lord* will be a day of salvation (Joel 2.21-32; 3.18; Obad. 15-21; Zech. 14.1-21). In the letters, this event is sometimes known as "the day of the Lord Jesus" (1 Cor. 1.8; 2 Cor. 1.14; and see Phil. 1.6, 10; 2.16), when he comes to execute the divine judgment (2 Thess. 1.6-10).

Since Jesus taught the disciples that it was impossible to know when this day would occur (Matt. 24.36; Mark 13.32-37; Acts 1.7), it was necessary to be ready for it at all times (cf. 1 Thess. 5.4-6; 2 Pet. 3.10-11). *The day of the Lord* will come suddenly at an unexpected moment, that is, *like a thief in the night*. This assertion finds its roots in the teaching of Jesus about his coming (Matt. 23.43-44; Luke 12.39-40) and was then incorporated into the instruction given to the church about the end (2 Pet. 3.10; Rev. 3.3; 16.15). The apostle never argued that there would be no signs before the end (see 2 Thess. 2.1-4); he only wanted to say that it was impossible to set the time of this event. This day should not surprise the church, although even believers do not know the "when," because they should always be prepared (v. 4). Although they do not know when the day will come, they will see it, and they will be ready.

3 In v. 3 Paul reminds the church that the "the day of the Lord will come like a thief in the night" (v. 2). His coming, like that of a thief, will be sudden and unexpected, and for that reason unbelievers will not find a way to escape from the day of judgment. The author explains, *While people are saying, "Peace and safety," destruction will come on them suddenly, as labor pains on a pregnant woman, and they will not escape.* With these words he refocuses part of Jesus' discourse on the last days (Luke 21.34-36)[160] to show how unbelievers will not be able to find refuge from the coming judgment. The implied subject of the declaration that there is *peace and safety* is the unconverted who persecute the Thessalonians (2.14) and who will suffer divine chastisement when the Lord Jesus ap-

---

about this subject than that which is presented in this passage. He does not lay out any detailed and speculative explanations about the final events.

159. BAGD, 347.

160. The two passages present the same idea that the day will surprise those who have embraced sin, and they also share certain key terms such as the verb *ephistēmi* ("to come"), the adjective *aiphinidos* ("sudden"), and the verb *ekphygō* ("to escape").

pears (2 Thess. 1.6-10). The whole passage is marked by the contrast between the Thessalonians and "the others" (vv. 3-6) as well as the union between this church and the larger Christian community, including the apostles ("we," vv. 5b-10). The deep desire that drove the Thessalonians to inquire about the "times and dates" welled up from the conflict between the church and the community. The apostle responds by reminding this church of their union with other churches and the common experience they shared.

From the start, the gospel preached in Thessalonica included the proclamation of the *parousia* of the Lord and his establishment as the one true Sovereign, a point that generated conflict between this city loyal to Rome and the apostles (Acts 17.6-7). The affirmation of *peace and safety* was possibly a summary of the response of the unconverted to the announcement that judgment would come upon them and upon the emperor whom they worshiped as divine (2 Thess. 1.6-10; 2.1-12).[161] Only one hundred years earlier the great orator Cicero was exiled in Thessalonica, during which time he complained bitterly about the city's lack of security.[162] The barbarians had taken control of the Via Egnatia, and the Thessalonians defended themselves behind the walls of the city. But with the establishment of the *pax Romana* under Augustus, *peace and safety* became the byword in the city as throughout the empire, and so the apocalyptic teaching of the apostles would have sounded decidedly strange. Numerous authors lauded this "peace,"[163] while the *Res gestae* of the emperor Augustus said that "the senate decreed that an altar of Augustan Peace should be consecrated for my return in the Campus Martius, on which the magistrates and priests and Vestal Virgins were ordered to make an annual sacrifice" (12.2).[164] The Thessalonians had benefited greatly from this peace and the Roman politic that favored the city, so the city responded by erecting a temple in honor of the divine Julius Caesar and of Augustus, "the son of god."[165] The word *peace* described a political reality that was both the absence of war and a social concord that consisted of a guarantee of tranquility that brought joy and

161. Most likely, the apostle is not quoting their exact words but rather employing the rhetorical technique of "impersonation," of which Quintilian (*Inst.* 9.2.30) says, "By this means we display the inner thoughts of our adversaries as though they were talking with themselves" (Margaret M. Mitchell, *Paul and the Rhetoric of Reconciliation* (Louisville: Westminster/John Knox Press, 1991), 86.

162. See the Introduction, p. 5. *In Pisonem* 34 (84).

163. For example, Ovid mentions the "peace of Augustus" (*Ex Ponto* 2.5.18), while Martial (7.80.1) and Tacitus (*Annals* 12.29) reflect on the *pax Romana*. Philo of Alexandria similarly called Augustus "the guardian of the peace" (*De Legatione ad Gaium* 147).

164. See Sherk, *The Roman Empire: Augustus to Hadrian*, 44.

165. *IT,* n. 31.

prosperity to a people.[166] The public and political *safety (asphaleia)* was the condition of those who were saved from any kind of harm and the security and stability under which people could live.[167] The two words appear together frequently in ancient literature. Diodorus Siculus, for example, spoke of "comfort in the time of peace and security in the time of war."[168] The Thessalonian population enjoyed both during the mid-first century AD.

But the apostle replies that in a time of political tranquility and social prosperity *destruction will come on them suddenly*. The Lord Jesus taught that the final judgment would come upon the inhabitants of the earth in a moment when it would be least expected (Matt. 24.36-39; Luke 21.34-35). The verb *will come* appears in contexts where an author wished to describe how calamities would come over people,[169] while the word translated *suddenly (aiphnidios,* an adjective modifying *destruction)* had a similar ominous tone, for it spoke of those sudden and unannounced events that would cause terror and anguish.[170] This is the way the final *destruction* will come, that time when people will lose "all that gives worth to existence"[171] (1 Tim. 6.9; 1 Cor. 5.5). In 2 Thessalonians 1.9 Paul describes in some detail how the Thessalonians' persecutors "will be punished with everlasting destruction and shut out from the presence of the Lord and from the majesty of his power." Those who rest in their *peace and safety* will lose all in this final conflict, without recourse or hope.

At this point in the argument, Paul does not discuss the nature of the *destruction* but only states that it will come *as labor pains on a pregnant woman*. In a number of inscriptions commemorating deceased women, the cause of death was inscribed as *labor pains (ōdin)*,[172] so this metaphorical way of speaking of the final *destruction* is not so strange as it first appears to those of us who live in a world where many of the dangers of childbirth have been minimized. The apostle may have in mind the time of great conflict before the coming of the Messiah that was known as "the labor pains of the Messiah," though this interpretation is far from certain.[173] The emphasis of our passage is on the way the final judgment,

---

166. *TDNT,* 1.424-25.

167. BAGD, 118; *TLNT,* 1.217; Josephus, *Antiquitates* 2.245 (2.10.2); Epictetus 1.9.7.

168. Diodorus Siculus 20.102.4; 4.14.3; Plutarch, *Antony* 40.4; Dio Chrysostom 74.4.

169. BAGD, 330-331; Luke 21.34; Sophocles, *Oedipus Tyrannus* 777; Wis. 19.1.

170. BAGD, 26; *TLNT,* 1.49-52; Wis. 17.14; 2 Macc. 14.17; 3 Macc. 3.24; Luke 21.34; and see Mark 13.36-37, where in light of the coming of the Lord at an unexpected moment, the disciples are exhorted to "Watch!"

171. MM, 445; BAGD, 536; Josephus, *Antiquitates* 17.38 (17.2.4); *Vita* 264 (51); *Sib. Or.* 3.327, 348.

172. *TDNT,* 9.668.

173. SB, 1.950; *TDNT,* 9.667-74; Matt. 24.8; Mark 13.8; Isa. 13.8; *1 Enoch* 62.4.

here compared to *labor pains,* comes at an unexpected moment. When this time comes, *they will not escape,* any more than a woman can escape from labor when her time is upon her. This final affirmation is extremely emphatic.[174] There will be absolutely no way for unbelievers to flee from that *destruction* (cf. Luke 21.36). Its coming is sure, though its time cannot be divined. And once it comes, there is no way to flee.

4 At this point the apostle contrasts the condition of the church in anticipation of the day of the Lord with that of the unbelievers in the city. The day of the Lord will come upon the unconverted at an unexpected time, that is, "like a thief in the night" (v. 2). On the other hand, the members of the church will be prepared for this event. The section from v. 4 through v. 10 may respond to a concern the Thessalonians held about their fate when the day of the Lord arrived. Paul reminds them that although the unbelievers "will not escape" (v. 3), God had not destined his own to suffer wrath (v. 9). To highlight the contrast between the fate of the believers and the unbelievers, the apostle begins with the emphatic, *But you, brothers, are not in darkness so that this day should surprise you like a thief.*[175] This statement does not mean that the church will know when *this day* will come but rather clarifies that Christians are those who are prepared for this final event (cf. Mark 13.35-37). They *are not in darkness.* The *darkness* is the dominion of sin that characterizes the life of the unconverted (John 3.19; Rom. 13.12; 2 Cor. 6.14; Eph. 5.11), whose understanding has been "darkened" (Rom. 1.21; Eph. 4.18), and who therefore live *in darkness* (Rom. 2.19). The association between the life of sin and darkness was well known in the OT as well as in the writings from Qumran and other Jewish literature.[176] Not surprisingly, authors could describe Christian salvation as the passage from darkness to light (Acts 26.18; Eph. 5.8; Col. 1.13; 1 Pet. 2.9) and redemption as "being enlightened" (Heb. 6.4; 10.32). The Christian is one who has left the sinful life of "the darkness" and who lives in the light of holiness (Rom. 13.12; Eph. 5.8-9; 1 John 1.6; 2.10). The believers in Thessalonica have been liberated from moral *darkness* and do not live in sin — they are not *in darkness* — and so are prepared for *this day.* The *darkness* is moral and does not refer to "ignorance" about the teaching on the day of the Lord.[177]

The brothers and sisters *are not in darkness so that this day should surprise you like a thief.* The verb *surprise* may mean simply "come upon," as

---

174. *Ou mē* with the subjunctive *ekphygōsin.* See 4.15.

175. Some mss. (A, B) have the plural "thieves" *(kleptas),* but the singular enjoys stronger textual support (ℵ, D, F, G, Ψ).

176. Pss. 74.20; 82.5; 112.4; Prov. 4.18-19; Isa. 2.5; 5.20; 1QM 13.15; 15.9; 1QS 1.1-10; 3.13–4.26; *T. Levi* 19.1; *T. Naph.* 2.7-10; *T. Ben.* 5.3. *TDNT,* 7.424-45; *NIDNTT,* 1.421-25.

177. Contra Wanamaker, *Commentary on 1 and 2 Thessalonians,* 181.

nightfall comes upon people,[178] but it could also be used where someone wished to describe how some disaster or death would suddenly befall or overtake a person, a sense that is reflected in our verse.[179] That is to say, *this day* of the Lord will not overtake Christians as some unexpected and disastrous event. Their preparedness is a function of their moral life. They can anticipate that day with assurance since they are *not in darkness* and, as we will see presently, that day will be for their salvation, not their condemnation (v. 9).

5   The reason why the apostle has confidence in saying that the brothers and sisters in Thessalonica "are not in darkness" (v. 4) is introduced in v. 5, which begins with the word "because" (*gar*, left untranslated in the *NIV*): *You are all sons of the light and sons of the day.* Paul includes *all* the members of the church as those who are *of the light* and *of the day* — no one is excluded (cf. 1.2; 4.10; 5.14, 26-27; 2 Thess. 1.3, 10; 3.18). The expression translated *sons of* would have embraced both the men and women of the congregation and should therefore be rendered "children of" *(NRSV)*. "Children of *x*" was both a Hebrew and a Greek expression[180] that meant that a person or group of people participated in something or were in close relationship with something (Matt. 8.12; 13.38; Mark 3.17; Luke 16.8; 20.34, 36; John 17.12; Eph. 2.2; 5.6; 2 Thess. 2.3). Those who are "children of light" are those who have been saved from darkness and now belong to the realm of "light" (Acts 26.18; Eph. 5.8; 1 Pet. 2.9). The members of the Dead Sea sect at Qumran called themselves by this very name (1QS 1.9; 2.16; 3.13, 24-25; 1QM 1.1, 3, 9, 11, 13), but the Christian use finds its roots in the teaching of Jesus (Luke 16.8; John 12.36). The Thessalonians are also called "children of the day" *(NRSV)*, or those who in the present time participate in the new era of God's order that is now being inaugurated (Rom. 13.12) and that will fully dawn when the Lord Jesus comes on the "day of the Lord" (5.2, 8; 2 Thess. 1.10). Their participation in *the light* and in *the day* has clear moral implications, as the apostle explains in the following verses (vv. 6-8).

Being children of light and of the day means, on the other hand, that *We do not belong to the night or to the darkness.* Starting at this point and going through v. 10, Paul couches his teaching and exhortation in the first person plural, moving from talking about what *they*, the Thessalonians,

---

178. Dionysius of Halicarnassus 2.51.3; Lucian, *Toxaris vel Amicitia* 31, 52; Josephus, *Antiquitates* 5.61 (5.1.17); *Vita* 329 (62).

179. Herodotus 2.66; 3.42; 4.11; 8.21; LSJ, 897; *TDNT*, 4.9-10.

180. Deissmann, *Bible Studies,* 161-66, brings together a number of Greek texts that use the expression "children of" but that show no Hebrew influence whatsoever. See BAGD, 834; BDF, §162.6.

do to what *we*, the Christians, do. The section is concerned, on the one hand, with the distinction between Christians and unbelievers (see v. 3 and comments) and, on the other, with the identification of the Thessalonians with this new order in which both they and the apostles participate. The shift to the first person plural stands at the head of the following moral exhortation and gently draws the Thessalonians into the common Christian life, reminding them of who *we* are and what *we* do. The structure of the verse is clearly chiastic, where the first and final elements are placed in contrast, as are the second and third:

    a *You are all children of the light*
      b *and children of the day.*
      b' *We are not of the night*
    a' *or of the darkness.*[181]

In this structure the elements *b'* and *a'* repeat the same ideas as *a* and *b* but in a negative form. The negative statements in the first person plural serve to highlight the Thessalonians' identification with the apostles in their moral life but at the same time underline the distance of the Christian community from the immoral practices that characterize unbelievers (Rom. 13.12; Eph. 5.8-11; John 8.12).

    6 The believers' existence as "children of the light and children of the day" has moral implications that the author begins to elaborate in this verse: *So then, let us not be like others, who are asleep, but let us be alert and self-controlled.* The imperative is put in the first person plural[182] and begins with the words *so then (ara oun)*,[183] which introduce the inference drawn from the previous statement (v. 5). Since Christians are "children of the light and children of the day," they should not *sleep* but rather *be alert and self-controlled.* This intimate relationship between their new existence and their new moral life touches a fundamental aspect of Christian ethics: What they are is what they should do. The moral exhortation finds its roots in the previous work of God in their lives. They have been made "children of the light and children of the day" via their salvation, and now they are to act according to that new state of being. The gift of grace *includes* within it the call to obedience. As V. P. Furnish states, "God's *claim* is regarded by the apostles as a constitutive part of God's *gift.* The Pauline concept of grace is *inclusive of* the Pauline concept of obedi-

---

181. See the commentary on 1.8 and n. 55, p. 103.
182. The subjunctive serves as an imperative.
183. See Rom. 5.18; 7.3, 25; 8.12; 9.16, 18; 14.12, 19; Gal. 6.10; Eph. 2.19; 2 Thess. 2.15. BAGD, 104.

ence."[184] Since the imperative is integral to the indicative, the summons of Christian ethics becomes, "Act what you are."

The imperative of the verse begins with the call "let us not sleep" (the imperative proper is not *let us not be like others*, as in the *NIV*).[185] While "sleep" may function as a metaphor for "death" in certain texts (see 5.10; 4.13, 15), it may also figuratively characterize the moral and spiritual indifference of those who are not converted (v. 7; Eph. 5.14). In the Gospels, the Lord calls the disciples to shun "sleep" by being "alert" so that they do not fall into temptation (Matt. 26.40-41; Mark 14.37-38; Luke 22.45-46) and so that they may be ready because they do not know the hour of the coming of the Lord (Mark 13.32-37). The same complex of ideas appears in this section of 1 Thessalonians, which suggests that the source of the instruction is the teaching of Jesus himself. The Christians' conduct should be distinct from that of "the others" (cf. 4.13), the unbelievers whose lives are marked by this "sleep" of moral indifference and sin.

Instead of being "asleep" in sin, the apostle exhorts the church, saying, *let us be alert and self-controlled*. To *be alert (grēgorōmen)*[186] means "to be awake," but figuratively it may mean either "to be alive" (5.10) or, as here, "to be alert and vigilant," spiritually and morally, especially in the face of a critical situation. The Lord called his own to *be alert* because they do not know when he is to come (Matt. 24.42-44; 25.13; Mark 13.32-37; Luke 12.35-40; and see Rev. 3.2-3; 16.15) and so that they do not enter into temptation (Matt. 26.40-41; Mark 14.37-38; and see 1 Pet. 5.8). Being "awake" is linked in Paul with standing firm (1 Cor. 16.13) and prayer (Col. 4.2). This is the moral state of having all systems "on" and functioning. But the apostle also calls the Thessalonians to be *self-controlled*. The verb means "to be sober" instead of drunk (cf. the use of the adjective in 1 Tim. 3.2 and Titus 2.2), but in the NT it always carries the metaphorical sense of exercising moral self-control or self-restraint and having clear thinking[187] in the face of adversity or danger (2 Tim. 4.5; 1 Pet. 5.8), especially as Christ's revelation and the end of all things approaches (1 Pet. 1.13; 4.7). According to Paul, Christian "self-control" or "self-restraint" means exercising the virtues of faith, love, and hope in light of the coming of the day of the Lord (v. 8). This is the way Christians remain alert and sober as children of light and of the day. The urgency of the call to

---

184. Victor Paul Furnish, *Theology and Ethics in Paul* (Nashville and New York: Abingdon, 1968), 225. See also Herman Ridderbos, *Paul: An Outline of His Theology* (Grand Rapids: Eerdmans, 1975), 253-58.

185. BAGD, 388; *TDNT*, 3.431-37; *NIDNTT*, 1.441-43.

186. BAGD, 167.

187. So Diogenes Laertius 10.132; Lucian, *Hermotimus* 47; Herodian 2.15.1; Josephus, *Bellum Judaicum* 4.42 (4.1.6); *Ep. Arist.* 209.

moral readiness and sobriety comes from the fact that the day of the Lord is truly coming at a time when he is least expected (v. 4). Christians stand prepared for the final event of history by having a sober and alert moral life and not by date-setting. Such is their nature, and so they do.

7 Continuing the metaphors of the previous verse, our author declares, *For those who sleep, sleep at night, and those who get drunk, get drunk at night.* The apostle describes two activities people engage in principally *at night:* sleeping and getting drunk. The normal time to sleep is *at night,* while those *who get drunk* do not commonly "tie one on" in the middle of the day. Not a few ancient texts reflect how scandalous it was to *get drunk* during the day (Isa. 5.11; Eccl. 10.16; *As. Mos.* 7.4; Acts 2.15; 2 Pet. 2.13). Sobriety characterizes life during the day (Rom. 13.13), while the *night* is associated with a variety of sins. Before the time when city streets were brightly illuminated by streetlights, the night was thought to be a horrible and sinister time. While we might talk excitedly about "going out for the night," they would speak about the night negatively and fearfully.[188] In the NT, for example, the night is the time when the Lord was betrayed and denied (Matt. 26.34; John 13.30). The night is the time when evil people do their deeds. As Chrysostom commented, "For it is just as corrupt and wicked men do all things as in the night, escaping the notice of all, and enclosing themselves in darkness. For tell me, does not the adulterer watch for the evening, and the thief for the night? Does not the violator of the tombs carry on all his trade in the night?"[189] These negative associations give rise to the metaphorical sense of *night* in this verse as the era of darkness that, as Paul says elsewhere, is already on its way out with the dawn of the gospel (Rom. 13.12). During this era, those who have not accepted the gospel *sleep,* an allusion to their moral and spiritual indifference (see v. 6 and commentary). Moreover, the apostle declares that during this *night* the unbelievers *get drunk.* Their drunkenness, just as the *sleep* referred to here, is a moral state that is not limited to the use and abuse of alcohol. This is the opposite of the sobriety of the Christians described in the previous verse (see commentary) and means embracing hedonistic desires and giving oneself over to vice instead of living soberly and giving oneself to Christian virtues. The thought driven home to the Thessalonians is that those who *sleep* and those who *get drunk* will not be ready for the day of the Lord (cf. Matt. 24.51; Luke 12.42-46).[190] Because of their condition the day of the Lord will come upon them *like a thief in the*

---

188. *NIDNTT,* 1.420; *TDNT,* 4.1123-26.

189. *Homilies on 1 Thessalonians* 9.

190. In Philo, *De Somniis* 2.101-6, the same contrasts between night and day, sleep and being awake, drunkenness and sobriety appear, but there with reference to the ignorant person.

night. On the other hand, the state of the Christian is different since Christians are of the day and are always prepared (v. 8).

8 Paul now compares the condition of those who "sleep" and who "get drunk" (v. 7) with that of believers. The stark contrast between Christians and unbelievers is introduced by the adversative *but (de)* and the emphatic *we (hēmeis): But since we belong to the day, let us be self-controlled.* The apostolic company has already made it quite clear that both they and the Thessalonians are of *the day* and that they should therefore be *self-controlled* or morally "sober" (vv. 5-6). Best has suggested an alternative reading that says that the call in v. 8 is not to moral sobriety but rather to the type of vigilance that characterizes a soldier, an interpretation prompted by the military imagery of the second half of the verse.[191] Under this reading, "be sober" has shifted in meaning to "be vigilant." However, Paul normally employs the verb "to be alert" (*grēgoreō,* as in v. 6) to express the idea of vigilance. The use of military imagery in the second part of the verse is somewhat surprising since, during the apostles' era, popular opinion of soldiers was not very favorable. Not a few ancient authors make special note of the lack of discipline among the troops during times of peace.[192] The expectation, however, is highlighted by the critique. A good soldier should be one who is disciplined and whose head is clear, or one who is "sober." In the same way, as an essential aspect of their preparedness for the coming of the "day of the Lord," the Christian should be "sober" (vv. 2, 4-6).

Believers are called to remain sober and ready for the coming day of the Lord, but they must also be armed with the fundamental Christian virtues, *putting on faith and love as a breastplate, and the hope of salvation as a helmet.*[193] At a number of points in his letters, Paul makes use of military metaphors to describe Christians and their conduct (Rom. 13.12; 2 Cor. 6.7; 10.3-5; Eph. 6.11-17; Phil. 2.25; 2 Tim. 2.3-4). The source of the teaching in v. 8 is Isaiah 59.17 (repeated in Wis. 5.17-20), where God himself is compared to a soldier, "He put on righteousness as his breastplate, and the helmet of salvation on his head." The apostle has reworked the meta-

---

191. Best, *First and Second Epistles to the Thessalonians,* 213.

192. Benjamin Isaac, *The Limits of the Empire* (Oxford: Clarendon Press, 1990), 24-25.

193. The aorist participle *endysamenoi* ("putting on") is placed after the principal verb. In the majority of cases where the verb precedes the aorist participle, the participle describes an action contemporary with the action of the verb and not before it. See Stanley E. Porter, *Verbal Aspect in the Greek of the New Testament, with Reference to Tense and Mood* (New York: Peter Lang, 1989), 381; BDF, §381; contra Wanamaker, *Commentary on 1 and 2 Thessalonians,* 185. The adverbial clause introduced by the participle may describe *how* the believer is to be sober ("by putting on . . .") or, as suggested here, may simply present a concomitant action.

phor so that it now refers to Christians who put on[194] the *breastplate* and *helmet.*" The idea of *putting on* virtues is not linked exclusively with military imagery, for in the *Testament of Levi* 8.2 the same verb describes the investiture of the priest as a metaphorical description of taking on justice, understanding, truth, faith, and prophetic power. But both here and in Ephesians 6.10-18 the military imagery from Isaiah prevails. The *breastplate* was either a coat of mail or could be made of either leather and metal, scales made from horse hooves stitched together, or even linen, while the *helmet* was fabricated from metal.[195] This armor was all defensive and therefore could be aptly used to describe the preparedness of the Christian soldier. In Ephesians 6.14, as in Isaiah 59.17, the *breastplate* represented "justice," but here the metaphor is changed so that it stands for *faith and love.* The *helmet* in Ephesians 6.17 and Isaiah 59.17 was "salvation," but the apostle again alters the metaphor somewhat so that it refers to *the hope of salvation.*

Paul tells this church that the fundamental Christian virtues of *faith, love,* and *hope* become the defensive armor that will insure that the Christians are prepared for the "day of the Lord," whenever it comes. The Thessalonian church showed clear evidences of these virtues (1.3 and commentary), so much so that Timothy was able to both witness them and tell his associates how this church lived in them (3.6, 8). In the second letter, Paul tells how these virtues kept abounding and growing in this church, and that the apostles boasted about them to other churches (2 Thess. 1.3-4). Their *faith* in God (1.8) and their *love* to other Christians and to all people (4.9-10), plus their *hope* in the coming of the Lord Jesus (1.3), enabled them to be completely prepared for the day of the Lord, without knowing when this event was going to occur. The *hope* they enjoyed is specifically linked with their future *salvation* (cf. Matt. 10.22; 24.13; Mark 13.13; Rom. 5.9-10; 1 Cor. 3.15; 2 Tim. 4.18), which here, as in Romans 5.9-10, is deliverance from the wrath of God, as the following verse shows. *The hope of salvation* is not a vague expectation but rather the settled assurance of future deliverance (see 1.10; Rom. 8.24).

9 Up to this point Paul's teaching has focused on the differences between the character of Christians and unbelievers in the time before the coming day of the Lord. The unconverted sleep and get drunk at night, but believers, who are of the day, keep themselves sober and alert. In v. 9 the focus shifts. Now the author explains the destiny of the two groups —

---

194. The verb "put on" (here the participle *endysamenoi*) appears in a number of texts, including Isa. 59.17, where the author describes how a soldier "puts on" his armor (Wis. 5.18; Josephus, *Antiquitates* 7.283 [7.11.7]; 13.309 [13.11.2]).

195. Ferguson, *Backgrounds of Early Christianity,* 51; Pausanias 1.21.6.

one will suffer divine wrath (implicit in v. 9) while the other will be saved from it. The reason why the Christians in Thessalonica could put on "the hope of salvation as a helmet" (v. 8) and have confidence in anticipation of the coming cataclysm is explained in this verse: *For God did not appoint us to suffer wrath but to receive salvation through our Lord Jesus Christ.*[196] Occasionally in these letters, the apostle reminds the Thessalonians of their election by God (1.4; 4.7; 2 Thess. 1.11; 2.13-14), a point to which he returns in the present verse. In both this and other texts where it appears, the principal verb of the first clause means "to destine or appoint someone to or for something"[197] (Acts 13.47; Rom. 4.17; 9.33; 1 Cor. 12.18, 28; 1 Tim. 1.12; 1 Pet. 2.6). Whenever the verb is used in this manner, the divine appointment is made so that God's purposes might be fulfilled. For example, Paul notes how he was appointed to carry out the divine service in 1 Timothy 1.12. For that very reason, the use of the verb in juxtaposition with *wrath* is striking. The Thessalonians should clearly understand that God has not destined his chosen *to suffer wrath* since his purposes for them spring from his love (1.4) and result in *salvation* (5.9; 2 Thess. 2.13). The church had been well instructed concerning how Christians would suffer for their faith and were even destined for this (3.3 and comments), but their portion did not include being subject to the *wrath* of God (cf. 1.10; 2.16 and comments). The fury of God's wrath is described graphically in 2 Thessalonians 1.6-10 and 2.8-10 as it is directed against those who do not obey the gospel. Paul assures the church that although they do not know when the day of the Lord will arrive (5.2), they need not be anxious since they will be alert, sober, and prepared as good soldiers (vv. 5-8), and God's plan for them is salvation and not destruction (v. 9b). This teaching responds to the Thessalonians' concerns about the time of the coming of that day (5.1). Their eschatological expectation was so vivid and their sufferings so profound and painful that later they were persuaded that the day of the Lord was right upon them (2 Thess. 2.1-2 and comments), a teaching the apostle then corrected (2 Thess. 2.3ff).

Paul explains that God has destined the Christians *to receive salvation through our Lord Jesus Christ.* The word translated *to receive* (*peripoiēsin*, a verbal noun), which means either "obtaining" or "possessing" something, appears with *salvation* in the OT (Isa. 31.5), apocryphal literature (1 Macc. 6.44), and the NT (Heb. 10.39).[198] In 2 Thessalonians 2.14

---

196. Wanamaker, *Commentary on 1 and 2 Thessalonians*, 186, argues that v. 9 presents the reason why Paul and his readers should be "vigilant and self-controlled," thus linking this verse with the principal verb of v. 8. However, v. 9 is linked more specifically with the last phrase of v. 9, which speaks of the future hope of the believer.

197. BAGD, 816.

198. BAGD, 650; *TDNT*, 3.102.

what is obtained is "the glory of our Lord Jesus Christ." The term thus points to that which the Christian will gain when the day of the Lord arrives — not *wrath* but *salvation*. While this salvation is multi-dimensional (see 1 Thess. 2.16; 2 Thess. 2.10), the present concern is with deliverance from the divine chastisement that will come upon those who rebel against God's way. Christians will not gain this salvation through any merit on their part; it becomes theirs because of God's gracious election. It is not obtained as if it were a salary. This message of grace is both implied in the verb and underlined by the final clause, *through our Lord Jesus Christ*. The Lord is the one who will deliver believers from the coming wrath (1.10 and commentary).

10 Salvation from the wrath of God is the fruit of the redemptive work of Christ on the cross: *He died for us so that, whether we are awake or asleep, we may live together with him.* This is one of the few texts in the Thessalonian letters where the author mentions the cross of Christ (see 2.15; 4.14), and the only place in these books where the purpose of Christ's death is explained (cf. Rom. 14.9; 2 Cor. 5.15, 21; Gal. 1.4). The death of Jesus was *for us,* words that point to his substitutionary death for our sins (see 1 Cor. 15.3). The absence of a fuller elaboration of the theology of the cross at this point implies that the first readers already understood the teaching about the death of Christ. This was part of the initial instruction the church had received (see Acts 17.3), and it became the foundation of the church's confession (1 Thess. 4.14). In this verse, the death of Jesus is inextricably linked with deliverance from wrath and obtaining salvation (v. 9), which is further defined as living *together with him.* He *died* for believers so that they in turn might *live together with him.* This exchange touches the heart of the gospel of God. Moreover, the confession that believers *may live together with him* implies that the very one who *died* for them was raised from the dead and is now alive.

The salvation Christ brings through his death is for all those who have believed in him, whether they remain alive or die, that is, *whether we are awake or asleep.* Previously in this section the author referred to Christians as those who were "awake" (v. 6) or morally "alert," using the same verb found in the present verse. On the other hand, unbelievers are classified as those who "sleep" because of their moral indifference (v. 7), again with the same verb found in v. 10. But although the terminology in v. 10 is identical to that found in vv. 6-7, the sense is entirely different. Paul is not saying that all people, whether or not they are believers, *live together with him.* This kind of universalism is distant from his thought and even denied by the previous argument, which distinguishes between the character and the destiny of the believer and the unbeliever. Rather, the argument of this and the following verse harkens back to the beginning of the

243

eschatological discourse in which the author discussed the destiny of the dead and living in Christ. In 4.13-15 "those who fall asleep" are the dead in Christ who will be resurrected.[199] Those who "are still alive, who are left till the coming of the Lord" (4.15), are referred to in 5.10 as those who are *awake*. This is the only place in the NT where "to be awake" becomes a way of saying "to be alive,"[200] although the combination "to sleep" *(katheudō)* and "to awake" *(egeirō*, a word related to *grēgoreō)* are used figuratively with reference to death and life (Mark 5.39, 41; Luke 8.52, 54).

This return to the discussion of the ultimate destiny of living and dead believers serves as an inclusio that ties in the inquiry about "day of the Lord" (5.1-2) with the Thessalonians' questions about deceased believers (4.13). The call in the final verse of this section (v. 11) for the believers to comfort one another also reiterates the conclusion of the previous section, "Therefore comfort each other with these words" (4.18). While the issue that precipitated the teaching of 5.1-11 was the Thessalonians' query about the time of the day of the Lord (vv. 1-2), this concern appears to have been generated primarily out of their grief and bewilderment when faced with the death of some beloved member or members of their community. Verse 10 returns to reassure them that the destiny of the dead in Christ is secure, since, *whether we are awake or asleep, we may live together with him* (cf. 4.15-17).

We may be lured at this point to understand the statement that both living and dead believers *live together with him* as a reference to their present existence. If this were the idea the author is trying to convey, it would mean that both the living and the dead are currently living *with him*. On this reading the declaration would be a clear statement about the intermediate state of deceased Christians — they are alive with Jesus! As attractive as this interpretation might be, we should observe that the immediately preceding argument brings to the forefront the eschatological hope of believers. They have put on the "hope of salvation" (v. 8) and anticipate salvation from the coming wrath through the Lord Jesus Christ (v. 9). This final salvation is now described in v. 10 as living *together with him*. As in 4.16-17, the theology of v. 10 has to do with the resurrection of the dead and the catching away of the living and the dead "to be with the Lord forever" (cf. the use of "to live" with reference to the resurrection in Acts 1.3; Rom. 14.9a; 2 Cor. 13.4a; Rev. 2.8; 20.4-5). The glorious declaration of hope in v. 10b that *we may live together with him* echoes the last part

---

199. The verb used to describe sleep in 4.13 *(koimeō)* is synonymous with the verb in 5.10 *(katheudō)*, which itself appears in the LXX of Dan. 12.2 and Ps. 88.5 to refer to the deceased.

200. BAGD, 167; *TDNT*, 2.339.

of 4.17, "And so we will be with the Lord forever." The portion that the believers await, whether they are the living or the dead in Christ, is the promise of the resurrection and life in union with him.

11 As in 4.18, Paul calls the members of the Christian community to use this teaching for mutual comfort as well as edification. While this comfort and edification are rooted in the apostolic teaching, the pastoral responsibility does not fall simply to the founders or even the leadership of this church. Their grief in the face of death and their confusion about the time of the day of the Lord (4.13; 5.1-2) find their answer in the fundamental apostolic doctrine and the mutual support of members in the church. The apostle concludes the section with the words, *Therefore, encourage one another and build each other up, just as in fact you are doing*. The first part of the exhortation is identical to 4.18 (see commentary), and, along with 5.9-10, implies that the Thessalonians' concern about the day of the Lord was linked with their questions about the dead in Christ. They are therefore to "comfort" one another, reminding each other that God has destined all of them, both the living and the dead, to salvation. This call to mutual comfort is tied in with the further exhortation to *build each other up*, a verb that appears for the first time here in the Pauline letters. It derives from the world of construction (Matt. 21.33; 23.29; Mark 14.58; Luke 12.18; Acts 7.47), but the apostle uses it metaphorically. It describes the way the apostle and other believers help each other grow and progress in the faith. Each individual in the community is responsible for the development of others and of the whole through this mutual building process. This term therefore becomes fundamental to Paul's understanding of the life of the church.[201] The goal of each member of the community is to build up other members of the church (Rom. 14.19; 15.2; 1 Cor. 14.3-5, 12, 17, 26; Eph. 4.12, 29; Col. 2.7) through the use of the gifts of the Spirit. Although Paul does not state explicitly that the church should use the teaching previously presented for mutual comfort and edification, as he did in 4.18 ("encourage each other with these words"), most likely he has their instruction in mind. But since the Thessalonian church was already practicing this mutual ministry, the apostle encourages them to continue in what they are already doing, *just as in fact you are doing* (cf. 4.9-10, 1). With these words he concludes his responses to the questions put to him by the church (4.9).

The purpose of eschatological teaching is not to fuel speculation about the dates and times of the final consummation. The time of the end is God's concern, and the "when" is a secret he has decided not to share.

---

201. See *TDNT*, 5.140-42; BAGD, 558. The metaphorical use of the word does not originate with Paul. MM, 441-42.

The future should not bring dread but call the believer to be prepared, whenever the day of the Lord may come. The Christian therefore "lives in the light of his coming," each day doing that which is good and just. The current trend toward speculation based on counting toes in Daniel or horns in Revelation and relating them to current events is somewhat misplaced. Whatever happens in Israel or the Middle East is, for us, beside the point. The Christian focus is always on readiness, but a readiness not based on an "accurate" reading of the times but on living in faith, hope, and love. In an age of comfort and materialism some Christians have let any thought of a final consummation and judgment become like so many dusty, unread books on the shelf. Concerns about their present well-being and prosperity drown out any biblical call to be mindful of the future. Genuine Christian faith has an "eschatological edge" that balances vivid hope about the future with stellar piety in the present.

4. "Respect those who work hard among you" — The Community and Its Leadership (5.12-13)

Occasionally in the letters we catch a glimpse of the way the NT authors made use of a common store of teaching to develop their thoughts or how one author would use the same, standard instruction in correspondence to different churches. For example, the teaching on reciprocal relationships, "house tables" as they are sometimes called (or *Haustafeln* in German), appears in more than one of Paul's writings as well as in 1 Peter (Eph. 5.21–6.9; Col. 3.18–4.1; 1 Pet. 2.18–3.7). The same general orientation about the Christian's responsibility toward the state is found in both Romans 13.1-7 and 1 Peter 2.13-17. Peter and James lay out almost identical instruction about the Christian's response to the devil in 1 Peter 5.5-9 and James 5.6-7. Similarly, the apostolic decree of Acts 15.29 is echoed in 1 Thessalonians 4.3. In the following section (5.12-22), the moral instruction Paul elaborates seems to be standard stuff that he turned around and used in his letter to the Romans as well (Rom. 12.3-17). This instruction may simply be part of what became Paul's own formal cycle of teaching for the churches, but it may also have enjoyed a wider circulation. One of the pioneering studies on the "form criticism of the epistles" was that of E. G. Selwyn, who, in his magisterial commentary on 1 Peter, outlines his observations on the common core of Christian teaching that had made its way into several letters.[202] In one of his comparative charts he not only shows the close relationship between this section in 1 Thessalonians and Romans, but also suggests that some of the following was integrated into

202. Selwyn, *The First Epistle of St. Peter*, 365-466.

1 Peter.[203] Such parallels signal that Paul and others considered this teaching to be fundamental for new Christians in any church as they sought to define their lives and conduct vis-à-vis the moral currents that surrounded them. What seems, then, to be simply a random collection of moral exhortations fired in a shotgun pattern is really part of a set outline of teaching. That outline touches on their social obligations toward church leadership (5.12-13), to various groups within the church (5.14), and to those outside the Christian community (5.15). The section then addresses the themes of proper Christian character before God (5.16-18) and the proper function of prophecy in the church (5.19-22).

After responding to the queries of the Thessalonians concerning fraternal love, the destiny of the dead in Christ, and the time of the day of the Lord (4.9–5.11), the apostle turns to address the question of leadership in the church. We are left wondering how these people came into positions of leadership in this congregation. Perhaps Paul and his companions appointed leaders during their short stay in the city in anticipation of their departure. On the other hand, the mission of Timothy may have included naming elders within the congregation during his trip to Thessalonica (cf. Titus 1.5; Acts 14.21-23), in which case the following exhortations would be calculated to affirm such people in the eyes of the other believers in the church. But it is also possible that we are looking in the window at those who emerged as leaders without being formally named to their position, whom the apostle now commends to the congregation. Although we cannot arrive at a definitive answer concerning the mechanism of their appointment, v. 12 suggests that the final hypothesis reflects how it occurred. But however these leaders were established, at this early date the young church in Thessalonica had in their midst those who gave direction in the church and who needed the support of the apostles so that their ministry might be effective.

12 Because of the absence of the founders, the establishment of leadership in the church was a primary concern. But who was qualified take on the responsibility for a congregation now that the founders were no longer with them? The pastoral letters include lists of qualifications designed to aid Timothy and Titus in appointing elders and deacons in Ephesus and Crete (1 Tim. 3.1-11; Titus 1.5-9). But in the case of the Thessalonian church, the text remains silent about how the new leaders were chosen. Verse 12 suggests that Paul and his associates did not lay out criteria to evaluate potential leaders but simply urged the church to

203. Ibid., 408-10; and see the comparative chart in Marshall, *1 and 2 Thessalonians*, 145-46. Selwyn suggests the possibility that Silvanus may have played a role in this adoption (1 Pet. 5.12).

recognize those who were emerging as congregational leaders. Their exhortation to the church was, *Now we ask you, brothers, to respect those who work hard among you, who are over you in the Lord and who admonish you.*

Paul signals the transition to a new section with the vocative "brothers and sisters" and the exhortation *we ask you.* What follows is not simply a polite request but rather a strong exhortation concerning how the church should respond to its new leadership. *We ask* is the same verb that appears in 4.1 and means "to beseech" or "to entreat." In this paragraph, as there, it is combined with "we urge" or "we exhort" (v. 14).[204] First, the believers are to *respect* these leaders, a word that means "to know" *(eidenai)*;[205] given this context, however, it might be an instruction either "to honor" them (so our translation) or "to recognize" them as the legitimate leaders of the church.[206] This second understanding of the verb is likely the one intended, for two reasons. First, if the call were "to respect" the new leaders, the following exhortation in v. 13 would be an unnecessary redundancy: "Hold them in highest regard." Second, Paul repeats the same exhortation in 1 Corinthians 16.15, where he calls the church to recognize the leadership[207] of those of the house of Stephanas because they were "the first converts in Achaia" and because of their service. For this reason the Corinthians should submit both to their leadership and that of "everyone who joins in the work, and labors at it" (1 Cor. 16.16; the verb "labors," *kopiōntas,* appears also in 1 Thess. 5.12b). Those who should be recognized as leaders and received the apostolic approval were those who did the work. What legitimized this leadership was not their status or social rank, as was commonly the case in both Greek and Roman society, but the labor they undertook among the members of the congregation, as the second part of the verse explains.[208]

The apostle describes the work of these leaders in three ways. In the Greek text, only one article links all three participles that clarify their function, and so we should not imagine that our author is thinking of three distinct types of persons. The true leaders who should be recognized as such by the church are first described as those who *work hard among you.* The verb has to do with engaging in difficult or exhausting labor, the same as

---

204. On the language of exhortation in 1 Thessalonians, see Malherbe, "Exhortation in First Thessalonians," 240-41. On the various types of exhortation, see Seneca, *Epistulae Morales* 94.

205. Used as a synonym for *ginōskō* during the Hellenistic period (*TDNT,* 5.116-19).

206. See BAGD, 555-56; MM, 440; *TDNT,* 5.116-19.

207. *Oidate* is probably an imperative. See the commentaries and Ignatius, *Smyrnaeans* 9.1. The same thought is found in 1 Cor. 16.18, which uses the verb *epignōskete.*

208. See Andrew D. Clark, *Secular and Christian Leadership in Corinth* (Leiden: Brill, 1993), 126.

the noun form of the word in 1.3. Over and again it designates ministerial labors (1 Cor. 3.8; 15.58; 2 Cor. 6.5; 11.23, 27; Col. 1.29; 1 Thess. 3.5; and 1 Cor. 15.10; 16.16; Gal. 4.11; Phil. 2.16; Col. 1.9; 1 Tim. 4.10; 5.17) and highlights the fact that true leaders are those who put forth great effort in their work for the benefit of the church. These various leaders *work hard among you,* in those affairs that are in the interest of the congregation, including teaching and the other aspects of their pastoral ministry.

Secondly, these leaders are those *who are over you in the Lord.* The translation of this word is problematic because it may highlight their leadership or point to those who protect and render aid to the church. The term frequently designated those who were leaders of communities or who functioned as guardians and heads of communities.[209] For example, an inscription from Thessalonica dedicated to Marcus Anius speaks of him as the one who presided over (*proistamenos,* as in 1 Thess. 5.12) the *koinon* in Macedonia.[210] The term similarly could be used to convey the meaning "to preside" or "govern" in 1 Timothy 3.4, 5, 12 and 5.17. On the other hand, the meaning "to protect" was quite common,[211] as were the related meanings of "to help" or "to be concerned about" (see Titus 3.8, 14). The verb arises in discussions about benefaction since benefactors are those who render aid. Paul uses the substantive form of this verb to talk about Phoebe, who was the deaconess and benefactor or patron of the church in Cenchrea, and of himself as well (Rom. 16.1-2). In the case of 1 Thessalonians 5.12 as of Romans 12.8, difficulties arise when we try to decide between the concepts of rendering aid on the one hand and leadership and authority on the other. But in antiquity, "leadership" and "rendering aid" were not neatly separated ideas. Those who exercised leadership within the towns and villages, as well as in the empire itself, were those who served the population as benefactors. Political responsibility went hand in hand with benefaction toward the community.[212] Given the common use of this term and the prominent place of patrons in the leadership of society at large, the most likely candidates for leaders in this young church were people like Jason, who served as both patron and leader within the church (Acts 17.5-9). Those who governed the church were at the same time the ones who sought her benefit and cared for her. In our text, the phrase *in the Lord* is linked specifically with this function of leadership. While leaders may have been benefactors, the authority

209. BAGD, 707; MM, 541; *TDNT,* 1.123; *NIDNTT,* 1.193, 194, 197.
210. *SIG*³ 700.7. On the Macedonian *koinon,* see p. 24.
211. For example, Epictetus 3.24.3; Josephus, *Antiquitates* 14.196 (14.10.3).
212. See *New Docs,* 4.82; David Braund, "Function and Dysfunction: Personal Patronage in Roman Imperialism," in *Patronage in Ancient Society* (ed. Andrew Wallace-Hadrill; London and New York: Routledge, 1989), 137-52.

and leadership they exercised derived from their relationship with the Lord (cf. 4.1; 2 Thess. 3.12). We should note that while Paul and his associates caution those in the church who would want to continue as dependent clients (4.11-12 and later in 2 Thess. 3.6-15), at the same time he commends true benefaction (4.9-10; 2 Thess. 3.13) toward those in genuine need (remember the offering for the needy believers in Jerusalem, which is discussed in 1 Cor. 16; 2 Cor. 8-9 and elsewhere).

Finally, the leaders of the church in Thessalonica are those who *admonish* the congregation, correcting their doctrinal and moral errors. An author would not employ this word to describe the task of imparting information, though it might be linked with teaching (Col. 1.28), but would rather take it up to point to giving advice and correction designed to change the conduct of a person (5.14; 2 Thess. 3.15). While personal correction has almost become anathema in the church today, ancient opinion was that correction by others was profitable for a person's well-being.[213] "To admonish" was considered one of the primary responsibilities of parents toward their children (e.g., Eph. 6.4; Philo, *De Specialibus Legibus* 2.232; Wis. 11.10), of leaders toward their congregations (Acts 20.31; 1 Cor. 4.14; Col. 1.28), and of the various members of the congregation toward their brothers and sisters in the faith (Rom. 15.14). In the Thessalonian church, those who were distinguished by their labors for the church, their leadership and provision, and their moral influence over others were those who should be recognized as the true leaders in the church. Neither their status nor their title but rather their service among the believers is what separated them for this ministry. True Christian leadership is not show but substance, not self-serving but self-sacrificial.

13 While v. 12 called the Thessalonians to recognize those who were the legitimate leaders among them, v. 13 takes the further step of exhorting the believers to be loyal both to them and their fellow Christians. With regard to those who exercise leadership in the church, Paul urges, *Hold them in the highest regard in love because of their work.* Some have suggested that the principal verb of the sentence *(hēgeisthai)* means "to respect" or "to esteem," but the word never appears with this sense in biblical literature, and this meaning is extremely rare in the wider body of Greek literature.[214] The verb normally signifies "to think" or "to consider" (2 Cor. 9.5; Phil. 2.25; 3.8; 2 Pet. 1.13), a definition that is most likely conveyed in the present verse. The combination of this verb "consider" with

213. Philo, *Legum Allegoriae* 3.193, "If you desire to become the slave of the wise person, you will accept your share of reprimands or corrections"; *De Congressu Eruditionis Gratia* 157, "What is good and profitable for those who need to be rebuked is admonition."

214. BAGD, 343; MM, 277; *TDNT,* 2.907. See Thucydides 2.89.9.

the adverb "quite beyond all measure" *(hyperekperissou)*[215] yields the sense reflected in the *NIV.* The Thessalonians should think about them in the highest way possible, and so *hold them in highest regard.* They should not only recognize the leaders among them but also respect them greatly. This esteem is expressed *in love* (cf. Eph. 4.2, 15-16). Their great regard for their leaders is not mere submission to a person of higher rank but is rather part of a relationship that is characterized by love. Just as love delimits the relationship between all the members of the congregation (1.3; 4.9-10), so it should be the seal of their relationship with their leaders. This *love* is closely related to the community harmony or *peace* that is called for in the exhortation of the second part of this verse. In fact, the first-century Latin author Lucan all but identifies love with *concordia,* "Be present now, thou that embracest all things in an eternal bond. Harmony, the preserver of the world and the blended universe! Be present, through hallowed Love that unitest the world!" *(Bellum Civile* 4.189-91). The apostle summons the congregation to this profound loyalty to their leaders *because of their work* and not because of their position or office. The honor they receive and the loyalty they enjoy are not given them because of their social status, either inside or outside the Christian community, nor is it because of their riches, family name, or title. While the leadership of the church may well have come from the higher classes who served as patrons of the church (v. 12), their social status was not to be the foundation of respect for them but rather the labor they engaged in for the benefit of the congregation.

But the relationship between the congregation and the leaders was not the only concern of the apostle. The Christians are called to a commitment of loyalty among themselves: *Live in peace with each other.* This call to peace among the members of the community is rooted in the teaching of Jesus (Mark 9.50), and the call to live in peace with everyone, both inside and outside the church, became a common element of Christian moral instruction (Rom. 12.18; 2 Cor. 13.11; Heb. 12.14; and see Rom. 14.17, 19; 1 Cor. 14.33; Jas. 3.18). *Peace* was considered one of the fruits of the presence of the Spirit in the life of the believer (Gal. 5.22; Eph. 4.3). The theme of *peace* was so important in antiquity that Aristotle could even say that it was one of the five principal themes of rhetoric *(Ars Rhetorica* 1.4.7). In the realm of interpersonal relationships, the verb *to live in peace* pointed to the absence of discord and the maintenance of harmony between persons (Sir. 28.9, 13).[216]

But although this exhortation *to live in peace* was a standard *topos* in moral instruction, in the case of the Thessalonians it responded specifi-

---

215. BAGD, 840; MM, 653; *TDNT,* 6.61-62; *NIDNTT,* 1.730. See 3.10 and commentary; Eph. 3.20.

216. *TLNT,* 1.424-38.

cally to certain elements of discord found in this community. Although the relationships between the members of this church were extremely good (1.3; 4.9-10), some of the believers were not working and their dependence as clients was a cause of social tension (v. 14; cf. 2 Thess. 3.6-15, where the discussion of the disorderly who were not working is concluded with a prayer for peace). Moreover, questions concerning the proper place of prophecy in the church generated division (vv. 19-22), while sexual immorality among certain members of the church had become a catalyst for tension (4.3-8). The call to *live in peace with each other* was especially important in light of the adversity this church suffered at the hands of their contemporaries (2.13). Community loyalty was the best defense against attacks from outside.

5. "Warn . . . encourage . . . help . . . be patient" — Life in Community (5.14)

14 Moving on from the theme of loyalty within the community (vv. 12-13), Paul exhorts the believers concerning how they are to respond to various persons within the congregation: *And we urge you, brothers, warn those who are idle, encourage the timid, help the weak, be patient with everyone.* This pastoral responsibility is not placed solely in the hands of the leadership but delegated to all the members of the church. Although the leaders played an important role within the congregation (v. 12), the task of maintaining the well-being of the Christian community did not fall to them exclusively. The members of the church shared a mutual responsibility to help one another for their building up in the faith (cf. 5.11; Eph. 4.16). The type of help extended to others was to respond to the particular needs of each. This kind of differentiation between people of various dispositions and the counsel concerning how to respond to each group that we find here was a theme touched on in Seneca as well.[217] Wisdom dictated that they should not "warn the weak" nor "encourage the idle."

---

217. *Epistulae Morales* 94.13-16. Seneca opens the discussion (94.1-2) by speaking about advice given to those of different positions, saying, "That department of philosophy which supplies precepts appropriate to the individual case, instead of framing them for mankind at large — which, for instance, advises how a husband should conduct himself towards his wife, or how a father should bring up his children, or how a master should rule his slaves — this department of philosophy, I say, is accepted by some as the only significant part, while the other departments are rejected on the ground that they stray beyond the sphere of practical needs — as if any man could give advice concerning a portion of life without having first gained a knowledge of the sum of life as a whole!" The so-called apostolic "house tables" or domestic code functions the same way (Eph. 5.21–6.9; Col. 3.18–4.1; 1 Pet. 2.13–3.7). Seneca's argument, however, goes on to embrace those of different dispositions.

The transition to this new instruction is signaled by the vocative "brothers and sisters" and the exhortation *we urge you* (see 4.1; 5.12 and comments). First, members of the church are called to *warn those who are idle*. The church is not to remain passive in the face of disorderly members but should respond to correct their conduct by admonishing them (the verb is the same as found in 5.12c; cf. Rom. 15.14; Col. 3.16; 2 Thess. 3.15). Those who are in need of this admonition are the *idle (ataktous)*, who are not the "lazy" but rather those who are "disorderly" or "undisciplined" in the community. The term appears in such places as the gymnasiarchal law of Berea that prescribes the disciplinary measures that should be taken to correct the conduct of those of the gymnasium who do not follow the rules and who are therefore "disorderly."[218] The "disorderly" members of the church are most likely those who had chosen to maintain their status as dependent clients and who had opted not to respond to the teaching and the apostolic example concerning the necessity of working to earn one's own bread (1 Thess. 4.11-12; 2 Thess. 3.6-15). In the extensive discussion of the problem in the second letter to this church, the ones who were doing no work are repeatedly spoken of as the "disorderly" (2 Thess. 3.6-7, 11). The fact that the apostles needed to return to this theme indicates that such people not only ignored the apostolic teaching but also refused to heed the correction that came from their leaders and fellow members of the community (1 Thess. 5.12, 14).

Second, the apostle exhorts the Thessalonians to *encourage the timid*. The *timid* are the "faint-hearted" or "discouraged" who were in danger of giving up.[219] Either the adversity they suffered (1.6; 2.14; 3.3-4) or the death of the loved ones in the community (4.13-18) would have been sufficient reason for some of the members of the church to become greatly discouraged. The responsibility of the rest toward these people was to *encourage* them (*paramytheisthe;* as in 2.12 and commentary) so that they would not lose heart in the midst of their worries. These people did not need to be admonished but persuaded not to give up.

Third, the church should take care to *help the weak*. We do not know exactly who the *weak* were in this congregation. They may have been Christians who were weak physically, such as the sick among them (Matt. 25.43-44; Luke 10.9; Acts 4.9; 5.15-16; 1 Cor. 11.30), but we would expect the apostles to call for prayer for these instead of only urging the church to *help* them (cf. Jas. 5.14-16). On the other hand, the *weak* may be those Christians who had very strict scruples with regard to the externals of re-

---

218. *New Docs*, 2.140; Cormack, "The Gymnasiarchal Law of Beroea"; Jewett, *The Thessalonian Correspondence*, 104-5; *TLNT*, 1.223-26; contra BAGD, 119.

219. *Oligopsychos*, only here in the NT. *TDNT*, 9.665-66; MM, 445; BAGD, 564.

ligion, such as eating certain foods and keeping certain days (Rom. 14.1-12; 15.1; 1 Cor. 8.7-13). Although there were tensions between "the weak" and "the strong" in more than one congregation, the Thessalonian letters give us no evidence that the church had such people in its midst. Alternatively, *the weak* may be those who had no social status or power since they were slaves or *libertini* (former slaves) or because of their economic situation. In 1 Corinthians 1.26-29 Paul uses the term in exactly this way, referring to the "weak" according to the world's standards as those whom God has chosen. Although there were members of the Thessalonian church who had both economic and social power,[220] we have evidence that some in the congregation faced genuine need (2 Thess. 3.13 and comments). Greek society did not consider weakness to be a virtue in any way (cf. 2 Cor. 13.4; 12.5, 9). Epictetus harshly degrades the weak, saying that "every faculty which is acquired by the uneducated and the weak is dangerous for them, as being apt to make them conceited and puffed up over it" (1.8.8).[221] But the church's response to the weak was to be different. The brothers and sisters were to *help* such people, which meant that they should take an interest in them, pay attention to them, and remain loyal to them (see Matt. 6.24; Luke 16.13; Titus 1.9).[222] Those whom society walks over and puts down are lifted up and given support by the church.

Finally, Paul exhorts the Thessalonians to *be patient with everyone*. How many churches would be transformed today by heeding this simple call? The exhortation is a call to be longsuffering and tolerant of others, whatever their condition or status.[223] This virtue, which is another fruit of the Spirit (Gal. 5.23; and see Eph. 4.2; Col. 1.11; 3.12; 2 Tim. 3.10), is the opposite of the irritability that characterizes so many human relationships. Within the church, the great diversity of social classes (slaves, *libertini*, and freeborn) and races (Macedonians, Greeks, Romans, Jews, and others) would have undoubtedly presented occasions in which *patience* needed to be exercised. In the case of the Thessalonians, the apostle may specifically have in mind the tolerance that was needed to respond in a charitable manner to the disorderly, the discouraged, and the weak. Each group had special needs that could generate reactions in others that would be out of harmony with the call to love one another. Patience was to be exercised at all times and toward *everyone*, whatever their situation or problem.

---

220. See the Introduction, p. 29.
221. See BAGD, 115; *TDNT*, 1.490-93; *New Docs*, 4.248; LSJ, 256.
222. BAGD, 73; MM, 46.
223. BAGD, 488; MM, 386; *New Docs*, 4.170; *NIDNTT*, 2.768-72.

6. "Make sure that nobody pays back wrong for wrong" — The Life of Nonretaliation (5.15)

15 *Make sure that nobody pays back wrong for wrong, but always try to be kind to each other and to everyone else.* Because of the hostilities the Christians in Thessalonica faced (2.14), there was sufficient motivation for the believers to seek ways to avenge themselves on their persecutors. Moreover, within the church itself there were members who did not completely conform to the moral standards of the community and who even took advantage of fellow believers (4.3-8; 5.14a), presenting another temptation to those affected to *pay back wrong for wrong* instead of correcting them for their benefit and building up (see, e.g., 2 Thess. 3.15). Paul shows the Thessalonians a different path to follow than resorting to personal vengeance. They are to do good to all, whether the person who did them ill is from within or outside the congregation. Teaching about vengeance was a standard theme in the moral orientation the apostles delivered to new congregations (Rom. 12.17-21; 1 Pet. 3.9), having its roots in the teaching of the Lord Jesus (Matt. 5.38-48; Luke 6.27-36).

The discussion about vengeance was carried out in other forums as well. In the OT, the *lex talionis*, "eye for eye, tooth for tooth, hand for hand, foot for foot" (Exod. 21.23-25; Lev. 24.19; Deut. 19.21) limited the degree of vengeance acceptable under the law. But in Proverbs the wisdom of ever seeking revenge was questioned (Prov. 20.22; 24.29; 25.21), counsel echoed in Sirach, which says, "The vengeful will face the Lord's vengeance, for he keeps a strict account of their sins. Forgive your neighbor the wrong he has done, and then your sins will be pardoned when you pray" (28.1-2, and see vv. 3-7). The ancient philosophers likewise reflected on vengeance, and a number of them, such as Socrates, warned against revenge (Plato, *Republic* 1.335; Seneca, *De Ira* 2.32.2-3) and even prescribed overcoming evil with good (Hierocles, *On Duties* 4.27.20). Hierocles referenced Socrates on this matter, saying, "With respect to every person, then, and especially a brother, we should imitate Socrates who, when someone said to him, 'May I die if I do not avenge myself on you,' replied, 'May I die if I do not make you my friend.'"[224]

But all these authors recognized that the natural tendency of humans and the culturally accepted way to respond to evil was to avenge oneself. Thucydides, for example, sanctioned it, stating that "where vengeance follows most closely upon the wrong, it best equals it and most amply requites it" (3.38.1). Seneca commented that vengeance was "legitimate" (*De Ira* 2.32.2). In the Roman world, just as in the Greek, avenging

---

224. Cited in Malherbe, *Moral Exhortation: A Greco-Roman Sourcebook*, 94.

oneself for a wrong done was necessary "because of the humiliation a Roman's prestige suffered, if he showed himself reluctant to respond and retaliate for hostile acts. A Roman, governed by a harsh ethos, simply could not afford to 'turn the other cheek' and expect to maintain his position in society."[225] The loss of social honor called for vengeance to be extracted in order to reestablish one's place in the community. Sometime before Paul's era, one Roman mother voiced the common and abiding belief in the necessity of vengeance as she counseled her sons, "You will say that it is beautiful to make revenge on your enemies. I consider revenge as important and glorious as anyone, but only if it can be attained without harm to the Republic."[226]

In this environment, the apostle presents the Christian teaching on revenge, *Make sure that nobody pays back wrong for wrong.* When someone did them *wrong,* harming them in some way, perhaps with evil intent (Acts 9.13; Rom. 12.21; 13.10; 2 Tim. 4.14),[227] the Christians were to be on their guard[228] against the tendency to respond in like manner. Interestingly, Paul does not present any theological justification for their call to nonretaliation in this verse. Jesus, on the other hand, says that by putting aside revenge his disciples would be acting like "sons and daughters of the Most High" (Luke 6.35-36; Matt. 5.45, 48), while Paul cites Proverbs 25.21-22 as he counsels the Romans against revenge, reminding them that God is the one who will repay those who do them wrong (Rom. 12.17-21). Seneca the philosopher entreated people to refrain from vengeance on more humanistic grounds, saying, "Only a great soul can be superior to injury" (*De Ira* 2.32.3). However, in 5.23 the apostle summarizes all the previous moral instruction by saying that this is the sanctification that God effects in their lives. Through his moral work in them they will "be kept blameless at the coming of our Lord Jesus Christ." This confidence in the divine working in the believers and the eschatological hope they bore are the anchors for the previous teaching on nonretaliation. They *can* refrain from vengeance because God is at work to sanctify them, and they *should* embrace nonretaliation so that they might be blameless before the Lord.

Instead of taking revenge, the Thessalonians should *always try to be kind to each other and to everyone else.* The *NIV's* rendering of the verb *try (diōkete)* does not communicate the force of this word, which does more

225. David F. Epstein, *Personal Enmity in Roman Politics 218-43 BC* (London, New York and Sydney: Croom Helm, 1987), 2.

226. Ibid., 20.

227. BAGD, 398.

228. *Horate.* Cf. Matt. 8.4; 18.10; Mark 1.44. The word is a Latinism. BAGD, 578; BDF, §362, 364.3.

than suggest that they should "at least make an effort" to do good to those who do them evil. They should rather "pursue" or "strive for" this type of conduct. The implication is that effort needs to be expended in order to reach this goal, even though it may be difficult to obtain (cf. Rom. 12.13; 14.19; 1 Cor. 14.1; 1 Tim. 6.11; 2 Tim. 2.22; Heb. 12.14; 1 Pet. 3.11).[229] The Thessalonians are to put in the effort to do "the good" *(to agathon,* translated *kind* in the *NIV)* to others who have done them ill, without defining what kind of "good" is in mind. Among the Jews, "good works" were deeds of charity such as hospitality to strangers, comfort for the destitute, and other works calculated to help those in need, especially the poor and afflicted. In the Greek environment, good works could be exercised toward family, friends, or the state. Doing good works was the virtue of extending aid to anyone in need, without distinction.[230] The teaching presented to the Thessalonians goes well beyond this Greek conception since they are to do good *to each other and to everyone else* (see the same expression in 3.12 and cf. Gal. 6.10), that is, to those inside and outside the church, even to those who have done them evil. By "doing good" Christians give concrete expression to their love for their enemies (Luke 6.27, 33, 35). But the Thessalonians are not called to do good only in response to injustices done to them but rather to strive to do good to everyone *always,* in every occasion and situation.

7. "Be joyful . . . pray . . . give thanks" — Communion with God (5.16-18)

In this group of three exhortations, Paul leaves the instruction about the social obligations of the believers (vv. 12-15) and turns to the habits that characterize Christians' relationship with God. The marks of a Christian laid out in these verses are joy (v. 16), prayer (v. 17), and gratitude (v. 18). The person so oriented lives according to the will of God (v. 18 and commentary). The apostle joins these three together, showing the Thessalonians that they should be constant in joy, prayer, and gratitude — at all times and in every situation ("always," "continually," "in all circumstances").

16 The first exhortation of the trilogy is, *Be joyful always.* Paul has already noted the joy the Thessalonians experienced, even in the face of suffering (1.6b; cf. Matt. 5.11-12; Luke 21.28; Acts 4.41; 2 Cor. 4.8-10; Col. 1.11, 24; 1 Pet. 1.6; 4.13), which was evidence of the fruit of the Spirit in

---

229. See BAGD, 201; MM, 166.

230. See the seminal article on doing "good" by van Unnik, "Teaching of Good Works in 1 Peter," 94.

their lives (1.6c; cf. Gal. 5.22; Rom. 14.17). This joy should *always* be in their lives, in whatever circumstances they found themselves (Phil. 3.1; 4.4). The apostles never encourage believers to deny that adversity brings sadness and grief (see 4.13; 1 Pet. 1.6; Rom. 12.15), but they recognize that in the midst of the most agonizing situations the presence of God through his Spirit can infuse the soul with hope and the heart with joy. This joy is rooted deeply in the gospel (Luke 2.10-11) and became one of the primary distinctives of the Christian community.

In contrast, joy was not a characteristic of other religions of the era. The church was unique in its proclamation that joy was at the heart of its faith (see Rom. 14.17).[231] Only Stoicism, with its dispassionate indifference, somewhat approached this Christian ideal. Epictetus (2.19.24) exclaimed, "Show me a man who though sick is happy, though in danger is happy, though dying is happy, though condemned to exile is happy, though in disrepute is happy. Show him! By the gods, I would fain see a Stoic!" The joy of the Stoic was not rooted in religion nor based on hope but arose out of the separation of people from their passions and the belief in the uncontrollable nature of fate. "Qué será, será, so why get ruffled?" The source of Christian joy was different. Christian joy, rooted in the gospel, is infused with hope, and grows in relationship with the Lord. The pessimism and lack of hope that generally characterized ancient society (see 4.13 and comments) found its answer in the salvation God offered through Jesus Christ.

17 The second exhortation of the trilogy is to *pray continually*. This imperative is sometimes understood as a call to pass each waking moment every day in prayer, a goal that is psychologically out of reach! As we have already observed in 1.2, where the word translated *continually* appears for the first time in this letter *(adialeiptōs)*, this adverb is a hyperbole that yields a sense similar to the Lord's command to his disciples that "they should always pray and not give up" (Luke 18.1) or Paul's exhortation to the Romans that they should "persevere in prayer" (Rom. 12.12 *NRSV*; Eph. 6.18; Col. 4.2), as the apostles themselves did for the churches (1 Thess. 1.2-3; 2.13; 3.10; 2 Thess. 1.11; and Rom. 1.9). Prayer was not to be limited to prescribed hours but should rather be a common and constant element in their daily life. At other points in these letters the apostle also called on the Thessalonians to keep him and his associates in their prayers (5.25; 2 Thess. 3.1).

Prayer was a common function of religion at that time, and the prayers of pagans included invocations of the deity, worship, and petitions. Along with sacrifices, prayers were commonplace in the pagan

231. *TLNT*, 3.498-99.

cult, but prayers were not limited to these occasions. Private prayers as well as public petitions were frequent in that world where the presence of the gods occupied a significant and fundamental place in the consciousness of the people.[232] But unlike pagan prayers, which sought to influence the gods to have a favorable disposition toward their suppliants,[233] Christian prayer began with confidence in a God who was their Father and whose desire was to do them good as his children (Matt. 6.9-13; 7.7-12). This familial relationship, not the manipulation that at times was symbolized by votive offerings in pagan rites, was the foundation stone of Christian prayer.

18 The third exhortation of the trilogy is: *Give thanks in all circumstances.* Although the one who receives the thanks is not specified, we may assume that the author is thinking about giving thanks to God. Frequently Paul heads his letters with thanks to God for the churches (Rom. 1.8; 1 Cor. 1.4; Phil. 1.3; Col. 1.3; 1 Thess. 1.2; 2.13; 2 Thess. 1.3). Now he encourages the Thessalonians also to give thanks to God as an essential part of their relationship with him. Giving thanks to God was a key element in Christian worship (Matt. 26.27; Mark 8.6; Luke 22.17, 19; 1 Cor. 11.24), but in v. 18 the focus is on the daily thanksgiving of believers. The call to *give thanks in all circumstances* does not mean that they should engage in thanksgiving every moment (see the nontemporal sense of *en panti* in 2 Cor. 4.8; 7.5; 9.8; Phil. 4.12), although Paul elsewhere understands prayer as a constant in the Christian's life. In Ephesians 5.20 believers are called to "always [give] thanks to God the Father for everything, in the name of our Lord Jesus Christ." Here the call is limited to thanksgiving in the midst of every situation, however good or adverse it might be. Thanksgiving should characterize a Christian (cf. Eph. 5.20; Col. 2.7; 3.17), just as joy and prayer are constants in their lives (vv. 16-17).

Offering thanksgiving to the gods was frequent and regular in ancient religions, in Judaism as in paganism. Many texts and inscriptions preserve the thanks offered to the gods for favors received.[234] The deities were considered to be the supreme benefactors of humanity, and the obligation of the one who received their bounty was to return thanks, always with the hope of receiving further benefits in the future. The law of reciprocity dominated the exchange of gift and thanks. But the apostle exhorts the believers to offer thanks to God *in all circumstances* and not simply when they become recipients of some boon or good from God. This exhortation, however, is not the same as calling the church to give thanks

---

232. Ferguson, *Backgrounds of Early Christianity,* 181-83.
233. See the Introduction, pp. 33-34.
234. See MM, 267; *New Docs,* 4.127-129; *IT,* nn. 79, 81, 85, 87.

for everything that comes their way, as if they were Stoics who believed that fate brought them what was destined to be their lot. That philosophy embraced the notion that the universe was rational and moved according to good purposes. Therefore whatever happened was precisely what was supposed to happen. The Stoic response was resignation to every situation that came their way. But the Christian approach is decidedly different since the believer trusts in a sovereign God who can turn any situation to their good (Rom. 8.28) and who can make someone more than triumphant in any adversity or other circumstance (Rom. 8.31-39).

Paul concludes this trilogy of Christian characteristics by explaining that joy, prayer, and thanksgiving are what God has called them to, *for this is God's will for you in Christ Jesus.* We should probably understand the antecedent of *this* (*touto,* neuter) as the three previous exhortations and not only the call to give thanks to God. As in 4.3 (see commentary), the will of God is the expression of the moral requirements to which he calls his people (Mark 3.35; Rom. 12.2; 2 Cor. 8.5; Eph. 6.6; Col. 4.12; 1 Thess. 4.3; Heb. 10.36; 1 Pet. 2.15; 4.2; 1 John 2.17). The reason for including the phrase *in Christ Jesus* is a bit difficult to ascertain. Is it linked with *you* who are said to be *in Christ Jesus?* Under this reading, *God's will,* outlined in vv. 16-18, is for those who are in relationship with Christ Jesus. Alternatively, is this phrase to be understood with *God's will?* While the syntax of the Greek sentence favors this reading, just what does *God's will . . . in Christ Jesus* mean? Frequently Paul speaks about the sphere in which the benefits of God are given to humanity as *in Christ Jesus,* such as his redemption (Rom. 3.24), eternal life (Rom. 6.23), the grace of God (1 Cor. 1.4), or inclusion in the people of God (Eph. 3.6). Under this reading, *God's will . . . in Christ Jesus* would not be *God's will* as demonstrated in Jesus' life or made known by Jesus. Rather, it is his gracious gift, the blessing of his will, which was given to the Thessalonians to follow. Understood in this way, God's call, expressed in his will, is part of his gift. They are blessed by being drawn into the sphere of doing his will *in Christ Jesus.* The reason the apostle gives for this call to joy, prayer, and thanksgiving is the strongest and highest imaginable for the Christian. These are not optional, secondary characteristics of the Christian's existence but stand at the center of God's plan for his people in Christ Jesus.

8. *"Do not put out the Spirit's fire"* — *Prophecy in the Community (5.19-22)*

The last group of imperatives Paul delivers includes five exhortations that concern the use and control of prophecy within the church. Some people in the congregation were prohibiting prophecy. The apostle counters this tendency by saying that although this manifestation of the Spirit should be regulated, prophecy should not be banned from the meetings of the assembly.

19 The cycle of exhortations about the use of prophecy begins with two exhortations that arrest attempts to impede the use of this gift within the church: *Do not put out the Spirit's fire; do not treat prophecies with contempt.* The verb of the first imperative *(sbennyte)* means "to extinguish the fire" (Wis. 16.17; Matt. 12.20; 25.8; Mark 9.48; Heb. 11.34) and then metaphorically "to annihilate" or "to cause to disappear" (2 Sam. 14.7; Job 18.5; Prov. 10.7; 13.9; Wis. 2.3).[235] At times the verb describes an action that makes something disappear completely, such as a person's very existence when death comes, but elsewhere it carries the more moderate meaning of "to attenuate" or "to restrict" something.[236] The exact nuance Paul has in mind is not easy to ascertain, but the first sense is the most likely in the context of prophecy (see the quotation from Plutarch below). Some Thessalonians appear to have attempted to prohibit[237] manifestations of the Spirit in their church. Since the presence of the Holy Spirit in the community is compared with fire (Jer. 20.9; Matt. 3.11; Luke 3.16; Acts 2.3; 18.25; Rom. 12.11; 2 Tim. 1.6; and John 5.35), the verb "to quench" would aptly describe the attempts to eliminate these manifestations. On the other side, Paul exhorts Timothy about the Spirit's activity in his life by saying, "Fan into flame the gift of God, which is in you through the laying on of my hands" (2 Tim. 1.6).

The manifestations of the Spirit's presence are for the good of the community and for that reason should not be eliminated. But where did this attempt to restrict the Spirit's activity originate? Interestingly, Plutarch, the priest of Apollo at Delphi, used the same vocabulary as found here in his apologetic against the diminished confidence in the oracle of that famous sacred city. The priestesses had ceased giving forth prophecies in verse, which led some to the conclusion "either that the prophetic priestess does not come near to the region in which is the godhead, or else that the spirit has been completely quenched *(tou pneumatos pantapasian apesbesmenou)* and her powers have forsaken her" *(Moralia* 402B). The "quenched spirit" had to do with the cessation of prophecy. The presence of the Spirit in the church was linked inextricably with prophecy among the people of God (Luke 1.67; Acts 2.17; 19.6; 28.25; Eph. 2.5; Rev.

235. BAGD, 745; MM, 570; *New Docs,* 3.50-51; *TLNT,* 3.242-43.
236. *TLNT,* 3.243, n. 13.
237. Although the present imperative with the negative *mē* does not necessarily mean "cease doing something," this is the apparent sense here, as the following imperative implies. On prohibitions in Greek, see especially Stanley E. Porter, *Idioms of the Greek New Testament* (Sheffield: JSOT Press, 1992), 224-26.

22.6); so it does not surprise in the least that our author should respond to any attempt to prohibit its use with the exhortation, "Do not quench the Spirit." This was not the first occasion, then, in which the people of God questioned prophecy, even those utterances that were legitimate (Num. 11.26-29; Amos 2.12; Mic. 2.6). We are not told why some members of the church wanted to curtail prophetic activity in the community, but we do know that during this era there was a rising scepticism about the validity of prophecy. Some hundred years earlier Cicero brought into question the validity of divination in general, of which prophecy was a subset. Scepticism about the oracles was fueled especially by the Epicureans, against whom Plutarch sets his defense of Delphi. But the tradition of scepticism goes back even further to the time of Xenophanes and Euripides (sixth and fifth centuries BC, respectively).[238] Paul later affirmed that prophecy would one day come to an end (1 Cor. 13.8-10), but only as an eschatological event.

20 The second exhortation repeats the idea of the first, with the difference that now we are given some insight into why some in the church wanted to extinguish the gift of prophecy. The apostles call on the community to engage in a more positive response to prophecies, saying, *do not treat prophecies with contempt*. The verb may mean either that they are not to despise prophecies or that they should not reject them contemptuously. The verb is used in both these ways in the NT (Luke 18.9; Rom. 14.3, 10; 1 Cor. 16.11; 6.4; Gal. 4.14; and cf. 1 Sam. 8.7; *Pss. Sol.* 2.5; *1 Enoch* 99.14; Acts 4.11), but this second sense is most likely in mind here.[239] Some not only despised but rejected prophecy in the meetings of the congregation. In an environment where oracular speech was under suspicion from a number of quarters (see v. 19), the church was a decidedly conservative body that affirmed prophecy while at the same time showing that the Spirit of God was the true source of divine speech and that other means of divination were invalid (Acts 2.17-18; 11.27-28; 13.1-2; 19.6; 21.9-10; Rom. 12.6; 1 Cor. 11.4-5; 12.1–14.40; 1 Tim. 1.18; 4.14; and

---

238. See Plutarch, *The Oracles at Delphi No Longer Given in Verse* and *The Obsolescence of Oracles;* Cicero, *De Divinatione; OCD,* 488; and Gene L. Green, "'As for Prophecies, They Will Come to an End': 2 Peter, Paul and Plutarch on the 'Obsolescence of Oracles,'" *JSNT* 82 (2001): 107-22. On the topic of NT prophecy, see Wayne Grudem, *The Gift of Prophecy in 1 Corinthians* (Washington, D.C.: University Press of America, 1982); idem, *The Gift of Prophecy in the New Testament and Today* (Westchester, Ill.: Crossway Books, 1988); David Hill, *New Testament Prophecy* (Atlanta: John Knox Press, 1979); Christopher Forbes, *Prophecy and Inspired Speech in Early Christianity and Its Hellenistic Environment* (Tübingen: J. C. B. Mohr [Paul Siebeck], 1995); Thomas W. Gillespie, *The First Theologians: A Study in Early Christian Prophecy* (Grand Rapids: Eerdmans, 1994).

239. *New Docs,* 2.83, records a letter in which the verb is used in relationship to the rejection of prophecy; BAGD, 277.

Acts 13.4-12; 16.16-18). Evidently there were those within the Thessalonian church who were engaging in prophetic speech. According to Paul's teaching on this subject to the Corinthians, the main purpose of Christian prophecy was not to divine the future but rather for "strengthening, encouragement and comfort," with special emphasis on its role in building up the community (1 Cor. 14.1-5, 12, 26). But there were problems in more than one congregation with false prophecies, and for that reason measures were put in place to help the church distinguish between genuine and bogus manifestations of the Spirit (1 Cor. 14.29; 1 John 4.1-3; also 1 Cor. 14.39). One of the gifts of the Spirit, "distinguishing between spirits" (1 Cor. 12.10), was given to some within the church for the purpose of judging between true and false prophecies.[240] After the writing of 1 Thessalonians, this church embraced a false teaching regarding the day of the Lord, and Paul suspected that a prophecy had possibly been the source of this erroneous belief (see 2 Thess. 2.2 and comments).

We are not left with clear evidence, however, concerning the cause of the rejection of prophecy in the Thessalonian church by some of its members at this early date. It could have been that suspicions arose that certain prophecies were of questionable origin, or possibly some became enamored with the more spectacular gifts, as was the case with the Corinthians, and so provoked a negative reaction in others. Another conceivable interpretation is that those who prophesied went into a state of ecstasy when they exercised the gift, causing embarrassment in others. It may be that the apocalyptic nature of the prophecies was reason enough for rejecting them. But as previously intimated, a better approach would be to examine this phenomenon in light of the prevailing attitudes about oracular speech in general. We have already noted that Plutarch found it necessary to defend the oracle at Delphi against its detractors, especially the Epicureans. The critique was not limited to that city's oracle since doubting the validity of oracles and divination in general was part of common philosophical discussion. Cicero comes out firmly on the side of those who questioned all forms of divination (De Divinatione). Against the posture of the Stoics he concluded, "Then let dreams, as a means of divination, be rejected along with the rest. Speaking frankly, superstition, which is widespread among the nations, has taken advantage of human weakness to cast its spell over the mind of almost every man" (2.72.148). In a similar manner the Epicureans, such as Lucretius, questioned whether any type of prophecy was valid (The Nature of Things

240. See James D. G. Dunn, *Jesus and the Spirit* (Philadelphia: Westminster Press, 1975), 233-36.

5).[241] In the city of Thessalonica, oracular manifestations were associated with the cult of Isis and Serapis,[242] and so, given the general questions about oracles that existed at this time plus the way the church had distanced itself from pagan cults (1.9), we can well identify the conditions in the environment that would have provoked some people to reject prophecy.[243]

21 The apostle's counsel is that the reaction of the church should be more balanced than simply rejecting prophetic utterances: *Test everything. Hold on to the good.* The adversative "but" (*de*, not translated in the *NIV)* signals that these imperatives are linked to the preceding exhortations. The *everything* that they are to put to the test is precisely the prophecies that some within the church had rejected. The first verb in the imperative, the same one that is found in 2.4 (see commentary),[244] here means "to test in order to verify the character of something" (1 Cor. 3.13; 11.28; 1 Tim. 3.10; 1 Pet. 1.7). John uses the same verb to inform his readers that they should put the content of prophetic speech to the test (1 John 4.1-2). Paul recognized that the church had the responsibility of verifying whether prophetic utterances were genuine or not (1 Cor. 14.29; 12.10; 1 John 4.1-3) because of the presence of false prophets and prophecies that promoted heterodox doctrines in the primitive church (Matt. 24.24; 1 Cor. 12.1-3; 2 Thess. 2.2; 1 John 4.1). The apostle does not explain how the Thessalonians were to evaluate prophecies to test their validity, but both Paul and John appeal to the apostolic doctrine as the rule by which the utterances should be measured (1 Cor. 13.3; 1 Thess. 2.5, 15; 1 John 4.1-3). Some fifty years later the writing known as the *Didache* instructed the church to evaluate the character of those who put themselves forward as prophets within the church: "But not everyone who speaks in a spirit is

---

241. The Epicurean stance is stated by Lucretius:

Likewise, thou canst ne'er
Believe the sacred seats of gods are here
In any regions of this mundane world;
Indeed, the nature of the gods, so subtle,
So far removed from these our senses, scarce
Is seen even by intelligence of mind.
And since they've ever eluded touch and thrust
Of human hands, they cannot reach to grasp
Aught tangible to us. For what may not
Itself be touched in turn can never touch.

242. *IT*, n. 92, *kat' epitagēn*, "according to the command or divine oracle."
243. The reconstruction of Donfried, "The Cults of Thessalonica," 342, that "the Apostle does not wish the gift of the Spirit to be confused with the excesses of the Dionysiac mysteries" does not convince.
244. Also *TLNT*, 1.353-61; BAGD, 202; MM, 167.

a prophet, except he have the behavior of the Lord" (*Did.* 11.8 and vv. 9-12). The test of character and not just content resonates with the call of Jesus, "Watch out for false prophets. . . . By their fruit you will recognize them" (Matt. 7.15-20).

Having submitted the prophecies to testing, the believers were to *Hold on to the good.* The caution they exercised in evaluating the various utterances would result in the rejection of those thought not to be divinely inspired, a point made in the following verse. But having judged that a prophecy was truly divine and genuine, it was their duty to take it seriously and hold on to it. The verb *hold on to* was a technical term that authors would use if they wanted to emphasize the necessity of holding firmly to inspired tradition or authentic doctrine (Luke 8.15; 1 Cor. 11.2; 15.2; Heb. 3.6, 14; 10.23).[245] In this context, *the good (to kalon)* they should hold firmly is the prophecies they have tested and found to be genuine. Xenophon, for example, uses the same adjective with the article to describe those coins that have been tested and found genuine.[246] Tested prophecies are likewise *the good.* Such prophecies would serve for the building up and not the tearing down of the church.

22 The Thessalonians were to embrace those prophetic messages that were found to be genuine, but they were also called to reject those that were otherwise. The call to reject the inauthentic prophecies is the final exhortation of this cycle: *Avoid every kind of evil.* The language is strikingly similar to that of Job 1.1, 8, where Job is described as a man who "shunned evil."[247] While the exhortation to separate themselves from evil had wide applicability, in this context the command is put into service to guide their reaction to prophecies that were considered false. They should shun *every kind of evil,* whatever its nature, including false prophecy.[248] The term translated *kind* appears in other contexts with the meaning "appearance," but only in the sense of external appearance that reflects internal reality.[249] But it frequently is found alongside the word *every,* and in these contexts it means *every kind,* giving us the rendering of

245. *TLNT,* 2.288; BAGD, 422-23.

246. Xenophon, *Memorabilia* 3.1.9. The normal way this procedure was done was to make a banker's mark with a sharp instrument such as a knife either on the edge or the face of the coin to see whether the metal, either silver or gold, was what it appeared to be on the outside. See Milligan, *St. Paul's Epistles to the Thessalonians,* 76.

247. Job 1.1 (LXX), *apechomenos apo pantos ponērou pragmatos;* 1 Thess. 5.22, *apo pantos eidous ponērou apechesthe.*

248. The same expression is found in Josephus, *Antiquitates* 10.27 (10.3.1), where he speaks of how Manasseh exhibited "every form of wickedness in his conduct" (*pan eidos ponērias*).

249. The *KJV* understands the word this way, "Abstain from all appearance of evil." See *NIDNTT,* 1.703-4.

the *NIV*.[250] The verb, which means "to keep away from" or "to abstain from" something, appears in ethical contexts such as this and 4.3 (see the comments there and Acts 15.20, 29; 1 Tim. 4.3; 1 Pet. 2.11). This exhortation is quite similar to an inscription from Sardis that calls the guardians of the temple of Zeus to keep themselves apart from other mysteries.[251] In the same way, Christians should keep away from any kind of inspired revelation that the community deems to originate from a source other than the Holy Spirit. The church should not treat true prophecies lightly, nor should they adhere to revelations that are patently false.

IV. "MAY GOD HIMSELF" — THE FINAL PRAYER, GREETINGS, AND BLESSING (5.23-28)

A. "May God . . . sanctify you through and through" (5.23-25)

Paul has come to the end of the first letter to the Thessalonian Christians. In the letter's closing, the author includes a blessing expressed in the form of a prayer (v. 23) and assures the believers that God will faithfully carry out his work in their lives (v. 24). He then requests that the Thessalonians pray for them (v. 25). To mark the closing of their letters, Greek and Roman correspondents commonly penned a wish that the recipient would enjoy health, while Semitic authors would include a blessing of peace to signal that they had reached the end. The apostle concludes with a prayer blessing in which the "God of peace" is invoked, elements that signal that the author has transitioned from the main body of the letter to the closing of the correspondence.[1]

23 The blessing of v. 23 is presented as a prayer expressed as a wish lifted up before God: *May God himself, the God of peace, sanctify you through and through.* Paul is emphatic in his affirmation that *God himself* is the ultimate source of their sanctification (see 3.11 and commentary, where the same expression is found). Although the believers must conform their lives to his will in this ongoing process of sanctification (4.3), in no way should they assume that they are left on their own to attain that goal. God is the one who called them and will carry out his work in their

---

250. MM, 182.

251. *New Docs*, 1.21-22; see also *TLNT*, 1.166-67; BAGD, 85.

1. Jeffrey A. D. Weima, *Neglected Endings: The Significance of the Pauline Letter Closings* (Sheffield: JSOT Press, 1994), 175, 100.

lives through the agency of the Holy Spirit (v. 24; 4.7-8 and comments). He is identified here as *the God of peace,* a name that appears frequently in Paul's peace blessings (Rom. 15.33; 16.20; 2 Cor. 13.11; Phil. 4.9) but that is used only sparingly elsewhere (Heb. 13.20; *T. Dan* 5.2; cf. "the Lord of peace" in 2 Thess. 3.16). At the head of this and the following letter (1.1; 2 Thess. 1.2), Paul expresses his desire that the brothers and sisters receive grace and peace, and these two, which summarize Christian salvation, appear once again at the end of the correspondence (5.23, 28; 2 Thess. 3.16, 18). *Peace* in this context is almost synonymous with Christian "salvation" (1.1; Acts 10.36; Rom. 2.10; 5.1; 8.6; 14.17; Eph. 6.15).[2] Some authors have suggested that the appeal to the *God of peace* is the counterpoint to the discord that existed within the Thessalonian church (5.13b),[3] but the focus of v. 23 is on the complete sanctification of the believer in anticipation of the coming of the Lord. The God of this salvation or *peace* is the one who will carry out this work. While it is certainly true that their sanctification will include the resolution of conflicts among the members of the Christian community, the emphasis in the present verse falls on the entire work of God in their lives.

The apostle's desire is that God will *sanctify you through and through.* We have already noted that the moral sanctification of the church was a principal concern of its founders (4.3, 4, 7, 8), especially as they stood in anticipation of the coming of the Lord (3.13). The current petition is that they may be sanctified *through and through,* or "entirely," so that they reach "the full end or goal" for which they were saved,[4] which Paul explains in more precise terms in the following clause. The prayer is extraordinary in that it anticipates that they will be found *blameless* in their moral conduct at the time of *the coming of our Lord Jesus Christ,* since they have patterned their lives according to the will of God (see also 3.13; 1 Cor. 1.7-8; Phil. 1.10-11). Obviously, the confidence the apostle had in God's work transcended the believers' moral weaknesses of which he and his associates had so recently become aware (v. 24).

What this entire sanctification means is explained in the following clause, which appeals to God, saying, *May your whole spirit, soul and body be kept blameless at the coming of our Lord Jesus Christ.* The word translated *whole* (*holoklēron*) is an adjective that may either function as a substantive ("your whole being") or may modify the three following nouns, as the *NIV* translates, although the Greek adjective itself is singular. The combination of a

---

2. BAGD, 227.

3. Weima, *Neglected Endings,* 185; Marshall, *1 and 2 Thessalonians,* 161.

4. *Holoteleis,* found only here in the NT. This is a rare term in both classical and Hellenistic Greek. *TDNT,* 5.175; BAGD, 565; MM, 447.

singular adjective with a string of connected substantives would not be un-usual for Greek since in such constructions the adjective normally agrees in number with the nearest substantive.[5] The *NIV* gives the proper sense. The adjective *whole*, which appears only here and in James 1.4 in the entire NT, conveys the quality of being "complete" or "entire," similar to the word "entirely" of the previous clause. James explains the sense of the word in his desire that his readers "may be mature and *complete, not lacking any-thing.*" This term could, in other contexts, describe a sacrificial victim that was preserved complete and not mutilated, or the mind of a person that was intact.[6] Understood this way, the adjective would describe how their *spirit, soul and body* would be preserved morally complete.

However, in the papyri and inscriptions of the era this adjective was synonymous with the words "good health." For example, a votive was offered to Artemis "for the wholeness of my feet."[7] In Acts 3.16 a related word *(holoklēria)* refers to the "complete healing" the lame person en-joyed after being healed. During the third century AD, the very word of our text appears frequently in letter closings where the author wishes the reader good health.[8] During the first century, the inclusion of a prayer or wish for good health was quite common in letter closings, though most commonly expressed with other vocabulary. However, the verbal form of the word *whole (holoklērein)* is attested in such contexts.[9] The author of our letter most likely adapted this convention to his purposes and offers this wish prayer that the Thessalonians' *spirit, soul and body* may enjoy moral health or wholeness. That the type of health he has in mind is moral is un-derlined by the prayer for their sanctification (v. 23a) and the desire that they might be found blameless before the Lord in his coming (v. 23c).

So that the Thessalonians may understand that this sanctification embraces their whole being, Paul specifies its scope by including the an-thropological terms *spirit, soul and body.* This is the only place in the Pau-line letters where the apostle uses these three terms to describe the total-ity of human nature. During that era, there was an ongoing debate concerning whether the human person consisted of two or three parts,[10] a discussion that continues down to our day. We should not, however, sim-ply conclude that Paul was falling out on the side of those who embraced

---

5. BDF, §135.3.

6. *TLNT*, 2.578-79; MM, 446; BAGD, 564.

7. *TLNT*, 2.579; and see *New Docs*, 4.161-62.

8. Ibid.

9. *Papyrus Oxyrhynchus* 1670, cited in Weima, *Neglected Endings*, 37. On the wish for health in letter closings, see ibid., 34-39; White, *Light from Ancient Letters*, 194-97, 200-201.

10. Note the discussion in Plutarch, *Moralia* 943A; and see Marcus Aurelius 12.3, 14; Plato, *Timaeus* 30B.

the tripartite view. In 1 Corinthians 7.34 Paul summarizes the totality of human nature with the bipartite description "body and spirit." Jesus, on the other hand, spoke of humans as "soul and body" (Matt. 10.28), while on another occasion he summarizes human nature as "heart, soul, mind and strength" (Mark 12.30; cf. Deut. 6.4-5; Matt. 22.37; Luke 10.27). While these terms may describe different *aspects* of a human's nature, in the present context the apostle's appeal to God is simply that his sanctification may extend to the *entirety* of their being.[11] Paul's prayer is that God would sanctify the Thessalonians so that their whole being, everything that they were as humans, would be *kept blameless at the coming of our Lord Jesus Christ,* a prayer they previously offered in almost identical terms in 3.13 (see commentary). Their firm hope is that God will keep[12] them blameless so that they can stand before him without shame or guilt. The work of salvation, planned in their election and effected in their calling and conversion, will be brought to completion at *the coming of our Lord Jesus Christ.*

24 If this goal seemed unattainable, the apostle added a note of confidence in the one who brings about this sanctifying work: *The one who calls you is faithful and he will do it.* What God began in the election and calling of the Thessalonians (1.4; 2.12; 4.7; 2 Thess. 2.13-14) he will complete at the time of the coming of Jesus Christ (cf. Rom. 8.30). They had received a call from God to sanctification, and the apostle expresses his complete confidence that God will continue this sanctifying work in them to the very end. The perseverance of the saints is founded on this divine initiative. The same overflowing confidence in the work of God being carried on in believers is found in Philippians 1.6, where the apostle proclaims with unleashed faith, "being confident of this, that he who began a good work in you will carry it on to completion until the day of Christ Jesus." The source of this confidence is not only the divine initiative witnessed in their election but also the character of God. He is *faithful* (1 Cor. 1.9; 10.13; 2 Cor. 1.18; 2 Thess. 3.3; 2 Tim. 2.13; Heb. 10.23; 11.11; 1 John 1.9). The faithfulness of God is understood here as the surety that he will fulfill the promise extended to his people. Knowing that such is the nature of God, the apostle can declare that *he will do it* — their sanctifi-

---

11. On NT anthropology, see George Eldon Ladd, *New Testament Theology* (revised by Donald A. Hagner; Grand Rapids: Eerdmans, 1993), 499-520; Robert Jewett, *Paul's Anthropological Terms* (Leiden: Brill, 1971); Robert H. Gundry, *Soma in Biblical Theology* (Cambridge: Cambridge University Press, 1976); Mario Veloso, "Contenido antropológico de 1 Tesalonicenses 5,23," *RB* 41 (1979) 129-40.

12. The verb appears in this moral sense in Marcus Aurelius 6.30, "So keep thyself a simple and good man, uncorrupt, dignified, plain, a friend of justice, god-fearing, gracious, affectionate, manful in doing thy duty." MM, 633.

cation will be complete and extended to the entirety of their being. He is able to bring about this sanctifying work within their lives, whatever their past and whatever situation they face in the present (cf. Eph. 1.19; 3.20).

25 Having prayed for the Thessalonians, the author now asks for prayer from the church for him and his associates: *Brothers, pray for us.* This petition is part of a common set of exhortations that appear in the closings of Paul's letters (5.25-27; Rom. 16.17-19; 1 Cor. 16.13-16, 22; 2 Cor. 13.1; Gal. 6.17; Phil. 4.8-9; Phlm. 20, 22).[13] Some Greek manuscripts include the word "also," omitted in the *NIV*. The manuscript evidence for this textual variant is divided, although it slightly favors its inclusion.[14] The call to the church to "also" pray for the apostles underlines the reciprocal relationship between them and the congregation — as they prayed for the church, so, too, they hoped that the church would pray for them. Reciprocity was a fundamental element in the relationship between the apostle and the church, being expressed principally in prayer (Rom. 15.30-32; 2 Cor. 1.11; Eph. 6.19-20; Phil. 1.19; Col. 4.3-4, 18; 2 Thess. 3.1-2; and Phlm. 22), although it was not limited to this act of devotion (Rom. 1.11-12; 1 Thess. 3.8-9). The author does not explain why prayer was requested, but possibly he desired prayer for the mission, including the return visit to Thessalonica, and for security in the face of so much persecution (1 Thess. 2.16; 3.7, 10-11; 2 Thess. 3.1-2; and cf. Rom. 15.30-32; Eph. 6.19-20; Col. 4.3-4). The prayers Paul and his associates offered for them served as a model that they were to imitate (1.2-3; 3.9-13).

B. "Greet all the brothers and sisters" (5.26-27)

26 The exhortations in both this and the following verses presuppose that the church gathered for the reading of this letter so that all might receive the instruction, even the illiterate among them (cf. Col. 4.16; 1 Tim. 4.13). At the end, they should engage in a mutual greeting that would express their solidarity: *Greet all the brothers with a holy kiss* (Rom. 16.16; 1 Cor. 16.20; 2 Cor. 13.12; and the equivalent "kiss of love" in 1 Pet. 5.14). In the ancient world, a kiss could symbolize a number of sentiments, such as love between family members, honor and respect, or friendship (Mark 14.44-45; Luke 7.36-47; 15.20; Acts 20.37). Kissing on the mouth,

---

13. Weima, *Neglected Endings,* 145-48. Although vv. 25-27 are all exhortations, v. 25 is linked to the previous section with the word "also." See the following discussion.

14. The word *kai* is found in p[30], B, D, but is absent from ℵ, A, D, F, G, Ψ. It appears in brackets in the critical editions of the Greek text.

which expressed erotic love, was not the most common form of kissing. Much more common was the kiss on the forehead or the cheek in greetings and good-byes between family members, friends, and respected people, or on official occasions such as games or when contracts were made. People also kissed when they were reconciled to each other.[15] In the early Christian communities, which embraced all social classes (slaves, *libertini,* and free) and various races (Greeks, Romans, Macedonians, and Jews), the *holy kiss* would serve as an affirmation of their filial unity as "brothers and sisters" in the common faith. In the case of the Thessalonians, the tensions that existed between the brothers and sisters (5.13-15, 19-20) would be another reason why the apostle urged that *all* should be greeted with a kiss. This kiss is described as *holy,* not necessarily to distinguish it from the erotic kiss but rather to identify it with the common life of those who were "holy ones" or "saints." As such, the adjective *holy* reinforces the bond between them that the kiss itself symbolizes and separates this symbol of their unity from the kisses they would exchange with others in their world.[16] In the following centuries, the church permitted the liturgical kiss to be exchanged only between persons of the same sex because of the abuses of decorum that had arisen.[17]

27 At the end of this letter, Paul steps out from the group to add a final exhortation (cf. 2.18; 3.5 and comments),[18] and so the narrative changes from the first person plural to the singular. Possibly Paul himself added this final exhortation in his own hand (cf. 2 Thess. 3.17),[19] but it is just as possible that he dictated it in the same way that he added his own personal comments previously in this book. The language of the command is exceedingly strong: *I charge you before the Lord to have this letter read to all the brothers.*[20] The verb translated *I charge (enorkizō)* means that the author wants to cause them to swear by or before *the Lord* that they will read this letter to all the members of the church.[21] They are bound by an oath to make sure the content of this letter is communicated to everyone. The reason for such a strong exhortation is most likely found in the tensions that existed between certain members of the congregation (4.6;

15. *TDNT,* 9.118-27, 138-46; *NIDNTT,* 2.549; Keener, *IVP Bible Background Commentary,* 448.

16. See Best, *First and Second Epistles to the Thessalonians,* 245-46.

17. Ibid.; Bruce, *1 and 2 Thessalonians,* 134; *Apostolic Constitutions* 2.57.17.

18. On the authorship of this letter, see the Introduction, pp. 56-59.

19. See Wanamaker, *Commentary on 1 and 2 Thessalonians,* 208.

20. Some mss. read "to all the *holy* brothers" (ℵ^c, A, K, P, Ψ), but the evidence favors the shorter reading reflected in the *NIV* (ℵ, B, D, F, G). See Metzger, *Textual Commentary,* 565-66.

21. BDF, §155.7; BAGD, 267; MM, 217-18; *New Docs,* 3.67. Note that the verb takes a double accusative object *(enorkizō hymas ton kyrion).*

5.13-14, 20), especially between the majority of the believers and the disorderly among them (4.3-8 and 5.14). Paul understood the necessity of gathering together "all the brothers and sisters" of the city to hear the message of this letter, and this included the members who had crossed Christian moral bounds. In this gathering not even the illiterate among them would be excluded from the encouragement, instruction, and correction contained in this letter, while at the same time this collective hearing would underline the community's solidarity. The public reading would also bind the apostle again with this young church. The letter stood in the place of the apostle and was representative of his presence and authority. The word translated *read* means "to read publicly." As the Law was read publicly for the Jewish people gathering in the synagogue (Luke 4.16; Acts 13.15, 27; 15.21; 2 Cor. 3.14-15; Josephus, *Contra Apionem* 2.175 (2.19); Philo, *De Vita Mosis* 2.215-16), so now the Christians gather to hear not only Scripture (1 Tim. 4.13) but also the apostolic letters (Col. 4.16). The practice of reading letters out loud to their recipients was a known custom (Diodorus Siculus 15.10.2), as was the public reading of discourses of philosophers (Epictetus 3.23.6), so the recitation of this letter in the gathering of the church would not be out of the ordinary. No doubt the church read this letter on more than one occasion.

C. "The grace of our Lord Jesus Christ be with you" (5.28)

28 Like all the Pauline letters, 1 Thessalonians ends with a blessing of grace: *The grace of our Lord Jesus Christ be with you*[22] (cf. Rom. 16.20; 1 Cor. 16.23; 2 Cor. 13.13; Gal. 6.18; Eph. 6.24; Phil. 4.23; 2 Thess. 3.18; 1 Tim. 6.21; 2 Tim. 4.22; Titus 3.15; Phlm. 25). This final benediction is a modification of the formal closings found in Hellenistic letters where the author included a wish for the recipient to "Be strong" or "Prosper." At times a prepositional phrase was tacked on that said "with all of you," "with you all," or "in [your] whole household."[23] The apostle does not simply wish strength or prosperity on the readers but rather invokes a blessing on them for what they needed most: the grace that comes from the Lord Jesus Christ. This letter began with this desire for grace, plus that for peace (1.1), and here, as there, it summarizes the essence of the faith the Thessalonians have received. The person of Jesus, the Lord and Christ, is the

---

22. Some manuscripts include a final "amen" (ℵ, A, Dᶜ, K, L, P), but it is absent from significant mss. of the Alexandrian and Occidental families (B, D, F, G, 333, 424ᶜ). See Metzger, *Textual Commentary*, 566.

23. Weima, *Neglected Endings*, 29, 32. See the discussion on 29-34 and 78-87.

fountain from which the grace of God flows out to them. This benediction is far from being a formality tacked to the end of the letter. The blessing of grace from the Lord Jesus Christ embraces the fullness of the salvation that comes from the one who is the sole Sovereign and Savior.

2 THESSALONIANS

I. "PAUL, SILVANUS, AND TIMOTHY, TO THE CHURCH OF THE THESSALONIANS" — THE EPISTOLARY SALUTATION (1.1-2)

1 The second apostolic letter to the Thessalonians begins almost exactly like the first correspondence.[1] As was the custom in ancient letters, the authors identify themselves first *(Paul, Silas[2] and Timothy)*, after which the recipients are named *(to the church of the Thessalonians in God our Father and the Lord Jesus Christ)*. The only difference between this ascription and that found in 1 Thessalonians 1.1 is the inclusion of the description of God as *our* Father. This echo of the prayer the Lord taught the first disciples can be heard throughout Paul's letters (cf. Matt. 6.9, "Our Father in heaven," and Rom. 1.7; 1 Cor. 1.3; Gal. 1.3-4; Eph. 1.2; Phil. 1.2; 4.20; Col. 1.2; 1 Thess. 1.2; 3.11, 13; 2 Thess. 1.2, 2.16; Phlm. 3). God is not viewed simply as the one to whom humans owe their existence and who sustains all human life (Acts 17.28), but as the God with whom these former pagans have come into intimate familial relationship. At the same time, the designation of God as *our* Father draws the Thessalonian believers into one family and joins them together with Paul and his associates, as well as with the church throughout the world. The foundation of the Christian family and of Christian unity finds its bedrock in this prayer/confession.

2 As in the first letter to the Thessalonians, Paul inserts a blessing for the church at the head of the correspondence: *Grace and peace to you from God the Father and the Lord Jesus Christ.* The form of this blessing is almost identical with that of 1 Thessalonians 1.1 with the exception that the source of *grace and peace* is spelled out here instead of being implied. Some Greek manuscripts indicate that this *grace and peace* come from *God*

---

1. See the commentary on 1 Thess. 1.1 for the details. While Wanamaker and others contend that 2 Thessalonians was the first correspondence sent to this church, this commentary follows the traditional view concerning the order of the letters (pp. 64-69). On the issue of authorship, refer to pp. 59-64.

2. As in 1 Thess. 1.1, the Latinized form of his Semitic name is transliterated in the Greek *(Silouanos)*, which emphasizes his Roman citizenship.

our Father, but the textual evidence is balanced between the inclusion and exclusion of *our,* making our determination of what the Paul dictated quite difficult at this point.[3] In any case, the expanded form of the blessing of *grace and peace* conforms to that of other Pauline letters that underscore that these divine benefits proceed not only from *God the Father* but also, together with him, from *the Lord Jesus Christ* (see Rom. 1.7; 1 Cor. 1.3; 2 Cor. 1.2; Gal. 1.3; Eph. 1.2; Phil. 1.2; Col. 1.2; 1 Tim. 1.2; 2 Tim. 1.2; Titus 1.4; Phlm. 3). The apostolic author names both as the source of these divine blessings, a point with clear christological implications. *The Lord Jesus Christ* is not viewed as inferior to *God the Father* in the work of salvation.

Although the words *grace and peace* summarize the totality of the saving benefits thast these and the rest of the Christians enjoyed (see the comments on 1 Thess. 1.1), in 2 Thessalonians they acquire special significance in light of the situation that beset this church. 2.16 signals "God our Father" as the one who "by his grace gave us eternal encouragement and good hope." This eschatological hope, which proceeds from divine grace, allows believers to stand face to face with death (see the commentary on 2.16). Moreover, the blessing of *peace* appears again at the end of the letter where the apostle expresses the desire that "the Lord of peace himself give you peace at all times and in every way," an allusion to the persecution that assailed them (3.16 and comments; and 1.3-10). As they stand against every kind of adversity, whether in life or in death, these believers can rest in the security of receiving *grace and peace . . . from God the Father and the Lord Jesus Christ.*

II. "YOUR FAITH IS GROWING AND YOUR LOVE IS INCREASING" — THANKSGIVING AND PRAYERS FOR THE FAITH, LOVE, AND STEADFASTNESS OF THE PERSECUTED THESSALONIANS (1.3-12)

At the beginning of the second letter to the Thessalonians, Paul offers a thanksgiving to God for the church (vv. 3-4a). After touching on the theme of persecution (v. 4b), he discusses the final judgment that will come upon the persecutors and introduces the rest God will give to his own people

---

3. *Our* (Gk. *hēmōn*) is included in mss. ℵ, A, F, G, and I but is excluded from B, D, and P. We do not know whether the word was excluded from the original for stylistic reasons (cf. v. 1 — *our Father*) or if *our* was included to harmonize with the headings in other Pauline letters (compare Rom. 1.7; 1 Cor. 1.3; 2 Cor. 1.2). See Metzer, *Textual Commentary,* 567.

(vv. 5-10). The introduction concludes with a prayer for the church that "the name of our Lord Jesus may be glorified in you" (vv. 11-12).[1]

A. "We must always give thanks to God for you" — The First Thanksgiving (1.3-5)

3 2 Thessalonians begins with a thanksgiving to God for the church, as does the first letter to this congregation (vv. 3-4; 1 Thess. 1.3ff.). The first words of the thanksgiving are almost identical to 1 Thessalonians 1.3. Paul states, *We ought always to thank God for you, brothers, and rightly so.* As in the first correspondence, these words inform the brothers and sisters of the apostles' thanksgiving to God for them, but here they add that offering such thanksgiving is a duty or obligation *(we ought, opheilomen).* Similar language appears in Jewish literature where the necessity of giving thanks to God is emphasized. The inclusion of the language of obligation should not therefore be construed as an indication that their present thanksgiving was somehow less warm or genuine than that offered in 1 Thessalonians. Philo of Alexandria, for example, spoke of the "necessary obligation" *(anankaiōs opheilei)* of offering to God "hymns and benedictions and prayers and sacrifices and the other expressions of gratitude as religion demands" because of the protection God gives a person.[2] The following phrase in our verse, *and rightly so,* adds that such thanksgiving to God is also fitting and proper *(axios)*[3] precisely because we owe God such honor (cf. 1 Thess. 2.12). In the case of the Thessalonians, the apostle recognized the necessity of offering thanksgiving to God for the growing faith and love demonstrated by this church (v. 3b). The presence of such virtues in the congregation was the result of God's activity among them, and for that reason he is the one who is worthy of their thanks (see 1 Thess. 1.1 and commentary). Both this verse and the second thanksgiving,[4] which begins in 2.13, let the Thessalonians know that Paul and his associates offered their thanks to God for them at every opportunity *(always).*

1. On the rhetorical analysis of this letter, see pp. 69-72. Discussion of Paul's opening thanksgivings is found on pp. 86-87 and in O'Brien, *Introductory Thanksgivings in the Letters of Paul,* 167-84.

2. Philo, *De Specialibus Legibus* 1.224. Roger D. Aus, "The Liturgical Background of the Necessity and Propriety of Giving Thanks according to 2 Thes. 1:3," *JBL* 92 (1973) 432-38, examines the Jewish use of this kind of language and argues from these parallels that the background of the present thanksgiving is the liturgy of the church. However, in the Jewish texts that Aus presents, the expressions of obligation arise from a recognition of the goodness of God and do not presuppose a liturgical context.

3. BAGD, 78; LSJ, 171. See Philo, *De Specialibus Legibus* 1.173; 4 Macc. 17.8.

4. Cf. the three thanksgivings in 1 Thess. 1.3; 2.13; 3.9.

The reasons why the apostle believed they were under obligation and thought it was proper to give thanks to God for the church was *because your faith is growing more and more, and the love every one of you has for each other is increasing.* As in 1 Thessalonians 1.3, the reality of the Thessalonians' faith and love moves him to offer thanks. Although he makes no mention in the present verse of their hope (cf. 1 Thess. 1.3c), the presence of this virtue is implied in the following verse, which praises their perseverance in the midst of "persecutions and trials." While the thanksgiving in 1 Thessalonians is based on the active character of their faith and love ("your *work* produced by faith, your *labor* prompted by love"), what moves the apostle here is the way this church's faith and love are growing and not in any way static or attenuated. In describing how their *faith is growing more and more,* Paul employs a verb that is found only here in the NT, an intensive form of "grow" (cf. 2 Cor. 10.15, where Paul speaks of his hope for the Corinthians' growth in faith). The Thessalonian believers were noteworthy for their faith in God (1 Thess. 1.3; 3.2, 5-7; 5.8; 2 Thess. 1.11; and cf. 3.2), which is defined as their confidence both in him (1 Thess. 1.8) and in his gospel (2 Thess. 2.13), demonstrated in the face of all the adversity that had come upon them (1.4). Likewise, the apostle notes that the mutual love of the Thessalonian Christians *is increasing.* This love characterized the believers' relationships among themselves, as the apostle observed over and again (1 Thess. 1.3; 3.6, 12; 4.9-10; 5.8, 13). However, Paul had previously exhorted the church to exhibit love toward one another "more and more" (1 Thess. 4.10) and had even prayed that their "love [might] increase and overflow for each other" (1 Thess. 3.12, a verse that uses the same verb found here, *pleonazō,* "to increase abundantly"). A fair conclusion would be that God responded to Paul and his associates' prayers and that the Thessalonians had taken the exhortation to heart! The mutual care and concern of this congregation were inclusive (*the love every one of you has for each other;* cf. 1 Thess. 3.12; 4.9), as was the encouragement they gave each other (1 Thess. 4.18; 5.11) and the good works they demonstrated toward one another (1 Thess. 5.15). No member of this church was excluded from either giving or receiving love. The reciprocal care among the members of this congregation moved the founders to give thanks to God and stands as an exhortation to those of us who belong to fragmented Christian communities.

4 The growing faith and love of the Thessalonians were the reasons for thanksgiving to God (v. 3), but their good progress also resulted in the founders' recital of their story to other congregations.[5] Paul relates

---

5. *Therefore (hōste)* introduces the actual result of the preceding. See BAGD, 900.

this activity to the Thessalonian believers: *Therefore, among God's churches we boast about your perseverance and faith in all the persecutions and trials you are enduring.* The Greek text begins with the emphatic "we ourselves" *(autous hēmas),* which appears to introduce a contrast — but with what? Is the idea that "We ourselves, in contrast to our normal practice of not boasting in the churches, boast about you"? This understanding is unlikely since Paul unashamedly boasts about the churches, as they do about him (2 Cor. 7.14; 8.24; 9.3; and 5.12). Paul even boasted about the generosity of the Macedonian congregations (2 Cor. 8.1-5). An alternate reading would understand the contrast as the apostle's response to what other believers were saying about the Thessalonians (cf. 1 Thess. 1.9). But nothing in the immediate context implies that Paul was comparing his thoughts about the Thessalonians with those of others. On the other hand, the Thessalonians themselves may have had a rather low conception of themselves, especially in light of the shame they endured as a persecuted people, and so the apostle contrasts the praise of the church with the shame these believers felt. But once again, while they may have suffered under the burden of shame, this is not expressed explicitly or implied by the author.[6] The most likely conclusion is that the emphatic "we ourselves" was simply a way of underlining the author's strong sentiments about the church without putting them in contrast with anything or anyone (cf. the similar grammatical construction in Rom. 7.25; 15.14; 2 Cor. 10.1; 1 Thess. 4.9).

Paul boasted about this church, as well as the other Macedonian congregations (2 Cor. 8.1-5), and was careful to speak out about the good of this and other churches (2 Cor. 7.14; 8.24; 9.3). The verb translated *boast (enkauchasthai)* appears only in this verse in the whole of the NT, clearly with a positive meaning. The same word principally carries a pejorative sense in the LXX (Pss. 52.1 [51.3]; 74.4 [73.4]; 97.7 [96.7]). On the other hand, one may properly boast in God (Ps. 106.47 [105.47]). While boasting in oneself is not an acceptable practice in either Jewish, Christian, or Greek morals (e.g., Prov. 27.1; 1 Cor. 1.29; Plutarch, *Moralia* 539A-B, D),[7] with certain notable exceptions (*T. Judah* 13.3; Plutarch, *On Inoffensive Self-Praise*), Plutarch states that the praises that come from others are pleas-

---

6. See the summary of the various opinions in Best, *First and Second Epistles to the Thessalonians,* 252; Marshall, *1 and 2 Thessalonians,* 171; Wanamaker, *Commentary on 1 and 2 Thessalonians,* 218.

7. See the discussion in *TLNT,* 2.295-302; *TDNT,* 3.645-53; *NIDNTT,* 1.227-29. The verb is equivalent to *kauchaomai.* See also the comments on "boasting" in Timothy B. Savage, *Power through Weakness* (Cambridge: Cambridge University Press, 1996), 19-64; Scott J. Hafemann, "'Self-Commendation' and Apostolic Legitimacy in 2 Corinthians: A Pauline Dialectic?" *NTS* 36 (1990) 66-68.

ant.[8] But more than being pleasant, they can strengthen resolve and stimulate hope; as Plutarch notes, praise "arouses and spurs the hearer, and not only awakens his ardor and fixes his purpose, but also affords him hope that the end can be attained and is not impossible" (*Moralia* 544E). Most likely the boasting the apostle did among the other congregations, which now rings in the Thessalonians' ears, became a fountain of great encouragement for them in the midst of the adversity they faced. Paul gave them a strong affirmation in the eyes of *God's churches* (see 1 Thess. 2.14; 1.1 and commentary; 1 Cor. 11.16), honoring the Thessalonians in the presence of their peers. By mentioning these churches, he opens the Thessalonians' consciousness once more to their participation in a wider movement that includes all those who responded to the call of the only God, to whom they have converted (1 Thess. 1.9). What is more, through such boasting the Thessalonians were held out as an example for the other congregations to emulate (1 Thess. 1.7). The purpose of this boasting and the narrative of such activity were calculated to strengthen both the Thessalonians and the other Christian congregations. There is nothing of vanity here; rather, such boasting buttressed the churches as they faced assault, and served clear didactic ends (cf. 2 Cor. 8.1-5, where boasting of Macedonian generosity is calculated to spur the Corinthians on to the same).

The second part of the verse explains the content of the boasting among the other churches, which was *about your perseverance and faith in all the persecutions and trials you are enduring.* The Thessalonian church's endurance of persecution stood as an example to the believers in the provinces of Macedonia and Achaia (1 Thess. 1.6-7), and now the author reveals that this was, in part, due to the report he had spread abroad. These believers had displayed a truly noteworthy tenacity, and this perseverance was rooted deeply in the hope in the coming of the Lord Jesus Christ that they held (1 Thess. 1.3 and commentary). Paul had become extremely concerned about their resolve to continue in the faith and had sent Timothy "to find out about" their faith (1 Thess. 3.5) and "to strengthen and encourage" them in their faith (1 Thess. 3.2). The founders entertained the fear that the Thessalonians might have abandoned the faith due to the overwhelming social pressure against them motivated by the tempter himself (1 Thess. 3.3, 5 and commentary). But after his visit, Timothy brought the team good news of their steadfastness in the faith (1 Thess. 3.6-8). 2 Thessalonians now presents evidence that this

---

8. *Moralia* 539D, citing Xenophon, *Memorabilia* 2.1.31, says, "For while praise from others, as Xenophon said, is the most pleasant of recitals, praise of ourselves is for others most distressing."

church continued firm in the faith despite the *persecutions and trials* they faced.

The *persecutions* (*diōgmois;* see Mark 10.30; Acts 8.1; 13.50; 2 Cor. 12.10; 2 Tim. 3.11) were those that they suffered at the hands of their contemporaries and that were motivated by Satan (1 Thess. 1.6; 2.14; 3.3-5). The plural, strengthened by the adjective *all,* most likely indicates that these outbreaks of hostility arose on various occasions and in a variety of ways. The author also describes their sufferings as *trials* (*thlipsesin;* in combination with *diōgmos* in Matt. 13.21; Mark 4.17; Rom. 8.35), which may indicate any type of suffering a human may endure, whether external attack or internal distress. But in these letters *trials* refers exclusively to the hostility they endured as Christians and as such is synonymous with the word *persecutions* (1.6-7; 1 Thess. 1.6; 3.3, 7; and cf. the verb in 1 Thess. 3.4; 2 Thess. 1.6-7; and see 2 Cor. 8.1-2). These believers were not simply distressed emotionally but buffeted by great hostility.[9] The following verses imply that the persecution of the church had in no way abated but had rather intensified. In spite of their *persecutions and trials,* these believers were *enduring* the situation in which they found themselves (cf. 1 Cor. 4.12).[10] This virtue of endurance was an ideal of Stoic ethics as well. The well-known Stoic dictum was "Endure and abstain."[11] But whereas the Stoic ideal was generated by the belief in fortune's inevitable control over events (we might say, "Why fuss if you can't do anything about it?"), Christian endurance was rooted in God, who was the object of both their hope and faith. He is the one who has ultimate control of their situation (vv. 5-10).

5 The following verses (vv. 5-10) constitute an expansion of Paul's thoughts on the persecutions the Thessalonians endured and the destiny of both the believers and their persecutors.[12] The present verse is of particular importance since it presents the church with an important aspect of the theology of suffering. In the divine plan, the suffering of God's people plays a central role and should not be construed as a sign of God's rejection or neglect of his own. In fact, the apostle presents an extraordi-

---

9. See the comments on 1 Thess. 1.6; 3.3, 7 and the discussion in Todd D. Still, *Conflict at Thessalonica: A Pauline Church and Its Neighbors* (Sheffield: Sheffield Academic Press, 1999), 208-12.

10. On the use of the present tense in this verse and its implications with regard to the order of the letters, see the Introduction, pp. 64-66.

11. *Anechou kai apechou* (see *apechō* in 1 Thess. 4.3; 5.22); MM, 42; *NIDNTT,* 2.764-67; *TNDT,* 1.359-60; BAGD, 65.

12. Although the *NIV* places a paragraph break between vv. 4 and 5, these verses are part of one continuous sentence in the Greek text. Since v. 5 continues the thought of the previous verse, a paragraph break should not be placed between them.

nary perspective on their sufferings by saying, *All this is evidence that God's judgment is right.* Exactly what is this clear *evidence*[13] that *God's judgment is right?* The Greek sentence is an elliptical construction that demands that the reader supply the words *all this* or something similar ("This is" in the *NRSV,* which would convey the sense of a supplied *ho estin*). Alternatively, the first word of the Greek sentence, *evidence,* may be understood as an accusative in apposition to some element in the previous verse.[14] However the construction is understood, the *evidence* of this just *judgment* is found in the previous verse. The *evidence* of just *judgment* may be the "the perseverance and faith" of the Thessalonians, or it may be the sufferings themselves. What does Paul have in mind?

The ideas presented in this verse are strikingly similar to those in Philippians 1.27-28, where Paul speaks of the steadfastness of the church in the face of opposition, "without being frightened in any way by those who oppose you. This is a sign to them that they will be destroyed, but that you will be saved — and that by God." In those verses their perseverance in the midst of persecution is the "sign of salvation" for the Philippians. But the perspective of 2 Thessalonians 1.5 is somewhat different. The "sign" or *evidence* here does not point to the salvation of the Thessalonians but rather that *God's judgment is right.* Moreover, the immediate antecedent in v. 4 is not the "perseverance and faith" of the Thessalonians but rather their "persecutions and trials." In fact, v. 5 continues the discussion about the trials of the Thessalonians, not their reaction to their situation. Because of these observations, Bassler suggests that the clear *evidence* that *God's judgment is right* is precisely the persecutions themselves![15] Understood in this way, the verse would be part of the theology of suffering that flourished both in Christianity and in Judaism. Peter, for example, in his explanation of the persecutions the believers in Asia Minor were enduring, stated, "For it is time for judgment to begin with the family of God; and if it begins with us, what will the outcome be for those who do not obey the gospel of God?" He goes on to declare that they are suffering "according to God's will" (1 Pet. 4.17, 19).[16] *God's judgment is right,* or, rather, "just" *(dikaias)* (cf. Rom. 2.5; 2 Tim. 4.8; 1 Pet. 2.23; Rev. 16.7; 19.2; Pss. 19.9 [18.9]; 119.137 [118.137]; Jer. 11.20) because in the end he will give to each what he or she deserves (2 Thess. 1.6-

---

13. *Endeigma,* only here in the NT. See Plato, *Critias* 110B; Demosthenes 19.256 ("and in a manner I think that even the events of this scrutiny furnish the commonwealth with a new *example* of the divine favor"); BAGD, 262; LSJ, 558.

14. BDF, §480.6.

15. Jouette M. Bassler, "The Enigmatic Sign: 2 Thessalonians 1:5," *CBQ* 46 (1984) 496-510; and see Wanamaker, *Commentary on 1 and 2 Thessalonians,* 220-23.

16. See Green, *1 Pedro y 2 Pedro,* 264-74.

10). This *judgment* has already begun (Rom. 1.18; 1 Pet. 4.17) in anticipation of its full realization in the future, as the following verses describe.

Within Judaism, the theology of suffering appears in a number of writings, as Bassler demonstrates (*Gen. Rab.* 33.1; *Pss. Sol.* 13.9-10; 2 Macc. 6.12-16; *2 Bar.* 13.3-10; 52.5-7; 78.5). According to this literature, the judgments of God are truly just, and he, in due time, will change the fortune of his people and their oppressors. Bassler observes, "Thus the temporal suffering is no longer a sign of rejection by God. In this theological framework it is viewed somewhat paradoxically as a sign of *acceptance* by God insofar as he offers through it an opportunity for his elect to receive in this age the punishment for their few sins, thus preserving the full measure of their reward in the age to come"[17] (cf. vv. 6-10). The perspective that is presented in this theology is the exact opposite of the interpretation of history that Polybius presents. This second-century-BC writer explained the defeat of the Macedonian Empire by the Romans as clear evidence of the corruption inherent in that kingdom (Polybius 36.17.13-15; 38.3.8-13). For him and most in his day, to suffer ill was a sign of internal decay. The message of the apostle to these Macedonian Christians is strikingly different. The Christian paradigm is always the cross.

In his theology of suffering, Peter explains that one purpose of the suffering that comes with persecution is to test the character of the believer (1 Pet. 1.7; 4.12). Paul offers a similar perspective in 1.5b. They do not come close to saying that persecutions have a purifying effect, but affirm that *as a result you will be counted worthy of the kingdom of God, for which you are suffering.* In the city of Thessalonica, the Christians had suffered rejection and dishonor at the hands of their contemporaries (1 Thess. 2.14), but in the plan of God the source of social shame is transformed into a sign of honor. God counts them *worthy of the kingdom of God* (Luke 20.35; Acts 5.41), and their sufferings are a mark of that dignity. Just as a person had to be "counted worthy" in order to become a citizen of the great city Alexandria in Egypt (3 Macc. 3.21),[18] so these believers are *counted worthy of the kingdom of God* because of their *suffering.*[19] So intimate is the relationship between the *kingdom of God* and the *suffering* of the people of God that Paul included the teaching that "We must go through many hardships to enter the kingdom of God" (Acts 14.22) as part of his basic instruction of new Christians. The future significance of their entrance to this kingdom is explained in the following section (vv. 7-

17. Bassler, "The Enigmatic Sign: 2 Thessalonians 1:5," 502.
18. On the word *kataxiōthēnai* see 2 Macc. 13.12; *Ep. Arist.* 175; Josephus, *Antiquitates* 15.76 (15.3.8); 4.281 (4.8.36); Polybius 1.23.3; Diodorus Siculus 2.60.3; BAGD, 415; MM, 330; *TDNT*, 1.379-80; *NIDNTT*, 3.348-49.
19. Comments on the *kingdom of God* can be found at 1 Thess. 2.12.

10). But even in the present moment, these who had been rejected from being worthy members of their community are now considered *worthy* to participate in the *kingdom of God* (see 1 Thess. 2.12).

B. "It is indeed just of God to repay with affliction those who afflict you" — The Destiny of the Persecutors (1.6-10)

6 Verse 6 begins with a word that the *NIV* leaves untranslated (*eiper*, "if indeed" or even "since"), which introduces additional information about the "judgment of God" declared in v. 5.[1] Paul returns to the theme of the just judgment of God and assures the Thessalonians that *God is just: He will pay back trouble to those who trouble you*. Rather than presenting a frank statement about God's just character, the Greek text suggests that it is just in God's sight *(dikaion para theō)*[2] to recompense the persecutors with divine chastisement (vv. 6, 8-9) and to grant rest to the persecuted Thessalonians (vv. 7-10). God is all about just outcomes. Over and over biblical and extrabiblical literature declares that God's judgment is in accordance with his justice (Gen. 18.25; 1 Kings 8.31-32; 2 Chr. 6.22-23; Pss. 7.8-9, 11 [7.9-10, 12]; 9.4, 8 [9.5, 9]; 35.24 [34.24]; Tob. 3.2; 2 Macc. 12.6; Sir. 35.18; 2 Tim. 4.8; Rev. 18.6-7; 19.1-2). God is not capricious but rather judges justly. Hence those who mount the opposition against the church will suffer for their opposition, while the community of God will receive its rightful recompense. God considers it a *just* thing to *pay back trouble to those who trouble you*. Scripture addresses frequently the theme of divine recompense, at times using the same verb that the apostle employs in this verse *(antapodounai;* see Ps. 137.8 [136.8]; Isa. 66.4, 6;[3] Rom. 12.19; Heb. 10.30 [Deut. 32.35]). The author claims that it would be unjust for God to allow the persecutors to escape their deserved judgment.

---

1. BAGD, 220; MM, 182; BDF §454.2. See Rom. 3.30; 8.9, 17; 1 Cor. 8.5; 15.15. Although the term introduces a conditional clause, the function of the clause is to present a fact about which there can be no doubt.

2. See BAGD, 610, and the similar construction in Rom. 2.13; 1 Cor. 3.19; Gal. 3.11; Jas. 1.27; 1 Pet. 2.4. The *NRSV* gets close to the sense with the translation, "For it is indeed just of God to repay with affliction those who afflict you."

3. Roger D. Aus, "The Relevance of Isaiah 66.7 to Revelation 12 and 2 Thessalonians 1," *ZNW* 67 (1976) 252-68, demonstrates the intertextual echoes of Isa. 66 in this passage:

2 Thess. 1.6	Isa. 66.6
2 Thess. 1.8a	Isa. 66.15
2 Thess. 1.8b	Isa. 66.4, 15
2 Thess. 1.12	Isa. 66.5

In Romans Paul contrasts the vengeance a person may wish to extract with the retribution God brings on the enemies of his people (Rom. 12.17-19). But Paul's purpose here is not to call the Thessalonians to abstain from revenge by giving place to divine vengeance. Rather, the emphasis on the vengeance of God is calculated to encourage the brothers and sisters in the face of great adversity, supplying them with an eschatological perspective that will enable them to evaluate their present situation rightly. As they, the Christians, presently suffer (see v. 4 and commentary), so in the future *God will pay back trouble to those who trouble you.* This is one of the few texts that calls the result of God's judgment "suffering" (*thlipsin,* translated *trouble* in the *NIV;* see Zeph. 1.15; Rom. 2.9),[4] although the idea is commonplace enough. The author graphically details the nature of this suffering in the following verses (vv. 8-9), and so returns to a theme that the church already understood due to the previous apostolic instruction (1 Thess. 2.14-16; 5.3, 9). The NT knows nothing of the Epicurean denial of future divine judgment nor of its rejection of providence, but affirms strongly both God's providential care of his own and the inevitable execution of his wrath.[5] Christians will escape the oppression of their persecutors in that day (v. 7), but those who are disobedient to the gospel will find no relief (vv. 8-9). In a world that clamors for justice, the present teaching continues to serve as a source of hope. But our modern glib rejection of the notion of divine intervention and judgment stands corrected by these words.

7 The second part of that which God considers just (v. 6) is presented in this verse. Having explained what will happen to the persecutors in the previous verse, the apostle turns his attention to the believers and assures them that they will receive liberation from their oppression when the Lord Jesus is revealed. The assurance offered the church is that he will *give relief to you who are troubled, and to us as well.* The promise given to these believers who have suffered so much at the hands of their persecutors (see v. 4) is that God will reward them with *relief* at the time of the revelation of the Lord Jesus (v. 7b). The principal verb is carried over from the previous verse *(antapodounai),* a term that is there linked to divine retribution or punishment but here points to the divine reward.[6]

---

4. BAGD, 362; *NIDNTT,* 2.807-9. See the use of the term as a description of the persecution or oppression the Thessalonians and the apostles endured in 1 Thess. 1.6; 3.3, 7; 2 Thess. 1.4; and 1.6b.

5. Plutarch's work entitled *On the Delays of the Divine Vengeance (De Sera Numinis Vindicta)* is an instructive starting point to understand the well-known Epicurean and Stoic debate on this issue.

6. BAGD, 73. See the positive sense in Prov. 25.22; Sir. 30.6; 1 Macc. 10.27; Luke 14.14; Rom. 11.35.

The word that describes their promised reward could be translated "rest" (the *KJV* rendering of *anesin*),[7] but in the NT it commonly denotes *relief* from some type of affliction.[8] The apostle holds out the promise of the longed-for *relief* from persecution and affliction. These believers will not be disadvantaged in any way but will experience the same *relief* that Paul and his companions will enjoy *(and to us as well)*. As the apostles suffered, so did the Thessalonian believers (1 Thess. 2.1, 16; 3.7; 2 Thess. 3.2). So, too, they could anticipate sharing with them in the liberation (cf. 2 Cor. 1.7). This liberation is an aspect of the full Christian hope that included resurrection and rapture (1 Thess. 4.13-18) as well as the glory or honor they will enjoy when Christ returns (2 Thess. 2.14; 1.10). The expectation of this eschatological *relief* in no way implies that Christians may not rightly pray and hope for the intervention of God in the present to ameliorate their situation (3.2; Phil. 1.19-26; 2 Tim. 4.16-18). What is more, in the present believers know that their lot includes affliction and that they can rest in the firm promise that God will empower them to overcome even in the midst of the adversity they face, whatever its source (Rom. 8.31-39). In the end, God's guarantee is that the injustices they presently endure will reach their conclusion. Hope sends its roots deep into this soil.

In the second part of the verse, the apostle elaborates on the time when the events described in vv. 6 and 7a will come to pass: *This will happen when the Lord Jesus is revealed from heaven in blazing fire with his powerful angels.* In the other texts in these letters that speak of the coming of the Lord Jesus, the author refers to the event as the *parousia* (1 Thess. 2.19; 3.13; 4.15; 5.23; 2 Thess. 2.1), but here it is described as his "revelation" (*apokalypsei*; see 1 Cor. 1.7; 1 Pet. 1.7, 13; 4.13; and the verb in Luke 17.30). The term means "the removal of the veil"[9] and is frequently employed in those contexts where the biblical author wishes to talk of some kind of divine "revelation," such as the unveiling of truths previously hidden (Luke 2.32; 1 Cor. 14.6, 26; 2 Cor. 12.1, 7; Gal. 1.12; Eph. 1.17; 3.3). But the present declaration is not about the unveiling of some aspect of the mystery of God but of a person, *the Lord Jesus.* This affirmation was of great importance for these Christians who had neither a temple nor a visible god as did their pagan contemporaries. He whom neither they nor their

---

7. So Josephus, *Antiquitates* 3.254 (3.10.6), 281 (3.11.3).

8. 2 Cor. 8.13; 2.13; 7.5; and see 2 Chr. 23.15; 1 Esdr. 4.62; Diodorus Siculus 19.26.10. Acts 24.23 is an exception in that it conveys the idea of "liberty." A later Christian inscription from Thessalonica speaks of the "relief and forgiveness of sins" (*IT,* n. 786.5). See BAGD, 65; MM, 42; *TDNT,* 1.367.

9. Milligan, *St. Paul's Epistles to the Thessalonians,* 149-51; *TLNT,* 2.247-50; *TDNT,* 3.563-92; BAGD, 92; *NIDNTT,* 3.310-16.

pagan persecutors could see will be revealed in all his glory and power, and on that day all will see him (Matt. 24.30; cf. 1 Pet. 1.8). *The Lord Jesus* is hidden, but not absent. The hope they held was that he would be *revealed from heaven*, the place to which he had gone in his ascension and from which he would come upon his return (1 Thess. 1.10; 4.16 and commentary). Marshall rightly adds that the declaration that he will be *revealed from heaven* "does not merely indicate his origin but also stresses his authority. He comes from the dwelling place of God with the authority of God to execute judgment and recompense."[10]

This revelation will be *in blazing fire* (words that relate to the following verse but are part of this sentence in the Greek text), a further point that highlights the consequences of the unveiling for the Thessalonians' persecutors. These words, which literally mean "in flame of fire," constitute an intertextual allusion either to the revelation of the presence of God (Exod. 3.2-3) or to his judicial power (Isa. 66.15-16). The repeated references in this passage to Isaiah 66[11] and the description of judgment in v. 8 direct the reader's attention to the fire of judgment.[12] In this theophany the Lord Jesus "will punish those who do not know God" (v. 8).

In his revelation, the Lord Jesus will be accompanied *with his powerful angels*, or "the angels of his power" (*angelōn dynameōs autou*). A number of texts describe how these beings will accompany the Lord in his coming (1 Thess. 3.13; Matt. 16.27; 24.30-31; 25.31; Mark 8.38; and Zech. 14.5). Although they are powerful in themselves (2 Pet. 2.11), the point of the present verse is that they are the executors of the Lord's judicial power. Paul is not thinking about some special class of angels such as those that occasionally appear in the intertestamental literature (e.g., *1 Enoch* 61.10; *T. Judah* 3.10).[13] The Lord Jesus, who was so despised in Thessalonica, will come with great authority and judicial power, accompanied by the those who will aid in the execution of divine judgment.

8 In v. 8 Paul explains the purpose of the Lord Jesus' powerful judicial revelation: *He will punish those who do not know God and do not obey the gospel of our Lord Jesus.* The language of the verse is taken from Isaiah 66.15 in the Greek version ("he will return vengeance in wrath") in combination with Isaiah 66.4 ("Because I called them and they did not obey

---

10. Marshall, *1 and 2 Thessalonians*, 176.

11. See n. 3.

12. Judgment by fire is a reality described in both Testaments and in Jewish literature: Deut. 32.22; Isa. 29.6; 30.27, 30, 33; 33.14; 66.24; Joel 2.30; Nah. 1.6; Zeph. 1.8; 3.8; Mal. 4.1; Acts 2.19; 2 Pet. 3.7, 10; Rev. 9.17-18; 16.8; 20.9; *Sib. Or.* 2.196-213; 3.80-93; 4.171-82; 5.155-61, 206-13; *Pss. Sol.* 15.4; *1 Enoch* 1.6-7; 52.6; 1QH 3.19-36; Josephus, *Antiquitates* 1.70 (1.2.3); *Adam and Eve* 49.3.

13. See Frame, *Epistles of St. Paul to the Thessalonians*, 232.

me"), which describe the wrath Yahweh visits on the disobedient.[14] The expression translated *he will punish (didontos ekdikēsin)* may refer either to divine punishment (2 Cor. 7.11; 1 Pet. 2.14) or, as here in 1.8, to divine vengeance or retribution (Luke 18.3, 5; 21.22; Acts 7.24; Rom. 12.19; Heb. 10.30 [Deut. 32.35]; and *1 Enoch* 25.4). This "vengeance" is the result of a judicial decision and disposition against those who have rejected God and his gospel.[15] The nature of God's vengeance is described more fully in the following verse. Those who have rejected God and his message will not escape judgment — God is the Avenger (1 Thess. 4.6 and commentary). This vengeance is not simple retaliation nor an irrational outburst of anger but an execution of God's just judgment (vv. 5-6).

The ancients understood that the coherence of society was in part due to the promise of rewards and the threats of punishment. In these societies, where reciprocity was at the heart of both private and public social intercourse, the notion of retribution and reward was deeply embedded in their ideas of justice. The frustration of the Thessalonian believers would have been to suffer such injustices without any hope of recourse or vindication. But the promise held before them is that those who are presently under no threat of human justice will not escape the just vengeance of God, because the root cause of the believers' suffering is the unbelievers' rejection of God himself. The issues at stake go well beyond the personal.

Those who are the objects of divine vengeance are described as *those who do not know God and do not obey the gospel of our Lord Jesus.* Marshall and others have suggested that two groups are in mind: the Gentiles *(those who do not know God)* and the Jews (those who *do not obey the gospel of our Lord Jesus).*[16] Although Marshall is correct in pointing out that sometimes the Gentiles are described as those who are ignorant of God (see 1 Thess. 4.5; and Ps. 79.6 [78.6]; Jer. 10.25) and the Jews as those who are disobedient (Isa. 66.4; Acts 7.39; Rom. 10.16), Paul also accuses both groups of being disobedient (Rom. 11.30-32). Also, both the OT and the NT occasionally describe the Jews as those who are ignorant of the true God (Jer. 4.22; 9.3, 6; Hos. 5.4; John 8.55).[17] A preferable reading of the second part of v. 8 would be to understand the statement as a two-part description of those who are subjects of divine vengeance. They are, in the first place, *those who do not know God.* In the OT, God declares his judg-

14. See n. 3.
15. MM, 193; BAGD, 238; and see Philo, *Legum Allegoriae* 3.106 (where the ideas of punishment and vengeance appear together); Polybius 3.8.10. *1 Enoch* 25.4 speaks in a similar way of "the great judgment, when he shall take vengeance on all and conclude (everything) forever."
16. Marshall, *1 and 2 Thessalonians*, 177-178.
17. So Wanamaker, *Commentary on 1 and 2 Thessalonians*, 227.

ment on those who do not know him (Jer. 10.25; Ps. 79.6 [78.6]). This ignorance is not merely failing to recognize his existence but rather the rejection of his person as he is revealed to both nations and individuals (see
1 Thess. 4.5 and commentary; Rom. 1.18-32). As the knowledge of God is
linked with obedience to his law (Ps. 36.10 [35.11]), so also the ignorance
of God is understood as disobedience to his call. What follows is therefore closely parallel to the preceding thought. Those who suffer divine
vengeance are, secondly, those who *do not obey the gospel of our Lord Jesus*
(cf. Rom. 2.8; 1 Pet. 4.17). The NT frequently describes the act of conversion as obedience to the *gospel* (Acts 6.7; Rom. 1.5; 6.17; 10.16; 15.18; 16.26;
Heb. 5.9; 1 Pet. 1.2, 14, 22). Such a description of the event cues us to the
fact that the *gospel* is both the promise and offer of salvation and the demand of obedience to its call. It calls humans to respond to the good news
of God, but if the divine initiative is rejected, the very same gospel becomes the criteria by which God will judge the person (Rom. 2.16). In
fact, in the judicial sphere the word *obey (hypakouousin)* means "strict obedience to an order or a law."[18] God calls humans through his gospel
(2.14), and those who do not respond can only hope for judgment. In the
divine scheme, disobedience to the gospel is elevated to the status of a
criminal offense, a thought quite different from the modern notion that
the gospel should be received simply for personal benefit. Those in
Thessalonica who had rejected the gospel were like those of Isaiah 66.4
(LXX), "Because I called them and they did not obey me, I spoke and they
did not hear."

9 Paul continues with a description of the character of the Lord's
vengeance against those who have rejected God and the gospel of the
Lord Jesus: *They will be punished with everlasting destruction and shut out
from the presence of the Lord and from the majesty of his power.* The words
translated *they will be punished* (NRSV, "These will suffer the punishment," *hoitines dikēn tisousin*) come from the world of jurisprudence and
mean "to pay the consequences" for some action. This is the "punishment" that the guilty suffer for the evil they have done.[19] Jude speaks of
"those who suffer the punishment of eternal fire" (Jude 7); in the present
passage the apostle understands the execution of the final judgment in a

---

18. *TLNT*, 1.447. For example, "Since Cathytes, summoned before men, has not responded *(ouch' hypēkousen)* I have decided that for his disobedience *(apeithias)* he shall
pay 250 denarii" (cited in ibid.).

19. See the expression in Epictetus 3.24.4; 3.26.20; Plutarch, *Moralia* 553F, 559D,
561B, and 592E; Philo, *De Vita Mosis* 1.245; *De Specialibus Legibus* 3.175. The word *dikē*
originally conveyed the idea of "justice" in the tribunal but came to mean "punishment"
or the execution of the judicial verdict. MM, 163, 636; BAGD, 198, 818; and see 2 Macc.
8.11; Wis. 18.11; Jude 7.

similar way (v. 7b). He further describes this as *everlasting destruction*. The term *destruction* (*olethron,* the same word encountered in 1 Thess. 5.3) frequently appears in those texts that speak of eschatological ruin or destruction (1 Tim. 6.9; Jer. 25.31 [32.31]; 48.3 [31.3]; Hag. 2.22; Wis. 1.14-15; 4 Macc. 10.15 [in combination with "eternal"]; and see Jer. 22.7; Ezek. 6.14).[20] The duration of this *destruction* is *everlasting* or "eternal," a terrible reality that is highlighted in other NT texts (cf. Matt. 18.8; 25.41 ["eternal fire"], 46 ["eternal punishment"]; Jude 7 ["the punishment of eternal fire"]). The apostle by no means implies that those who have rejected God will be annihilated eternally, a notion that appears to take the edge off the severity of divine judgment. Rather, the punishment will endure and will not end.[21] While the gospel brings the promise of "eternal encouragement" (2.16) to those who receive it, rejection of God's initiative will bring eternal perdition. This state to which the judged are assigned is variously described in the NT as a place of "unquenchable fire" (Matt. 3.12), a "fiery furnace" (Matt. 13.42, 50), the "blackest darkness" that "has been reserved forever" (Jude 13), and a "fiery lake of burning sulfur" (Rev. 21.8). The graphic language appears inadequate at each point to describe the horrid nature of this state. No hope is held out for a second opportunity to escape or obtain salvation. The verdict, as its execution, will be final.

This punishment *with everlasting destruction,* beyond being permanent and irrevocable, also means being *shut out from the presence of the Lord and from the majesty of his power.* While the preposition that begins this clause in the Greek text *(apo)* is construed in the *NIV* as signaling that the judged will be excluded from the *presence of the Lord,* the thought is rather that the *presence of the Lord* is the source from which the judgment proceeds.[22] This part of the verse is a nearly exact citation of Isaiah 2.10, 19, and 21 from the Septuagint ("And now go into the rocks, hide in the ground, from the presence of the terror of the LORD and from the glory of his strength"). The *Lord* in the Isaiah texts is Yahweh, who executes his judgment in the "day of Yahweh" against those who worship idols instead of the Lord himself: "Their land is full of idols; they bow down to the work of their hands, to what their fingers have made. So man will be

---

20. BAGD, 563; *TDNT,* 5.168-69; *NIDNTT,* 1.465-67.

21. Marshall's observation is instructive, "In favour of everlasting punishment it can be argued: (1). Jesus believed in it, and Paul will have shared his outlook (Matt. 5:29-30; 12:32; 18:8-9; 25:41, 46; Lk. 16:23-25); (2). Jewish teaching of the time accepted the fact of eternal punishment (1QS 2:15; 5:13; *Pss. Sol.* 2:35; 15:11; 4 Macc. 10:15); (3). In the present context the reference to separation from the Lord is of little significance if those punished are not conscious of their separation." (*1 and 2 Thessalonians,* 179).

22. See Isa. 2.10, 19, 21; and BAGD, 86-87, *apo* II.1.

brought low and mankind humbled — do not forgive them" (Isa. 2.8-9). The pride and arrogance of those who have rejected Yahweh is the cause of this horrible judgment (2.11-12, 17). They did not exalt Yahweh, but "the LORD alone will be exalted in that day, and the idols will totally disappear" (2.17b-18). In no way will anyone escape that judgment (Isa. 2.10, 19-21). The apostle presents the terrible promise that those who disobey the call of the gospel, the persecutors of the Thessalonian Christians, will by no means escape. Their hubris and pride, linked to their adherence to false worship, will in the end cause their demise.

As in 1.9, *the presence of the Lord* is associated in a number of texts in the OT and the book of Revelation with the judgment of God (Num. 16.46; Judg. 5.5; Pss. 34.16 [33.17]; 96.13 [95.13]; Jer. 4.26; Ezek. 38.20; Rev. 6.16; 20.11), and, as Isaiah notes, his presence is fearful. John was given a glimpse of the final judgment and exclaimed, "Then I saw a great white throne and him who was seated on it. Earth and sky fled from his presence, and there was no place for them" (Rev. 20.11). The idea that 1.9 conveys is not merely that the disobedient will be excluded from the Lord's *presence* but that from this *presence* the *everlasting destruction* comes forth. Moreover, the *destruction* they suffer will be *from the majesty of his power*. This *majesty* is the visible "glory" *(doxēs)* of God and is synonymous with his *presence* (Rom. 1.23; Jude 24). Christ is himself called the "Lord of glory" (1 Cor. 2.8), while on the other hand "glory" at times describes God's power (Rom. 6.4; Col. 1.11). The present verse highlights precisely this idea *(ischyos, power,* speaks of the power of God in Eph. 1.19; 6.10). The *Lord* Jesus comes in the divine *power* and is able to execute judgment. *The majesty of his power* is both the measure and the source of this judgment.

Paul gears this long discussion about the final judgment (vv. 5-10) to encourage the Thessalonian believers in their suffering for the faith (v. 4) and to assure them that justice will truly be done. But the passage also takes a side in the debate that was boiling during that era concerning the inevitability of divine judgment. The Epicureans questioned any notion of future divine judgment, and they were not alone in such speculation.[23] The argument against divine retribution revolved around the apparent tardiness of its execution. The fictive debate Plutarch sets up around the issue begins with the comments of Patrocleas, who says, "The delay and procrastination of the Deity in punishing the wicked appears to me the most telling argument by far. . . . Yet that feeling dates from long ago, when it would chafe me to hear Euripides say: 'Apollo lags; such is the

---

23. See, e.g., Juvenal, *Satirae* 2.149-53; Lucian, *De Luctu;* Zeus, *Juppiter Confutatus* 16-19. See Meeks, *The Origins of Christian Morality,* 177.

way of Heaven'" (*Moralia* 548C-D and 549B-D; and cf. 1 Pet. 3.3-13). So popularized was the Epicurean notion that Plutarch, a priest of Apollo at Delphi at the end of the first century, felt compelled to write a whole trac-tate to defend the traditional view *(De Sera Numinis Vindicta)*. In this cli-mate, the sufferings of the Thessalonians and the lack of any apparent in-tervention by God to bring an end to their undeserved suffering would be enough reason for the apostles to have presented such lengthy and de-tailed reassurances of the certainty of future judgment. This church suf-fered an enormous amount of confusion regarding eschatological subjects (see 1 Thess. 4.13–5.11; 2 Thess. 2.1-12), and their concerns do not surprise us given the diverse body of public opinion that circulated at that time about these topics.[24] The apostle lays down an argument revolving around the character of God and his justice (vv. 5-6) and the promise of the coming of the Lord as Avenger who has all power to execute the verdict (vv. 7b-9). Judgment is certain, and it will be supremely powerful.

10 Although the revelation of the Lord will result in judgment for those who have rejected God and who persecute the church (vv. 7b-9), the significance of this event for believers is completely different (cf. v. 7a). The terror described in vv. 7b-9 will occur *on the day he comes to be glorified in his holy people and to be marveled at among all those who have believed*. The temporal note "on that day" *(en tẹ̄ hēmerạ ekeinẹ̄)* echoes Isaiah 2.11, 17 (LXX), the same chapter quoted in v. 9. This *day* is none other than the "day of the Lord" (1 Thess. 5.2, 4; 2 Thess. 2.2), the time when the wor-shipers of idols will be humbled and God will be exalted, according to the prophecy of Isaiah. The author finds the fulfillment of the prophecy in the Lord Jesus, a fact that has clear christological implications. Who is this Jesus but the Lord himself? He will "come" (an alternative way of speaking of his "revelation" in v. 7) *to be glorified in his holy people*. Once more the apostles appeal to the OT, taking this citation from the Greek version of Psalm 89.7 (88.8), which says, "God will be glorified in the council of the saints." The "saints" in 1 Thessalonians 3.13 are the angels who will accompany the Lord in his coming (see commentary), but here the reference is rather to the believers (as in Rom. 1.7; 1 Cor. 1.2; 2 Cor. 1.1; Eph. 1.1; Phil. 1.1; Col. 1.2; and cf. 1 Thess. 5.27), as the parallelism with the second part of the verse implies *(those who have believed)*. The Thessalonians themselves will take part in this glorification of the Lord, along with the great company of Christians, as v. 12 suggests and the last part of the present verse states: *This includes you!*

---

24. It is not necessary, as Jewett does, to recur to the model of a radical millenarian community to understand the eschatological confusion that prevailed in the Thessalo-nian church. See Jewett, *The Thessalonian Correspondence*, 161-78.

The grammar of v. 10a may imply that the *holy ones* are instruments of this glorification (*en tois hagiois;* so the *NRSV*'s "by his saints"), or that he will be glorified "in the midst of his saints." Another possible reading is that the glory of the Lord will be reflected in them (cf. 1 Thess. 2.12). The citation of Psalm 89.7 (88.8) favors the second interpretation, and the parallelism with the second part of the verse (itself taken from Ps. 68.35 [67.36]) supports this reading as well. However, the thought of the passage moves us in the direction of the first reading. *Those who have believed* will marvel at him and *the holy ones* (the same group) will glorify him, in stark contrast to the rejection he and his people suffered (v. 8). In his revelation, his people will give him the glory and honor he deserves because of the execution of his judgment on that *day* (cf. Exod. 14.4, 17, 18; Ezek. 28.22; 38.23).[25]

The second affirmation of the verse is that he will *be marveled at among* ("by") *all those who have believed,* an allusion to the Greek version of Psalm 68.35 (67.36), "God will be marveled at among his saints." In citing the Psalm, Paul substitutes one of his favorite designations of Christians, *those who have believed,* for "saints" (see 1 Thess. 1.7; 2.10, 13 and comments). The verb "to marvel" (*thaumasthēnai,* passive voice) in certain contexts meant "to be astonished at," but elsewhere, as here, it conveys the idea of "admire" or "honor." "To marvel at" appears in Greek literature as a human response to the revelation or miracles of a deity that evoke admiration and wonder (cf. Luke 8.25; 11.14; John 7.21; Acts 3.12; Rev. 13.3).[26] The Thessalonians are among those who will admire him, as the explanation of the following clause reveals: *This includes you,*[27] *because you believed our testimony to you.* The *testimony* is nothing less than the apostolic proclamation of the gospel (Matt. 24.14; Luke 21.13; Acts 4.33; 1 Cor. 1.6; 2 Tim. 1.8), to which the Thessalonians responded in faith at the time of their conversion (cf. 1 Thess. 2.13). This reaction to the divine initiative in the gospel (cf. 2.13-14) places the members of the church in contrast with "those who do not know God and do not obey the gospel of our Lord Jesus" (v. 8). The ultimate destiny of a person or a group of people at the time of the final revelation of the Lord depends on their response to the message of the gospel delivered by the apostolic witnesses. The importance of this *testimony,* and of one's response to it, transcends the boundaries of debate and opinion. Eternal destiny is bound inextricably with one's response to the gospel of Christ.

---

25. *TDNT,* 2.254-55.

26. *TDNT,* 3.28; *NIDNTT,* 2.625-26. The combination "glory" and "marvel at" appears in Exod. 34.10; Judg. 16.13; Sir. 38.6.

27. The *NIV* brings out the implicit sense by adding these words.

C. "To this end we will always pray for you" — The Remembrance of Prayers to Be Worthy of God's Call (1.11-12)

After giving thanks to God for the Thessalonian church (vv. 3-10), Paul informs the church of his and his associates' prayers for them (vv. 11-12).[1] This prayer links specifically with the issues addressed in vv. 6-10, which touched on the revelation of the Lord Jesus and the implications of his unveiling for the church and its persecutors. The Thessalonians received the promise that they would find "relief" at that time (v. 7) and that the Lord would be glorified by them (v. 10), while the persecutors would pass through the horrors of divine judgment (vv. 6, 7b-9). But the future promise given to believers brings with it obligations in the present time, and these become the theme of the apostles' prayers. Their future hope is wound together with their present conduct.

11 Meditating on the previous declarations concerning the revelation of the Lord Jesus and the final judgment,[2] Paul makes known his concerns for the Thessalonian church in this first prayer of the letter: *With this in mind, we constantly pray for you*. The language of the prayer is quite similar to that of 1 Thessalonians 1.2. His prayers for the church, as well as his offerings of thanks to God, were not sporadic or occasional but rather constant and faithful (cf. 1.3; Col. 1.3, 9). His investment in prayer for this church was robust and rigorous. Since the final judgment would be so severe and the revelation of the Lord so glorious, the apostle prays in the first place *that our God may count you worthy of his calling*. Although Bauer's lexicon understands the verb translated *count you worthy (axiōsē)* to mean "make you worthy,"[3] in many other texts it suggests the meaning reflected in the *NIV* (Luke 7.7; 1 Tim. 5.17; Heb. 3.3; 10.29; and Diodorus Siculus 16.59.2; 17.76.3; Josephus, *Antiquitates* 2.258 [2.11.2]).[4] These citations speak to us of those who are evaluated and found *worthy* of some kind of honor. While it is certainly true that in the end God is the one who makes believers *worthy of his calling* (1 Thess. 5.23-24), this thought about God's powerful working in their lives does not enter until the second part of v. 11. Paul had already exhorted the Thessalonians "to

---

1. On the function of prayers in ancient letters, see pp. 86, 175.

2. The prayer begins with *eis ho*, which is well understood in the *NIV* as *with this in mind*.

3. BAGD, 78; so, too, *TDNT*, 1.380.

4. The meaning of the verb is the same as *kataxiōthēnai* in 1.5, which is translated "you will be counted worthy." The sole exception is the *Diogn.* 9.1, where the meaning of "make worthy" is attested. In unrelated contexts, the verb may also mean "consider suitable, fitting," as in Acts 15.38; 28.22. See MM, 51; *NIDNTT*, 3.348.

live lives worthy of God, who calls you into his kingdom and glory" (1 Thess. 2.12 and comments; cf. Eph. 4.1; Phil. 1.27; Col. 1.10). The present prayer anticipates the evaluation of their conduct in light of *his calling* (cf. 1 Thess. 2.12; 4.7; 5.24; 2 Thess. 2.13-14), while it rests on the security of knowing that God is the one who enables them to do what is good and right (1 Thess. 5.23). This *calling* was to a lifestyle that conformed to God's will. The divine initiative in their *calling* carried with it "great responsibilities"[5] (Eph. 4.1; 2 Pet. 1.10).

Paul frames the prayer that the Thessalonians would be "counted worthy" within God's purposes for them (election and calling) and God's present power in their lives. In the second part of the prayer, the apostle petitions *that by his power he may fulfill every good purpose of yours and every act prompted by your faith.* The verb translated *may fulfill* could be used in other contexts to mean "to pay a debt," but here the sense is rather to complete or finish something already initiated (Rom. 15.19; 2 Cor. 10.6; Gal. 5.14; Phil. 2.2; Col. 1.25; 4.12).[6] This prayer recognizes that God is the ultimate source of the good they do and that the complete fulfillment of what they ought to do as those who are called depends on God's intervention in their lives. This in no way minimizes the need for responsible volition and action on their part (cf. 2.13-15)! The apostle desired that *every good purpose of yours* might be complete. This *purpose (eudokian)* could alternately be understood as either a "desire" (as in Rom. 10.1) or "goodwill" (as Phil. 1.15), whether the desire or goodwill was that of humans (Rom. 10.1; Phil. 1.15) or of God (Eph. 1.5, 9; Phil. 2.13).[7] But what is in mind in the present verse is not the "goodwill" of God but rather the attitude of the Thessalonians. The adjective *good (agathōsynē,* used exclusively of human conduct) may describe an object to obtain, their "desire to do the good."[8] But if *good* is interpreted as the source or motivation from which their conduct flows, the phrase could be understood as "the goodwill which is the fruit of the good."[9] This second alternative is preferable since the words stand in a grammatical construction parallel to the following phrase *every act prompted by your faith (ergon pisteōs).* The "goodwill" the Thessalonians demonstrated to others was the fruit of the *good* that characterized them as Christians (see Rom. 15.14; Gal. 5.22; Eph. 5.9).[10] This *purpose* or "goodwill" issues in their labors on behalf of others, whether they be within or outside the community of faith (1 Thess. 3.12).

---

5. Milligan, *St. Paul's Epistles to the Thessalonians,* 93.
6. BAGD, 671; MM, 520.
7. See *TLNT,* 2.104-6.
8. Understood as an objective genitive.
9. Understood as a subjective genitive. See BAGD, 319.
10. *TLNT,* 1.3-4; BAGD, 3.

Under this reading, Paul offers the prayer that God will complete this "goodwill" *by his power* (Rom. 15.13; Col. 1.29). In an environment of social hostility, the Thessalonians could realize their good intentions because God gave them the ability to do so. They were not simply dependent on their own resources or resolve to accomplish that which was pleasing to God and beneficial to others. In the same way, the apostle prays that *by his power* God would complete *every act prompted by your faith.* The expression here repeats that found in 1 Thessalonians 1.3 (see commentary). These "good works" arise out of true *faith* and are undertaken for anyone's benefit. This community was already demonstrating the fruit of these works, and the apostle's concern was that they brought to fulfillment what they had already begun, and this by the *power of God.*

12 Having prayed that God would bring their goodwill and work to completion (v. 11), Paul now explains the purpose[11] of the progress he and his companions prayed for: *We pray this so that the name of our Lord Jesus may be glorified in you, and you in him.* The first part of this verse echoes the Greek version of Isaiah 66.5 (cf. 24.15 as well), a section from the prophet that the authors have already quoted in vv. 8-9.[12] Isaiah 66.5 is a word directed at those faithful people of God who are despised by the rest. Those who mockingly rejected the ones who tremble at God's word said to his people, "Let the LORD be glorified, that we may see your joy!" These are mocking words, yet Isaiah turns and proclaims that the mocking ones who hate and detest them will be brought to shame. But in the hands of the translator of the LXX, the words are placed in the mouth of the despised and rejected[13] and become the answer to the persecutors. Paul uses the text in harmony with the LXX reading. In the end, the name of the *Lord Jesus* will *be glorified* instead of being despised and rejected as it was in Thessalonica (see Acts 17.7). This point was already made in v. 10 ("he comes to be glorified in his holy people"). But in the present verse Jesus' glorification is specifically linked with the attitude and conduct of the Thessalonian believers (v. 11), which, in the end, will result in the final eschatological glorification of the Lord (v. 10). As Jesus said in his prayer,

11. The verse does not begin with *We pray this* but rather with the word *hopōs* ("in order that"), which introduces the purpose of the previous statement (BDF, §369.4; BAGD, 576).

12. See the commentary and n. 3, p. 286. Contra Wanamaker, *Commentary on 1 and 2 Thessalonians,* 234-35, who overemphasizes the change in the verb from *doxasthē* (Isa. 66.5) to *endoxasthē* (2 Thess. 1.12).

13. "Hear the words of the LORD, the ones that tremble at his word; speak, our brothers, to those that hate you and detest you, that the name of the LORD might be glorified, and may be seen in gladness; but they shall be put to shame." On the LXX of Isa. 66 see David A. Baer, *When We All Go Home: Translation and Theology in LXX Isaiah 56–66* (Sheffield: Sheffield Academic Press, 2001).

"And glory has come to me through them" (John 17.10). At this very time, not only will the Despised and Rejected One be glorified, but so, too, those who have followed him will be glorified: *and you in him* (cf. 2.14; 1 Thess. 2.12; Rom. 5.2; 8.17-18, 21; Col. 3.4; Heb. 2.10).

Paul places special emphasis on the way the *name of our Lord Jesus* will be glorified. The *name* of a person in that era was much more than a way to distinguish him or her from others. The name often became a symbol of all that a person was, his or her qualities and power, and revealed that person's fundamental character.[14] For that reason, the name was intimately linked with a person's reputation and honor, much as we would speak about a person's "good name" or "bad name" (Mark 6.14; Rev. 3.1; 1 Macc. 8.12). So for these persecuted followers of the one mocked as "another king, one called Jesus," the promise that the *name of the Lord Jesus* would be glorified had great social importance. In fact, the glorification of deities was a common theme in the literature of the day. One prayer offered to the Egyptian goddess Isis shows striking similarities to the present verse. The worshiper prayed, "Lord Isis, glorify me as I glorify your son Horus."[15] The idea is that the deity is to be honored and respected, and the worshiper will be glorified as well.[16] In fact, this is the particular domain of the deity. So one inscription dedicated to Isis (a list of her virtues) places in the mouth of the goddess the following declaration,[17] "No one is glorified without my consent." While the name of Jesus and his followers suffered dishonor in the sight of those who were disobedient to the call through the gospel, the Thessalonian church could anticipate the day when they as well as their Lord would be publicly honored. This glorification would be mutual: he in them and they *in him.*[18] The rest will have no part in this grand event.

At the end of this verse and section, the eschatological glorification or honor of the church is conceived as the fruit of God's grace: *according to the grace of our God and the Lord Jesus Christ.* This *grace* is the source[19] of their salvation and hope (see 1.2; 2.16; 3.18; 1 Thess. 1.1; 5.28), as also their glorification. Grace comes from *our God and the Lord Jesus Christ,* which

14. See the discussion is BAGD, 571; *NIDNTT,* 2.648-56; Deissmann, *Bible Studies,* 146-48, 196-98; O'Brien, *Introductory Thanksgivings in the Letters of Paul,* 182-83; Milligan, *St. Paul's Epistles to the Thessalonians,* 94.

15. Cited in BAGD, 204; MM, 169.

16. See *TLNT,* 1.58-59.

17. Called an aretalogy. One such aretalogy to Isis was found in Thessaloniki (*IT,* n. 254).

18. Although according to v. 10 Jesus will be glorified "among" his holy ones (*en tois hagiois*). But here the Lord and the church are presented as the agents of glorification (*en hymin, en autǭ*), he by them and they by him, as the parallel construction suggests.

19. Cf. the same grammatical construction in Rom. 4.4, 16; 12.6; 1 Cor. 3.10.

the note in the *NIV* indicates may be translated, our "God and Lord, Jesus Christ." A single definite article governs both the words *God* and *Lord* in the Greek text[20] and unites the two titles in an ascription to the same person, *Jesus Christ* (see also Titus 2.12; 2 Pet. 1.11).[21] The translation contained in the *NIV* note is preferable. They will glorify and be glorified by no less than the most exalted *God and Lord,* the one who stands as the true source of all things.

III. "AS TO . . ." — THE BODY OF THE LETTER (2.1–3.15)

Paul brought to a conclusion the introduction to the letter, which included the thanksgiving and the proclamation of the revelation of the Lord and his judgment (vv. 3-10), followed by a prayer for the church (vv. 11-12). The new section he now begins introduces the eschatological and moral themes that constitute the body of the letter (2.1–3.16).[1] The first section of the body of the letter (2.1-17) discusses the time of the coming day of the Lord (2.1-12), gives thanks to God for the election of the Thessalonians (2.13-14), exhorts the church (2.15), and offers a blessing that centers on Paul's concern for the establishment and stability of the congregation (2.16-17).

A. "As to the coming of our Lord Jesus Christ" — The Time of the Day of the Lord (2.1-17)

1. Do not "be quickly shaken" — False Teaching about the Day of the Lord (2.1-12)

1 The apostle introduces the first section of the body of the letter by exhorting (vv. 1-2) the Thessalonians not to *become easily unsettled or alarmed* over a false teaching that had infiltrated the community and proclaimed

20. *Tou theou hēmōn kai kyriou Iēsou Christou.*

21. Porter, *Idioms of the Greek New Testament,* 110-11; Nigel Turner, *Grammatical Insights into the New Testament* (Edinburgh: T&T Clark, 1965), 16. It has been argued on the other side that often the name "Lord Jesus Christ" frequently appears without the article (as in 1.2) and therefore such great theological significance should not be attached to the absence of the article. However, the ascription of the title "God" to Jesus was sufficiently common in the NT that its use here is hardly unusual (see John 1.1, 18; 20.28; Rom. 9.5; Heb. 1.8-9; 1 John 5.20).

1. On the structure of the letter, see pp. 69-74.

that *the day of the Lord has already come* (v. 2). The Greek text puts the beginning of the exhortation at the head of the sentence in v. 1, *we ask you, brothers,*[2] using the same verb as that found in 1 Thessalonians 4.1 and 5.12, which introduce an exhortation in the form of a request (*erōtōmen;* see 1 Thess. 4.1 and commentary; 5.12; Phil. 4.3; 2 John 5). We could properly render the imperative "we beseech" or "we entreat" (*NRSV,* "we beg you"). There is an urgency in the request as well as a call to pay heed to the teaching they are about to receive.

The concern raised is expressed at the beginning of the English translation of v. 1: *Concerning the coming of our Lord Jesus Christ and our being gathered to him.* The coming of Christ in his royal *parousia* is linked inextricably with two events, those being the "day of the Lord" (v. 2b) and the *gathering* of the whole church to him, a complex of occurrences that were previously brought together in 1 Thessalonians 4.15–5.2. The word *concerning* (*hyper* plus the accusative; cf. John 1.30; 2 Cor. 8.23; 12.8; Demosthenes 21.121)[3] introduces the principal concerns of the author at this moment, which had to do with how the false understanding of the "day of the Lord" affected their understanding of the *coming of the Lord Jesus Christ* and the gathering of the church *to him.* Most likely the false doctrine about "the day of the Lord" that v. 2 elaborates caused such anguish in the church precisely because it distorted their understanding of the *parousia* of Christ and the rapture/resurrection of the church. These events are aspects of the same eschatological consummation and cannot be separated temporally or theologically, as some have suggested.[4]

The first part of the fallout from the false teaching concerning the "day of the Lord" had to do with *the coming of our Lord Jesus Christ,* a theme the apostle had addressed repeatedly (1 Thess. 2.19; 3.13; 4.15; 5.23; and 2 Thess. 1.7-10). Most likely Paul had taken up this topic with them while he was in the city (2.5). In the present letter, the author refers to this event as the time "when the Lord Jesus is revealed from heaven"

---

2. Or "brothers and sisters," as the *NRSV* renders *adelphoi,* since both male and female members of the congregation are addressed at this point.

3. BAGD, 839; BDF, §231.

4. Since the 1830s not a few biblical expositors have tried to propose a two-stage coming of Christ that separated his advent for his church from the final "day of the Lord" when he will return with his church. However, as 1 Thess. 4.13-18 shows, only one coming is discussed in the NT and this event will be at the very time of the "day of the Lord" (cf. 1 Thess. 5.1ff.). The present verse brings to grief the popular notion that the rapture of the church will somehow take place before the tribulation. See, e.g., George Eldon Ladd, *The Blessed Hope* (Grand Rapids: Eerdmans, 1956); Robert H. Gundry, *The Church and the Tribulation: A Biblical Examination of Posttribulationalism* (Grand Rapids: Zondervan, 1973); Richard R. Reiter et al., *The Rapture: Pre-, Mid- or Post-tribulational?* (Grand Rapids: Zondervan, 1984).

(1.7). He also speaks of the "the splendor of his coming" (2.8). Christ's *parousia* is the counterpoint to the "revealing" and the "coming" of the "lawless one" (2.6, 8-9). While this figure, the incarnation of evil, will have his own *parousia*, the Lord Jesus Christ will destroy him when he comes (2.8). The second theme related to the coming "day of the Lord" is the church's *being gathered to him* at the very time of his *parousia* (the focus of the discussion in 1 Thess. 4.13-18). The gathering of the dispersed people of God was a piece of the fundamental hope of the Jewish people that this verse, like many others, recasts in terms of the church. Due to exiles and wanderings, the people of Israel found themselves dispersed throughout the ancient world (the "diaspora").[5] The hope of the final gathering of God's people into the land of promise is described repeatedly using the same verb the author employs at this point in 2 Thessalonians (*episynagōgēs*, and also its verbal form, as in Pss. 106.47 [105.47]; 147.2 [146.2]; Isa. 52.12; Tob. 14.7; *T. Asher* 7.6-7). God will "assemble the righteous from among the nations" (*T. Naphtali* 8.3). The oppressed people of God will be gathered, and so they offer the prayer, "Gather together our scattered people, set free those who are slaves among the Gentiles, look on those who are rejected and despised" (2 Macc. 1.27). Their hope of the great gathering burned bright: "We have hope in God that he will soon have mercy on us and will gather us from everywhere under heaven into his holy place, for he has rescued us from great evils and has purified the place" (2 Macc. 2.18). This gathering is linked with the glorious revelation of God. Jesus' teaching converts this hope into the expectation that all his dispersed people will be gathered at the time of his coming (Matt. 24.31; Mark 13.27). The gathering of Christians in worship anticipates and symbolically rehearses this grand eschatological event (Heb. 10.25).[6] The apostle earnestly desires that the vital hope of the *coming of the Lord Jesus* and the gathering *to him* do not become distorted by some erroneous teaching about the "day of the Lord."

2 Paul exhorts the Thessalonians not to *become easily unsettled or alarmed by some prophecy, report or letter supposed to have come from us, saying that the day of the Lord has already come.* In some unknown way or another, the Thessalonians had received an erroneous teaching about the *day of the Lord.* This novel teaching had moved them away from what

---

5. See Schürer, *History of the Jewish People in the Age of Jesus Christ,* 2.530-31; George Foote Moore, *Judaism in the First Centuries of the Christian Era* (3 vols. in 2; Peabody, Mass.: Hendrickson, 1997), 2.366-69; *TDNT,* 2.99-101; John M. G. Barclay, *Jews in the Mediterranean Diaspora* (Edinburgh: T&T Clark, 1996); James M. Scott, ed., *Exile: Old Testament, Jewish and Christian Conceptions* (Leiden and New York: Brill, 1997).

6. Cf. also Jesus' desire to gather the inhabitants of Jerusalem to himself (Matt. 24.37; Luke 13.34).

they already knew and provoked acute confusion and strong emotional distress among the members of the Christian community. The exhortation that they *not become easily unsettled* means that they should "not be moved so quickly from their understanding." The expression does not refer to being emotionally unsettled. The verb used could mean either "be shaken" or, as here, "be made to waver" (*saleuthēnai,* which in other contexts could be used literally as well as figuratively), and appears in those contexts in ancient literature where an author wanted to talk about people who were unstable in their opinions. Philo, for example, said that the wise person or the one with understanding was firm in his opinion and would not be moved (*asauleuton*); therefore, his understanding did not waver.[7] The apostle similarly exhorts the Thessalonian believers not to be moved in their "understanding" (*noos*),[8] that is, that they should not change their opinion so quickly (*tacheōs*),[9] leaving to one side the teaching they had previously received from the apostles (vv. 5, 15). This false teaching, which they had swallowed in the short lapse of time since the exit of the Christian heralds from the city and the present, had come to replace the apostolic instruction and had also caused great emotional anguish for the Thessalonians, as the following exhortation suggests. Paul calls the church not to be *alarmed* or frightened (cf. Matt. 24.6; Mark 13.7; Luke 24.37)[10] by this theological novelty, which had brought not only doctrinal confusion but also emotional instability to the congregation.

As noted previously, the apostle did not know for certain what was the source of the false teaching, and so he called the church not to abandon what they had been taught, whatever mode the propagators had chosen to infect the church: *by some prophecy, report or letter supposed to have come from us.* The word translated in the *NIV* as *prophecy* is simply "spirit" (*pneumatos*). Both Paul and John employ the term as shorthand to speak about prophecies (cf. 1 Cor. 12.10; 1 John 4.1-3).[11] Already certain tensions existed in this congregation that centered on the use of this gift (1 Thess. 5.19-22). The apostle seems to suspect that despite the teaching he had given concerning the necessity of examining all prophetic utterances, the possibility still existed that a heresy could have escaped this net and entered the church by this means. Another possibility is that the

---

7. Philo, *Quod Omnis Probus Liber Sit* 28-29; BAGD, 740; MM, 568; LSJ, 1581; *TDNT,* 8.65-70.

8. BAGD, 544-45.

9. The term usually carries the negative sense of doing something "too soon." See Prov. 25.8; Wis. 14.28; Gal. 1.6; 1 Tim. 5.22; and BAGD, 806-7; MM, 627.

10. BAGD, 364.

11. Fee, *God's Empowering Presence,* 74; Charles H. Giblin, *The Threat to Faith* (Rome: Pontifical Biblical Institute, 1967), 148-49; Dunn, *Jesus and the Spirit,* 233-36.

error regarding the *day of the Lord* entered by some *report*. The term used is "word" *(logou)*, which in a variety of contexts can refer to a message preached, a teaching, or a discourse (2.15; Luke 4.32; 10.39; John 4.41; 17.20; Acts 2.41; 4.4; 10.44; 15.32; 20.2; and Diodorus Siculus 40.5a.1).[12] We know from other NT writings that itinerant preachers circulated among the churches and promoted heterodox teachings (2 John 7; 2 Tim. 2.17-18). The apostle recognized that someone who was not established in the apostolic teaching could have been the source of the error that so greatly troubled the Thessalonians. Alternately, Paul guessed that false teaching might have come via a letter that was written under his name: *or letter supposed to have come from us*. In order to guard against the falsification of his letters, which had been composed with the aid of an amanuensis, Paul included a final greeting as a sign of authenticity (3.17). The final words here, *supposed to have come from us*, should be read exclusively with the last word of the group, *letter*. The source of a false prophecy or preaching would have been evident, but a letter could be forged.

Some authors have questioned this analysis of the situation. The argument runs that the problem was not the entrance of a false doctrine from the outside but rather the misreading of doctrinal instruction that Paul himself had given them. Those who follow this view observe that the words *supposed to have come from us (hōs di' hēmōn)* do not refer to the mode of communication but rather to the content or authority behind the communications. Taking this line, Fee states that Paul wishes to make the point that "what they are now believing about the Day of the Lord did not come through him."[13] On the surface the expression seems somewhat awkward, at least until we recognize that this was the common way in which ancient authors spoke of writings that were composed by someone other than the person indicated.[14] Although the preposition translated *from (dia* plus the genitive) normally points to instrumentality and not origin, it can be understood as indicating the direct agency of an action (1 Pet. 2.14). Finally, the concern of the apostle at this point is not the misunderstanding of their teaching but the *means* of communication of the false teaching. Not every prophecy, sermon, or letter could be considered reliable. In fact, prophecies as well as teachings must be examined in light of the apostolic doctrine they are called to remember and adhere to (vv. 5, 15). The Thessalonians had accepted the content of the false teaching

12. BAGD, 477; MM, 379.

13. Fee, *God's Empowering Presence*, 74; Giblin, *The Threat to Faith*, 149-50; and see the summary of interpretations in Jewett, *The Thessalonian Correspondence*, 181-86.

14. *Hōs* followed by the genitive. See Diodorus Siculus 33.5.5 ("they sent a letter which purported to come from the emissaries," cited in BAGD, 898); Diogenes Laertius 10.3; cf. Rom. 9.32; 2 Cor. 10.2; 11.17; 13.7.

merely because of the means by which it came to them. We might caution modern Christians to understand that the message of every radio or television preacher, or even every person who stands behind a pulpit, needs to be examined through the lens of apostolic teaching as contained in Scripture.

The false teaching that had moved the Thessalonians away from their apostolic foundations and that caused them great anxiety was that *the day of the Lord has already come*. Because the believers had already received instruction about the *day of the Lord,* they knew something of its nature and were firm in the hope of its coming (1 Thess. 5.2, 4; 2 Thess. 1.10; 2.5, 15; and see Acts 2.20; 1 Cor. 1.8; 5.5; 2 Cor. 1.14; 2 Pet. 3.10). A certain amount of confusion about the time of this event circulated in the church, as is evidenced by the query they put to Paul that he answered in his first letter (1 Thess. 5.1-11). Despite the previous clarification, the questions continued, and the Thessalonians were open to receive a distorted teaching on this issue that stated that this day had *already come*.[15] The *NIV's* rendering of the verb (*enestēken,* perfect tense) implies that the doctrine the apostle had to face was some form of overrealized eschatology, something akin to the teaching Paul and Timothy confronted in Ephesus according to 2 Timothy 2.18 ("They say that the resurrection has already taken place, and they destroy the faith of some"). But in some contexts the verb we find here may mean that an event is impending and imminent (2 Tim. 3.1; 1 Cor. 7.26; Josephus, *Antiquitates* 4.209 [4.8.12]). Was the idea that the *day of the Lord* was to come at any moment? Oepke argues that the error was not a "spiritualization" of the idea of the *day of the Lord;* thus the present perfect carries future significance: "the day of the Lord is in process of coming."[16] This latter interpretation has the merit of explaining why the apostle did not simply present the fact that Jesus had not returned as evidence that *the day of the Lord* had not arrived. His coming was so tied with the advent of the *day of the Lord* (vv. 1-2; 1 Thess. 4.15-16; 5.1-2) that reminding them of the *absence* of Jesus means that the *day of the Lord* could not be present or have come. The following discourse on the signs before the end (vv. 3ff.) itself indicates that the concern was not about whether the day had already come but its imminence.

15. BAGD, 266. See the use of the verb in Rom. 8.38; 1 Cor. 3.22; Gal. 1.4; Heb. 9.9; Josephus, *Antiquitates* 12.175 (12.4.4).

16. *TDNT,* 2.544; BDF, §323.3; Ernst von Dobschütz, *Die Thessalonicher-Brief* (Göttingen: Vandenhoeck & Ruprecht, 1974), 267-68; and Bruce, *1 and 2 Thessalonians,* 165, present this option. Cf. the use of the perfect in Acts 22.10; 2 Tim. 4.6; John 17.22; Jas. 5.2-3. Porter, *Verbal Aspect in the Greek of the New Testament,* 265-67, explores the present and future use of the perfect tense in the Greek of the era.

The burning question of this church concerned the timing of the *day of the Lord* (1 Thess. 5.1-11), and the false teaching responded to that issue, despite the fact that the church had received instruction on that matter (teaching that they may have deemed unsatisfactory). The implications of the error were evident. The new doctrine provoked insecurity regarding their part in the coming glory (vv. 13-17), just as the death of beloved members of the church provoked grave concerns (1 Thess. 4.13-18). Once more the apostle reminds the church that they will not be excluded on that day because they have been chosen by God himself (v. 13).

3 With deep concern over the error about the day of the Lord that had entered the church through some unknown source, Paul presents his correction with the exhortation, *Don't let anyone deceive you in any way.* Whatever the means of communication (v. 2b), they should not be duped by the error. The call not to be deceived was a relatively common exhortation in ancient literature. The warning could be against the teachings of false prophets (Josephus, *Antiquitates* 10.111 [10.7.3]) or against certain erroneous opinions of philosophers (Epictetus 2.20.7). "Self-deception" also appears as a concern (Lucian, *De Mercede Conductis* 5).[17] In the case of the Thessalonians, the error had come through some supposedly "reliable" source, and the church had been taken in by the error. In order to rescue them from this false teaching and its consequences, the apostles make an appeal to hold on to what the church had already been taught (vv. 5, 15).

Certain events were going to precede the day of the Lord, and the apostle puts forward the fact that these had not occurred as evidence that they were not on the very verge of its advent. He explains: *for that day will not come until the rebellion occurs and the man of lawlessness is revealed, the man doomed to destruction.* The first part of the verse is elliptical in the Greek text (an anacoluthon); for that reason the translators have included here ideas taken from the previous verse that, though not expressed, are implicit. The *NIV* adds *that day will not come* (cf. v. 2b). Giblin, on the other hand, argues that what is implied should be supplied from the following verses and not the previous context. He would understand the implied idea as something like, "the judgment of God will not have been executed against the power of deception, removing them once and for all" *until* etc. The other suggestion he makes to supply the missing apodosis is, "The Lord will not have come in judgment to end definitively the deception that is the work of Satan" *until* etc.[18] But despite the rather de-

---

17. Note how the verb is used in Rom. 7.11; 16.18; 2 Cor. 11.3; 1 Tim. 2.14; Josephus, *Antiquitates* 13.89 (13.4.3); Epictetus 2.22.15; and see BAGD, 273.

18. Giblin, *The Threat to Faith*, 122-39.

tailed nature of Giblin's argument, the more natural and simple way to understand the anacoluthon is with reference to information the readers already knew and not to thoughts that are yet to be introduced. The matter at hand was the time of the "day of the Lord" (v. 2). In order that their understanding might not be distorted, we must assume that the author would have allowed the omission only if the sense was immediately accessible from the preceding context.

Paul is keen to emphasize the order of future events throughout this section (vv. 3, 6-8). At the head they declare that "first" (*prōton*, rendered loosely in the *NIV* as *until*);[19] that is, before the day of the Lord, two events will occur: *the rebellion occurs and the man of lawlessness is revealed.* In ancient writings a *rebellion (apostasia)* could be understood as being against any kind of established authority, be it political (1 Esdr. 2.21; Josephus, *Vita* 43 [10]) or religious and against God (Josh. 22.22; 2 Chr. 29.19; 33.19; 1 Macc. 2.15).[20] In the NT it frequently appears with this second sense of "apostasy" (Acts 21.21; 1 Tim. 4.1; cf. the verbal form in Heb. 3.12), and this is the most likely thought here. In the present verse, as in 1 Timothy 4.1, Paul explains that some form of "rebellion" is a sign of the last times. Similarly, part of the Jewish eschatological expectation was that before the end there would be apostasy against God (*1 Enoch* 93.9; 90.26; *4 Ezra* 5.1-13; *2 Bar.* 41.3; 42.4),[21] a perspective that appears again in the teaching of Jesus (Matt. 24.11-13). It is unlikely that the apostle has in mind the rebellion of the Jewish people against the gospel (cf. 1 Thess. 2.14-16) since the term itself implies that a person was once a participant in something and then separated or apostatized. Both Jesus and Paul indicate that Christians could anticipate deserters from the faith before the end (Matt. 24.11-24; 1 Tim. 4.1). We should recognize that in the face of the great persecution the church endured in the first century and the temptations their former life presented, not a few people abandoned the faith, and their apostasy became a paradigm for what was expected in the last times (see 1 Thess. 3.5 and commentary). The hope of the apostle is that the church in Thessalonica would in no way participate in the apostasy (vv. 13-15).

The other event that will occur before the day of the Lord is that *the man of lawlessness is revealed, the man doomed for destruction.* The verb *is re-*

---

19. "First" may be understood with both the *rebellion* and *the man of lawlessness is revealed,* as in the *NIV,* or it may refer exclusively to the *rebellion.* But the absence of some statement about the revelation of the *man of lawlessness* being the second event (such as "then") argues in favor of the present reading. These are the events that must first take place.

20. *TDNT,* 1.512-14; *NIDNTT,* 1.606-8.

21. SB, 3.637.

vealed is the verbal form of the noun "revelation" in 1.7; it appears not only here but also in vv. 6 and 8 in reference to the revelation of this evil figure. Using a variation of a name that comes from the OT (see Ps. 89.22 [88.23] — "son of lawlessness"; Isa. 57.3-4 — "lawless sons," in combination with "children of destruction"), Paul characterizes this person as someone who is without law and whose character is therefore the personification of sin. In fact, in v. 8 the person is simply called "the lawless one." This ascription *(anomias)* could mean "without [the] law" or "against [the] law," but it came to be a synonym for "sin" or "iniquity" (see Rom. 4.7; 2 Cor. 6.14; Titus 2.14; Heb. 1.9; 10.17).[22] Among the Jewish people, the "lawless ones" is a title ascribed to the Gentiles (Wis. 17.2; 1 Macc. 2.44), but though the figure here described by the apostle is most likely a Gentile, the name brings into view something more than his ethnic origin. Wanamaker observes that "the lawless one" is a title that was given to the Roman general Pompey in the *Psalms of Solomon* 17.11, who led the Roman troops to subjugate Palestine in 63 BC, an event that led to Jewish apostasy. He argues that the "lawless one" to whom Paul refers recalls this person.[23] As will be seen presently, the imperial power of Rome as embodied in the emperor who received divine accolades is the prototype of the figure here described as *the man of lawlessness.* The identification of Pompey as the figure who anticipates this *man of lawlessness* is questionable since the name was used more generally and the text in *Psalms of Solomon* 17.11 is in no way secure (the manuscripts read "the wind" [*anemos*] instead of "the lawless one" [*anomos*]).[24] The most we can say at this point is that the figure described here embodies all that the Lord opposes and, as will be seen, will attempt to usurp the place of God himself (v. 4).

This figure is also described as *the man doomed for destruction,* or, more literally, "the son of destruction" *(huios tēs apōleias).* This is the very title that Judas received in John 17.12. The expression "son of" was a common Semitism that indicated that which was characteristic of a person (see 1 Thess. 5.5 and commentary). The term *destruction (apōleias)* may carry either a transitive sense ("the one who causes destruction" — Matt. 26.8; Mark 14.4) or an intransitive one ("destruction that one experiences" or "annihilation" — 1 Tim. 6.9; 2 Pet. 3.16).[25] In the NT the term commonly has to do with the destruction of those who oppose God and

22. *TDNT*, 4.1085-87; *NIDNTT*, 2.440, 447; BAGD, 71-72.

23. Wanamaker, *Commentary on 1 and 2 Thessalonians*, 245.

24. See Herbert Edward Ryle and Montague Rhodes James, *Psalms of the Pharisees, Commonly Called The Psalms of Solomon* (Cambridge: Cambridge University Press, 1891), 132-33.

25. BAGD, 103; *TDNT*, 1.396-97; *NIDNTT*, 1.462-66.

his purposes (Matt. 7.13; Rom. 9.22; Phil. 1.28; 3.19; Heb. 10.39; 2 Pet. 3.7; Rev. 17.8, 11). This passage in 2 Thessalonians emphasizes the destruction of this *man of lawlessness* (v. 8) and not the destruction that he causes. The Thessalonians would have derived great comfort from the beginning, knowing that the very one who exalted himself in his opposition to God, as powerful as he might be (v. 9), was destined for destruction. This powerful one who incarnates sin will meet his end on the day of the Lord.

4 The apostle continues the discourse concerning the signs before the day of the Lord by giving a fuller exposition of the character of the "man of lawlessness": *He will oppose and will exalt himself over everything that is called God or is worshiped, so that he sets himself up in God's temple, proclaiming himself to be God.* Paul fixes his attention on the unbridled pride of this figure. *He will oppose* any and every other deity, whether the God of the Christians or any other object of adoration in the ancient cities. The term implies that he will set himself up in the position of an adversary (Exod. 23.22; Esth. 9.2; 8.11; Isa. 41.11; 45.16; 66.6;[26] 2 Macc. 10.26; Luke 13.17; 21.15; 1 Cor. 16.9; Phil. 1.28) against anyone or anything that would claim people's religious devotion. The description of the "man of lawlessness" as an adversary should also be understood in the light of the social reality of the church. They suffered greatly at the hands of their adversaries. The title likewise serves as a prelude to the following explanation that the power behind this figure is Satan himself (v. 9; cf. 1 Thess. 2.18; 3.5), who himself is called "the adversary" (1 Tim. 5.14; 1 Pet. 5.8).[27]

The "man of lawlessness" will *exalt himself over* every object of worship. This figure is not only adversarial but also raises himself up in self-exaltation over God and all the gods (2 Macc. 5.23; 2 Cor. 12.7; and cf. the idea in Dan. 11.36-37).[28] This is more than pride and hubris. This figure places himself in a position above all others as he presses his claim to be the legitimate and proper object of worship. Milligan demonstrates that this verb *(hyperairomenos)* appears in legal contexts where the plaintiff raises up his claim against another.[29] The implication may be that this one resorts to legal means to assert his position.

The opposition that the man of lawlessness raises is against *everything that is called God or is worshiped.* This figure does not simply exalt himself over the God of the Christians. The expression *everything that is called God (panta legomenon theon)* is echoed in Paul's first letter to the Corinthians, where he speaks of the "so-called gods" *(legomenois theoi* in 8.5).

---

26. The apostles allude to Isa. 66 in 1.8-9, 12, and so it is possible that the Isa. 66.6 influences their thought at this point.

27. BAGD, 74; *TLNT*, 1.128-30.

28. BAGD, 839; MM, 652; LSJ, 1858; and see SIG^3, 747.20, 21, 25, 33, 35, 66.

29. MM, 652.

The man of lawlessness will oppose every object that is called divine, even though they are really false deities and not the true God.[30] Daniel 11.36-37 is in the back of the author's mind. The prophet denounces a figure whom a number of commentators have identified as Antiochus Epiphanes, who profaned the temple in Jerusalem during the time of the Maccabees:[31] "He will exalt and magnify himself above every god and will say unheard-of things against the God of gods. He will be successful until the time of wrath is completed, for what has been determined will take place." The pride of this figure leads him to take a place above the gods, even the God of Israel.

His exaltation also extends over *everything . . . that is worshiped (sebasma)*, which designates any sanctuary, idol, or person that receives adoration (Acts 17.23; Wis. 14.20; 15.17).[32] In the year 27 BC, the ruler of the Roman Empire, Octavian, received the name "Augustus" in Latin and its Greek equivalent *Sebastos*, a word that shares the same root as *worshiped* and so was replete with religious and divine associations. The divinization of Augustus was celebrated throughout the empire, while even in Thessalonica a temple was erected to honor him and his father, the divine Julius Caesar. This was the hub of the imperial cult in the city during the first century, although the primary responsibility for maintaining the emperor cult in Macedonia was in the hands of Berea, the seat of the Macedonian *koinon*.[33] The divine claim of the emperor celebrated in the imperial cult was thus the prototype of the "man of lawlessness," and the Thessalonian believers would have understood this allusion well.

The audacity of the "man of lawlessness" is demonstrated in the establishment of the cult to himself: *so that he sets himself up in God's temple.* The text indicates that he "sits" in the *temple*, as on a throne, to symbolize his authority.[34] This is not a position that anyone appoints him to but one that he takes for himself. The thought may be that this "man of lawlessness" either will take his place in the temple or will put his own image there to be worshiped (as through the practice described in Wis. 14.17-

---

30. See Epictetus 4.1.5; Dio Chrysostom 13.11; 77/78.34; Josephus, *Antiquitates* 12.125 [12.3.2]; *Corpus Hermeticum* 2.14; and BAGD, 470; Bruce W. Winter, "In Public and in Private: Early Christians and Religious Pluralism," in *One God, One Lord* (ed. Andrew D. Clark and Bruce W. Winter; Grand Rapids: Baker Book House, 1991), 144, n. 58.

31. 1 Macc. 1.10-28; 2 Macc. 4.7-17; 5.11–6.17. On the date of Daniel and whether this is a prophecy (as the present author believes) or history in the guise of prophecy, see the commentaries.

32. BAGD, 745.

33. See the Introduction, p. 24; and *IT*, nn. 31, 133.

34. See the uses in MM, 312-13; BAGD, 390.

21).[35] He establishes his own cult and expects that others will ascribe divine honors to him, and exclusively to him.[36] The "man of lawlessness" establishes himself in the *temple* because he is *proclaiming himself to be God.* He exhibits himself[37] to be *God,* or "a god," or "divine." In Ezekiel 28.2-10 the prophet announces an oracle against one who has exalted himself in precisely the same way, "In the pride of your heart you say, 'I am a god; I sit on the throne of a god; I sit on the throne of a god in the heart of the seas.' But you are a man and not a god, though you think you are as wise as a god. . . . Will you then say, 'I am a god,' in the presence of those who kill you?" The "man of lawlessness" who exalts himself as a god will likewise meet his doom at the hands of the Lord Jesus (v. 8).

The identification of the *temple* where the "man of lawlessness" sits has been the theme of no little discussion. The most common interpretation, which is followed by the *NIV,* is that the reference to the *temple of God* is to the temple in Jerusalem. As noted above, Antiochus Epiphanes profaned that temple (169 BC) in an event that Daniel described as the "abomination which causes desolation" (Dan. 9.27; 11.31; 12.11; 1 Macc. 1.54). This event prefigured the profanation of the temple that Jesus anticipated before his coming (Matt. 24.15; Mark 13.14). Antiochus had taken to himself divine honors that have been preserved for us in a tetradrachm that has his image and the ascription, "Of King Antiochus, god made manifest and victorious."[38] This one may have served as the prototype for the figure Paul describes as the "man of lawlessness." However, the identification cannot be pressed since Antiochus IV did not establish himself or his image in the Jewish temple. His profanation of the temple consisted of sacrificing swine on the altar and identifying the God of Israel with Dionysus. A closer parallel arose during the period of Roman occupation when the emperor Caligula (Gaius) tried to have his own image placed in the temple in Jerusalem during AD 40 (Josephus, *Antiquitates* 18.261-309 [18.8.2–18.8.9]; Philo, *De Legatione ad Gaium* 203-346). His design was to turn the Jerusalem temple into a sanctuary for his own cult as one who designated himself "the new god manifest" (*theos epipanous neou;* cf. 2 Thess. 2.8). Fortunately, the Syrian legate stalled

---

35. "When people could not honor monarchs in their presence, since they lived at a distance, they imagined their appearance far away, and made a visible image of the king whom they honored, so that by their zeal they might flatter the absent one as though present. . . . The multitude . . . now regarded as an object of worship (*sebasma*) the one whom shortly before they had honored as a human being."

36. On the introduction of new cults, see Bruce W. Winter, "On Introducing Gods to Athens: An Alternative Reading of Acts 17.18-20," *TynBul* 47 (1996) 71-90.

37. 1 Cor. 4.9; *T. Jos.* 2.7; and BAGD, 89.

38. See Ferguson, *Backgrounds of Early Christianity,* 382.

when given the order to set up the image there, and the whole event never came to pass due to the rather timely death of the emperor by assassination in AD 41. These events, which Paul would have known well, may have served as the prototype for the way the "man of lawlessness" will seek divine accolades.

As attractive as the identification of the *temple* in 2 Thessalonians 2.4 with the temple in Jerusalem may be, we should ask whether the Thessalonians themselves would have understood the allusion in this way. The events in Jerusalem previously described occurred far from Thessalonica and would have been of little interest to the Macedonians and Romans in that city, even those who had become Christians (the vast majority of the members of this church were Gentiles — 1 Thess. 1.9). It may be that the *temple* here referred to is the heavenly sanctuary, which is mentioned a number of times, especially in apocalyptic literature (Ps. 11.4 [10.4]; *1 Enoch* 14.8-25; *2 Bar.* 4.3-6; *T. Levi* 5.1-2). But once more the question arises as to whether the Christians in Thessalonica would have understood this rather opaque reference. Moreover, that sanctuary is the domain of the God of Israel, and we have no explanation concerning how the "man of lawlessness" could establish his cult in relationship to that realm.

Another alternative reading is to understand the *temple* as a reference to the church where the "man of lawlessness" enthrones himself (1 Cor. 3.16; 2 Cor. 6.16; Eph. 2.21).[39] This identification is unlikely since the apostle describes a cult center where people go to offer worship and where this figure proclaims himself to be a god against every other deity. Moreover, the orientation of the divine claims of the "man of lawlessness" is toward the world at large and not the church. A much more fruitful line of interpretation is to understand the present description against the backdrop of the imperial cult in the city of Thessalonica and other cities of the empire.[40] Archaeologists have discovered an inscription that names the person responsible for the construction of the Thessalonian temple dedicated to the divine Julius and Augustus. This temple was fully functioning during the first century, complete with the priesthood. Understood in light of this and similar institutions, the reference to *God's temple* could be to "the temple of [the] god," that is, the structure dedicated to the one who asserted himself as a god (v. 4b). The Thessalonians would have readily understood the allusion in light of the presence of the

---

39. Giblin, *The Threat to Faith*, 76-80, takes this position.

40. See the Introduction, pp. 38-43; and Duncan Fishwick, *The Imperial Cult in the Latin West* (Leiden: Brill, 1987); Dominique Cuss, *The Imperial Cult and Honorary Terms in the New Testament* (Fribourg: The University Press, 1974); Horsley, *Paul and Empire*, 140-223.

imperial cult in the city. The superb relationships the city had with Rome led the Romans to shower Thessalonica with many benefits. Part of the city's gratitude and response to Rome's benefaction was the establishment of the imperial cult.[41] In such an environment, the Christians who would take no part in this cult would undoubtedly have suffered for their lack of loyalty and civic commitment. We should be cautious, however, about fully identifying the "man of lawlessness" with the proceedings of the imperial cult since the apostle asserts that this figure had not yet been revealed(vv. 3, 6-8). The reference is to events in the present: "the secret power of lawlessness is already at work" (v. 7). This is what the Thessalonians could witness daily in the imperial cult, a civic institution that anticipated the final revelation of the "man of lawlessness" (see the comments on v. 7).

5   The explanation of the events that will precede the day of the Lord was not new information for the first readers of this letter. During his stay in the city Paul had given them specific instruction about these matters. So in the midst of the response concerning the false teaching about the day of the Lord (v. 2), he reminds them of the things they had learned by asking, *Don't you remember that when I was with you I used to tell you these things?* The question implies that the church already had sufficient instruction to evaluate and reject the teaching that had so moved them and put them in turmoil. What they needed to do was simply to remember and apply the apostolic instruction, as is frequently the case in the battle against error (Jude 3). Over and again in these letters, the Thessalonians are called to remember what they already know (1 Thess. 2.9; 3.4; 4.1; 5.1-2; 2 Thess. 3.10). The author repeatedly reaffirmed the truths they had received (1 Thess. 1.5; 2.1-2, 5, 11; 3.3-4; 4.2; 5.2; 2 Thess. 3.7).[42] The form of this call to remember is most similar to 1 Thessalonians 3.4 and 2 Thessalonians 3.10, which specifically mention the apostolic visit, but with one significant difference. Instead of using the first person plural, in the present verse Paul comes forward from the group and puts his own question to them using the first person singular *I* (cf. 3.17; 1 Thess. 2.18; 3.5; 5.27 and commentaries).[43] The change in person serves

41. See Hendrix, *Thessalonicans Honor Romans.*

42. As Marshall, *1 and 2 Thessalonians,* 192-93, observes, the fact that in 2.5 Paul does not appeal to the teaching of the previous letter is not a significant factor in the discussion of authorship. The themes discussed in this chapter are not those that were elaborated in the previous letter but rather those gave Paul when he was first in the city and when he instructed the new believers. Similarly, the appeal to previous teaching in 2.5 says nothing about the order of the letters (contra Wanamaker, *Commentary on 1 and 2 Thessalonians,* 249).

43. On the authorship of these epistles, see pp. 56-59.

to remind us that of all the members of the apostolic team, Paul was the principal teacher. The change to the first person singular, apart from its appearance in the closing greetings of these letters, also occurs at those places where Paul touches on the activity of Satan, whether against his own ministry (1 Thess. 2.18), against the church (1 Thess. 3.5), or in the world at large through the "man of lawlessness" (2 Thess. 2.3, 8-9). Likely Paul was acutely conscious of the battle against Satan in his ministry and expresses and inserts his strongest sentiments precisely at those points in these writings that discuss themes touching on the core of the battle.

6 The Thessalonians had already received instruction about the apostasy and the coming of the "man of lawlessness" (v. 5). They are now reminded of another aspect of the initial apostolic teaching: *And now you know what is holding him back, so that he may be revealed at the proper time.* The practice of reminding a pupil of what was already known was common among ancient moralists (see the comments on 1 Thess. 2.1). Unfortunately for us, the author does not explain many aspects of the knowledge he shared with the Thessalonians. For that reason v. 6 remains quite opaque to us as observers of their conversation. To what is Paul referring to when he speaks of that which is *holding him back* and *the one who now holds it back* (v. 7)? This Gordian knot has been nearly impossible to cut!

The first thing the apostle wants to underline is the contrast between present and future realities. *Now* they *know what is holding him back* (v. 6); "the secret power of lawlessness is *already* at work" and "will continue to do so *till* he is taken out of the way" (v. 7); "*And then* the lawless one will be revealed" (v. 8a). In light of the problem concerning the time of the coming "day of the Lord" (v. 2 and comments), Paul clarifies which elements are present and which are future in their discussion on the timing of the day of the Lord. Yes, there are aspects of the end that are already at work, but, no, the final consummation is still a future event.

Second, the Thessalonian brothers and sisters understood that there was something *holding back* this "man of lawlessness." The author first identifies this agent as a force (v. 6 — *to katechon*, neuter participle) and then as a personal figure (v. 7 — *ho katechōn*, masculine participle). We do not know with any certainty what power or person Paul had in mind. The suggestions, however, are legion, including God himself (possibly in the person of the Holy Spirit),[44] the Roman Empire and the emperor,[45] the

44. Charles Caldwell Ryrie, *First and Second Thessalonians* (Chicago: Moody Press, 1959), 111. "Most premillennialists further identify the restrainer as the third person of the Godhead, the Holy Spirit."

45. This interpretation was followed in the third century by such authors as Tertullian and Hippolytus, but has found little acceptance among modern commentators.

rule of law and government in general,[46] or the preaching of the gospel and the apostle Paul himself (note that in Mark 13.10 Jesus stated that the end would come only after the gospel was preached to the nations).[47] Every one of these interpretations understands *to katechon/ho katechōn* as a power that opposes the "man of lawlessness." The proposal that suggests that this refers to God the Father or the Holy Spirit fails to explain why the author would make such an opaque reference to God. As the verse is commonly understood, it would also not explain in what way and by whom he would be "taken out of the way" (v. 7, although see the comments on that verse). The interpretation that points to the restraining power as the empire or the emperor is unlikely as well since this very imperial power prefigures the "man of lawlessness" in the imperial cult. We may also properly ask how the power of Rome could be "taken out of the way," unless the reference is to the final fall of the empire. The interpretation that points to the rule of law or government in general is also unlikely since it does not take into account the change from the neutral to the masculine participle (vv. 6, 7) and does not explain how the law or government at that time could restrain "the man of lawlessness." If we understand this figure as someone prefigured by the emperor and the cult practiced in his honor, it would be difficult to see how Roman law could be understood as a force somehow contrary to his power. The shocking reality was that the mechanisms of the state supported this rule, including the imperial cult.[48] The other interpretation, which argues that the preaching of the gospel, especially by Paul, is the power that restrains the revelation of the "man of lawlessness," does not take into account the social reality of the church in the first century. In that era the gospel was not a strong social force, whatever it was to become in later centuries. Paul never styles himself as one whose preaching is holding the fort against the breakout of the personification of evil. His letters do not betray that he understood his ministry in this manner. Moreover, we would

---

46. As in Morris, *First and Second Epistles to the Thessalonians*, 227.

47. Marshall, *1 and 2 Thessalonians*, 199-200, suggests a variation of this interpretation that states that the reference is to the preaching of the gospel and an angel of God, not Paul.

48. Cohesion within the empire was based largely on the system of patronage. Only through the almost interminable nexus of patron/client relationships was Rome able to maintain control of the empire. Those in the provinces, for example, gained access to the senate and the emperor through patrons, and those who had central power made their presence felt in the provinces through those who served as their clients. In other words, the exercise of power and control was not due simply to military presence. The imperial cult was another part of the system of *clientela*. In such a context, it is hard to imagine how state power could be generated against one such as the "man of lawlessness," whose model emerges out of this context.

have to ask why Paul would refer to himself in such a veiled way as "the one who restrains" and who then will be "taken out of the way."

The problem all of these interpretations have in common is that they all understand *to katechon/ho katechōn* as a power contrary to "the man of lawlessness." However, v. 7 explains something about the nature of this power: *For the secret power of lawlessness is already at work.*[49] This context appears to indicate that *to katechon* is a power that is in some way or another aligned with "the man of lawlessness." Some commentators adopt this line of interpretation. Frame, for example, identifies that which "is holding him back" (v. 6) with Satan and interprets the words *to katechon* as that which "is holding sway" or rules over the forces of evil.[50] Running along a similar line, Giblin argues that *to katechon* is not a power that restrains the "man of lawlessness" but rather one that exercises his power on behalf of Satan.[51] This is a power that "seizes" or "possesses" and may imply some form of demonic possession such as that which was found in the cults of Dionysus and Serapis (both of which were quite popular within the city of Thessalonica). The use of the term to describe demon possession, along with its frenetic activity, was quite common and can be found both in the active voice ("the one who seizes") and the passive ("the one who is possessed").[52] On this reading, *to katechon* would be a power aligned with "the man of lawlessness" and who is identified with the "secret power of lawlessness" in the following verse. This power that "seizes" or possesses is manifested particularly in the one so possessed (v. 7). Giblin suggests that this false inspiration that prefigures the revelation of "the man of lawlessness" is the same one that is responsible for the doctrinal confusion of the Thessalonians (v. 2). Understood in this way, the role of the "one who possesses" would be similar to that of the false prophet in Revelation 13.

The purpose[53] of this power that "seizes" is *so that he* ("the man of

---

49. Verse 7 begins with *gar*, which, in this case, introduces an explanation concerning what was stated previously.

50. Frame, *Epistles of St. Paul to the Thessalonians*, 258-63.

51. Giblin, *The Threat to Faith*, 167-242; Charles H. Giblin, "2 Thessalonians 2 Reread as Pseudepigraphal: A Revised Reaffirmation of *The Threat to Faith*," in *The Thessalonian Correspondence* (ed. R. F. Collins; Leuven: Leuven University Press, 1990), 459-69; and MM, 336, who note the way the word is used to describe possession by a god.

52. MM, 336; *TLNT*, 2.290; *TDNT*, 2.829; and see *New Docs*, 3.27-28. Also Xenophon, *Symposium* 1.10; Philo, *Quis Rerum Divinarum Heres* 69; *De Somniis* 1.254. Both Best (*The First and Second Epistles to the Thessalonians*, 299) and Wanamaker (*Commentary on 1 and 2 Thessalonians*, 252) object by saying that the term was never understood this way when found in the active voice, but they fail to take into account *PLit. Lond.* 52.12, which speaks of "the god which seizes" (LSJ, 926) and Justin, *2 Apologia* 6.6.

53. *Eis to* plus the infinitive. See BAGD, 229.

lawlessness") *may be revealed at the proper time.* The presence of this power in the city that anticipates the revelation of that one is described again in the following verse. The apostle depicts the coming of "the man of lawlessness" as his "revelation" both here and in vv. 3 and 8. Although the Thessalonian believers could already witness the presence of this demonic force that anticipated "the man of lawlessness," his revelation would be detained until *the proper time* or "his own *(heautou)* time." The NT understands many events to occur at a divinely appointed time (1 Tim. 2.6; 6.15; Titus 1.3). God is the one who brings them about when he wills (Mark 1.15; Acts 17.26). This verse presents a striking contrast with that order. This "man of lawlessness" is *revealed* in his "own" time. Though a strong note of self-determination on the part of this figure is sounded here, the Thessalonians are assured that this time has not yet come.

7   Paul now explains[54] how this power that "seizes" operates: *For the secret power of lawlessness is already at work.* Previously the author noted that the Thessalonians knew of the existence of a power that was "seized" or "possessed" (v. 6). Now he moves on to observe that this power, here described as the *secret power of lawlessness,* is not simply a future threat but a present reality. The verb *at work (energeitai)* is the same one that is found in 1 Thessalonians 2.13 and implies some kind of supernatural activity, whether it be divine (Matt. 14.2; Mark 6.14; 1 Cor. 12.6, 11; Gal. 2.8; 3.5; Eph. 1.11, 20; 3.20; Phil. 2.13; Col. 1.29) or evil (Eph. 2.2; 2 Thess. 2.9). Paul does not suggest that this *secret power* is divine but only that it is supernatural, and, according to the context, malignant and satanic (v. 9). For this reason, the apostle calls this power *the secret power of lawlessness.* This *secret power* aligns itself with "the man of lawlessness" (v. 3) and represents his power in the world before the time of his revelation (cf. 1 John 2.18, which speaks of the antichrists who prefigure the antichrist). Paul normally uses the term translated *secret power* (or "mystery," *mystērion*) to refer to the "mystery of God" that is now revealed in the gospel (1 Cor. 2.1; 4.1; Eph. 1.9; 3.3, 4, 9; 6.19; Col. 1.26, 27; 2.2; 4.3), but in the present verse the "mystery" refers to an evil and satanic power (cf. Rev. 17.5, 7). Jewish literature occasionally uses similar terminology to describe the mysterious machinations of Satan or of some person (e.g., 1QM 14.9, "In all the mysteries of his [Belial's] enmity"; Josephus, *Bellum Judaicum* 1.470 [1.24.1], "so that Antipater's life might have been not incorrectly described as a mystery of iniquity [*kakias mystērion*]").

However, the term "mystery" was also commonly employed to speak of the secret and sacred rites of various religions of that era, and it is likely that Paul has some such cult in mind. Such religions were quite common

---

54. *Gar* is a conjunction that in this case explains the preceding. See BAGD, 344.

and attracted many devotees, who were made to pass through initiation rites under the promise of receiving salvation, especially from the enslaving power of fate or destiny.[55] These "mysteries" formed part of the religious environment of Thessalonica, as numerous inscriptions from the city bear witness, referring to such local cults as those of Osiris, Isis, and Dionysus.[56] During that period, mysteries were celebrated in relation to the imperial cult,[57] although we have no archaeological or textual evidence that would confirm the presence of such a practice in Thessalonica. The fact that "the man of lawlessness" presents himself as a religious figure who demands worship (vv. 3-4) implies that the "mystery *of lawlessness*" has to do with the cult that anticipated his revealing. The "one who seizes" would most likely participate in this cult as the one who is demonically possessed and who, most likely, has prophetic powers as a result (vv. 6, 7b).

Before the revelation of "the lawless one" (v. 8) one more event must take place: *but the one who now holds it back will continue to do so till he is taken out of the way.* Here the power that "seizes" (*to katechon* of v. 6) is presented as a person, "the one who seizes" or "the one who is possessed" (*ho katechōn* — masculine), the *reference* being to the one demonically possessed or the one who possesses, that being Satan himself (v. 9).[58] This figure does not "hold *it back*" but rather prefigures and anticipates the revelation of "the lawless one." The apostle underlines the limited nature of the work of the "one who seizes" by stating that he will be *taken out of the way.* The *NIV* implies that some other power will take him *out of the way* (passive voice). There is no indication within the immediate context that tells them or us the identity of the agent that undertakes his removal. What person or power are the apostles talking about? Since no agent is indicated, it may be just as possible that we should understand the expression as active and not passive. The same expression is found in Plutarch in his life of Timoleon (5.4), who "made up his mind to live by himself, apart from the world *(ek mesou genomenos).*"[59] If the sense in the present verse is active, "the one who seizes" retires from the scene of his

<hr>

55. See Marvin W. Meyer, ed., *The Ancient Mysteries: A Sourcebook* (New York: HarperCollins, 1987; Helmut Koester, *Introduction to the New Testament, 1: History, Culture, and Religion of the Hellenistic Age* (2 vols.; Berlin and New York: Walter de Gruyter, 1982), 1.196-203.

56. See *IT,* nn. 107, 259, 260, and 254. From earlier times the mysteries of the Cabiri from Samothrace were known in the city, a cult mentioned in Herodotus 2.51. Giblin, *The Threat to Faith,* 193-97, refers to the mysteries of the cult of Serapis but does not recognize how popular this cult was in the city. See the Introduction, pp. 43-46.

57. H. W. Pleket, "An Aspect of the Emperor Cult: Imperial Mysteries," *HTR* 58 (1965) 331-47.

58. So *Plit. Lond.* 52.12, *ho theos estin ho sas katechōn phrenas.* See LSJ, 926.

59. H. W. Fulford, "*Heōs ek mesou genētai,* 2 Thes. 2:7," *ExpTim* 23 (1911-12) 40-41.

318

own will in order to permit the revelation of the more terrifying figure of "the lawless one."[60] The text in no way indicates where "the one who seizes" retires but only emphasizes that he will give way to "the lawless one." Whatever the sense, this observation would signal to the Thessalonians that the end was not immediately on them (v. 2) because "the one who seizes" was still active, as they themselves could witness. That which prefigured the coming of "the lawless one" was still present. Whether we understand the final clause of v. 7 as active or passive, the verse in no way indicates that the Holy Spirit or the church will in some way be taken out of the world. This is hardly an adequate foundation for the commonly held teaching that the rapture of the church will happen sometime before the antichrist is revealed!

8 After the "one who seizes" retires from the scene, *the lawless one will take center stage: And then the lawless one will be revealed* (cf. vv. 3, 6), the same figure who is called "the man of lawlessness" in v. 3. The verb that describes his coming denotes that the veil will be taken off so that he will be revealed to everyone. Normally Paul uses this verb in his discussions about the revelation of God (see 1.7 and comments); the term was used generally during that time to speak of the revelation of a deity.[61] This verse and vv. 3 and 6 are the only places in Pauline literature where the verb is applied to some figure who is not God.

But as soon as the apostle declares that *the lawless one will be revealed*, he informs the Thessalonians of this figure's final destruction: *whom the Lord Jesus will overthrow with the breath of his mouth and destroy by the splendor of his coming.* In spite of the divine pretensions of *the lawless one* (v. 4) and his supernatural power that supposedly accredits him (v. 9), the *Lord Jesus* will triumph over him and will strip him of all power. The first part of the description of this judgment is an allusion to Isaiah 11.4 (LXX) that proclaims the final judgment of God on the earth. This judgment is attributed to *the Lord Jesus:*[62] "he shall judge the cause of the lowly, and shall reprove the lowly of the earth: and he shall smite the earth with the word of his mouth, and with the breath of his lips shall he destroy the ungodly one." In the allusion to this oracle, the apostle uses the word *breath*[63] and

---

60. This interpretation allows us to understand *ho katechōn* as the subject of *genētai* instead of interpreting the sentence as elliptical and forcing readers to supply the verb from the context. For a discussion of the grammatical possibilities, see Wanamaker, *Commentary on 1 and 2 Thessalonians*, 255-56.

61. See *NIDNTT,* 3.310.

62. Some manuscripts read simply "the Lord" (B, D², K, Textus Receptus), but the evidence slightly favors the inclusion of "Jesus" (ℵ, A, D, G, P, Ψ).

63. Cf. Ps. 32.6 (LXX), which speaks of creation "by the Spirit (breath) of his mouth."

the verb *destroy* from the second clause in Isaiah 11.4, and he also changes the object of the judgment from "the ungodly one" to *the lawless one*. Paul highlights the utter power and effectiveness of this judgment. At that time the *Lord Jesus will overthrow* the *lawless one*, an expression that indicates that he will kill him violently[64] and so break his power. The point is not merely that he will be overthrown from his position, as the *NIV* may imply. Moreover, the author adds that the Lord will *destroy* this *lawless one*. Paul uses this verb again and again when describing the final judgment (1 Cor. 2.6; 6.13; 15.24, 26; 2 Tim. 1.10; and see Heb. 2.14); it signifies that the power of the one who is judged will be annulled and destroyed.[65] The *Lord Jesus* will effect this judgment *by the splendor of his coming*, an event that is mentioned repeatedly in these letters (1 Thess. 2.19; 3.13; 4.15; 5.23; 2 Thess. 2.1).

At times the *coming* of Jesus is described as his "epiphany" *(epiphaneia)*, as in the present verse (1 Tim. 6.14; 2 Tim. 1.10; 4.1, 8; Titus 2.13). In the ancient world, a god's epiphany was the manifestation of the deity by revealing himself or by some demonstration of his power. This event would be particularly associated with the *coming (parousia)* of the deity.[66] The ancients could even speak of the epiphany of the emperor as a component of the imperial cult.[67] The epiphany of a deity was frequently associated with the manifestation of his divine power to rescue or save a community or an individual, and it was an important component in the accreditation of the god and the establishment of worship in his honor.[68] The epiphany of the *Lord Jesus* will be so powerful that it will *destroy* the *lawless one* and his power (v. 9) and will establish the way of the afflicted Christians as the one, true superior religion. This despised faith will receive glorious honor (1.9-10).

9 The mention of the "coming" *(parousia)* of the Lord Jesus and his glorious epiphany that will spell the destruction of "the lawless one" (v. 8) reminds the author that "the lawless one" will come accompanied by signs and wonders: *The coming of the lawless one will be in accordance*

64. So the verb *anaireō* in Matt. 2.16; Luke 22.2; Acts 2.23; and see BAGD, 54-55; MM, 34; LSJ, 106.

65. BAGD, 417; *TDNT*, 1.452-54. So also LXX 2 Esdr. 4.21, 23; 5.5; 6.8.

66. BAGD, 304; MM, 250; *TLNT*, 2.67; *New Docs*, 4.74-76, 80-81; *LAE*, 370-73. An inscription from Epidaurus says, "Asclepius manifests his coming." See Dionysius of Halicarnassus 2.68; Dio Chrysostom 32.41; 2 Macc. 2.21; 3.24; 5.4; 12.22; 14.15; 15.27.

67. A coin from Actium minted at the time of Hadrian commemorates the "epiphany of Augustus" *(LAE, 373)*.

68. *New Docs*, 4.74-76, 80-81. An inscription from Ephesus dedicated to Artemis says, "everywhere her shrines and sanctuaries have been established, and temples have been founded for her and altars dedicated to her because of the visible manifestations *(epiphaneias)* effected by her."

with the work of Satan displayed in all kinds of counterfeit miracles, signs and wonders. The advent of "the lawless one"[69] is called his *parousia,* which is his own royal/divine entrance (see the comments on the *parousia* of Jesus in 1 Thess. 2.19; 3.13; 4.15; 5.23; 2 Thess. 2.1, 8). The power that will be demonstrated in his coming will be satanic, *in accordance with the working of Satan.* The term translated *working* implies some form of supernatural activity[70] (2.11; and the verb in 1 Thess. 2.13; 2 Thess. 2.7), which in this case is not inherent in "the lawless one" but rather is energized by *Satan,* the same one who opposed this church and its apostle (1 Thess. 2.18; 3.5). The satanic purpose is to accredit "the lawless one" in his *parousia* by means of supernatural signs that will deceive those who have not accepted the gospel (v. 10; cf. Mark 13.22; Rev. 13.13-15). Paul deeply desires to guard the Thessalonians from this type of deception, especially in light of the error concerning the day of the Lord that had already entered the church (v. 2) and the presence, possibly prophetic, of the "one who seizes" (vv. 6-7).

The miracles "the lawless one" will manifest in his *parousia* are described as *all kinds of counterfeit miracles, signs and wonders.* The combination of *miracles, signs and wonders* appears in various NT texts (Acts 2.22; 2 Cor. 12.12; Heb. 2.4), but only here do they refer to satanic activity. *Miracles* is the same term that is found in 1 Thessalonians 1.5 (see comments) and denotes any type of miracle. *Signs* also can refer to "miracles" but with emphasis on the way they provide evidence showing the nature of the one who manifests them.[71] Moreover, these miracles of "the lawless one" are called *wonders,* a word that appears over and again in combination with *signs* (e.g., Matt. 24.24; John 4.48; Acts 2.19, 43; 4.30; 5.12). It points to some kind of portent or prodigy, "terrible appearances which elicit fright and horror."[72] Although our author affirms that the power that is behind these *wonders* is *Satan* himself, he calls them *counterfeit,* that is, a lie.[73] A number of ancient texts testify that false miracles accompanied a number of cults, and such were even characteristic of the imperial cult.[74]

---

69. The *NIV* supplies "the lawless one" from the context, whereas the Greek text states simply, "whose coming etc." The *NIV* also adds the word *displayed.*

70. The term in the NT always points to the activity of supernatural beings (BAGD, 265). Diodorus Siculus (15.48.1) speaks, e.g., of "some divine force *(energeias)* which brings destruction and ruin over humanity."

71. See Matt. 12.38-39; 16.1, 4; Mark 8.11, 12; 16.17, 20; and of various ancient divinities in Diodorus Siculus 5.70.4; 16.27.2; Strabo 16.2.35; Polybius 3.112.8; Plutarch, *Alexander* 75.1; and see LSJ, 1593; *TLNT,* 3.252-54.

72. *NIDNTT,* 2.633; LSJ, 1776; BAGD, 812.

73. BAGD, 892.

74. See Lucian, *Alexander the False Prophet;* Athenagoras, *Plea on Behalf of Christians* 26-27; Hippolytus, *The Refutation of All Heresies* 4.28-41; Stephen J. Scherrer, "Signs and

Such *wonders* included images that could talk and move as well as the production of thunder and lightning. Although the apostle recognized the tricks that "the lawless one" would play, according to the religious conventions of the day, he is careful to note that real satanic power was working in him (cf. 1 Cor. 10.19-20).

10 This verse describes the deception of "the lawless one," the reaction of unbelievers, and the ultimate consequences of rejecting the gospel. Continuing the thought of the previous verse, the author describes "the lawless one's" advent as also *in every sort of evil that deceives those who are perishing. They perish because they refused to love the truth and so be saved.* Not only does "the lawless one" come with "counterfeit miracles, signs and wonders," but also with any other method that will forward his deception. He employs "every kind of . . . deception" *(NRSV; apatē)*, a term that describes his deceitfulness and the seduction, which the ones who have rejected the truth of the gospel will embrace.[75] The same term could refer of the delights of pleasure (see Mark 4.19 with Luke 8.14),[76] but the coordination with the false miracles (v. 9) and the contrast with the *truth* in the present verse indicate that the seducing power has deception as its goal. The deception is further described as *evil* or "wicked" *(adikias)*.[77] This adjective, which is frequently found in contrast with "truth" (2.10b, 12; John 7.18; Rom. 2.8; 1 Cor. 13.6), underlines the error of the deception that "the lawless one" promotes. The deception is wicked, unrighteous, or *evil* in the sense of being lying, false, or untruthful.[78] The ones who will embrace the seductive error of "the lawless one" are *those who are perishing,* that is, those who are not saved (vv. 10b, 13) but eternally lost (1 Cor. 1.18; 2 Cor. 2.15; 4.3; John 3.16; 10.28; 17.12).[79] Eternal destiny is bound up with truth. To embrace error, however powerfully and plausibly it may be presented, is dangerous business. In our age, when truth is increasingly viewed as relative and personal, thoughts about the power and consequences of embracing error move to the periphery. The apostolic

---

Wonders in the Imperial Cult: A New Look at a Roman Religious Institution in the Light of Rev 13:13-15," *JBL* 103 (1984) 599-610.

75. BAGD, 82; LSJ, 181. According to ancient mythology, even the gods could employ deception to further their ends. The same term could speak of the delights of pleasure (see Mark 4.19 with Luke 8.14; and *TLNT*, 1.153-55; *TDNT*, 1.385). Both ideas of "deception" and "(sexual) pleasure" are joined in Strabo 11.2.10.

76. *TLNT*, 1.153-55; *TDNT*, 1.385. Both ideas of "deception" and "(sexual) pleasure" are joined in Strabo 11.2.10.

77. Some Greek manuscripts (א[2], D, Ψ) place the definite article before the adjective. In this case the reading would be "the Unjust One" *(tēs adikias)*, Satan himself. However, the weight of the manuscript evidence favors the exclusion of the article.

78. *TDNT*, 1.154.

79. BAGD, 95.

perspective is that there is a right way and a wrong way, and that the power of Satan is and will be powerfully operative to assure that people, in the end, will be eternally lost. The stakes in the battle for truth and against error could not be higher.

The reason why these people eternally *perish* is *because they refused to love the truth and so be saved.* The apostle's conviction is that a person's ultimate destiny is bound up with his or her relation to the *truth.* The *truth* to which the author refers is not some abstract concept but rather the gospel itself that had been proclaimed in Thessalonica (vv. 12-14; Gal. 2.5, 14; Eph. 1.13; Col. 1.5; 2 Tim. 2.15). The thought is not that they had rejected any and every form of truth but the truth that was contained in the gospel. Instead of "receiving" *(edexanto)*[80] *the truth,* these people did not obey the gospel that was preached to them (1.8). But, curiously, the text states that such people do not receive "the love of *the truth.*" Milligan suggests that these people "had not only not 'welcomed' . . . this truth, but had no *liking* for it, no *desire* to possess it."[81] Their lack of interest and indifference to the proclamation of "Christ crucified," manifested in their rejection of the message, was a reality the believers confronted on every side (cf. 1 Cor. 1.23). In our time the situation is not much different. Those who do not receive *the truth* will not obtain the benefit offered in the gospel. They will not *be saved* (see 1 Thess. 2.16; 5.8-9; 2 Thess. 2.13 and comments). Eternal salvation, which is the only answer for those *who are perishing,* is not found apart from the reception of the gospel (v. 13). Offers of salvation were numerous in that age, but none was effective to save. In any era of pluralism, the exclusivity of the gospel is a scandal. But the line between life and death, between being saved and perishing, is drawn by the gospel of the Crucified One.

11 As a result of their having rejected the truth of the gospel, God begins to execute his judgment on the unbelievers in what, to us, is a very surprising way: *For this reason God sends them a powerful delusion so that they will believe the lie.* What God sends them in this judicial act is, first, *powerful,* a term that describes some kind of supernatural and powerful action (2.9 and the verb in 2.7; 1 Thess. 2.13). This "power" produces in them a great *delusion.*[82] Since they did not receive the truth of the gospel, God sends them confusion so that they cannot distinguish between the truth and *the lie* and, in the end, they believe *the lie* as if it were the truth.

---

80. The verb frequently describes the reception of the gospel (see 1 Thess. 1.6; 2.13 and comments; Acts 8.14; 11.1; 17.11; Luke 8.13; and BAGD, 177).

81. As Milligan observes, "God gives the wicked over to the evil which they have deliberately chosen" (*St. Paul's Epistles to the Thessalonians,* 105). See Marshall, *1 and 2 Thessalonians,* 203.

82. BAGD, 665 and see the comments on 1 Thess. 2.3.

As strange as this kind of judgment may seem to us, it is in harmony with the biblical witness, which shows the way God gives sinners over to the very sin and error they have embraced (Ps. 80.12-13 [81.12-13]; Rom. 1.24, 26, 28; 11.8; 2 Tim. 4.4).[83] The thought is similar to that in those texts in the OT that describe how God uses malignant spirits to execute his judgments and will even employ the inspiration of false prophets (2 Sam. 24.1/1 Chr. 21.1; 1 Kgdms. 22.19-23; Ezek. 14.9).

Thus, those who have rejected the truth of the gospel *will believe the lie*, that very *lie* which was propagated by "the lawless one" (v. 9) and which stands in terrible contrast to the truth (vv. 10, 12-13). The power to persuade was a fundamental theme in Greek and Latin rhetoric. In fact, the goal of rhetoric was to persuade the hearer of the position of the one who spoke.[84] But these people who *believe the lie* disseminated by "the lawless one" are persuaded because of a strong delusion that overtakes them as a result of having rejected the truth of the gospel. To reject the truth results in the judgment of embracing the most distorted *lie*.

12 In vv. 10-11 Paul explained how "the lawless one" will deceive unbelievers and how they will accept the lie and be lost. In v. 12 the author continues the explanation of the character of the divine judgment that will come upon them. According to v. 11, they have believed the lie of "the lawless one." The result is now spelled out: *and so that all will be condemned who have not believed the truth but have delighted in wickedness.* The word translated *will be condemned* comes from the world of jurisprudence and points beyond the legal decision to the consequences of a conviction, that being condemnation.[85] The nature of that condemnation has already been described in the most graphic apocalyptic terms in 1.6-9 (see comments). None of those who embrace error will escape this condemnation, but *all* will experience it. This condemnation is inclusive; there will be no exception clause.

The objects of this condemnation are ones *who have not believed the truth,* that is to say, those who have rejected the message of the gospel (v. 10 and comments) and who have embraced the lie of "the lawless one" (v. 11). Such people not only reject the gospel but also *have delighted in wickedness. Wickedness* is the same word the apostle used in v. 10 *(adikia);* it appears in Greek literature as the opposite of "the truth" (cf. v. 10b). The word should be understood along this line in the present verse; as such it

---

83. Milligan, *St. Paul's Epistles to the Thessalonians,* 105.

84. Aristotle, *Ethica Nicomachea* 1.2.8; 3.13.1, 4. Litfin, *St. Paul's Theology of Proclamation.*

85. *TDNT,* 3.921-41; *NIDNTT,* 2.362-67; BAGD, 451-52. See Rom. 2.1; Heb. 10.30; 13.4; 1 Pet. 4.6.

is the equivalent of "the lie" of v. 11b. The verb that describes their embrace of the error commonly means "to accept" or "to consent" to an idea after having been persuaded by it.[86] Understood in this way, the thought expressed is quite similar to v. 11b, that is, these people "believe the lie" since they have been persuaded of its validity. The error will have its adherents, but the Thessalonian believers are to be stable and unmoved since they have accepted the truth (cf. v. 2). This is the theme of the following section in which the apostle expresses thanksgiving to God for the way the gospel came to them and for their reception of its truth (vv. 13-14).

2. "But we must always give thanks to God for you" — The Second Thanksgiving (2.13-14)

13 The second thanksgiving of the letter begins almost exactly like the first (1.3 and comments) as it expresses the obligation Paul and his companions felt to give thanks to God. The motive for the first thanksgiving was the growing faith and love that were abundantly evidenced in the Thessalonian believers. But in this second thanksgiving Paul remembers the divine election of the Thessalonians that resulted in their salvation. This thanksgiving for those who responded to the gospel should also be read in light of the rejection of the call to salvation by others who had heard it in Thessalonica and who, as a result, became subjects of God's judgment (vv. 10-12). The author signals this contrast between the two groups in v. 13, which begins with the adversative "but" *(de)*. In fact, the apostle contrasts the action of God toward the two (v. 11, God sent them "powerful delusion"; v. 13, *God chose you*), the means used to bring about his purposes (v. 11, "powerful delusion"; v. 14, "through our gospel"), and the ultimate destiny of both (v. 12, "all will be condemned"; v. 13, *to be saved*).[87]

In this thanksgiving, Paul says, *But we ought always to thank God for you, brothers loved by the Lord, because from the beginning God chose you to be saved through the sanctifying work of the Spirit and through belief in the truth.* Here, as in 1 Thessalonians 1.4 (see comments), the divine election of the Thessalonians is embedded deeply in God's love for them. The way the author speaks of this election is unique. He uses a verb that means "to take for or to oneself" and that in other contexts in the NT does not refer to divine election but rather to the selection of something or making a de-

---

86. *TLNT,* 2.99-103; MM, 260; BAGD, 319; Diodorus Siculus 14.110.4; Polybius 1.8.4; 2.38.7; 1 Macc. 1.43; 1 Esdr. 4.39; 2 Cor. 12.10.
87. O'Brien, *Introductory Thanksgivings in the Letters of Paul,* 185.

cision because it is preferred (cf. Phil. 1.22; Heb. 11.25).[88] We might say that God's election of these Thessalonians was not only *unto* salvation but also *for* himself (cf. Deut. 26.18). Apart from this, the apostle does not discuss *why* God loved and *chose* the Thessalonian brothers and sisters but only offers thanksgiving for that fact. Paul declares that this election was *from the beginning (ap' archēs)*, although various principal Greek manuscripts of the letter read "as first-fruits" (*aparchēn*, a reading followed in the *NRSV*). Although the evidence is strong in favor of *from the beginning*,[89] this expression is not found in any other book of the Pauline corpus. Whenever the apostle uses the term *archēs* in other contexts, it rarely bears the meaning found in 2.13, conveying rather the sense of "ruler" or "authority" (with the exception of Phil. 4.15). On the other hand, "first fruits" is quite common in Paul, and the manuscript evidence in favor of this reading is substantial.[90] The scribal tendency was to change *aparchē* to *ap' archēs* (Rev. 14.4; Rom. 16.5), the most likely scenario being that the same tendency is at play in the present verse.[91] Following the reading reflected in the *NRSV*, the Thessalonians are the "first fruits," an allusion to the first part of the harvest or even the first offspring of animals that are dedicated exclusively as sacred to God (Exod. 23.19; Num. 15.17-21; Deut. 12.6, 17). Here the readers of the letter are viewed as the first converts from Thessalonica (cf. *1 Clem.* 42.4).[92] Paul's custom was to speak about the first converts from a region in this way (Rom. 16.5; 1 Cor. 16.15), and he probably views the members of the already established church as the first of many who will be converted to God. The evangelistic flame was not extinguished by the rejection of the gospel, its messengers, and the first converts in that metropolis. Hope for the city still burned bright.

The purpose of God's election was that they might *be saved* (see 1 Thess. 5.8-9 and comments), and this *through the sanctifying work of the Spirit and through belief in the truth*. In 1 Thessalonians Paul exhorted the believers again and again to dedicate themselves to sanctification (1 Thess. 4.3, 4, 7),[93] reminding them that sanctification was God's will for them and that God called them to the same. But he also assured the Thessalonians that sanctification was a work of God (1 Thess. 5.23) that he effects through the agency of the Holy Spirit (1 Thess. 4.8). The process

---

88. In fact, the verb *haireō* can mean simply "to prefer." BAGD, 24; *TDNT*, 1.180; *NIDNTT*, 1.533; and see Homer, *Iliad* 10.235. It is used in the OT, however, of God's election (Deut. 26.18).

89. ℵ, D, K, L, Ψ.

90. B, F, G, P.

91. See Metzger, *Textual Commentary*, 636-37.

92. BAGD, 81.

93. On the term, see *TDNT*, 1.113; BDF, §109.1; *NIDNTT*, 1.223-32; BAGD, 9.

of sanctification began at their conversion (1 Pet. 1.2) and is being worked out throughout their lives so that the believers might be blameless before the Lord at his coming (1 Thess. 5.23; and see Rom. 15.16; 1 Cor. 6.11; 1 Pet. 1.2). Far from its being auxiliary to their salvation, the apostle understands the *sanctifying work* as the action *of the Spirit* of God that brings about salvation. It may be possible to understand *Spirit* as the human "spirit," the object of sanctification as in 1 Thessalonians 5.23, but the focus of this verse is rather the powerful divine operation in their lives by means of the Holy *Spirit* and *the truth*. These Christians entered into the realm of salvation *through belief in the truth*, that is, through their faith in the gospel that was proclaimed to them (see vv. 10, 12).[94] Although the divine decision and activity in bringing about salvation are the primary focus, the apostle does not lose sight of human responsibility in this process, which is indicated by the word *belief*.

14 Having chosen the Thessalonians for salvation, God then called them by means of the preaching of the gospel: *He called you to this through our gospel, that you might share in the glory of our Lord Jesus Christ*. That to which they were *called (this)* is found in v. 13: "God chose you to be saved through the sanctifying work of the Spirit and through belief in the truth."[95] The God who chose them to be saved is the same God who made sure that the message of salvation reached them by means of the apostolic proclamation of the gospel. God is the one who gave Paul the night vision to preach the gospel in Macedonia (Acts 16.9-10), and when he and his associates arrived in the city the proclamation the Thessalonians heard and received was the very message of God. They heard his voice through the proclamation (1 Thess. 2.15; cf. 1.5)! So the apostle is now able to say that God *called you to this through our gospel* (see 1 Thess. 2.12; 4.7; 5.24; and 2 Thess. 1.11). They were not persuaded by the rhetorical abilities of the heralds; rather, God was active in the apostolic preaching, and he *called* them through this message (cf. 1 Thess. 1.4-5; Gal. 1.6-7).

The call to salvation is a common theme in the NT, which is always understood as the activity of God and not of some human agent, though a human messenger may be employed (Rom. 8.30; 1 Cor. 1.9; Gal. 1.6, 15; 5.8; Eph. 4.1, 4; Col. 3.15; 1 Tim. 6.12; 2 Tim. 1.9; Heb. 9.15; 1 Pet. 1.15; 2.9; 5.10; 2 Pet. 1.3). Jesus assumes this divine privilege (Matt. 4.21; Mark 2.17), while in the OT it is attributed to Yahweh (e.g., Isa. 41.9; 42.6; 48.12, 15; 51.2), who takes for himself those whom he calls. Despite the fact that

---

94. The *NIV* understands the genitive *pneumatos* as subjective *(of the Spirit)* and the genitive *alētheias* as objective *(in the truth)*.

95. The antecedent to *eis ho* (neuter, translated *to this*) is not *sōtērian* ("salvation"), *hagiasmǭ* ("sanctification"), nor *pistei* ("belief"), all of which are feminine.

the majority of believers in the Thessalonian church were Gentiles and not Jews,[96] their previous religious training allowed them to understand the idea of "being called" by some deity, an idea that was common especially in the mystery religions.[97] For example, Pausanias speaks of those called by the Egyptian goddess Isis, saying, "No one may enter the shrine except those whom Isis herself has honored by inviting *(kalesē)* them in dreams" (10.32.13). But the way God chose to call the Thessalonians was quite different. He called them *through our gospel,* which in other places in these letters is called "the gospel of God" (1 Thess. 2.2, 4, 8, 9) or "the gospel of Christ" (1 Thess. 3.2; 2 Thess. 1.8). The message and the agency are divine, not simply human.

The purpose of this calling is that the Thessalonians *might share in the glory of our Lord Jesus Christ.* In the first letter, the apostle informed the church that God had "appointed [them] . . . to receive salvation" (1 Thess. 5.9), and the point made here is similar. The term there translated "receive" is the same as that which is rendered *might share (peripoiēsin),* which describes the process of obtaining or possessing "salvation" (Isa. 31.5; 1 Macc. 6.44) or "life" (Heb. 10.39). The verb appears in the writings of Philo of Alexandria, who notes that God permits a person "to obtain" that which was not previously possessed.[98] What the Thessalonians will obtain is *the glory of our Lord Jesus Christ,* which will be revealed in his coming (Matt. 16.27; 19.28; 24.30; 25.31; Mark 8.38; 13.26; Luke 9.26; 21.27; Titus 2.13). This promise of receiving *glory* became one of the great hopes of the Christian faith (1 Thess. 2.12; Rom. 5.2; 8.17, 18; Col. 1.27). In fact, both Paul and Peter announce that Christians are called to this *glory* (Rom. 8.30; 1 Pet. 5.10). *Glory* is frequently associated with "honor" in honorific inscriptions, and obtaining such honor was one of the chief concerns in ancient Mediterranean "honor/shame" cultures.[99] For the Christians in Thessalonica, the promise of receiving this exalted honor would have been a great comfort and encouragement in light of the dishonor they suffered in their communities because of their adherence to the One who was humiliated on the cross (1 Thess. 2.14). God *called* them to this *glory,* which is *of our Lord Jesus Christ,* the one who was also exalted.

96. See pp. 107-8.

97. *TDNT,* 2.490.

98. *Legum Allegoriae* 3.136; *Quod Deus Sit Immutabilis* 86. See BAGD, 650; *TLNT,* 3.102.

99. *TLNT,* 1.362-79. On honor in the Mediterranean world see, e.g., Bruce J. Malina, *The New Testament World* (Louisville: Westminster/John Knox, 1993), 28-62; Jerome H. Neyrey, ed., *The Social World of Luke-Acts,* 25-65.

3. "Stand firm and hold fast to the traditions" — Exhortation to Steadfastness (2.15)

15 In this verse Paul returns to the principal concern of this section: the stability of the Thessalonian Christians in the face of the false teaching, which came from an unknown source (2.2). As a consequence of every-thing previously stated concerning the events preceding the day of the Lord (see vv. 3-12, especially v. 5) and concerning their election, calling, and destiny (vv. 13-14), the apostle exhorts them, saying, *So then, brothers, stand firm and hold to the teachings we passed on to you, whether by word of mouth or by letter.* The call to be constant and stable *(stēkete)*[100] reflects one of the principal concerns of the apostles in their pastoral ministry to new Christians (see Rom. 14.4; 1 Cor. 16.13; Gal. 5.1; Phil. 1.27; 4.1). This exhortation could be understood as a call to stability and faithfulness in the light of the persecution they experienced (see 1 Thess. 3.8 and comments). But in the context of chapter 2 his concern is rather their constancy in the teaching they had received from the apostles (vv. 2, 5, 15b; cf. 1 Thess. 4.1-2). They should continue faithfully in that teaching, holding on to it without wavering in any way even in the face of contrary opinion (the verb *krateite* is used in the same way in Mark 7.3; Heb. 4.14; 6.18; Rev. 2.14-15, 25; 3.11).

The Thessalonians should hold fast to the *teachings* received from the apostles. Paul here calls these *teachings* "the traditions" *(paradoseis)*, a term that could have a pejorative sense in the NT (Matt. 15.2-3, 6; Mark 7.3, 5, 8-9, 13; Col. 2.8) or a positive meaning (3.6; 1 Cor. 11.2; and the verbal form of the term in Rom. 6.17; 1 Cor. 11.23; 15.3; Jude 3).[101] In this text the sense is clearly positive as the word denotes the authoritative apostolic traditions the founders of the congregation had handed over to the members of the church. In both the Jewish and Greek worlds the transmission of the sacred traditions of a people's forebears was considered a high obligation. Such traditions were considered to be of divine origin and, therefore, authoritative.[102] By means of these traditions people were integrated as members of the group to which they belonged. In fact, in collectivist cultures the process of passing on and maintaining the traditions of the group was a principal concern (note how the Pharisees se-

---

100. BAGD, 767-68; *TDNT*, 7.636-38.

101. The combination of *krateō* ("hold to") and *paradosis* ("tradition") is found in Mark 7.3, 8.

102. Josephus, *Antiquitates* 13.297 [13.10.6]; Wis. 14.15; Plato, *Philebus* 16C, says, e.g., "The ancients, who were better than we and lived nearer the gods, handed down the tradition *(paredosan)* that all the things which are ever said to exist are sprung from one and many and have inherent in them the finite and the infinite."

verely criticized Jesus for not holding to the traditions in Mark 7.1-3).[103] When the apostles confronted the threat of heterodox doctrine, they reoriented the church back to the apostolic traditions that had been handed down to them (cf. Jude 3). In the case of the Thessalonian church, these sacred and authoritative traditions were those that *we passed on to you* ("you were taught" NRSV), *whether by word of mouth or by letter. Word of mouth* is a reference to the teaching the apostle gave when they were in the city (1 Thess. 3.4; 4.1-2; 5.1-2; 2 Thess. 2.5; 3.10), while the *letter* refers to the first correspondence sent to the Thessalonian church.[104] These teachings that they had already received were the antidote for the destabilizing confusion that had entered the church "by some prophecy, report or letter supposed to have come from us, saying that the day of the Lord has already come" (2.2). This theological novelty was rejected in favor of the "traditions" the apostle had taught them.

4. "Now may our Lord Jesus Christ himself and God our Father" — The First Prayer (2.16-17)

16-17 After the exhortation to "stand firm" and to "hold fast" the apostolic traditions the church was taught (v. 15), Paul offers the first prayer of the letter in the form of a wish or desire (cf. 2 Thess. 3.16 and 1 Thess. 3.11-13; 5.23). The prayer begins, *May our Lord Jesus Christ himself*[105] *and God our Father,* making both *God our Father* and *our Lord Jesus Christ* the objects of the petition and so placing them on the same plane. The christological implications are evident. But unlike the majority of the verses where both the *Father* and *Jesus Christ* appear together, the name of the *Lord Jesus Christ* is placed in first position (see Rom. 1.7; 1 Cor. 1.3; 2 Cor. 1.2; Gal. 1.3; Eph. 1.2; Phil. 1.2; 2 Thess. 1.2; Phlm. 3; and cf. Gal. 1.1; 2 Cor. 13.13, where the order is the same as in the present text). Although many commentators attribute the following description *(who loved us and by his grace gave us eternal encouragement and good hope)* to both *God our Father* and *our Lord Jesus Christ,*[106] the grammar favors the

---

103. See Malina and Neyrey, *Portraits of Paul,* 164-169.
104. Contra Wanamaker, *Commentary on 1 and 2 Thessalonians,* 269. See the Introduction, pp. 64-69.
105. On the use of the pronoun *himself* in liturgical texts, see the comments on 1 Thess. 3.11.
106. See, e.g., Frame, *The Epistles of St. Paul to the Thessalonians,* 286; Maarten J. J. Menken, *2 Thessalonians* (London and New York: Routledge, 1994), 123; Marshall, *1 and 2 Thessalonians,* 211; Bruce, *1 and 2 Thessalonians,* 196; Best, *The First and Second Epistles to the Thessalonians,* 320.

interpretation that understands these words as an extended ascription of *God our Father.*[107]

God is, in the first place, the one *who loved us.* The aorist participle most likely points us to some event in which *God our Father* demonstrated his love, a possible allusion to his election of the Thessalonians (2.13; and see 1 Thess. 1.4), to the incarnation (John 3.16), or to the act of sending his Son to die for our sins (Rom. 5.8). The way in which the apostle links God's love with election in these letters favors the first interpretation. But whatever act of love the author has in mind, their concern is to encourage and strengthen the Thessalonians in the midst of their persecutions and their battle against erroneous teaching (v. 17). In the presence of these adversaries the love of *God our Father* would be the foundation of their hope (the thought is similar to Rom. 8.37-39, where God's love is the counterpoint to the believers' sufferings).

God is also known here as the one who *by his grace gave us eternal encouragement and good hope.* In Romans 15.4 Paul combines the ideas of *encouragement* and *hope* as in this verse, but there they are understood as the fruit of the message contained in the OT Scripture: "For everything that was written in the past was written to teach us, so that through endurance and the *encouragement* of the Scriptures we might have *hope.*" In that text the apostle's thoughts about *encouragement* and *hope* are bound up with his concern for community harmony, especially that between Jews and Gentiles in the church. But the issue here in v. 16b is the final destiny of the believers, their eschatological *hope,* which should become the lens through which they seek to face their present circumstances. This destiny is described, on the one hand, as *eternal encouragement* and, on the other, as *good hope.* This last expression was quite common in ancient literature and frequently referred to "high hopes" that were firm and ripe with the expectation of being fulfilled.[108] But it could also refer to life after death, and even the happiness associated with it.[109] Since the expression *good hope* here appears in combination with *eternal encouragement,* the thought most likely points to the Christian *hope,* which transcends this life and carries with it the promise of bliss in the life hereafter. The theme of *hope* permeates the first letter to this church (1 Thess. 1.3; 2.19; 5.8) and is understood as a particular virtue that distinguishes the Christian from the rest of humanity (1 Thess. 4.13). Among the Greeks, "hopes" could be

---

107. So Wanamaker, *Commentary on 1 and 2 Thessalonians,* 270-71. The singular participles *ho agapēsas . . . kai dous* are decisive.

108. For example, Plato, *Phaedo* 67C; *Leges* 1.649B; Thucydides 4.81.3; Xenophon, *Cyropaedia* 1.5.13.

109. *TLNT,* 1.483, 486; Best, *The First and Second Epistles to the Thessalonians,* 321; Wanamaker, *Commentary on 1 and 2 Thessalonians,* 271.

nothing more than negative thoughts about the future,[110] but the destiny and end of the Christian is a *good hope.*

The future *hope* is alternately described as *eternal encouragement.* The encouragement *(paraklēsin)* is that which a person may have in the face of adversity (so the verbal form of the word in 1 Thess. 3.2), and so the word was commonly used in military contexts to speak of the encouragement given to soldiers.[111] This church suffered greatly at the hands of their contemporaries (1.3-10) and desperately needed the *encouragement* that came from *God our Father.* But the adjective *eternal* may point to an alternative understanding of *encouragement* in this verse. This term also appears in those contexts where a person attempts to console another in the face of the pain and sadness that fills the soul when confronted with death. Understood this way, the term could be translated as the *NRSV* does, "comfort." Now the "comfort" that was offered in Greek society lacked genuine *hope,* and not a few ancients echoed the words of Theognis, "Best of all for mortals is never to have been born, but for those who have been born to die as soon as possible."[112] Whatever hopes there were regarding immortality were vague and uncertain. But the "comfort" that *God our Father* gives is *eternal* and transcends death, offering something more than the grave as the goal of life. What the Thessalonians already enjoyed was "comfort" in the face of death and *hope* that was firm because *God our Father* gave it to them *by his grace,* that is, through his free gift (see 1 Thess. 1.1; 5.28; 2 Thess. 1.2, 12; 3.18). The prayer to be offered is rooted in the *grace* of God, which holds promise beyond the limits of death.

Their future is certain and full, but what of the present? The way in which *God* extended his love in the past in their election and gave them a firm *hope* for the future, even to eternity, forms the base of the prayer for the Thessalonians in this present time. The founder of the church prays that *God our Father and our Lord Jesus Christ . . . encourage your hearts and strengthen you in every good deed and word* (v. 17). The plural subject of the prayer is properly *God our Father and our Lord Jesus Christ,* but the verbs are placed in the singular *(encourage . . . strengthen).* This grammatical phenomenon is not unknown in the NT (see, e.g., Matt. 6.19; 24.35; John 1.17; 1 Cor. 15.50) and does not carry any theological significance. The desire[113] expressed in the petition to the *Lord Jesus Christ* and *God our Father* is that they might *encourage* and *strengthen* the Thessalonians, a concern that echoes Timothy's mission when he visited the church soon after

---

110. LSJ 537.
111. *TDNT,* 5.775.
112. Ibid., 787.
113. The verbs are in the optative mood which expresses a wish or desire.

its founding "to strengthen and encourage" them in their faith (1 Thess. 3.2). The verbs in both verses are the same (see the comments on 1 Thess. 3.2), but the order is reversed in the present text. In the absence of the members of the apostolic team, Paul appeals to the *Father* and the *Lord* of the church to *encourage* and "establish" them.

The first verb of the wish prayer may mean "to console" (1 Thess. 4.18), but in combination with *heart* it normally means to encourage or to exhort (Acts 11.23; Eph. 6.22; Col. 2.2; 4.8). In the present context it may communicate the idea of *encourage* (as in 1 Thess. 3.7), but most likely the apostle has the moral sense of "to exhort" in mind (as in 1 Thess. 2.12; 3.2; 4.1, 10; 5.11, 14; 2 Thess. 3.12; and see 2 Cor. 4.20, which speaks of God's exhortation). Understood in this way, the petition would be that the *Lord Jesus Christ* and *God our Father* would "exhort" their *hearts,* the center of their moral life (as in 1 Thess. 3.13; see comments). The idea is not simply that they might have internal encouragement[114] but that they might experience divine moral exhortation. The prayer also expresses the desire that God may *strengthen* them or their *hearts,* a word that most likely serves as the object of both verbs in the absence of any other expressed object in the Greek. The same words appear in 1 Thessalonians 3.13 ("strengthen your hearts"; see comments and Jas. 5.8), where the apostle prays that the *heart* of the Thessalonians, the center of their moral existence, might be established in holiness in anticipation of the time when they shall stand "in the presence of our God and Father when our Lord Jesus comes." He expresses the concern that the Thessalonians will do the will of God and stand firm in this. The apostle wants their morality to be comprehensive (cf. 1 Thess. 5.23) *in every good deed and word.* The combination of *deed and word* is found in other NT texts (Luke 24.19; Acts 7.22; Rom.15.18) and was also quite common in ancient literature, whether the reference was to good[115] or evil[116] words and deeds. The prayer is that everything they do and say will be *good* and not evil (cf. Col. 3.17; 2 Thess. 1.11-12). What orients their conduct and their communication in the present time, according to this prayer, is the past and future work of God (v. 16). The importance of this prayer is highlighted by the agonizing adversity this congregation faced daily. The prayer not only presents a petition to God but also serves as an implicit exhortation to the Thessalonians to live lives that are in harmony with the desire expressed in the prayer.

---

114. Contra Wanamaker, *Commentary on 1 and 2 Thessalonians,* 272.
115. For example, Plato, *Leges* 647D; Xenophon, *Memorabilia* 1.2.59; 2.3.17.
116. For example, Plato, *Leges* 879D-E, 885B, 909D; Xenophon, *Memorabilia* 2.3.6.

B. "Finally, brothers and sisters" — Final Instructions (3.1-15)

Paul begins this final section of the letter by soliciting the prayers of the Thessalonian believers (3.1-2), a request followed by a confession that the Lord is faithful to establish this congregation (3.3-5). Both the petition and the declaration are framed by references to the hostile opposition both the apostles and the Thessalonians faced. The second major concern of the section revolves around labor and patronage (3.6-15), a theme Paul had already addressed while they were in the city and had taken up again in his first letter to this church (1 Thess. 4.11-12; 5.14).

1. "Pray for us" — Mutual Prayers (3.1-5)

a. "So that the word of the Lord may spread rapidly" — The Prayer Request of the Apostles (3.1-2)

1 The paragraph begins with two words, translated *Finally (to loipon)*, that mark the transition to a new section in the argument (as in 1 Thess. 4.1). This Greek expression could serve as a rhetorical marker that signaled that an author had arrived at the end of his writing (Gal. 6.17), or it may simply signal the introduction of a new theme (Phil. 3.1; cf. Eph. 6.1; Phil. 4.8).[1] As in 1 Thessalonians 5.25, the author requests the brothers and sisters of the church to pray for him and his companions, an appeal that follows the assurance of their prayers for the church (2.16-17; cf. 1 Thess. 5.23-24): *Finally, brothers, pray for us.* Repeatedly Paul not only made known his prayers for the churches but also his need of the congregations' prayers (Rom. 15.30-32; 2 Cor. 1.11; Phil. 1.19; Phlm. 22). Such mutual concern of believers and leaders is characteristic of the church. They are bound together both by their sufferings for Christ and their mutual prayer support. Unlike 1 Thessalonians 5.24, where the apostle does not specify why they needed prayer, the petition here is for the wider reception of the gospel (v. 1b; cf. Eph. 6.18-19; Col. 4.3-4) and for deliverance from the persecutions they faced at the hands of unbelievers (v. 2).

The first prayer request the apostle sets before the Thessalonians is *that the message of the Lord may spread rapidly.* The *message* or "word" *of the Lord* is the gospel he and his associates proclaimed (1 Thess. 1.8; 4.15; cf. Acts 8.25; 13.44, 48-49; 15.35-36; 19.10). Paul wants divine intervention so that the gospel may *spread rapidly* or "run" *(trechē),*[2] giving it rapid or per-

1. MM, 380.
2. LSJ, 1814; BAGD, 826-27; *TDNT,* 8.226-33. The figurative use of the verb "to run" was not unknown in Greek literature (Hesiod, *Opera et Dies* 219).

haps unimpeded progress (see v. 2). The request echoes the words of Ps. 147.15 (147.4).[3] In the imagery of the psalm, God sends his word to the earth, and it runs like a messenger. God is clearly in control of this diffusion in the same way that he spreads snow on the land and sends the irresistible winter weather (147.16-18 [147.5-7]). But the present verse appears to fuse the allusion of the psalm with the contemporary imagery of the games. Paul commonly used running the race as a metaphor for the apostolic mission (1 Cor. 9.24-26; Gal. 2.2; Phil. 2.16).

The second request of the prayer suggests this imagery, asking that the word of the Lord may *be honored, just as it was with you*. The apostle has in mind the reception of the gospel as it was preached in the cities of the empire and so became *honored (doxazētai)*.[4] Acts 13.48 speaks of the reception of the gospel in precisely the same way. The combination of "run" and *be honored* suggests that the apostles visualize the word as a runner who competes in the games and wins the prize, and so receives the honor that is due.[5]

We learn from Acts and the Pauline letters that in city after city Paul and his associates met with great opposition, and from the depth of these experiences Paul solicits this request for the Thessalonians' prayers. This message and its messengers had been dishonored by the tumult and riots that frequently ensued when it was proclaimed, as in the case of Thessalonica. On other occasions the gospel was simply rejected as so much foolishness (1 Cor. 1.23), or mocked as it was in Athens (Acts 17.32). In light of the dishonor the gospel received, Paul asks this church to pray that the gospel would *be honored, just as it was with you*, that is, by being received as the message of God. The Thessalonians were reminded of the exemplary manner in which they received the message as the word of God (1 Thess. 1.6, 9-10; 2.13). The optimism expressed in this petition does not arise out of the apostle's present experience of rejection and opposition but rather out of confidence in the power of God who sends his word running.

2 The second part of the petition is for the security of the apostolic team: *And pray that we may delivered from wicked and evil men*. In Romans 15.31 and 1 Corinthians 1.8-11 Paul solicited the same prayers from other congregations. By reading the catalogs of adversities that Paul and other Christian messengers endured we can well understand why this was a pressing concern (e.g., 2 Cor. 6.3-10; 11.23-26). The apostle previously

---

3. LXX, "He sends his word to the earth: his word will run swiftly *(tachous drameitai)*."

4. On the verb, see 1.10, 12; LSJ, 444; BAGD, 204; *TLNT*, 1.363.

5. Contra Marshall, *1 and 2 Thessalonians*, 213; Best, *The First and Second Epistles to the Thessalonians*, 324.

mentioned their sufferings in the first letter to this church (1 Thess. 1.6; 2.15-16), and the Thessalonians knew full well what type of sufferings they had endured in Philippi before coming to Thessalonica (1 Thess. 2.2). The petition expressed here echoes Isaiah 25.4 (LXX), which affirms that God is the one who rescues his people from danger.[6] The verb "may be delivered" (*rhyomai*) is used in many ancient texts, both Greek and Jewish, to describe the way a deity preserves someone from danger.[7] Paul and his companions recognize that God is the only hope in the face of such overwhelming opposition to their message and persons. The ones from whom they need divine protection are described as *wicked and evil men*. The first adjective, a term that is the antonym of "good" or "kind" (*chrestos*; Luke 23.4), depicts these characters as morally evil (*atopōn*).[8] The second adjective, *evil (ponērōn)*, is almost synonymous with the first as it labels them as "wicked" or "malevolent" (1 Thess. 5.22; 2 Thess. 3.3).[9] Both adjectives describe the evil aggression of these people and not simply some passive character flaw.[10] The messengers of the gospel experienced active antagonism against them from both their Jewish opponents (1 Thess. 2.14-16; 2 Cor. 11.26) and their Gentile persecutors (2 Cor. 11.26).[11]

The root of the opposition against Paul and fellow heralds is the rejection of their message, the gospel: *for not everyone has faith*. Faith may refer to the positive response to the preaching of the gospel (cf. 2.11-12, where the unconverted are described as those who "believe the lie" and "who have not believed the truth"), or it may be understood as the gospel itself, "the faith" (Rom. 1.5; Gal. 1.23; Jude 3). Since the apostle spoke extensively about the rejection and reception of the gospel in the previous context (2.10-15), the first interpretation suggested here is preferable. These people have not embraced the message of God in *faith*. This *faith* is something more than adherence to the doctrine they preached; it is understood as loyalty to the message and, in turn, to its messengers. For that reason they have come to oppose the messengers of the gospel who seek to spread the word abroad (cf. the Thessalonians' response in 2.13-15).[12] The presupposition underlying the observation that *not everyone has*

6. "You will deliver them from wicked men."
7. For example, Homer, *Iliad* 17.645; 15.290; Exod. 6.6; 14.30; 2 Sam. 12.7; 22.18, 44, 49.
8. LSJ, 272; BAGD, 120; MM, 90.
9. LSJ, 1447; Milligan, *St. Paul's Epistles to the Thessalonians*, 110.
10. Ibid.
11. Marshall, *1 and 2 Thessalonians*, 214, wrongly limits the reference to their Jewish opponents.
12. See Malina and Neyrey, *Portraits of Paul*, 167-68.

faith is that the response to the gospel determines the conduct of a person and that person's relationship to its messengers.

b. "But the Lord is faithful; he will strengthen you" — Confidence in the Lord (3.3-4)

3 Paul spoke to the Thessalonians briefly about his and his companions' needs as they carried out the Christian mission (v. 2); now he returns to the desperate situation of the Thessalonians. They were suffering persecution generated by their contemporaries (1 Thess. 2.14; 3.3-4; 2 Thess. 1.4-6), the prime mover behind the hostilities being Satan himself (1 Thess. 3.5; and see 2.18; 2 Thess. 2.9). Having mentioned the struggle the founders of the church faced at the hands of those who did not have "faith" (*pistis*) as they sought to spread the gospel (v. 2), Paul now reminds the Thessalonians of something they already know: *But the Lord is faithful* (*pistis*, which, as in the previous verse, embraces the idea of "loyalty"). In the first letter the founders of the church reminded the Thessalonians of the fidelity of God (1 Thess. 5.24; and 1 Cor. 1.9; 10.13; 2 Cor. 1.18; 2 Tim. 2.13; Heb. 10.23; 11.11; 1 John 1.9). But while that confession underscored God's faithfulness in completing his work in the lives of the believers, here his faithfulness is tied to the protection of the Thessalonians in the midst of their sufferings: *he will strengthen and protect you from the evil one*. In the ancient system of patronage, which defined many social relationships as well as religious and governmental institutions, the patron was expected to demonstrate fidelity toward his or her clients, which was understood, at least in part, as the patron's "protection" of the client. A person or even a nation could be under the protection (Gk. *pistis* or Lat. *fides*) of another.[13] In the present text, *the Lord* is viewed as the patron/protector in his faithfulness to the persecuted believers. As such, *he will strengthen* them, that is, he will establish them in the midst of their trials so that they do not fall (see 1 Thess. 3.2, 13; 2 Thess. 2.17 and comments; cf. Luke 22.32; Acts 18.23; Rom. 16.25; 1 Pet. 5.10; 2 Pet. 1.12; Rev. 3.2).

The promise the apostle extends is also that *the Lord* will *protect* them *from the evil one*, Satan (Matt. 13.19; John 17.15; Eph. 6.16; 1 John 2.12-13), words that echo the prayer Jesus taught the disciples (Matt. 6.13). Most likely this church had already learned to pray the same way.

---

13. Livy 8.1.10; 25.16.14; Polybius 3.15.5. See John Rich, "Patronage and Interstate Relations in the Roman Republic," in *Patronage in Ancient Society*, 123-32. See section 3.6-15 on the negative aspects of *clientela*. While Paul heartily affirmed benefaction (1 Thess. 4.9-10; 2 Thess. 3.13) and viewed God as the ultimate Benefactor, he was set against dependency as clients for those who were able to earn their own living (2 Thess. 3.6-15).

The verb translated *protect* could mean "watch over," as shepherds guard their sheep (Luke 2.8), or "keep under custody," as one would do a criminal (Luke 8.29; 11.21; Acts 12.4; 23.35; 28.16). Clearly the former sense is in mind here as God watches over his people to *protect* them (2 Tim. 1.12; 2 Pet. 2.5; Jude 24).[14] Although the church enjoys no social power, the believers are not without defense. God is with them, and so *the evil one* will in no way triumph over them. This promise is hardly meant to convey to the church that they will not suffer but rather affirms that in the midst of their sufferings their faithful Patron will strengthen them so that they will not fall. He will shield them from the ultimate shame of succumbing to the wiles of their adversary (cf. 1 Thess. 3.5 and comment).

4 Having expressed confidence in the way God will establish the Thessalonians in the midst of their persecutions (v. 2), the apostle also trusts in the Lord that the Thessalonians both are and will be obedient to the moral instruction passed on to them. Paul declares, *We have confidence in the Lord that you are doing and will continue to do the things we command.* The verb translated *we have confidence* means "to persuade," but in the perfect tense it communicates the idea of conviction and certainty that something is the case (*pepoithamen*; see Rom. 8.38; 15.14; 2 Cor. 2.3; Phil. 1.6, 25; Phlm. 21).[15] The root of this certainty about the good conduct of the Thessalonians is not the effectiveness of the missionaries nor the resolve of the Thessalonians but rather *the Lord* himself (as in Rom. 14.14; Gal. 5.10; Phil. 2.24; and cf. 1 Thess. 5.24). This church suffered hostility and persecution (1.4-7), faced false teaching (2.2), and some had even rejected the Christian teachers' exhortations about labor (3.6-16). However, in spite of these grave problems, the recognition of the divine work in their lives irresistibly persuaded the apostle of the Thessalonians' continuance in the practice of the Christian way of life. But this expression of confidence also serves a parenetic end. In ancient literature, those in authority at times used the verb "to have confidence" to express their confidence that their subjects would obey their decrees. One example of this is the declaration of Tiberius Julius Alexander, who states, "I am persuaded that in the future no one will any longer recruit farmers or tenants by force"[16] (cf. Gal. 5.10; Phlm. 21). The indicative of Paul's confidence in God is, at the same time, an imperative to the church.

This confidence is that the brothers and sisters of this church *are doing and will continue to do the things we command.* Previously, in the first letter, Paul commended the church for their fidelity to the moral instruction

---

14. LSJ, 1961; BAGD, 868.
15. BAGD, 639-40; *TLNT*, 3.66-79.
16. *BGU* 1563.37, cited in *TLNT*, 71. See also 76.

handed down to them (1 Thess. 4.1, 10; 5.11 and comments). In the literature of the era that touched on ethics, this type of praise served as a stim-
ulus to action and obedience.[17] The verb Paul uses to describe the moral
instruction means more than "to teach"; it conveys the strong imperatival
force "to command," as correctly reflected in the *NIV* (see 1 Thess. 4.11
and comments; cf. 4.2). The same verb permeates the following section
(3.6, 10, 12), and therefore this note of confidence also serves as a prelude
to the teaching on the necessity of working for one's food (3.6-15). Paul's
confidence in their obedience to the apostolic commands presented in the
letter (*we command*, present tense) has, it appears, two aspects. The first is
that most members of the church have not only obeyed (*are doing*) but
also will *continue to do* so (hence the *NIV* rendering of the future tense).
They are obeying the teaching they had already received about work. In
the first letter to the church, as well as during the initial oral instruction of
the new believers, the messengers outlined the Christian ethic about labor (1 Thess. 4.11-12; 5.14; 2 Thess. 3.10). The affirmation here indicates
that the majority of the members of the church heeded these commandments and obeyed them. The apostle praises them for their obedience
and expresses confidence that they *will continue to do* the same. But there
are also those who clearly had not obeyed (vv. 6-15) but who, being subject to the church's and the apostle's admonitions, "will do" what is being
commanded. Paul's *confidence in the Lord* is also for the moral progress of
some and moral change in others.

c. "May the Lord direct your hearts to the love of God" — The Second Prayer (3.5)

5 In v. 5 the author presents the second prayer in the form of a wish (cf.
2.16-17) before launching into his exhortation concerning work. The
prayer is, *May the Lord direct your hearts into God's love and Christ's perseverance.* The prayer asks that the *Lord* Jesus Christ (cf. 1.1-2, 7-8, 12; 2.1, 8, 14,
16) *direct* their *hearts* in the moral life, echoing a common Jewish expression (cf. 1 Chr. 29.18; 2 Chr. 12.14; 20.33; 30.19; Prov. 21.2; 23.19; Sir. 49.3;
and see Luke 1.79).[18] As in 2.17 and 1 Thessalonians 3.13, the *heart* is the
center of their lives; the *Lord* guides their hearts so that his purposes are
accomplished in them.

17. Cicero, *Epistulae ad Familiares* 6.10b.4; Seneca, *Epistulae Morales* 1.1; 25.4; 94.39.
Letters, as a form of epideictic rhetoric, were generally concerned with "praise" and
"blame." On the issue of praise and blame, note Aristotle, *Ars Rhetorica* 1358b and see
p. 70. This and the following section are wrapped in these dual themes.
18. In 1 Thess. 3.11 the petition is that God the Father and the Lord Jesus Christ
may "guide" the messengers again to the church. See comments.

The teacher defines the conduct he wants to see in the Thessalonians as *God's love and Christ's perseverance* (NRSV, "to the love of God and to the steadfastness of Christ"). The interpretation of these expressions is problematic. Is the "love of God" that which has God as its object (*May the Lord direct your hearts* to love God)?[19] Or is the idea rather that the *love* God demonstrates toward them becomes a model that they follow (*May the Lord direct your hearts* to love as God loves)?[20] When Paul speaks about the "love of God" in other letters, he always has in mind the love God demonstrates towards humanity or his people (Rom. 5.5; 8.39; 2 Cor. 13.13; and cf. 1 John 4.7, 9; Jude 21). Moreover, in these letters the author reminds the church of the way God has loved them (1 Thess. 1.4; 2 Thess. 2.13, 16). However, in the writings of other NT authors "the love of God" can mean "love toward God," while John uses the expression to communicate both ideas (Luke 11.42; John 5.42; 1 John 2.5; 3.17; 5.3). The same problem of interpretation presents itself in the following words, *Christ's perseverance*. Is the *perseverance* or "steadfastness" (*hypomonēn*; see 1 Thess. 1.3; 2 Thess. 1.4 and comments) that which they have as those who hope in Christ ("steadfastness hoping in Christ"; cf. 1 Thess. 1.3)?[21] Or is the thought that the *perseverance* or "steadfastness" that Christ demonstrated on the cross becomes an example for them to follow ("perseverance that Christ showed"; cf. Heb. 12.2-3; and see Rom. 15.4-5).[22] In light of the fact that these letters emphasize God's love for the Thessalonians and taking into account how Paul speaks of God's love for humans, the second interpretation of *God's love* is preferable (*May the Lord direct your hearts* to love as God loves). Although the second phrase is more difficult to understand, the grammatical parallel with the previous expression favors the interpretation that puts forth Christ as a model for their steadfastness ("perseverance that Christ showed"). The apostle's request is that the *Lord* direct the Thessalonians' moral life in such a way that they exhibit *love* and *perseverance* (1 Thess. 1.3; 2 Thess. 1.3-4) that imitate these virtues of God the Father, who loved them, and Jesus Christ, who was steadfast in his sufferings for them. "Act as God acts!" is the principal exhortation in Jewish and Christian ethics.

19. *Tēn agapēn tou theou*, objective genitive.
20. *Tēn agapēn tou theou*, subjective genitive.
21. *Tēn hypomonēn tou Christou*, objective genitive.
22. *Tēn hypomonēn tou Christou*, subjective genitive.

2. "Now we command you" —
The Problem of the Disorderly (3.6-15)

When Paul and his associates were in Thessalonica, they instructed the church in the basic contours of the Christian way of life, which included teaching on the Christian ethic of work (1 Thess. 4.11; 2 Thess. 3.10). They not only gave them the command that "If a man will not work, he shall not eat" but also instructed the believers by working with their own hands, thus leaving the church an example to follow (3.7-9). In spite of this moral instruction given by word and conduct, some members of the Thessalonian church ignored them. As a result, in the first letter Paul returned to this theme and reminded the church of the necessity of working "with your hands" and called on the believers to warn those who had not taken heed of the apostolic instruction (1 Thess. 4.11-12; 5.14).[23] But before writing the second letter, the apostle heard that the situation in Thessalonica had remained static. Some members of the congregation continued the practice of not working but depending instead on others for their daily bread (2 Thess. 3.11). Since the situation was not resolved, Paul sends an extensive and strongly worded teaching on the course of action the church should take to correct the conduct of the disorderly members of their community. But he also directly addresses those who were not working, admonishing them that they should work and eat their own bread, not that of others. Since this letter was read publicly before all (cf. 1 Thess. 5.27), we can only imagine the shame the disorderly must have experienced before their brothers and sisters.

The question naturally arises concerning why some members of the church refused to support themselves and depended on others. As we saw in the comments on 4.11-12, a number of authors attribute their behavior to the overblown eschatological expectation of the Thessalonians. Their view is that the Thessalonians believed the day of the Lord was upon them (2.2), and so they left off working as they waited expectantly for this great event. In the meantime, hunger ruled, and they were forced to depend on the resources of others. But in the present text and the others that deal with this problem, the eschatological expectation is not addressed, and Paul does not imply that this is the source of their rejection of labor. Although this and the previous letter are deeply concerned with eschatology, the author does not link this teaching with the problem of labor. In fact, the discussion on labor in 3.6-15 is not even juxtaposed with the eschatological concerns addressed previously. Alternately, it has been

---

23. On the order of the letters, a point that bears on the historical reconstruction of the problem, see the Introduction, pp. 64-69.

argued that some members of the congregation had adopted the apostolic privilege of not working but receiving their support from the church.[24] However, it is hard to understand how members of the Thessalonian church would have adopted this perspective since Paul and his associates worked with their hands during their stay in the city (3.8), despite the fact that they had received some support from the Philippian church (Phil. 4.16).

Another and more suitable explanation of the problem is to understand it against the backdrop of the institution of patronage that was pervasive in the ancient world.[25] Clients depended on their rich patrons, receiving benefits from them such as food, money, and representation, while the patrons enjoyed the public honor that accrued to their account for having so many clients. In this relationship the patron was under social obligation to continue the economic and social support of his or her clients. To cut a client off would place the patron in a relationship of enmity with the client.[26] Paul, on the other hand, taught Christians who were clients that they should not depend on their patrons for their support, whether or not the person was a Christian (1 Thess. 4.11-12), and he reminded Christian patrons that they were not under any obligation to continue their support of those in the congregation who simply did not want to change their status and work. At the same time, the apostles encouraged the patrons to continue to act as benefactors to those who were in true need (2 Thess. 3.13). In fact, God himself is a Patron, and as such a Protector, of his people, though this fact is never understood as license for not doing what was one's social duty, that being to work for one's own food.

24. See Jewett, *The Thessalonian Correspondence,* 104-5. On the history of interpretation of the passage, see Ronald Russell, "The Idle in 2 Thess. 3.6-12: An Eschatological or Social Problem," *NTS* 34 (1988) 105-7. Russell rejects the eschatological interpretation, which, on the other hand, is argued by Maarten J. J. Menken, "Paradise Regained or Lost? Eschatology and Disorderly Behavior in 2 Thessalonians," *NTS* 38 (1992) 271-89.

25. So Winter, *Seek the Welfare of the City,* 41-60; Wanamaker, *Commentary on 1 and 2 Thessalonians,* 282; and see Wallace-Hadrill, *Patronage in Ancient Society;* Saller, *Personal Patronage under the Early Empire.* A description of the institution, although idealized, is found in Dionysius of Halicarnassus, *Antiquitates Romanae* 2.9-11. Dionysius says, e.g., that the duty of the patron was "to secure for them both in private and in public affairs all the tranquility of which they particularly stood in need" (2.10.1). Patronage is a concern in many modern cultures as well. Little reflection has been undertaken to unpack the significance of the NT teaching on this matter and to bring it to bear on modern practices.

26. Winter, *Seek the Welfare of the City,* 47.

a. "Keep away from believers who are living in idleness" — The First Exhortation (to the Community) (3.6)

6 The apostle signals a change in theme by using the direct address "brothers and sisters" *(adelphoi)* at the head of the section: *In the name of the Lord Jesus Christ, we command you, brothers,* etc. The following instruction is not presented as a suggestion that the church may wish to follow but rather as a command *(parangellomen;* see 1 Thess. 4.11 and comments). The apostle leads up to this section by indicating his confidence that the Thessalonian believers would do all that he commanded (3.4), and he strengthens their sense of obligation by repeating the very same verb two more times in the following verses (3.10, 12). The verb *command* appears in those texts where a person in authority gives orders (as the Lord Jesus does in Matt. 10.5; Luke 8.29; 9.21; Acts 1.4; 10.42), and so it was employed frequently in military contexts (e.g., Jdt. 7.1; 1 Macc. 5.58; 2 Macc. 5.25; 13.10). At a number of points the apostle Paul uses the verb in his moral teaching (1 Cor. 7.10; 11.17; 1 Tim. 6.13-14), clearly indicating the importance of obedience as the proper response. In this verse, as in 1 Thessalonians 4.2 (also see 4.3, 6, 8), the authority behind the command is not the apostle's own but is rather derived: *in the name of the Lord Jesus Christ* (Acts 3.6; 16.18 [with *parangellō*]; 1 Cor. 1.10; 5.3-4; Phil. 2.10; and cf. 2 Thess. 1.12). In the first letter the apostle did not see the need to present the divine backing for this teaching (1 Thess. 4.11), but now the situation calls for the warrant to be invoked. The commands that follow are authoritative, and the apostle expects everyone in the community, both the "disorderly" and the rest, to obey.

The first command is directed to the whole church, instructing them how they should respond to the "disorderly": *keep away from every brother who is idle and does not live according to the teaching you received from us.* As in 1 Thessalonians 5.14, the problem is with those members of the church who "walk" or conduct themselves[27] in a disorderly manner *(ataktōs)* and not in accordance with the apostolic teaching on work. The term translated *idle* does not mean "lazy" but rather tags these people as those who conduct themselves in a way that is "out of order" or "disorderly" because they do not follow the rule of the community (vv. 7, 11).[28] In this

---

27. The participle *peripatountos* is from the same verb as that found in 1 Thess. 2.12; 4.1, 12; 2 Thess. 3.11. See comments.

28. See LSJ, 267, and the discussion of the term in the comments on 1 Thess. 5.14. The context determines what kind of disorderly conduct the author has in mind. In this case, the disorderly were not working; hence the *NIV* translation *idle*. However, the primary emphasis is not on their lazy character but rather their unwillingness to conform to the apostolic rule.

case the rule has to do with labor (v. 10). The end result of their disorderly conduct was that they did not work. The standard to which they refused to conform is *the teaching you received from us*. This *teaching* is the authoritative apostolic "tradition" *(paradosin)* that the founders had handed down to the church and to which the church was to adhere (2.15 and comments). In his commentary Menken argues that the "tradition" regarding work finds its roots in Genesis 3.17-19 (LXX) and various Jewish interpretations of the passage. *Targum*[29] *Pseudo-Jonathan* on Genesis 3.19, for example, says, "From the work of your hand you will eat food."[30] Menken makes a strong case that the apostolic teaching on labor is rooted in the Jewish interpretation of Genesis 3. Paul underscores that the "disorderly" themselves had received this tradition about labor (*NRSV*, "the tradition that *they* received from us"; see 1 Thess. 2.13; 4.1 and comments), but had paid no attention to it. (There is a textual variant in the Greek manuscripts at this point, and the reading "they received" has stronger support than the *NIV's you received*.)[31] This tradition was handed down to them not only by oral instruction and letter (3.10; 1 Thess. 4.11-12) but also by means of the heralds' example as they labored with their own hands while in the city (2 Thess. 3.7-9).

The apostle commands the church to *keep away* from any believer who does not obey this tradition. As we will see further on, the community should not consider this person to be an "enemy" or somehow outside the fold but should "warn him as a brother" (v. 15). These persons continue to be members of the family of faith, although they are subject to the correction and discipline of the community. They had already received the apostolic tradition on more than one occasion, and now in light of their continued disobedience more drastic measures need to be taken. The verb translated *to keep away from (stellesthai)*, which appears in the NT only in this verse and in 2 Corinthians 8.20, means "to stand aloof" or even "avoid." As an imperative the term would mean, "Be-gone!"[32] The composite verb based on the same root *(hypostellō)* conveys the same idea and is found in Galatians 2.12 and Hebrews 10.38. Social separation was the principal means the primitive church employed to correct those members who did not conform to Christian moral teaching

---

29. The targumim were Aramaic translations of the Hebrew Scriptures.

30. See Menken, *2 Thessalonians*, 130-33; idem, "Paradise Regained or Lost? Eschatology and Disorderly Behavior in 2 Thessalonians," 279.

31. *Paralabosan*, third person plural. Various manuscripts read *parelabon* (third person singular; א[2], D[2], Ψ), while others have the reading *paralabete* (second person plural; B, F, G). The reading *parelabosan* is preferable (א, A) due both to the textual support and the way this reading explains how the others arose.

32. BAGD, 766; MM, 587; LSJ, 1637.

(see Matt. 18.17; Rom. 16.17; 1 Cor. 5.9-13). In extreme cases, this separation meant excommunication of the member from the community of faith, but the apostle does not contemplate such drastic measures in this instance. In vv. 14-15 he advises the church on the limits of the discipline: "Take special note of him. Do not associate with him. . . . Yet do not regard him as an enemy, but warn him as a brother."

Although further on in this chapter Paul directs the correction to the disorderly themselves (v. 12), at the beginning he orients the church regarding the Christians' corporate responsibility to initiate disciplinary action to correct the behavior of errant members. The community itself was responsible for doing what was necessary to assure that the members lived in harmony with the apostolic tradition. This was not simply the obligation of the leadership but of the whole church. In a collectivist culture like this one, the control of an individual's conduct and the correction of those who departed from the norms were always taken up by the community. While personal responsibility was in no way minimized, there was also a keen sense that the group was in some way responsible to insure the good conduct of the individual. Such social control received support from the traditions of the community, and censure (blame) was employed to bring those who did not conform back in line. Such dishonor in an honor/shame culture was strong motivation to act as one should. If we also understand that in these cultures the identity of a person was bound up intimately with the group to which he or she belonged, the force of this social control becomes evident.[33] Moreover, these Christians lived as social pariahs in the city of Thessalonica and had come into the new Christian family, the church. Therefore, the separation of the disorderly believer from the new family would have been devastating. It is hard to imagine a more forceful way of bringing these people into harmony with the apostolic teaching. The censure of separation would cause them shame (v. 14), and was done with the hope of repentance. This discipline was redemptive at its heart and was not designed to destroy the person (v. 15).

b. "We were not idle when we were with you" — The Example of the Apostles (3.7-10)

7 In this and the following verses, Paul reminds the church of the example he and his companions gave them (vv. 7-9) and the teaching they delivered (v. 10) concerning the believers' responsibility to work for their food. At a number of other points in these letters, the author reminds the

---

33. See Malina and Neyrey, *Portraits of Paul*, 183-87.

church of what they already knew (see 1 Thess. 1.5; 2.1, 2, 5, 9, 10, 11; 3.3, 4; 4.2; 5.2; 2 Thess. 2.5, 6 and comments), a well-known practice in ancient instruction (see Dio Chrysostom 17.1-11). The apostle begins, therefore, by saying, *For you yourselves know how you ought to follow our example*. In his first letter to the church, Paul spoke about how this church had become imitators of the Lord, the churches in Judea, and the apostles themselves in their sufferings (1 Thess. 1.6; 2.14 and comments). Now he intimates that the church is obliged to imitate their conduct with regard to work (*dei*, "it is necessary," signals this obligation, as in 1 Thess. 4.1). Both the apostolic teaching and the example presented to the believers taught them how to conduct themselves, and so the example itself becomes authoritative (cf. 1 Cor. 4.16; 11.1; and see 2 Thess. 3.9). Teaching by the example of a person's life was well known in antiquity. Hierocles, for example, declared the value of imitation by stating, "we should imitate the man of intellect in those things we can" (*On Duties* 4.22.21), and Plutarch is of the same opinion, saying, "So, I think, we also shall be more eager to observe and imitate the better lives if we are not left without narratives of the blameworthy and the bad" (*Demetrius* 1.6). Seneca was even of the opinion that "the living voice and the intimacy of a common life will help you more than the written word. You must go to the scene of action, first, because men put more faith in their eyes than in their ears, and second, because the way is long if one follows patterns. Cleanthes could not have been the express image of Zeno if he had merely heard his lectures; he shared in his life, saw into his hidden purposes, and watched him to see whether he lived according to his own rules" (*Epistulae Morales* 6).[34] The Christian messengers worked with their own hands, giving these new believers something to see, and did not become clients of any of the Thessalonians during their stay in the city (v. 8). The members of the church should imitate what they saw.

The example they should imitate is defined more closely in the second part of the verse: *We were not idle when we were with you*. The word translated "to be idle" (*ētaktēsamen*) is the verbal form of the adverb "disorderly" in 3.6 and 11 and of the adjective "disorderly" in 1 Thessalonians 5.14. The word means "to be undisciplined" or "to live in a disorderly manner" and is used to describe those who do not fulfill their obligations.[35] In this case, the obligation had to do with working for one's own food. The heralds themselves had lived according to the "tradition" about labor (v. 6), and therefore their conduct was not "disorderly." There

---

34. Quotations taken from Malherbe, *Moral Exhortation*, 110, 138, 65.
35. LSJ, 267; *TLNT*, 1.223-26. See Xenophon, *Oeconomicus* 7.31; Lysias, *Against Alcibiades* 14.18; and the adjective in moral contexts in *T. Naph.* 2.9; Diodorus Siculus 1.8.1.

was complete harmony between what they taught (2.15) and what they did, and so Paul could say that their conduct was completely orderly, conforming to the Christian ethical tradition. Therefore, they could present themselves to the church as examples to follow.[36]

8 The apostle continues explaining how he and his companions did not live in a disorderly manner while in Thessalonica, saying, *nor did we eat anyone's food without paying for it*. In the first letter Paul declared that they were not motivated by avarice (1 Thess. 2.5) and that they were not a financial burden to anyone (1 Thess. 2.9). Paul did teach elsewhere that to receive financial support for Christian service was an acceptable practice, although he did not make use of this privilege (v. 9; 1 Cor. 9.7-14; Gal. 6.6; 1 Tim. 5.17-18; cf. Matt. 10.10). On the other hand, he raised his voice against those who engaged in ministry simply for financial gain (Acts 20.33; 1 Tim. 3.3, 8; Titus 1.7; and see 1 Tim. 6.9-10; Heb. 13.5; 1 Pet. 5.2; 2 Pet. 2.3). Here the apostle reminds the church that they paid for their own food or "bread," and nobody in the church supported them ("bread," *arton*, means *food*,[37] and "to eat bread" was a Semitic expression that simply meant "to eat," as in 1 Sam. 20.34; 28.20; 1 Kings 21.5; Pss. 41.9; 102.9). The messengers of the gospel managed to support themselves both by their own labors (v. 8b) and by means of the offerings sent to them by the Philippian church (Phil. 4.15-16). By these means they avoided eating anyone's bread *without paying for it*. This expression translates the adverb "freely" (*dōrean*; see Matt. 10.8; Rev. 21.6; 22.17), a term that appears in a number of contexts where the author wished to speak of the benevolence given by a benefactor.[38] In other words, the founders did not receive bread gifted to them as a client would receive bread from his or her benefactor or patron. The point is not that they did not pay for their keep but that they did not act as clients act, waiting for handouts.

Far from being dependent clients, Paul and his companions worked hard to sustain themselves, even in the midst of the Thessalonian mission: *On the contrary, we worked night and day, laboring and toiling so that we would not be a burden to any of you*. This affirmation is exactly the same as the one previously made in 1 Thessalonians 2.9, using the same vocabulary found in that verse (see comments). But unlike 1 Thessalonians 2.9 where the apostle reminds the church of their integrity as they labored and toiled so that they could preach without being a financial burden (unlike many of the itinerant philosophers of the day; see 1 Thess. 2.1-12),

---

36. The clause that begins with *hoti* ("*because* we were not disorderly when we were with you," v. 7b) presents the reason why the Thessalonians should follow their example (v. 7a).

37. BAGD, 110-11.

38. MM, 174.

here the point is rather that this conduct serves as an example for the believers to imitate (vv. 7a, 9). More than one factor motivated Paul and company to refrain from seeking to support themselves through the preaching of the gospel.

9 Having explained how they maintained themselves without becoming dependent clients of the Thessalonians, Paul now includes a parenthetical comment on their right to receive their support from the congregation and an explanation concerning why they did not make use of this right. The grammatical construction in the Greek is elliptical,[39] and so the translators of the *NIV* complete the sense by adding the words *We did this.* The preachers labored and did not receive benefits as clients *not because we do not have the right to such help, but in order to make ourselves a model for you to follow.* To *have the right* was an expression that frequently appeared in legal contexts and documents where someone wished to declare the legal rights that a person possessed.[40] Clearly the Thessalonians were under no legal obligation to maintain the apostolic band while they were in the city, but the legal use does underscore the level of obligation implied by the expression. Paul argues in 1 Corinthians 9.1-18 that the apostles did have the *right* to receive their support from the churches (1 Cor. 9.4, 6, 12), basing his argument on the common norms of labor and salary (1 Cor. 9.7), the Law (1 Cor. 9.9-10), the practice in the temple (1 Cor. 9.13), and the teaching of the Lord Jesus himself (1 Cor. 9.14). The Thessalonians may have understood these rights more in line with the demands of reciprocity intrinsic in the relationship between patrons and clients.[41]

In spite of the common practice of many philosophers to look for patrons to maintain them, there was a certain social reservation about such arrangements that served as a motivation to avoid *clientela*.[42] Paul argues that the Thessalonians should avoid it as well, and so he puts himself, Silvanus, and Timothy forward as examples that the members of the church should follow. He declares that they refrained from adopting client status *in order to make ourselves a model for you to follow.* A person or a group of persons could be a moral *model* for others to *follow* (see 1 Thess. 1.7 and comments), as the messengers were. In this way he reinforces the

---

39. The verse begins, *not because we do not have the right.*

40. MM, 225; BAGD, 277-78; *TDNT*, 2.562-74.

41. Bruce Winter, *Philo and Paul among the Sophists: A First-Century Jewish and a Christian Response* (Cambridge: Cambridge University Press, 1997), 172-74; Peter Marshall, *Enmity in Corinth*, 101-5, 165-77.

42. Avoiding *clientela* is a theme that appears in such diverse authors as Hesiod (*Opera et Dies* 352-69, 405-14, 453-57) and Jesus (Acts 20.35). See Paul Millett, "Patronage and Its Avoidance in Classical Athens," in *Patronage in Ancient Society*, 15-47.

teaching of vv. 7-8. In 1 Corinthians 9.1-18, Paul explains that he did not make himself a client of that congregation so as not to "hinder the gospel of Christ" (v. 12b), but the motivation presented to the Thessalonians is different. His and his companions' example becomes an imperative for the disorderly of the congregation.

10 The apostle not only reminds the Thessalonians of the example of how one ought to work (vv. 7-9), but he also returns to the teaching delivered to the church when the heralds were in the city: *For even when we were with you, we gave you this rule: "If a man will not work, he shall not eat."* In the first letter the apostle reminded the congregation of the teaching he had previously given about suffering (1 Thess. 3.4; cf. 4.1-2; 5.1-2), using the same vocabulary found in the first clause of this verse. In 2 Thessalonians he also reminds the church of the teaching they had already received (2.5, 15). The author makes no mention of the teaching about work that they had briefly included in the first letter (1 Thess. 4.11-12), reminding them rather of the oral instruction that, according to many Roman and Greek authors, was more potent than written communication.[43] As previously noted, this instruction came in the form of an authoritative command (3.4, 6, 12; and see 1 Thess. 4.11): "We gave you this command" (*NRSV; parēngellomen*). The verb is in the imperfect tense, which suggests that the teachers had given this command on various occasions during their rather short stay in Thessalonica. The disorderly who continued to hold on to their client status did so in the face of repeated commands to break off from patronal relationships. These people were disobedient, not simply ill informed or confused.

The command given over and again to the church was, *"If a man will not work, he shall not eat."* The necessity of working formed part of the ethical tradition of the church (cf. Eph. 4.28; 1 Thess. 4.11-12), finding its roots both in the OT (see Gen. 3.17-19; Ps. 128.2; Prov. 10.4; 12.11; 19.15) and in Jewish literature (e.g., *Gen. Rab.* 2.2, "If I do not work, I have nothing to eat").[44] The same idea appears in Greek literature (Phaedrus, *Fabulae* 4.25.17, "You don't work? For this reason you don't have anything when you need it")[45] as well as in later Christian instruction (*Did.*

---

43. See Seneca, *Epistulae Morales* 6, 33.5-9; Plutarch, *De Audiendo* 37F-38D; 2 John 13-14.

44. See SB, 3.641-42.

45. Cited in Menken, *2 Thessalonians*, 135. See *LAE*, 314, where Deissmann conjectures, "As a matter of fact, St. Paul was probably borrowing a bit of good old workshop morality, a maxim applied no doubt hundreds of times by industrious workmen as they forbade a lazy apprentice to sit down to dinner." Assembled parallels are found in J. J. Wettstein, *Novum Testamentum Graecum cum Lectionibus Variantibus et Commentario Pleniore Opera Jo. Jac. Wetstenii* (Amsterdam: Dommerian, 1752), 314.

12.1-5). The *Didache* says that if a traveler comes, the church may help him for a few days, "And if he wishes to settle among you and has a craft, let him work for his bread" (12.3). The church should reject anyone who is unwilling to work (12.4). Russell has argued that the root of the problem was the situation of the urban poor who could not find adequate work in the cities.[46] But the circumstance in this church was rather that the "idle" did not *want* to work (*ou thelei*, "Anyone *unwilling* to work should not eat," *NRSV*). The apostle reminds the congregation that they were not under any obligation to sustain such people, and even commanded them not to feed them. *He shall not eat (esthietō)* is a third person singular imperative in the Greek that embraces the responsibility of the church not to feed the person ("Let him not eat!"). With these words Paul liberates the patrons of their patronal responsibility, which, under normal circumstances, was considered to be a perpetual obligation if the client responded to the patron with thanks and honors.[47]

c. "Work quietly and earn your own living" — The Second Exhortation (to the Disorderly) (3.11-12)

11 For the first time in this section, Paul explains the exact nature of the problem that motivated him to prescribe disciplinary action against the disorderly (v. 6), although what is at issue is easily deduced from the foregoing argument. They introduce the theme, saying, *We hear that some among you are idle.* We do not know how the apostle was apprised of the fact that the church's problem with the disorderly had continued (cf. 1 Thess. 4.11-12; 5.14). Some messenger (Timothy?) had taken 1 Thessalonians to the church, and perhaps that person returned to Paul and reported that the disorderly had not taken heed to the teaching contained in the letter. Alternately, one of the Thessalonians who became a travel companion of Paul, such as Aristarchus or Secundus, may have brought information when he came from the city.[48] Whatever the source of the information, the apostle notes that *some*, not all, of the members of the church *are idle.* The expression is the same as that found in v. 6 and means that such people lived disorderly lives, not in accordance with the apostolic teaching regarding labor (see comments). The end result was that they did not work for their bread.

The following clause presents the exact nature of the disorderly

---

46. Russell, "The Idle in 2 Thess. 3.6-12," 112.
47. See Winter, *Seek the Welfare of the City*, 46.
48. These two men from Thessalonica traveled with Paul (Acts 19.29; 20.4; 27.2; Col. 4.10; Phlm. 24). See the Introduction, p. 7, and the comments on 1 Thess. 1.8.

conduct: *They are not busy; they are busybodies* (NRSV, "mere busybodies, not doing any work"). The problem of the disorderly was not simply that they did not *want* to work (v. 10) but that they *refused* to work (v. 11b). The NIV's translation *They are not busy*, while catching the play on words in the original (see below), somewhat obscures the sense of the Greek, which says simply that they were not working *(mēden ergazomenous)*. These people maintained their status as dependent clients of either richer members of the congregation (v. 13) or unconverted patrons. We do not know the exact reason why they opted to continue to live as clients. Manual labor was, as we have seen, despised by not a few, especially the social elite, but some philosophers and others considered such labor noble.[49] On the other hand, Juvenal discusses *clientela* and notes that certain people made themselves clients because of hunger and because they did not want to beg.[50] We can only say for sure that some of the Thessalonians decided to remain clients and were not forced into the situation against their will. Their decision and not their lack of options motivated them (v. 10). With a play on words, the author says that such persons "are not working" *(mēden ergazomenous)* but are rather busybodies *(periergazomenous)*. This second participle appears only here in the entire NT (although the noun form is found in Acts 19.19 and 1 Tim. 5.13) and means "to meddle" in that which is not one's concern.[51] The idea is not that these people had too much time on their hands and wasted other people's time, interrupting their work by their talking.[52] Neither is the thought that they get in among their neighbors, giving them unwanted advice, nor that they are causing disturbances in the popular assembly.[53] The problem is rather the involvement of the clients in public assembly where they supported the causes of their patrons, entangling themselves in issues that were properly none of their concern. At issue is their political participation in favor of their patron, as 1 Thessalonians 4.11-12 implies (see comments). These people should rather learn to be "quiet" and withdraw from such activity (see 3.12 and comments).[54]

12 Paul insisted that the first letter should be read publicly to all the members of the church (1 Thess. 5.27 and comments), and we may

---

49. See Malherbe, *Moral Exhortation*, 150-52, 98-99, and the comments here on 1 Thess. 1.8.

50. Juvenal, *Satires* 5.11.

51. Sir. 3.23; *T. Reub.* 3.10; Plato, *Apology* 19B; Demosthenes 10.72; 18.72; 26.15; 32.28; *New Docs*, 3.21, 26; MM, 505.

52. Contra Marshall, *1 and 2 Thessalonians*, 224-25.

53. Contra Russell, "The Idle in 2 Thess 3.6-12," 108.

54. See Epictetus 2.22.97; Demosthenes 10.72; Winter, *Seek the Welfare of the City*, 48-72.

suppose that the same was expected when this letter arrived in their hands. In the assembly the apostle speaks through the letter directly to the disorderly, saying, *Such people we command and urge in the Lord Jesus to settle down and earn the bread they eat.* The two verbs of exhortation *(command and urge)* have already appeared in the moral teaching of these letters *(command* in 1 Thess. 4.11; 2 Thess. 3.4, 6, 10; *urge* in 1 Thess. 4.1, 10; 5.14 and comments). The combination of the two underscores the authority behind the exhortation and the necessity of obedience.[55] Moreover, as noted in the comments on 1 Thessalonians 4.1, the formula that is employed to present the exhortation is modeled after official commands and so itself communicates the authority of what follows. The formula consists of the verb *urge* with another verb of exhortation *(command and urge)*, the identification of the persons to whom the command is addressed *(such people)*, a prepositional phrase *(in the Lord Jesus)*, and a command that begins with *hina (to settle down and earn the bread they eat)*.[56] Paul constructed the exhortation to the disorderly in the strongest terms possible. The authority behind the exhortation is that of *the Lord Jesus* (cf. 1 Thess. 4.1-2; 2 Thess. 3.6). To ignore this exhortation was not simply a rejection of apostolic authority but the authority of the *Lord* himself (cf. 1 Thess. 4.8).

The exhortation is that the disorderly *settle down and earn the bread they eat.* The vocabulary of this verse is almost identical to that in 1 Thessalonians 4.11, where the apostle exhorts certain Thessalonian believers to adopt a "quiet" life (here *meta hēsychias*) and "work with your hands." In ancient Greek literature, the "quiet" life was contrasted with life involved in public and meddlesome activity. In this context, as in 1 Thessalonians 4.11, it means that those who were in the position of clients should not take up the cause of their patrons in public assembly and so should not occupy themselves in political causes (see comments on that verse). Philo commented on this type of person who was meddlesome and did not lead a quiet life, saying, "Besides, the worthless man whose life is one long restlessness haunts market-places, theatres, law-courts, council-halls, assemblies, and every group and gathering of men; his tongue he lets loose for unmeasured, endless, indiscriminate talk, bringing chaos and confusion into everything, mixing true with false, fit with unfit, public with private, holy with profane, sensible with absurd, because he has not been trained to that silence *(hēsychian)* which in season is most excellent. They keep their ears open in meddlesome curiosity

---

55. Cf. 1 Thess. 4.1 and comments. In that verse, as here, two verbs of exhortation are combined.

56. See the comments on 1 Thess. 4.1 and Bjerkelund, *Parakalō,* 109-11, 188-90.

(*polypragmonos periergias*[57])."[58] Instead of living in this way, Christians should "work" (*ergazomenoi,* translated *settle down* in the *NIV*) with their hands (1 Thess. 4.11b) and so "eat their own bread," which they earn, not depending on others for their food.

d. "Do not be weary in doing what is right" — The Third Exhortation (to the Community) (3.13)

13 Paul turns from addressing the disorderly and speaks directly to the other members concerning what they are to do in the face of the disobedience of those who refused to abandon client status. The first exhortation is positive (v. 13), while the following verses outline the disciplinary measures the church is to take (vv. 14-15). The apostle exhorts, *And as for you, brothers, never tire of doing what is right.* The command *never tire (mē enkakēsēte)* does not mean simply that they should not become weary with *doing what is right* but rather that they should not give up or abandon their efforts (cf. Luke 18.1; 2 Cor. 4.1, 16; Gal. 6.9; Eph. 3.13).[59] Although the apostle had absolved the patrons of their responsibility to those who did not want to work (v. 10), this in no way implied that they should quit doing what was correct on behalf of those in genuine need. They should not give up on *doing what is right (kalopoiountes),* a composite verb that appears only here in the NT. It is not the term that would have been used if they wished to say that the Thessalonians should not cease doing works of benefaction (in which case the term would have been *agathapoiountes).*[60] Rather, the word suggests doing that which is correct or noble (the meaning of the uncompounded *kalos* or *to kalon poieō,* as in Phil. 4.14; 3 John 6; Gal. 6.9). In this context the correct or noble thing would be to help those who had true need by means of benefaction. Paul brings these two ideas together in Galatians 6.9-10 where in v. 9 he makes the same appeal as in the present verse: "Let us not become weary in doing good *(to de kalon poiountes mē enkakōmen).* . . . Let us do good to all people *(ergazōmetha to agathon)."*

---

57. Cf. 2 Thess. 3.11b, where the participle of the same verb appears (*periergazomenous).*

58. *De Abrahamo* 20-21; cf. *De Vita Mosis* 1.49.

59. See Polybius 4.19.10, who says, "The Lacedaemonians had *culpably omitted* (*enekakēsan)* to send the stipulated contingent of men." *TLNT,* 1.398-99; LSJ, 469; BAGD, 215.

60. See Milligan, *St. Paul's Epistles to the Thessalonians,* 116.

e. *"Take note of those who do not obey"* — *Discipline in the Community (3.14-15)*

14 The disorderly had rejected the teaching about labor that the Christian messengers had given them while in the city (v. 10) and had also not responded when the same instruction was repeated in the first letter (1 Thess. 4.11-12). They did not change their client status even when admonished by other members of the congregation (1 Thess. 5.14, assuming that the rest of the church heeded this instruction). Therefore, Paul now takes more drastic measures to insure their conformity, publicly giving the community further authoritative commands. He addresses the church first by saying, *If anyone does not obey our instruction in this letter, take special note of him.* The apostle expected that the believers would *obey* the moral teaching (v. 12; cf. Phil. 2.12; and 2 Cor. 7.15; Phlm. 21), here called *our instruction* (*tọ logọ hēmōn,* "our word," meaning "rule of conduct" or "command").[61] The rule given *in this letter* can be found in the previous verses (vv. 6-12). They should have obeyed the apostle's command since such teaching was the authoritative tradition he handed down to the church (vv. 6, 10). The written word in this letter therefore carries the same weight as the authoritative tradition (v. 6).

First, the church should *take note of him,* recognizing who the person was and taking special note of him.[62] Having identified and marked who the disorderly are, the next step that the church should take is: *Do not associate with him* (cf. 1 Cor. 5.9, 11). The command means that they should not mingle with such people. At times this verb appears in contexts where a group is exhorted not to associate with others so they will not be defiled morally or cultically.[63] But here the church is called to disassociate from the unrepentant brothers with a redemptive goal in mind (vv. 14b-15). These people continue to be considered members of the family of faith (v. 15) and not outside the pale of salvation. The discipline prescribed is not the same as excommunication (cf. the more drastic measures of Matt. 18.17; Rom. 16.17-19; 1 Cor. 5.9-11; Titus 3.10-11; 2 John 10-11). The concern that motivated this call to separation is not that the rest of the church will be infected by the behavior of the unruly, but that the

61. See Wanamaker, *Commentary on 1 and 2 Thessalonians,* 288-89. See Rom. 13.9; Gal. 5.14.

62. Depending on the context, the term could be used to imply disapproval (as in Polybius 5.78.2, where it means "to take note" of a sinister omen) or approval (as in Josephus, *Antiquitates* 11.208 [11.6.4], where people "take note" of a person who is worthy). See BAGD, 748; MM, 573; *TDNT,* 7.266.

63. Hos. 7.8; Exod. 20.18; *Ep. Arist.* 142; Philo, *De Vita Mosis* 1.278; *Did.* 15.3; cf. 1QS 8.21.26; and see Plutarch, *Philopoemen* 21.4; Josephus, *Antiquitates* 20.165 (20.8.5). BAGD, 784; *TDNT,* 7.852-55.

unruly will respond to the discipline. This separation implies that other members of the church should not meet with the disorderly; therefore they would be excluded even from the common meal of the assembly (1 Cor. 5.11; 11.17-34). Moreover, the members of the church are not to engage them socially, although the call to admonish them implies that they would not be cut off from all communication (v. 15).

They are to disassociate from the disorderly *in order that he may feel ashamed (entrapē;*[64] cf. 1 Cor. 4.14 and Titus 2.8). In a society oriented primarily toward the group rather than the individual and in which honor and shame were fundamental motivations for human action, the prescribed social separation that provoked shame would have been a powerful discipline. Honor in Mediterranean societies came from the group to which one belonged, and the loss of honor resulted in shame.[65] To be dishonored by the community was a strong moral condemnation. The censure of the body to which one belonged would have been one of the most effective ways to assure conformity to the standards of the group. Regarding the control of deviation from the norms of a collectivist society, Malina and Neyrey comment, "Onlookers control behavior with full force of custom, which grants honor (praise) or withholds it (blame)."[66] In the case of the Christians, separation from the group would throw the disorderly brother into a precarious social situation. He had already experienced rejection and dishonor from his contemporaries in the city (1 Thess. 2.14), and now he would not be in communion with the new society to which he belonged and in which he found his new identity as a member of the family of God. He would have lost his honor both in the society at large and within the new family. The resultant shame would be a forceful motivation to conform to the rule of the community (vv. 6, 10, and 12).

But there is an amazing redemptive approach in the apostle's teaching since socially dishonoring behavior was generally crushing and by no means redemptive. In his discussion on *hubris* Aristotle says, "Similarly, he who insults another also slights him; for insult consists in causing injury or annoyance whereby the sufferer is disgraced, not to obtain any other advantage for oneself besides the performance of the act, but for one's own pleasure; for retaliation is not insult, but punishment. The cause of the pleasure felt by those who insult is the idea that, in illtreating others, they are more fully showing superiority. That is why the

64. MM, 219; BAGD, 269; Xenophon, *Hellenica* 2.3.33; Polybius 2.49.7.
65. On the values of honor and shame, see J. G. Peristiani, ed., *Honor and Shame: The Values of Mediterranean Society* (Chicago: University of Chicago Press, 1966); Malina, *The New Testament World*, 28-62; deSilva, *Despising Shame*.
66. Malina and Neyrey, *Portraits of Paul*, 187.

young and the wealthy are given to insults; for they think that, in committing them, they are showing their superiority. Dishonor is characteristic of insult; and one who dishonors another slights him; for that which is worthless has no value, either as good or evil" (*Ars Rhetorica* 1378b). As the following verse shows, shame is calculated to bring positive change and not to condemn and provoke enmity. The one subject to shame is not considered worthless but rather "a brother" (v. 15).

15 In the world of the author and the readers of this letter, the announcement that one was no longer welcome in a house was normally accompanied with the declaration that the person had gone from the status of being a "friend" to being an *enemy* (a process that finds its highest expression in the *amicitiam renuntiare*, the renunciation of friendship, by which the emperor would express his discontent with one of his subjects). In fact, an *enemy* could be defined as a person separated from friendship. The word *enemy* is derived from the adjective that meant "hated"[67] (*echthros*), and such a person was viewed as someone hated and feared. In relationships characterized by enmity some form of hostile action was anticipated that would begin with breaking off social relations and culminate in attacks against "his honour, his property and his civic rights."[68] The apostle warns the church in Thessalonica not to express hostility toward the disorderly, attacking them because of their lack of conformity to the norms of the group. He exhorts, *Yet do not regard him as an enemy, but warn him as a brother.* Although the person is excluded from the community, some contact continues that gives the members of the church further opportunity to "admonish" him in the hope that such warnings will correct his conduct (see 1 Thess. 5.12, 14 and comments).[69] The person continues to be a member of the community of faith, or *a brother.* This designation, which appears repeatedly in these letters (see 1 Thess. 1.4 and comments), marks him out as one who is part of the Christian family. Paul is deeply concerned for the well-being of such people and for change in their behavior.

---

67. LSJ, 768; BAGD, 331; *TDNT,* 2.811-14; *NIDNTT,* 1.553-55.

68. Epstein, *Personal Enmity in Roman Politics 218-43 BC,* 76, and see 75, 2-4.

69. J. Moffatt, "2 Thessalonians iii.14, 15," *ExpTim* (1909-10) 328, refers to Marcus Aurelius (6.20), who says that if someone does not conduct himself properly in the gymnasium, "Still we do keep an eye on him, not indeed as an enemy, or from suspicion of him, but with good-humoured avoidance."

IV. "NOW MAY THE LORD OF PEACE HIMSELF GIVE YOU PEACE" — THE THIRD PRAYER AND FINAL GREETINGS (3.16-18)

A. "Now may the Lord of peace himself give you peace" — The First Benediction (3.16)

16 The closing of this letter begins in this verse with the blessing of peace that commonly serves as the heading of the Pauline letter closings.[1] The blessing starts with a prayer, *Now may the Lord of peace himself give you peace at all times and in every way.* Unlike the prayer in 1 Thessalonians 5.23, where the petition is addressed to "the God of peace" (see comments), here it is offered to Jesus Christ, who is *the Lord of peace.* And while the prayer of 1 Thessalonians 5.23 petitions God for the sanctification of the church, this appeal is that Jesus Christ *himself give you peace at all times and in every way.* The prayer echoes the blessing of peace in Numbers 6.26 (LXX) ("The LORD lift up his countenance upon you, and give you peace") but also finds its roots in Jesus' blessing of peace upon the disciples that is recorded in John 14.27 (assuming that Paul was familiar with this event in which Jesus said, "Peace I leave with you; my peace I give to you"). *Peace* is not an internal emotional state of tranquility but rather refers to a political or social reality. *Peace* could be the state of a nation that is not involved in war (cf. Acts 24.2; Rev. 6.4), but in the social sphere it consists of the absence of discord and conflicts between citizens. As such it was the key term used to describe public order or social concord.[2] Taking into account the hostility the Christians suffered at the hands of their compatriots, a principal concern of this and the previous letter (1.4-10; 1 Thess. 2.14), this prayer should be understood as a petition that the *Lord* would bring an end to this conflict. A number of commentators link the prayer for *peace* with the internal situation of the church, seeing it as a counterpoint to the discord between the disorderly and the other members of the church (3.6-15).[3] However, in the previous section the apostle does not indicate that the problem of the disorderly provoked serious division within the congregation. Moreover, the final blessing of peace stands as the closure to the entire letter and is not linked exclusively with the previous section. This all-encompassing prayer asks

---

1. So Weima, *Neglected Endings*, 187, 175, and comments on 1 Thess. 5.23-24.
2. Plato, *Leges* 1.628B; Isocrates, *Areopagiticus* 51 (7.51); Epictetus 3.13.13; 4.5.24, 25. See *TLNT*, 1.424-38; BAGD, 227.
3. For example, Marshall, *1 and 2 Thessalonians*, 230; Weima, *Neglected Endings*, 189; and cf. Wanamaker, *Commentary on 1 and 2 Thessalonians*.

that they be granted *peace at all times and in every way* (cf. Luke 24.53; Acts 2.25; 10.2; Rom. 11.10; Heb. 9.6; and Rom. 3.2; Phil. 1.18; 3 Macc. 7.8).[4] The grand nature of the prayer stands in contrast with the agonizing situation that assailed this church. In the face of a social reality that appeared out of control, the founder of the church raises his eyes to the only one who is able to intervene and give the believers *peace.* The ancients recognized that it was the role of the gods to establish *peace,*[5] but the apostle affirms that only Jesus Christ is truly *the Lord of peace.*

The prayer ends with a blessing, *The Lord be with all of you.* This blessing, which anticipates the final benediction of the letter (v. 18), reflects the consciousness that permeated the ancient church that *the Lord* was always with them (Matt. 28.20; Acts 18.10; 2 Tim. 4.22); for that reason Paul could pray and hope for his presence in every situation (Rom. 15.33; Phil. 4.9; 2 Tim. 4.22). In the midst of conflicts and confusion, Christians are never alone. The Lord is always "Emmanuel" — "God with us" (Matt. 1.23).

B. "I, Paul, write this greeting" —
The Apostolic Greeting and Guarantee (3.17)

17 Although Silvanus and Timothy contributed in some manner to the composition of this letter,[1] Paul was the principal author; for this reason he adds this final greeting: *I, Paul, write this greeting in my own hand, which is the distinguishing mark in all my letters. This is how I write.* Although ancient authors were known to write letters in their own hand,[2] it was common practice to engage the services of a secretary (amanuensis) who wrote the letter as it was dictated by the author.[3] In fact, some amanuenses learned a technique of taking dictation using a form of shorthand that allowed them to write as fast as someone could speak (Seneca, *Epistulae Morales* 90.26). In the same way, Christian authors such as Paul and Peter used amanuenses and at times included the secretary's name in the letter (Rom. 16.22; 1 Pet. 5.12). When authors made use of this services of an amanuensis, it was customary for them to include a greeting in their own

---

4. BAGD, 179 and 827.

5. Epictetus 3.13.12.

1. On the authorship of this and the previous letter, see the Introduction, pp. 54-64.

2. See, e.g., the comments of Cicero, *Ad Atticum* 7.3, 12.

3. The writing would have been done on wooden tablets that had an indentation filled with wax. Two or more of these tablets could held together with leather thongs. A stylus was used to write on the wax, and thus a letter could easily be corrected before the composition was transposed onto papyrus.

hand at the end of the letter (1 Cor. 16.21; Gal. 6.11; Col. 4.18; Phlm. 19). At times this greeting would be written without any indication that it was the author himself who added it by hand. A number of ancient letters that have survived include a final note in a hand other than that which wrote the body of the letter, with no indication that the author took the pen apart from the change in the handwriting.[4] This was the most common practice. The change was evident to anyone who read the letter. However, Paul frequently included a note about the change in his hand because his letters were read publicly in the assembly of the Christians.[5] Not everyone could see the greeting in his handwriting, but everyone could hear it.

Ancient authors included subscriptions in their own hands for a number of reasons. At times it served as a means to insure that the agreements and content of the letter were legally binding,[6] but in other cases the author included a note in his own hand to give the writing a personal touch. In other instances authors included it either to deal with a personal subject they did not want to dictate or to guarantee the authenticity of the correspondence.[7] In each case, the context indicates the author's purpose. In 2 Thessalonians, Paul included this subscription as his *distinguishing mark (sēmeion)*, which means that it served as a sign that "authenticates the letter."[8] The last words of the verse underscore this point: *This is how I write.* In light of the presence of letters falsely ascribed to Paul (2 Thess. 2.2 and comments), it became necessary to authenticate his genuine correspondence in this way in order to help keep the new congregations from being seduced by false doctrine. Much more than being a personal note, the subscript was a weapon in the war against heresy.

C. "The grace of our Lord Jesus Christ be with you all" — The Final Benediction (3.18)

18 The second letter to the Thessalonians ends almost identically to the first with the blessing of grace: *The grace of the Lord Jesus Christ be with you all* (see 1 Thess. 5.28 and comments). Unlike the benediction in 1 Thessalonians, this one is pronounced over *you all*, perhaps taking up again the theme of 3.15 concerning the way the church should respond to the disor-

4. See the examples in *LAE*, 170-73, 179-80; Weima, *Neglected Endings*, 119; Stowers, *Letter Writing in Greco-Roman Antiquity*, 60-61.

5. Ibid.

6. Gordon J. Bahr, "The Subscriptions in the Pauline Letters," *JBL* 87 (1968) 31.

7. Weima, *Neglected Endings*, 47-50, 118-35.

8. *TLNT*, 3.251; *TDNT*, 2.259.

derly. They are still brothers, and for that reason the blessing is pronounced over all members of the church. By means of this grace the church can continue in the faith the apostles handed down to them and can remain firm in the face of so much opposition against their allegiance to *our Lord Jesus Christ. Grace* was the summary of everything they needed (1.2). In the midst of their sufferings and in their struggle against false teaching, they could not get by without God's *grace.* In matters of morality and community, divine *grace* was needed. For any Christian, at any time in history and in any place, *the grace of our Lord Jesus Christ* brings the full blessings of salvation day by day. *Grace* brought them and us safe thus far. *Grace* will lead us home.

The grace of the Lord Jesus Christ be with you all.

Index of Modern Authors

Ackroyd, P. R., 149
Alcock, S. E., 206
Aune, D. E., 73, 82
Aus, R. D., 279, 286

Badian, E., 39
Baer, D. A., 298
Bahr, G. J., 359
Bailey, J. A., 60, 61, 63
Balch, D. L., 185, 203
Bammel, E., 149, 161
Barclay, J. M. G., 302
Barr, J., 231
Bassler, J. M., 284
Bauer, W., 296
Baur, F. C., 55
Beauvery, R., 196
Beekman, J., 103
Bell, A. A., Jr., 189
Benjamin, A., 40
Best, E., 83, 85, 92, 93, 96, 101, 108, 157,
    158, 162, 163, 166, 169, 206, 209, 210,
    214, 221, 223, 240, 271, 281, 316, 330,
    331, 335
Beutler, J., 70
Bjerkelund, C. J., 183, 352
Boers, H., 74
Braund, D., 249
Bruce, F. F., 64, 82, 85, 96, 101, 121, 140,
    149, 156, 157, 189, 192, 209, 271, 305,
    330
Buck, C., 64

Burton, Ernest De Witt, 126
Butcher, K., 38

Calderone, S., 89
Callow, J., 103
Carrington, P., 185
Casson, L., 158
Cavanagh, W. G., 10
Chow, J. K., 26, 29, 211
Clark, A. D., 248, 310
Collart, P., 4
Collins, R. F., 70, 143, 316
Cormack, J. M. R., 23, 253
Cosby, M. R., 224, 227
Crawford, C., 127
Cullmann, O., 231
Cuntz, O., 4
Cuss, D., 312

Danker, F. W., 41, 207
de Gruyter, W., 318
Deissmann, A., 82, 137, 157, 219, 236,
    299, 349
De Jonge, M., 148
Dell, H. J., 10, 39
deSilva, D. A., 194, 355
Donfried, K. P., 21, 32, 36, 45, 70, 71,
    143, 264
Doty, W. G., 57, 73, 74
Drummond, A., 27
Dunn, J. D. G., 263, 303

Edgar, C. C., 57, 81
Edson, C., 4, 10, 16, 32, 37, 38, 43, 44, 45, 48
Eisenstadt, S. N., 26
Elgvin, T., 192
Ellingworth, P., 105, 220
Ellis, E. E., 159
Epstein, D. F., 256, 356

Fee, G., 93, 95, 96, 193, 303, 304
Ferguson, E., 23, 24, 35, 37, 38, 42, 213, 218, 241, 259, 311
Finley, M. I., 207
Finn, T. M., 32
Fisher, N. R. E., 116
Fishwick, D., 312
Fitzmyer, J. A., 86
Foakes-Jackson, F. J., 31
Forbes, C., 262
Fowl, S., 127
Frame, J. E., 56, 59, 94, 111, 119, 140, 147, 209, 289, 316, 330
Fredricksmeyer, E. A., 39
Fulford, H. W., 318
Furnish, V. P., 159, 237-38

Garnsey, P., 29
Gaventa, B. R., 107, 127
Gelzer, M., 211
Giblin, C. H., 303, 304, 306, 307, 312, 316, 318
Gillespie, T. W., 262
Gilliard, F. D., 143
Gilmore, D. D., 194
Gold, B. K., 26
Gow, A. S. F., 1, 3, 9, 20, 30, 33, 34, 35, 36, 37, 40, 43, 188, 189, 219
Green, G. L., 66, 262, 284
Grudem, W., 262
Gruen, E. S., 15, 16, 89
Gundry, R. H., 269, 301

Hafemann, S. J., 281
Hagner, D. A., 129, 269
Hammond, N. G. L., 2, 3, 4, 5, 6, 10, 48
Hanson, A. T., 110
Harrison, R. K., 37
Hawthorne, G. F., 41
Helliesen, J. M., 15
Helly, B., 21

Hemberg, B., 36, 43, 45
Hemer, C. J., 29, 48, 82, 83, 157
Hendrix, H. L., 16, 17, 18, 21, 36, 37, 38, 39, 40, 41, 42, 43, 44, 313
Hengel, M., 82
Herman, G., 26, 207
Hill, D., 262
Hock, R. F., 30, 130, 131, 210, 211
Hoffmann, E., 218
Holland, G. H., 70, 71
Hollander, H. W., 148
Horbury, W., 118, 161
Horsley, R. A., 94, 312
Hughes, F. W., 70, 71
Hunt, A. H., 57, 81

Isaac, B., 240

James, M. R., 308
Jensen, J., 190
Jeremias, J., 222
Jewett, R., 26, 30, 62, 64, 70, 71, 92, 143, 149, 163, 175, 253, 269, 294, 304
Johanson, B. C., 70, 204
Jones, A. H. M., 23, 38
Judge, E. A., 22, 50

Keener, C. S., 271
Kemmler, D. W., 95
Kennedy, G. A., 69
Kinman, B., 223, 224
Knox, A. D., 161
Koester, H., 204, 318
Kortē-Kontē, S., 35, 43
Koukouli-Chrysanthaki, C., 22

Ladd, G. E., 129, 269, 301
Lake, K., 31
Lattimore, R., 217
Levinskaya, I., 31, 32, 48, 49
Lightfoot, J. B., 55, 93, 140, 142, 157
Litfin, A. D., 69, 324
Loubser, J. A., 58
Lund, N. W., 103
Lünemann, G., 56, 94, 101

Makaronas, C. I., 5
Malherbe, A., 72, 73, 74, 81, 98, 112, 113, 114, 115, 116, 118, 119, 124, 127,

129, 130, 135, 151, 168, 185, 195, 205, 212, 213, 216, 230, 248, 255, 346, 351
Malina, B. J., 89, 93, 177, 190, 328, 330, 336, 345, 355
Manson, T. W., 64, 189
Marshall, I. H., 60, 63, 70, 71, 92, 96, 108, 109, 110, 132, 142, 148, 157, 159, 166, 173, 176, 200, 206, 209, 210, 214, 223, 231, 247, 267, 281, 289, 290, 292, 313, 315, 323, 330, 335, 336, 351, 357
Marshall, P., 116, 348
McNeil, B., 161
Meeks, W., 93, 142, 203, 207, 295
Menken, M. J. J., 330, 342, 344, 349
Mercati, G., 161
Metzger, B. M., 126, 181, 271, 272, 278, 326
Meyer, M. W., 318
Miller, K., 4
Millett, P., 122, 348
Milligan, G., 54, 56, 93, 101, 104, 119, 120, 121, 133, 134, 140, 142, 152, 155, 172, 173, 180, 223, 265, 288, 297, 299, 323, 324, 336, 353
Mitchell, M. M., 233
Moffatt, J., 356
Moore, G. F., 302
Morris, I., 207
Morris, L., 94, 104, 119, 130, 152, 157, 161, 214, 315
Mott, S. C., 41
Moule, C. F. D., 221
Moulton, J. H., 124
Munck, J., 106
Murphy-O'Connor, J., 32, 82
Mylonas, G. E., 5

Nestle, E., 161
Neyrey, J. H., 89, 93, 177, 194, 328, 330, 336, 345, 355
Nida, E. A., 105, 220
Nigdelis, P. M., 47
Nilsson, M. P., 36
Nock, A. D., 43, 48, 107, 218
Nygren, A., 92

O'Brien, P., 86, 140, 175, 279, 299, 325
O'Sullivan, F., 4, 5
Okeke, G. E., 143, 148
Oliver, J. H., 22

Orchard, J. B., 148
Osiek, C., 203
Otto, W. F., 36
Overman, J. A., 32

Page, D. L., 1, 3, 9, 20, 30, 33, 34, 35, 36, 37, 40, 43, 188, 189, 219
Papazoglou, F., 15, 17, 19, 20, 24, 25, 26, 37, 38, 40
Parry, R. St. John, 161
Pearson, B. A., 143
Peristiani, J. G., 355
Peterson, E., 227
Pfitzner, V. C., 117
Pleket, H. W., 318
Plevnik, J., 215
Porter, S. E., 240, 261, 300, 305
Purvis, J. D., 47

Raditsa, L. F., 196
Raubitschek, A. E., 40
Reiter, R. R., 301
Resch, A., 222
Reynolds, J., 32
Rich, J., 10, 89, 207, 337
Richard, E. J., 214
Richards, E. R., 57
Richards, K. H., 42
Ridderbos, H., 238
Rigaux, B., 54, 56, 59, 60
Romiopolou, C., 4
Roniger, L., 26
Rousselle, A., 189
Rowley, H. H., 92
Russell, D. A., 105
Russell, R., 342, 350, 351
Ryle, H. E., 308
Ryrie, C. C., 314

Sakellariou, M. B., 1, 15
Saller, R. P., 26, 27, 207, 342
Sanders, J. T., 74
Savage, T. B., 281
Schaefer, P., 146
Scherrer, S. J., 42, 321-22
Schippers, R., 148
Schlier, H., 93
Schlueter, C. J., 143
Schmidt, D. D., 143
Schmidt, J. E. C., 60

Schmithals, W., 111, 112, 200, 214
Schrader, K., 55
Schubert, P., 74, 86
Schuler, C., 21, 22, 25
Schürer, E., 302
Scott, J. M., 143, 302
Selwyn, E. G., 186, 190, 246, 247
Sevenster, J. N., 146
Sherk, R. K., 41, 233
Sherwin-White, A. N., 51
Sivignon, M., 1
Spencer, A. B., 58
Spicq, C., 92, 96
Still, T. D., 283
Stowers, K. S., 73, 82, 151, 168, 174, 185, 216, 359
Stroker, W. D., 222

Tannenbaum, R., 32
Tasker, R. V. G., 110
Taylor, G., 64
Theissen, G., 178
Thurston, R. W., 64
Touratsoglou, I., 38
Treggiari, S., 188, 189, 196
Trilling, W., 60, 61, 62, 63
Turner, N., 124, 300

Vacalopoulos, A. E., 7, 10, 22, 24, 36, 37, 38, 45
van Unnik, W. C., 90, 257
Veloso, M., 269
Veyne, P., 128, 134
Vickers, M., 10, 40
Vokotopoulou, J., 40

von Dobschütz, E., 305

Wainwright, A., 157
Walbank, F. W., 6
Wallace-Hadrill, A., 10, 26, 27, 29, 89, 122, 207, 249, 342
Walton, S., 70
Wanamaker, C. A., 53, 54, 62, 64, 65, 66, 68, 70, 71, 83, 92, 94, 101, 104, 123, 132, 133, 136, 140, 149, 156, 157, 163, 169, 178, 192, 200, 204, 206, 207, 211, 214, 223, 229, 230, 235, 240, 242, 271, 277, 281, 284, 290, 298, 308, 313, 316, 319, 330, 331, 333, 342, 354, 357
Weatherly, J. A., 143
Weima, J. A. D., 266, 267, 268, 270, 272, 357, 359
Weiss, J., 64
West, J. C., 64
Wettstein, J. J., 349
White, J. L., 66, 72, 73, 74, 81, 268
Wikenhauser, A., 60
Wilcox, M., 31
Wiles, G. P., 175, 176
Winter, B. W., 29, 41, 69, 105, 113, 114, 124, 207, 209, 210, 211, 310, 311, 342, 348, 350, 351
Wistrand, E., 223
Witherup, R. D., 107
Witt, R. E., 36, 37, 44, 45, 48, 93
Witton, J., 192
Woolf, G., 29
Wrede, W., 60

Yarbrough, O. L., 189, 192, 193

Index of Subjects

Alexander (III) the Great, 8-12, 18, 24, 39, 102, 139
Andriscus, 14-17
Antipater of Thessalonica, 1, 3, 9, 20, 33-36, 188, 219
Aristarchus, 7-8, 29, 102, 350
athletic imagery, 117, 154, 165, 335
Augustus (Octavian), 18-19, 24, 28, 39-41, 48, 50, 94, 196, 233, 310, 312, 320
authorship: of 1 Thessalonians, 54-59; of 2 Thessalonians, 59-64

Barnabas, 83

Caesar, Julius, 18, 20-22, 39-40, 171-72, 233, 310, 312
Cassander (king of Macedonia), 2, 10, 45
chronological order of 1-2 Thessalonians, 64-69
client/patron relationship. *See* patron/client relationship
Cynic philosophers, 112-16, 124

"day of the Lord." *See* second coming of Christ
death, as a church concern, 47, 68, 73, 108, 213-29, 244-45, 253, 306

flattery, 121-22

greed, 122-23

honor, as sociocultural value, 163, 194, 208, 256, 328, 345, 355

idolatry, 31-33, 36, 47, 49, 102, 104-8, 140, 144, 195, 292-94

Jason, 7-8, 20-21, 29, 50-51, 102, 131, 153, 249
Jews: community of, in Macedonia, 31, 46-49, 108; opposing the gospel, 49-50, 111, 138, 142-50, 153, 290, 307, 336; suffering under Romans, 149, 308
Judas, 58, 83
judgment: final, 54, 110-11, 147-49, 155, 179-80, 197, 230, 232-35, 246, 289-96, 306, 319-20, 323-25; for sin, 197-98, 284-87

kiss, holy, 270-71

Luke, 1, 5, 48

Macedonia, Roman rule of, 12-29
"man of lawlessness," 32, 42, 53, 306-13, 314-17, 319-22, 324
marriage: and contemporary customs, 187-89; Paul's teaching on, 190-93
military imagery, 152, 225, 240-42, 332

patron/client relationship: Paul's teaching on, 28-31, 131, 208-12, 334, 347-

53; as social institution, 26-29, 89, 208-12, 249, 315, 337, 342, 348

Paul: as author of 1 Thessalonians, 52-59, 67, 82-83, 152; as author of 2 Thessalonians, 52-53, 59-64, 67, 358-59; boasting about the Thessalonians, 154-56, 241, 281-82; and opposition, 20, 50-51, 112, 115-16, 145, 149-50, 168-70, 335-36; as parental figure, 126-29, 133-35, 150; travels of, 1, 3, 5, 6, 7, 46, 47-48, 84, 102, 152, 157, 166, 174

Perseus (king of Macedonia), 11-15, 44, 48, 102

Philip II (king of Macedonia), 2, 3, 8-10, 12, 39, 48

Philip V (king of Macedonia), 10, 11

Philip of Thessalonica, 29, 30, 33, 35, 36, 40, 219

prayer: as component of ancient letters, 73-74, 86; Paul's requests for, 54, 270, 334-35; Paul's teaching on, 238, 257-60, 277, 337; for the Thessalonians (in 1 Thess.), 52-53, 86-88, 91, 152, 155, 168, 173-81, 252, 266-69; for the Thessalonians (in 2 Thess.), 279, 280, 296-300, 330-33, 339-40, 357-58

prophecy: false, 263-65, 306, 316, 324; given to Thessalonians, 162-64, 198; Old Testament, 9, 108, 144, 147-48, 231, 294, 298, 310-11; Paul's teaching on, 52, 203, 205, 247, 252, 260-66, 302-4, 330

resurrection: of Christ, 109-10, 126, 213, 216, 219-21, 229; of the dead, 110, 213-29, 244-45, 288, 301, 305

revenge, warnings against, 66, 255-57, 287

Satan, 51, 58, 91, 151-53, 156, 164-65, 173-74, 283, 306, 309, 314-18, 321, 323, 337

second coming of Christ, 47, 52-53, 56, 63, 91, 108-9, 154-55, 180-82, 209, 213-36, 238, 244-46, 256, 288-89, 294-95, 301-7, 313, 320, 341

Secundus, 7-8, 102, 350

sexual purity: contemporary practice, 187-89, 194-96; Paul's teaching on, 36, 52-53, 118-19, 158, 175, 182, 187, 189-202

Silas (Silvanus): background of, 83; and composition of 1 Thessalonians, 54-59, 152; and composition of 2 Thessalonians, 59, 358; and opposition, 48-51, 115-16; as prophet, 48, 162, 221; travels of, 1, 5, 47-48, 51, 130, 157, 166

thanksgiving: exhortation to, 259-60; as part of a standard letter, 73; for Thessalonian church (in 1 Thess.), 52, 86-88, 91, 111, 138-39, 166, 168, 171-73; for Thessalonian church (in 2 Thess.), 61, 278-80, 296, 300, 325-26

Thessalonians: church leaders of, 247-51; persecution of, 42, 51, 53, 61-66, 68-69, 82, 88-91, 98-100, 109-12, 138, 141-45, 148, 156, 160-65, 168-70, 209, 211, 213, 222, 229, 232-34, 255, 280-85, 307, 329-38; role of, in spreading the gospel, 8, 101-5, 208

Thessalonica: as metropolitan center, 8, 10, 20-21, 32, 100-102, 207-8; physical description of, 1-6, 25

Timothy: background of, 83-84; and composition of 1 Thessalonians, 54-59, 152; and composition of 2 Thessalonians, 59, 358; report of, about the Thessalonians, 52, 82, 88-89, 112, 165-77, 182, 187, 202, 241, 282; sent to Thessalonica by Paul, 65-66, 136, 151-52, 156-64, 179, 213, 247, 282, 332-33, 350; other travels, 1, 5, 7, 47, 51-52, 84, 157, 166

vengeance, divine, 148, 197, 287, 289-94

Via Egnatia, 2-7, 16, 25, 44, 46, 48, 50, 51, 100, 102, 115, 233

work, as a church concern, 28-31, 54, 67-68, 89-90, 206-13, 253, 339, 341-53

Index of Scripture References

OLD TESTAMENT

Genesis
1.28	213
2.7	129
3	344
3.17-19	349
3.17-19 (LXX)	344
6.11-13	147
14.18	47
14.18 (LXX)	47
15.16	147
18.25	286
31.50	123
37.35	169
46.4	149
47.30	217

Exodus
2.11	93
3.2-3	289
6.6	336
10.2	135
14.4	295
14.17	295
14.18	295
14.30	336
20.18	354
21.23-25	255
23.19	326
23.22	309
23.33	108

34.10	295

Leviticus
19.2	189
19.18	205
21.7-8	181
24.19	255

Numbers
6.26 (LXX)	357
11.26-29	262
15.17-21	326
16.5	181
16.7	181
16.46	293
23.27	145
26.54	177

Deuteronomy
4.9	135
4.37	92
5.26	108
6.4-5	269
6.7	135
7.7-8	92
9.10 (LXX)	84
9.13	152
10.15	92
11.19	135
12.6	326
12.17	326
15.2	204

17.6	123
18.6 (LXX)	84
19.15	123, 132
19.21	255
26.18	326
28.64	108
30.2 (LXX)	107
31.16	217
31.30 (LXX)	84
32.8	47
32.8 (LXX)	47
32.22	289
32.35	197, 286, 290
32.46	135
33.2	181

Joshua
3.10	108
8.24	149
22.22	307

Judges
4.22 (LXX)	227
5.5	293
9.23	200
10.13	108
11.10	123
16.13	295
20.2 (LXX)	84

Ruth
4.10	192

1 Samuel

6.12	176
7.3 (LXX)	107
8.7	200, 262
8.8	108
9.14 (LXX)	227
12.5	123
13.10 (LXX)	227
16.7	121, 151
17.36	108
17.39	152
20.34	347
20.42	123
21.5	192
25.20 (LXX)	227
25.32 (LXX)	227
25.34 (LXX)	227
28.20	347

2 Samuel

12.7	336
14.7	261
19.15 (LXX)	227
19.16 (LXX)	227
19.20 (LXX)	227
19.24-25 (LXX)	227
22.18	336
22.44	336
22.49	336
24.1	324

1 Kings

2.10	217
3.10	145
8.14 (LXX)	84
8.31-32	286
8.33 (LXX)	107
11.43	217
17.1	108
19.10	144
19.14	144
21.5	347

2 Kings

1.1	200
4.26 (LXX)	227
5.21 (LXX)	227
8.8-9 (LXX)	227
18.7	200
19.4	108

20.3	137

1 Chronicles

5.25	200
21.1	165, 324
28.9	121, 149
29.11	138
29.18	339

2 Chronicles

6.22-23	286
6.26	107
12.12	149
12.14	339
15.2 (LXX)	227
15.3	108
19.2 (LXX)	227
20.33	339
23.15	288
28.9 (LXX)	227
29.19	307
30.19	339
31.5	177
33.19	307

Ezra

7.32	217

Nehemiah

9.26	144
10.34	231
13.20	152
13.31	231

Esther

1.4	138
3.13 (LXX)	126
8.11	309
9.2	309

Job

1.1	265
1.1 (LXX)	265
1.8	265
2.9	109
3.21	128
5.1	181
7.2	109
15.15	181
15.24	169

16.19	123
18.5	261

Psalms

5.8	176
7.8-9 (7.9-10)	286
7.9	121
7.11 (7.12)	286
9.4 (9.5)	286
9.8 (9.9)	286
9.18	149
11.4 (10.4)	312
12.3	154
18.5	104
19.9 (18.9)	284
25.5	205
32.6 (LXX)	319
34.2	154
34.16 (33.17)	293
35.24 (34.24)	286
36.10 (35.11)	291
41.9	347
42.2	108
42.8	173
44.8	154
47.4	92
49.6	154
52.1	154
52.1 (51.3)	281
63.6	173
68.35 (67.36)	295
69.31	145
71.17	205
71.21	177
74.4	154
74.4 (73.4)	281
74.20	235
77.2	173
77.8	149
78.68	92
79.6	195
79.6 (78.6)	290, 291
80.12-13 (81.12-13)	324
82.5	235
88.5 (LXX)	244
89.5	181
89.7	181
89.7 (88.8)	294, 295
89.22 (88.23)	308
94.1	197

94.3	154	**Ecclesiastes**		43.17		217
96.13 (95.13)	293	3.1	231	45.16		309
97.7 (96.7)	281	10.16	239	48.12		327
102.9	347	11.9	137	48.15		327
106.47 (105.47)	281, 302			49.4		165
111.8	160	**Isaiah**		49.6		147
112.4	235	1.2	200	51.2		327
116.12	171	1.10	221	52.7		95
118.5	176	2.3	205	52.12		302
119.137 (118.137)	284	2.5	235	53.1		140
119.143	169	2.8-9	293	54.13		205
119.157	145	2.10	293	57.3-4		308
128.2	349	2.10 (LXX)	292	59.11		109
137.8 (136.8)	286	2.11 (LXX)	294	59.17	240, 241
139.23	121	2.11-12	293	61.1-2		95
143.10	205	2.17	293	63.9 (LXX)		224
145.11-12	138	2.17 (LXX)	294	65.16		108
147.2 (146.2)	302	2.17-18	293	65.23		165
147.15 (147.4)	335	2.19 (LXX)	292	66	286, 289, 309
147.16-18 (147.5-7)	335	2.19-21	293	66 (LXX)		298
		2.21 (LXX)	292	66.4	286, 290
		5.11	239	66.4 (LXX)		291
Proverbs		5.20	235	66.5		286
4.18-19	235	6.10 (LXX)	107	66.5 (LXX)		298
4.26-27	176	11.4	320	66.6	286, 309
5.15-18	192	11.4 (LXX)	319	66.14		289
6.22	137	13.6	232	66.15	286, 289
8.20	137	13.8	234	66.15-16		289
9.15	176	13.19	138	66.24		289
10.4	349	14.8	217			
10.7	261	21.2 (LXX)	200	**Jeremiah**		
12.11	349	24.15 (LXX)	298	1.4		221
13.9	261	24.16	200	4.22		290
16.31	154	25.4 (LXX)	336	4.26		293
17.3	121	26.13	192	9.3		290
19.15	349	27.13	225	9.6		290
20.22	66, 255	29.6	289	9.23-24		154
21.2	339	30.27	289	10.10		108
23.19	339	30.30	289	10.25	195, 290, 291
24.22	171	30.33	289	11.20	121, 284
24.29	255	31.5	242, 328	12.1		200
25.14	154	33.1	200	12.3		121
25.21	255	33.14	289	13.16		109
25.21-22	256	37.4	108	17.7 (LXX)		153
25.22	287	37.17	108	17.10		121
25.8	303	40.9	95	20.9		261
27.1	281	41.9	327	22.7		292
27.19	154	41.11	309	24.7 (LXX)		107
29.27	176	42.1	92	25.31 (32.31)		292
		42.6	327	29.23		123

31.33-34	205	2.1-2	93	1.14	232
42.5	123	5.4	290	9.1-8	9
48.3 (31.3)	292	7.8	354	9.14-16	225
51.39	217	14.2	107	14.1-9	181
				14.1-21	232
Ezekiel		**Joel**		14.5	181, 289
1.3	221	1.1	221		
6.14	292	1.15	232	**Malachi**	
13.5	232	2.1	225, 232	3.18 (LXX)	107
14.9	324	2.11	232	4.1	289
16.12	154	2.12-14 (LXX)	107	4.5	232
18.25	176	2.19	107		
23.42	154	2.21-32	232		
28.2-10	311	2.30	289	**NEW TESTAMENT**	
28.22	295	3.14	232		
30.3	232	3.18	232	**Matthew**	
36.27	201			1.21	147
37.6	201	**Amos**		1.23	358
37.14	201	2.12	262	2.16	320
38.20	293	4.8	107	3.7	110
38.23	295	5.1	221	3.11	261
39.23	200	5.18	232	3.12	292
		5.20	232	3.17	109
Daniel				4.1	165
2.21	231	**Obadiah**		4.3	164
2.39	9	15-21	232	4.21	174, 327
4.13	181			4.25	141
4.36	138	**Micah**		5.4	169
6.26	108	1.1	221	5.8	180
7.6	9	1.2	123	5.11-12	99, 257
7.12	231	1.3	224	5.28	195
7.13-14	226	2.6	262	5.29-30	292
7.14	138	4.2	104, 205	5.32	190
8.5-8	9			5.38-48	255
8.13	181	**Nahum**		5.43-48	178
8.21	9	1.6	289	5.45	256
8.23 (LXX)	148			5.48	256
9.27	311	**Zephaniah**		6.7	88
11.3	9	1.7	232	6.9	176, 277
11.31	311	1.8	289	6.9-13	259
11.36-37	309, 310	1.14	232	6.10	138
12.2	217	1.15	287	6.13	337
12.2 (LXX)	244	1.15-16	225	6.19	332
12.6	231	3.8	289	6.24	254
12.11	311			6.26	184
12.12	223	**Haggai**		7.7-12	259
		2.22	292	7.13	309
Hosea				7.15-20	265
1.1	221	**Zechariah**		7.21	189
1.2	204	1.3 (LXX)	107	8.4	256

8.12	236	19.28	328	26.54	185
8.18-22	98	20.12	125	26.64	109
9.26	104	21.17	157	27.11	180
9.38	173	21.25	109	27.52	217
10.5	343	21.31	189	28.20	358
10.8	347	21.33	245		
10.9	192	22.37	269	**Mark**	
10.10	347	22.39	178	1.1	94, 160
10.21	203	23.8	204	1.13	165
10.22	241	23.14	122	1.14	117
10.22-25	98	23.29	245	1.15	138, 317
10.23	145	23.31	144	1.19	174
10.28	269	23.31-32	148	1.28	104
10.37-38	137	23.34	144, 145	1.44	256
11.12	138, 226	23.37	144	2.17	327
12.18	92	23.43-44	232	3.6	144
12.20	261	24.3	231	3.17	236
12.28	148, 223	24.6	185, 303	3.27	192
12.29	192, 226	24.8	234	3.32-35	204
12.32	292	24.11-13	307	3.35	189, 260
12.38-39	321	24.11-24	307	4.10	157
12.50	189	24.13	241	4.11	212
13.15	107	24.14	295	4.12	107
13.19	226, 337	24.15	311	4.17	283
13.21	283	24.24	264, 321	4.19	195, 322
13.38	236	24.29-31	222	5.23	170
13.41	181	24.30	226, 289, 328	5.39	244
13.42	292	24.30-31	289	5.39-42	217
13.50	292	24.31	224, 225, 302	5.41	244
14.2	140, 317	24.35	332	5.43	164
14.35	207	24.36	231, 232	6.5	96
15.2-3	329	24.36-39	234	6.14	140, 299, 317
15.6	329	24.37	302	6.21	49
15.19	190	24.40-41	222	6.26	200
16.1	109, 321	24.42-44	238	6.55	207
16.4	157, 321	24.51	239	7.1-3	330
16.16	49	24.64	226	7.3	329
16.25-26	129	25.6	226	7.4	139
16.27	289, 328	25.8	261	7.5	329
17.5	226	25.13	238	7.8-9	329
17.10	185	25.31	289, 328	7.9	200
17.11	111	25.32	180	7.13	329
17.12	163	25.41	292	7.21	190
17.22	163	25.43-44	253	7.22	119, 122
18.8	292	25.46	292	8.6	259
18.8-9	292	26.8	308	8.11	321
18.10	256	26.10	131	8.11-12	123
18.17	345, 354	26.27	259	8.12	321
18.33	184	26.34	239	8.34	98
19.9	190	26.40-41	238	8.38	181, 289, 328

9.1	138	2.49	184	11.14	295
9.2	157	3.7	110	11.16	109, 123
9.7	226	3.11	128	11.20	138, 148, 223
9.11	185	3.16	261	11.21	338
9.48	261	3.18	118	11.42	340
9.50	251	4.2	165	11.47-51	144
10.29-30	129	4.14	104	12.15	122
10.30	283	4.16	272	12.18	245
10.32	163	4.32	304	12.24	184
11.16	192	4.43	185	12.32	128
12.30	269	4.44	141	12.35-40	238
12.31-33	178	6.22-23	99	12.39-40	232
12.40	122	6.24	118	12.42-46	239
13	63	6.27	257	12.47	189
13.7	185, 303	6.27-36	255	12.48	123
13.8	234	6.33	257	12.51-53	129
13.10	185, 315	6.35	257	13.17	309
13.12	203	6.35-36	256	13.33-34	144
13.13	241	6.40	174	13.34	302
13.14	311	6.43-45	90	14.4	210
13.22	321	7.1-5	49	14.14	171, 287
13.26	226, 328	7.7	296	14.19	119
13.27	181, 302	7.17	104	15.20	270
13.32	231	7.30	200	15.32	184
13.32-37	232, 234, 235,	7.36-47	270	16.8	236
	238	8.12	165	16.11	120
14.1	144	8.13	98, 151, 323	16.13	254
14.4	308	8.14	322	16.19-31	217
14.6	131	8.15	265	16.23-24	292
14.36	176	8.16	192	16.28	198
14.37-38	238	8.25	295	17.20	231
14.44-45	270	8.29	338, 343	17.30	288
14.58	245	8.52	244	17.31	192
14.62	226	8.54	244	18.1	88, 184, 258, 353
15.14-15	144	9.18	157	18.3	290
16.17	321	9.21	343	18.5	131, 290
16.20	321	9.26	328	18.7	131
		9.31	163	18.9	262
Luke		9.34-35	226	18.12	192
1.1	96	9.44	163	20.34	236
1.5	141	10.2	173	20.35	285
1.6	180	10.9	253	20.36	236
1.19	166	10.16	200	20.47	122
1.67	261	10.21	99	21.9	185
1.75	133	10.27	269	21.13	295
1.79	339	10.27-37	178	21.15	309
2.8	338	10.39	304	21.16	203
2.10-11	258	11.2	176	21.19	91, 192
2.32	288	11.7	131	21.22	290
2.34	162	11.13	109	21.27	226, 328

21.28	99, 257	6.31-33	109	20.28	300
21.34	234	6.45	205	21.23	104
21.34-36	232, 234	7.1	144		
21.36	155, 180, 235	7.17	189	**Acts**	
22.2	320	7.18	123, 156, 322	1.3	244
22.15	151, 195	7.21	295	1.4	343
22.17	259	7.39	163	1.6	231
22.19	259	8.9	157	1.6-7	222
22.32	160, 337	8.12	237	1.7	231, 232
22.45-46	238	8.50	123, 156	1.8	96
23.4	336	8.55	290	1.9	226
23.5	141	8.59	144	1.11	109, 110
23.39-43	217	9.4	185	1.16	185, 198
23.56	210	9.31	189	1.18	192
24.18	164	10.12	226	1.24	121
24.19	333	10.16	185	2.2	109
24.26	162	10.28	322	2.3	261
24.37	303	10.28-29	226	2.15	239
24.45-46	49	11.11-14	217	2.17	261
24.46-49	96	11.19	136	2.17-18	262
24.53	358	11.31	136	2.19	289, 321
		11.45-53	144	2.20	232, 305
John		11.51	163	2.22	96, 321
1.1	300	12.26	228	2.23	144, 320
1.17	186, 332	12.28	200	2.25	358
1.18	300	12.33	163	2.34	109
1.30	301	12.36	236	2.36	144
1.32	109	12.38	140	2.40	118, 198
1.47	119	12.40	107	2.41	304
3.13	109	13.30	239	2.43	321
3.14	185	13.34-35	178, 205	3.6	343
3.16	110, 205, 322, 331	14.3	111	3.7	109
3.19	235	14.27	357	3.12	295
3.27	109	15.12	178, 205	3.13-15	144
3.30	185	15.17	178, 205	3.15	109
3.31	109	15.18-21	98	3.16	268
4.21	111	16.6	218	3.19-21	231
4.38	131	16.20	218	3.21	185
4.41	304	16.33	98	4.4	304
4.48	321	17.3	108	4.9	253
4.50	170	17.10	299	4.10	109, 144
4.51	170	17.12	236, 308, 322	4.11	262
4.53	170	17.15	337	4.12	185
5.18	144	17.20	304	4.13	116
5.35	151, 261	17.22	305	4.30	321
5.42	340	17.24	228	4.31	173
5.44	123, 156	18.32	163	4.33	295
6.6	165	19.21	207	4.41	257
6.15	226	19.29	192	5.12	321
6.22	157	20.9	185	5.15-16	253

INDEX OF SCRIPTURE REFERENCES

5.28	186	11.29	141	15.28	125
5.29	184	12.1-5	143	15.28-29	58
5.30	109, 144	12.3	143	15.29	190, 193, 246,
5.41	99, 285	12.4	338		266
6.3	132	12.24	221	15.30-31	58
6.7	291	13.1-2	262	15.31	118
7.22	333	13.4-12	263	15.32	48, 58, 66, 83,
7.24	290	13.9	82		160, 162, 221, 304
7.38	84	13.10	119	15.35-36	334
7.39	290	13.15	272	15.38	296
7.47	245	13.22	189	15.40	47, 83, 86, 190
7.52	144	13.26	147	16	115
7.55	109	13.27	272	16.1	83, 115, 157
7.55-60	217	13.30	109	16.1-3	47
7.60	217	13.36	217	16.2	83
8.1	145, 283	13.37	109	16.3	58, 157
8.1-3	143	13.44	101, 334	16.4	190
8.2	218	13.45	145	16.6-7	48, 152
8.3	143	13.46	116, 195	16.6-10	48
8.4	140	13.47	147, 242	16.9	1
8.14	98, 140, 323	13.48	335	16.9-10	327
8.20	192	13.48-49	101, 334	16.10	48
8.24	173	13.48-51	146	16.11	43, 46, 48
8.25	101, 198, 334	13.49	207, 221	16.11-12	5, 7
8.39	226	13.50	49, 145, 283	16.11-18	115
9.1	143	13.52	99	16.12	14
9.3	109	14.2	145, 146	16.15	46
9.13	256	14.3	116	16.16-18	263
9.15	192	14.4-6	145	16.16-40	48
9.15-16	98, 168	14.5-6	145	16.18	343
9.16	162	14.11-18	106	16.19	83
9.22	49	14.14	126	16.22	116
9.23-25	145	14.15	106, 107, 108	16.22-24	168
9.24	131	14.19	146	16.24	186
9.27-28	116	14.19-20	145	16.25	83
9.28-30	145	14.21-22	98	16.29	83
9.29	145	14.21-23	247	16.35	116
9.31	118, 141, 143, 207	14.22	66, 98, 141, 160,	16.37	83, 116
10.2	49, 358		161, 162, 168, 285	16.37-38	116
10.36	267	14.35-36	221	16.39	145
10.37	141, 207	15	142	16.40	48, 160
10.40	109	15.8	121, 201	17	31, 56
10.42	198, 343	15.9	180	17.1	6, 14, 46, 48
10.44	304	15.19	107	17.1-4	46
11.1	98, 140, 141, 323	15.19-21	58	17.1-9	47
11.9	109	15.20	190, 193, 266	17.2-3	49
11.17	201	15.21	272	17.3	108, 162, 220,
11.18	195, 210	15.22	83, 190		243
11.23	66, 160, 333	15.23-29	57, 58, 81	17.4	29, 49, 58, 83,
11.27-28	262	15.27	83		108

374

17.5	20, 22, 49, 108, 111, 131, 138, 145, 157	18.26	116	23.26	22
		18.28	49	23.35	338
		19.6	261, 262	24.2	357
17.5-7	29, 131	19.8	116	24.3	22
17.5-9	19, 20, 22, 23, 98, 142, 143, 249	19.8-10	48	24.4	152
		19.9	145	24.23	288
17.5-10	146	19.10	101, 221, 334	26.18	107, 235, 236
17.6	20, 21, 116	19.12	130	26.22	136
17.6-7	20, 28, 50, 155, 233	19.19	351	26.23	220
		19.21-22	152, 174	26.25	22
17.6-9	7, 42	19.22	7, 83	27	3
17.7	41, 46, 131, 138, 298	19.23-41	106	27.2	7, 102, 350
		19.27	207	27.30	122
17.8	20, 21, 51	19.29	7, 29, 102, 350	28.11	3
17.9	20, 29, 51, 131, 153	19.31	24	28.15	226
		19.32	84	28.16	226, 338
17.10	4, 7, 14, 20, 51, 83, 145, 150, 168	19.39	84	28.22	296
		19.41	84	28.23	198
17.11	98, 323	20.1	7, 160	28.25	261
17.12	49	20.1-3	7	28.27	107
17.13	145	20.1-6	48, 152, 174	28.28	147
17.13-14	168	20.2	7, 304	28.31	96
17.14	83, 145, 157	20.4	7, 29, 84, 102, 350		
17.14-15	7, 47, 51			**Romans**	
17.15	83, 100	20.5-6	7	1.1	82, 117
17.16	33	20.20	135	1.4	180
17.16-34	166	20.21	198	1.5	56, 164, 291, 336
17.19	120	20.24	198	1.7	85, 92, 277, 278, 294, 330
17.22	120	20.26	136		
17.22-31	106	20.28	142	1.8	87, 104, 207, 259
17.26	317	20.31	131, 135, 250	1.9	87, 123, 258
17.28	277	20.33	347	1.9-10	87
17.32	168, 310, 335	20.33-35	130	1.10-11	170
17.34	120	20.34	211	1.11	128, 167
18.1	102, 157, 166	20.35	179, 221, 348	1.11-12	270
18.1-4	130	20.37	270	1.11ff.	144
18.2	149	20.43	123	1.13	152, 216
18.5	49, 52, 58, 83, 130, 157, 166, 198	21.9-10	262	1.15	166
		21.14	210	1.16	46, 144, 147
18.5-6	48	21.21	307	1.16-17	48, 146, 203
18.6	100, 145	21.25	190, 193	1.18	110, 111, 149, 285
18.9-10	168	21.34	164	1.18ff.	144, 150
18.10	358	22.3	82, 130	1.18-32	195, 291
18.11	52	22.10	305	1.21	235
18.12-13	19	22.25-29	82	1.22-25	106
18.12-17	23, 145	22.28	192	1.23	293
18.15	226	22.30	164	1.24	118, 194, 195, 199, 324
18.19	157	23.10	226		
18.23	66, 160, 337	23.11	198	1.26	324
18.25	261	23.25-30	81	1.27	185

1.28	324	7.11	306	10.15	166
1.29	119, 122	7.25	237, 281	10.16	290, 291
2.1	324	8.1	85	10.16-17	140
2.5	110, 180, 284	8.3	109	10.18	104
2.7	123, 194	8.4	137, 201	11.1-5	144
2.8	291, 322	8.6	267	11.3	144
2.9	287	8.8	121, 145, 185	11.5	92
2.10	267	8.9	201, 286	11.7	144
2.13	286	8.11	109, 213, 220	11.8	324
2.16	291	8.12	237	11.10	358
2.18	119	8.15	93	11.11	144, 147, 195
2.19	235	8.17	98, 162, 286, 328	11.11ff.	144
2.20	126	8.17-18	138, 299	11.15	144
3.2	120, 358	8.18	328	11.23-26	144
3.4	108	8.18-25	147	11.25	216
3.8-9	56	8.21	299	11.25-27	149
3.22	100	8.23	56	11.28	92
3.24	85, 86, 260	8.24	147, 241	11.30-32	290
3.30	286	8.25	91	11.33-38	175
4.4	299	8.27	121	11.35	171, 287
4.7	308	8.28	93, 260	12.1	135, 183
4.16	299	8.29	109	12.1-2	183, 189
4.17	242	8.30	269, 327, 328	12.2	260
4.21	96	8.31	171	12.3-17	246
4.24	109	8.31-39	260, 288	12.5	85
5.1	86, 104, 267	8.32	109	12.6	262, 299
5.1-5	89	8.34	109	12.8	249
5.2	138, 299, 328	8.35	98, 169, 283	12.10	178, 194, 204,
5.3	168	8.36	170		205
5.3-4	91	8.37-39	331	12.11	261
5.3-5	70, 91	8.38	305, 338	12.12	99, 169, 258
5.5	205, 340	8.39	340	12.13	257
5.7	167	9–11	143	12.15	218, 258
5.7-8	92	9.1	137	12.17-19	287
5.8	205, 331	9.1-5	144	12.17-21	255, 256
5.9	110, 111, 147	9.3	93	12.18	251
5.9-10	241	9.5	300	12.19	171, 286, 290
5.10	109	9.11	92	12.21	256
5.15	86	9.16	237	13.1-7	246
5.18	237	9.18	237	13.4	197
6.4	109, 137, 293	9.21	194	13.8	178
6.6	108	9.22	309	13.8-10	178, 179
6.9	109	9.27	144	13.9	354
6.16-20	108	9.31	148, 223	13.10	206, 256
6.17	184, 291, 329	9.32	304	13.12	235, 236, 237,
6.19	119, 190, 199	9.33	242		239, 240
6.22	190	10.1	144, 297	13.13	137, 212, 239
6.23	260	10.8-13	146	14.1-12	254
7.3	237	10.9	109	14.3	262
7.7-8	195	10.12	178	14.4	329

14.5	96	16.21	7, 83, 90, 102, 159	3.22	305
14.9	243, 244	16.22	358	4.1	317
14.10	262	16.23	84	4.3	232
14.12	237	16.25	160, 337	4.8	164
14.14	183, 338	16.26	291	4.9	311
14.15	137, 206			4.11	130
14.17	99, 138, 251, 258, 267	**1 Corinthians**		4.12	90, 123, 130, 211, 283
14.18	119	1.1	82, 84, 159	4.14	129, 250, 355
14.19	237, 245, 251, 257	1.2	84, 142, 181, 294	4.14-15	134
		1.3	85, 277, 278, 330	4.15	134
14.22	119	1.4	87, 139, 259, 260	4.16	98, 179, 183, 346
15.1	254	1.6	295	4.17	83, 129, 158, 179
15.1-3	121, 185	1.6-7	95	4.18-19	158
15.2	245	1.7	108, 288	4.19	95
15.4	91, 331	1.7-8	267	4.20	138
15.4-5	340	1.8	232, 305	4.21	179
15.5-6	175	1.8-11	335	5.1	195, 196
15.13	175, 177, 298	1.9	109, 269, 327, 337	5.3	151
15.14	250, 253, 281, 297, 338	1.10	135, 174, 183, 186, 343	5.3-4	343
				5.5	232, 234, 305
15.16	117, 327	1.17	95, 166	5.9	354
15.17-18	154	1.18	140, 146, 322	5.9-11	354
15.18	291, 333	1.21	100, 128, 146, 195	5.9-13	345
15.18-19	95			5.11	106, 354, 355
15.19	16, 297	1.22	201	5.12-13	178, 212
15.22	152	1.23	49, 323, 335	6.4	262
15.22-23	152	1.26-29	254	6.9	106, 138
15.23	90, 167	1.29	281	6.9-10	197
15.26	100	1.30	190, 199	6.11	327
15.26-27	142, 207, 208	1.31	154	6.12-20	193
15.30	183, 186	2.1	317	6.13	320
15.30-32	183, 270, 334	2.1-5	95, 114	6.14	109, 220
15.31	335	2.3	168	6.15	109
15.33	267, 358	2.4	95, 96, 119	6.15-20	201
16.1	100	2.4-5	96	7	193
16.1-2	206, 249	2.6	320	7.1	202
16.3	90, 159	2.8	293	7.2	193
16.5	84, 101, 203, 326	2.14	140	7.2-7	193
16.6	90	3.1	126	7.5	151, 153, 165
16.8	179	3.3	137	7.8-9	193
16.9	90, 159	3.8	90, 131, 249	7.10	222, 343
16.10	120	3.9	159	7.14	199
16.12	90	3.10	299	7.17	137
16.16	270	3.13	90, 119, 264	7.25	202, 222
16.17	183, 345	3.13-15	154	7.26	305
16.17-19	270, 354	3.15	147, 241	7.32	145
16.18	306	3.16	312	7.32-34	121, 185
16.19	154, 172	3.19	286	7.34	269
16.20	153, 267, 272			7.35	212

7.39	217	12.11	140, 317	15.31	170
8.1	202	12.18	242	15.32	36
8.5	32, 107, 286, 309	12.28	242	15.34	195
8.7-13	254	13.2	167	15.35-37	228
9.1	126	13.3	264	15.46	225
9.1-18	348, 349	13.6	322	15.50	138, 332
9.4	348	13.8-10	262	15.51	217
9.6	90, 348	13.11	126	15.51-52	222
9.7	348	13.13	89, 167	15.52	225
9.7-14	131, 347	14.1	257	15.58	90, 115, 165, 177,
9.9-10	348	14.1-5	263		249
9.12	125, 348	14.3	118, 136	16	250
9.13	348	14.3-5	245	16.1	202, 207
9.14	222, 348	14.6	288	16.2	179
9.15-18	125	14.12	177, 245, 263	16.3	119
9.17-18	120	14.17	245	16.5	152, 174
9.19	130	14.23	84	16.7	158
9.22	121	14.26	245, 263, 288	16.9	309
9.24-26	335	14.29	263, 264	16.9-10	90
9.25	154	14.31	162	16.10	83
10.1	216	14.33	251	16.10-11	158, 166
10.1-2	226	14.36	104, 157	16.11	262
10.1-13	197	14.37	186	16.12	158, 159, 202
10.5	128	14.39	263	16.13	170, 238, 329
10.6	100	14.40	212	16.13-16	270
10.13	269, 337	15	56, 213	16.15	101, 183, 248,
10.14-22	106	15.1	139, 184		326
10.19-20	322	15.1-11	220	16.15-16	183
10.32	142	15.2	265	16.16	248, 249
10.32-33	147	15.3	139, 184, 243,	16.18	248
10.33	121, 185		329	16.19	84, 101, 203, 207
11.1	98, 179, 346	15.3-4	49	16.20	270
11.2	265, 329	15.3-7	62	16.21	359
11.4-5	262	15.5	126	16.22	270
11.16	282	15.6	217	16.23	272
11.17	343	15.6-7	225		
11.17-34	355	15.7	126	**2 Corinthians**	
11.22	142	15.9	142	1.1	82, 100, 101, 126,
11.23	139, 184, 329	15.10	90, 115, 154, 165,		142, 159, 181,
11.23-25	222		249		207, 294
11.23-26	62	15.12-28	220	1.2	85, 278, 330
11.24	259	15.14	114	1.4	169, 228
11.28	119, 264	15.15	286	1.4-7	118
11.30	214, 217, 253	15.18	217, 225	1.5	98, 162
12.1	202, 216, 217	15.20	110, 217	1.6	91, 163, 169
12.1-3	264	15.22	85	1.7	169, 170, 288
12.1–14.40	262	15.23	225	1.8	101, 169, 216
12.2	195	15.23-24	180	1.11	270, 334
12.6	140, 317	15.24	320	1.14	232, 305
12.10	263, 264, 303	15.26	320	1.15–2.4	152

1.16	152, 168, 174
1.18	269, 337
1.19	83, 109
1.23	123
1.24	159
2.3	154, 338
2.4	169, 179, 221
2.8	183
2.11	153, 165
2.13	96, 152, 288
2.15	322
3.3	108
3.14-15	272
3.16	107
4.1	353
4.2	137
4.3	94, 159, 322
4.7	192
4.8	163, 259
4.8-10	99, 257
4.10-11	170
4.13	118
4.14	109, 220, 222
4.16	170, 353
4.17	125, 169
4.20	333
5.1	222
5.2	167
5.6-9	228
5.6-10	217
5.7	137
5.10	88, 155, 173, 180, 185
5.12	151, 281
5.15	243
5.20	140
5.21	243
6.1	115, 140, 165, 183
6.3-10	168, 335
6.4	91, 168, 169
6.5	90, 130, 131, 165, 249
6.6	179
6.7	95, 240
6.10	130
6.11-13	134
6.14	235, 308
6.16	108, 312
7.1	180

7.4	96, 99, 154, 169, 172
7.5	152, 163, 259, 288
7.6	166, 169
7.6-7	169, 228
7.7	118, 154
7.8	151
7.11	290
7.13	169
7.14	281
7.15	354
8–9	206, 250
8.1	86, 129
8.1-2	8, 100, 131, 206, 283
8.1-5	206, 281, 282
8.2	99, 169, 177, 208
8.4	118, 173
8.5	129, 260
8.6	158
8.7	86, 167
8.8	206
8.10-11	206
8.13	288
8.16	151
8.17	140
8.18	94
8.20	344
8.20-21	123
8.22	119
8.22-23	159
8.23	159, 301
8.24	154, 206, 281
9.1	204
9.2	100
9.3	281
9.4	100
9.5	122, 250
9.8	90, 259
9.14	167
10.1	183, 281
10.1-2	183
10.2	304
10.2-3	137
10.3-5	240
10.6	297
10.11	97
10.13	154
10.14	148, 223

10.14-15	131
10.15	280
10.18	119
11.2	153
11.3	153, 306
11.4	140
11.7	117, 130
11.8	130
11.9	125
11.11	179
11.14	153
11.16	142
11.16-29	168
11.17	304
11.20	131
11.23	90, 131, 165, 249
11.24	145
11.25-26	3
11.26	145, 336
11.27	90, 130, 131, 165, 249
11.28-29	164
12.1	288
12.2	226
12.4	226
12.5	254
12.7	153, 288, 309
12.8	301
12.9	254
12.10	97, 128, 168, 283, 325
12.12	95, 96, 321
12.13	125
12.15	129, 179
12.16	119
12.18	137, 158, 159, 166
12.21	118, 199
13.1	123, 132, 270
13.2	162, 198
13.3	123
13.4	244, 254
13.5	119
13.7	119, 304
13.11	174, 182, 251, 267
13.12	270, 272
13.13	330, 340

Galatians

1.1	82, 109, 120, 330
1.2	207
1.3	85, 278, 330
1.3-4	277
1.4	243, 305
1.6	303, 327
1.6-7	327
1.9	139, 184
1.10	121, 145, 185
1.11-12	140
1.12	139, 184, 186, 288
1.13	142
1.15	120, 327
1.15-16	128
1.16	109, 195
1.16-18	120
1.17-24	142
1.22	141, 142
1.22-23	143
1.23	164, 336
2.1-10	142
2.2	165, 335
2.5	151, 323
2.7	120
2.8	140, 317
2.9	86
2.10	206, 207
2.12	344
2.14	323
2.16	85
2.21	200
3.2	140
3.5	140, 201, 317
3.11	286
3.14	195
3.22	100
3.23	203
3.26-28	85
4.1	126
4.3	126
4.4	109
4.6	93, 109
4.8	108, 195
4.9	107
4.11	249
4.12	98
4.14	140, 262
4.19	127

4.20	151
5.1	329
5.3	136
5.5-6	89
5.6	89, 167
5.7	152
5.8	137, 327
5.10	338
5.13	178, 199
5.14	297, 354
5.14-15	178
5.16	137, 201
5.16-17	195
5.19	118, 199
5.20-21	106
5.21	138, 162, 198
5.22	205, 251, 258, 297
5.23	254
6.1	165, 174
6.2	125, 205
6.4	119
6.6	347
6.9	353
6.9-10	353
6.10	29, 90, 178, 237, 257
6.11	359
6.14	154
6.17	131, 270, 334
6.18	272

Ephesians

1.1	82, 181, 294
1.2	85, 277, 278, 330
1.4	92
1.5	92, 297
1.9	297, 317
1.11	140, 317
1.13	146, 323
1.15	167
1.16	87
1.17	288
1.19	270, 293
1.20	109, 140, 317
1.20-21	109
1.22	84
1.23	84
2.2	137, 140, 153, 228, 236, 317

2.3	218
2.5	147, 261
2.6	109
2.8	86
2.8-9	89
2.10	89, 90, 137, 199
2.12	91, 218
2.19	237
2.20	144
2.21	312
3.3	288, 317
3.4	317
3.6	260
3.9	317
3.13	169, 353
3.17	167
3.20	140, 173, 251, 270, 317
3.20-21	175
4.1	135, 137, 183, 297, 327
4.2	178, 251, 254
4.3	251
4.4	199, 327
4.11-12	174
4.11-16	175
4.12	90, 245
4.14	118, 126
4.15-16	251
4.16	90, 252
4.17	136, 137, 195
4.17-18	195
4.18	235
4.19	119, 122, 199
4.24	133
4.27	153
4.28	128, 200, 349
4.29	245
5.1	98, 129
5.1-2	205
5.2	137
5.3	191, 193, 199
5.5	106
5.6	110, 111, 114, 236
5.8	137, 235, 236
5.8-9	235
5.8-11	237
5.9	297
5.10	185
5.11	235

5.13	118
5.14	238
5.15	137
5.20	87, 139, 259
5.21–6.9	246, 252
5.29	128
6.1	334
6.4	250
6.5-9	31
6.6	189, 260
6.8-10	241
6.10	293
6.10-17	153
6.11	153
6.11-12	164
6.11-17	240
6.14	241
6.15	267
6.16	337
6.18	221, 258
6.18-19	334
6.19	116, 317
6.19-20	270
6.20	116
6.22	333
6.24	272

Philippians

1.1	84, 126, 181, 294
1.2	85, 277, 278, 330
1.3	259
1.3-4	87
1.4-5	172
1.6	232, 269, 338
1.7	151
1.8	123, 167
1.9	177, 184
1.10	180, 232
1.10-11	267
1.12	184
1.15	297
1.16	162
1.17	169
1.18	122, 358
1.19	201, 270, 334
1.19-26	288
1.20	96, 116, 179
1.20-24	217
1.22	326
1.23	151, 195, 228

1.25	338
1.27	65, 137, 170, 297, 329
1.27-28	284
1.28	65, 147, 309, 309
1.29	162
1.30	115, 117, 168
2.1	118, 136
2.2	154, 172, 297
2.6-11	62
2.10	343
2.12	129, 354
2.13	140, 297, 317
2.15	180
2.16	154, 165, 232, 249, 335
2.17	99, 129
2.19	83, 158, 166
2.19-22	83
2.19-24	158
2.20-22	158
2.22	90
2.24	158, 338
2.25	159, 160, 240, 250
2.25-30	153
2.26	167
2.27	218
3.1	182, 258, 334
3.3	154
3.4	184
3.6	180
3.8	250
3.10	98
3.14	85
3.16	148, 223
3.17	98, 99, 179
3.17-18	137
3.19	309
3.20	108, 109
3.20-21	228
4.1	129, 154, 170, 172, 179, 329
4.2	135, 183
4.3	183, 301
4.4	258
4.5	222
4.6	87
4.8	182, 334
4.8-9	270

4.9	139, 179, 184, 267, 358
4.10-19	125
4.12	130, 259
4.14	169, 353
4.14-16	206
4.15	101, 326
4.15-16	130, 347
4.16	125, 342
4.20	277
4.23	272

Colossians

1.1	82, 84, 126
1.2	85, 87, 277, 278, 294
1.3	87, 259, 296
1.4-5	89, 167
1.5	91, 118, 323
1.9	249, 296
1.9-10	189
1.10	90, 121, 137, 145, 297
1.11	91, 254, 257, 293
1.13	138, 235
1.18	84, 220
1.24	99, 169, 257
1.25	297
1.26	317
1.27	138, 153, 317, 328
1.28	153, 250
1.29	117, 140, 249, 298, 317
2.1	117, 151
2.2	96, 317, 333
2.5	151
2.6	137, 140
2.6-7	184
2.7	245, 259
2.8	114, 118, 329
2.12	109
2.23	194
3.3-4	228
3.4	299
3.5	106, 118, 122, 193, 194, 199
3.6	110, 111
3.7	137
3.11	203

3.12	92, 254	1.4	87, 90, 91-93, 97,	2.1	74, 105, 113, 114-
3.15	327		129, 131, 177,		15, 117, 121, 124,
3.16	253		182, 198, 231,		129, 133, 161,
3.17	259, 333		242, 242, 269,		165, 185, 231,
3.18–4.1	246, 252		331, 340, 356		288, 314, 346
3.22–4.1	31	1.4-5	93, 327	2.1-2	96, 114, 313
3.22	121	1.4-10	73	2.1-9	132
4.2	87, 238, 258	1.5	58, 62, 86, 93-97,	2.1-10	111
4.3	317		105, 106, 114,	2.1-12	52, 53, 73, 95, 96,
4.3-4	270, 334		115, 117, 128,		105, 106, 111-38,
4.5	137, 178, 212		132, 138, 140,		139, 140, 150, 347
4.8	333		160, 185, 199,	2.1–3.10	71, 175, 179
4.9	159		231, 313, 321, 346	2.1–3.13	111-81
4.10	7, 102, 350	1.5-6	97	2.1–5.22	111-266
4.11	159	1.6	51, 52, 65, 86, 91,	2.2	48, 62, 94, 98,
4.12	260, 297		95, 97-99, 105,		105, 115-17, 118,
4.15	203		113, 140, 141,		120, 128, 129,
4.16	270, 272		161, 168, 169,		132, 146, 160,
4.17	90, 184		171, 179, 197,		163, 168, 185,
4.18	88, 270, 359		253, 257, 258,		231, 328, 336, 346
5.22	99		283, 287, 323,	2.2-12	115
			335, 336, 346	2.3	117-19, 199, 323
1 Thessalonians		1.6-7	101, 282	2.4	55, 62, 105, 119-
1.1	47, 54, 56, 71, 81-	1.6-10	95, 97, 111, 138		21, 123, 128, 132,
	86, 142, 176, 197,	1.6–3.13	71		145, 146, 151,
	267, 272, 277,	1.7	8, 98, 99-101,		160, 180, 185,
	278, 279, 282,		133, 142, 282,		264, 328
	299, 332		295, 348	2.4-6	125
1.1-5	71	1.7-8	86, 208	2.5	96, 114, 121-23,
1.1-10	71	1.8	7, 56, 87, 89, 100,		131, 132, 185,
1.2	61, 86, 87-88, 91,		101-5, 120, 140,		231, 264, 313,
	138, 139, 171,		146, 167, 167,		346, 347
	176, 236, 258,		178, 197, 207,	2.5-6	119
	259, 277, 296		221, 237, 241,	2.6	121, 123-24, 125,
1.2-3	73, 173, 258, 270		280, 334, 350, 351		156
1.2-4	91	1.9	32, 47, 49, 58, 85,	2.6-7	123
1.2-10	71, 86-111, 138		86, 93, 104, 105-	2.6-8	125, 313
1.3	31, 52, 86, 87, 88-		8, 106, 108, 109,	2.6-12	97
	91, 92, 109, 110,		113, 114, 133,	2.7	47, 58, 82, 116,
	129, 140, 155,		155, 155, 180,		124-28, 129, 131,
	165, 167, 171,		185, 195, 264,		134
	173, 176, 177,		281, 282, 312	2.8	62, 94, 128-29,
	180, 197, 202,	1.9-10	49, 56, 86, 102,		132, 157, 160,
	206, 241, 249,		109, 140, 186,		179, 328
	251, 252, 279,		187, 335	2.9	30, 58, 62, 90, 94,
	280, 282, 296,	1.10	41, 47, 87, 91,		114, 117, 123,
	298, 325, 331, 340		108-11, 148, 213,		125, 128, 129-32,
1.3-4	139		214, 224, 241,		135, 160, 165,
1.3-5	111		242, 243, 289		173, 211, 313,
1.3ff.	279	2	114, 138		328, 346, 347

2.10	100, 114, 123, 132-33, 136, 141, 180, 295, 346	2.17-20	52, 114, 150-56, 156		139, 152, 153, 154, 156, 157,
2.10-12	132, 133	2.17–3.13	53, 61, 73		158, 159, 160,
2.11	96, 114, 127, 129, 133-35, 137, 185, 191, 231, 313, 346	2.18	54, 56, 58, 151-53, 156, 159, 164, 173, 174, 176, 271, 309, 313, 314, 321, 337		161, 164-65, 166, 167, 169, 170, 171, 174, 249, 271, 282, 307, 309, 313, 314, 321, 337, 338
2.11-12	134				
2.12	113, 135-38, 160, 183, 185, 198, 198, 212, 228, 253, 269, 279, 285, 286, 295, 327, 328, 333, 343	2.19	88, 91, 108, 109, 110, 138, 153-55, 156, 173, 180, 197, 213, 222, 288, 301, 320, 321, 331	3.5-7	280
				3.6	31, 52, 58, 68, 81, 82, 83-84, 88, 89, 112, 129, 152, 160, 165, 166-68, 170, 171, 177, 200, 202, 241, 280
2.13	47, 52, 56, 61, 63, 87, 92, 95, 96, 98, 100, 106, 108, 118, 133, 138-41, 139, 171, 176, 184, 186, 199, 200, 205, 252, 317, 321, 323, 335, 344	2.19-20	172		
		2.20	153, 154, 155-56, 172, 173	3.6-8	52, 282
		3	114	3.6-9	52, 139
		3.1	51, 128, 151, 152, 156-58, 160, 164, 166, 170	3.6-10	52, 165-75
				3.6-12	114
		3.1-2	51, 58	3.7	98, 129, 135, 158, 161, 162, 164, 167, 168-70, 183, 228, 270, 283, 287, 333
2.13-14	295	3.1-3	164		
2.13-16	73, 111, 138-50	3.1-5	52, 66, 69, 91, 114, 156-65		
2.14	42, 49, 51, 64, 65, 85, 88, 91, 93, 98, 107, 111, 129, 129, 138, 141-43, 162, 170, 203, 211, 222, 232, 253, 255, 282, 283, 285, 328, 337, 346, 355, 357	3.1-10	65	3.8	65, 82, 88, 89, 91, 109, 161, 165, 167, 170-71, 197, 241, 329
		3.2	51, 62, 65, 66, 83-84, 94, 129, 132, 135, 136, 156, 157, 158-60, 161, 164, 165, 167, 169, 171, 174, 179, 183, 228, 280, 282, 328, 332, 333, 337		
				3.8-9	270
				3.9	88, 138, 153, 154, 155, 156, 169, 171-73, 174, 176, 180, 279
2.14-16	52, 111, 143, 287, 307, 336			3.9-10	88
		3.2-4	65, 156	3.9-13	270
2.15	110, 121, 143-46, 185, 197, 243, 264, 327	3.2-5	88, 160, 167	3.10	81, 131, 151, 158, 164, 167, 173-75, 216, 251, 258
		3.3	65, 66, 98, 161-62, 163, 169, 185, 231, 242, 282, 283, 287, 346		
2.15-17	138, 144, 147, 150, 153, 336			3.10-11	52, 152, 158, 167, 168, 179, 270
2.16	105, 111, 120, 144, 145, 146-50, 223, 242, 243, 270, 288, 323	3.3-4	51, 52, 98, 114, 141, 164, 204, 253, 313, 337	3.11	81, 129, 175-76, 177, 180, 266, 277, 330, 339
		3.3-5	283	3.11-12	71
2.17	68, 87, 129, 150-51, 152, 156, 161, 166, 173, 180, 195	3.4	64, 114, 115, 161, 162-64, 185, 198, 231, 283, 313, 330, 346, 349	3.11-13	62, 71, 175-81, 176, 197, 330
				3.12	31, 90, 167, 176-79, 184, 202, 208, 229, 257, 280, 297
2.17-18	51, 81, 112, 167, 168, 173, 174	3.5	51, 56, 58, 90,		

3.13 66, 74, 88, 91,
    109, 110, 129,
    138, 150, 155,
    160, 173, 176,
    179-81, 190, 213,
    222, 224, 267,
    269, 288, 289,
    294, 301, 320,
    321, 333, 337, 339
4   47
4.1 121, 129, 135,
    136, 137, 140,
    145, 160, 177,
    182-85, 186, 189,
    195, 208, 212,
    228, 245, 248,
    250, 253, 301,
    313, 333, 334,
    339, 343, 344,
    346, 352, 352
4.1-2 63, 136, 182-87,
    189, 190, 197,
    205, 216, 329,
    330, 349, 352
4.1-8 52
4.1-12 73
4.1–5.3 71
4.1–5.22 71, 174,
    181-266
4.2 114, 135, 182,
    183, 185-87, 189,
    193, 204, 231,
    313, 339, 343, 346
4.2-8 158
4.3 180, 183, 187,
    189-91, 193, 194,
    201, 246, 260,
    266, 267, 283,
    326, 343
4.3-4 193, 199
4.3-5 195
4.3-8 36, 53, 175, 182,
    187, 187-202,
    203, 252, 255, 272
4.4 180, 187, 189,
    190, 191-94, 267,
    326
4.4-5 193
4.5 183, 185, 187,

    189, 193, 194-95,
    200, 201, 290, 291
4.6 129, 135, 162,
    180, 183, 187,
    189, 190, 195-98,
    199, 200, 201,
    203, 216, 271,
    290, 343
4.7 118, 137, 180,
    183, 187, 189,
    190, 194, 198-99,
    242, 267, 269,
    297, 326, 327
4.7-8 267
4.8 183, 186, 187,
    190, 199-202,
    267, 326, 343, 352
4.9 8, 52, 67, 90, 158,
    167, 177, 178,
    182, 202-5, 206,
    208, 216, 217,
    229, 230, 245,
    280, 281
4.9-10 29, 30, 31, 53, 56,
    67, 90, 93, 129,
    177, 178, 182,
    202, 241, 245,
    250, 251, 252,
    280, 337
4.9-12 202-13
4.9–5.11 202-46, 247
4.10 29, 30, 100, 129,
    135, 142, 177,
    178, 182, 183,
    184, 186, 202,
    205-8, 211, 228,
    236, 280, 333,
    339, 352
4.10-12 183
4.11 29, 30, 54, 67, 90,
    186, 206, 208-12,
    339, 341, 343,
    349, 352, 353
4.11-12 28, 31, 52, 54,
    131, 175, 182,
    187, 202, 203,
    207, 209, 250,
    253, 334, 339,
    341, 342, 344,
    349, 350, 351, 354

4.12 124, 137, 178,
    185, 212-13, 343
4.13 51, 52, 67, 68, 91,
    129, 143, 158,
    162, 163, 175,
    202, 213, 214,
    215, 216-19, 221,
    223, 228, 229,
    230, 238, 244,
    245, 258, 331
4.13-14 222
4.13-15 244
4.13-18 53, 55, 56, 62,
    63, 108, 182, 202,
    213-29, 253, 288,
    301, 302, 306
4.13–5.11 60, 73, 294
4.14 109, 110, 133,
    213, 216, 219-21,
    243
4.14-15 217
4.14-17 214, 216
4.14-18 110
4.15 91, 109, 138, 140,
    148, 155, 170,
    180, 213, 221-23,
    225, 228, 229,
    235, 238, 244,
    288, 301, 320,
    321, 334
4.15-16 220, 305
4.15-17 197, 214, 216,
    222, 244
4.15–5.2 301
4.16 41, 50, 55, 109,
    181, 213, 217,
    222, 223-25, 289
4.16-17 220, 227, 244
4.17 109, 223, 225-28,
    245
4.18 135, 169, 213,
    215, 216, 223,
    228-29, 230, 244,
    245, 280, 333
5   47
5.1 67, 68, 129, 158,
    163, 202, 209,
    217, 230-31, 242
5.1-2 52, 53, 175, 182,
    204, 216, 222,

	229, 244, 245, 305, 313, 330, 349		197, 231, 247-50, 251, 252, 253, 301, 356	5.23-24	175, 198, 199, 296, 334, 357	
5.1ff.	301			5.23-28	71, 266-73	
5.1-11	56, 63, 108, 202, 228, 229-46, 305, 306	5.12-13	52, 90, 182, 203, 246-52	5.24	137, 266, 267, 269-70, 297, 327, 334, 337, 338	
		5.12-15	257			
5.1-12	182	5.12-22	71, 246	5.25	258, 266, 270, 334	
5.2	114, 185, 197, 230, 231-32, 235, 236, 240, 242, 294, 305, 313, 346	5.12-23	73	5.25-27	129, 270	
		5.13	31, 55, 90, 167, 173, 202, 248, 250-52, 267, 280	5.26	81, 270-71	
				5.26-27	85, 178, 207, 236, 270-72	
5.2-3	50	5.13-14	272	5.27	56, 59, 72, 84, 152, 175, 200, 271-72, 294, 313, 341, 351	
5.3	229, 230, 232-35, 237, 287, 292	5.13-15	271			
		5.14	52, 54, 67, 129, 135, 136, 182, 183, 203, 207, 228, 236, 247, 248, 250, 252-54, 255, 272, 333, 334, 339, 341, 343, 346, 350, 352, 354, 356			
5.3-6	233			5.27-28	197	
5.4	109, 129, 232, 235-36, 239, 294, 305			5.28	267, 272-73, 299, 332, 359	
5.4-6	232, 240			**2 Thessalonians**		
5.4-8	230			1	47	
5.4-10	230, 235			1.1	56, 59, 62, 83, 84, 142, 277, 278	
5.4-11	71					
5.5	236-37, 308	5.14-15	52, 53	1.1-2	71, 176, 277-78, 339	
5.5-6	240	5.14-22	182			
5.5-8	242	5.15	66, 178, 229, 247, 255-57, 280	1.1-12	71	
5.5-10	233			1.2	85, 86, 267, 277-78, 299, 300, 330, 332, 360	
5.6	218, 237-39, 240, 243	5.16	257-58			
		5.16-17	259			
5.6-7	243	5.16-18	247, 260	1.3	31, 61, 87, 90, 139, 164, 167, 176, 177, 178, 191, 202, 207, 236, 259, 279-80	
5.6-8	109, 236	5.17	55, 87, 88, 257, 258-59			
5.7	139, 238, 239-40, 243					
		5.18	189, 257, 259-60			
5.8	31, 89, 91, 167, 202, 236, 238, 240-41, 242, 244, 280, 331	5.19	261-62	1.3-4	71, 89, 100, 104, 177, 241, 278, 279, 340	
		5.19-20	52, 203, 271			
		5.19-22	205, 247, 252, 260-66, 303			
5.8-9	323, 326			1.3-5	53, 279-86	
5.9	110, 111, 147, 148, 181, 197, 199, 230, 235, 236, 241-43, 244, 287, 328	5.20	262-64, 272	1.3-10	229, 278, 296, 300, 332	
		5.21	119, 264-65	1.3-12	61, 71, 278-300	
		5.22	190, 265-66, 283, 336	1.4	59, 61, 64, 69, 91, 98, 142, 154, 161, 167, 169, 278, 280-83, 284, 287, 293, 325, 340	
5.9-10	110, 245	5.23	55, 91, 109, 110, 138, 155, 175, 176, 180, 190, 194, 197, 201, 213, 222, 256, 266-69, 288, 297, 301, 320, 321, 326, 327, 330, 333, 357			
5.10	217, 228, 236, 238, 243-45					
5.11	66, 135, 182, 184, 208, 228, 229, 230, 244, 245-46, 252, 280, 333, 339			1.4-6	337	
				1.4-7	64, 98, 338	
5.12	129, 182, 183,			1.4-10	163, 357	

1.4-12   161
1.5   64, 138, 283-86, 296, 327
1.5-6   290, 294
1.5-9   180
1.5-10   41, 279, 283, 293
1.5-12   63, 71
1.6   64, 98, 161, 169, 171, 286-87, 288, 296
1.6-7   283
1.6-9   59, 324
1.6-10   53, 110, 111, 232, 233, 242, 284-85, 286-96
1.7   61, 64, 109, 163, 181, 224, 287-89, 292, 294, 296, 302, 308, 319
1.7-8   339
1.7-9   197, 294, 296
1.7-10   91, 108, 138, 149, 285-86, 301
1.8   62, 94, 160, 195, 286, 289-91, 295, 323, 328
1.8-9   286, 287, 298, 309
1.9   138, 197, 234, 291-94
1.9-10   138, 320
1.10   100, 133, 181, 236, 288, 294-95, 296, 298, 299, 305, 335
1.11   89, 90, 137, 164, 167, 242, 258, 280, 296-98, 327
1.11-12   53, 176, 279, 296-300, 333
1.12   286, 294, 298-300, 309, 332, 335, 339, 343
2   28, 32, 47, 60, 68, 329
2.1   91, 108, 138, 155, 180, 183, 222, 228, 288, 300-302, 320, 321, 339

2.1-2   53, 71, 108, 229, 242, 300, 305
2.1-4   232
2.1-11   63
2.1-12   60, 61, 62, 63, 67, 108, 180, 222, 230, 233, 294, 300-325
2.1-17   71, 300-333
2.1–3.16   300
2.2   61, 65, 67, 68-69, 163, 209, 232, 263, 264, 294, 301, 302-6, 307, 313, 314, 316, 319, 321, 325, 329, 330, 338, 341, 359
2.3   53, 59, 236, 306-9, 313, 314, 317, 319
2.3-4   59, 318
2.3ff.   242, 305
2.3-8   50
2.3-12   329
2.3-15   71
2.3-17   71
2.3–3.5   71
2.4   32, 43, 59, 308, 309-13, 319
2.4-8   53
2.5   53, 56, 59, 67, 68, 129, 152, 162, 230, 231, 301, 303, 304, 305, 306, 313-14, 329, 330, 346, 349
2.5-6   114
2.6   204, 231, 302, 314-17, 318, 319, 346
2.6-7   321
2.6-8   307
2.7   140, 313, 314, 315, 316, 317-19, 321, 323
2.8   41, 59, 108, 138, 155, 180, 222, 302, 308, 309, 311, 314, 317,

318, 319-20, 321, 339
2.8-9   302, 314
2.8-10   242
2.9   153, 309, 317, 318, 319, 320-22, 323, 324, 337
2.9-12   53, 59
2.10   98, 140, 243, 321, 322-23, 324, 327
2.10-11   324
2.10-12   325
2.10-15   336
2.11   139, 321, 323-24, 325
2.11-12   336
2.12   128, 133, 322, 324-25, 327
2.12-13   324
2.12-14   323
2.13   61, 87, 90, 92, 93, 139, 147, 164, 167, 176, 177, 180, 190, 198, 199, 242, 279, 280, 306, 322, 323, 325-27, 331, 340
2.13-14   61, 92, 181, 198, 242, 269, 297, 300, 325-28, 329
2.13-15   297, 307, 336
2.13-17   54, 306
2.14   47, 94, 128, 137, 138, 140, 160, 184, 242, 288, 291, 299, 325, 327-28, 339
2.15   63, 65, 68, 81, 170, 237, 300, 303, 304, 305, 306, 329-30, 344, 347, 349
2.16   86, 90, 118, 176, 176, 177, 277, 278, 292, 299, 339, 340
2.16-17   71, 176, 300, 330-33, 334, 339

2.17	65, 66, 135, 160, 169, 183, 337, 339	3.9	98, 99, 141, 346, 347, 348-49	2.6	317
3	206	3.10	28, 52, 54, 60, 90,	2.14	306
3.1	59, 61, 101, 140,		162, 186, 206,	2.15	167, 190
	182, 221, 258,		212, 313, 330,	3.1-11	247
	334-35		339, 341, 343,	3.2	238
3.1-2	54, 270, 334-37		344, 345, 349-50,	3.3	123, 347
3.1-5	61, 62, 334-40		351, 352, 353,	3.4	249
3.1-13	71		354, 355	3.5	142, 191, 249
3.1-15	71, 334-56	3.11	185, 212, 253,	3.6-7	153
3.2	59, 98, 164, 280,		341, 343, 346,	3.7	212
	288, 334, 335-37,		350-51, 353	3.8	347
	338	3.11-12	67, 350-53	3.10	119, 264
3.3	160, 269, 336,	3.12	30, 135, 183, 186,	3.12	249
	337-38		210, 250, 333,	3.13	96
3.3-4	337-39		339, 343, 345,	3.15	142
3.3-5	54, 98, 334		349, 351-53, 354,	4.1	307
3.4	184, 186, 208,		355	4.3	266
	212, 338-39, 343,	3.13	29, 30, 206, 211,	4.10	249
	349, 352		250, 254, 337,	4.12	98, 99, 158, 167
3.5	59, 167, 175, 176,		342, 351, 353	4.13	118, 270, 272
	177, 202, 339-40	3.14	345, 354-56	4.14	262
3.6	136, 137, 140,	3.14-15	71, 345, 353,	4.20	153
	184, 185, 186,		354-56	5.5	131
	212, 329, 339,	3.15	59, 250, 253, 255,	5.10	163
	343-45, 346, 349,		344, 345, 354,	5.12	200
	350, 352, 354, 355		355, 356, 359	5.13	351
3.6-7	253	3.16	175, 176, 177,	5.14	309
3.6-10	67		267, 278, 330,	5.17	249, 296
3.6-12	354		357-58	5.17-18	131, 347
3.6-13	28, 131	3.16-18	71, 357-60	5.19	123
3.6-15	54, 61, 62, 67, 71,	3.17	56, 59, 61, 67, 68,	5.21	198
	131, 206, 207,		152, 271, 304,	5.22	303
	208, 209, 212,		313, 358-59	5.23	158
	250, 252, 253,	3.18	236, 267, 272,	6.5	123
	334, 337, 339,		299, 332, 358,	6.9	195, 234, 292,
	341-56, 357		359-60		308
3.6-16	338			6.9-10	347
3.7	98, 114, 141, 204,	**1 Timothy**		6.11	89, 91, 167, 257
	231, 313, 343,	1.1	82, 153	6.12	198, 327
	345-47, 348	1.2	83, 86, 278	6.13	144
3.7-8	349	1.3	84, 152, 158, 174	6.13-14	343
3.7-9	54, 179, 211, 341,	1.5	167, 186	6.14	320
	344, 345, 349	1.11-12	120	6.15	317
3.7-10	345-50	1.12	242	6.21	272
3.7-12	29	1.13	143		
3.8	30, 90, 123, 125,	1.14	167	**2 Timothy**	
	131, 342, 346,	1.15	147	1.1	82
	347-48	1.18	186, 262	1.2	83, 278
3.8-9	130	2.1	87, 183	1.3	87, 131
				1.4	167, 172

INDEX OF SCRIPTURE REFERENCES

1.5	83	1.7	123, 347	3.12	180, 307
1.6	261	1.8	133	3.14	265
1.8	295	1.9	254	4.2	140
1.9	92, 327	1.11	123, 184	4.12	140
1.10	320	2.2	91, 167, 238	4.14	109, 329
1.12	338	2.4-10	212	5.9	291
1.13	167	2.5	167	6.4	235
1.18	84	2.7	98, 99	6.10	90
2.2	221	2.8	355	6.11	96
2.3-4	240	2.12	300	6.12	98
2.4	121, 145, 185	2.12-13	109	6.18	329
2.8	109	2.13	108, 320, 328	8.7	180
2.11-12	91	2.14	308	9.6	358
2.13	269, 337	3.1-2	212	9.9	305
2.14	198, 199	3.2	178	9.14	108
2.15	120, 323	3.3	195	9.15	327
2.16-18	222	3.5	147	9.24	109
2.17-18	304	3.8	249	10.6	128
2.18	305	3.10-11	354	10.8	128
2.20	192	3.14	249	10.17	308
2.21	90, 193	3.15	167, 272	10.22	96, 180
2.21-22	194			10.22-24	89
2.22	167, 193, 257	**Philemon**		10.23	265, 269, 337
2.24	126, 178	1	84, 159	10.25	302
2.26	153	2	203	10.28	123
3.1	305	3	85, 277, 278, 330	10.29	296
3.10	89, 167, 254	4	87, 139	10.30	286, 290, 324
3.10-11	83	5	167	10.32	235
3.11	283	7	118, 154, 172	10.36	189, 260
3.12	162	9-10	183	10.38	128, 344
3.13	118	10	134	10.39	129, 242, 309,
4.1	138, 198, 320	15	151		328
4.4	324	16	129	11	98
4.5	238	19	359	11.7	165
4.6	305	20	270	11.8	163
4.8	154, 155, 284,	21	208, 338, 354	11.11	269, 337
	286, 320	22	168, 174, 270,	11.25	326
4.9	166		334	11.34	261
4.13	166	24	7, 102, 159, 350	12.1	91, 117, 199
4.14	256	25	272	12.2-3	340
4.16-18	288			12.5	118
4.18	138, 241	**Hebrews**		12.14	190, 251, 257
4.22	272, 358	1.8-9	300	13.1	204
		1.9	308	13.4	324
Titus		2.3-4	95	13.5	347
1.1	82	2.4	96, 321	13.7	98
1.3	120, 317	2.10	299	13.17	172
1.4	278	2.14	320	13.19	183
1.5	157, 247	3.3	296	13.20	267
1.5-9	247	3.6	265	13.20-21	175

13.21	174, 189	2.13–3.7	252	1.10	297
13.22	183, 221	2.14	290, 304	1.11	300
13.23	84	2.15	260	1.12	160, 337
		2.17	93	1.13	250
James		2.18	167	1.17	128
1.2	99	2.18–3.7	246	1.18	109
1.3-4	91	2.20-21	162	2.3	122, 347
1.4	268	2.21	98	2.5	338
1.21	140	2.22	119	2.9	191
1.27	286	2.23	284	2.11	289
2.5	167	3.3-13	294	2.13	239
2.8-9	178	3.7	152, 192	2.14	122, 180
2.20	114	3.9	66, 255	2.18	118
3.18	251	3.10	119	2.22	107
4.5	167	3.11	257	3.4	217
4.17	191	3.17	162	3.7	289, 309
5.2-3	305	3.17-18	98	3.10	232, 289, 305
5.6-7	246	3.20	129	3.10-11	232
5.8	179, 333	3.22	109	3.16	308
5.14-16	253	4.2	260	3.17	118
		4.2-3	195		
1 Peter		4.3	106, 195	**1 John**	
1.2	85, 190, 291, 327	4.6	324	1.4	172
1.6	99, 162, 218, 257,	4.7	238	1.5	235
	258	4.8	178	1.9	269, 337
1.7	194, 264, 285,	4.11	175	2.5	340
	288	4.12	162, 163, 285	2.10	235
1.8	167, 172, 289	4.12-13	98	2.12-13	337
1.10-11	162, 231	4.13	154, 172, 257,	2.17	189, 260
1.12	96		288	2.18	317
1.13	238, 288	4.13-14	99	2.26	118
1.14	195, 291	4.17	117, 284, 285, 291	2.27	205
1.15	327	4.19	162, 284	2.28	179
1.15-16	189, 198	5.1	135, 183	3.7	118
1.17	176, 180	5.2	123, 347	3.11	178, 205
1.18	133	5.3	98, 99	3.17	29, 340
1.21	109	5.4	154	3.17-18	206
1.21-22	89	5.5-9	246	3.21	179
1.22	178, 204, 205,	5.8	152, 165, 238,	3.22	121, 145
	291		238, 309	3.23	167, 178, 205
2.1	119	5.9	93, 141	3.24	201
2.4	286	5.10	66, 137, 160, 327,	4.1	264
2.6	242		328, 337	4.1-2	264
2.7	194	5.12	83, 247, 358	4.1-3	263, 264, 303
2.9	235, 236, 327	5.14	270	4.6	118
2.11	135, 183, 190,			4.7	178, 205, 340
	195, 266	**2 Peter**		4.9	340
2.11-17	212	1.2	85	4.11	205
2.12	29, 195	1.3	327	4.11-12	178
2.13-17	246	1.7	202, 204	4.13	201

4.17	204	21	340	11.18	110
5.3	340	23	226	12.5	226
5.20	108, 300	24	154, 293, 338	12.10	131
5.21	106			13	316
		Revelation		13.3	295
2 John		1.1	185	13.13-15	321
2-4	170	1.4	85	14.4	326
3	86	1.7	226	14.11	131
4	172	2.2	89, 131	14.13	131, 225
5	178, 183, 205,	2.2-3	91	14.14-16	226
	301	2.8	244	16.7	284
7	304	2.10	165	16.8	289
10-11	354	2.14-15	329	16.15	232, 238
12	168, 172, 174	2.19	167	16.19	110
13-14	349	2.23	121	17.5	317
		2.24	125	17.7	317
3 John		2.25	329	17.8	309
3	172	3.1	299	17.11	309
4	172	3.2	160, 337	18.6-7	286
6	353	3.2-3	238	19.1-2	286
11	98	3.3	232	19.2	284
13-14	174	3.10	207	19.7	154
14	168, 174	3.11	329	19.15	110
		4.1	185	20.4-5	244
Jude		4.8	131	20.9	289
1	92, 93	4.10	154	20.10	131
3	183, 313, 329,	6.4	357	20.11	293
	330, 336	6.9-11	217	21.6	347
7	291, 292	6.16	110, 293	21.8	106, 292
9	224	6.16-17	110	22.6	185, 261-62
11	123	7.15	131	22.15	106
13	292	9.17-18	289	22.17	347
14-15	181	11.12	226	22.20	222

Index of Extrabiblical Literature

JEWISH LITERATURE

APOCRYPHA

1 Esdras
2.21	307
4.39	325
4.62	288

2 Esdras
4.21	320
4.23	320
5.5	320
6.8	320
20.35	231
23.31	231

Judith
7.1	186
7.12	109
7.28	136
8.17	109
12.8	176

1 Maccabees
1.1-7	9
1.10-28	310
1.43	325
1.54	311
2.15	307

2.44	308
3.30	152
5.58	186
6.2	9
6.44	242, 328
8.5	13
8.12	299
10.27	171, 287

2 Maccabees
1.1	85
1.27	302
2.1	93
2.3	135
2.18	302
2.21	320
3.17	155
3.24	320
4.7-17	310
5.4	320
5.11–6.17	310
5.23	309
5.25	186
6.12	135
6.12-16	285
6.14	109, 148
7.5	135
7.20	167
7.21	135
8.11	291
8.16	135
9.26	135

10.26	309
12.6	286
12.22	320
12.42	135
12.45	217
13.10	173
13.12	285
13.14	136
13.19–14.1	204
14.15	320
14.17	234
15.8	136
15.8-9	136
15.14	204
15.17	136
15.27	320

3 Maccabees
1.4	136
3.2	101
3.21	285
3.24	234
5.36	136

4 Maccabees
1.11	91
6.2-3	225
6.19	100
8.17	136
10.1	136
10.15	292
12.6	136, 222

13.9	97	4.7	223	25.4	290
13.18	222	4.10-11	226	52.6	289
13.23	204	5.17-20	240	61.10	289
13.26	204	5.18	241	62.4	234
14.1	204	6.13	223	90.26	307
16.24	136	7.13	128	93.9	307
17.4	91	7.15	137	99.14	262
17.8	279	8.8	231	100.5	217
		11.10	250		
Sirach		12.19	184	**2 Enoch**	
2.7	109	14.15	329	3.1	226
3.23	351	14.17-21	310-11		
5.3	197	14.20	310	**Epistle of Aristeas**	
5.7	109	14.28	303	79	210
6.19	109	15.17	310	142	354
13.21	160	16.17	261	175	285
14.9	123	16.28	184, 223	188	97
14.11	137	17.2	308	209	238
22.23	192	17.14	234	210	97
23.23	190	18.11	291	280-81	97
24.10	160	19.1	234		
28.1-2	255				
28.3-7	255			**4 Ezra**	
28.9	251	**OLD TESTAMENT**		4.33	231
28.13	251	**PSEUDEPIGRAPHA**		5.1-13	307
29.5	231			13.24	223
30.6	171, 287	**Adam and Eve**			
30.19	145	49.3	289	**Psalms of Solomon**	
35.18	286			2.5	262
36.24	192	**Assumption of Moses**		2.35	292
38.6	295	1.15	217	13.9-10	285
38.34	160	7.4	239	15.4	289
40.13	101	10.14	217	15.11	292
40.19	160			17.11	307
42.17	160	**2 Baruch**		17.32	205
49.3	339	4.3-6	312	17.50	223
		13.3-10	285		
Tobit		41.3	307		
3.2	286	42.4	307	**Sibylline Oracles**	
4.12	190, 193	52.5-7	285	2.196-213	289
12.1	184	52.6	99	3.80-93	289
14.7	302	78.2	85	3.327	234
14.61	107	78.5	285	3.348	234
				4.171-82	289
Wisdom of Solomon		**1 Enoch**		5.155-61	289
1.14-15	292	1.6-7	289	5.206-13	289
2.3	261	1.9	181		
3.5	137	10.11	199	**Testament of Asher**	
4.2	97	14.8-25	312	4.3	97
4.4	151	20.1-7	224	7.6-7	302

Testament of Benjamin
3.1	97
4.1	97
5.3	235

Testament of Dan
5.2	267

Testament of Joseph
2.7	311
7.8	195
10.1	91
17.5	173
20.4	217

Testament of Judah
3.10	289
13.3	281
18.4	145

Testament of Levi
5.1-2	312
6.11	148, 149
8.2	241
9.9-10	190, 193
19.1	235

Testament of Naphtali
2.7-10	235
2.9	346
8.3	302
8.6	192

Testament of Reuben
3.10	351

DEAD SEA SCROLLS

1QH
3.19-36	289

1QM
1.1	236
1.3	236
1.9	236
1.11	236
1.13	236
13.15	235

14.9	317
15.9	235

1QS
1.1-10	235
1.9	236
2.15	292
2.16	236
3.13	236
3.13–4.26	235
3.24-25	236
5.13	292
6.6-8	173
6.10	93
6.22	93
8.21.26	354

RABBINIC LITERATURE

m. Aboth
2.2	130

m. Berakhot
5.5	126

m. Ketubot
3.4-5	192

b. Pesahim
112a-b	192

Qiddushin
29a	130

b. Sanhedrin
152a	192

Genesis Rabbah
2.2	349
33.1	285

Targum Pseudo-Jonathan
on Gen. 3.19	344

PHILO

De Abrahamo
20	210
20-21	352-53
27	210
116	224
216	210

De Confusione Linguarum
131	107
146	224

De Congressu Eruditionis Gratia
157	250

De Congressu Quaerendae Eruditionis Gratia
58	160

De Fuga et Inventione
49	160

De Hypothetica
7.14	134

De Josepho
87	107

De Legatione ad Gaium
87	204
147	233
203-346	311

De Praemiis et Poenis
30	160
117	224
121	123

De Somniis
1.157	224
1.254	316
2.11	160
2.101-6	239
2.174	107

De Specialibus Legibus
1.173 279
1.224 279
2.15 190
2.31.1 150
2.202 160
2.228 134
2.232 135, 250
2.256 107
3.175 291

De Virtutibus
163 190

De Vita Mosis
1.49 210, 352-53
1.245 291
1.278 354
1.300 190
2.50 136
2.215-16 272

In Flaccum
39 101
64 156
141 186

Legum Allegoriae
1.102 190
3.106 290
3.136 328
3.193 250

*Quod Deterius Potiori
Insidiari Solet*
34 211

*Quod Deus Sit
Immutabilis*
17 107
86 328

*Quod Omnis Probus
Liber Sit*
28-29 303

*Quis Rerum Divinarum
Heres*
69 316
205 224

JOSEPHUS

Antiquitates
1.20 190
1.70 289
1.102 190
1.160 141
1.284 192
2.53 195
2.67 168
2.245 234
2.258 296
3.71 120
3.80 155
3.203 155
3.207 210
3.254 288
3.281 288
4.26 204
4.108 169
4.130 195
4.209 305
4.281 285
5.61 236
7.247 223
7.283 241
7.327 228
7.346 159
8.318 196
9.55 155
10.27 265
10.53 107
10.104 136
10.111 306
10.142 184-85
11.208 354
11.329-36 227
12.125 310
12.175 305
13.89 306
13.297 329
13.309 241
14.196 249
14.212 171
15.76 285
15.330 210
16.241 186
16.253 168
16.301 122
17.38 234

17.199 224
18.261-309 311
20.105-12 149
20.165 354
20.183 120

Bellum Judaicum
1.206 210
1.470 317
2.102 159
2.142 190
2.224-27 149
2.285 192
2.313 190
4.42 238
4.231 122
5.377 197
5.571 168
7.68-72 227

Contra Apionem
1.35 222
1.164 190
1.292 145
2.121 146
2.175 272

Vita
43 (10) 307
264 (51) 234
329 (62) 236
421 (75) 170
429 (76) 19

**EARLY CHRISTIAN
LITERATURE**

Athenagoras
*Plea on Behalf of
Christians*
26-27 321

Chrysostom
*Homilies on 1
Thessalonians*
2 100, 101, 103
4 177
9 239

1 Clement
9–12	98
17–18	98
19	98
34.4	162
42.4	326
53.3	152

2 Clement
2.6	160

Clement of Alexandria,
Exhortation to the Heathen
ch. 2	35, 36, 44

Stromata
5.3	59

Didache
11.5-6	123
11.8	264-65
11.9-12	264-65
11.12	123
12.1-5	349-50
12.3	350
12.4	350
15.3	354
16.6	55

Diognetus
9.1	296

Eusebius
Historia Ecclesiastica
3.3.5	54-55

Eustathius
364.16	142

Hermas
Mandates
4.1.5	190
5.1.2	192

Hippolytus
The Refutation of All Heresies
4.28-41	321

Ignatius
Ephesians
10.1	55

Romans
2.1	55
10.3	59

Irenaeus
Against Heresies
3.7.2	59
5.6.1	55

Justin
2 Apology
6.6	316

Dialogue with Trypho
32.12	59
110.6	59

Martyrdom of Polycarp
19.1	141

Polycarp
Philippians
8	98
9	98
11.3	59

Shepherd of Hermas
Vision
3.9.10	55

Tertullian
Against Marcion
5.15	55
5.16	59

De Anima
57	59

On the Resurrection of the Flesh
24	55

PAPYRI

Oxyrhynchus Papyri
294.28	183
774.6	183
1670	268

Tebtunis Papyri
276	37

GRECO-ROMAN LITERATURE

Achilles Tatius
7.15.3	228

Aeschylus
Eumenides
664	132

Apollodorus
1.5.1	226

Apollonius Rhodius
3.1114	226

Appian
Bella Civilia Romana
1.71	162
2.85	197
2.139	162
5.30	223
5.40	168

Aratus
Phaenomena
5	127

Aristophanes
Equites
643	166

Aristotle
Ars Rhetorica
1.2.1	69
1.3.3-4	70
1.4-10	70
1.4.7	251
2.2.5-6	116
2.2.16-17	172
3.9.1-3	134
3.12.1-3	72
3.12.5-6	70
3.14-19	71
1358b	339

1378b 355-56

Ethica Nicomachea
1.2.8 324
3.13.1 324
3.13.4 324
1127a 122
1160b 134

Historia Animalium
612b.12 145

Arrian
Anabasis
4.21.10 194

Augustus
Res Gestae Divi
Augusti 42
12.2 233

Catullus
5.4-6 217

Cicero
De Divinatione 262
1.19.37-38 164
2.72.148 263

De Inventione
1.19 71

De Partitione Oratoria
27 71

De Provinciis
Consularibus
2 4
2.4 5

Epistulae ad Atticum
3.14 5
7.3 358
7.12 358
8.14.1 72, 202
9.10.1 72
11.5.1 57
12.53 72

Epistulae ad Familiares
1.4.3 185
2.4.1 81

6.10b.4 184, 339

In L. Calpurnium Pisonem
40 5

In Pisonem
34 (84) 17, 18, 233

Pro Caelio
18.42 187

Pro Cnaeo Plancio
41 3, 24

Pro Fonteio
20 (44) 17

Pro Rabirio Perduellionis
Reo
12 116

Corpus Hermeticum
2.14 310

Demetrius
De Elocutione
223 72
224 72
226 72

Demosthenes,
Orationes
10.72 351
18.72 351
19.256 284
21.121 301
26.15 351
32.28 351
59.122 188

Against Midias
21.111 120

De Corona
323 166

Dio Cassius
21.38 15
41.18.4-6 18
41.43.1-5 18
56.25.5-6 50
57.15.8 50
60.24 19

60.27.4 210
62.4.1-2 227
71.35 122

Dio Chrysostom
7.103-32 211
7.125 212
7.150 188, 194
8.33 124
12.5 124
12.9 116
13.11 310
17 123
17.1-6 114
17.1-11 185, 346
17.2 185, 186, 230
17.6 123
17.7 123
17.8 196
17.16 123
32.10 115
32.11 112-13, 116, 122, 123, 124
32.11-12 119
32.41 320
34.52 210
35.1 123
47.22 106
74.4 234
77/78.27 124
77/78.34 310
77/78.38 135
77/78.42 135

Diodorus Siculus
Historical Library
1.8.1 346
2.60.3 285
4.12.3 186
4.14.3 234
4.43.1-2 44
4.61.9 125
5.10.2 72, 272
5.49.5-6 44
5.70.4 321
10.4.6 168
14.110.4 325
15.16.4 223
15.48.1 321
16.27.2 321

16.59.2	296	2.20.22	107	219	334
16.69.4	225	2.22.15	306	352-69	348
17.76.3	296	2.22.36	231	405-14	348
19.26.10	288	2.22.97	351	453-57	348
19.33.2	212	3.13.12	358		
19.52.1	10	3.13.13	357	**Hesychius**	
19.70.8	125	3.22.82	135	*Lexicon*	128, 161
20.102.4	234	3.23.6	272	2368.1	142
31.8.8-9	14	3.23.23-24	124		
31.8.9-12	13	3.23.27-28	118	**Hierocles**	
32.9	15	3.23.32	124	*On Duties*	
33.5.5	304	3.24.3	249	4.22.21	346
34.1.1-2	145	3.24.4	291	4.27.20	204, 255
37.5	16	3.26.20	291		
40.3.4-5	145	4.1.5	310	**Homer**	
40.5a.1	304	4.1.163	212	*Iliad*	
		4.5.24	357	9.319	194
		4.5.25	357	9.501	196
Diogenes Laertius		4.11.5	199	10.235	326
2.136	160	18.20	137	11.241	217
5.64	231			14.206	190
8.31-32	228			14.305-6	190
10.3	304	**Eupolis**		15.290	336
10.132	238	236-37	122	17.645	336
Dionysius of		**Euripides**		*Odyssey*	
Halicarnassus		*Hecuba*		2.46-47	127
Antiquitates Romanae		149	150	4.817	129
2.9-11	29, 208, 342			9.281	165
2.10	211	*Helena*		15.250-51	226
2.10.1	342	426	222		
2.11.1	28			**Isocrates**	
2.27.1-5	134	**Herodian**		*Areopagiticus*	
2.51.3	236	2.1.7	222	51	357
2.68	320	2.14.3	197		
9.7.1	196	2.15.1	238	**Juvenal**	
		7.4.5	197	*Satires*	
Epictetus				2.149-53	293
Dissertationes		**Herodotus**		5	208
1.4.1	107	*History*		5.11	351
1.4.18-21	107	1.18	172	14.96-106	145
1.4.31-32	139	1.53	162	15.96-106	49
1.8.8	254	2.51	318		
1.9.7	234	3.89	127	**Livy**	
1.9.29	165	4.141	224	*Annals*	
1.10.2	210	7.32	231	8.1.10	337
1.27.17	231	8.53	184	25.16.14	337
2.8.12-13	199			42.32.6	11
2.14.12-13	97	**Hesiod**		42.50.7	11
2.19.24	258	*Opera et Dies*		42.51.1-11	12
2.20.7	306	90-105	218	44.46	2

44.46.6-7	2	7.66	133	1.649B	331
45.18	14	12.3	268	6.765C-D	120
45.18.1-2	13	12.14	268	8.847A	176
45.18.3-5	6			10.906C	196
45.29.9	14	**Martial**		11.945D	180
45.29-30	14	7.80.1	233	647D	333
45.30	14			829C	191
45.30.4	6	**Musonius Rufus**		879D-E	333
		frag. 12	195	885B	333
Periochae				909D	333
53	16	**Ovid**			
		Ex Ponto		*Phaedo*	
Lucan		2.5.18	233	67C	331
Bellum Civile					
4.189-91	251	**Pausanias**		*Philebus*	
		1.21.6	241	16C	329
Lucian		10.32.13	328		
Alexander the False		10.38.7	44	*Republic*	
Prophet	321			1.335	255
		Perseus		2.366A	196
De Luctu	293	1.54-55	208	4.433A	210
				6.496D	210
De Mercede Conductis		**Phaedrus**			
5	306	*Fabulae*		*Symposium*	
17	194	4.25.17	349	182D	196
Demonax		**Philodemus**		*Timaeus*	
1-2	97	*De Libertate*		30B	268
		23.3	137		
Hermotimus				**Pliny the Elder**	
47	238	**Philostratus**		*Naturalis Historia*	
		Vita Apollonii		2.5.27	110
Lucius or The Ass		5.33	145	4.10	9, 13, 19
46.5	6				
		Pindar		**Pliny the Younger**	
Timon		*Pythian Odes*		*Epistulae*	
10	145	4.167	132	8.13	97
				8.24	185, 204
Toxaris vel Amicitia		**Plato**		10.96	50
31	236	*Apology*			
52	236	19B	351	**Plutarch, *Lives:***	
		31B-C	132	*Aemilius Paulus*	
Lucretius				19.4-5	12
The Nature of Things		*Critias*		38.4	49
5	263-64	110B	284		
				Agis and Cleomenes	
Lysias		*Gorgias*		3.1	123
Against Alcibiades		507B	133	16.1	123
14.18	346	527C	122		
15.6	120			*Alexander*	
		Leges		1	157-58
Marcus Aurelius		1.628B	357	7.2	174
6.20	356				
6.30	269				

7.5　　　　　　139
33.2　　　　　176
75.1　　　　　321

Antony
40.4　　　　　234

Brutus
46　　　　　　18

Catone Minore
1.4　　　　　　125
20.1　　　　　125

Demetrius
1.4-6　　　　　97
1.6　　　　　　346
49.5　　　　　136

Othone
2.2　　　　　　199

Pericles
1.4–2.2　　　　211
37　　　　　　125

Philopoemen
21.4　　　　　354

Sulla
35.5　　　　　180

Timoleon
5.4　　　　　　318

Titus Falmininus
9.5　　　　　　11
10.3-5　　　　11

Plutarch, *Moralia:*
53B　　　　　210
78A　　　　　124
131A　　　123, 124
138E　　　　192
144B　　　　188
144E　　　　190
169C　　　　153
189D　　　　192
274B　　　　228
352B　　　　45
402B　　　　261
509F　　　　197
525A-B　　　195
539A-B　　　281

539D　　　281, 282
544E　　　　282
548C-D　　　293-94
549B-D　　　293-94
553F　　　　291
559D　　　　291
561B　　　　291
591C　　　　226
592E　　　　291
798E-F　　　210
943A　　　　268

Consolation to Apollonius
102C　　　　218
102C-D　　　218

De Audiendo
37F-38D　　　349

De Fraterno Amore
478E-F　　　204
479D　　　　204
482E-F　　　204

De Iside et Osiride
351F　　　　45
358A-B　　　36
365C　　　　36
372E　　　　45
376C-D　　　46

De Liberis Educandis
8F-9A　　　　134
13A-B　　　　122
13D　　　　134
14A　　　　134

*De Sera Numinis Vindicta.
See On the Delays of the
Divine Vengeance*

*Obsolescence of Oracles,
The*　　　　262

*On Inoffensive
Self-Praise*　　　281

*On the Delays
of the Divine
Vengeance*　287, 294
550E　　　　97

*Oracles at Delphi No
Longer Given in Verse,
The*　　　　262

*Quomodo Adulator ab
Amico Internoscatur*　122
65F　　　　117
70F　　　　135

*Quomodo Quis Suos in
Virtute Sentiat Profectus*
81C-D　　　117

Polybius
Histories
1.8.4　　　　325
1.23.3　　　285
1.78.8　　　128
2.38.7　　　325
2.49.7　　　355
3.8.10　　　290
3.15.5　　　337
3.112.8　　　321
4.19.10　　　353
4.32.7　　　125
5.2.11　　　174
5.26.8　　　227
5.26.8-9　　　227
5.78.2　　　354
6.27.1　　　186
13.5.7　　　192
13.8.6　　　136
15.25.1　　　192
18.25.4　　　156
27.9-10　　　12
29.16　　　　12
29.17.1　　　12
31.25.6-7　　　13
34.12.8　　　4
36.10　　　　15
36.17.13　　　15
36.17.13-15　　285
36.17.14　　　15
36.17.15　　　13
38.3.8-13　　　285

Pseudo-Demetrius
"Epistolary Types"　73

Pseudo-Diogenes
32   185

Pseudo-Libanius
"Epistolary Styles"
2   81
4   73

"Epistolary Types"
92   74

Quintilian
Institutio Oratoria
9.2.30   233

Quintus Smyrnaeus
11.289-90   226

Seneca
De Beneficiis
2.24.4   172
2.31   172
2.33.1-2   172
2.35.1   172
3.1.1   172

De Ira
2.32.2   255
2.32.2-3   255
2.32.3   256

Epistulae Morales
1.1   184, 339
6   346, 349
13.15   185
25.4   184, 339
33.5-9   349
40.1   81, 168
75.1   72, 81
90.26   358
94   248
94.1-2   252
94.13-16   252
94.39   184, 339

Sophocles
Antigone
425   150

Electra
509   217

Oedipus Tyrannus
777   234

Strabo,
Geography
7, frag. 10   2
7, frag. 11   9
7, frag. 20   2
7, frag. 21   2, 10
7, frag. 24   2, 10
7, frag. 47(48)   14
7, frag. 50(51)   43, 48
7.7.4   4, 5, 16
7.20-21   6
8.8.5   4
8.6.21   5
11.2.10   322
16.2.35   321

Suda
1411.1   142

Suetonius
Claudius
25.4   149

Nero
16.2   50

Tacitus
1.76.4   19
1.180.1   19

Annals
12.29   233
15.44.2-8   50

Histories
5.5   145
5.9   141

Themistocles
2.5-6   174

Theocritus
Idyll
4.42   218

Thucydides
Histories
1.43.2   172
2.89.9   250

3.38.1   255
3.57.4   153
4.19.3   172
4.81.3   331

Xenophon
Anabasis
2.5.38   194
3.2.27   225
5.6.12   157

Cyropaedia
1.5.13   331
7.3.10   180

Hellenica
2.1.4   186
2.3.33   355

Historia Graeca
3.4.18   154

Memorabilia
1.2.55   136
1.2.59   333
1.6.3   97, 192
2.1.31   282
2.2.11   185
2.2.13-14   139
2.3.6   333
2.3.17   333
2.9.1   210, 211
3.1.9   265
3.5.30   120

Oeconomicus
7.31   346

Symposium
1.10   316
2.10   192
4.35   177

Zeus
Juppiter Confutatus
16-19   293

Zonaras
9.28   15